PROUST'S
NARRATIVE
TECHNIQUES

B. G. ROGERS

PROUST'S
NARRATIVE
TECHNIQUES

GENÈVE
LIBRAIRIE DROZ
8, RUE VERDAINE

1965

CONTENTS

PREFACE

It is fashionable to divide up the ever-growing mass of Proustian criticism into two general phases: the first, growing concurrently with the actual composition and publication of *A la Recherche du Temps Perdu,* which did not appear in entirety until 1927, five years after Proust's death, and gradually assimilating all the main implications of the work; while the second takes into account the increasing knowledge of Proust's career as a writer, made available by the steady trickle of biographical material which has flowed unstemmed since the *Nouvelle Revue Française's Hommage à Marcel Proust* [1], and the often very revealing light cast upon *A la Recherche du Temps Perdu* by the successive publication of earlier, fragmentary works. [2] It is within this second phase that the study of Proust's narrative techniques inevitably falls, first because it is only in the light of the preceding experiments that the final work can be properly understood as stemming from a series of attempts to reconcile constantly-recurring problems of composition and 'genre'; second, because the study of narrative techniques can only be undertaken when the main aesthetic and psychological implications of the work are firmly established, and third, because not until recently has a critical text of the unrevised final sections of *A la Recherche* been made available, [3] replacing the faulty fifteen-volume edition much of which, published posthumously, contained a considerable number of errors [4]. With the provision of new material, then, it was time that the new phase of Proustian criticism began to 'clarify the pattern of Proust's evolution as a writer, his quest for a style and his position in the history of the novel'. [5]

Among serious works by eminent critics, those preoccupying themselves with technical problems of construction and composition have

---

[1] *Nouvelle Revue Française,* No. 112, 1st. January, 1923.

[2] Notably *Jean Santeuil,* (1952) and *Contre Sainte-Beuve,* referred to as *C.S.-B.* (1954). For details of publication see *Jean Santeuil,* by Georges Bataille, *Critique,* July 1952; *Jean Santeuil,* by Maurice Blanchot, *Nouvelle Revue Française,* 1st September 1954; *Proust, Contre Sainte-Beuve,* by A. Rousseaux, *Le Figaro Littéraire.*

[3] The Pléiade edition of *A la Recheche du Temps Perdu,* afterwards referred to as *ARTP,* appeared in 1954.

[4] Cf. the preface to *ARTP,* Paris, Gallimard, 1954.

[5] Walter A. Strauss : *Proust and Literature,* Harvard University Press, 1957.

been in the minority, and a glance at a current Proust bibliography reveals the lack of attention that this aspect of *A la Recherche* has received. While, from the days of the first volumes of *A la Recherche,* interest in the plan of the work has been manifest, too often critics have been content to paraphrase Proust's own remarks in *Le Temps retrouvé,* or to resort to extravagant claims on the author's behalf. *Swann* has been seen as a literary transcription of the musical sonata-form, while the whole work has been 'proved' to have been based architecturally on the deliberate repetition of 'la scène que Proust appelle sadique', the entire narrative tone dictated by his 'hypermnésie'.[6]

In 1949, Professor Green published his book on Proust[7], raising many problems of narrative technique, the most interesting perhaps being his interpretation of Proust's conception of drama in the novel, while some of the peculiar problems of retrospective first-person narrative were explored in a fascinating article by Louis Martin-Chauffier.[8] No work, however, discusses the related problems of experimentation in 'genre' and technique in the early works and the conclusions of such experimentation in *A la Recherche.* Similarly, the various, isolated problems, raised in the stimulating articles of Elizabeth Jackson,[9] W.L. Hodson[10] and Autret's book on Proust and Ruskin[11] are rarely applied to the most important of all the works, *A la Recherche* itself. Only in one article do we find any attempt, moreover, to analyse the characteristic narrative 'patterns' of *A la Recherche*[12], while its author himself speaks of the lack of material so far collected on this subject.[13]

The object of this study is to examine Proust's whole output in the light of the two opposing tendencies which characterise it, dictating choice both of 'genre' and technique; the one consisting of reflexions, aphorisms and general conclusions in the manner of La Bruyère and classical moralists—a strain which dispenses altogether with fiction-alisation, or subordinates it to the secondary role of illustration and

---

[6] See Kneller: *The Musical Structure of Proust's Swann,* Yale French Studies II, No. 2, pp. 55-62; and M.A. Cochet: *L'Ame proustienne,* Brussels, 1929.

[7] F.C. Green: *The Mind of Proust,* Cambridge, 1949.

[8] *Proust and the Double 'I', Partisan Review,* October 1949, pp. 1011-1027.

[9] *The Genesis of the Involuntary Memory in Proust's early works. PMLA;* December 1961.

[10] Proust's methods of Character Presentation in *Les Plaisirs et les Jours* and *Jean Santeuil, Modern Language Review,* January 1962.

[11] Jean Autret: *L'Influence de Ruskin sur la vie, les idées et l'œuvre de Marcel Proust.* Droz, Geneva, 1955.

[12] J.P. Houston: Temporal Patterns in *A la Recherche du Temps Perdu, French Studies,* January 1962.

[13] *Ibid.,* p. 33: 'The guiding themes, ideas and images of *A la Recherche du Temps Perdu* have often been analysed; an aspect of Proust's work which has, however, received little attention is narrative technique: the ordering of events in a temporal fiction'.

example; the other comprising all the traditional preoccupations of the novelist, with conventional attitudes and techniques which place the ordering of a fictional story above comment and observations. We shall try to trace the influence of these two trends on the *choice* of genre before the writing of *A la recherche,* attempt to evaluate Proust's evolving attitudes towards fiction and straightforward observation and commentary, and in the light of both enquiries examine in detail the techniques embodied in the final work. In doing so, we shall hope not to lose sight of the critic's fundamental task, once summarised as being to *stimuler l'admiration en révélant les procédés par lesquels l'écrivain de génie transpose une réalité transitoire et personnelle en un réalisme permanent et universel.* [14]

Proust's narrative techniques are therefore discussed from three different viewpoints. First, that of the early works, with their background of seventeenth-century observation and nineteenth-century fiction. Second, in the light of the technical mastery they reveal in Proust, and his consequent search for new and original forms. Third, the final novel is presented as the gradual interlocking of individual techniques with these new forms.

Before being adapted to the formula of *A la recherche,* Proust's techniques clashed with all attempts to create a fictional hero in the centre of his writing—his instinctive approach being rather to concentrate on general commentary and to sacrifice coherent narrative forms to psychological analysis and speculation. A permanent proccupation with dialogue and dramatic presentation in all forms, none the less, indicates a strong interest in conventional fiction.

Proust came gradually to create new techniques to replace conventional plot and action, and turned increasingly to the first-person narrative, which he embodied at first in an unseen but personalised narrator, and later in a highly subjective 'hero'. Objective description, too, began gradually to be attached to this central figure, who stemmed both from the conventional hero and from the observer of manners. Plot, hero and drama not surprisingly became a structural convenience. The sometimes shadowy Marcel embraces investigations and demonstrations of the most varied kind, and exists to support a fiction based on his own life-story. Retrospective self-examination allowed Proust to manipulate both narrative and time-perspectives, while time itself, memory and character-portrayal all began to benefit from an almost continual interplay of subjective and objective reporting. What incoherence remains in the final structure is directly related to Proust's early experiments, as well as to the inevitable confusion of a concept of reality based on involuntary memory and associations. Proust's striving for artistic 'salvation', eventually achieved by the reproduction of personal thought-processes in a search for truth, went hand in hand

---

[14] Godin, review of Gilbert Mayer's edition of *Illusions perdues, French Studies,* 1, p. 364, 1947.

with his pursual of an instinctive method of composition which ignored rules, and followed the paths of a cultivated imagination, which was made to reveal the 'essence' of experience. Proust's quest for a form, therefore, almost parallels Marcel's search for artistic salvation in *A la recherche du temps perdu.*

Trinity College,
Cambridge,
June 1964.

PART ONE

———

THE BACKGROUND AGAINST WHICH
A LA RECHERCHE DU TEMPS PERDU
EVOLVES

LES PLAISIRS ET LES JOURS

The plan of *A la Recherche du Temps Perdu* aroused interest among discerning readers of Proust long before the final, decisive volumes of *Le Temps Retrouvé* appeared. The controversy surrounding the two main critical attitudes towards the problems of composition is well summed up in Crémieux' *Débat avec M. Louis de Robert,*[1] and shows no signs of abating today, more than a quarter of a century later.[2] Much of the confusion[3] seems to arise from the two main trends discernible throughout Proust's writing, to which we have already referred: the attitude of the moralist and the attitude of the novelist in Proust, and it is with these influences in mind that the question of narrative techniques must be examined.

First, what is known of the background against which *A la Recherche* evolved, the kind of influences brought to bear on the final work? Its author's admiration for the seventeenth century is well known and frequently expressed, but with the exception of Racine, Proust seems to have been drawn mostly towards the moralists and memorialists of that period, particularly La Bruyère, La Rochefoucauld and Saint-Simon. The reason is probably an admiration for their combination of simplicity and clarity with a deep understanding of human problems— the same qualities which attracted him to Racine—and a profound, natural affinity with them, which L.A. Bisson sums up as follows:

> Like all French novelists and nearly all Frenchmen, (Proust) was a moralist, a moralist with a gift of precise observation, and mastery in the heightened, significant notation of what he observed; rich powers of comic invention and intense, intuitive perceptions were allied in him

---

[1] *Du côté de Marcel Proust,* by Benjamin Crémieux, Paris, Lemarget, 1929, pp. 65-94.

[2] See, for instance, Jean-François Revel's stimulating and controversial pamphlet *Sur Proust, Remarques sur A la Recherche du Temps Perdu.* Paris, Julliard, 1960.

[3] e.g. Robert's remark: 'Et je ne crois pas m'abuser en pensant que le tort de cette formule "composition en rosace" est de nous donner une impression géométrique, de nous faire croire à une méthode rigoureuse. L'art de Proust était plus capricieux, plus détendu, plus lâche dans sa trame. Chaque logette, chaque alvéole était extensible selon la substance dont il l'emplissait.' Crémieux, *op. cit.,* p. 69.

with a faculty of penetrating analysis and delicate description of psychological and emotional states. [4]

The affinity with La Bruyère appears in the earliest works, notably the *Fragments de Comédie Italienne* in *Les Plaisirs et les jours* [5] and Proust adopts with remarkable ease the whole technique of symmetrical construction and lapidary epithet which characterises the 17th century moralists. [6] The preoccupation with individual episodes and the virtual absence of a plan to provide a link between the scattered portraits and general observations, moreover, reappear, as we shall see, in most of Proust's writings, even when these are conceived on a fictional basis. With La Rochefoucauld, Proust shares an affinity of a different kind; though both have an interest in general observation, Proust's natural scepticism and cynicism find a perfect counterpart in the tone of the *Maximes,* with their systematic unmasking of human motives and weaknesses, while the mordant aphorisms which characterise the analyses of love in *A la Recherche,* for example, proclaim the extraordinary similarity of the two writers. [7] Proust was also an ardent reader of Saint-Simon's *Mémoires* and attention has often been drawn to the similarity between the 'mécanisme' of the courts of Louis XIV and the Duc d'Orléans who succeeded him as Regent, and the portrayal of the Guermantes and Verdurin societies in *A la Recherche.* Again, the absence of a real plan, the creation of the celebrated portraits, and the inclusion of a personal narrative tone all leave their mark upon Proust who, while denying that he intended to write the '*Mémoires* de Saint-Simon d'une autre époque', [8] nevertheless assimilated many of the latter's attitudes and techniques. Proust, then, belongs to the great French classical tradition and is the continuation, in the twentieth century, of a whole set of reflexes, instincts and attitudes carefully matured over more than three hundred years.

At the same time, Proust is 'firmly rooted in the French literary tradition' as a whole, [9] and parallels have been drawn between the author of *A la Recherche* and Stendhal, Balzac, Flaubert and Fromentin. [10] Stendhal and Flaubert undoubtedly furnished ample material for reflexion, if only for their widely-differing conceptions of the novel,

---

[4] Proust in 1947, *French Studies,* I, 1947, p. 217.

[5] *Les Plaisirs et les Jours,* Paris, Gallimard, 1928, pp. 69-67. Afterwards referred to in these notes as *P. et J.*

[6] See also Mouton, *Le Style de Marcel Proust,* Paris, Corrêa, 1948, pp. 39-40.

[7] See also Rivière's allusion to Proust's 'immense et tranquille scepticisme naturel', quoted by Chardon, who adds 'Mais le fond désolé de son âme était le pessimisme. Il ne croyait pas à grand chose quant aux sentiments humains et il le laisse voir à la fin dans ses lettres'. *Expliquez-moi Marcel Proust,* Paris, 1949, p. 21.

[8] *ARTP,* III, 1044.

[9] J.M. Cocking, *Proust, Studies in Modern European Literature and Thought,* London, Bowes and Bowes, 1956, p. 28.

[10] *Ibid.,* pp. 27-28.

their techniques, styles and methods of composition. Proust, from *Les Plaisirs et les Jours* onwards, found himself inescapably drawn towards fictional forms and we shall see the sometimes dazzling virtuosity he displays in his early attempts to evolve fictional techniques; from Stendhal Proust inherited the conception, at least in part, of what he calls a 'novel of motives'[11], though transforming and developing Stendhal's method of demonstrating them, while from Flaubert he learned many invaluable lessons on the use of tense in fictional presentation, the inclusion of time through technical devices and the importance of an individual style, even if he deplores the absence in Flaubert of metaphor[12]. At times similarities are apparent between Proust and a minor writer like Barbey d'Aurevilly, whose work Proust is known to have liked—mostly in the complicated structures both affect to introduce the main elements of their stories, structures sometimes arbitrary and clumsy, often flatly conventional. But it is by studying the relationship between Proust and Balzac that one realises the extent to which the former owes his development as a writer of fictional novels to the literary tradition of the 19th century. References to Balzac abound in *A la Recherche,* and the relationship between the two novelists has been examined by Abraham[13], Fernandez[14], and Harry Levin[15]. We shall attempt to show the role played by Balzac in the evolution of Proust's narrative techniques, both before *A la Recherche* and in the final work itself. It is clear that the *Comédie Humaine* deeply influenced Proust's attitude to fiction and his use of traditional techniques; it is worth nothing, too, at this point that while Proust drew extensively on Balzac, he never possessed the latter's sheer technical skill in handling events on the gigantic scale demanded by the *Comédie Humaine*; though it would be unfair to say of Proust what Balzac himself says of Félicien in *Illusions Perdues* (Paris, Garnier, page 382):

> Félicien est incapable de concevoir une œuvre, d'en disposer les masses, d'en réunir harmonieusement les personnages dans un plan qui commence, se noue et marche vers un fait capital ...

nonetheless we shall see how Proust's ambition as a novelist sometimes exceeds his technical ability, particularly when it is compared with Balzac's mastery in dealing with similar situations. We shall refer at length to the methods of character presentation in the two writers, but an even more significant similarity exists in the presence both in the *Comédie Humaine* and in *A la Recherche du Temps Perdu* of the author's voice, giving his comments and explanations: the introduction

---

[11] *C.S.-B.,* pp. 413-416.
[12] See also Strauss: *op. cit.,* pp. 105-123.
[13] Pierre Abraham, *Proust, Recherches sur la création intellectuelle,* Paris, Rieder, 1930.
[14] See Fernandez's preface to Daudet's *Répertoire des Personnages: La Vie sociale dans l'œuvre de Marcel Proust.* Paris, Gallimard, 1928.
[15] *Balzac et Proust,* H. Levin, in the UNESCO *Hommage à Balzac,* Paris, Mercure de France, 1950.

of an external commentator is also a distinguishing feature of George Eliot whom Proust greatly admired, and it is obvious that he is attracted to those kinds of fiction which attempt to combine in this way the traditional techniques of the novelist and the reflexions and observations of the classical moralists. It would be interesting to know whether Proust had read the novels of Marivaux and, if so, what his opinion of them was, for Marivaux, much closer in time to the great moralists of the 17th century, and situated near the very beginnings of the novel in France, faced the same problems which confronted Proust, with his direct, personal link with the 17th century some one hundred and fifty years later, notably that of combining a fictional story with a moralist's observations and commentary. Though the 18th century writer occasionally uses his aphorisms to enhance the character of the heroine, nevertheless a whole commenting strain is introduced generally quite baldly, and superimposed unsubtly on the story—a fact which Marivaux does not attempt to hide:

> (Marianne) ne s'est refusé aucune des réflexions qui lui sont venues sur les accidents de sa vie; ses réflexions sont quelquefois courtes, quelquefois longues, suivant le goût qu'elle y a pris. [16]

—and the result is that the narrative thread often disappears for long intervals.

Proust belongs then to a special part of the tradition of the novel— *A la Recherche* being the amalgam of two sometimes complementary, sometimes quite opposite techniques and attitudes; he helps inaugurate the tradition of the international European novel, already taking shape at the end of the last century and to which writers such as Mann, Dostoevsky and Gide belonged, the tradition that Joyce entered with *Ulysses*. This demanded fresh techniques, a new way of combining intellectual inquiry and the traditional forms of the novel. But before discovering either these techniques or the final 'genre' represented by his novel, Proust grappled for a long time unsuccessfully with fictional writing, and it is the result of this experimentation, carried out under the shadow of the two great traditions Proust was conscious of having inherited, that we propose now to examine and apply to *A la Recherche du Temps Perdu*.

Proust's output divides conveniently into three main stages, the first being marked by the publication in 1896 of *Les Plaisirs et les Jours,* which continues in some measure the articles and reviews he had been contributing to *le Banquet,* collected and published with later material in 1927 under the title *Chroniques.* At the same time they announce *Jean Santeuil,* a work of fiction, since Proust in this early period is attracted both by fictional and non-fictional forms, and a study of *Les Plaisirs et les Jours* and *Chroniques* illustrates clearly the simultaneous pull towards and away from fictional forms.

---

[16] Marivaux, *La Vie de Marianne,* Paris, Stock, 1947, p. 23.

The failure of *Jean Santeuil* is followed significantly by a complete withdrawal from any further experiments in this field, and Proust concentrates on translation and commentary, producing in 1904 *La Bible d'Amiens* and in 1905 *Sésame et les Lys,* and then turning aside to pastiche. A transitional period which has aroused much critical interest [17] is represented by the writing in 1908 and 1909 of the essays now known and published as *Contre Sainte-Beuve,* where again the attitude towards fiction is curiously ambiguous.

The third and final period is entirely centred around *A la Recherche,* begun probably by the end of 1910 and well on its way to completion, in the first, Grasset, version, by early 1912. Thus the writer's whole career is strongly marked by a series of changing attitudes towards fictional 'genres', doubtless influenced by the doctrines of artists like Ruskin, who tended to lead Proust away from the long-contemplated novel form, and by the seeming failure which marked his attempts at composition, particularly in *Jean Santeuil.* The emphasis changes according to the 'reigning' influence of the moment, for Proust seems to have had a series of literary infatuations—notably for Ruskin and Balzac—which oriented his approach to literature in sometimes completely opposite directions. We shall attempt to trace these different orientations and show how first the 'moraliste' in Proust and then the novelist who lurked never far below the surface, approach, advance, retreat, and finally converge, sometimes uneasily, in *A la Recherche.*

An examination of the six fictional stories in *Les Plaisirs et les Jours* [18], reveals immediately Proust's interest in 'conventional' fictional forms and techniques. Yet at the same time, the pull away from such forms and techniques is startlingly apparent in the experiments in other 'genres', represented by the remaining, and larger part of the collection; moralising and fragmentary episodes in the manner of La Bruyère in *Fragments de Comédie Italienne* [19], attempts at a Musset-like 'spectacle dans un fauteuil' in *Scénario* [20], flattering compliments addressed to a lady, describing a salon painted on a fan and operating simultaneously in reality in *Evantail* [21]. All take their place beside more straightforward evocations of mood and place, with no attempt at transformation into dramatic or even fictional scenes, and patterns adopted wholesale from other novelists, like the cameo *Mondanité et Mélomanie de Bouvard et Pécuchet* [22]. This diversity of mood and style reveals occasional originality and considerable uncertainty about the form and even the 'genre' most suited to the ideas Proust wished to

---

[17] See particularly Henri Bonnet's meticulous *Marcel Proust de 1907 à 1914,* Paris, Nizet, 1959.

[18] *La Mort de Baldassare Silvande; Violante ou la mondanité; Mélancolique villégiature de Madame de Breyves; La Confession d'une jeune fille; Un Dîner en ville; and La Fin de la jalousie.*

[19] See note 5, p. 16.

[20] *P. et J.,* pp. 83-87.

[21] *P. et J.,* pp. 87-91.

[22] *P. et J.,* pp. 99-112.

express, but it will be noticed that beside the sometimes glittering array of techniques and pastiches in *Les Plaisirs et les Jours* the six fictional stories contain themes which are to recur throughout Proust's entire output, and which find their first expression in an unmistakably fictional setting. Thus despite the evidence of Proust's attraction to widely-differing 'genres' we may consider *Les Plaisirs et les Jours* as the first real attempt to use traditional techniques and to build a narrative around the central considerations of plot, character and situation.

At first sight, the fictional transpositions of *Les Plaisirs et les Jours* are disappointing. Technically they show a mixture of astonishingly sure fictional devices [23] and, at times, an almost complete ignorance of the basic necessities of the writer's craft. The general impression is often one of heavy immobility, aggravated by the unquestionably static and episodic quality of many of the stories. *La Mort de Baldassare Silvande,* for example, besides being fundamentally episodic in construction, is strikingly bare of movement and action. The tendency is always to present a ready-made situation, where the relationships between the various characters, or between characters and situations, are previously established. When Proust wishes to indicate change, he does so by stopping the narrative short, listing all the events supposed to have taken place in order to bring about the change in circumstances, and then proceding with the static description of the new state of affairs. The pushing of the action back into the pluperfect tense is particularly noticeable:

Le lendemain de la visite d'Alexis, *le vicomte de Sylvanie était parti* pour le château voisin ...
>   *(La Mort de Baldassare Silvande,* II, p. 27).

Les courses incessantes sur le cheval que son oncle lui *avait donné,* en développant ses forces *avaient lassé* tout son énervement.
>   *(ibid.,* III, p. 30).

Les émotions, les fatigues de Baldassare pendant la maladie de sa belle-sœur *avaient précipité* la marche de la sienne.
>   *(ibid.,* IV, pp. 39-40).

... on *avait dressé* son lit dans la vaste rotonde où Alexis l'*avait vu* le jour de ses treize ans, l'*avait vu* si joyeux encore.
>   *(ibid.,* V, p. 43).

This refusal to report action directly is noticeable not only at the beginning of each section or episode, but also within the episodes themselves; to show the passage of time, for example, Proust simply leaves

---

[23] See also the remark in Anatole France's laudatory though conventional preface to *P. et J.* (p. 9): 'Soudain, dans l'air lourd et délicieux, passe une flèche lumineuse, un éclair qui, comme le rayon du docteur allemand, traverse les corps. D'un trait le poète a pénétré la pensée secrète, le désir inavoué. C'est sa manière et son art. Il y montre une sureté qui surprend en un si jeune archer'.

a blank in the narrative, describes a later scene, and finds himself once again forced to list, in the pluperfect tense, the events separating the two moments in time [24].

Just as the pluperfect tense is often the sign of Proust's desire to furnish a brief résumé of events which do not interest him particularly, so the imperfect tense generally appears when Proust is occupied in his favorite exercise of describing static, psychological situations. Again using *La Mort de Baldassare Silvande* as an example, we are introduced almost immediately in the opening paragraphs into the realm of Alexis' psychological relationship with his uncle and although the dialogue with which the whole story opens makes some attempt to situate the narrative at a particular time, nonetheless it remains slight and receives much less attention than the description of Alexis' feelings about Baldassare [25].

The result, then, of the importance placed upon psychological analysis and commentary (which is not, at this stage, always of a very high order [26]) is to draw the emphasis away from the events *producing* the successive situations, until they either become the equivalent of stage directions, or are drained of their inherent dramatic potential. In *Violante ou la Mondanité,* written two years earlier than *La Mort de Baldassare Silvande,* Violante's unhappy infatuation for Laurence, 'un jeune Anglais', although used as the basis [27] of one of the décisive disillusionments in the story, is dismissed briefly:

> Violante était éprise, elle fut dédaignée. Laurence aimait le monde, elle l'aimait pour le suivre. Mais Laurence n'y avait pas de regards pour cette campagnarde de vingt ans. [28]

and the dramatic change in Honoré is related in so calm and un-impassioned a tone that it is scarcely credible [29].

If the reporting of action, situation and plot suffer from a reluctance to adopt the necessary fictional techniques, and the preference for analytic observation inserted within a fictional mould tends to annul the impact of the stories, characterisation also suffers from the evidently divided interest that Proust continues to reveal in *Les Plaisirs et les Jours.* The disdain that constantly shows itself in Proust's writing for the tools of the writer's craft may be traced to the tradition embodied by writers like Saint-Simon [30], but the shadowy characterisation in the

---

[24] *La Mort de Baldassare Silvande,* section II, p. 28.
[25] *La Mort de Baldassare Silvande,* section I, pp. 17-19.
[26] For example, the superficiality of Alexis' reaction to his uncle's imminent death in section III, p. 31.
[27] 'Elle avait depuis longtemps pris son parti de (la méchanceté) des hommes.' *Violante ou la Mondanité,* chapter V, p. 63.
[28] *Violante ou la Mondanité,* chapter III, p. 57.
[29] *Violante ou la Mondanité,* chapter V, pp. 60-61.
[30] A point made by Mouton (*op. cit.,* p. 61), and echoed by Cattaui, *Marcel Proust,* Paris, Julliard, 1952, who sees Proust essentially as an 'ennemi des procédés littéraires' (p. 226).

six stories of *Les Plaisirs et les Jours* owes something too to Proust's lack of experience and uncertainty as to the role the characters should play in fiction. What could be less convincing than the 'portrait', far removed in technique from the striking, living portraits of Saint-Simon, of Violante and her parents?

> La vicomtesse de Styrie était généreuse et tendre et toute pénétrée d'une grâce qui charmait. L'esprit du vicomte son mari était extrêmement vif, et les traits de sa figure d'une régularité admirable. Mais le premier grenadier venu était plus sensible et moins vulgaire. Ils élevèrent loin du monde, dans le rustique domaine de Styrie, leur fille Violante, qui, belle et vive comme son père, charitable et mystérieusement séduisante autant que sa mère, semblait unir les qualités de ses parents dans une proportion parfaitement harmonieuse. [31]

In fact, as W.L. Hodson remarks, [32] Violante is not a character at all, 'but a peg on which Proust has hung certain reflexions on the awakening of love and the invasion of the soul by boredom and routine'. This, of course, is true of Proust's whole attitude towards fiction in *Les Plaisirs et les Jours,* and the result it has on all the techniques is clear: Proust is not really interested in creating characters, any more then he is concerned with portraying convincing action or detail; his conception of fiction is one that will perform the technical function of providing a framework for his observations on life and death. To say, therefore, that *Violante ou la Mondanité* is about 'mondanité and not Violante,' and *La Mort de Baldassare Silvande* about dying and not about Baldassare [33] is simply to point out the overwhelming emphasis placed upon non-fictional considerations in a fictional framework, the conflict, showing itself in a particularly concrete way in character presentation, between the techniques of the moralist and those of the novelist.

The basic attitude towards fiction, then, in *Les Plaisirs et les Jours,* is ambivalent and the use of fiction in a secondary, illustrative role recalls immediately the cameos and portraits which adorn *Les Caractères,* proving a point or emphasising a moral, but rarely existing in their own right. However, Proust has chosen to use a fictional framework with certain curious results. Preferring to neglect a completely fictional transposition of experience, his stories take on a didactic character, and much of the narration is handled directly by commentary and explanation. Though all but one of the stories are written in the third person, we are present here at the first concrete example of the emergence of a first-person narrator—foreshadowing the developments in the later *Jean Santeuil*—who has to deal with narration in a way that will compensate for Proust's lack of concern for traditional techniques.

---

[31] *Violante ou la mondanité,* chapter I, pp. 49-50.
[32] W.L. Hodson, *op. cit.,* p. 41.
[33] *Ibid.,* pp. 41-42.

Action, when called for by the pattern of the story, is either stripped to its bare essentials, as we have seen, until it appears in the light in which Proust himself evidently considered it, or characterisation and the exploitation of dramatic possibilities are swept aside and reaction, in which Proust is really interested, is conveyed by reported speech and explanation provided by an unseen 'narrator'. Having chosen to concentrate on analysis and explanation, Proust finds himself naturally resorting to a commenting narrator, to reinforce the thread of the story, which suffers from a lack of dynamism. This is the impression gained from an examination of the passage in *La mort de Baldassare Silvande* were Alexis' mother is dangerously injured. As usual the necessary action is introduced simply, and in fact reads like a newspaper report of an accident [34]. The Viscount's reaction is presented straightforwardly, and then the whole episode is given its real interpretation by the narrator who retells the story in new and different terms:

> Quand la mort était venue à lui peu à peu il n'avait pas voulu la voir; maintenant il s'était trouvé subitement en sa présence. Elle l'avait épouvanté en menaçant ce qu'il avait de plus cher; il l'avait suppliée, il l'avait fléchie. [35]

The consequences of the emergence of this new element, compensating for the lack of self-explanatory, visual scenes, are clear. Proust is no longer obliged to remain a neutral observer; he can infuse his own personal sentiments into the fictional narrative—he emits judgments:

a) The humorous comment on Alexis' decision to withdraw to a desert refuge:

> Heureusement, plus puissante que leurs moqueries (his parents), la vie dont il n'avait pas encore épuisé le lait fortifiant et doux tendit son sein pour le dissuader. [36]

b) The moral judgment contained in the sententious, Balzacian remark of the narrator:

> Les anges exterminateurs qu'on appelle Volonté, Pensée, n'étaient plus là pour faire rentrer dans l'ombre les mauvais esprits de ses sens et les basses émanations de sa mémoire. [37]

c) The cynical amusement on defining a love affair:

> Violante fut amoureuse, c'est-à-dire qu'un jeune Anglais qui s'appelait Laurence fut pendant plusieurs mois l'objet de ses pensées les plus insignifiantes, le but de ses plus importantes actions. [38]

---

[34] 'Un après-midi qu'elle allait voir le vicomte, presque au moment d'arriver chez lui, ses chevaux prirent peur; elle fut projetée violemment à terre, foulée par un cavalier, qui passait au galop, et emportée chez Baldassare sans connaissance, le crâne ouvert.' *La Mort de Baldassare Silvande*, p. 37.

[35] *Ibid.*, p. 38.

[36] *Ibid.*, p. 26.

[37] *Ibid.*, p. 44.

[38] *Violante ou la mondanité*, chapter III, p. 57.

d) The criticism of society, placed in the present tense:

Les personnes du monde sont si médiocres que Violante n'eut qu'à daigner se mêler à elles pour les éclipser presque toutes. [39]

e) Generalisations, [40] and an open invitation to the reader to read on, if he wishes to see a change in Violante:

Nous verrons qu'elle peut considérer un peu plus tard que l'amour sensuel était moins encore. [41]

This development may be considered as the first step towards the 'double vision' technique of *A la Recherche,* which we shall examine later. Here, the narrator is left vague, his personality and place in time left unspecified. Yet already Proust is beginning to make him the vehicle for certain reflexions, often of a 'moraliste' nature, which transform his neutral role as the 'ideal' third-person narrator into one of a more personal and individual nature.

The interest in first-person narration is not confined, however, to the development and individualisation of the 'ideal' narrator of third-person narrative. Two further stories, *Mélancolique villégiature de Madame de Brèyves* [42] and *La Confession d'une jeune fille* illustrate the way in which first-person narrative is brought to the aid of a writer torn between two conflicting attitudes towards fictional composition. Evident in the first twelve pages of *Mélancolique villégiature*—a little over half the narrative—is a considerable attempt to fulfil all the exigencies of 'traditional' fiction, notably in the creation of characters and situations sufficiently convincing to hold the reader's attention and to order the course of events. The effort is not sustained, for the author's interest in Françoise de Brèyves' psychological state soon outweighs all other considerations—pages 124-134 dispensing entirely with all attempts to write visual or dramatic narrative [43]. It is at this point that Proust introduces a new, independent but characterised narrator, who helps add a new dimension to the person of Françoise, but who quickly assumes the function of commentator and interpreter. He is not the same person as the invisible narrator of the preceding sections, since, while the latter had been led to comment and generalise, from time to time, [44] he was never associated as the new 'je' is with the fictional situation. He remarks:

C'est à Trouville que je *viens de trouver* Madame de Brèyves, que *j'avais connue* plus heureuse. Rien ne peut la guérir. [45]

---

[39] *Ibid.,* chapter IV, p. 59.
[40] *Ibid.,* chapter IV, p. 61.
[41] *Ibid.,* chapter IV, p. 60.
[42] Written in July 1893.
[43] This dual treatment of material is far from being unconvincing since the psychological examination of Françoise can be seen to arise directly from the train of events preceding it.
[44] For example, *Mélancolique Villégiature,* section III, p. 119.
[45] *Ibid.,* section V, p. 129.

But then the narrator's purpose changes, and the pull between fiction and abstract commentary breaks out afresh. For here Proust has provided himself with an opportunity to add a new dimension to his central character, adding to the viewpoints already projected by Geneviève, M. de Laléande and even M. de Grumello. The new 'je', who has been observing Françoise in her Trouville retreat, seems to be on the point of adding a new testimony to complete our knowledge of Proust's heroine but instead prefers to rationalise about the phenomenon of love, shifting the emphasis away from Françoise altogether.

In *La Confession,* the first person narrator is placed in the foreground and acts as both heroine and commentator. By making her tell her past history to provide the key to her attempted suicide, moreover, Proust invests the observations and commentary in which she indulges with great significance, successfully combining a commentary on the action with the presentation of the action itself. Here, then, is a step-forward in narrative presentation, resulting from the ingenious use of the first-person narrator: the point of view, the perspective through which the whole narrative is seen, is that of the dying narrator. The story thus presented is coloured by the addition of subsequent experience which adds a second layer of meaning, the technique which, after many trials and experiments, Proust will turn to again in *A la Recherche du Temps Perdu.*

Les Plaisirs et les Jours illustrate the uncertain attitude towards the whole question of fiction versus abstract commentary and analysis, the confrontation of Proust's two instinctive tendencies in composition. Significantly, this clash produces the first and probably most important technique which will leave its mark on the whole plan and ordering of *A la Recherche*—that, as yet little exploited, though handled carefully, of retrospective first-person narration. Yet the fact that probably at about the same time that he was writing *La Confession* Proust was planning a long novel in the third person suggests that its 'discovery' in *Les Plaisirs et les Jours* had not assumed the same significance for the young Proust that it has for the critic looking back over the writer's early works for 'revealing' tendencies. Indeed, while it is legitimate perhaps to see in *Les Plaisirs et les Jours* a conscious attempt to discover suitable forms to fit preoccupying themes, it must be remembered that these very themes were in a state of flux, and it is not until the later stages of *Jean Santeuil* that they seem to take a permanent form [46].

We have seen how Proust's interest in analysis leads him to extend, and in some cases to distort the fictional patterns into which he inserts observation and commentary. At the same time, it must be pointed out that his interest in fictional techniques was growing rapidly, and that

---

[46] See *The Genesis of the Involontary Memory in Proust's early works,* by Elizabeth Jackson, *PMLA,* Dec. 1961. It is sometimes as well to remember that scholars, as Saintsbury once remarked, are
"Priests that slay the slayer
And shall themselves be slain."

his skill in handling purely narrative forms shows a marked development in *Les Plaisirs et les Jours*. Once again the ambivalence is noticeable, not only in the conception of fiction, but in the skill with which fictional techniques are put to work.

First, Proust evolves techniques to bind together more closely the two sides of his writing in the person of a 'chorus', whose function it is to point out the meaning and possible dangers of the action. In *Violante ou la Mondanité*, Augustin, steward to Violante, points out to her the errors of her behaviour and interprets her actions to herself. The need to provide a constant commentary which we have already drawn attention to, is here transformed into a technical device, becoming part of the narrative texture instead of giving rise to a second and symbolic interpretation of events by an external commentator. Thus Augustin combines the role of confidant, [47] chorus [48] and omniscient even ubiquitous onlooker, with a distinctly dramatic function in the development of the story, for each exchange marks a new stage in the development of Violante's love of society and her subsequent disillusion [49].

Second, Proust pays considerable attention to the creation of dialogue and situation. Many of the conversations between Augustin and Violante are eminently dramatic:

> ... Je reviendrai dans notre Styrie, vivre auprès de toi, mon cher.
> — Le pourrez-vous? dit Augustin.
> — On peut ce qu'on veut, dit Violante.
> — Mais vous ne voudrez peut-être plus la même chose, dit Augustin.
> — Pourquoi, demanda Violante.
> — Parce que vous aurez changé. [50]

—and with the greatest simplicity of style and language, Proust uses a series of related conversations to form the entire framework of the story, a device he repeats in *Mélancolique Villégiature*.

Third, Proust shows a preoccupation with questions of form, shape, symmetry and balance. The scene, for example, where Violante is instructed by Henri in the secrets of love [51] is balanced by a corresponding scene between Violante and the princesse de Misène, in which her education is completed [52]. This scene is carefully constructed with a preparatory introduction, exposition and conclusion. The same attention to detail and its relationship to the overall plan is evident, too, in the device used to emphasise the change in Violante. It consists of two passages, separated by a page and a half, presenting two opposite situations in identical terms:

---

[47] *Violante ou la Mondanité*, p. 43.
[48] *Ibid.*, pp. 57-58.
[49] *Ibid.*, pp. 53, 58, 60, 61-62.
[50] *Ibid.*, chapter III, p. 58.
[51] *Ibid.*, pp. 51-52.
[52] *Ibid.*, pp. 62-63.

Bientôt elle dit chaque soir à son mari:
— Nous partirons après-demain pour ma Styrie et nous ne la quitterons plus.

and:

— Partirons-nous demain? demandait le duc.
— Après-demain, répondait Violante.
Puis le duc cessa de l'interroger. [53]

Fourth, Proust shows much skill in varying the pace and tempo of his narrative. Françoise's efforts in *Mélancolique Villégiature* meet with failure again and again, but the pull of her fascination creates new emotional rhythms all the time. Similarly he is adept at introducing dramatic changes of event, like, for example, the unexpected advances M. de Laléande makes to Françoise, which are all the more surprising for the sharp contrast they provide with his former lack of reaction to her previous, delicate manœuverings [54]. He makes efforts to remain in strict control of his material, insisting on concision, cutting parentheses and explanations to a minimum [55], shaping each section with great care and often introducing a note of significant detail to sharpen a point [56], even quoting Baudelaire to do so [57].

The most significant experiments in fictional techniques are those where Proust begins to consider the possibility of working into a fictional story the passage of time, and the consequent interest he develops in the problems of chronology. We have already referred to the construction of *La Confession d'une jeune fille,* where time plays an integral part in the plan and narrative tone. In this story, the use of the 'flash-back' technique, introducing the reader dramatically to the narrator—heroine, permits him to re-live her past as she meditates on the attempts leading up to her attempt on her life. She begins by recalling the park known as *Les Oublis,* and it is not hard to see in the jolt this memory gives the narrator's train of thought the more polished, though basically similar device of the *madeleine* in *Combray* [58]. The impression Proust gives of moving freely and confidently within this framework is strengthened by the ingenious way in which he exploits the 'flash-back' technique to the full. It is perhaps by surveying the overall time-structure of *La Confession* that we can best appreciate Proust's intention: as in *Mélancolique Villégiature,* the preoccupation is with the growth and development of a passion. The methods of approach and interpretation which characterise the two stories differ

---

[53] *Ibid.,* pp. 63 and 65 and cf. *Mélancolique Villégiature,* pp. 115-116, where the same device is repeated.
[54] *Mélancolique Villégiature de Madame de Brèyyes,* section II, p. 116.
[55] *Ibid.,* section I, p. 114; section II, p. 117.
[56] *Ibid.,* pp. 114, 118, 121-122.
[57] *Ibid.,* section IV, p. 128.
[58] *La Confession d'une jeune fille,* p. 142.

profoundly, however, since in *La Confession* the growth of passion is clearly related to time and time plays a role in the story, whereas in *Mélancolique Villégiature* this is not the case. In *La Confession* the narrator is situated straightaway in the present, and the whole time progression centred around the growth of remorse in the narrator at different, earlier, stages in her life. These are continuously related to the moment of narration (by means of commentary and explanation [59]) with the result that past and present are juxtaposed throughout, throwing up new perspectives as the narrative progresses, and the narrator's story moves nearer to the present. Not only is this progression of time recorded, then, but a natural climax is achieved, when the narrator's life and the moment of narration fuse:

> Alors tandis que le plaisir me tenait de plus en plus, je sentais s'éveiller, au fond de mon cœur, une tristesse et une désolation infinies... ce n'est pas la dernière fois que je vous le raconte: je vous l'ai dit, je me suis presque manquée... [60]

It can be seen how perfectly this technique provides Proust with the opportunity of experimenting with the confrontation of past and present. Here the device is scarcely exploited at all, except in the evocation of the flowers which somehow survive the journey from past to present [61]; the whole theme of 'psychologie dans le temps' would fit in well and, indeed, seems to suggest itself for an instant [62].

It is clear that chronology in fictional narrative presents a fascinating challenge to Proust, even as early as 1896, the year in which *Les Plaisirs et les Jours* were published. He is never afraid to experiment boldly and risks the presentation of doubly-past time without hesitation. In general, apart from the passage mentioned above, where the narrative becomes incomprehensible, Proust always appears sure of himself, and in the main his experiments succeed.

Les Plaisirs et les Jours illustrate the influence on Proust of techniques and attitudes reflecting both the moralist, in the meaning implied in the French 'moraliste' [63], and the novelist. Not only is there hesitation in choosing a 'genre', but the treatment of fictional forms is often curiously ambivalent. At the same time, Proust shows a real interest in the technical possibilities of 'traditional' fiction, and experiments with chronological and a-chronological narrative presentation. He shows, by his indecision about whether to use first or third-person forms an aesthetic conscience often in conflict with a moral conscience,

---

[59] *Ibid.*, pp. 143, 144, 145, 146.
[60] *Ibid.*, pp. 157-158.
[61] *Ibid.*, p. 147.
[62] 'Hélas! en même temps qu'en moi, c'est hors de moi que *mon âme de quatorze ans se réveille encore. Je sais bien qu'elle n'est plus mon âme et qu'il ne dépend plus de moi qu'elle la redevienne.' Ibid.*, p. 147.
[63] That is to say, a tradition embodying not only moralising commentaries on life, but also lively portraits, disconnected aphorisms, striking observations, all recorded in a more or less critical vein, but not necessarily adding up to a consistent, or even damaging view of humanity.

which tries at all times to shift the obsessions and preoccupations he feels within himself onto the shoulders of fictional characters, whose substance he is incapable of filling out, while writing all the time in a form verging on the confessional first-person narrative. The need to provide a continuous commenting element is also evident in Proust's attempts to compromise between this form and straightforward third-person narrative: the introduction of characters who will take over one of the techniques for a few pages and then disappear, the creation of a personal narrator in objective narrative.

Concurrently with the writing of *Les Plaisirs et les Jours,* Proust was contributing non-fictional articles to Parisian newspapers and seems to have been far more at ease with the absence of technical problems these allowed him. It will therefore be illuminating, in the following chapter, to examine the considerable influence they exert on the still rapidly-evolving narrative techniques of Marcel Proust.

CHRONIQUES

Chroniques, published with the final volumes of *A la Recherche du Temps Perdu* in 1927, contains a set of articles which Proust had contributed to the *Figaro, le Banquet, Littérature et Critique, La Revue Blanche* and *La Nouvelle Revue Française,* and covers the period ranging from 1892 to that marked by the critical studies which continued to appear up to a year before his death. By concentrating on the pieces written between 1892 and 1904, we shall be able to see Proust, this time writing essentially non-fictional articles which allow him all the freedom he needs to develop his sometimes rambling observations, being pulled inexorably to a fictional, even dramatic form of presentation. In his introduction to *Chroniques,* Robert Proust remarks:

> Nous avons pensé que les lecteurs d'*A la Recherche du Temps Perdu* seraient heureux de connaître de Marcel Proust jusqu'aux plus reculées de ses œuvres et de pouvoir ensuite suivre pas à pas l'évolution de sa pensée. [64]

The articles of *Chroniques* reveal also a further step-forward in the evolution of his narrative techniques.

Contre l'obscurité, written in 1896 and appearing that year in *La Revue Blanche,* contains valuable information about Proust's evolving attitude towards fiction, and the techniques it necessarily implies. He states that purely symbolic works, if they do not contain convincing characters and situations, tend to lose both in *vraisemblance* and in real depth, and take on the form of allegory [65]. Now this, as we have just seen, is precisely the fault of most of the stories in *Les Plaisirs et les Jours,* where characterisation is poor and little attention paid to the creation of situations. The theory is clearly defined, and it is only the lack of experience that is preventing Proust from putting it into practice. At the same time, significant attempts are noticeable in some of the articles, including *Contre l'obscurité,* to remedy this problem

---

[64] Robert Proust, Introduction to *Chroniques,* Paris, Gallimard, 1927, p. 8.
[65] 'Les œuvres purement symboliques risquent donc de manquer de vie et par là de profondeur. Si, de plus, au lieu de toucher l'esprit, leurs 'princesses' et leurs 'chevaliers' proposent un sens imprécis et difficile à sa perspicacité, les poèmes, qui devraient être de vivants symboles, ne sont plus que de froides allégories.' *Chroniques: Contre l'obscurité,* p. 143.

and to create convincing characters, even during the course of purely
intellectual argument. The introduction, into the texture of a theoretical
and explanatory text on modern poetry, of a form of dramatic dialogue
between the author and the school of *'jeunes poètes'*, whose obscurantist
tendencies he is denouncing, is thus particularly interesting. Beginning
with a question supposedly addressed by *tout monsieur de cinquante
ans* to *tout étudiant de vingt ans qui fait de la littérature,* the article
develops into a cameo containing the former's comments on the literary
scene, whose lively and almost visual nature will be repeated later:

> "Etes-vous de la jeune école?" demande à tout étudiant de vingt ans
> qui fait de la littérature tout monsieur de cinquante ans qui n'en fait
> pas. "Moi, j'avoue que je ne comprends pas, il faut être initié... D'ail-
> leurs, il n'y a jamais eu plus de talent: aujourd'hui presque tout le monde
> a du talent". [66]

For Proust's method of denouncing the fundamental aesthetic mis-
conception of his opponents is to present their viewpoint in the form
of reported dialogue, during which what might have remained shadowy,
'allegorical' figures really come to life. The innovators' preliminary
argument, for example, that all new poetry seems at first obscure, is
refuted by Proust who, addressing them directly, after congratulating
them on their clever way of dodging the issue, retorts:

> Ne voulant pas sans doute faire allusion aux écoles précieuses, vous avez
> joué sur le mot 'obscurité' en faisant remonter si haut la noblesse de
> la vôtre... [67]

This draws forth the immediate reply:

> Vous vous étonnez que le maître soit obligé d'expliquer ses idées à ses
> disciples. Mais n'est-ce pas ce qui est toujours arrivé dans l'histoire de
> la philosophie...? [68]

Having thus established the two fundamentally opposed theories, Proust
breaks off from his dramatic dialogue to develop at length the objections to obscurantism in poetry. However, the conception of the
exchange of ideas in dialogue form is never far away, nor the idea of
personalised examples of tendencies and literary schools, for at one
point he addresses another reproach directly to the 'jeunes prêtres' [69],
and, at another, evokes the type of philosophising novelist whom he
singles out for attention [70]. In *Silhouette d'artiste,* the process is carried
a stage further; in evoking the kind of theatrical critic who is subject
to *la nécessité d'aller souvent au théâtre et l'illusion de s'y sentir
regardé* [71], Proust begins naturally to create the critic himself, capturing

---

[66] *Ibid.,* p. 137.
[67] *Ibid.,* p. 139.
[68] *Ibid.,* p. 139.
[69] *Ibid.,* p. 141.
[70] *Ibid.,* p. 140.
[71] *Silhouette d'Artiste,* p. 11.

his style, language and vocabulary, and presenting a living example of his subject's literary and social mannerisms. Though never introducing dialogue, or stopping to draw a visual portrait of his victim, a character nevertheless clearly emerges from the wealth of quotations which show the shallowness of the critic and the superficiality of his judgments; he uses conventional, meaningless phrases:

> Sarah Bernhardt un jour 'cherchait visiblement à se surpasser'. Le lendemain, elle était 'au-dessus d'elle-même' et 'n'a pas donné ce qu'elle aurait pu'. [72]

and speaks in a precious, pretentious style:

> S'il échappe au critique une locution telle que 'tandis que M. Worms s'esbigue', il ajoute plaisamment 'comme dirait feu Royer-Collard' ou 'si j'ose m'exprimer ainsi'. [73]

The impression created by *Silhouette d'artiste* is that Proust has set down his observations with obvious delight, with the intention of doing no more than to record certain impressions of the world of dramatic criticism, but that in doing so he has almost accidentally created a living character who has transformed a *froide allégorie* into a *vivant symbole,* for what might easily have been a general denunciation of superficiality and affectation in dramatic criticism has been made to come vividly alive by the use of fictional techniques.

Another indication that Proust is preoccupying himself with the problem of the transference of a 'sentimental' reality to a fictional background is contained in his article reviewing Louis Ganderax's novel *Les Petits Souliers* [74]. Here he states that fictional reality cannot be obtained without transferring much of the simple, accessory detail of everyday reality into that fiction. Again, this illuminates *Les Plaisirs et les Jours* where detail is left on one side, and points to the coming change in attitude in *Un Amour de Swann,* for example, where the love-affair is closely related to the 'accessory' evolution of the Verdurin salon [75]. Thus, the reviewing of works by other writers gives Proust the opportunity to reconsider some of the basic problems connected with the art of fiction. But even more significant, perhaps, is the unexpected appearance, within journalistic articles in fashionable newspapers, of certain unmistakable fictional techniques.

Le Salon de la Princesse Mathilde [76] provides a clear example of the introduction of fictional techniques into journalism. In order to

---

[72] *Ibid.,* p. 12.
[73] *Ibid.,* p. 12.
[74] *Un conte de Noël, Chroniques,* pp. 125-129, written in 1892.
[75] *Ibid.,* p. 128: 'C'est que l'art plonge si avant ses racines dans la vie sociale que dans la fiction particulière dont on revêt une réalité sentimentale très générale, les mœurs, les goûts d'une époque ou d'une classe ont souvent une grande part, et peuvent même en aviver singulièrement l'agrément'.
[76] *Chroniques,* pp. 14-27; written in February 1903.

evoke the 'essence' of the Princess, Proust deliberately refuses to analyse or generalise; instead he recreates the visual scene offered every evening to the guests at the Princess' house in the rue de Berri:

> Mais pourquoi analyser le charme de cet accueil? *J'aime mieux essayer de vous le faire sentir en vous montrant la princesse en train de recevoir.* [77]

The maximum amount of reality is aimed at; Proust invites the reader to accompany him to the rue de Berri where the soirées are held [78], the scene is set as though the author were describing a theatrical decor, with explanations of the situation as it was before the curtain went up [79]; the action is set in the present, and the stage indications about the position of doors and vestibules carefully indicated [80]. The curtain up, the author begins to point out the figures in the tableau which stands revealed:

> A côté de la princesse, une ou deux des habituées de ses dîners de la rue de Berri: la comtesse Benedetti, si spirituellement jolie et si joliment spirituelle; Mme Espinasse, dame d'honneur de la princesse ... [81]

—a tableau where the actors are tensed with expectation, as they wait for the after-dinner guests to arrive. The technique, as can be seen, is dramatic, and effectively so: from a general catalogue of the Princess' *bons mots,* we have suddenly been transported to one of her receptions, and are now introduced into her presence as though we too were among her guests for the evening. This approach is repeated in *Le Salon de Mme Madeleine Lemaire* [82] where again the method is one of raising a curtain and displaying the activity, this time in Mme Lemaire's *atelier,* putting names to the figures who from time to time move across the stage and commenting on their conversations and actions. In the same way as in the Princesse Mathilde article, Proust sets the scene, [83] describes the room, its portraits and the roses Mme Lemaire has been painting, describes the guests' arrival, points to latecomers' efforts to perch on stools and chairs [84]; Mme Lemaire's own attempts to make room for Jean Béraud who has arrived too late

---

[77] *Ibid.,* p. 15. My italics.
[78] *Ibid.,* p. 15: 'Suivez-moi rue de Berri et ne nous attardons pas trop, car la soirée n'y commence pas tard.'
[79] 'On a dîné de bonne heure. Pas aussi tôt peut-être qu'à l'époque où Alfred de Musset vint...' *Ibid.,* p. 15.
[80] '... un grand fauteuil qu'on aperçoit à droite en venant du dehors, mais au fond de la pièce. En venant du grand hall, ce fauteuil serait au contraire à gauche, et fait face à la porte de la petite pièce, où, tout à l'heure, seront servis les rafraîchissements.' *Ibid.,* p. 15.
[81] *Ibid.,* p. 16.
[82] *La Cour aux lilas et l'atelier des roses: Chroniques,* pp. 28-38.
[83] 'La soirée vient de commencer au milieu du travail ininterrompu de l'aquarelliste... A côté (des roses), un portrait commencé, déjà magnifique de jolie ressemblance, d'après Mme Kinen...' *Ibid.,* p. 31.
[84] *Ibid.,* p. 32.

to find a seat [85], punctuating the narrative all the time with humorous comments and comparisons, like the one he makes between M. Mézières and Prince Antoine Bibesco and a high priest consulting Apollo. [86]

Equally present in the articles destined for social and literary journals is Proust's tendency, noticed earlier in fictional contexts, to experiment with chronology. *Le Salon de la Princesse Mathilde* contains a kind of dialogue between past and present, in which scenes from the past, retold vividly in dialogue and often very amusingly, illuminate the present, where, apart from the arrival of the guests, no action is reported, no anecdote recounted and no character sketched in. He calls up, for example, the memory of Count Benedetti, and of the amusing companion who provides the remark about 'les tables tournantes' for the later *Un Amour de Swann,* effecting a transition by neatly making an object in the room the point of departure for an evocation of the past [87]. It is a technique with clear affinities, again, with the Combray *madeleine* episode. The transition back to the present is managed equally skilfully, by making the activity of the arriving guests disturb the train of thought conjured up by memory [88].

Particularly significant is the evolution in a journalistic article of a fictional technique, which in *A la Recherche* recurs constantly, becoming part of its basic construction. The soirées of the later work owe much to the evocation of actual evenings spent in the houses of fashionable society hostesses and collected in *Chroniques*. Not only do many of the anecdotes appear there for the first time [89] but the very pattern of the long soirées of *A la Recherche* is evolved too. To take once again the article on Madeleine Lemaire as an example, the symmetry and attention to form which always underline the great soirées of *A la Recherche* is immediately apparent. First the reader is presented with the scene before the majority of the guests arrive; he is then carried along on a rapid crescendo which leads to the climax of Reynaldo Hahn's performance, after which the guests depart, and finally a diminuendo movement takes him back to a scene, placed in symmetrical opposition to the first, leading to the vision of Mme Lemaire seeing off the last of her guests:

Puis, tout s'éteint, flambeaux et musique de fête. [90]

The idea of crowning a society function with a musical item seems to have been developed naturally from the accounts of real soirées, though it should be noticed that the effect desired, and obtained, in this article is quite different from that apparent in *A la Recherche*. For

---

[85] *Ibid.,* p. 33.
[86] *Ibid.,* p. 34.
[87] *Le Salon de la princesse Mathilde,* p. 16.
[88] *Ibid.,* p. 18.
[89] The whole of *Le Salon de la princesse Mathilde* is constructed round a string of such anecdotes; see pp. 14-27.
[90] *La Cour aux lilas,* p. 38.

here the object of ordering the narrative around a central episode is clearly meant as a compliment to the singer, not to the aesthetic or emotive value of the music he is performing. We are forced to the conclusion that many of the techniques which will reappear refined and developed in *A la Recherche* were evolved early [91], but their possibilities not always recognised. Proust's musical appreciation is, as yet, so shallow as to appear ludicrous [92] and it is clear from the very closely observed portrait of Proust's friend Reynaldo Hahn that here is the centre of the author's attention [93]. To use Painter's terms [94], Proust is still in Time Lost, but his techniques are often already those of Time Regained [95].

The attraction of fictional devices, then, continues to exert an influence over Proust, even to the extent of transforming newspaper articles into miniature sketches of *A la Recherche du Temps Perdu,* and encouraging him to continue in a new and non-fictional setting experiments, particularly in Time transposition, which had already been a feature of *Les Plaisirs et les Jours.* However, if fictional techniques are introduced into non-fictional writing, it is also possible to detect a very clear influence upon later fictional writing of the experiments embodied in the articles of *Chroniques.*

When the *NRF* produced its *Hommage à Marcel Proust,* one of the most penetrating remarks to come from its distinguished list of contributors was the following comment by Stephen Hudson on the very particular relationship Proust somehow sets up between himself and his reader:

> Lorsque je me demande, he wrote, ce qu'il y a de spécifiquement indivi-duel dans l'œuvre de Proust, la première chose qui me vient à l'esprit, c'est que peut-être aucun autre écrivain n'a forgé des liens aussi étroits entre lui et son lecteur.

It is in *Chroniques* that this intimate relationship begins for the first time to develop, and it owes much to the easy way Proust projects into these articles, many of whose probable readers he knew personally, even intimately, the best of his own personality. This is a characteristic scarcely discernible in *Les Plaisirs et les Jours,* in which, indeed, Proust often deliberately hides behind the objectivity of third-person nar-rative [96]. Freed from the problems of conventional fictional composition,

---

[91] Cf. *La Confession d'une jeune fille.*
[92] *La Cour aux lilas,* p. 36.
[93] *Ibid.,* pp. 36-37.
[94] George D. Painter: *Marcel Proust, a biography,* Vol. I, London, Chatto and Windus, 1959.
[95] Particularly in the effect of the music upon the audience, — an effect remarkably similar to that created by Vinteuil's sonata, while the poetry of the narrator's reaction is foreshadowed in the magnificent '... silencieuse et solennelle ondulation des blés sous le vent' — p. 37.
[96] Mouton, *op. cit.,* p. 43, also remarks on 'cet éloignement de son texte' and adds: 'Cette attitude se révèle particulièrement sensible dans *Les Plaisirs et les Jours* où le moule un peu rigide de la phrase isole en quelque sorte le narrateur de son récit.'

Proust immediately establishes an intimate relationship with the reader, while at the same time remaining sufficiently detached to impose on him opinions and generalisations. This is the tone that Proust continually seeks to rediscover and translate into a fictional setting.

What are the consequences of this narrative tone? First, Proust's still-present snobbery projects itself unfortunately from time to time, in the pretentious little joke about the Duc de Luynes' christian name, for example [97], and in the flattering remarks addressed to Mme Lemaire and her guests. He can also be ironically detached, however, as he observes Mlle Suzette Lemaire listening to Grosclaude [98], or the chagrin of Francis de Croisset's companion when his hostess bids him be quiet and listen to Reynaldo Hahn singing *Le Cimetière* [99]. Most characteristic, though, is the marked tendency to let the article follow the whims and fancies of the cultivated, unseen but strongly personalised narrator, who is none other than Proust himself. The sketch of the Count and Countess d'Haussonville in *Le Salon de la comtesse d'Haussonville* [100] is generally recognised to be the first attempt at recording two of the originals (there are many others) of the duc and duchesse de Guermantes. Now, Proust's real interest lies, not in their salon, as the title of the article might suggest, but in his two subjects, whom he knew personally, and in the literary and social themes they suggest, in any order, to his imagination. Since the only limitations imposed by the *Figaro* on Proust were presumably clarity and space, he could not have felt any obligation to limit himself to straightforward portraits of his sitters, but instead was free to embroider at will on the central theme, sometimes disappointingly, as in *Le Salon de la princesse Edmond de Polignac* [101], at others with more success, as in *Le Salon de la comtesse d'Haussonville*. The articles on the Princesse de Polignac, the Comtesse Potocka and the Contesse de Guerne [102] develop, with the help of Proust's new narrative tone, into discursive essays, in which literary allusions, social comments, the presence of time and history all find a place, refracted through the narrator's personality, around the central theme. There is generally no attempt to introduce symmetry or balance. For example, in the *Salon de la comtesse d'Haussonville* the introduction of the Count and Countess themselves is preceded by reflexions on Renan, quotations from his *discours de réception* at the Académie Française and a comparison between France and Germany [103]. In order to include M. d'Haussonville's attachment to his ancestral home, Coppet, anecdotes about the communist Jaurès appear [104]. Still by way of introduction, Proust criticises M. d'Hausson-

97 *La Cour aux lilas,* pp. 33-34.
98 *Ibid.,* p. 36.
99 *Ibid.,* p. 37.
100 *Chroniques,* pp. 47-54.
101 *Chroniques,* pp. 39-46.
102 *Chroniques,* pp. 39-46, 55-61, 62-66.
103 *Chroniques,* pp. 47-49.
104 *Chroniques,* p. 49.

ville's early works on his ancestress Mme de Staël, includes more anecdotes, this time about visitors to stately homes, tenuously linked with
an imagery tour *sous la conduite des Cook* of Coppet itself,[105] and
finally turns to the composition of the d'Haussonville salon. He soon
breaks off to meditate on Time, however,[106] and indulges in his favorite
device of confronting past and present in a single symbol. Eventually,
after listing more society 'names', he begins an appreciation of the
Countess and the Count—in that order, but still with digressions on
etymologies, Balzac, *Hercule* (an operetta by Gaston de Caillavet and
Robert de Fers), and referenes to the anti-catholic laws[107]. The
narrative tone, the presence of a cultivated, witty, urbane voice accompanying and directing the reader emerges through the loosely-knit
texture of the article—a tone which is to reappear in *A la Recherche,*
but with several important modifications. It is, indeed, strongly remi-
niscent of the essayist who, following an individual train of thought,
moves without difficulty from one topic to another, determined to pursue all the paths his imagination opens up, regardless of the logicality
of his argument. In fact, there is little attempt at argument proper,
Proust's method of proving his point being to multiply quotations and
anecdotes, which themselves suggest other topics often far removed
from the main theme. Allusions are often literary: Balzac occurs frequently in *Le Salon de la comtesse Potocka*[108], where references are
made both to entire works, like *Les Secrets de la princesse de Cadignan,*
or to particular figures in the *Comédie Humaine,* and quotations of
passages which spring to Proust's mind[109]. References to Saint-Simon,
Victor Hugo and Stendhal appear[110]; topical events are included 'en
passant', while the tendency to generalise is given a very wide rein,
as the narrator pursues his different flights of fancy.

We may conclude that it is precisely the lack of a recognisable
technique which characterises the essays of *Chroniques,* a lack of
technique which suddenly enriches the narrative by unleashing the
full force of Proust's many-sided personality and culture. As Bernard
de Fallois has more than half suggested, the development of a narrative
form which is so constituted as to allow Proust's personality to
emerge, instead of being stifled by the artificiality of the early stories,
is one of the most significant steps in Proust's career :

> Il s'agit moins d'un personnage que d'un ton. Et c'est pourquoi il faut
> y voir l'acquisition capitale de cette période. A travers les articles, les
> essais, les lettres, les comptes rendus, Proust a été amené, presque par
> force, à adopter cette première personne qui désormais va conduire tous
> ses récits.[111]

---

[105] *Chroniques,* p. 50.
[106] *Chroniques,* p. 51.
[107] *Chroniques,* pp. 52-54.
[108] *Chroniqesu,* p. 55.
[109] *Chroniques,* pp. 56, 57.
[110] *Chroniques,* pp. 55, 59, 64.
[111] Bernard de Fallois, preface to *Contre Sainte-Beuve,* Paris, Gallimard,
1954.

The period of writing covered by *Les Plaisirs et les Jours* and the articles we have been discussing is wide, and an evolution in many spheres is noticeable between the earliest pieces, printed in *Les Plaisirs* and dating from 1892, and the later ones in *Chroniques* written about 1904. A comparison between the articles which were appearing between 1904 and 1905 and this work reveals another 'acquisition capitale' whose presence it is interesting to trace in most of Proust's writings. When he first began to contribute articles to reviews and newspapers, Proust's method was, as we have seen, in *Contre l'obscurité, Silhouette d'artiste, Le Salon de S.A. La princesse Mathilde* and *Le Salon de Mme Madeleine Lemaire,* to adapt the techniques of fictional writing to journalism; later in the 1904-05 articles, *Le Salon de la comtesse d'Haussonville, Le Salon de la comtesse Potocka,* and *La comtesse de Guerne,* he seems to have abandoned this approach, and to have accepted the freedom, offered by the 'genre' of literary and fashionable journalism, to allow his fancy, imagination and literary culture direct his flow of thought—and his pen. A comparison between the same articles and the rich texture of *A la Recherche du Temps Perdu,* on the other hand, suggests that Proust has profited from the sudden increase of warmth and complexity in his style, following the 'abandoning' of the traditional techniques of fictional composition for the free style of the essayist, and has somehow incorporated this richness into *A la Recherche.* What is in fact happening during the whole period covered by *Les Plaisirs et les Jours, Jean Santeuil* [112] and the articles of *Chroniques* is the gradual transformation of the 'non-fictional technique' which is an instinctive way of writing for Proust, into a new and consistent method of narrative presentation—where the lack, or apparent lack of logical links, a deeply personal style, a close relationship between author (or narrator) and reader and the nourishment of the material with all the resources of a vast culture combine to create a new narrative technique. This development can be traced in *Les Plaisirs et les Jours, Chroniques* and *Jean Santeuil,* and its gradual perfection is one of the most interesting developments reflected in these works.

One of the earliest appearances of a method of composition, differing profoundly from the conventional techniques Proust nevertheless greatly admired in novelists like Balzac, occurs in a passage in *La Confession d'une Jeune Fille;* having established the framework of his story, the author introduces an image—the *parc des Oublis*—which, through memory and association, recalls a moment of past time when the narrator and her mother would meet there for a few days during the summer holidays, the mother's goodnight kiss remaining as a general impression. The memories, *tant de doux moments,* as the narrator calls them [113], are vague and unconnected, but evoke a mood and establish

---

[112] *Jean Santeuil,* whose probable dates of composition, 1895-1900 (?), place it in the central part of the period under discussion.
[113] *La Confession d'une jeune fille,* p. 143.

an emotional atmosphere to form a bakcloth, against which another memory begins to focus more sharply—the fourteen-year old girl's first taste of sexual experience. The vividness with which the memory is recalled presents affinities with the Combray *baiser du soir* episode which, too, detaches itself from a vague background of half-remembered scenes and incidents. The technique is simply that, eminently dramatic, of evoking a setting, extracting and throwing into relief a significant event and finally concentrating the essence of both by injecting it, along with the comment it draws forth from the more experienced narrator, into a symbolic representation of the past: the narrator evokes the pansies in the garden which contain the different subjective meanings grafted on them by Time [114]. Within a tight and carefully thought-out framework, then, Proust inserts a number of small dramatic scenes, whose only connecting link is memory, but which together serve to create atmosphere and tension. In *La Fin de la jolousie* a similar 'technique' is employed. As Honoré lies dying, he thinks back, like Baldassare Silvande, to scenes in his past life and compares different moments in time; significantly, the goodnight kiss is again introduced, while other dramatic scenes, briefly taking shape against the hazy background of memory and association, include phrases spoken earlier by other characters and transposed directly into a new context [115]. In both cases the essence of the composition is the adoption of an individual train of thought, with the vagaries and complicated cross-references provided by memory and sense-association as the basic thread upon which to hang scenes and passages of dialogue. In *Jean Santeuil,* this preference for the ordering of narrative around personal reminiscence, instead of around a chronological, rationalised schematisation of events, is more marked, though it still bears the mark of an almost unconscious way of writing, rather than being a deliberately adopted technique. The unconscious element is reflected in the way Proust slips from the 'fictional' attitude to that of personal reminiscence, in *Le Jardin des Oublis,* for example, [116] but where the tendency to group the narrative is the same as in *La Fin de la Jalousie.* Experience is arranged around the passage's central preoccupation, Jean's spiritual development. The paragraph opens with an evocation of a boat ride down the Loir; then the emphasis changes and we see the banks slipping away, not through Jean's eyes, but through those of the narrator—who now assumes precisely the same function as that shown in the articles in *Chroniques,* directing the narrative according to his own individual and sometimes idiosyncratic thought and memory processes; the interest switches from external description to internal psychological analysis [17], examples for which lead Proust to vary tenses considerably, evoking states, habits, events in past, present and even future time [118], and

---

[114] *Ibid.,* p. 146.
[115] *La Fin de la Jalousie,* p. 263.
[116] *Jean Santeuil,* Part II, chapter IV, pp. 189-213.
[117] *Jean Santeuil,* Vol. I, p. 207.
[118] *Jean Santeuil,* ibid.

disregarding the 'conventional' chronology of the episode which provides the 'excuse' for this analysis. At some point during the writing of *Jean Santeuil,* Proust must have realised how again and again he was being led to experiment with narrative patterns, instinctively creating fictional scenes and particular moods which form a continuous chain built from sense and memory association, rather than concentrating on a developing narrative thread, dependent upon rational and chronological considerations. A more conscious use of this tendency can be seen in the two episodes which jointly make up the chapter *Les Dimanches d'Etreuilles* [119] ; the scene evoked in both is that created by the inhabitants of Etreuilles—or, as Proust inadvertantly calls them, the Illiersois going to church on Sundays, the only difference being in the perspective through which each is viewed. The structure of the first version shows Proust busy with the problems of chronology; essentially it is another experiment in successive backward steps in time, counterbalanced by a movement forwards again to the moment of narration. It is almost perfectly conceived and the only discrepancy occurs in the tense at the end.

We shall see, when we come to examine in detail Proust's approach to a work of full-length fiction, that he constantly uses frameworks which jar with the material they are intended to contain. The deliberate intention of casting *Jean Santeuil* in a conventional mould, in fact, jars with many of the natural evolutions which are taking place in Proust's attitude towards writing, and his instinctive method of composition which we can see taking shape in *Les Plaisirs et les Jours, Jean Santeuil* and *Chroniques* is influenced by the heavy reliance placed unthinkingly on the 'traditional' techniques of the novel. These, as we shall show, are largely abandoned in *A la Recherche,* but as *Jean Santeuil* progresses, Proust for a while adapts his essentially antifictional 'technique' of scene and mood painting to the formal exigencies of the conventional novel.

Two episodes illustrate this point, showing, moreover, how instinctive and natural to Proust was a method of composition which dispensed with rational and chronological plans, since it underlies even conventional experiments of fictional writing. The purely objective reporting, closely associated with third-person narrative, is a feature, for example, of *Une Séance à la Chambre* [120], and provides much of the chapter's structural framework: the narrative follows the action of what is essentially a dramatic scene, expectancy, climax and conclusion being provided by the interval before Couzon's speech, the speech itself, graphically reported, and the reaction it produces [121]. Yet despite its conventional structure, the chapter in fact provides an indication of Jean's sensitive reactions to injustice in all its forms, and once again the linking theme is emotional. By working this motive into the

---

[119] *Jean Santeuil*, Part II, chapter V.
[120] *Jean Santeuil*, Part. III, chapter VIII.
[121] *Jean Santeuil*, ibid., pp. 316-317, 320-321, 321-323.

dramatic texture of the narrative, Proust combines his instinctive a-chronological and anti-rational narrative composition with traditional techniques. In order to indicate fully the emotional significance of Jean's state of mind, Proust illustrates his feelings by including incidents which occured, chronologically, much earlier, and compares them with his present attitude [122], and with the eventual reactions his feelings of injustice will provoke in the future [123]. We have already seen the beginnings of this technique in *Journées de dimanche*, where the simple description of Jean's state of mind is graphically heightened by relating it to a past episode. Here, too, the simple comment:

> Et quand Couzon se décide à faire de son gros bras court ce petit geste de convention au-dessus de sa tête, c'est comme un signal qui retentit longuement dans le cœur de Jean. [124]

is invested with more than the explicit meaning of the words themselves by the inclusion, earlier, of the description of Jean during previous debates, and his reaction to Couzon's own attitude. Particularly interesting is the way in which the confrontation of traditional techniques and Proust's own instinctive 'technique' leaves no doubt as to Proust's own attitude: not only does he depart from the actual story to pursue themes which interest him more than the simple 'arranging' of experience in a dramatic way, but he also leaves the visual scene—so carefully prepared in the beginning—hanging in mid-air, as his attention becomes engrossed in the general implications of the narrative which, now that it has served its purpose as an illustration, is totally forgotten. From visual comments like *Et Jean aussi était heureux, s'essuyait le front en souriant,* Proust shifts his attention to a more general interpretation:

> On pourrait peut-être dire que malgré le courant de cette figure, la justice n'est pas une personne, et que sa manière toute particulière de périr c'est précisément d'être armée, sans s'occuper de quelle manière. Mais on vous répondra que si les grands révolutionnaires y avaient tant regardé, jamais la justice n'eût remporté de victoire. [125]

A similar example, though worked into a much longer and more complicated episode, occurs in Chapter VII: *Querelle de Jean avec ses parents.*

Action, although treated with due respect, is nonetheless subordinated to the central, psychological and emotional theme, and as such appears in a new perspective.

To return now to the articles of *Chroniques,* which mark the final stage of Proust's 'first period', it is clear that the reliance on a personal and idiosyncratic thought-process has entirely different reper-

---

[122] *Jean Santeuil,* ibid., p. 317.
[123] *Jean Santeuil,* ibid., p. 319.
[124] *Jean Santeuil,* ibid., p. 317.
[125] *Jean Santeuil,* ibid., p. 323.

cussions on Proust's journalistic writing. They also illustrate the dangers involved in too heavy a reliance upon the vagaries of the invisible narrator when he ignores for long a recognisable structural pattern. *Le Salon de la princesse Mathilde* was written some three years after the probable abandoning of *Jean Santeuil,* and emphasises the tendency which will reappear in *A la Recherche* to over-develop the narrator's commenting role at the expense of his other functions. The most obvious feature of this article, for example, is the eventual break-down of the original framework which was to show the Princess, it will be remembered, *en train de recevoir.* For, by letting his imagination work on the stories and anecdotes that he has heard about the brilliant literary salon once grouped under the Princess' aegis, Proust's interest wanders visibly away from the evening he has evoked for the reader towards other evenings, situated in the past, when great literary and artistic figures reigned in the place of the less interesting M. Pichot of the *Revue Britannique,* and Charles Ephrussi, from the *Gazette des Beaux-Arts.* The balance between past and present, in such circumstances, can no longer be held. First, the anecdotes, which are firmly kept under control at the beginning of the article, begin to increase in length. The quarrels between the Princess and Taine and Heredia give way to long evocations of the second Empire's injustice towards the Royal Princes, and the forty-year old quarrel between the Princess and the Duc d'Aumale. Their treatment becomes less and less anecdotic and more and more developed [126], until they cease eventually to be treated as anecdotes any longer, and whole extracts from correspondence are quoted, along with reports on Mathilde's relations with her uncle and cousin, the Tzars Nicholas I and II. With the shift of emphasis from present to past, Proust's control over his narrative wanes: many of the faults, characteristic of *Jean Santeuil,* reappear; he indulges in extensive comments—on litterature, Sainte-Beuve's critical method, the misunderstanding of genius and the artist's attitude to social rank. As a shaped and controlled piece of writing, the article is an obvious failure, but its real interest lies in the illustration it provides of the effect upon narrative, not submitted to the tight control of plan and structure, of a characteristic tendency of Proustian composition, which can be seen evolving throughout all the early works. It is accompanied, as we have suggested, by the emergence of a new narrative tone, and it is the unsuccessful attempt to reconcile this narrative tone with the creation of a separate fictional hero, that we now propose to demonstrate, by examining Proust's first full-length fictional work, posthumously entitled *Jean Santeuil.*

---

[126] The final reconciliation between the Duc d'Aumale and the Princess, for example, is developed into a long pathetic scene: *Chroniques,* p. 23.

JEAN   SANTEUIL

So far, we have noticed Proust's interest in portraits, sketches, in fictional, quasi-allegorical stories and in journalism. All the works represented by this diversity of interest are short, some are successful, others leave the impression that Proust is still casting about for a suitable form in which to write comfortably. One of the successful attempts was *La Confession d'une jeune fille,* written in the first-person singular, and one might expect that Proust's attempt at a full-scale novel would continue to use this narrative form. The fact that Proust is attracted to the novel form is, in itself, hardly surprising, given the extreme interest he takes in the whole tradition of the novel. Strauss [127] notes that in all the stages of Proust's career literary criticism, generally of other novelists, plays an important role in his development as a writer. But it is clear from *La confession* that the use of the first-person is limited, so far, to the inclusion of certain revelations, and that it is insufficient for the novelist undertaking a work likely to developed on the scale which *Jean Santeuil* finally assumed; for the internal portrait of the 'jeune fille' in question, though suitable for certain descriptions of the type which constitute the entire substance of *La Confession,* is foreign to the personality of Proust himself who, as we have seen, prefers to let his character blossom out in the richness and diversity allowed him by commentary and observation. At this stage, then, (and it is as well to remember that *Jean Santeuil* was abandoned as early as 1900), first-person narration is too limiting to be used as a basis for a full-scale novel. The fundamental lesson of *Jean Santeuil* will be to show how that basis can be broadened into a suitable form, capable of accomodating most of his themes and preoccupations, and how the projection of a 'confession' into objectively-observed characters (for Jean is not the sole repository of Proust's self-revelations) clash with the still developing narrative tone, which allots more and more importance to the unseen narrator.

At the same time, the interest in the 17th century tradition of portrait, observation and generalisation continues to manifest itself throughout *Jean Santeuil,* and the fact that Proust has chosen to write a novel does not necessarily imply that he was able to do so. The

---

[127] *Op. cit.,* p. 6.

second lesson that Proust learns from *Jean Santeuil* is that he is unable to creat a hero, but is forced to create a narrator, changing third-person narrative into first-person narrative.

The Introduction to Jean Santeuil

The introduction to *Jean Santeuil,* according to all available research[128], was written early in 1896 (March), after Proust had taken the decision to use third-person narration for the sections he had already begun[129]. It is therefore interesting to examine the introduction which, unlike the work it precedes, is written in the first-person, since, with the exception of *Un Amour de Swann*[130], this is the narrative method finally adopted in *A la Recherche du Temps Perdu.* We shall see that not only is Proust's use of first-person narrative, as we saw in *La Confession,* limited to one kind of personal revelation, but that technically he is embarrassed by the peculiar restraints it imposes on the writer, especially on the writer with a lively, moralist's eye for observation and comment, without being able to exploit the equally peculiar advantages it offers the writer interested in psychological analysis and introspection.

Although the purpose of the introduction is manifestly that of creating a pretext for publishing the remainder of the text[131], its twenty-old pages (a composite of three distinct sections pieced together by the editor) cast a significant light on Proust's conception and use of first-person narrative at this time.

> J'étais venu passer avec un de mes amis le mois de septembre à Kerengrimen ... [132]

So begins the introduction to *Jean Santeuil,* plunging us immediately into the world of the first-person narrator. The point of narration is later in time then the events being recounted, the narrator's viewpoint retrospective. Retrospective first-person narrative, as in *La Confession,* provides the basis for a kind of double narrative, a 'dual vision' through which events are seen and related. True, a number of judgments and generalisations appear; the narrator has learned, for example, that the Duchess he used as a means of introducing himself to the novelist C was totally unknown to the latter, and in the light of this knowledge, comments on his actions[133]. He generalises, too, about

---

[128] See particularly Painter, *op. cit.*
[129] i.e. Part I (1-7); some of part VI, and part VII (5).
[130] And even *Swann* contains, as we shall see, a retrospective commentary.
[131] The introduction is, in fact (in this respect), similar to that of *Adolphe,* where a mysterious stranger's manuscript is accidentally discovered and subsequently published, or, as André Maurois remarks in his introduction to *Jean Santeuil* to 'tant de manuscrits "trouvés dans une bouteille", voire "dans une cervelle" dont l'existence fictive donne à l'auteur l'illusion qu'il se décharge sur un être imaginaire de toute responsabilité'.
[132] *Jean Santeuil,* Part one, section I, p. 33.
[133] *Jean Santeuil,* Vol. I, p. 36.

human nature and not only comments on his actions but rearranges them to suit a new, logical explanation, which was not apparent at the time, but which has now become evident to him as he looks back over a span of (unspecified) time. But the possibilities thus offered him to portray simultaneously two different moments in time are largely ignored. Proust gives no indication that he is aware of the potentialities of the technique he is employing. Again, the possibility of showing the same character—the narrator/hero—at two different points in time, contrasting and comparing his two 'personalities', is hardly apparent. It is evident that, if this is to be done, the characterisation of the narrator must receive particular attention. Now, it is evident, too, that this is far from being the case in *Jean Santeuil* and that, as we have pointed out, the 'two personalities' of the narrator are contrasted only insofar as their opposition gives Proust the opportunity to develop moral and psychological judgments on human nature. The number of interpolations of all kinds, inserted by the narrator, has been noted by Justin O'Brien, who remarks:

> Still in his early twenties, then, Marcel Proust already possessed a gift for generalisation and frequently mastered a lapidary form of expression. [134]

Clearly the influence of La Bruyère is still very strong, strong enough in fact, to direct the technical resources at Proust's disposal towards the embracing of humanity on an intellectual, rather than on a realist level. The concept of the narrative is still ambiguously suspended between Proust's moralist and novelist selves, first-person narrative merely emphasising the difference between them.

Third-person narrative in Jean Santeuil

Proust, still pulled strongly towards the objective study of reality, chose to write the rest of *Jean Santeuil* in the third person. Here again, we shall see that his efforts met with no more success than in the introduction, however, for the subjective, introspective emphasis of the work grows, over the five years devoted to its composition, out of all proportion to the 'moralist' strain already firmly established in *Les Plaisirs et les Jours*. The result, as we shall see, is the conversion of third-person narration into first-person narrative for certain kinds of material, just as in the Introduction the reverse takes place for other kinds of material. Proust has yet to find a technique, or, perhaps, a construction which allows him to handle with ease the two very different aspects of his developing genius in one comprehensive form.

In many ways, the discarding of the subjective 'I' in third person narrative seems to leave Proust free to conduct his 'novel' with greater

---

[134] *The Wisdom of the Young Proust,* by Justin O'Brien, *Romanic Review,* April 1954, p. 123.

ease, and to indulge in stylistic innovations arising from the detached, ironical attitude afforded him by the presence of the omniscient narrator. Part One is an excellent example of the perfect way Proust manages to assimilate all the techniques implied by the use of an objectively-described fictional form [135]. Third-person narration is given its traditional rôle of recounting a chronological series of events; there is no attempt, in the overall structure, to juxtapose two positions in time, or to experiment with a comprehensive time-pattern. The presence of a personalised narrator, the case in the introduction, who can impose a kind of unity upon the moralist and novelist tendencies, is no longer a technical necessity and many of the problems associated with his presence consequently disappear. The opening scene of *Jean Santeuil*, then, shows Proust no longer confined to the convention which demands that the personalised narrator cannot report any subjective reaction but his own, but instead describing the attitudes and intimate reactions of all the characters he cares to introduce. The opportunity for psychological analysis is therefore greatly increased, when describing each person's thoughts *from within,* sketching in their respective attitudes, and gaining considerably in *vraisemblance* as compared to the techniques he finds himself obliged to alopt, not always successfully, in the introduction, in order to achieve the same effect in first-person narrative. Mme Santeuil's psychological motives for keeping silent in answer to the doctor's question about the composition of the garden soil [136] give the author an opportunity to display his already penetrating observation of human behaviour, and by doing so opens what will prove to be a rich vein of humour.

Similarly M. and Mme Santeuil's intimate relationship is also indicated by the freedom which allows the omniscient narrator to put himself in the place of M. Santeuil, after having done the same for Mme Santeuil [137]. The unspoken thoughts of all three, as they sit in the garden, are sketched in, providing a delicate, exquisitely drawn scene where the absence of dialogue and external observation (techniques demanded by first-person narrative to achieve the same effect) particularly suit the mood being conveyed [138].

In his valuable article on the manuscripts of *Jean Santeuil*, Claude Mauriac remarks:

Dans *Jean Santeuil*, au contraire, le narrateur et l'enfant, puis l'adolescent, puis le jeune homme coïncident — alors que l'adulte (et pour cause)

---

[135] The whole of Part One, with the possible exception of the section Le Lycée Henri IV, was certainly written during September and October 1895. It therefore forms a fairly comprehensive sequence which, from the point of view of composition, may be studied as a whole, rather than as a series of unconnected episodes, the case in later sections. *Jean Santeuil*, Vol. I, pp. 61-131.

[136] *Jean Santeuil*, Vol. I, p. 63.

[137] *Jean Santeuil*, Vol. I, p. 63.

[138] *Ibid.*

demeure absent. Il n'y a que le minimum de recul exigé par l'art d'écrire entre le temps où le récit est rédigé et celui où il est censé se passer.[139]

While it is true to point to the absence of the mature Proust in this, most immature, work[140] it is less so to imply that the narrator's position in time is no near that of the events taking place, that only the technical time division, necessary for retrospective narration, separates them. On the contrary, an examination of Proust's use of third-person narrative in *Jean Santeuil* illustrates clearly the stylistic advantages, that Proust has great pleasure in exploiting, in the distinct separation of narrator and hero. M. Mauriac has perhaps not taken fully into account the complexity of the narrator's rôle vis-à-vis the hero of *Jean Santeuil*—a complexity which lays the foundations for a far more intricate relationship in *A la Recherche* between the 'two Marcels'. Section Three of *Jean Santeuil*, for example, illustrates how Proust uses the separation of narrator and hero to underline the vocational 'theme' of the work, as well as to insert humour, irony, poetry and general comment into the narrative. Chapter V: *Monsieur Duroc*[141] is mainly concerned with the vocational theme of *Jean Santeuil* and it is underlined neatly by the separation of hero and narrator; the latter remains detached, not only from the personality of Jean himself, but from the very circumstances of his story. From this viewpoint, he is able to underline certain aspects of the situation which he views with mild irony. This is evident in the description of Jean's reaction to Duroc's baroque definition of poetry:

> (Jean) ... ne s'était jamais représenté la poésie comme un assaisonnement auquel on a recours à volonté pour mettre un peu de piquant dans les affaires sérieuses ...[142]

the malicious description of Duroc's studied greeting:

> ... comme la fête que la femme brillante d'un Garde des Sceaux modéré prépare avec des artifices qui n'arrivent à donner un plaisir d'art dans les salons pourtant spacieux et beaux du ministère[143].

and the explicit condemnation of his remarks as 'tant de spécieuses raisons'[144]. The most frequently observed effect of the distance between narrator and hero is irony: irony directed towards Jean himself[145],

---

[139] Claude Mauriac: Jean Santeuil de Marcel Proust, *La Table Ronde,* August 1952.

[140] M. Antoine Adam has pointed out in *La Revue des Sciences Humaines* (October-December 1952, pp. 356-365), the backward step represented, in some ways, by *Jean Santeuil*.

[141] *Jean Santeuil,* Vol. I, pp. 276-288.

[142] *Jean Santeuil,* Vol. I, p. 279.

[143] *Jean Santeuil,* Vol. I, p. 278.

[144] *Jean Santeuil,* Vol. I, p. 281.

[145] *Jean Santeuil,* Vol. I, p. 280.

towards Henri [146], towards the Desroches's social climbing [147]. It is the source of much humour [148], still detached when describing the flames in the ancestral Réveillon fireplace devouring the republican *Temps,* 'comme une offrande agréable et une victime expiatoire', and of poetry, when the newspaper is changed into a source of beauty:

> La flamme alerte tissait rapidement une cendre plus légère que la tapisserie de la duchesse ... [149]

Proust also uses the separation of hero and narrator to introduce sometimes quite cynical comments on the action, which could not possibly emanate from the hero, and which once again recall La Bruyère and La Rochefoucauld. The dry comment on love [150] and the brilliant pastiche of La Bruyère on the two kinds of snob [151] are two examples of the way the ever-present moralist vein is neatly inserted into the narrative by the separation of hero and narrator. The result upon the hero of this viewpoint is well summed up by Cattaui:

> Le héros, Jean Santeuil, n'est pas encore tout à fait ce que sera le narrateur de la Recherche; il a beau être le porte-parole de l'auteur, nous sentons bien qu'entre Proust et lui subsiste un certain écart; si les événements de sa vie sont — à peine transposés — ceux que Proust a vécus, en revanche, il nous est peint du dehors, avec un curieux mélange de complaisance et d'ironie, ce qui le fait paraître plus égoïste, plus léger, plus vaniteux, plus cynique et, tout ensemble, moins vivant que 'Marcel' [152].

It would seem therefore that Proust has found in third-person narrative an excellent means of presenting the story of his hero, Jean, a set of conventions and techniques which he is thoroughly in control of, a narrative technique, in short, which suits his every purpose. It is only by examining the rôles allotted to hero and narrator that we realise how totally false an impression this is.

Hero and Narrator in third-person narrative

In all the examples quoted above to illustrate the separation of hero and narrator, there is at no time any confusion between them. It is the fact that they are two separate personalities which allows certain effects of irony and detachment to be achieved. But how few such examples are in the three lengthy volumes of *Jean Santeuil* ! Far more characteristic is the chapter immediately following *Monsieur Duroc*: chapter VI: *Portrait d'un ami* [153]. Here the confusion, which

---

[146] *Jean Santeuil,* Vol. I, p. 287.
[147] *Jean Santeuil,* Vol. I, p. 250.
[148] *Jean Santeuil,* Vol. I, p. 266.
[149] *Jean Santeuil,* Vol. I, p. 269.
[150] *Jean Santeuil,* Vol. I, p. 251.
[151] *Jean Santeuil,* Vol. I, pp. 253-256.
[152] Georges Cattaui, *Marcel Proust,* Ed. Universitaires, Paris 1958, pp. 52-53.
[153] *Jean Santeuil,* Vol. I, pp. 289-298.

often arises in the respective rôles of hero and narrator, is fully illustrated. Three distinct stages can be noticed. The first is that the detached, impersonal narrator is personalised. He identifies himself with the circumstances of Jean's youth and childhood, creating an initial feeling of confusion between hero and narrator. Introducing the 'portrait' of Bertrand de Réveillon, the narrator unexpectedly remarks:

> Il y a un ami de Jean dont je voudrais fixer les traits. C'est Bertrand de Réveillon. *Même si je ne l'avais pas beaucoup aimé, j'aurais le désir de le faire.* [154]

— introducing an element hitherto absent, the relationship of the omniscient narrator himself to the events he is recounting. He also begins to include his personal opinions in the narrative, whereas before he had remained the passive intermediary between Jean and the reader. The result is seen in the second stage, where a whole shift in the emphasis from Jean to the narrator occurs. What now begins to emerge is not the Jean/Réveillon relationship, but, and unexpectedly, the Réveillon/narrator relationship [155]. The narrator ceases to be the technical intermediary, while Jean's function vanishes altogether. It should be noticed that, by the time this shift of emphasis is complete [156], far from Jean and the narrator merging to form a single unit, their separation now becomes extreme. The generalisations are solely those of the narrator and, through the testimony they give of a wide experience of life, could not possibly belong to Jean, at this stage of his career [157]. The final step involves discarding not only the fictional hero, but the whole fictional cadre as well. The narrator now addresses Réveillon directly:

> Pardon, Bertrand, d'avoir ce soir-là aimé en vous une beauté dont ne pouvait s'enorgueillir votre amour-propre, et qui ne pouvait entrer dans notre affection [158].

It is not difficult to see in this barely-disguised autobiographical episode, that not only is the fictional element discarded with the 'abolition' of the hero, but that the very convention of literature is abandoned when the reader himself is ignored, and the author directly addresses another person. This prompts the reflexion that the autobiographical material is not yet assimilated—an impression strengthened by the unexplained change in Réveillon's name from Henri to Bertrand [159]. The general conclusion which the startling evolution of the

---

[154] *Jean Santeuil*, Vol. I, p. 289. My italics.
[155] i.e. La société de ces nobles supérieurs est infiniment plus agréable que ceux dont Bertrand de Réveillon reste pour moi le type: *Jean Santeuil*, Vol. I, p. 290.
[156] *Jean Santeuil*, Vol. I, p. 295.
[157] *Jean Santeuil*, ibid.
[158] *Jean Santeuil*, Vol. I, p. 298.
[159] A transformation easily explained, however, by Proust's biographers. See particularly Painter, *op. cit.*, pp. 296-313.

narrator's rôle suggests is that Proust in writing *Jean Santeuil,* while occasionally able with considerable success to control the translation of autobiographical material into a fictional narrative, is manifestly unable to create a hero, and is forced instead to rely upon an increasingly personalised narrator, whose introduction demands less technical manipulation, who is nearer to the 'raw state' of the experiences Proust feels unable to split successfully between hero and narrator, and whose inclusion automatically suppresses conventional third-person narrative.

The chaotic state of the work which follows is due in the main to the radical opposition of narrator and hero. Whether the narrator is used to project commentary, or simply to act as the vehicle for autobiographical material, there can be no doubt that in rôle, function and personnality he totally eclipses the hero Jean. Proust, in choosing third-person narrative, committed himself to transfering the major part of his own experience to an objectively-observed fictional character. In the introduction, the result of Proust's psychological observation of objectively-presented characters is clear : a personalised narrator immediately appears, changing the centre of interest and adopting some of the functions proper to the hero. As the work progresses, this tendency leads to what threatens to be the complete breakdown of the fictional structure: for the unity necessary to combine the two tendencies in Proust's writing—novelist and moralist, dynamic and static respectively—a unity which ought to proceed from the character of Jean himself, is almost totally lacking. Proust cannot decide which should be the centre of attention: the fictionalised story of Jean, or the barely-transposed experience and commentary of a more and more personalised narrator, who is really Proust himself. To take a typical episode from Part Two of *Jean Santeuil* we can observe a development which recurs time and time again: it can be summed up as follows:

> *fictional scene,* giving way to *generalisation,* and the appearance of the narrator

or, more simply:

> *Jean* > generalisation: *narrator.*

For example, the episode relating the magic lantern sessions in Jean's bedroom provides a characteristic illustration of the continual shift of emphasis from Jean to the narrator. We are first introduced to the fictional scene of Jean's room at Etreuilles [160], and a fictional situation is created as the reader follows through Jean's eyes the jerky movements of the images projected..., 'fantômes, apparitions et glissements de vitraux impalpables' [161]. However, the presence of the narrator is felt throughout, despite the emphasis on the fictional hero, in the latter's

---

160 *Jean Santeuil,* Vol. I, p. 181.
161 *Jean Santeuil,* Vol. I, p. 182.

commentary [162]. Next follows a period of transition where the narrator comes to the fore and begins to explain certain of the hero's reactions— a technique whose evolution may be traced back to the earliest stories of *Les Plaisirs et les Jours*. Finally, the hero, Jean, 'disappears' altogether and it is the narrator who monopolises the reader's attention, developing themes and reflexions which Jean and Etreuilles have simply been the pretexts for introducing. The tone becomes more general and new examples are drawn from Proust's own experience as illustrations, though having little to do with Jean Santeuil, who is by now completely forgotten [163]. We shall see later how the habit of creating new examples to illustrate general comments, suggested by Jean's story, but in reality having little relationship to it, will be carried to extreme lengths. We may notice, too, the change of tense which marks the development of the narrator's rôle: the imperfect tense is abandoned for the present, as the narrator's personality obliterates that of Jean. Beginning with impersonal formulae like 'Il peut être bien pour l'esprit...' and 'il est plus troublant peut-être encore de voir...', Proust soon moves to the more personal 'nous' and 'vous' variants of the general 'on' [164]. Gradually Proust himself takes over the narration, and the 'nous' becomes 'je', the 'notre' 'mon':

> ... dans la froideur qu'il y avait alors à Etreuilles entre le maire radical qui pourtant était un vieil ami de *mon* oncle et *notre* vieil ami le curé, dans le nom du pâtissier que *je vois* au bout de la grande rue sur son enseigne, et dans la voix de *ma* mère quand elle *me* disait: "Il faut aller vite chez Mongeland chercher une tarte". [165]

It is evident that third-person narration, barely sufficient to convey a fictional story because of Proust's impatience with formal techniques, is completely out of place when he wishes to enrich the bare story with personal observations. A confusion in time and focus inevitably results, as the emphasis shifts from Jean in the past at Etreuilles [166] to Proust in the present. There is no corresponding shift of emphasis back to the fictional story of Etreuilles and Jean, and it is on one of the narrator's questions that the whole episode ends [167].

Even more critical is the clash between hero and narrator when Proust wishes to enrich the story with poetry and deeply felt impressions and sensations. Once again the same development occurs: fictional scene,>poetry and generalisation by narrator. The poetry of

---

[162] *Jean Santeuil,* Vol. I, p. 181.

[163] e.g. Vol. I, p. 183: '... ces tons verts que les tuyaux qui conduisent l'eau au fond du bassin ont pris... ce que vous avez senti, les heures mêmes que vous avez vécues... la statue de bronze de Pan dans le parc...' etc.

[164] e.g. Vol. I, p. 184: 'Nous les regardons avec amour, ces reliques mêmes de notre vie.'

[165] *Jean Santeuil,* Vol. I, p. 184.

[166] Even the fiction of Etreuilles is dropped, and it reverts to the autobiographical town of Illiers: *Jean Santeuil,* Vol. I, pp. 226, 228, 229 etc.

[167] *Jean Santeuil,* Vol. I, p. 185.

Jean Santeuil is for the most part not integrated into the narrative proper, but remains firmly attached to the personality of the author/narrator, thus distinct from the personality of the hero. A typical example is the passage describing Jean's delight in nature in *Journées de Vacances* [168]. First, Jean is the intermediary between the poetic description of nature and the reader [169]. Next, as he goes down to the garden, we still see the trees and flowers through his eyes:

> Il descendait au jardin... Feuilles et fleurs étaient là, ardentes et droites dans l'ombre, mais elles respiraient encore la douceur du soleil dans lequel elles ont quelques instants baigné... [170]

when suddenly the tense changes and the point of view radically alters. Once again the narrator has taken over from Jean—the time of narration is his, and the picture evoked arouses feelings in him and not in his fictional hero:

> Et ces papillons, les petits oiseaux surtout... font penser aussi aux ange-lots ailés du tableau *dont je parlais...* [171]

From here to the next stage of generalisation, the step is not great and is prepared by general comparisons on the narrator's part. Soon the characteristic 'nous' appears, indicating a relationship between the narrator and the reader which totally excludes Jean [172]. We are forced to ask to what extent is the narrator Proust and if he is Proust, what is his relation to the hero? It is clear that the latter is deprived of many chances to establish himself as a convincing character, because of the overwhelming importance given to the narrator. Not only, as we have shown [173] is it he who introduces most of the poetry into the narrative—in the description of the storm at Penmarch, the unexpected inclusion of a colour-picture as the sun floods the room with light, is remarkable for the complete absence of the hero [174]—but also, and more surprising perhaps, the literary discussions which are a feature of *Jean Santeuil* are far more closely identified with the narrator than with Jean. The latter is soon dispensed with in Section VI, chapter V, for example, where the serious reflexions on the pleasures of reading are made not by Jean, but by the narrator, who is far closer to the reader, whom he embraces in his generalisations, than to the hero:

---

[168] *Jean Santeuil*, Vol. I, pp. 143-171.
[169] *Ibid.*, p. 149.
[170] *Ibid.*, p. 149.
[171] *Ibid.*, p. 151.
[172] e.g. Vol. I, p. 151: 'Voilà le royaume heureux vers lequel les reflets du soleil faisant du ciel au jardin, du jardin à *notre* fenêtre, de *notre* fenêtre à *notre* vie une échelle heureuse, s'offraient à *nous* conduire'.
[173] Other examples include the view from the farm (Vol. II, p. 182), the colours of the apple trees (*ibid.*); the peninsula (Vol. II, pp. 185-7) etc.
[174] The reflexions are those of the narrator, as are those appearing in *Lectures de Plage*, when the narrator has supplanted Jean altogether: *Jean Santeuil*, Vol. II, pp. 205, 191.

Notre histoire comme hommes est moins variée et laisse si peu voir des périodes en désaccord avec les goûts que nous nous connaissons ... [175]

The emergence of a narrator

There can be no doubt that Proust was aware of the chaotic state of the narrative, and the abandoning of *Jean Santeuil* was not decided upon before he had made considerable efforts to redress the balance, upset by the continual emergence of a first-person narrator.

One of the reasons for the narrator's inflated rôle in *Jean Santeuil* is, of course, Proust's desire to insert the mass of reflexions and generalisations which occurred to him on practically every topic. It should be remembered, therefore, that technically, Proust has provided himself, in the introduction, with a ready-made excuse, as it were, for the inclusion of such 'extraneous' material: it is explicitly stated that C the novelist, whose story *Jean Santeuil* is supposed to be, would often interrupt the reading of his proofs and insert explanation and commentary for Jean and his friend's edification:

> Souvent son récit était interrompu par quelques réflexions, où l'auteur exprime son opinion sur certaines choses, à la manière de certains romanciers anglais qu'il avait autrefois beaucoup aimés [176]

Elsewhere he declares his own preference for digressions, admitting to a certain weakness for them, despite the threat they constitute to 'vraisemblance':

> Car un écrivain que nous adorons devient pour nous comme une sorte d'oracle que nous aimerions à consulter sur toute chose et chaque fois qu'il prend la parole pour donner ainsi un avis, exprimer une idée générale, parler, lui, de cet Homère, de ces dieux que nous connaissons, nous sommes ravis, nous écoutons bouche bée la maxime qu'il lui plaît de laisser tomber, désolés qu'elle soit si peu longue. [177]

As if realising, however, the inadequacy of such an 'excuse', Proust also takes practical steps to counteract the movement away from fiction, and the emergence of the narrator. Sometimes, carried away by the force of his reflexions, Proust substitutes, as we have seen, the narrator for Jean. When he realises this, he takes care to rectify the situation immediately. Insensibly slipping from Jean's to the narrator's reactions in the middle of a sentence [178], Proust carefully adds, by way of an explanation that the narrator's conclusions and observations are really those of the hero, and that the 'véritables chariots de Thespis où nous nous amusions *comme Jean venait de le faire tout à l'heure* à

---

[175] *Jean Santeuil*, Vol. II, p. 190.
[176] *Jean Santeuil*, Vol. I, p. 53.
[177] *Jean Santeuil*, Vol. I, pp. 178-9.
[178] *Jean Santeuil*, Vol. II, pp. 203-4.

reconnaître l'Isabelle, le pédant, la Zerbinette, acteurs tout grimés... [179], are to be retrospectively applied to Jean. Sometimes, Proust realises the disproportionately small place he has alloted to his hero, and attempts to redress the balance by inserting a passing reference to the, by now, forgotten fictional scene. After a long 'digression' on the pleasures of reading by the narrator, Proust abruptly turns back to the fictional jumping-off point—which has lost all importance. The sudden evocation of Jean reading after dinner destroys the unity of tone previously established by the narrator, and strikes the reader as confusing, even incomprehensible [180]. On other occasions Proust lets his imagination lead him, beyond the simple fictional basis, to a complicated exploration of all the implications it contains—perhaps the most frequently-recurring characteristic in both *Jean Santeuil* and *A la Recherche.* Once launched in this direction, he creates whole new fictional situations, which do not fit into the already existing fictional setting—of Etreuilles, for example. Proust completely forgets this initial scene, and goes on enthusiastically creating new scenes to illustrate his general ideas, regardless of the fact that they are incompatible with the first scenes [181]. After a long development in this vein, Proust then tries to work these secondary scenes into the original Etreuilles narrative, by ingeniously suggesting that we have really been witnessing a retrospective scene, suddenly recalled by the narrator [182]. The attempt is unsuccessful, since, by now, he has become manifestly more interested in his second, parallel fictional scenes, than his first ones, and he continues to develop them:

Ainsi, à cet instant dont nous parlions tout à l'heure... M. Albert, ses neveux et son petit-neveu restaient droits sur la chaise... [183]

—having realised that the details of the two scenes do not coincide, and giving up all further efforts to return to the original scene.

It is significant that the only way in which Proust tries to find a compromise solution is by introducing a personalised narrator. We may take the passage referred to above, the attempt to fit the narrator's illustrations retrospectively into the fictional story, as an indication of the way Proust will decide to present basically similar material when he rewrites *Jean Santeuil* in the form of *A la Recherche du Temps Perdu.* The problems raised by the fictionalisation of the 'hero's' spiritual and intellectual development still apply in the later work: however, one essential difference between the two versions is the change from the first to the third-person, and the use, as here, of a narrator to provide a means of reconciling fictional and moralist attitudes—in part

---

[179] *Jean Santeuil,* Vol. II, p. 204.
[180] *Jean Santeuil,* Vol. II, pp. 191-92.
[181] e.g. *Jean Santeuil,* Vol. I, pp. 154-162.
[182] Voilà comment *la vue rétrospective de la salle à manger à Illiers...* etc. Vol. I, p. 158.
[183] *Jean Santeuil,* Vol. I, p. 159.

at least. We may conclude, then, that whether he realised it or not, Proust had discovered the way to rewrite *Jean Santeuil* satisfactorily.

The hero-narrator relationship

It is in the chapters dealing with Mme Marmet that the hero/narrator relationship reaches its most complex stage of development. The hero becomes, at first, the projection of Proust's snobbish daydreams while the narrator acts as the intermediary, pointing out certain facts, arranging situations in which the 'hero' triumphs over his enemies. Here the latter is almost entirely passive: he behaves like a puppet in the hands of the author/narrator, his reactions are rarely recorded, and the 'vengeance' is usually contrived by other characters for him. Occasionally he shows normal reactions as, for example, when he shows his gratitude to his defenders in *Réparation,* but this is rare. Yet from time to time the narrator stands back and judges the hero; their personalities sometimes seem very distinct, and even when the situation has been contrived for Jean's benefit, the narrator is still capable of judging the latter's snobbery severely:

> ... il eut honte de sa bouche qui s'ouvrait ainsi dans une joie vulgaire, de sa parole satisfaite et de sa personne brusquement et laidement illuminée... (vol. III, p. 13)

Thus, as we suggested at the beginning, Proust is fully aware of the possibilities offered him by third-person narrative, but instinctively he tends to shie away from using them unless special factors like snobbery, or sexual confession [184] are involved. We may now take the opportunity to review rapidly the exceedingly complex relationship existing between hero and narrator in third-person narrative and the rôles each one assumes, a subject arising directly out of a consideration of autobiographical sources.

In the chapters dealing with the 'scandale Marie' [185], the impersonal, omniscient narrator gives way to a different, more personalised figure who assumes what is most accurately described as the rôle of a 'raconteur'. By this, we mean the individual choice of material, accompanied by reflexions, commentary, and above all—distinguishing these chapters from others where a personalised narrator introduces discussion and digression into the narrative—a certain obvious pleasure

---

[184] Proust already possesses the scrupulous attitude of the true artist towards his material and is determined to include references to Jean's sexual immorality at Réveillon. The fact that such scenes are attributed to Jean recalls *La Confession d'une jeune fille,* and we may briefly point out that here the apologetic tone of the narrator: ('Et ici nous avons à faire un aveu que beaucoup de gens ne trouveront pas favorable à notre héros.' Vol. II, p. 245) does not entirely coincide with the apparently objective attitude he seems to profess, and one concludes that certain links between narrator/hero survive their 'separation' in third-person narrative.

[185] Vol. II, pp. 69-115.

on the narrator's part as he recounts events. This may be seen as the corresponding development within a purely fictional framework of the narrative tone which so strongly emerges in the 1904-5 articles of *Chroniques.* The characteristic of the raconteur, attention to his audience rather than to his material, is once again particularly noticeable, and the narrator/reader relationship manifestly intimate. Cattaui remarks:

> Ayant toujours nié la valeur et la réalité même de l'amitié, Proust n'a qu'un ami: son lecteur; [186]

and it is in *Jean Santeuil,* far more than in *A la Recherche,* that Proust establishes his most intimate links between himself and his 'cher lecteur' [187]. The impression is always that of the narrator acting the part of a more experienced friend, lifting a curtain (as in *Chroniques*) pointing to a number of scenes being played, occasionally withdrawing to let us enjoy the spectacle alone, but generally interposing himself between the 'jours lointains' whose evolution he is permitting us to follow and ourselves, the readers:

> Aux jours lointains dont je te parle, lecteur, où M. Santeuil était ce monsieur à barbe noire... [188]

He appreciates the peculiar flavour of the situations he describes, adding his own corroboration of certain episodes with obvious relish [189], he enjoys keeping the reader in ignorance of the true causes for certain others, playing a kind of guessing game with his reader-confidant [190]. He nudges his reader's elbow to point out an amusing fact:

> Vous pensez si Augustin était fier de penser qu'il était plus au fait des affaires du gouvernement que le ministre de l'Agriculture [191]

and takes an obvious delight in speculating, for the reader's benefit, on the real facts behind Mme Marie's devotion to her husband [192]. Always ready to insert an interesting parenthesis (again, exactly as in *Chroniques*) his attitude is almost that of an after-dinner speaker, giving the latest information on the subject under discussion [193]: he turns aside to insert personal reflexions, asserts his honesty in giving his listeners the true facts, and includes amusing comparisons [194]. If we reflect upon the implications of the technique, we can see that, apart from the new flavour it imparts to the narrative, the function of the

---

[186] *Op. cit.,* pp. 18-19.
[187] Vol. II, p. 107.
[188] Vol. II, p. 69.
[189] Vol. II, pp. 72-73.
[190] Vol. II, p. 71.
[191] Vol. II, *ibid.*
[192] Vol. II, p. 74.
[193] Vol. II, p. 76.
[194] Vol. II, pp. 71 and 77.

narrator/raconteur has certain advantages. It allows Proust to work in generalisation and comment in a satisfactory and convincing way; he can also link explanation to the description of psychological states, by adopting a conversational tone: in short, the transformation of third-perosn narrative into something closely approaching first-person narrative solves many problems. The result, however, is not always to Proust's advantage, since the technique concentrates too much on the narrator/reader relationship, even to the detriment of the narrative itself. Proust is more interested in gauging his reader's reactions than in recounting the story [195] and too often turns aside from the narrative to engage the reader in a kind of dialogue:

> N'est-ce pas ce que vous voulez dire, cher lecteur, quand vous m'assurez que si vous vouliez parler vous sauriez rien qu'en disant des choses vraies écrire le plus dramatique, le plus incroyable, le plus romanesque des romans? [196]

Moreover, by placing himself between the reader and the narrative itself, the raconteur becomes interesting in himself and channels off much of the interest which belongs legitimately to the story; instead of being a passive intermediary, as in traditional third-person narrative, the narrator actually becomes a barrier. His interpolations and generalisations detract from the individuality of the 'hero', Marie, himself, and the whole technique of lifting a veil to disclose a carefully chosen sequence of episodes and tableaux belongs more to the moralist trend in Proust, illustrating his judgments on human behaviour by the Marie scandal, just as La Bruyère pin-pointed his observations by a portrait of Arias. Marie is hardly more than the counterpart in *Jean Santeuil* of 'le voyageur', in the abstract, 'le débauché', 'le paresseux', 'le gourmand' [197]. While the original link between Jean's spiritual and intellectual development and the Marie affair, originally intended to illustrate it, fades completely into the background.

Finally, the Dreyfus affair sums up the exceedingly complex relationship which exists between narrator and hero, and the confusion surrounding their functions. In this episode (chapters V-IV of section five) the narrator's rôle shows an astonishing flexibility:

(a) he disappears altogether
(b) he merges with the figure of the hero
(c) he co-exists beside the figure of the hero
(d) he ousts the hero altogether.

(a) *The narrator's presence is not felt at all* in the description of Boisdeffre's arrival at, and subsequent departure from the Palais de Justice in chapter V: *Premiers temps de l'affaire Dreyfus*: generalisa-

---

[195] Vol. II, p. 79: 'Vous vous étonnez peut-être que...'
[196] Vol. II, p. 107.
[197] Vol. II, *ibid.*

tion and comment disappear and the visual scene is made to speak for itself. It can be legitimately argued that in third-person narrative, the narrator figure can never be completely absent, since it is he who chooses the incidents we are reading, there indicating certain things about himself [198]. However, in these pages, there is a conscious attempt to reduce even this choice to a minimum: when Jean and Durrieux return after lunch to the Palais de Justice, they find it in a state of turmoil, indicated by prose which follows as closely as possible the penetration into their consciousness of the troubled situation [199] : there is no attempt to 'arrange' these impressions, the chronological order of events is discarded for that of the importance they assume in the eyes of the two young men. All the elements of confusion are present as though a tape-recorder had mechanically absorbed them. Then the scene expands; it is as though the spotlight had been directed solely on one corner of the room, and is now beginning to play over the whole assembly. Once again, this is exactly the technique required to reproduce the order and importance of the impressions for the reader, as they appeared to Jean and his friend. Thus, the rôle of the personal narrator is significantly reduced, his personality in fact, is stripped from him, and even his element of choice, though impossible to eliminate altogether [200] has been drastically cut.

(b) *Narrator and hero merge* when Jean's thoughts are attributed to the narrator, and vice-versa. Chapter V illustrates the resulting confusion in one very revealing sentence: the change-over from 'il' to 'nous' occurs half-way through the sentence:

> Mais il faudrait d'abord aller dehors, et dame il faisait froid, et on entendait le vent dans la cheminée. Mais Henri l'accompagnerait. Henri, n'était-ce pour lui le seul ami, si dans la figure de notre ami il faut que ce soit notre vie elle-même et non celle que nous ne connaissons pas, notre vie elle-même ardente, inconnue et joyeuse qui nous sourit? [201]

This again raises the whole problem of the hero-narrator relationship seen in the light of the fictionalisation of autobiographical material. It is evident from this isolated example that Proust has been unable to decide to which of his two 'porte-paroles' (hero or narrator) he should attribute his own opinions on friendship. It is also clear that their functions overlap considerably, to such an extent, in fact, that they become synonymous with each other without any difficulty. It further suggests that, as we mentioned before, the 'hero', much of whose life-blood is channelled off into the narrator's abstract generalisations, rarely comes sufficiently alive to sustain the weight of the narrative which accumulates around him and is, as such, a failure.

---

[198] Flaubert's 'objectivity' is a case in point.
[199] Vol. II, pp. 121-122.
[200] Despite the attempts of exponents of the so-called 'nouveau roman'.
[201] Vol. II, p. 119.

(c) *Narrator and hero co-exist* peacefully, however, when Proust deliberately uses their separation to obtain technical effects, as we have already abundantly shown.

(d) *The hero 'disappears'*, not only when the narrator concerns himself with generalities, as for example, in Chapter VI: *Le Colonel Picquart,* but also when the latter's attention wanders away from Jean to contemplate other actors in the Dreyfus affair. It is in such cases that we realise that Jean, far from being the unifying centre of these two episodes [202], originally both intended to provoke in him reactions about justice, heresay, guilt and so on, yields this important function to the narrator. In fact, there is a fundamental disparity, arising directly from the existence of a hero who is not at the same time the narrator, between Proust's desire to show Jean evolving in the light of the experience he gains from the 'scandale Marie' and the Dreyfus Affair, and his equally strong desire to create, by means of reference to a number of abstract 'laws', a formal construction based upon a series of generalisations, themselves illustrated by certain scenes from the 'affaire'. In the first conception, the narrator plays no part, in the second, the hero is likewise absent. The rôle of narrator and hero, then, as illustrated by *Jean Santeuil* prove that Proust's attitude to fiction is still bedevilled by the moralist and novelist tendencies he yields to simultaneously, never finally making up his mind between either of them.

The Suitability of Third-person narrative in Jean Santeuil

We can now review the choice of third-person narrative in the light of the various themes which run though the work. The greatest advantage offered by third-person narrative is the possibility of obtaining the overall view necessary for the moralist's observations of character and mœurs. In *A la Recherche* Proust will use the techniques of omniscient narration, despite his first-person narrator, for the portrayal of this element, and it is evident for *Jean Santeuil* that they suit his purpose admirably. The narrator transports his reader to a later period in time, for example, to point out some significant change; he can present any one character, as the subjective narrator cannot do, and indulge in satire—at the expense of Mme de Thonnes [203] in the poetic evocation of sensations [204], and in the observation of custom and habit [205], all because the omniscient narrator has a unique insight into the motives and reactions of the characters being discussed. This is, of course, one more reason why the narrator so often eclipses the hero, since the latter's viewpoint is necessarily limited, compared with the 'universal' knowledge of the omnicient narrator. The disadvantages

---

[202] The Dreyfus Affair and The Scandale Marie.
[203] Vol. III, p. 175.
[204] Vol. III, p. 169.
[205] Vol. III, pp. 174-175.

of third-person narrative appear as soon as we consider its effect upon the tratment of love, and on the evolution of the vocation theme. In the long and important chapter entitled *De l'Amour,* the most striking feature is the lack of fictionalisation, combined with the characteristic hesitation between narrator and hero, the continuous switch from one to the other indicating the lack of a focal point around which the episodes could be arranged. Thus there is considerable uncertainty in the handling of the episode, largely due to third-person narrative. This, at first, seems paradoxical, since the corresponding chapter in *A la Recherche, Un Amour de Swann,* is the only one where third-person narrative appears, but it would be a mistake to presume that the narrative of *Swann* is identical to that of *Jean Santeuil* as it would be to presume that the first-person narrative of the introduction to *Jean Santeuil* is the same as the immensely complex use of it in *A la Recherche.* Here, third-person narrative simply implies a continual struggle between hero and narrator, whereas in *A la Recherche* this is eliminated almost completely. Again, *De l'Amour* is a good example of the hesitation between a straightforward discussion of love in treatise form with no attempt to provide fictional settings and characters, and the normal exigencies of fictional narrative—caused by the split between narrator and hero. The thoughts Proust wishes to convey are attributed mainly to the former while Jean is introduced secondarily, as an illustration of the narrator's ideas. The narrator continually usurps the hero's primary function in this way; in no more than two pages, hero and narrator alternate at least five times, the generalisations which thus appear draw upon new fictional examples, retrospectively attributed to Jean, exactly as before. A particularly striking example [206] of the subordination of hero to narrator occurs towards the end of the chapter when Jean is referred to cryptically, and then totally forgotten as the situation is explored—by the narrator. There the choice and use of third-person narrative may be taken to be the primary reason why the love episodes in *Jean Santeuil* refuse to assume the same unity which is present not only in *Un Amour de Swann,* but also in *La Prisonnière* and *La Fugitive.* The duel between narrator and hero results in the subordination of the fictional element to the moralist and didactic trend, reducing the story of Jean and Françoise to a series of unconnected episodes, illustrating a treatise on the effects of love.

The vocation theme also suffers from the 'limitations' of third-person narrative. By limitations, we mean the inevitable separation of hero and narrator, and the circumscribed view that the hero always has of experience. For example, by opposing, in the chapter entitled *Les Tuileries,* two facets of his existence, Jean realises confusedly that activities like frequenting duchesses and shining in literary 'salons' are unimportant compared with the pleasures obtained from the con-

---

[206] Vol. III, pp. 141-142.

templation of natural beauty and the joy of unsollicited memories [207].
The rider, added by the narrator, shows that *Jean Santeuil* is orientated
in exactly the same direction as *A la Recherche,* for Jean never understands his vocation until later—the first novel remaining unfinished, of
course, Jean never understands it properly at all. Nonetheless, this
provokes certain comments; when the narrator adds:

> Mais toutes ces pensées n'apparurent que vaguement ce jour-là à Jean,
> suscitées seulement au fond de sa conscience parce que c'était par ces
> pensées qu'il répondait toujours intérieurement à la nouvelle d'un nou-
> veau succès de Grisard ou de Dubonnet [208] (two social climbers).

—we realise that, had Proust continued to write *Jean Santeuil* he could
never have combined the two elements of the vocational theme which
are ever present when it appears. They are, basically, Jean's inge-
nuousness and the narrator's full realisation that one day this inge-
nuousness will disappear. Now, however easily the personalities of the
two protagonists of *Jean Santeuil* merge into one, since each is a
different projection of an author uncertain how much to attribute to
one, and how much to the other, the hero can never *become* this more
knowledgable narrator, as he does in *A la Recherche.* In *A la Recherche*
the point of narration is superimposable on the final pages of *Le
Temps Retrouvé,* whereas in *Jean Santeuil* third-person narrative main-
tains the technically rigid separation of hero and narrator. The latter
must always remain external to Jean, for as we have seen, the reader
is much nearer to the narrator, while Jean is reduced at times, despite
efforts to gain the reader's sympathy for him, to no more than an
animated puppet or a passive symbol.

Only in the treatment of the 'novelist' vein of *Jean Santeuil* does
third-person narrative offer decided advantages. For the love and
vocation themes, first-person seems more natural, and the experience
of writing *Jean Santeuil* brings this fact to Proust in no uncertain
manner, for when we see him actively engaged in composition after
the abandoning of *Jean Santeuil* the narrator's intimate tone becomes
more and more prominent.

---

[207] Vol. III, p. 163.
[208] Vol. III, p. 164.

CHAPTER IV

THE BEGINNINGS OF FORM AND CONSTRUCTION:
FROM JEAN SANTEUIL TO CONTRE SAINTE-BEUVE

It is evident, in *Jean Santeuil* that Proust is being drawn inevitably to the first-person as the fundamental means of narrative presentation. However, it is equally clear that Proust writes naturally and easily in the framework of third-person narrative as his experiments in traditional techniques testify. His problem is now to find an overall form which will accommodate the advantages he sees in both third and first-person narrative, giving him the degree of omniscience he obviously requires—and which his technical manipulation of first-person narrative in the Introduction to *Jean Santeuil* points towards—and the degree of subjective reporting normally associated with the first-person—illustrated vividly by the *Dreyfus affair* and *Scandale Marie* chapters in the later sections of the work.

Proust knew that his work was formless. His letter to Marie Nordlinger referring to the writing of his book as an operation similar to that of Dorothea Brooke's husband in *Middlemarch,* 'amassing ruins' [209], shows that he was despairing of finding a suitable framework for his episodes, and the following year sees the abandoning of the work altogether. The well-known question 'Puis-je appeler ce livre un roman?' finds a partial answer in the examination of the two sources of technique employed in *Jean Santeuil*. The most superficial reading of this 'novel' shows both a strange disregard for fundamental considerations like chronology, continuous, developing situations and the presentation of action, combined nevertheless with a desire to present the story of Jean Santeuil in the form of traditional narrative, following his development from infancy to manhood, including visual scenes, the presentation of character and the creation of a certain kind of fictional situation. The framework, such as it is, expresses a tendency, in fact, which the actual treatment belies: a paradoxical situation summed up in Proust's own words:

Ce livre n'a jamais été fait, il a été récolté.

---

[209] Marcel Proust: *Lettres à une amie*: Manchester 1942, dated Thursday Dec. 5, 1899.

The circumstances are somewhat complex: Proust in writing *Jean Santeuil* seems to have been obeying two impulses. First, he wanted to write, and particularly to write in novel form, as the experimental *Les Plaisir et les Jours* and the fictional elements of *Chroniques* both testify. Second, the particular experiences he wanted to record concerned mainly his own intellectual and artistic development which, as an examination of the close link between *Jean Santeuil* and *A la Recherche* indicates, had evolved remarkably by the years between 1895 and 1900 [210]. What he only begins to realise as he works on *Jean Santeuil,* however, is the unsuitability for an inner, spiritual examination of personality, combined with extensive introspection and psychological analysis, of straightforward techniques proper to autobiography, where the fiction rests upon the transposition of Marcel Proust into Jean Santeuil. The technical problems involved are almost insuperable. For example, the traditional novel framework demands the retelling of a story, based largely, if not wholly, on a logical, chronological sequence, demands a care for detail, an eye for the particular. The re-creation of a spiritual development, on the other hand, dispenses with detail unless (as in the 'madeleine' episode or the 'drame du coucher') the detail has special significance, and it is more interested in the general than in the particular. The development of attitudes towards experience, rather than an insistence on experience itself, of an interest in psychological analysis rather than the portrayal of physical actions demands examples drawn more or less at random from many different stages of the physical, as distinct from the mental development which necessarily accompanies it, but not necessarily at the same pace: the formality of chronology and of spacial restriction is consequently of less importance. The two sides of the question are linked, since the setting of Jean's childhood ceases to be a passive framework and becomes a factor of the latter's evolution, and ideally they should be so *closely* linked that unity is imposed in the person of Jean himself. However all our examinations of the hero/narrator relationship have shown Proust's complete inability to create and maintain that unity, and his confusion when he attempts to fit narrative techniques, more suited to objective reporting, to a subject demanding subjective introspection.

Contre Sainte-Beuve, unlike *Jean Santeuil,* represents an effort to write an 'ouvrage suivi'. It is therefore revealing to examine the different and sometimes contradictory experiments in composition and structure which it contains, and to try to discover what progress has been made in this direction, as compared with the remarkable step-forward in the authoritative tone and assurance of the material, much of which is reproduced fundamentally unchanged in *A la Recherche.*

---

[210] 'L'auteur de Jean Santeuil possède déjà la clef qui lui ouvrira les portes du temps, mais il ne sait pas encore s'en servir.' Claude Mauriac, *op. cit.*

The Preface to Contre Sainte-Beuve

Bernard de Fallois' interesting preface to *Contre Sainte-Beuve*
refers to Proust's letter to Georges de Lauris in 1908 in which Proust
'lui fait part de son désir d'écrire sur Sainte-Beuve une étude pour
laquelle il hésite entre deux types 'd'article' and the author quotes the
relevant passage:

> L'un est un article de forme classique, l'essai de Taine en moins bien.
> L'autre débuterait par le récit d'une matinée, maman viendrait près de
> mon lit, et je lui raconterais l'article que je veux faire sur Sainte-Beuve
> et je le lui développerais [211]

Two quite distinct questions arise from this desire to discover the
ideal formula for his attack on the critic Sainte-Beuve: the success or
failure of the techniques Proust decides to use, and the introduction
of fiction into the article. These two points may seem connected.
Proust did, after all, consider as one of the possible formulae the
conversation with his mother, which is a kind of fiction, but we shall
show that this idea never really took root and, moreover, that Proust
was incapable of keeping the article on two different planes at the
same time.

Proust's own preface to *Contre Sainte-Beuve* indicates from the
very beginning the tendency which persists throughout towards a
rational basis of argument, on to which examples of involuntary
memory are grafted, as part of a logical demonstration. The argument
is easy to follow:

(a) 'chaque jour j'attache moins de prix à l'intelligence'—followed
by examples of the biscuit dipped in tea, and the uneven stones
of the pavement [212]

(b)   'Non seulement l'intelligence ne peut rien pour nous pour ces
résurrections, mais encore ces heures du passé ne vont se
blottir que dans des objets où l'intelligence n'a pas cherché
à les incarner' —

followed by three specific examples [213].

(c) the conclusion that the intelligence is restricted, followed by
the general example of the examination of Sainte-Beuve's
critical method.

Not only is the plan entirely rational in outline, but it bears a
striking resemblance to the overall plan of *A la Recherche*. Not that
the preface foreshadows the eventual dramatisation of the involuntary
memory episodes to form a framework for the novel; on the contrary,
though the basic elements will appear again at the beginning and end

---

[211] B. de Fallois, Préface to *Contre Sainte-Beuve*, p. 16.
[212] *Contre Sainte-Beuve*, pp. 53-55.
[213] *Contre Sainte-Beuve*, pp. 55-58.

of *A la Recherche,* their arrangement is totally *un*dramatic. What is interesting, however, is the way in which the individual elements of the overall plan tend to develop organically within the framework which contains them. Not only is example followed by example, but each incident organically introduced to add weight to the basic argument [214], takes on an importance which all but threatens the balance of the reasoning. This is important as one of the perennial criticisms levelled against the construction of *A la Recherche* is precisely that the individual elements develop organically, but become so distended as to harm the overall structure, and consequently the aesthetic meaning of the work. On the drastically-reduced scale of Proust's preface to *Contre Sainte-Beuve,* it is easy to see one of the reasons for this characteristic of Proust's composition, and, since the essence of what the author says here is reproduced in a more or less different form in *A la Recherche,* the same reason holds good both for the preface and for the later work. For both represent a paradoxical situation, just as *Jean Santeuil* represented a paradoxical attitude towards fiction. We have seen that the basis of the preface is an intellectual argument— against intelligence. The examples Proust furnishes to this end depend entirely for their effect, however, not upon reasoning but upon the recreation of *sensation.* Their development therefore obeys laws foreign to those of intellectual reasoning, and consequently threatens to destroy the framework which supports them, and which their very presence contradicts. Though in *A la Recherche* the framework is transformed from that of reasoned argument to a dramatic and largely fictional basis, nevertheless the same paradox exists. As it has been noted 'the speculations of (Proust's) intelligence were not, as Baudelaire's, carried on outside the work of art, but as part of its very substance. The coherence of *A la Recherche* is planned and established by the intelligence' [215]. Thus, the problem which continually faces Proust in *A la Recherche,* the fundamental disparity between the essence of the experience conveyed and the structure conceived to convey it, is present at an early stage.

The fictional element in Contre Sainte-Beuve

What is Proust's attitude to fiction, when he decides to accord supreme importance to the *form* of the work of art? Faced with the probem of finding a suitable plan for his article on Sainte-Beuve, Proust has two ideas: one, that he should abjure any attempt to introduce a fictional element, and two, that it should be firmly subordinated to an intellectual criticism of the critic's method. Thus, even when the conversation idea is envisaged, it is easy to see that Proust never intends it to be anything more than a technical device upon which to 'hang' the article. We are immediately reminded of the attitude to

[214] i.e. 'chaque jour j'attache moins de prix à l'intelligence', p. 53.
[215] J.M. Cocking: *op. cit.,* p. 23.

fiction which we found in *Jean Santeuil,* where often the fictional element is introduced as an excuse for the author's pet ideas. In the second plan, the mother is to be given precisely the same technical function as that of Jean in *Jean Santeuil.* Evidently, despite the severe lesson of his abandoned novel, Proust still cherishes the idea of creating both a narrator and a hero.

Yet it is apparent that Proust, in order to introduce the intimate, conversational tone he has been developing in articles and criticism between 1900 and 1908, resorts this time to fiction. For the technical advantages of the second, conversation, project, the alliance, in fact, of a conversational, familiar narrative tone with a carefully-conceived attack upon a complicated critical method based upon multiple references and quotations, are dubious. The reason for risking them is without any doubt Proust's liking for an informal first-person narrative tone—a form which suits him perfectly and which he has near-perfected in the articles. The view that Proust, consciously or unconsciously, always desired to substitute the ideal figure of his reader for the disappointing experiments in friendship which he made throughout his life seems very just and probably explains the origin of some of the difficulties Proust encountered wherever, before *A la Recherche,* he tried to write objectively, remaining in the background and trying to capture his audience through the more indirect and tortuous means of character and situation-creation. Proust's claim that he had no creative imagination, when he discusses realism, and his complaint that superfluous detail always escaped his notice is no jest. He never acquired the novelist's technique to the degree that Balzac did, and he was obliged to proceed in a different direction.

Before proceding to examine the experiments in construction represented by *Contre Sainte-Beuve,* we must first mention briefly the state of the work as we possess it. As Henri Bonnet has pointed out, we are very much in the dark as to the criteria which prompted M. Fallois to choose certain fragments for publication and to reject others. The result is that it is often difficult to discover which of the two 'schemes' we are dealing with, and whether what appears to be a confusion on Proust's part is not perhaps due to faulty editing. We may be reasonably sure, however, that the chapter entitled *La Méthode de Sainte-Beuve* [216] is part of the first, or classic plan for the article, although the cross-reference to Bourget, whose name had previously appeared solely in connection with the second, or conversation project, is at first misleading [217]. The Gérard de Nerval article, too, is conceived on the first plan and it is only with *Sainte-Beuve et Baudelaire* and *Sainte-Beuve et Balzac* that we have what seem to have been chapters destined originally to fit into the conversation scheme with the author's mother. If we reconstruct, as far as the published text allows, the essence of this second project, we can see that not only is Proust's

---

[216] *Contre Sainte-Beuve,* pp. 131-156.
[217] *Contre Sainte-Beuve,* pp. 130 and 132.

treatment of the fictional element once again ambiguous, but that at times he literally forgot the device he was at such pains to introduce. We may assume that the second attempt to introduce fiction, this time making it the centre of the work [218], is a direct result of the failure of chapters 10 and 11.

It is towards the end of chapter VII, *Conversation avec Maman,* that the project for the article based upon conversation is introduced [219]. The whole is built upon a dialogue between mother and son, and it is noticeable that the quotations with which they address ane another continue a pattern already set up during the course of that chapter, and do not prefigure the attack on Sainte-Beuve exclusively [220]. Detail consistent with the fictional cadre is carefully introduced [221] and the greatest care is taken to ensure that the device contains the maximum impression of reality. The 'conversation' continues in *Sainte-Beuve et Baudelaire* and in the following chapter. In *Sainte-Beuve et Baudelaire,* it is immediately apparent that the narrative tone is somewhat less formal than in the classic project of *La Méthode de Sainte-Beuve* where questions of personality are rigorously avoided [222]. Here the narrator quotes personal experiences:

> Mais que de fois je l'ai entendu citer, et pleinement goûté, par une femme d'une extrême intelligence ... [223]

and speaks readily of himself:

> — mais ici ce n'est pas pastiche, c'est une remarque que j'ai faite, où les noms me viennent à la mémoire ou aux lèvres, et qui s'impose à moi en ce moment [224]

all the time maintaining a conversational tone:

> Il a donné de ces visions qui, au fond, lui avaient fait mal, j'en suis sûr, un tableau si puissant ... [225]

Similarly, the personality of the mother is carefully sketched in, her preferences are quoted [226], and we learn that her memory is as prodigious as her son's [227]. We are also continually reminded that the basis of the article is a conversation between two people, and are constantly aware of their physical presence, as for example, in passages like the following:

---

[218] *Contre Sainte-Beuve,* chapters 12-15.
[219] *Ibid.,* pp. 128-130.
[220] *Ibid.,* p. 129.
[221] *Ibid.,* ibid.
[222] *Ibid.,* p. 132.
[223] *Ibid.,* p. 181.
[224] *Ibid.,* p. 180.
[225] *Ibid.,* ibid.
[226] *Ibid.,* pp. 170 and 179.
[227] *Ibid.,* p. 187.

J'ai passé les tropiques, comme un aspect trop connu de son génie, au moins trop connu de nous deux, puisque j'ai eu tant de mal à t'habituer à *La chevelure...* [228]

But if we stop to examine the relationship between speaker and listener we are surprised to discover that it is exactly the same as that already established in *Jean Santeuil* between narrator and reader. For the mother, despite the several reference to her artistic preferences [229] is a fiction in the worst sense of the word, a device in fact chosen by Proust to allow him to adopt the conversational narrative tone which he found so natural a medium for his thoughts and ideas. We soon realise, moreover, that once Proust has established this tone, he immediately abandons the attempts he made at the outset to sustain the minimum fictional setting in which to place the conversation. The impression of a localised place is lost, the mother's figure becomes blurred ; the familiar 'nous' which appears every time the narrator, in whatever work he may figure, begins to embrace his audience in his general conclusions and observations, becomes more and more frequent. Consequently the object of the author's attention imperceptibly changes and, instead of trying to expose his ideas on Sainte-Beuve to the fictional character created expressly for the purpose, the narrator turns his attention to his readers. In exactly the same way that Jean is abandoned in *Jean Santeuil,* so the mother figure is now abandoned in *Contre Sainte-Beuve.*

It is interesting to follow the movement away from the fictional starting-point, towards a more general treatment of the theme. Three stages can be noticed: the sketching in of a fictional framework for the criticisms which is soon abandoned; a nominal adherence to the 'conversation' by referring from time to time to the mother as 'tu', but where the narrator has already veered away from the fictional conversation and is addressing his readers. This interesting stage is continued for a long time with a certain difficulty, for when Proust for reasons of his demonstration needs to include many references and quotations, he adopt a tone which suits the essays of *Chroniques,* but which fails to take into account the mother. It is extremely literary, and it is possible that Proust himself forgot at times the convention he had imposed upon himself, since he corrects himself only just in time when he refers precisely to the question of reference:

... où les noms me reviennent à la mémoire ou aux lèvres [230]

The reader receives a slight jolt, too, when the mother is directly addressed, so completely has her presence been forgotten, and certain details, notably references to Montesquiou, indicate that Proust is addressing his readers [231]. The third and final stage is the complete

---

[228] *Contre Sainte-Beuve,* ibid.
[229] All incidentally, general and included 'en passant'.
[230] *Contre Sainte-Beuve,* p. 180.
[231] *Contre Sainte-Beuve,* pp. 215, 221.

abandoning of the fictional element, so that what has originally formed two quite different projects in Proust's mind, so opposed to each other that he found it necessary to seek the advice of friends, in order to choose between them, fuse quite naturally into a single technique combining elements of both. For the conversational tone of the second plan takes the place of the coldly analytical approach of the beginning of the 'classical' article, while at the same time, the more generally literary aspect of the latter replaces the fictional setting of the bedside conversation, so that, in reality, the third and final stage combines conversation—with his reader—and general comment, but abandons fiction to do so. Thus, while Proust turns to the resources of fiction to create settings and constructional frameworks for his writing, not only does he still write more naturally in an abstract, intellectual and argumentative pattern, but even when he creates fictional scenes, he is still incapable, as he was in *Jean Santeuil,* of sustaining them effectively.

But the pull towards fiction manifests itself in another way. If the fictional settings are unsuitable, nevertheless the elements of fictional writing which were already present in Proust continue to assert themselves, with sometimes curious results. We shall consider their effect upon the chapters constructed, first on a rational and, second, on a fictional basis.

Allowing for the fact that we are not sure whether all the manuscripts date from the same period, nevertheless there is still a large element of confusion in the text even of a single chapter, like, for example, *Le Balzac de M. de Guermantes.* The narrative tone for the first few lines is that of the classic article on Sainte-Beuve:

> Balzac naturellement, comme les autres romanciers, et plus qu'eux, a eu un public de lecteurs qui ne cherchaient pas dans ses romans une œuvre littéraire, mais de simple intérêt d'imagination et d'observation ... [232]

Suddenly, fictional elements appear, accompanied by a change to the vivid present tense:

> Dans la petite bibliothèque du second, où, le dimanche, M. de Guermantes court se réfugier au premier coup de timbre des visiteurs de sa femme, et où on lui apporte son sirop et ses biscuits à l'heure du goûter, il a tout Balzac... [233]

—and although details of the duke's Sunday afternoon activities are included, it is still Balzac who occupies the centre of the stage, and the 'il' of page 227, for example, is not M. de Guermantes, but Balzac. The whole relationship between the fiction and the literary critic's tone is curious. Proust seems to be captivated by his characters, and begins to describe them for their own sake, forgetting all about the novelist on whom he is writing. We learn instead of the duke's

---

[232] *Contre Sainte-Beuve,* p. 227.
[233] *Contre Sainte-Beuve,* ibid.

passion for showing colour slides of Australia [234], of his friend the 'baronne de Tape's' scorn for such vulgar pleasures [235], and of the poor relation's envy because she is never invited [226]. The attitude towards these evolving fictional creations is clearly that of the moralist, and not the novelist proper, however, for the characteristic of them all is the author's obvious delight in observing human reactions and seeking to find the general in the observation of the particular. Consequently the thread connecting the various remarks on the ducal family's behaviour is extremely tenuous, the episodes themselves have a distinctly anecdotic flavour, and the noting of M. de Guermantes' 'tics' and traits leads us far away from the 'bibliothèque du second' where the fiction originally began. Not only are we suddenly transported, moreover, from the library to the salon, or the courtyard, we are also confronted with various allusions to characters whose presence within the original narrative construction is hard to explain. Brief allusions to the sound of rain falling—a hypothetical situation [237]—serve as an excuse to call up the image of Chopin, 'ce grand artiste maladif, sensible, égoïste et dandy' [238]; references to the duke's habit of exercising his horses are simple pretexts to observe the sociological phenomenom of the florist, who reacts to having his window periodically broken as a result, in a decidely revolutionary manner [239]. All this recalls the 'construction' of the literary articles of *Chroniques,* with Proust once again deliberately working into the narrative anecdotes and 'bons mots' collected in fashionable society. At times, he tries to bring the narrative back into the limits of the fictional construction but always without success [240]. Yet as the article progresses it becomes evident that the fictional characters, like the illustrations of involontary memory in the preface, are there to serve as examples for a rational argument, concerning certain attitudes towards literature. The marquise de Villeparisis is given the task of exemplifying a 'mondaine' with her superficial attitude towards Balzac [241]:

'... c'était un homme très commun, qui n'a dit que des choses insignifiantes, et je n'ai pas voulu qu'on me le présente'.

while the marquise de Cardaillac (née Forcheville, incidentally) exemplifies another [242]:

'Si vous voulez, vous viendrez demain avec moi à Forcheville, me dit-elle, vous verrez l'impression que nous produisons dans la ville... et vous verrez en l'honneur de toutes ces personnes allumer le lustre, ce qui causa, vous vous en souvenez, tant d'émotion à Lucien de Rubempré'.

---

234 *Contre Sainte-Beuve,* p. 228.
235 *Ibid.*
236 *Ibid.,* p. 229.
237 *Ibid.*
238 *Ibid.,* p. 230.
239 *Ibid.,* p. 232.
240 *Ibid.,* pp. 229-231.
241 *Ibid.,* p. 241.
242 *Ibid.,* pp. 245-246.

Thus once again the fictional element assumes a secondary rôle, and at one point [243] the narrator banishes the characters altogether, continuing the tone of the more straightforward articles on Sainte-Beuve, Balzac, Baudelaire, Nerval, and so on.

But perhaps the most curious feature is still to come. The creation of fictional characters as elements of a rational demonstration is clear: indeed we can even say that Proust has discovered a formula which allows him to exercise his talents as moralist, novelist and narrator, although the fundamental basis is an argument and not a novel. For it is by concentrating solely on one aspect of his characters, their attitude to Balzac, that Proust manages to keep the narrative more or less under control, and when he is led from anecdote to anecdote, and digression to digression, it is only the overall—and distinctly rational—framework which holds the work together. Yet as soon as the narrator is re-introduced as the vehicle for this rational framework, the original confusion between the two types of article which one supposed to have been eliminated in the earlier chapters, reappears. The narrator's rôle then becomes exceedingly complex: he continues his conversation with his mother [244], he serves as the argumentative but strongly personalised basis of the criticisms addressed to Sainte-Beuve, and combines the functions of the narrator and Jean in *Jean-Santeuil*, in his capacity as hero/narrator, for not only does he stand in the wings to observe his characters, he also takes the stage himself [245]. But whereas he referred to himself in the more autobiographical sections like the *Article dans 'Le Figaro'* as Marcel Proust [246], here the identity of the narrator changes. He lives next door to the Guermantes, and pays them long visits [247]—this is no longer Marcel Proust, but a projection of the author and the essence of his personality into a fictional creation, serving as a link between different episodes. For the first time, the narrator's function assumes the importance it will eventually have in *A la Recherche.*

Construction

On three different occasions Proust links a series of episodes by creating a fictional setting into which they are inserted. These are interesting for two reasons: the importance that Proust obviously attaches to a rigorous plan, using, as we shall see, a number of key-words on which to build the edifice of the overall construction; and the different ways in which he experiments with dialogue.

---

[243] *Contre Sainte-Beuve,* pp. 238-239.

[244] *Contre Sainte-Beuve,* p. 238.

[245] i.e. *La Race Maudite,* pp. 248-249 and *Le Balzac de M. de Guermantes,* p. 229.

[246] Cf. 'M. Marcel' *Contre Sainte-Beuve,* pp. 108 and 99: 'Ça y est, je vois bien les deux dernières colonnes, *mais pas plus de Marcel Proust que s'il n'y en avait pas'.*

[247] *Retour à Guermantes,* passim, pp. 284-300.

Though it is not particularly evident at first sight, chapter V of *Contre-Sainte-Beuve, L'article dans 'Le Figaro'*, is constructed on a very similar basis to that used in the 'overture' to *La Recherche*. it begins: 'Je fermai les yeux en attendant le jour'; a little later on we read: 'je rouvris les yeux, le jour avait paru' [248]. Two and a half pages further on Proust writes: 'l'idée de ma gloire se levant sur chaque esprit m'apparaît plus vermeille que *l'aurore innombrable qui rosit à chaque fenêtre*, while three pages before the end of the article he adds: 'Maintenant sous le ciel rose on sentait que le soleil s'était formé et que par sa propre élasticité, il allait jaillir' [249]. The final paragraph is a prose-poem addressed to the sun, now fully risen in all its glory [250].

Within this framework is carefully interwoven a complicated pattern of sensations which, though they create and obey their own rules, dispensing with the conventional calendar, reducing distance to nothing, nevertheless on a wider scale, still fit perfectly into an individualised and physically particularised setting. We know exactly how long Marcel Proust has been lying in bed musing on his article and his visit to Chartres, for Proust has evolved a construction capable of including two notions of time, one individual, the other conventional, and supporting them on their parallel courses. This is by no means all, however. The internal pattern is not merely created within the extremely delicate framework of dawn, but as part of the framework itself, linked inevitably with the drama of sunrise. Had the carefully-placed reference to the sun been merely an indication of the passing of time, Proust could just as easily have substituted a ticking clock, or the chime of a church bell [251], but instead the image of the 'ciel rose' is so subtly evoked into the pattern of memory and sensation, that not only is the final paragraph a hymn to the sun, but an appeal to the past, and all the memories that have come flooding back:

> Il faisait maintenant grand jour, je voyais à cette terre ces lueurs fantastiques d'or qui indiquent à ceux qui ouvrent leurs fenêtres que le soleil n'est pas levé depuis longtemps, et qui font frémir les grands soleils du jardin, le parc en pente et au loin la Loire immobile, dans cette poussière d'or qu'ils ne reverront plus qu'au coucher, mais qui n'aura plus alors cette beauté d'espérance, qui les fait se hâter de descendre dans le chemin encore silencieux [252].

The second example of a passage built around a fictional setting is also based upon the recurrence of 'key' phrases. The arrival of the article at the beginning of chapter V [253] prompts the following reflexion: 'Si un mot me paraît mauvais, oh ! ils ne s'en apercevront

---

[248] *Contre Sainte-Beuve*, p. 94.
[249] *Ibid.*, p. 101.
[250] *Ibid.*, p. 104.
[251] Cf. *Combray, ARTP*, I, pp. 87-88.
[252] *Contre Sainte-Beuve*, p. 104.
[253] *Ibid.*, p. 94.

pas; et puis ce n'est déjà pas mal comme cela...' [254]. Twenty pages further on we read:

Et après avoir lu des pages où les pensées les plus hautes et les plus beaux sentiments sont exprimés, et avoir dit "ce n'est pas mal"...' [255]

Within the framework created by the repetition of two 'key' phrase Proust fits in a fictional scene intended to support the reflexions and memories caused by certain sensations. Here again we can notice a curiously ambiguous attitude towards the fictional structure of the episode. For the latter is encompassed in a series of thoughts—on the quality of the *Figaro* article—and as such is hardly fictionalised. Within this setting, on the other hand, is a very tenuous fictional scene, meant to support the narrator's memories, but at times pratically invisible. Basically it is as follows: Marcel goes to ask his mother her opinion of his article and finds Félicie with her, brushing her hair [256]. A conversation follows, broken off, however, as Marcel becomes engrossed in the play of light on the window [257]. The tone changes and the fictional scene completely disappears while the narrator/hero discourses, in a new section, on the disparity between impressions and our descriptions of them, calling up a series of memories centred around the Champs Elysées, the house of a childhood friend, and the old anxiety which the sunlight on the balcony brings back [258], when suddenly we are transported back to Marcel's mother's 'cabinet de toilette'. The abruptness of the change from the fictional and temporal to the abstract and immaterial comes as a shock to the reader. Thus this 'fictional' setting, based on two 'phrases-clés' stands mid-way between the wholly analytical argument of the preface, and the wholly fictional basis of *A la Recherche*.

The completely fictional construction which heralds the approach of *A la Recherche* can be found in chapter XV: *Retour à Guermantes*. The techniques involved are straightforward. Proust is faced, as always, with the problem of finding a form to contain a number of loosely-connected episodes. Though the nature and even direction of the material now being used by Proust has changed since *Jean Santeuil*, even there the problem of conveying sensations and sense-associations had become acute. Now, by making the hero/narrator the central pivot around which memory and sensation are both ordered, the difficulties we observed in the early novel largely disappear. The realisation of the narrator/hero's technical superiority (for Proust) over a separate fictional hero is closely related to the gradually increasing tendency to construct upon a fictional basis. Since the narrator figure is the depository of the subjective emotions Proust wishes to convey, it is

---

[254] *Contre Sainte-Beuve*, p. 97.
[255] *Ibid.*, p. 114.
[256] *Ibid.*, p. 105.
[257] *Ibid.*, pp. 109 and 113.
[258] *Ibid.*, pp. 112-113.

natural that he should, finally, take the central position in the story, and by placing him in a completely fictional setting, the author is able to solve another of the problems which kept recurring in *Jean Santeuil*: the references, by means of memory and association, to other periods of time. The recounting of the central figure's life will always contain built-in 'points de repère' to which later phenomena of sense association can refer, without having to create past and future episodes to suit the demands of the moment. Once again conversation and dialogue are used as devices to support the narrative, but this time there is no attempt to mix fictional and non-fictional techniques as in *Rayon de soleil sur le balcon*.

We may note, at the beginning, a certain hesitation in the narrative tone, in which the chapter is recounted. Proust begins as we have noticed before, in a literary style, but the tone soon adopted to recount his stay at Guermantes to his mother is conversational and intimate, [259] often bold and figurative [260]. At time the mother asks a question [261], but the trick serving to unite the two different planes of existence leaves the conversation far behind. For not only does the convention of dialogue disappear, once the impetus of the cloud-formation resembling Chartres is given, but new, fictional scenes come to take its place. The key-phrases are now the 'clochers' of Chartres, introducing a new plane and a new narrative tone, where the narrator addresses his readers, explaining, reasoning, commenting, observing [262]. Thus, side by side with the evocation of the past, with its accompanying poetry, Proust can fit in the moralist side of his genius, besides including favorite anecdotes. All are held within the narrative framework, all suspended from the same thin wire, formed by the repetition of the belfry theme. The technique used to introduce the departure from Combray in this way is clear:

> Moi je ne voyais au contraire jamais sans tristesse les clochers de Chartres, car souvent c'est jusqu'à Chartres que nous accompanions Maman quand elle quittait Combray avant-nous. Et la forme inéluctable des deux clochers m'apparaissait aussi terrible que la gare [263]

From time to time the conversation is taken up again, though the links between the different parts of the dialogue it represents are not always very clear, and the editor has found it necessary to add an explanatory footnote [264]. But the important point to note in this whole chapter is the way Proust has managed at last to combine all the different facets of his genius in one construction. For *Retour à Guermantes* is in the best sense of the word, a demonstration. We have no need of the

---

[259] 'Hé bien, ce que je cherchais à Guermantes, je ne l'y ai pas trouvé. Mais j'y ai trouvé autre chose...' *Contre Sainte-Beuve*, p. 285.
[260] *Ibid.*, p. 287.
[261] *Ibid.*, p. 288.
[262] *Ibid.*, pp. 290-291.
[263] *Ibid.*, p. 291.
[264] *Ibid.*, p. 298.

explanations he gives us via the narrator's mother, for Proust has made the scenes, the compilation of impressions, the confrontation, and not simply the cohabitation, of two different levels of narrative, all speak clearly for themselves. It is with a clear conscience that Proust can say of Balzac:

> Quand il y a une explication à donner, Balzac n'y met pas de façons; il écrit "voici pourquoi": suit un chapitre [265].

for Proust has found a way of avoiding the explanations that abound interminably in *Les Plaisirs et les Jours* and *Jean Santeuil,* just as he has found a way of avoiding the résumés he finds so irritating in Balzac [266], and which also recur in *Jean Santeuil.* In fact, we may conclude that Proust has discovered the formula he will use to write *A la Recherche.*

Before turning our attention wholly to *A la Recherche,* in order to examine the techniques used to fit in with the final plan and conception of the work as a whole, we may notice in *Contre Sainte-Beuve* several more examples of individual construction which will later have a bearing on the final work.

The evolution of individual constructions to contain the dreams and memories that sensation can conjure up has the effect of immobilising the narrative. *Contre Sainte-Beuve* is essentially a static work, there being no progression in either the physical or the intellectual and spiritual situation of the narrator. Each episode, provided with its particular, independent plan is static. In *Sommeils,* and *Chambres* the narrator lies half asleep in bed, or is presented as musing on various themes, unaccompanied by physical movement. In *Journées,* far from showing an active narrator going about his business, Proust again creates a static scene: the narrator stands at his window once again allowing sensations, this time allied with observations, to control the direction of his thoughts and memories. Thus the transposition into a fictional construction of the individual thought processes which we discovered asserting themselves in all of the early works still lacks the final perfection it will receive in *A la Recherche* where measures will be taken to counteract the immobility of the narrative.

We have already mentioned different attempts made by Proust to find a satisfactory construction to hold together the different elements of the narrative. If we examine the early chapters closely, we can see that the experiments in unifying the narrator's impressions do not centre only around the latter, but that Proust invents other methods—which will reappear as individual constructions within the framework of *A la Recherche*—methods which are more directly poetic. For instance, in *Journées* the unifying structure is the internal extended metaphor of a symphony [267], while in *Noms de Personnes* the whole

---

[265] *Contre Sainte-Beuve,* p. 210.
[266] *Ibid.*
[267] *Ibid.,* pp. 75-79.

chapter is based on an exquisitely-developed image of a stained-glass window. Evoking the 'noms colorés et pourtant transparents' of great medieval families anachronistically surviving into the twentieth century, Proust insensibly transforms the implicit image into a complicated evocation of a vast window, containing coloured, transparent figures, representing the genealogy of the families of France:

> A gauche un œillet rose, puis l'arbre monte encore, à droite une églantine, puis l'arbre monte encore, à gauche un lys, la tige continue, à droite une nigelle bleue; son père avait épousé une Montmorency, rose France, la mère de son père était une Montmorency-Luxembourg, œillet panaché, rose double, dont le père avait épousé une Choiseul, nigelle bleue, puis une Charost, œillet rose [268].

The delicate, veined arches of the window form a support for the whole chapter, which ends upon the transcription of the last panel:

> ... la chambre où la reine reçoit les ambassadeurs qui la supplient de fuir dans le vitrail avant qu'elle parte sur la mer, dont le reflet tragique éclairait pour moi sa silhouette, comme sans doute, de l'intérieur de sa pensée, il lui éclairait le monde [269].

Synthesis

The synthesising process will have a profound influence on Proust's style. The constantly-recurring difficulty created by the parallel sets of examples, demanded by moralist demonstrations, but clashing with the initial narrative scheme of *Jean Santeuil* through an ambiguous attitude to fiction in general, disappears in *A la Recherche*. This can, we believe, be partially explained by the development in style which is noticeable throughout the period between *Jean Santeuil* and *Contre Sainte-Beuve*. During this period the characteristic metaphor-laden phrases of *A la Recherche* are developing, through Proust's contact with other writers and particularly with Ruskin. We hope to show that many of the comparisons and parallels, which Proust the moralist cannot resist, are transferred from their ambiguous position alongside the fictional story of *Jean Santeuil* into the actual style used to present the more positive fictional story of *A la Recherche*. Thus, instead of adding new scenes which jar with the narrative plan of the narrator's life-story, Proust transfers many of his examples of types and characters into his richly-imaged style. In this way the fictional creations dependent upon the moralist attitude,—Proust's equivalents of Arias, shall we say,—are integrated into the style. This is not completely the case, as we shall show in the case of the Courvoisier family, for example, and in the later portions of the work where other exceptions can be found. Nevertheless there can be no doubt that the change-over from a half-fictional, half-moralist and analytical basis to a wholly fictional conception of a work with certain accessory

---

[268] *Contre Sainte-Beuve,* p. 280.
[269] *Ibid.,* p. 283.

moralist elements, has profound repercussions on the style of that work.

Let us now sum up the progress Proust has made during the years 1892-1909, years which see the gradual evolution of most of the basic ideas, images and themes of the work he was to begin in earnest the following year.

From the beginning, first-person narrative appeared as the most natural form of expression for the nature of Proust's writings. Yet, as the moralist and novelist emphasis waxed and waned, the author found himself casting about, often desperately for a convenient form in which to fit his experience and ideas. At no time we should note, is there any question of the material itself being influenced by an artificially imposed plan. Even when Proust's natural, even idiosyncratic way of composing found itself face to face with traditional forms and techniques, it was the latter which eventually gave way, in *Une séance à la Chambre.* Another early indication of the kind of solution Proust was to find much later to the problem of form and 'genre', was the discovery in *La Confession d'une Jeune fille* of the utility presented by a carefully thought-out construction which created, by means of built-in time transference, new perspectives which modify the material. However, such indications as these did not coincide with Proust's technical mastery of the methods needed to support them, and his efforts to use first-person narrative, and his method of using complicated time constructions remained drastically limited by a fundamental lack of experience. It was by continuing to experiment, that Proust evolved what is obviously, for readers of *A la Recherche,* his personal and highly characteristic method of narrative presentation, based upon the links of sensation and memory, yet at the same time making use of concrete fictional scenes, inserted against a backcloth of associations and dreams. The beginnings of this technique can be traced back to *Chroniques* and it is there that they rapidly develop. By freeing himself of the formal constructions he had used both in *Les Plaisirs et les Jours* and in *Jean Santeuil,* Proust allows his thought and memory processes to dictate a new narrative technique which, for a while, unfortunately, leads him only to a mass of chaotic, episodic fragments. Gradually, however, as he gains confidence and uses techniques with increasing surety, he begins to evolve ideas for a construction which will contain his material, as it is, instead of trying to write within a ready-made mould, which he rapidly outgrows. *Contre Sainte-Beuve* is a vivid illustration of Proust's preoccupation with the problem of combining a coherent form with his narrative presentation techniques, and the kind of experience and observation he wishes to record, and it is fair to say that it was during the writing of *Contre Sainte-Beuve,* that he came nearest, as far as we can tell, to the final conception of the form and consequent narrative techniques of *A la Recherche du Temps Perdu.* For without form, his material is obscure and dilatory, within a rational framework it is comprehensible, but remains too much like a tract or a philosophy, when all his instincts

drove him to create character and situation. A compromise solution, the essay form of certain chapters of *Jean Santeuil,* for a while seemed a possibility, but again technical difficulties prevented Proust from extending its scope to embrace an entire work. All that was needed was a plan, a plan which would continue the synthesising processes already beginning, which would allow for dramatic scenes and the creation of character (techniques, which, as we shall see, had been evolved simultaneously with the overall narrative methods), and which would present in as vivid a form as possible the intellectual argument which forms the basis of Proust's preface to *Contre Sainte-Beuve,* using, if possible, the same autobiographical material, but translated into a living demonstration, freed from the characteristics both of parable and of 'froide allégorie', yet at the same time giving Proust the opportunity to carry out his moralist observations and rationalisations.

The examination of this plan, its implications, the narrative techniques it uses and gives rise to, will be the object of the second part of our study of Proust's narrative techniques.

PART TWO

THE COMBINATION OF THE DIFFERENT
ELEMENTS IN A NEW FORM

CHAPTER I

PROUST AND BALZAC,
THE DEVELOPMENT OF TRADITIONAL TECHNIQUES

Proust's contact with Balzac, unlike that with Ruskin, is confined to the realms of the novel; at one point in *A la Recherche* it is observed that addiction to a fault or a vice makes one particularly observant of its presence in others. Ironically, during his long acquaintance with the *Comédie humaine,* Proust came to observe in himself some of the failings that Balzac exhibited as a writer, and set about remedying them in characteristically individual ways. Proust owed far more to Balzac than the latter's ideas on successive character-presentation. [1] It will be interesting, at this point, therefore, to review Balzac's influence on the now maturing narrative techniques of Proust.

First, it is immediately apparent that Proust's fascination with Balzac is closely bound up with questions of narrative technique. Mouton [2] remarks that in his Balzac pastiche, Proust reproduces not so much the style of the *Comédie Humaine,* but its method of composition:

> Dans son Balzac, Proust s'est attaché surtout à reproduire les thèmes et les procédés de composition, plus que le style proprement dit.

The second illumination of all the early works, showing the path subsequetly to be taken by *A la Recherche,* comes from the relationship existing between the author and the creations of his imagination. This, as we have seen, is one of the reasons for the failure of *Jean Santeuil,* and Proust inevitably notices the same fault in Balzac:

> Lucien parle trop comme Balzac et il cesse d'être une personne réelle, différente de toutes les autres. Ce qui, malgré la prodigieuse diversité entre eux et identité avec eux-mêmes des personnages de Balzac, arrive tout de même quelquefois pour une cause ou une autre. [3]

He has already, independently, acknowledged the necessity of creating 'live' characters in *Jean Santeuil,* but has been unable to create situa-

---

[1] One pararaph only is devoted to what Proust terms the 'admirable invention de Balzac d'avoir gardé les mêmes personnages dans tous ses romans', in *Contre Sainte-Beuve,* p. 219.

[2] *Op. cit.,* p. 41.

[3] *Contre Sainte-Beuve,* p. 204.

tions in which they can move and act convincingly, without imposing his own explanations as a kind of commentary. The problem of a continuous commentary, present throughout the whole of Proust's work, acting in conjunction with 'normal' narrative procedures is now on the verge of being solved, as the plan of *A la Recherche* takes shape in Proust's mind. Already he shows he is aware of the problem as it appears in another author: the characters of a novel must be strongly differentiated, unlike the case in Balzac where

> Par moments, Mme de Langeais semble être Mme de Cadignan, ou M. de Mortsauf M. de Bargeton [4].

Insofar as the narrator appears as a character in *Jean Santeuil,* with his own personality, his decided opinions, his humour and irony, there is very little difference between him and the character intended to serve as a hero. At times, indeed, the reproach Proust addresses to Balzac is particularly appropriate to himself. What difference is there for example, between Henri, in *Daltozzi et les Femmes* and Jean the hero? Here is another case where Proust for reasons of sexual confession and revelation, has simply switched the names of Henri and Jean, just as Balzac sometimes called what was essentially the same character M de Mortsauf, sometimes M de Bargeton.

The general influence on Proust of certain, specific works belonging to the *Comédie Humaine* which he often read and re-read, may be briefly indicated by a short comparison between Balzac's *Illusions Perdues* and Proust's *Jean Santeuil.* Both tend, at times, to place life and literature on the same level. H. R. Janss [5] calls the latter a work 'dans la promiscuité entre la vie et une forme composée du roman', while Proust himself remarks that:

> Balzac met tout à fait sur le même plan les triomphes de la vie et de la littérature [6].

Both, as we have mentioned, tend to fail in their attempts to create highly individual variants of the same type. Lucien's 'vengeance scene', his passivity in the hands of other characters like Vautrin, are exactly paralleled by Jean's encounter with Mme Marmet, and his dependence on the Duchesse de Réveillon, and Balzac's habit of putting words into his characters' mouths, which neither go with the personality they embody nor with the situation in which they are described, is remarkably similar to Proust's own habit of using Jean as a tool for the narrator, manipulating him in such a way that the narrator can calmly pick up the essential problems of the situation in which the former is cursorily described, and develop them rationally. Another problem, still concerned with the creation of 'live' characters is raised in *Sainte-Beuve*

---

[4] *Contre Sainte-Beuve,* ibid.
[5] See H. Bonnet: *Une Etude allemande sur Proust à la recherche de la conception du roman. Revue d'Esthétique* 1956, pp. 312-321.
[6] *Contre Sainte-Beuve, p.* 196.

et Balzac, and casts light on another point of similarity between Proust and Balzac. Referring again to the latter's presence in his characters' conversations, Proust notes:

> A ces traits, nous reconnaissons Balzac et nous sourions, non sans sympathie. Mais à cause de cela, tous les détails destinés à faire ressembler davantage les personnages des romans à des personnes réelles, tournent à l'encontre [7].

Now Proust himself, it will be remembered, had tried, in some of the articles collected in *Chroniques,* to introduce into what is virtually a fictional setting characters whom he compares with people actually existing at the time Proust was writing about them. The comparison between the two techniques, (on the one hand Balzac, who creates a *ficttonal* world and, to make it seem more vivid, refers to its different elements as though they were actually existing in real life; on the other Proust, who refers to *actually-existing* characters in an attempt to bring vividness to a scene presented in brilliant though often conventional fictional terms) is illuminating, since each represents an extreme view. Proust, finally, as we shall show, makes the inevitable compromise between wholly fictional and completely non-fictional characters by composing a fictional superstructure upon a basis of reality [8].

In conclusion, the 'illumination' of certain of Proust's faults, by his reading of novels like *Illusions Perdues,* is best summed up in the following passage where the tone indicates that not only did Proust find in Balzac examples of his own shortcomings as a writer, but that he also discovered at the same time a means of remedying them. For it shows quite clearly that Proust has now realised the more or less unconscious ambition underlying *Jean Santeuil,* and the existence there of elements conflicting with it:

> Aussi continuerons-nous à ressentir et presque à satisfaire, en lisant Balzac, *les passions dont la haute littérature doit nous guérir.* Une soirée dans le grand monde décrite dans Balzac [9] y est dominée par la pensée de l'écrivain, notre mondanité y est purgée comme dirait Aristote; dans Balzac, nous avons presque une satisfaction mondaine à y asssiter [10].

With the help both of Ruskin and of Balzac, Proust has, without doubt, realised at the same time the faults of his attempts to write before *A la Recherche,* and the function of literature in general.

As Proust's ideas about 'genre' and form begin to clarify, under the influence of Balzac, and thanks to his own experiments in writing fiction and non-fiction, many of the conclusions reached by the writer

---

[7] *Contre Sainte-Beuve,* p. 205.
[8] As in the case of Céleste Albaret: *ARTP,* II, pp. 846-850.
[9] "Lapsus probable. Sans doute faut-il lire un autre nom. Tolstoï par exemple." Note by B. de Fallois.
[10] *Contre Sainte-Beuve,* p. 206.

over the period leading up to the actual composition of *A la Recherche* fall into place. We have already mentioned the case of dialogue, which reflects Proust's uncertainty as to form and technique, and how its use will later be modified in the final perfection of his own characteristic technique in *A la Recherche*. But evolving concurrently with the general conception of the work of art, with the utility and purpose of character and situation, with the general problems of composition, allegory, parable, autobiographical transposition and the degree of fictionalisation to be adopted, evolving concurrently with all these questions are a number of techniques, some more 'traditional' than others, which Proust inherited from the novelist tradition he consciously tried to continue.

We shall now attempt to trace the evolution of such techniques up to the date of composition of *A la Recherche,* showing how they are affected by Proust's hesitations about 'genre' and fictional writing in general. Then, with the final elaboration of the plan, construction and new techniques evolving in their wake in *A la Recherche* itself, we shall show how all the experiments find their place in the later work, which manages to incorporate all the different facets of the author's writing from formal composition to journalism and anecdote.

Dramatic Techniques

Part of the very obvious attraction exerted on Proust by the traditional techniques of "19c." fiction is seen in his constant tendency to use methods of heightening tension, of creating climax and of introducing anti-climax. To take but one, recurrent theme as representative of this tendency, the "involuntary memory" scenes and their precursors, it soon becomes evident that Proust simply adopted a whole range of traditional, dramatic narrative techniques, and used them with great skill in whatever form he was writing.

Elisabeth Jackson [11] remarks that the various potentials of the involuntary memory scenes were gradually discovered, but not all fully integrated until the writing of *A la Recherche,* repeating in different terms Claude Mauriac's conclusion that 'L'auteur de *Jean Santeuil* possède déjà la clef qui lui ouvrira les portes du temps, mais il ne sait pas encore s'en servir [12]. Yet if we look at some of the different appearances of the involuntary memory theme, we shall see that dramatic treatment is more often the rule than the exception. In chapter VII of *Jean Santeuil* [13], *La Mer à la montagne,* Jean's realisation of the power of memory and sensation is handled in a strikingly dramatic way. Not only is this realisation given an important position in the pattern of the whole section, but it also assumes a dramatic

---

[11] *Op. cit.,* p. 594.
[12] Cf. p. 63, note 210.
[13] Section VI, Vol. II.

function in the development of Jean's sensibility. Its appearance is carefully prepared beforehand: it is to perform a revolution in Jean's attitude to the 'vallée qu'enfermaient de hautes montagnes' [14], and the passages preceding it lay the foundation of this revolution. Jean dislikes the countryside which he finds depressing [15] and feels no desire to see his former friend there again. When, suddenly, everything changes. A climax is built up stage by stage as Jean watches the effect of light and shadow playing on the lake, and the culminating point is reached when, unexpectedly, memories of Begmeil come flooding back:

> Aussitôt Jean se revit sur le chemin de la forêt où si souvent un pâle soleil qui s'essayait à traverser la brume jaunissait les feuilles sans se montrer, comme si les feuilles fussent plus claires qu'elles n'étaient en réalité, ou plus tard dans cet automne où il allait en voiture à côté de l'aubergiste à Begmeil [16]

Now his attitude towards the countryside undergoes a radical transformation, and later he comes to realise certain facts about existence, the ephemeral quality of love, and the value of artistic revelation [17]. There is a conscious use of tension and climax which creates the same kind of excitement for the reader as that experienced by Jean. The same conclusions must be drawn from the very striking chapter one of the third section of *Jean Santeuil: La classe de Philosophie*. Once again Proust exhibits a complete mastery of the traditional novelist's techniques, combined with a certain confidence in handling originally a technique which may have been suggested to him by Flaubert. For the entry of the new philosophy master, M. Beulier, is handled with all the care of the traditional novelist, bent on creating suspense and climax. The stage is set with precision, the curtain goes up on the noisy scene of boys waiting expectantly [18], and indirect references to M. Beulier as 'l'esprit le plus profond qu'aient jamais connu les plus intelligents de ses camarades' [19] considerably heighten the sense of tension. Having presented the imminent arrival of the professor through the eyes of the class as a whole, Proust now narrows his spotlight onto the troubled figure of Jean, who, to be placed in M. Beulier's division, has had to overcome his parents' opposition, references to which increase the boy's expectancy as he tries to imagine what the next hour or so holds in store for him:

> ... il essayait vainement, dans une attente passionnée, avec un grand espoir qu'il ferait du bien à sa pensée lasse de s'analyser sans cesse, de se figurer le grand homme qui tardait tant à venir [20].

---

[14] *Jean Santeuil,* Vol. II, p. 214.
[15] *Ibid.*
[16] *Ibid.*, p. 215.
[17] *Ibid.*, p. 220.
[18] *Ibid.*, Vol. I, p. 239.
[19] *Ibid.*, p. 240.
[20] *Ibid.*, p. 239.

The whole of the first, preparatory section, with its neat and effective contrast between Jean's rêveries and the pandemonium reigning around him, is carefully rounded off by the advice of the form dunce [21]. The climax is an anticlimax: a technique which we shall see reappearing in *A la Recherche* whenever imagination creates a situation which reality cannot sustain. It is extremely revealing to note its appearance here in a purely dramatic, externally-reported passage; a page and a half of careful preparation leads us to the spectacle of

> ... un monsieur roux très essouflé, le cou dans un foulard, avec des lunettes et une serviette [22].

The disappointment created by his physical appearance is the beginning of a real climax, consisting of Beulier's handing back of vacation essays, an episode ending in a diminuendo movement with M. Beulier quietly disappearing for lunch. The preparation for this, second, climax is cleverly contrived in a mute dialogue between Jean's hopeful imagination and M. Beulier's devastating criticisms: the aim is clearly to create ironical humour at Jean's expense while doing so:

> ... 'Aucun de ces devoirs d'ailleurs ne vaut la peine que nous nous arrêtions bien longtemps', Jean ajoute mentalement: 'Mais j'ai tenu à mettre à part, car ce ne sont pas à proprement parler des devoirs... Je n'ose pas affirmer que ce sont des chefs-d'œuvre mais j'y vois la messe'. 'Ils sont bien faibles' reprit M. Beulier... [23]

The final episode, consisting of M. Beulier's quiet refusal to remove the punishment he had set Jean, marks the relaxing of the emotional tension created before. Throughout, Proust remains perfectly in control of his material, the attention to detail, like the description of M. Beulier's departure [24], and the scrupulous attention to dramatic effect show Proust's complete mastery of the dramatic and dynamic techniques of conventional narrative presentation.

THE TREATMENT OF CHARACTERS

The confident handling of dramatic techniques places Proust fairly and squarely in the 19th century "novelist" tradition, and their continued use in *A la Recherche* is a proof of Proust's solid attachment to this tradition. A different set of techniques which had been evolving during the year leading up to 1910 stems both from this same "novelist" tradition and from the fictional element of moralist observation-namely portrait. Three different trends can be seen developing

---

[21] *Jean Santeuil,* ibid.
[22] Recalling the first sight of Bergotte in *ARTP. Jean Santeuil,* Vol. I, p. 239 and cf. *ARTP,* I, p. 547 ff.
[23] *Jean Santeuil,* Vol. I, p. 243.
[24] *Jean Santeuil,* Vol. I, p. 246.

in the works preceding *A la Recherche*. First, the re-introduction of characters previously used in different contexts: this dates, possibly, from *Les Plaisirs et les Jours,* where characters who had figured in certain stories, notably the lovers Françoise and Honoré, reappear in *La Fin de la Jalousie,* a story which also sees the re-introduction of a Monsieur de Breyves whose name had already been mentioned in *Mélancolique villégiature de Madame de Breyves.* Second, the gradual introduction of characters, revealing often unexpected peculiarities: a method largely developed in *Jean Santeuil*; and third, the inclusion of portraits, demonstrating attitudes to life or observations on humanity, a tradition, as we have seen, which Proust always seems to have followed from his earliest works.

Compared with the techniques of character presentation used in *Les Plaisirs et les Jours,* those rapidly evolving in *Jean Santeuil* mark a significant step-forward. If we compare the formal description of the vicomtesse de Styrie and the vicomte her husband, in *Violante ou la Mondanité*:

> La vicomtesse de Styrie était généreuse et tendre et toute pénétrée d'une grâce qui charmait. L'esprit du vicomte son mari était extrêmement vif et les traits de sa figure d'une régularité admirable [25].

with the infinitely more subtle and gradual way in which we are introduced to C. the novelist, we are immediately aware of a fundamental difference in technique. The first appearance of C is in no way a list of abstract qualities [26], but a picture of the novelist in action and, exactly as in reality, we learn no more about his character than the conclusions we may reach by observing his appearance and habits. C, then, is introduced to us gradually, his character unfolds slowly. When we discover the generous streak in his nature, it is through having seen him give, in return for a few moments shelter from the rain, a far larger sum than was ncessary [27] ; the discovery of his sadism, and his weakness for elegant society is managed in similar fashion. The key to this new-found technique, seen in use here for the first time, is to be traced to Proust's curiosity as to the 'rapports secrets, les métamorphoses nécessaires qui existent entre la vie d'un écrivain et son œuvre, entre la réalité et l'art' [28], and the resulting adaptation of reality into fiction, using characters [29]; but Proust's use of his new technique is still uncertain. He tends to overemphasise: when C is presented, returning to Kerengrimen from the Princess's castle less happy then after a day spent writing in the light-house keeper's lodge, the point Proust wished to make is clear. Yet, to drive it home, the

[25] *Violante ou la Mondanité : Les Plaisirs et les Jours,* pp. 49-50 and cf. chapter one.
[26] *Jean Santeuil,* Vol. I, p. 35.
[27] *Ibid.,* pp. 37-38.
[28] *Ibid.,* p. 54.
[29] *Ibid.,* p. 53.
[30] *Ibid.,* p. 39.

narrator timidly upbraids C, emphasising the point [30], and underlines C's displeasure by a comparison whose implications could not be more obvious [31]. Similarly, there is a tendency to 'balance' good points against bad points. C is generous, we learn, but we are told immediately afterwards that he is sometimes sadistic. Two more had points are counted against him—his apparent ingratitude and his snobbery, and then the artistic qualities ('good') are resumed. So, in fact, though having gone a long way to bring about the 'métamorphoses nécessaires' which exist between reality and art, Proust has still not freed himself, in 1896, from trying to present a balanced picture of a character, and summing him up in the space of a few pages.

Turning from some of the earliest drafts of *Jean Santeuil* to some of the latest, we can appreciate fully the development of Proust's character presentation techniques, and see how they are now ready to fit into the master-plan of *A la Recherche*. Proust's debts to La Bruyère and Balzac in this field are particularly noticeable.

Section VIII [32] illustrates two main aspects of the technique. The first concerns the reappearance in *Jean Santeuil* of the same characters, and the way their function consequently changes. If we consider this technique in the light of Balzac's own methods of re-introducing characters—often in minor rôles—who have previously figured in earlier works, we can see that there is a remarkable similarity between the methods both writers employ. To take an example from *A la Recherche,* the revelation that the ruined nobleman at Balbec whom Marcel enjoys inviting to dinner is really Odette Swann's first husband [33] recalls the fitting together of a complicated, but circumscribed jig-saw puzzle, where the element of surprise is uppermost. This is often the same effect produced by the *Comédie Humaine,* though there the canvas is so vast that Balzac is able to avoid unlikely 'convergences', like the extraordinary Mlle de Forcheville and her physical and symbolic genealogy. This jig-saw element, with its accompanying effects of surprise, is already being worked out in the final sections of *Jean Santeuil*. Such, for example, is the reaction felt by the reader in chapter XIII: *La salle de garde de la Pitié,* where the brilliant young surgeon Servais turns out to be none other than the young man with a bicycle, glimpsed earlier in the train at Penmarch; the conversation between Jean and Servais illustrates this element of surprise:

'— Où donc étiez-vous, à Penmarch? non dans le petit train? dans le petit train... vous étiez le bicycliste!' [34]

Though the two novelists' reasons for using the same technique are very different (Balzac wishing to recreate a microcosm of society, Proust wishing rather to illustrate the fallibility of the intelligence),

[31] 'Il fronça les sourcils *comme quelqu'un sur la plaie de qui on aurait mis le doigt...' Jean Santeuil,* ibid.
[32] *Jean Santeuil,* Vol. III, pp. 9-118.
[33] *A la Recherche,* III, p. 301.
[34] *Jean Santeuil,* Vol. III, p. 108.

nonetheless the basic method is the same, and it is clear that, once set upon his course by Ruskin, Proust will make definite use of this essentially Balzatian technique, and adapt it for his own purpose. Meanwhile, the similarity is manifest: the reactions of surprise and pleasure, provoked by the chance mention of a familiar name in the *Comédie Humaine,* are present in Proust who adopts the same habit of making casual references to characters belonging to a different period in Jean's life. Such is the case with the reappearance of Mlle Kossichef, now a young lady [35], the passing references to the 'trois élèves intelligents' [36], the mention of M. Beulier, by now almost completely forgotten [37], and the inclusion of Daltozzi's name [38].

Where Proust's character-presentation technique differs radically from Balzac's is in the way characters are first introduced to the reader. The introduction of Mme Marmet continues the trend set with the novelist C, in the introduction; presentation of character is indirect, instead of starting from basic moral judgments, as, for example, the revelation in the first pages of *Le Père Goriot* of the latter's miserliness. Condemnation is present, but is implicit instead of being explicit. We see Mme Marmet in action, registering her faults and virtues with the hero. She is insultingly condescending in her manner, but she is beautiful [39]—two remarks which have little logical connection, but which strike the hero at the same time. It is only then that, with a kind of flourish, Proust provides a tiny visual glimpse of Mme Marmet, whom we know so well, but could not describe. The same technique is repeated later in Chapter V: *L'affront* where Mme Marmet's anxious attempts to keep Jean happy and at the same time parade him before her other guests are trascribed in a few lines of conversation and, as though to draw a line under this portrait of a society hostess, a little visual glimpse of her is included:

> Et elle disparut courant à petit pas, majestueusement suivie par sa longue traîne... [40]

A reproach which might be made of Proust is that, as yet, his characters are not the real-life figures they become in *A la Recherche.* Mme Marmet, for example, is 'tout d'une pièce', and the scenes where she and Jean confront each other from opposing boxes at the Opéra tend to 'use' them both as demonstrations of good versus evil, white versus black [41].

We are compelled to note, on the other hand, that character-presentation techniques are clearly progressing towards the complexity and sureness they assume in *A la Recherche.* Characters are presented

[35] *Jean Santeuil,* Vol. III, p. 15.
[36] *Ibid.,* p. 63.
[37] *Ibid.,* p. 108.
[38] *Ibid.,* p. 105.
[39] *Ibid.,* p. 9.
[40] *Ibid.,* p. 82.
[41] *Ibid.,* pp. 68-69.

in different perspectives, revealing what appear to be contradictory facets of one composite personality. Servais, in chapter XIII is a good example. Proust deliberately creates one impression, and nuances it by superimposing upon it a second. First presented as the man with the bicycle, Servais now reveals a disturbing callousness:

> — Et votre malade, comment va-t-il?, demanda Jean à Servais.
> — Il est mort, lui répondit Servais — Oui? — Vous entendez, Félicie, du champagne... [42]

In direct contrast with this attitude, however, is a quite opposite characteristic: he is gentle with his patients and extremely delicate in his treatment of them:

> Jean fut étonné et ravi d'entendre Servais parler au malade avec douceur, d'un ton presque tendre: 'Eh bien, mon pauvre petit, ça ne va donc pas? Votre abcès vous fait mal? Voyons, mon vieux, laissez-moi faire, je ne vous ferai pas de mal'. [43]

Finally we are transported to a period later in time when this brilliant young student has become a provincial doctor, respected but narrow-minded, rarely giving a thought to the past:

> ... il pensait aux mieux aimés sans tristesse, sans désir de les revoir, et s'ils lui eussent annoncé leur visite il aurait été très ennuyé, très pressé de les voir partir pour se retrouver tranquille au milieu de ceux au milieu desquels se mouvait commodément sa vie, comme elle l'avait fait jadis avec eux [44].

Here, then, is the technique in miniature, which will take us from Odette de Crécy, 'cocotte', mistress of unprincipled archdukes, to Mme de Forcheville, Saint-Loup's mother-in-law, with the lion of Parisian society as her secret lover. Only one difference can be detected in the techniques: though Servais is introduced earlier and then re-introduced, the progression from one personality to another is abrupt, and contained in the space of a single chapter. The effect of time is not yet introduced, by spacing out the successive transformations, as it will later be in *A la Recherche*.

THE CLASH OF DIFFERENT TECHNIQUES

An example of the way different evolving techniques begin to clash with each other, when not set in the framework of an overall plan, just as the narrative itself becomes unmanageable without a similar external, restricting element, is evident in one aspect of Proust's

---

[42] *Jean Santeuil*, Vol. III, p. 108.
[43] *Ibid.*, pp. 110-111.
[44] *Ibid.*, p. 113.

character presentation methods. The reappearances of Mlle Kossicheî, unlike those of Servais, are well spaced-out, indicating that Proust was well on the way to conceiving the long-range development of character which takes its place so naturally in the conception of thematic construction which he adopts from Ruskin [45]. References to her are found in the Champs-Elysées section of volume One, in the recollection of Normandy at lake Geneva, when she is staying near Jean, and again in Mme Marmet's salon. However, a brief comparison with the similar appearances of Odette and their relationship to the Swann-Odette love-affair of *Un Amour de Swann* shows how Proust tries to use two techniques at the same time, with little success. In the latter episode, there is little or no attempt to show the passage of time by interspersing extraneous material between the successive reapparances of Swann and Odette. On the contrary, the reader is surprised to discover how long the affair lasted, since no reference to time is made, and the chronology of the episode is not that registered by clocks, but that registered by emotion. In this way Proust can draw parallels between the beginning and end of what is, in some respects, a self-contained episode, emphasising, by turning a particular motif upside-down, the changes that gradually take place in the relations of Odette and Swann. Now, the same comments about the evolution of love are present in the earlier Jean-Marie Kossichef affair, but because the episode is spread untidily over three volumes, reflecting the character-presentation techniques being evolved, their force is lost, and attempts to draw revealing parallels between the beginning of Jean's adoration of Marie and his later indifference are largely unsuccessful. The reference to long-forgotten 'jours de pluie' as a significant change in his feelings comes so long after the isolated episode it recalls, that the force of the memory is weakened, and the violent emotional reaction which follows seems hard to understand:

> Quelquefois en passant devant l'hôtel il se rappelait les jours de pluie où il emmenait jusque-là sa bonne en pèlerinage. Mais il se les rappelait sans la mélancolie qu'il pensait alors devoir goûter un jour dans le senti-ment de ne plus l'aimer. Car cette mélancolie, ce qu'il projetait ainsi d'avance sur son indifférence à venir, c'était son amour [46].

It is therefore possible to conclude that Proust, in order to convey certain truths and observations about the behaviour of people in love, found himself obliged to abandon, in the *Amour de Swann,* techniques which are present in experimental form in *Jean Santeuil,* preferring, in the former, symmetry and classic form to techniques designed especially to demonstrate the falsity of patterns imposed upon

---

[45] Cf. particularly Proust's remark in the avant-propos to the *Bible d'Amiens*: 'Nous retrouvons dans un second livre, dans un autre tableau, les particularités dont la première fois nous aurions pu croire qu'elle appar-tenaient au sujet traité autant qu'à l'écrivain ou au peintre'. *La Bible d'A-miens,* av.-pr., p. 4.

[46] *Jean Santeuil,* Vol. III, pp. 15-16.

experience which conforms to no set pattern in particular, and very rarely assumes the shape created for it by the imagination.

THE NEED FOR A PLAN

All the works prior to *A la Recherche* show a gradual movement both in thought and technique, towards the finished product of *La Recherche*. The question of first and third person narrative in the experimental *Jean Santeuil* and *Contre Sainte-Beuve,* have been carefully explored and significant conclusions reached. Proust's decided preference for an easy conversational, even intimate tone, which his direct addressing of the reader permits, confirms finally the other technical advantages of first-person narration. One important difference, however, separates all the earlier works from *A la Recherche* itself : the decision, evident in the latter, to dramatise the story of Proust's vocation in the recounting of the 'adventures' of a fictional hero. In *Contre Sainte-Beuve,* attempts to fictionalise the writer's attacks on Sainte-Beuve had been half-hearted; moreover the difficulty of continuing the concept of a conversation with an almost academic attack on critical methods proved to be considerable. In *A la Recherche* all the lessons of the earlier works combine in creating a form which owes much to, but completely resembles none of the preceding experiments. The introduction of a dramatic element into *A la Recherche,* and not simply its introduction, but its function as a demonstration of values, sets the final work spart.

Two points suggest themselves immediately. The transformation of an argument, presented in an almost wholly rational and intellectual form in *Contre Sainte-Beuve* into a fictional story recalls Proust's earlier attempts to fictionalise his own life and to include, significantly, descriptions and transcriptions of his 'moments privilégiés' in *Jean Santeuil*. Though, as this early work progresses, there are signs that the spiritual uplifting of the hero is assuming more importance than hitherto, nevertheless it never becomes, as in *A la Recherche,* the basis of a fictional drama. Its greater or lesser importance, according to the degree of dramatisation involved, never influences the overall construction, which simply follows loosely the chronological story of Jean's early years, ending with the old age of his parents.

Thus, although Proust had carefully considered the use of both fictionalisation and dramatisation in *Jean Santeuil,* he had never conceived of the advantages of the latter as a means of providing an important demonstration. As he added more and more pages to the unfinished first novel, his ideas on character presentation and other important questions which were to re-appear in the final work, like the basic opposition between society and the claims of individual experience, began to mature. Consequently, the 'demonstrations' of character development gain in complexity. Under the continuing influence of Ruskin and Balzac, and the rejection of the 'poor guide'

Sainte-Beuve, Proust's ideas on art and technique focussed, a plan emerged, a plan which meant that the element of drama, present in the earliest descriptions of the 'baiser du soir' and the moral parables of *Les Plaisirs et les Jours,* itself took on the function of a demonstration, providing both an external form for the work as a whole, while springing organically from the many-sided character of the material it was to contain.

THE PLAN OF **A LA RECHERCHE** AND ITS ADVANTAGES

THE PLAN

Proust's strange work, as L. Cazamian has observed [47], is put together in a peculiar way. An identity-less narrator, twice in the course of the novel referred to as "Marcel", recalls the story of his past life, from a point somewhere in middle age; he does not follow a strict chronological plan, but begins and ends with two significant episodes, one of which is examined more fully than the other. By taking, in this way, the sensations of involuntary memory and using them as the pillars of the work [48], Proust centres the retracing of his narrator's career around his intellectual and spiritual life. Implied, too, in the construction is the revelation of what this life is to bring to the narrator, who passes from stage to stage apparently unaware of the outcome of his discoveries and disenchantments. For the first involuntary memory episode is used to introduce a whole section of his childhood, conjured up from the past by associations connected with one particular sensation—the famous 'madeleine' sequence [49]. The rediscovery of the past, effected but not fully understood in the first involuntary memory passage, is to be the result, made permanent this time in the writing of a book, of the second involuntary memory episode, at the end of the work [50]. Finally, the narrator examines all the implications of his experience and evolves an 'aesthetic' drawing upon the events and lessons of the life he has lived.

The outline of the work is clear: Proust continues to use involuntary memory as part of a 'demonstration', and the whole of *A la Recherche* becomes a 'demonstration' of the argument set forth in Proust's preface to *Contre Sainte-Beuve*: 'Chaque jour j'attache moins de prix à l'intelligence'.

---

[47] L. Cazamian: *A History of French Literature*, Oxford 1955, p. 433.

[48] 'Comme (*A la Recherche*) est une construction, forcément, il y a des pièces, des piliers, et dans l'intervalle des deux piliers je peux me livrer aux plus minutieuses peintures.' Proust to Jacques Rivière, 3-12 July 1920.

[49] *ARTP*, I, pp. 43-48.

[50] *ARTP*, III, pp. 866-869, 883-886.

Yet, like the preface to *Contre Sainte-Beuve, A la Recherche* is conceived and constructed by a master intelligence, and the work is a masterpiece of complex planning. For the narrator's life story is presented in a variety of different 'tones', which nevertheless preserve the underlying personality of the narrator: Marcel's career is presented in a subjective light, as through the eyes of the latter, who, inexperienced and often wildly romantic, goes through life misunderstanding, misinterpreting events and experiences which only later he realises to have been distorted by his imagination. At the same time, the same narrator, from his position in middle life, looking back over his past, continually makes his presence felt in the narrative, by dropping hints at intervals about the meaning and interpretation *he* attaches to the same events and experiences. The difference between his valuation of them and the earlier Marcel's is often great, and gives Proust the opportunity to introduce conclusions about life, irony, humour and so on. The final, synthetised, conclusion is saved until the end, the mystery of Marcel's seemingly useless life dramatically swept away in a series of lightening revelations and conclusions in *Le Temps Retrouvé.* Continually present, then, is what critics have called Proust's 'double vision' and this important part of Proust's elaborate narrative technique will receive particular attention.

Part of Proust's plan, to present demonstrations of the superiority of sensation over intelligence, involves the creation of a series of separate 'worlds' in which the narrator had lived, which he abandoned for other 'worlds' and which he eventually rediscovers living and intact within himself. In order to invest the final rediscovery of Combray, Balbec, the Champs Elysées, the world of the Guermantes and Doncières—the world of military society, in order to recreate these in the mind of the disillusioned narrator of *Temps Retrouvé,* they had first to be created in 'reality', in the way that Marcel first came in contact with them. Proust therefore evolves a technique (which we shall see to be the outcome of his experiments in the earlier works) to create a series of 'worlds' describing typical scenes, characters and events which created the atmosphere, lost and found again. Once again, the presence and active cooperation of a master intelligence is apparent behind the technique, whose function is to show, paradoxically, the inferiority of intelligence to sensation.

So long, and so complex is *A la Recherche,* that its general outline becomes blurred from time to time. A factor contributing to this over-complexity is the author's careful avoidance of conventional 'sign-posts' in the work. Events are often presented in a disconcertingly off-hand manner; for example, Swann, who is to play so large a part in Marcel's emotional life, both directly and indirectly, is a case in point. Not until after his influence has been exerted does Marcel make direct reference to it [51]. Balzac, on the other hand, represents the

---

[51] *ARTP,* III, pp. 915-916.

opposite tendency: his 'sign-posts' are always clearly marked, and the direction the narrative is taking is always clear [52].

Combray constitutes a symbolic ordering of Marcel's emotional attitude to life: the creation of the first of a series of worlds sets the pattern he will follow throughout his life. Within this world, two ways, or walks, which left a deep impression on the narrator as a boy, come to represent, as he grows older, the projection of a number of deeply-held beliefs and illusions. His life is shown as the methodical following of all the associations of the two ways, symbolised by Swann and the Guermantes family, until all illusions gone, all associations dispersed, they merge into a flat nothingness which immediately precedes the final revelation. Then the 'vases clos' which are the worlds of Marcel are rediscovered intact, the magic and charm of memory and sense-association demonstrated, and meaning restored to life in art. The work, it will be appreciated, was planned on symmetrical lines and, as J.M. Cocking remarks:

> If the middle sections of the novel had not been so inflated during the years of the war when publication was suspended, the abstract symmetry of the plan would have been reflected in the symmetry of the book; distributed over two or three volumes, we should have had *Du côté de chez Swann* and *Le côté de Guermantes,* in roughly equal dimensions, preceded by Combray and rounded off with the account of Marcel's revelation, originally to be called *l'Adoration perpétuelle* [53].

Symmetrically planned, the story is 'arranged', in order to provide the dramatic effect of *Temps Retrouvé* and many carefully-prepared passages, providing the kind of interest and suspense which the traditional novel derives from plot, prepare the final revelation. The traditional narrative techniques, which we have seen Proust perfecting, naturally take their place in the new scheme. At the same time, the later narrator's evocation of past states not seen in the final perspective of *Temps Retrouvé* allows Proust to include and develop his characteristic method of evoking atmosphere and sensation. Finally, the continual presence of the later narrator, whose attitude to life owes something both to his 'pre-revelation' and to his 'post-revelation' personality, gives the author every opportunity to include the element of commentary which earlier experiments showed to be indispensable to him.

This plan and narrative framework allows Proust to solve most of the problems which had beset him in earlier works, and most important, gives him the opportunity to combine ingeniously moralist and novelist aims and techniques.

---

[52] i.e. a typical example is the introduction to the reader of Mlle Sophie Gamard in *Le Curé de Tours,* where her function and rôle are clearly indicated: 'Telle était la personne destinée à exercer la plus grande influence sur les derniers jours de l'abbé Birotteau'. *Le Curé de Tours,* Nelson 1958, p. 427.

[53] J.M. Cocking, *op. cit.,* p. 38.

A la recherche du temps perdu — THE ALLEGORICAL DEMONSTRATION
OF *Contre Sainte-Beuve*

One of the difficulties Proust had to face in *Jean Santeuil,* for example, was the fact that he had evolved no satisfactory method of translating the demonstration of certain laws into a fictional form. *A la Recherche,* on the other hand, contains a variety of examples of the re-thinking of abstract observations, and their transformation into continuous fiction, using all the techniques proper to the novel. *Le côté de Guermantes,* beginning as it does with the account of Saint-Loup's infatuation with Rachel, provides a good illustration of the methods Proust used to transfer the theoretical judgments about love in *Jean Santeuil,* whose inadequately-prepared scenes succeed one another haphazardly, into the polished fiction of *A la Recherche.*

A single theory underlines the subjectivity of love and infatuation: this is the basic thread running through a number of scenes, from the introduction of Rachel to Marcel to the end of the sequence in the theatre [54]. Each one drives home the author's point in a different way; thus, the scene where Marcel meets Rachel, whom he has known as a prostitute, throws light on the general law, announced at the beginning:

> Je me rendis compte de tout ce qu'une imagination humaine peut mettre derrière un petit morceau de visage comme était celui de cette femme, si c'est l'imagination qui l'a connue d'abord [55].

—while the chance meeting with Rachel's friends demonstrates the fact that the victim of the illusions created by love can sometimes see beyond the stereotyped image created by his imagination [56]. Similarly, the presence of Rachel on the stage serves to illustrate for a third person, an objective observer (as Marcel is, of Saint-Loup's infatuation with Rachel), the nature of the subjective illusion in another person, even if he does not personally share it:

> Mais le commencement de cette représentation m'intéressa d'une autre manière. Il me fit comprendre en partie la nature de l'illusion dont Saint-Loup était victime à l'égard de Rachel... [57]

Thus, all the various nuances, characteristic of Proust's reasoning, are made the basis of a number of consecutive scenes, where the actors manipulated to reveal certain 'laws' remain the same throughout and exist in their own right, instead of being, as they so often are in the early novel, X and Y, or colourless 'types' introduced for their illustrative power and never reappearing. With the introduction of an overall plan, where a narrator/hero provides a focus for the mass of

---

[54] *ARTP,* II, pp. 152-183.
[55] *ARTP,* II, p. 159.
[56] *ARTP,* II, pp. 161-2.
[57] *ARTP,* II, p. 174.

observations Proust wishes to make, such demonstrations are incorporated into the fabric of the work, and are translated into fictional terms.

This transformation into consecutive fiction of purely abstract reasoning, moreover, depends largely upon the existence within the novel of many of its traditional ingredients: situation, character and 'plot'. On a larger scale, the conception of *A la Recherche* as a fictional demonstration, built upon a carefully reasoned plan, reveals the same kind of transformation that we have observed in the Saint-Loup/Rachel episodes. By means of convincing *characters,* like the Combray figures or the Duchesse de Guermantes, of carefully planned *situations,* like Marcel's successive contacts with different aspects of life which nearly all prove disappointing, and by means of *plot,* the unexpected revelation of art as the key to Marcel's vocation, *A la Recherche* is an allegorical demonstration of an argument, carried out in fictional terms. Within the framework provided by the plan, Proust uses two main techniques, corresponding to his two principal objectives. First, he evokes the 'essence' of the narrator's past, in a series of static descriptions of emotion and sensation ; this, he states in *Temps Retrouvé,* is the artist's foremost duty. Second, within the overall painting of a mood, or a particular atmosphere, Proust demonstrates 'laws' of human behaviour, drawing upon the traditional elements of the novel. Thus moralist and novelist aims and techniques figure in the final conception of *A la Recherche.*

Of equal importance is the working into the plot of *A la Recherche* of the commenting element which is characteristic of all Proust's writing. The first person narrator, whose intricate function we shall shortly examine, provides this necessary element, by being at one and the same time involved and detached; for though telling his own story, he is nonetheless placed after the dramatic revelation of *Temps Retrouvé* and possesses, even if he does not always project it, an entirely new and different point of view.

The experiments in time, carried out in a vaccuum in the early works, now assume a proper function within the work, largely owing to the plan evolved. Just as the whole of Marcel's experience is dramatically reviewed and re-evaluated in *Temps Retrouvé,* so the presence of time is dramatically introduced into the framework of the narrator's personal drama. Since *A la Recherche* is largely based on an a-chronological narrative technique, the passing of time is largely unnoticed. Yet, in the final period of depression, both reader and narrator are made aware of the vast wastage of the life which has gone before. In this way, a second perspective in which time is viewed results from the outline of the plan. Third, in the light of the revelation of *Temps Retrouvé,* time is shown to be an intellectual concept which must be revised to fit in with new theories of sensation and memory. Finally, time is made to precipitate the drama: it becomes a tool, as well as an ingredient, in the search for values. The realisation that little time is left to Marcel urges him on and contributes to the excitement and

drama of *Temps Retrouvé*: as the narrator remarks: '... celle du Temps... était un aiguillon, elle me disait qu'il était temps de commencer...' [58].

Thus the fictionalisation of experience, the moralist element, the interest in traditional techniques, the need to comment and the desire to experiment with time and chronology—all find their place in the new narrative scheme.

FIRST-PERSON NARRATIVE

What are the advantages of the retrospective first-person narrative form which Proust decided to use in *A la Recherche*? Although we have seen Proust being continuously and instinctively drawn towards the first-person, it would, theoretically, have been easy to write *A la Recherche* in the third person, objectively, so that the revelation of the ending could be achieved without the difficulties attendant on the choice of subjective narration. The author could have pointed out all the values of life that the hero had been living, without resorting to the creation of a situation, which, as Germaine Brée has pointed out, provides 'une réalité que (le narrateur) ne voit pas, et ne découvrira qu'à la fin, mais qui a une existence de fait dans son récit' [59]. In this way, the retrospective viewpoint of the hero, when he finally discovers his vocation, could have been successfully maintained, and through his reflexions we could have had a new illumination of the work which had preceded, having first, ourselves, come in contact with the true nature of the experience which the hero finally recognises. There are two main objections to this choice of third-person narration.

(1) *The moralist element in A la Recherche du Temps Perdu*

The lesson of *Jean Santeuil,* where the narrator, separated technically from the hero, is left with the observations on humanity, while the latter is reduced to the fictional tool necessary to provide the fictional basis to support such observation, was sufficient, as we have seen, to convince Proust of the advisability of creating a narrator/hero. In first-person narrative, the moralist element of *A la Recherche* is drawn closely into the main body of the work, since Proust makes use of it by fitting it into the aesthetic progression of the novel. For, by attributing not only the hero's progress, but also the simultaneous commentary to the same fictional character, Proust can incorporate into the plot a whole side of his genius which had remained, in *Jean Santeuil,* a more or less artificial addition to the story of Jean.

---

[58] *ARTP*, III, p. 1032.

[59] G. Brée : *Du Temps Perdu au Temps Retrouvé*, Paris, *Les Belles Lettres*, 1950, p. 29.

(2) *The Drama of the Plan*

We would remain to some extent *outside* the hero's experience if we could judge his reactions to life only through the intermediary of a separate narrator; the presence of such a narrator in *Jean Santeuil,* far from allowing us a complete view of the hero's individual personality, and an understanding of the values according to which he judges life, is an encumbrance to the direct communication of both. Had Proust nonetheless continued with both a hero and a narrator, he would necessarily have had to create two sets of judgments, two standards by which to measure the value of experience. For in order to reveal the intrinsic value of Marcel's life, and at the same time to show the reader that the latter was not reacting to it, Proust would have been forced to admit at an early stage that Marcel's life did in fact have an intrinsic value, and that all that remained to reveal was the moment when Marcel would sooner or later come to realise this fact, that he, the narrator, had understood it from the beginning.

This would be quite contrary to the calculated drama of the construction. In fact, the reader finds a succession of worlds unfolding before his eyes, which are founded on certain assumptions judged according to certain criteria which, even if he does not personally agree with them, he nonetheless accepts as representing a valid point of view, to which the presence of characters like Charlus add irresistible weight. It is only by reversing the whole set of values that the drama of the revelation can be transmitted to the reader. In this way Proust achieves the direct transmission of experience which is for him the only function of art. He does not wish merely to describe the hero's experience from the outside, as third-person narrative would oblige him to do, but rather to communicate that experience by recreating it. Such is the function and validity of the first-person narrative of *A la Recherche,* without which the ingenious structure would be meaningless. As Professor Brée points out, 'cette expérience ne pouvait être racontée par un tiers' [60].

THIRD-PERSON NARRATIVE IN *Un Amour de Swann*

Nevertheless, one episode is recounted in the third-person, objectively: *Un Amour de Swann.* It is known that an original version of *A l'ombre des jeunes filles en fleurs,* also in the third person, was rewritten in the first person, and it is interesting to try to discover the reasons why the same treatment was not given to Swann's story. Swann's role in *A la recherche* is summed up in *Le temps retrouvé:* it is his influence, presence and example which have always inspired and directed Marcel:

---

[60] G. Brée : *op. cit.,* p. 29.

En somme, si j'y réfléchissais, la matière de mon expérience, laquelle serait la matière de mon livre, me venait de Swann... [61].

Swann is Marcel's avatar, his doppelgänger. Now, in order to draw up a parallel of sufficient importance to highlight this function, it was not enough for Proust to describe Swann through the eyes of another person: his character-presentation theories and techniques all tend to show that such a viewpoint is likely to be distorted or, at the best, incomplete. Proust must present Swann from exactly the same viewpoint as that from which he judges Marcel: from within. Since it is Marcel who describes his own psychological reactions, Proust must be able to describe those of Swann in similar fashion, in order to point out their similarities, and to show at what stage Swann falls short of the ideals necessary for the making of an artist. It is obvious that Swann could have been made to tell his own story, but if we consider what the consequences of having two first-person narrators would involve, it is not hard to see why Proust did not adopt, if indeed he ever thought of, this solution. Not only has he been unable to make hero and narrator co-exist in *Jean Santeuil*; but the aesthetic consequences to the structure and meaning of *A la Recherche* of such dualism would have been fatal. Marcel can only look back upon his loves for Gilberte and Albertine, as he explains in *Temps Retrouvé,* because he has discovered his vocation. The whole point of Swann's rôle is that a similar 'illumination' never came. Therefore, not only would unity of construction have had to be sacrificed to allow Swann to share exactly the same technique as that used to describe Marcel's inner life, but the whole meaning of *A la Recherche* would have been jeapordised. Proust could not present Swann's story through the eyes of an observer, nor could he present it through Swann's own eyes. Both third and first-person narrative are automatically ruled out.

Proust eventually discovered a compromise solution; he decided to recount Swann's story both through Marcel's eyes, and in the third-person singular, thus having what can only be described as the best of both worlds. For it is Marcel who tells of *Un Amour de Swann* and by doing so, he solves a problem which Proust had been unable to cope with successfully in *Jean Santeuil*; Proust makes a narrator, whose commentary forms one of the most interesting parts of the story, coexist with a fictional hero, Swann. This feat is achieved by suppressing the appearance within the narrative of Marcel himself [62], while in *Jean Santeuil*, it will be remembered, the narrator frequently refers to himself as having personally known Jean's friends, insinuating that he remembers the same things as Jean, and merging to form one composite personality with the latter. This never occurs in *Un Amour de Swann*: unity is maintained since the same voice narrating *A la Recherche* is relating *Un Amour de Swann*. So cleverly is the time

[61] *ARTP*, III, p. 915.
[62] Technically, the 'affaire' took place before Marcel's birth: cf. *ARTP*, I, p. 186.

manipulated that the physical character present in the narrative is absent from this particular episode, and hero and narrator coexist peacefully. Aesthetic unity, too, is preserved because the lessons drawn from Swann's affair could be drawn only by the narrator, Marcel, and could only apply later to the hero, Marcel again.

In a similar episode in *Jean Santeuil* [63], Proust using objective narration centred all his attention on the main figure, Bastille, and forgot Jean, the real hero. In *A la Recherche,* Proust combines first-person narrator and third-person omniscience in *Un Amour de Swann* in the following way:

> C'est ainsi que je restai souvent jusqu'au matin à songer au temps de Combray ... à ce que, bien des années après avoir quitté cette petite ville, j'avais appris au sujet d'un amour que Swann avait eu avant ma naissance, avec cette précision dans les détails plus facile à obtenir quelquefois pour la vie de personnes mortes il y a des siècles que pour celle de nos meilleurs amis... [64]

The basis of the narrator's information is exactly that indicated in the introduction to *Jean Santeuil,* where Proust is also conscious of the limitations of subjective narration, and of the need to supplement by later knowledge the necessarily limited viewpoint of the first-person narrator. In the introduction, Proust's impatience with this viewpoint was manifest, and he tended to emigrate into the personality of the novelist C, describing his emotions which no amount of subsequent knowledge could have indicated at that moment. In *Un Amour de Swann,* Proust commits the same 'mistake', but immediately covers himself by adding that the detail of the story is often easier to obtain about others than about people we think we know well. Under cover of this explanation, Proust allows Marcel to describe Swann's most intimate psychological reactions, as though he had become the omni-scient third-person narrator of a novel like *Jean Santeuil.* Thus by striking a balance between first and third-person narrative, Proust has subtly introduced into an episode, told by a first-person narrator, all the advantages of omniscient third-person reporting.

We may conclude, therefore, that *Un Amour de Swann* is a special case, standing apart from the rest of *A la Recherche,* and demanding special treatment. But if we look closely at the use of first-person narrative in the main sections of the work, we see that, if whole episodes, like *Un Amour de Swann,* do not benefit from a special treat-ment, at least certain themes and subjects do; first-person narrative is not always entirely suitable for all of Proust's aims, notably the survey of society and the detached observation of manners. In order to include these elements satisfactorily, Proust resorts to a technical manipulation of the narrative which bears considerable similarity to that used in *Un Amour de Swann.* By carefully concentrating on one or other of

---

[63] *Jean Santeuil,* III, pp. 298-302.
[64] *ARTP,* I, p. 186.

the 'tones' which the presence of the narrator at two distinct moments in time affords him, Proust can convert first-person narration into omniscient third-person reporting, whenever it suits him to do so. This resulting 'double vision' is therefore one of the most interesting technical features of the work.

DOUBLE VISION

Let us rapidly sum up the basis of this 'double vision'. Thanks to the plan and structure of *A la Recherche,* two main narrative viewpoints are present throughout. The later position in time of the overall narrator gives Proust almost all the advantages of the 'ideal' third-person narrator, while preserving the limited viewpoint of Marcel, at the time of experience, by deliberately adopting his, sometimes distorted or incomplete, conclusions. Thus both viewpoints are present and alternate continually; yet since *A la Recherche* is based upon a dramatic structure, the final narrator though 'omniscient' withholds essential information whose inclusion before *Temps Retrouvé* would destroy the plot. Many passages indicate the presence throughout of the 'post-revelation' narrator, and from the beginning it is the Marcel who has learned the lesson of Art who speaks in the first person. The 'baiser du soir' episode, for example, provides an illustration of the possibilities offered by the coexistence of two different viewpoints, and the ease with which one can be substituted for another.

Before the first evocation of Combray [65] there is no doubt that it is the final narrator who is addressing us. Having lived through the experiences recounted in *Temps Retrouvé,* he is fully aware of the special powers of involuntary memory, and their implications:

> ... *mais alors le souvenir* — non encore du lieu où j'étais, mais de quelques-uns de ceux que j'avais habités et où j'aurais pu être — *venait à moi comme un secours d'en haut pour me tirer du néant d'où je n'aurais pu sortir tout seul* [66];

and he can judge the limitations of memory unaided by dreams or sensations:

> ... et mon corps, le côté sur lequel je reposais, gardiens fidèles d'*un passé que mon esprit n'aurait jamais dû oublier,* me rappelait la flamme de la veilleuse de verre de Bohême... [67]

When this final narrator recalls an earlier self, a stage in his development as an artist when many of his ideas were incomplete or mistaken, the two necessary elements of the 'double vision' are present. The sometimes imperceptible change from one viewpoint to another is made

---

[65] *ARTP,* I, pp. 9-43.
[66] *ARTP,* I, p. 5.
[67] *ARTP,* I, p. 6.

without warning and the consequent ambiguity of the narrative exploited to 'prove' various theories. In this episode, chosen solely to illustrate the possibilities of the double vision technique, it is character development which benefits particularly from the alternating viewpoints. The final narrator's retrospective viewpoint allows Proust to include reference to Swann's double life, a fact never suspected by the earlier Marcel. At other times the latter's subjective viewpoint alone is projected, and the perspectives radically altered. In a passage referring to his 'nuits d'insomnie', the final narrator mentions that one of the topics with which he would while away the time was the story of Swann and Odette. Yet here this knowledge is absent . Odette is referred to in the terms with which she was labeled at Combray: 'une femme de la pire société, presque une cocotte, que, d'ailleurs, (Swann) ne chercha jamais à présenter [68]. Similarly, the Guermantes, whose intricate story the narrator knows well, are introduced with all the naïveté of the child, whose only knowledge of the ducal family is dependent on his grand-mother's remark that the nephew of her friend, the marquise de Villeparisis, is a man of great vulgarity [69]—a comment paralleled by another about Jupien and his daughter, two of the least attractive characters in *A la Recherche,* as 'des gens parfaits':

> ... elle déclarait que la petite était une perle et que le giletier était l'homme le plus distingué, le mieux qu'elle eût jamais vu [70].

There is no attempt to correct the error of this partial vision for the same reason that the scattered hints and comments, belonging to the final narrator, are never presented together until the occasion of the dramatic climax in *Le Temps retrouvé.* The calculated effect of surprise in character presentation and in the plot of *A la Recherche,* forbids such rectification.

At one point, the childhood vision of experience is confronted with the narrator's more complete view, when Proust places the first important links between the childhood experience recounted in the 'baiser du soir' episode and the later torments of jealousy which spring from it. The description of the painful evening drama is seen through the eyes of the neurotic child:

> Aussitôt mon anxiété tomba; maintenant ce n'était plus comme tout à l'heure pour jusqu'à demain que j'avais quitté ma mère, puisque mon petit mot allait, la fâchant sans doute (et doublement parce que ce manège me rendrait ridicule aux yeux de Swann), me faire entrer invisible et ravi dans la même pièce qu'elle, allait lui parler de moi à l'oreille; [71]

but immediately rectified, at least partially, by the older narrator:

---

[68] *ARTP,* I, p. 20.
[69] *ARTP,* I, ibid.
[70] *ARTP,* I, ibid.
[71] *ARTP,* I,p. 30.

L'angoisse que je venais d'éprouver, je pensais que Swann s'en serait bien moqué s'il avait lu ma lettre et en avait deviné le but; or, au contraire, comme je l'ai appris plus tard, une angoisse semblable fut le tourment de longues années de sa vie, et personne aussi bien que lui peut-être n'aurait pu me comprendre [72].

Such direct confrontation of the two viewpoints is rare, and the passage from one to the other is generally more casual. One great advantage is that Proust is able to introduce an ironical, mocking tone into the narrative, without in any way impairing the intensity and sincerity of the original experience. Thus many of the images take on a double meaning. The several references to death, as the young Marcel 'buries' himself in the winding sheet of his bed, far from his mother, are at once the faithful transcription of his state of mind and the commentary on it of an older man who does not share it [73]. Many of the comparisons introduced as accompaniments to early events give the same impression. The narrator likens the child he once was to 'des maniaques qui s'efforcent de ne pas penser à autre chose pendant qu'ils ferment une porte' [74], amusedly refers to the grandfather's order to go to bed as violating 'la foi des traités', while the epithet 'férocité inconsciente' exactly pinpoints the double attitude, subjective and objective presentation being equally present in the narrative [75].

The 'baiser du soir' episode, then, is the retelling of the past through the double perspective of Time, deliberately manipulated to throw into relief certain themes and ideas which Proust intends to develop at length elsewhere. The insistence upon the subjective viewpoint, despite the continual presence of an objective and wiser narrator [76], is deliberate and carefully planned. The Bois de Boulogne passage [77], although itself added to form a conclusion to one section of the work, as it was originally published by Grasset, nevertheless is typical of the deliberate 'misleading' of the reader,—a device made necessary by the presence both of an 'enlightened' narrator and of the dramatic structural pattern.

The Bois de Boulogne passage, since Proust refers in his correspondence to its specific function as projecting one perspective only, is particularly relevant to our examination of Proust's double vision technique. Recalling childhood memories of Combray, the narrator expresses, at the end of *Du côté de chez Swann,* his regret that so much has altered since, delicately operating as he does so a complete optical illusion, by projecting the subjective element of his dual vision rather than his later, and different, conclusions. He gives the reader a transcript of the emotions a chance return to the Bois evokes...

---

[72] *ARTP,* I, ibid.
[73] *ARTP,* I, p. 28.
[74] *ARTP,* I, p. 23.
[75] *ARTP,* I, p. 27.
[76] Other passages include *ARTP,* I, pp. 3-9, 43-48, 186-187 ; II, 93, 394, 397 etc.
[77] *ARTP,* I, pp. 421-427.

emotions belonging to the earlier period before the illumination of *Temps Retrouvé*. And just as in the return to the past of Combray, the narrator projects the reactions of his earlier self. The section, and with it the whole of *Du côté de chez Swann,* comes to an end on the note of bitter dissappointment associated with the early Marcel— the effect Proust intended to create. Writing to Jacques Rivière about this passage, which, as Vigneron has shown, is a new ending demanded by the division of the work into two by his publishers [78], Proust revealed that not only did the passage form an ideal conclusion, but that he wished it to leave the impression that it contained his final judgment on life. It is a 'simple paravant' intended to mark

> ... une étape, d'apparence subjective et dilettante, vers la plus objective et croyante des conclusions. Si on en induisait que ma pensée est un scepticisme désenchanté, ce serait absolument comme si un spectateur ayant vu, à la fin du premier acte de Parsifal, ce personnage ne rien comprendre à la cérémonie et être chassé par Gurnemantz, supposait que Wagner a voulu que la simplicité du cœur ne conduit à rien.

It is not from the attitude of the narrator as it is here expressed, implies Proust, that his final conclusions can be deduced. Nevertheless this intermediary stage is necessary in the design of the work:

> Mais cette évolution d'une pensée, je n'ai pas voulu l'analyser abstraitement mais la recréer, la faire vivre. *Je suis donc forcé de peindre les erreurs, sans croire devoir dire que je les tiens pour des erreurs*; tant pis pour moi si le lecteur croit que je les tiens pour la vérité [79].

The narrator's 'conclusion' then, that 'les maisons, les routes, les avenues sont fugitives, hélas ! comme les années [80], is the projection of one viewpoint, while the other, present in the text [81], is deliberately restrained and kept in the background. This deliberate manipulation of viewpoint and perspective is the basis of the 'double vision' technique.

Double vision and the presentation of situation

The dual perspective in which the narrative is presented allows Proust to present every possible aspect of a situation. Thus, in order to comment on Marcel's efforts, during his 'affair' with Gilberte, to obtain entry into the Swann household, the narrator stands back from the

---

[78] Vigneron : "Prétentions et défaillances: *Structure de Swann*", *Modern Philology,* 1946, where the author remarks that, while accepting 'la division dès lors inévitable du reste de l'ouvrage en deux volumes', he, at the same time, adds a new ending, 'où il oppose au Bois de Boulogne d'autrefois et aux élégances des équipages et des toilettes du temps de Mme Swann, les vulgarités et la mélancolie du Bois de Boulogne d'aujourd'hui', p. 125.

[79] Marcel Proust to Jacques Rivière, 7 February 1914. My italics.

[80] *ARTP*, I, p. 427.

[81] i.e. *ARTP*, I, pp. 423, 424.

situation, and places it in a context of later knowledge available from his retrospective viewpoint [82]. On other occasions, the narrator moves closer to his subject, to emphasise a significant incident, either for the comic effect this produces, or for the heightening of a grotesque situation. In this way, he suddenly directs the spotlight of his attention on the figures of M. and Mme Verdurin, simulating helpless laughter [83]. But more often it is through the wider perspective belonging to the commenting narrator that such effects are produced. In order to emphasise Françoise's severity towards the most famous Paris restaurants, it is the narrator who supplies the name of the only one for which she will admit a grudging admiration:

> 'Ça travaillait beaucoup. Ah! on ramassait des sous là-dedans... Madame connaît bien là-bas, à droite, sur les grands boulevards, un peu en arrière...' *Le restaurant dont elle parlait avec cette équité mêlée d'orgueil et de bonhomie, c'était... le Café Anglais* [84].

Thus again, one of the most immediately apparent results of the dual vision is humour. Other examplles of Proust's comprehensive use of the resources of his technique illustrate the ways in which he sometimes confronts objective and subjective accounts of the same, or similar, incidents for the purposes of demonstration. It is in this light that Proust can show the reader the 'revers de la médaille', by deliberately altering the perspective in which the incident is seen, by changing what he himself refers to as 'la différence d'optique' [85] Saint-Loup's disappointment on seeing Albertine's photograph, and Marcel's corresponding amazement on meeting Rachel represent the same scene, turned inside out. Each illustrates the same 'law', but from a different point of view, and the analyses following each incident reflect first the objective and dispassionate view of the situation, and then the subjective and emotionally-involved view. In the first instance, Marcel remarks objectively:

> Ce visage, avec ses regards, ses sourires, les mouvements de sa bouche, moi je l'avais connu du dehors... [86]

while in the second, the truth he had observed 'from without' is suddenly presented to him from within when Saint-Loup's reaction is exactly that which Marcel had originally had about Rachel:

> "Elle est sûrement merveilleuse", continuait à dire Robert, qui n'avait pas vu que je lui tendais la photographie. Soudain il l'aperçut, il la tint un instant dans ses mains, sa figure exprimait une stupéfaction qui allait jusqu'à la stupidité. "C'est ça, la jeune fille que tu aimes?... [87]

[82] *ARTP*, I, pp. 479-480.
[83] *ARTP*, I, p. 262.
[84] *ARTP*, I, p. 486.
[85] *ARTP*, III, p. 439.
[86] *ARTP*, II, p. 159.
[87] *ARTP*, III, p. 437.

The situation is therefore seen from every possible angle, just as it might have been if the whole narrative had been cast in the third person, and the 'ideal' narrator had been able to explain the attitudes of the people concerned. But by deliberately altering the perspective of the narrator, not by artificial means, but by arranging the material so that it naturally invokes a 'différence d'optique', with the narrator himself viewing the same situation from a number of different angles, presenting it to the reader in a variety of narrative perspectives, Proust obtains a perfect equivalence of omniscience in first person narrative without betraying the limited viewpoint of the narrator. This is only made possible by the presence within the narrative of a 'subjective' hero and an 'objective' narrator, and by the permutations their presence makes possible.

Optical illusions of this kind are found throughout *A la Recherche,* but it should be noticed that the relationship between the two elements, hero and narrator, which make the 'double vision' possible, does not remain constant. This is to be explained by personal reasons: Proust's own attitude to much of the material he wished to include varied according to the intensity of emotion it could still arouse in him. The writing of the Albertine episode, particularly, reflects the way Proust modified his technique, consciously or unconsciously, since the death of Agostinelli still hangs over the narrative, which is infinitely more tortured than, for example, the parallel Gilberte affair.

In *A l'Ombre des Jeunes Filles en Fleurs,* there is much humour, the later narrator often points out the absurdities in his earlier self, not only in respect of his high ideals, but of his almost total ignorance of life in general. But it is the recounting of Gilberte's indifference towards Marcel—a situation which calls up in *La Prisonnière* a series of anxious and painful self-examinations on the narrator's part—that the essential difference in the presentation of two parallel situations is most noticeable. In the earlier episodes, the two elements of the dual perspective are present, and their subtle manipulation enhances the story of Marcel and Gilberte. The final scene, their last afternoon together, is, because of this dual perspective, among the funniest in the book, because, present at the same time as the painful undertones of the situation, is the later narrator's emphasis of the utter absurdity of his remarks:

> Et à tous nos propos une sorte de dureté suprême était conférée par le paroxysme de leur insignifiance paradoxale, lequel me consolait pourtant, car il empêchait Gilberte d'être dupe de la banalité de mes réflexions et de l'indifférence de mon accent. C'est en vain que je disais: "Il me semble que l'autre jour la pendule retardait plutôt", elle traduisait évidemment: "Comme vous êtes méchante!" [88]

This tone vanishes in *La Prisonnière,* where the atmosphere is much more tense, and the comparative absence of the second, objective ele-

---

[88] *ARTP,* I, p. 583.

ment of the narrator's double vision is perfectly summed up by Proust himself, when, referring to jealousy as an ingredient in his work, he emphasises the subjective element which naturally takes first place:

Les pinceaux, ivres de fureur et d'amour, peignent, peignent ... [89]

It is clear, therefore, that despite Proust's detachment from his work, his apologies to friends for treating them objectively [90], his conception of his book as a cemetery for former acquaintances [91], nevertheless, the actual treatment of material shows that he was not always able to maintain his unique blend of objective and subjective narrative presentation.

Double vision and the moralist element

Just as Proust's double vision of experience, projected simultaneously through Marcel and the later narrator, allows him to present every aspect, subjective and objective, of situations, so, from time to time, his refusal to adopt solely an objective view of events, (eschewing the omniscient narrator's rigorous conclusions), allows the moralist in Proust to advance a variety of theories and explanations. In this way, many situations are analysed and 'explained' in every possible light, as the narrator turns slowly around them, scrutinising them from all angles, with great care and exactitude. For example, of the various explanations of the 'marquise's' unwarranted benevolence towards Marcel, in A l'Ombre des jeunes filles en fleurs, ("Cette marquise me conseilla de ne pas rester au frais et m'ouvrit même un cabinet en me disant 'Vous ne voulez pas entrer? en voici un tout propre, pour vous ce sera gratis'.") [92], the narrator finally chooses none, after having reviewed the list of possible reasons for her conduct and motive in true moralist fashion, and is content to add that, whatever her motive, she did not have much success.

Proust, then, is not content to effect simply the amalgamation of the two sides of any given situation, according to whether it is seen subjectively or objectively. His 'double vision' allows him also to contrast the results of their confrontation to demonstrate theories of human behaviour and manners. The discovery, for example, that Albertine had lied about the origin of her rings [93] gives Proust an opportunity to comment on the relationship between lying, suffering and jealousy.

One of the characteristics we have noticed, in tracing the moralist element in Proust's writings, is the abundance of 'portraits' designed to illustrate attitudes to life, or typical examples of humanity. By

---

[89] *ARTP*, III, p. 917.
[90] *ARTP*, III, p. 902.
[91] *ARTP*, III, p. 903.
[92] *ARTP*, I, p. 492.
[93] *ARTP*, III, pp. 463-4.

switching adroitly from one viewpoint to the other, Proust can include such portrait painting in the fictional story of Marcel's vocation.

Many of the characters included in the Balbec episodes, for example, are 'portraits', executed in the manner of La Bruyère or Saint-Simon. The manager of the Grand Hôtel is drawn in a perfectly objective way by the narrator, although Marcel's contact with him is subjective. Throughout the episode, however, he never changes, and his basic personality is set out so carefully that the reader has the impression he is reading a prepared description:

> ... Le directeur, sorte de poussah à la figure et à la voix pleine de cica-trices... au smoking de mondain, au regard de psychologue prenant géné-ralement, à l'arrivée de l'"omnibus", les grands seigneurs pour des râleux et les rats d'hôtel pour des grands seigneurs [94].

Similarly, the pertinent psychological and sociological observations which accompany the portraits of the 'bâtonnier et ses amis' [95], inter-calated in Marcel's fictional career by the later narrator, reveal in Proust the 'amateur d'ichtyologie humaine' that he refers to a few pages later [96]. An example of a perfect 'portrait', drawn for its own sake, for the sheer pleasure Proust certainly had in mounting it with such care, is that of the Princesse de Luxembourg. Her entry on the scene is prepared:

> ... je vis de loin venir dans notre direction la princesse de Luxembourg, à demi appuyée sur une ombrelle... [97]

—her main interest, the rectification she tries to achieve between her own social position and that of the rest of humanity, is deliberately brought into focus:

> ... elle plaça sans doute notre niveau un peu moins bas dans l'échelle des êtres, car son égalité avec nous fut signifiée par la princesse à ma grand'mère par moyen de ce tendre et maternel sourire qu'on adresse à un gamin quand on lui dit au revoir comme à une grande personne [98]

whereupon, her function performed, she moves out of sight:

> Enfin, nous ayant quittés tous trois, la princesse reprit sa promenade sur la digue ensoleillée en incurvant sa taille magnifique qui comme un ser-pent autour d'une baguette s'enlaçait à l'ombrelle blanche imprimée de bleu que Mme de Luxembourg tenait fermée à la main [99].

Portraits such as this do not translate the vision of Marcel, they are the work of his later self, viewing past experience in a new perspective,

---

[94] *ARTP*, I, p. 662.
[95] *ARTP*, I, p. 677.
[96] *ARTP*, I, p. 681.
[97] *ARTP*, I, p. 699.
[98] *ARTP*, I, p. 700.
[99] *ARTP*, I, ibid.

yet the transition from one Marcel to the other is so casual and unexpected, that we accept the magnificent descriptions almost as part of the young Marcel's experience.

A broad distinction can be made in the treatment of characters between those who are to play an important rôle in Marcel's life, and those, who, like the Princess, are simply part of an isolated episode. The alternation of viewpoint, the manipulation of the dual narrative perspectives varies significantly with the characters involved and their rôle in the overall construction. Thus, the hotel manager, many of his clients, the Princess—all receive the same treatment: the listing, often in a humorous way, of their physical and moral qualities, never with a view to criticising them from any definitive standpoint (either social or moral), but always bathed in the light shed by the narrator's detached, ironical tone, one of the most marked characteristics he shares with the 17th century moralists. Characters who reappear to play a continuous part in Marcel's development, like the wealthy industrialist's son, receive different treatment. It is clear that the perspectives created by the double vision technique influence and reflect Proust's methods of character portrayal and that the substitution of Marcel's subjective and imperfect vision for the omniscient moralist, observer of human types, is the main criterion in their subsequent development.

In general, then, the moralist element, commentary, explanation and portrait-painting, is adroitly accommodated by Proust's double vision technique.

Double vision and Character Presentation and Development

We have seen how Proust incorporates the later narrator's portraits into the body of the narrative by his double perspective. Yet so complex is the whole technique of character presentation in *A la Recherche,* and so closely bound up with the double vision of the narrator, that we find certain elements of portrait painting in most of Proust's major characters.

If we turn to two of the most interesting of such characters, Saint-Loup and Charlus, we can see at once the close relationship between the dual perspective in which the narrative is presented and Proust's character presentation techniques.

First, Saint-Loup typifies three major aspects of character presentation. He first appears as the subject of a portrait which is carefully prepared. Like the Princesse de Luxembourg, he advances into the narrator's vision, occupies it wholly for a short space of time, and then departs. During this time, the reader is introduced to his physical appearance [100], his mode of dress [101] and to certain of his moral

---

[100] 'Je vis, grand, mince, le cou dégagé, la tête haute et fièrement portée, passer un jeune homme aux yeux pénétrants et dont la peau était aussi blonde et les cheveux aussi dorés que s'ils avaient absorbé tous les rayons du soleil.' *ARTP,* I, pp. 728-729.

[101] '... vêtu d'une étoffe souple et blanchâtre comme je n'aurais jamais cru qu'un homme eût osé en porter....' *ARTP,* I, p. 279.

characteristics [102]. Second, onto the basis of this initial 'character', another is grafted, that created by the subjective and limited vision of Marcel, whose adolescent imagination further distorts this image. Thus Saint-Loup is successively an 'insolent' full of 'dureté naturelle' [103], the victim of an hereditary code of manners [104], and finally undergoes a complete transformation to become 'Le plus aimable, le plus prévenant jeune homme que j'eusse jamais rencontré' [105]. Third, this subjective portrait is supplemented by objective elucidation by the later narrator, who knows about and hints at later characteristics which for the moment he is unwilling completely to disclose. The later narrator's viewpoint, then, is introduced to add information about certain aspects of Saint-Loup unknown to the Marcel of Balbec—but not to such an extent that they are permitted radically to alter the latter's overall impression. For instance, Saint-Loup's relations with socialist intellectuals are mentioned, but other characteristics are witheld for a 'coup de théâtre'. [106]

The three major aspects of character presentation, the portrait, the subjective, changing evaluation of Marcel, and the final objective summaries all reflect Proust's habit of presenting characters in the kaleidoscope of different narrative viewpoints. Each is seen in the dual perspective of time which the two Marcels possess, and the amalgam of the different optical illusions created in this way acts upon character as upon situation. Sainte-Beuve is presented, not systematically, but simultaneously, in a variety of perspectives, some of which alter, some of which remain incomplete and some of which are constant.

The unannounced change of perspective is even more carefully manipulated in the case of Saint-Loup's uncle, the baron de Charlus. Proust provides the reader, once again, with a sum of knowledge about the Baron, in order to provide the basis for the gradually emerging personality of the pederast. This equivalent of Saint-Loup's portrait is transmitted this time not by an omniscient narrator, but by Saint-Loup himself, introducing the character to the reader and laying down the foundations for the subsequent modifications of personality, since this initial information is subjective [107]. But the main advantage of the double vision technique is the opportunity it gives Proust of describing Charlus from as many different angles as possible; this is important since the personalised narrator/hero must not be implicated in the Baron's questionable activities, for fear of alienating the reader's sympathy [108]. By choosing first to present Charlus through the subjective viewpoint of Marcel, Proust is able to accentuate the inco-

---

[102] *ARTP*, I, ibid.
[103] *ARTP*, I, p. 732.
[104] *ARTP*, I, ibid.
[105] *ARTP*, ibdi.
[106] *ARTP*, I, p. 737.
[107] *ARTP*, I,p. 749.
[108] As, in fact, Proust does in the case of Charlus himself in *Le Temps Retrouvé*.

herence and absurdity of the homosexual's behaviour when observed by an uncomprehending observer. To Marcel's puzzled mind, even the most painstaking observation of the baron's behaviour fails to explain the latter's conduct towards him. The description of Charlus, then, is minute and detailed in the extreme. Take for example the observation of his penetrating stare:

> Avec la rapidité d'un éclair son regard me traversa ainsi qu'au moment où je l'avais aperçu, et revint, comme s'il ne m'avait pas vu, se ranger, un peu bas, devant ses yeux, émoussé, comme le regard neutre qui feint de ne rien voir au dehors et n'est capable de rien lire au dedans ... [109]

By next choosing to present the baron through the eye of a completely-informed observer, Proust can then, without difficulty, present an inner, psychological description of Charles and explain and comment on his real motives [110].

The discovery of Charlus' real character in *Sodome et Gomorrhe* further illustrates the effectiveness of Proust's double vision in creating characters. Proust is always prepared to present the narrative in such a way as to accentuate the objective and impersonal, when the subjective and personal is not required, and vice-versa when it is the narrator's changing viewpoint he wishes to illustrate. In the Charlus/Jupien scene, the coexistence of two narrative standpoints is particularly marked. Marcel's attitude is, at first, one of incomprehension. As he explains, from his later position in time, when he watched the activities of the Baron and the waistcoat maker:

> Dans les yeux de l'un et de l'autre, c'était le ciel, non pas de Zurich, mais de quelque cité orientale dont je n'avais pas encore deviné le nom, qui venait de se livrer [111].

Nevertheless, Proust is anxious at the same time to show how 'le Charlisme' is typical of a whole set of laws, and in order to do so, requires more knowledge at his disposal than the young Marcel evidently has. Thus, much 'informed' comment is injected into the description from later in time, and even some of Marcel's direct reporting bears the imprint of this later knowledge. While it is Marcel's imperfect viewpoint that is deliberately used to show Charlus and Jupien in 'cette sorte de scène des deux muets, qui... semblait avoir été longuement répétée [112], the references to the 'perfection' of the incident suggest a viewpoint considerably wider than that of Marcel's. Of the two perspectives possible, subjective [113] and objective [114], it is the second

---

[109] *ARTP*, I, p. 753.
[110] i.e. *ARTP*, III, p. 302 ff.
[111] *ARTP*, II, p. 606.
[112] *ARTP*, II, p. 605.
[113] i.e. II, pp. 609, 610, 604 and summed up "je trouvais la mimique, d'abord incompréhensible pour moi, de Jupien et de M. de Charlus aussi curieuse que ces gestes tentateurs adressés aux insectes, selon Darwin, par les fleurs dites composées", II, p. 630.
[114] i.e. II, p. 607.

which Proust tends to use more and more, until in certain passages, first-person narration becomes identical with third-person.

It is clear, therefore, that the dual perspective of the narrative, created by the plan and construction of *A la Recherche* provides Proust with many advantages in character presentation, and in the particular case of Charlus, with the problems his character portrayal raises.

There is little point in repeating the already well-known Proustian technique of successive character revelations in the build-up of personality. The process is most adequately summed up by Professor Guichard, who writes:

> En laissant ses personnages se développer d'eux-mêmes, leurs portraits se composer, se déformer, se reformer, se contredire successivement dans le temps, Proust a détruit ou contribué à détruire une des conventions les plus tenaces du roman [115].

Nevertheless, as we have already seen in Proust's presentation of Saint-Loup and Charlus, the author retains much of the traditional, accepted view of the multiple personality. Once again, this brings out the full force of the dual vision technique, and allows Proust to insert unspoken implications into the narrative by means of the contrast which he thus achieves. M. de Norpois is seen in two perspectives, for example. The basis of explanation, considered as the necessary foundation for the scenes to follow, is presented by the later narrator, as is the ambassador's quizzical examination of the small boy:

> Aussi, tout en me parlant avec bonté et de l'air d'importance d'un homme qui sait sa vaste expérience, il ne cessait de m'examiner avec une curiosité sagace et pour son profit, comme si j'eusse été quelque usage exotique, quelque monument instructif ou quelque étoile en tournée [116].

Yet, suddenly the perspectives change, the optical illusion is performed, and we see a different Norpois, through the anxious gaze of the boy himself:

> M. de Norpois... devait détenir cette vérité que je n'avais pas su extraire du jeu de la Berma, il allait me la découvrir ; en répondant à sa question, j'allais le prier de me dire en quoi cette vérité consistait [117].

The two viewpoints are continually present and manipulated, as here, with great discretion. Proust can also achieve ingenious technical effects, by switching from one viewpoint to another: the narrator remarks, at one point, as he looks back over his life, that it was a pity he did not appreciate the fund of career phrases which made up Norpois' conversation, for had he done so, he would have achieved an effect of local colour which is now impossible. But in fact, since Nor-

---

[115] Guichard: *Introduction à Proust,* Paris, Nizet, p. 55.
[116] *ARTP,* I, p. 452.
[117] *ARTP,* I, p. 456.

pois is originally presented both through the later narrator's eyes and the young Marcel's, this fund of career-phrases has been safely recorded, along with other objective observations [118].

The whole question of objective observation and the predominance of the later narrator in the presentation of certain themes is raised again in the application of the double vision technique to the society element of *A la Recherche*. Before turning to this, however, there is one theme which is perfectly suited to the advantage of double vision.

Double vision and the vocation theme

One of the most noticeable fields, in which the dual narrative perspectives are operated with success, is in that dealing directly or indirectly with Marcel's vocation. The appearance of this theme within the narrative is nearly always marked by the immediate change-over to the young Marcel's limited viewpoint. This enables the rhythm of enthusiasm and doubt, exaltation and disappointment, to be followed without rectification by a later narrator; it is the fluctuation of the narrator's sensibility in his acquaintance with art and literature which constitutes the 'story of a vocation'. When Norpois, for example, reduces the importance of Bergotte's work to that of a 'simple joueur de flûte' [119] Marcel accepts this judgment, and the reader must too, since no rectifying agent, in the shape of the later narrator, is present in the narrative:

> (M. de Norpois) m'inspira sur ma propre intelligence des doutes plus graves que ceux qui me déchiraient d'habitude, quand je vis que ce que je mettais mille et mille fois au-dessus de moi-même, ce que je trouvais de plus élevé au monde, était pour lui tout en bas de l'échelle de ses admirations [120].

Similarly, the ambassador's rejection of Marcel's prose poem is received as just by the discouraged Marcel for whom Norpois is 'le connaisseur le mieux disposé et le plus intelligent' [121]. Again the later narrator is absent from the narrative, and Proust deliberately underlines Marcel's subjective reactions. In this way, his partial conclusions are presented as definitive; like the parenthesis on the Bois de Boulogne, Marcel's 'conclusion' that he fully deserves Norpois' disdain is, in fact, the opposite of what he will finally come to believe. The interplay of subjcive and objetcive reporting, then, is an important part of Proust's recreation of 'l'évolution d'une pensée' [122].

---

[118] *ARTP*, pp. 347, 460 ff.
[119] *ARTP*, I, p. 473.
[120] *ARTP*, I, ibid.
[121] *ARTP*, I, p. 475.
[122] Letter to Rivière, 7 Feb. 1914.

Double vision and the theme of society

All the early attempts to deal with the presentation of society saw Proust adopting instinctively an objective tone, despite his preference for first person narrative in the treatment of love and personal introspection. The second element of the double vision technique, the later narrator's retrospective viewpoint, allows Proust to maintain the objective tone, while at the same time using a subjective technique for other themes, like that of Marcel's vocation.

One of the most striking characteristics of Proust's presentation of society is the detached, ironical tone of the later narrator. This, coupled with the inclusion of portraits to illustrate that society, descending in direct line from Saint-Simon, strengthens Proust's tendency to ignore Marcel's subjective viewpoint and to exploit fully the later Marcel's more comprehensive viewpoint.

The best illustration of this narrative tone in *A la Recherche* is in the soirée given by the Princesse de Guermantes, which constitutes Marcel's complete initiation into Parisian society [123]. The attitude of the narrator is that of the well-informed observer, drawing upon a store of witicisms and anecdotes as illustrations of a scene being personally presented to the reader. Thus, while commenting on the presence of 'une duchesse fort noire', whose conduct has excluded her from certain closed societies, the narrator adds that, in fact, many incongruous personalities besides her were there; such remarks are in the form of interpolations, accentuated by their parenthetical construction:

> (des artistes)... (Marie-Gilberte en protégeait beaucoup, il fallait prendre garde de ne pas être abordé par quelque illustre chanteuse allemande) ... [124]

and again:

> ... (on faisait passer maintenant, pour glorifier l'état-major, un général plébéien avant certains ducs)... [125]

Such descriptions contain the same personal note which had crept in to many of Proust's journalistic essays and it is obvious that Proust takes advantage of the narrator's later position in time in order to introduce this favorite form of reporting, within the narrative plan. The narrator invites us, for example, to laugh with him at the old marquise de Citry, and asks us wonderingly what could be the reason for her strange behaviour:

> Cette parole était-elle d'une sainte furibonde, et qui s'étonne que les Gentils ne viennent pas d'eux-mêmes à la vérité, ou bien d'une anarchiste en appétit de carnage? [126]

---

[123] *ARTP*, II, pp. 633-725.
[124] *ARTP*, p, 672.
[125] *ARTP*, II, ibid.
[126] *ARTP*, II, p. 687.

The actors in the scenes presented for our amusement and edification are classed according to personal whims and fancies. The duc de Guermantes, he says, reminds him of a Rembrandt picture, 'le bourg-mestre Six' [127], and he takes obvious pleasure in pointing to the absurdity of many others, like Mme de Citry's substitution for the judgment this eloquent habit implies of stroking her chin ('elle ne se donnait même pas la peine de dire 'la barbe') [128]. Inevitably, the habit of nudging his reader's elbow to let him into a secret, or to share a joke, quickly develops into satire, and the later narrator's finished 'portrait' of the marquise has a strong Voltarian flavour:

> Bientôt, ce qui fut ennuyeux, ce fut tout. "C'est si ennuyeux, les belles choses! Ah! les tableaux, c'est à vous rendre fou... comme vous avez raison, c'est si ennuyeux d'écrire des lettres!" Finalement ce fut la vie elle-même qu'elle vous déclara une chose rasante, sans qu'on sût bien où elle prenait son terme de comparaison [129].

Thus predominating in the society episodes of *A la Recherche* is a detached, amused yet highly personal tone, which takes little account of the subjective narrator's viewpoint.

While this narrative tone predominates, Proust is still careful to put to good purpose the advantages of a shifting viewpoint, in pre-senting the 'mécanisme' of society. The final narrator's viewpoint, as in character-presentation, is alternated with that of the first Marcel, to obtain a dual perspective illustrating both the moralist's aim of examining society as an interesting human phenomenon and the voca-tion theme, the shedding of illusions and the acquiring of new 'values' in a subjectively-reported contact with 'le monde'.

Marcel' initial impressions of 'le tout-Paris' are thus presented in conjunction with the older and better-informed narrator's commentary. The first, as in the case of Charlus, creates a perspective admirably suited for the illustration of the aristocracy's often incomprehensible rules of conduct. Marcel's astonished description of the typical Guer-mantes 'salute' is the portrait of a phenomenon whose reasons and explanation are unsuspected:

> ... l'aspect de Mme de Guermantes qui avait profité de l'indépendance de son torse pour le jeter en avant avec une politesse exagérée et le ramener avec justesse sans que son visage et son regard eussent paru avoir remarqué qu'il y avait quelqu'un devant eux [130].

The second viewpoint is then introduced, and the reader, though registering the young Marcel's impressions, is presented in addition with a second and wider perspective through which to view the same phenomenon. This perspective X-rays, as it were, the social organisms

---

[127] *ARTP*, II, p. 679.
[128] *ARTP*, II, p. 688.
[129] *ARTP*, II, ibid.
[130] *ARTP*, II, p. 200.

such phenomena represent, and an inner view of society is grafted onto the external view of Marcel, without destroying it. The reader can rectify, to some extent, the ignorance (in which he would be plunged, if he were dependent on Marcel's information alone) of the background of society, and can examine, with the later narrator, the general conclusions and laws that society symbolises. This is sometimes done dogmatically and rationally, as when the narrator, starting from the general observation that 'chacun voit en plus beau ce qu'il voit à distance'[131], elaborates this theory:

> Or, l'une ou l'autre de deux lois de langage pouvait s'appliquer ici. L'une veut que... etc.[132].

Thus, the subjective and objective elements of the double vision technique are applied to the portrayal of society in general, with the same aims and results as in its application to character and situation presentation. Nevertheless, unlike these two elements, the society theme, developed extensively throughout *A la Recherche* never presents a balance of perspectives and Proust's tendency is to over-develop the final narrator's moralist viewpoint.

We have seen how the 'double vision' of Proust's narrator, placed at two different moments in time, reacts upon various aspects of his novel. The long meditation on art and literature in *Temps Retrouvé* highlights the importance Proust attaches to this technique, and the relationship it bears to the theoretical and aesthetic basis of *A la Recherche*. The function of art, for the narrator about to write his book, is to create a medium in which to

> ... recréer la vraie vie, de rajeunir les impressions[133]

—a process only possible for the artist re-interpreting his past life from a position later in time, distrusting intelligence as the sole criterion, and desiring to plumb the depths of every individual sensation and reaction. Now, the narrator's 'dual vision' allows Proust to present Marcel's life as he lived it, and to comment continually upon it from a different point of view; the living of experience, and the translation of experience into something of universal value are the two strends running through the meditation of *Temps Retrouvé*:

> Seul (l'art) exprime pour les autres et nous fait voir à nous-mêmes notre propre vie, cette vie qui ne peut pas s'"observer", dont les apparences qu'on observe ont besoin d'être traduites et souvent lues à rebours et péniblement déchiffrées[134].

Marcel does not observe his life, as he lives it, in the perspective which will show him the hidden beauties and values of his apparently

---

131 *ARTP*, II, p. 235.
132 *ARTP*, II, p. 236.
133 *ARTP*, III, p. 896.
134 *ARTP*, III, p. 896.

meaningless existence. The subjective presentation of experience, the first element of the dual vision technique, projects into the fictional story of *A la Recherche* Proust's conviction that experience and happiness are intangible and can only be seized in retrospect. The objective presentation of experience, the later narrator's commentary on Marcel's activities, addressed to the reader and excluding Marcel, provides the second half of Proust's theory, the translation, the deciphering of different signs and symbols—this is the function of the continuous commentary of the post-revelation narrator.

Earlier in the novel, the intangibility of experience is referred to at greater length. The narrator remarks that the coincidence of imagination and reality is extremely rare, and that its rarity is emphasised because the complete and unspoiled quality of experience cannot normally be preserved. The intelligence, for example, does not have time to appreciate fully the value of the final crowning of a long-unfulfilled desire:

> ... quand la réalité se replie et s'applique sur ce que nous avons si longtemps rêvé, elle nous le cache entièrement, se confond avec lui, comme deux figures égales et superposées qui n'en font plus qu'une... [135]

It is, in fact, the property of such situations, however rare they may be, to be incapable of analysis at the moment they occur, and later 'explanation' merely succeeds in distorting them:

> ... pour donner à notre joie toute sa signification, nous voudrions garder à tous ces points de notre désir, dans le moment même où nous y touchons — et pour être plus certain que ce soit bien eux — le prestige d'être intangibles. Et la pensée ne peut même pas reconstituer l'état ancien pour le confronter au nouveau, car elle n'a plus le champ libre... [136]

However, if we consider the properties of the double vision technique, which permits the author to present the significant moments of Marcel's experience in such a way that the latter never comes to realise their full importance, and yet allows the reader, through the commentary which accompanies the 'moments privilégiés' to do so, we realise that the double vision technique accurately conveys all the properties of existence: its intangibility and uniqueness. For by reading *A la Recherche* we both understand and even share the individual experience which is Marcel's, and realise the near-impossibility (save through the work of art, through *A la Recherche* itself) of being able to share it. Proust's conception of reality and of the past finds, in the double perspective of the 'two' narrators of *A la Recherche,* a method of translating a whole attitude to life, underlining his own assertion that *A la Recherche* is

'une affaire non de technique, mais de vision'.

---

[135] *ARTP,* I, p. 537.
[136] *ARTP,* I, ibid.

THE FIRST-PERSON NARRATIVE OF
A LA RECHERCHE DU TEMPS PERDU

The 'double vision' technique, made possible by the plan and construction of *A la Recherche,* gives Proust the advantages of a double, alternating narrative viewpoint. Despite the flexibility gained in this way, permitting the introduction of different narrative 'tones' into the work, Proust cannot always fit all his material into the framework of first-person narrative. Three distinct narrative viewpoints are used in the course of *A la Recherche*:

(i) the subjective view of experience, belonging to the hero, Marcel.

(ii) the objective view of experience, told in the first-person by a later Marcel.

(iii) a completely objective and omniscient presentation of narrative, grafted onto the personal narrator in his 'final' position, but technically indefensible in first person narrative.

The subjective and objective first-person accounts are manipulated for technical and aesthetic reasons, and form the basis of Proust's 'double vision' technique. The completely objective, omniscient narrative viewpoint emerges in the presentation of the society theme; it is the continuation in *A la Recherche* of the third-person narrative of *Jean Santeuil,* the narrator in both works being strongly personalised, but retaining, even in the first-person narrative of *A la Recherche,* the faculty of knowing all, and being omni-present.

At the same time, certain other autobiographical narrative tones appear in the later stages of the work, where revision was hasty, and the composition itself hurried.

OMNISCIENT REPORTING IN FIRST-PERSON NARRATIVE

We are sometimes surprised to find, in the first-person narrative of *A la recherche,* descriptions and analyses of characters, reflecting the views of a third-person, omniscient narrator, objective, impartial and detached. It is not only, for example, the subjective portrait of M. de

Norpois with which the reader is presented; he is given, in addition, a complete and objective account of the character's actions by the later narrator, who imperceptibly appropriates the functions and faculties of the 'ideal', omniscient narrator who enters into the thoughts and motives of his characters. Describing his over enthusiasm in thanking the ambassador for his offer to speak to Gilberte and her mother on his behalf, Marcel recalls that, even as he was speaking, he realised he had gone too far, and that Norpois mistrusted his intentions. This is the objective, personal view of recalled experienced, recounted by the older Marcel. Then, without warning, Proust continues: "In fact, that is exactly what Norpois thought at the time":

> Je me rendis compte aussitôt que ces phrases ... étaient peut-être ... les seules qui pussent avoir pour résultat de l'y faire renoncer. En les entendant en effet ... M. de Norpois ... pensa que le désir, normal en apparence, **que j'avais exprimé, devait dissimuler quelque pensée différente...** [137]

Swann, like Norpois, is constantly viewed objectively, even though the third-person narrative of *Un amoir de Swann* has been discarded in *A l'ombre des jeunes filles en fleurs*. We read his thoughts as he remembers he once read a letter entrusted in all confidence to him by Odette, and enter into all his emotions as he thinks back to his jealousy of Forcheville:

> Il se rappelait parfois qu'il avait, bien des années auparavant, essayé un jour de lire à travers l'enveloppe une lettre adressée par Odette à Forcheville. Mais ce souvenir ne lui était pas agréable... [139]

and thereby achieve a degree of knowledge about another personality which is denied to Marcel and, indeed, to us all, as Proust himself insists [140]. We adopt the omniscient narrator's viewpoint as we penetrate, with him, into Swann's reactions to Odette when she implies that Mme de Cambremer was in love with him [141], and at one point benefit from so objective and impartial a view of Swann and Marcel, that we are in the privileged position of sharing each one's reaction to the other:

> A ce moment Swann s'aperçut de l'application que je pouvais faire de cette maxime à lui et à Odette. Et comme, même chez les êtres supérieurs, au moment où ils semblent planer avec vous au-dessus de la vie, l'amour-propre reste mesquin, il fut pris d'une grande mauvaise humeur contre moi [142].

---

[137] *ARTP,* I, p. 479.
[139] *ARTP,* I, p. 523.
[140] '... nous existons seuls. L'homme est l'être qui ne peut sortir de soi, *qui ne connaît les autres qu'en soi,* et, en disant le contraire, ment'. *ARTP,* III, p. 450.
[141] *ARTP,* I, p. 534.
[142] *ARTP,* p. 563.

The above examples are all taken from *A l'Ombre des jeunes filles en fleurs* and it may be that traces of the original third-person treatment of many of the episodes it now includes [143] remain in the published text. Such external evidence cannot, on the other hand, account for Proust's transformation of first into third person narrative, when faced with the problem of presenting the relationship between two characters, not involving Marcel. In *Un Amour de Swann* where situations of this kind between two objectively-observed characters provide the entire basis of the story, third-person narrative is the natural medium; and in the rest of *A la Recherche,* whenever analogous situations appear, Proust tends to slip unconsciously into the third person. It would seem that Proust was aware of this danger, and he resorts to a number of technical devices to ensure that his omniscient reporting remains in accordance with the overall plan.

He turns direct, objective narration into a hypothesis, for example, thus creating the same effect as if he were writing third-person narrative, but retaining the framework of depending on the personal narrator. Robert de Saint-Loup's glimpse into a part of Rachel's life he really knows nothing about is reported as though the omniscient narrator had emigrated into the lover's personality and were describing his intimate sensations and reactions. Yet we discover that the whole passage is a supposition on Marcel's part, and though the general impression Proust wishes to create is that Saint-Loup's feelings about Rachel are being directly transcribed, from time to time the author is careful to remind us that they are no more than a hypothesis on his part. Instead of stating categorically: 'Robert eut l'idée alors...' he says instead: 'Robert eut *peut-être* l'idée alors...' and continues to enumerate the latter's suffering, anxieties and doubts [144]. Again, when Marcel finds himself describing Saint-Loup's reactions to himself, he is careful to explain his 'omniscience' by turning them into suppositions:

> ... Voilà ce que je crains aujourd'hui que Saint-Loup ait quelquefois pensé. Il s'est trompé en ce cas [145].

Sometimes, on the other hand, Proust so arranges the narrative that Marcel finds himself in a privileged position with regard to other characters, which places him unexpectedly in possession of a number of important facts. When Saint-Loup presents Rachel, his mistress, to Marcel, the latter enjoys a considerable technical degree of omniscience; he can comment on the situation in the same authoritative tone one expects from the 'ideal' narrator, and possesses all the answers to Saint-Loup's own questions about Rachel—to a degree, indeed, unsurpassed by his later investigations into Albertine's true personality. This is because he knows Rachel's past, accidentally,

---

[143] Especially the continuation of *Un Amour de Swann, ARTP,* I, p. 431 ff.
[144] *ARTP,* II, pp. 162-4.
[145] *ARTP,* II, p. 414.

... (parce que j'avais connu "Rachel quand du Seigneur" dans une maison de passe)... J'aurais pu apprendre bien des coucheries d'elle à Robert, lesquelles me semblaient la chose la plus indifférente du monde. Et combien elles l'eussent peiné! Et que n'avait-il pas donné pour les connaître, sans y réussir! [146]

This way of introducing, by a sleight of hand, narrative tones more usually associated with third-person writing into *A la Recherche* sometimes leads Proust into contradicting some of his own theories on personality, and he uses technically unjustifiable means of 'enlarging' the first person narrative viewpoint. The scene depicting Saint-Loup's quarrel with Rachel in the restaurant in Paris, for example, illustrates Proust's 'law' that a separate personality is an impenetrable mystery to a third person. Robert cannot understand Rachel's treatment of him [147]. Yet, by putting Marcel in complete possession of Saint-Loup's own feelings towards Rachel, Proust paradoxically contradicts his own 'law'. If the narrator finds Gilberte, Albertine, Charles and Mme de Guermantes all impenetrable mysteries, surely he should find Saint-Loup's real personality inaccessible too? Yet for the purposes of his demonstration Marcel completely enters Robert's character, switching suddenly from the later Marcel's viewpoint to that of the wholly omniscient observer.

There can be no doubt that even the flexible narrative framework proves too limiting for Proust. In order to carry out many of his demonstrations, he must include descriptions of externally and objectively observed situations, which first-person narrative is hardly capable of. He therefore transforms first-person narrative into third person narrative when it suits his purpose to do so.

There are many reasons, however, why Proust chose to write in a narrative form which cannot justifiably accomodate all his aims as a novelist-cum-moralist. We have already seen why first-person narrative is necessary because of the dramatic structure of *A la Recherche* and the incorporation into the plot of the moralist commentary. Proust's attempt to include the main themes of *A la Recherche* in the third-person narrative of *Un Amour de Swann* provides the final demonstration of its inferiority, in all ways except one, to the narrative form adopted for the bulk of *A la Recherche*.

THE DEGREE OF OMNISCIENT REPORTING IN "UN AMOUR DE SWANN"

In *Un Amour de Swann*, Proust's main advantage in using an omniscient narrator is in the latter's overall view of 'demonstration' scenes. The whole story is essentially a demonstration of the subjectivity of Swann's love for Odette, and is so presented that the

---

[146] *ARTP*, II, p. 158.
[147] *ARTP*, II, p. 122.
[148] *ARTP*, I, p. 296.

demonstration gains from the overall view of an objective narrator. Proust, through his omniscient narrator, can provide the reader with information that Swann does not possess, but would have given much to know; the tone is factual and informative:

> Ces paroles étaient mensongères; du moins pour Odette elles étaient mensongères... Mais dans l'esprit de Swann au contraire, ces paroles, qui ne rencontraient aucun obstacle, venaient s'incruster et prendre l'inamovibilité d'une vérité... [149]

and by embracing the whole situation—as he cannot when later describing his own jealousy of Albertine—the demonstration is clear, precise and orderly. Similarly, when indicating Swann's efforts not to see Odette, the reader is made aware of their futility, the strength of the demonstration being, of course, Swann's ignorance of this fact:

> Car (Odette) ne reconstituait pas les diverses phases de ces crises qu'il traversait et, dans l'idée qu'elle s'en faisait, elle omettait d'en comprendre le mécanisme... [150]

The advantages of the narrator's detached position are clear: he remains distinct from the events he is narrating, viewing them from a distance which allows him to appreciate certain nuances unsuspected by the actors themselves, and embracing whole situations, to draw significant conclusions from them, in his impassive glance.

Yet how are such advantages put to use in *Un Amour de Swann*? Examples of the detached narrative view in the third person narrative of this episode are surprisingly rare. It is true that the narrator often refuses to take sides, that, while reporting on Swann's admiration for the Verdurins, he adds significantly that it is a subjective reaction dependent upon his love for Odette [151]. It is true that the third-person narrator can switch from one scene to another, to underline the pathos and drama fo a situation [152]. Yet the far more usual procedure adopted by Proust is to identify the narrator with Swann, to disregard the former's detached omniscience, and to give him Swann's own subjective viewpoint. Clearly, though the advantages of precise and explicit demonstration are used, Proust is more instinctively drawn to the underlining of the individual's necessarily limited knowledge of others, by providing the reader with no point of comparison, by making him share the characters' frustrations and impotence, rather than by coolly and rationally pointing them out. In this way, the narrator of *Un Amour de Swann* comes more and more to share the principal character's one-sided view of situations, following his biased opinions, accepting his faulty and imperfect conclusions. With very few

---

[149] *ARTP*, I, p. 296.
[150] *ARTP*, I, p. 307.
[151] *ARTP*, I, p. 197.
[152] *ARTP*, I, p. 260.

exceptions, we know little of Odette's reactions to Swann's love [153], and the whole progress and decline of the affair is seen through the latter's eyes. By projecting only the hero's view point, Proust fuses narrator and hero into a single unity. The scenes which benefit most from this fusion are those dealing with Swann's jealousy: here we are shown only one side of the situation, we live with Swann through all his misgivings and tortured suspicions, with no corresponding insight into Odette's feelings. The only occasion on which the reader ever penetrates into the suffocating atmosphere of Odette's apartment in the rue La Pérouse is to accompany Swann there [154]. When Odette tries desperately to hide the fact that she is expecting a visitor, it is through Swann's anxious questioning that we suspect Odette of hiding something from him. And if he cannot discover all the facts about Odette, Proust makes no attempt to extend our knowledge beyond that of Swann himself. There is no answer to his question:

> Quel mensonge déprimant était-elle en train de faire à Swann pour qu'elle eût ce regard douloureux, cette voix plaintive qui semblait fléchir sous l'effort qu'elle s'imposait et demander grâce? [155]

Our only clues as to the truth of her statements are those which Swann himself possesses: her voice has an unnatural ring, her hurt look betrays a secret, but neither Swann nor the reader ever penetrates the mystery constituted by the enigma of another personality. So completely is the narrator's viewpoint adjusted to that of his hero, that the hallucinatory scenes magicked up by his jealousy become as real as the scenes where the two actually meet [156]. The soirée at Chatou to which Odette is invited without Swann is presented in exactly the same way as scenes which are not, like this one, the product of Swann's imagination [157], and when the Verdurins take Odette to Compiègne we accompany Swann there in imagination again, as he anxiously constructs hypothetical circumstances [158].

This method of combining the narrator's viewpoint with the hero's is tantamount to rejecting the implications of omniscient reporting and turning third person narrative into first-person narrative. Proust's demonstrations of the subjectivity of experience gain by being pre-

---

[153] Cf. André Maurois remark: "Ce qu'il cherche à peindre, ce sont les effets de l'amour dans l'âme du narrateur ou, plus généralement, dans l'esprit de celui qui aime... Selon Proust l'objet aimé n'existe pas sinon dans l'imagination de l'amant", *A la recherche de Marcel Proust,* Paris, p. 231.

[154] *ARTP,* I, p. 219.

[155] *ARTP,* I, p. 281.

[156] One of Proust's recurrent ideas: cf. "Même à un simple point de vue réaliste, les pays que nous désirons tiennent à chaque moment beaucoup plus de place dans notre vie véritable que le pays où nous nous trouvons effectivement", *ARTP,* I, p. 390.

[157] *ARTP,* I, p. 286.

[158] These imaginary circumstances become so 'real' that in the 1913 Grasset edition of *Du côté de chez Swann,* the hypothetical conditional tense is replaced by the more factual imperfect. See *ARTP,* I, notes, p. 962.

sented themselves subjectively, and it is particularly significant to note that even when Proust deliberately adopts third-person narrative, he injects techniques and attitudes into the recounting of his story which convert it back to first person narrative .

OMNISCIENCE AND THE THEME OF SOCIETY

Only one theme of *A la Recherche* benefits from the objective dispassionate tone of the omniscient narrator: the theme of society. A comparison between the presentation of society in *Un Amour de Swann* and the remainder of *A la Recherche* shows that Proust needed a wider viewpoint than that of either of the Marcels, that he found this viewpoint in third person narration, and instinctively or otherwise introduced it into all subsequent appearances of the society theme.

The Sainte-Euverte soirée in *Un Amour de Swann* shows how Proust prefers an objective tone to describe the phenomenon of Parisian society. The observation of the social gathering it represents is handled almost entirely by the omniscient narrator. As Swann, at the beginning of the evening, ascends the immense staircase leading to the marquise's salons, the description of the valets and attendants is presented at first through his eyes. The magnificence of his surroundings is deliberately contrasted with a sordid apartment where Odette is at that moment. But soon this technique is abandoned, and it is not Swann but the omniscient narrator who observes the spectacle. It is he who tells us what the marquise de Gallardon is not only doing, but thinking:

> ...la marquise de Gallardon, occupée à sa pensée favorite, l'alliance qu'elle avait avec les Guermantes... Elle songeait en ce moment qu'elle n'avait jamais reçu une invitation ni une visite de sa jeune cousine la princesse des Laumes, depuis six ans que celle-ci était mariée [160].

The princesse des Laumes, herself, is described by a narrator who knows the innermost thoughts and motives of her person:

> ...elle se tenait debout à l'endroit qui lui avait paru le plus modeste (et d'où elle savait bien qu'une exclamation ravie de Mme de Sainte-Euverte allait la tirer dès que celle-ci l'aurait aperçue), à côté de Mme de Cambremer qui lui était inconnue [161].

The same objective, detached tone allows Proust to colour his descriptions of society with humorous comparisons, like the parallel he draws between the marquise de Gallardon and the kinds of tree, which

> nés dans une mauvaise position au bord d'une précipice, sont forcés de croître en arrière pour garder leur équilibre [162].

[159] *ARTP*, I, pp. 328-329.
[160] *ARTP*, I, pp. 328-329.
[161] *ARTP*, I, p. 330.
[162] *ARTP*, I, p. 329.

—or to introduce a dry humour when pointing out the limitations of the pretentions aristocrats' artistic sensibility:

> Mais depuis que Mme de Gallardon avait signalé à sa cousine la présence de Swann, Chopin ressuscité aurait pu venir jouer lui-même toutes ses œuvres sans que Mme des Laumes pût y faire attention [163].

At all times, an objective narrative tone is used in which to present the spectacle of society. In the remainder of *A la Recherche,* written in the first person, Proust continues to adopt the same tone, which we may legitimately take to be his own adaptation of the 'memorialist' attitude —of a Saint-Simon, for example. Proust's description of society, like that of the duc de Saint-Simon, is remarkable for its many portraits— presented by an unseen narrator whom it is not always easy to reconcile with the later Marcel. It is rare for one of the characters themselves to be accorded the privilege, like Célimène, of 'drawing' a portrait. The duchesse de Guermantes' description of the Empress of Austria is a notable exception:

> ... un peu folle, un peu insensée, mais c'était une très bonne femme, une gentille folle très aimable, je n'ai seulement jamais compris pourquoi elle n'avait jamais acheté un râtelier qui tint, le sien se décrochait toujours avant la fin de ses phrasés et elle était obligée de les interrompre pour ne pas l'avaler [164].

For in general it is an omniscient narrator who delights in furnishing details of all kinds about the different elements who go to make up a fashionable gathering. The intention is sometimes to illustrate laws of behaviour, sometimes merely to indulge in 'gratuitous' portrait painting, but in either ease the objective tone of *Un Amour de Swann* is sustained throughout *A la Recherche.* The characters we are invited to laugh at or to ponder over are presented *absolutely,* their past history furnished and their intimate thoughts recorded. When M. de Bréauté meets Marcel for the first time at a Guermantes function, we are able, with the help of the omniscient narrative view point, to enter into his personality completely:

> ... M. de Bréauté, se demandant qui je pouvais bien être, sentait un champ très vaste ouvert à ses investigations. Un instant le nom de M. Widor passa devant son esprit... [165]

There is a marked tendency to describe from *within* instead of from the point of view of either of the two Marcels. To accentuate the difference between Marcel's romantic vision of the Guermantes and the reality of their snobbery and vulgarity, Proust refers to a mysterious higher and infallible source of knowledge, understandable in a third-person narrative, difficult to explain in a first-person one:

---

[163] *ARTP,* I, p. 335.
[164] *ARTP,* II, p. 510.
[165] *ARTP,* p. 430.

M. de Guermantes, heureux que (la duchesse) me parlât avec une telle compétence des sujets qui m'intéressaient, regardait la prestance célèbre de sa femme, écoutait ce qu'elle disait de Frans Hals *et pensait*: "Elle est ferrée à glace sur tout..." [166].

The list of examples could easily be multiplied. The introduction into an allegorical demonstration of the subjectivity of all experience and judgment, the introduction into *A la Recherche* in fact, of an absolute narrator, possessing absolute knowledge is contrary to all of Proust's theories on the individual's imperfect perception of knowledge, and is unexpected, coming from an author who bases so much of his work on the assumption that one person can never know another. We may conclude that, whereas in his demonstrations of the mystery of another personality Proust preferred to recreate the frustration of trying to know another person—as in the case of Swann, or Marcel and Albertine—nevertheless, his demonstrations of the subjectivity of the imagination, when applied to more concrete subjects like society, demanded a more concret and objective treatment. In this sphere alone, Proust abandons the 'limitations' of the first person narrative, (limitations which he so cleverly makes use of, and which he even introduces into objective reporting to support his theory of personality), and adopts the overall view allowed him by third-person narrative, even though he contradicts some of his deeply-held theories to do so.

The Limited Narrative Viewpoint and its use in "A la Recherche"

However, comparison between the third-person narrative of *Un amour de Swann* and the first-person narrative of *A l'ombre des jeunes filles en fleurs* illustrates in the clearest possible way why first-person narrative was, on the whole, ideally suited to the purposes of the novel. In addition to the construction and plan of *A la recherche,* the 'moralist' element incorporated into the plot, and the advantages of the subjective demonstration of theories, all of which demand first-person narration the analysis of characters and situations gains immeasurably in intensity by the exploitation of the peculiar qualities of first-person narration.

One of the most characteristic features of *A la Recherche* is the combination of emotion and penetrating self-analysis, the lucid examination of thoughts and feelings which occur simultaneously with a detached observation of them. From the beginning of the work the reader is made aware of this special quality of Proust's narrative:

Il est clair que la vérité que je cherche n'est pas en lui (le breuvage), mais en moi... remarks Marcels as he searches for the key to the sensation recalled by the 'madeleine' dipped in tea... Je pose la tasse et me tourne vers mon esprit. C'est à lui de trouver la vérité. Mais

---

[166] *ARTP,* II, p. 524.

comment? Grave incertitude, toutes les fois que l'esprit se sent dépassé
par lui-même; quand lui, le chercheur, est tout ensemble le pays obscu¹
où il doit chercher et où tout son bagage ne lui sera de rien [167]

Swann, in the early chapters written in the third person, is a perfect
example of the Proustian figure, sensitively registering his slightest
emotion, and analysing it as though it belonged to another person.
Devoured by jealousy, scarcely capable of acting rationally, Swann
nevertheless always remains in a certain measure detached from his
emotions,

> Considérant son mal avec autant de sagacité que s'il se l'était inoculé
> pour en faire l'étude... [168]

But Marcel is an even more perfect example, in the chapters written in
the first person. For in presenting Marcel's story through Marcel's
eyes from a later point in time, Proust not only gains an effect of
'double vision', but in doing so gains a new perspective in which to
place his character's self-analysis. We see the young Marcel of *A
l'Ombre des jeunes filles en fleurs* through the commentary of the older
Marcel, and through the spontaneous self-analysis of the boy himself,
sharing his arguments and conclusions as he himself observes *at the
time* his own emotion. Two degrees of analysis result: that of the
first Marcel, observing himself, like Swann, with clinical detachment;
and that of the second Marcel, who gives an often different analysis,
commenting from his later position in time not only on the original
situation but on the reasoning which accompanied it too. In third-
person narrative only the first of these degrees of self-observation is
possible, since the narrator is technically separated from the hero. An
example of this multi-tiered self-analysing process can be found in
the description of Marcel's reactions to the *Phèdre* notice just before
New Year's Day. The reader follows Marcel as he stops and wonders
whether he should go to see la Berma in *Phèdre* or in another play.
He cannot decide—but is acutely aware all the time of his own indecision:

> ... quand cette journée de théâtre, jusque-là défendue, ne dépendit plus
> que de moi, alors, pour la première fois, n'ayant plus à m'occuper qu'elle
> cessât d'être impossible, je me demandai si elle était souhaitable, si
> d'autres raisons que la défense de mes parents n'auraient pas dû m'y
> faire renoncer [169].

Onto this is grafted a second degree of detached observation, as the
second, later Marcel inserts his own comments on the situation and
on his earlier self's own detachment; two stages, therefore, of rational
analysis appear: the later narrator can now see that what finally

---

[167] *ARTP*, I, p. 45.
[168] *ARTP*, I, p. 300.
[169] *ARTP*, I, p. 443.

decided Marcel to opt for *Phèdre* was, characteristically, a quite irrational factor—a discovery only made possible by his later position in time:

> „, j'avais vu, tout humide encore, l'affiche détaillée de Phèdre qu'on venait de coller pour la première fois (*et où, à vrai dire, le reste de la distribution ne m'apportait aucun attrait nouveau qui pût me décider*). [170]

As always, Proust obtains some of his most successful comic effects by juggling with the two narrative positions, and the second degree of analysis being often different, if only implicitly from the first, Proust exploits his double analysis to obtain very amusing results:

> ... je ne fis qu'un bond jusqu'à la maison, cinglé que j'étais par ces mots magiques qui avaient remplacé dans ma pensée "paleur janséniste" et "mythe solaire": "Les dames ne seront pas reçues à l'orchestre en chapeau, les portes seront fermées à deux heures". [171]

There can be no doubt that, with the exception of the society theme, for which he still needed the objectivity and freedom of omniscient reporting, first person narrative provided Proust with many more advantages than third-person. Let us end our review of the first-person narrative of *A la Recherche* by considering some of the ways in which Proust tackled the challenging problem of omniscience in first-person reporting, and the rôle and personality of Marcel, the first-person narrator.

THE PROBLEM OF OMNISCIENCE IN FIRST-PERSON NARRATIVE IN "A LA RECHERCHE DU TEMPS PERDU"

In all themes, excepting the society theme, complete omniscience is deliberately avoided in order to prepare for the dramatic revelation of *Temps Retrouvé*. Love, art, vocation are all presented through the eyes of a Marcel who becomes more and more disillusioned as his life advances. Though a later set of values and judgments is continually referred to indirectly, there is no attempt to rectify Marcel's dejected conclusion that 'les maisons, les routes, les avenues sont fugitives, hélas ! comme les années [172]; the intervention of the later narrator whose omniscience is limited only by his personal contact with the past, (a past almost exclusively concerned with himself), is carefully manipulated to retain the 'secret' of *Temps Retrouvé*. It is in the treatment of society that this one limitation proves embarassing. Though the narrator's moralist attitude can provide the kind of omniscience implicit in final judgments on humanity, it cannot change the fictional basis of *A la Recherche*, which demands that the personal narrator be the vehicle for the story, the plot, and for all the observations arising

---

[170] *ARTP*, I, p. 444.
[171] *ARTP*, I, p. 445.
[172] *ARTP*, I, p. 427.

from them. The presentation of a relatively large-scale fresco of society, by which Proust intended to set himself beside Balzac, is, because of the plot of *La Recherche,* entirely dependent upon the particular contact with society achieved by the hero, who recounts everything in the first person.

Proust set out to remedy this situation; but his attempts to do so sometimes underline the technical inferiority he never rid himself of, when dealing with the fundamental tools of the novelist's trade. In creating devices to bridge the gap between the insufficiency of his fictional plot and the wide-reaching aims he cherished in building up a picture of a particular society, and human nature in general, Proust illustrates his chronic disregard for conventional fictional considerations.

The problem of omniscience in first-person narrative is perhaps best illustrated in *Le côté de Guermantes.* Here, it is clear that, to present the descriptions of society activities and functions relevant to Proust's plan, the limited contact of the narrator Marcel is insufficient. He cannot be everywhere, even if Proust endows the later narrator with facts suggesting that he knows everything. In what ways, therefore, does Proust manage to include scenes, and comment on activity both of which are outside the normal scope of Marcel's experience?

In order to comment on the Guermantes, for example, Proust transports Marcel and his family from their apartment to a new one, which has the unsurpassed advantage of overlooking,—not the Bois, but—the hôtel de Guermantes. This is a bold, simple and perfectly legitimate way of bringing the hero into daily contact with a whole section of the aristocracy. But the problem of showing the intimate scenes of this family's life, obviously unknown to Marcel, remains. Proust has, it should be remembered, already overcome a similar problem, though in the context of third-person narrative, in *Un Amour de Swann.* There Marcel came to share the every day life of the Swann household, even after he had broken with Gilberte, but the same device can hardly be used in connection with the Guermantes. The result is often curious. Proust so arranges the position of the hôtel de Guermantes in relation to Marcel's apartment, that it is possible for him to *spy* on the Duke and Duchess. He can see the duchesse de Guermantes coquettishly preparing her 'toilette' before going out in the afternoon, and does not find it strange that he should be able to do so:

> ... le matin, au moment où elle allait sortir à pied... je pouvais l'apercevoir devant sa glace, jouant, avec une conviction exempte de dédoublement et d'ironie, avec passion, avec mauvaise humeur, avec amour-propre... ce rôle, si inférieur à elle, de femme élégante [173].

The narrator and his mother are able to see into the Guermantes house whenever they leave the door open [174], and their kitchen window sur-

---

[173] *ARTP,* II, p. 29.
[174] *ARTP,* II, p. 30.

prisingly affords views not only of the Guermantes dining room, but also of their 'galerie obscure, aux meubles de peluche rouge' [175]. Sometimes, it is true, the fact that the Guermantes can easily be spied upon by their neighbours is made use of to illustrate certain of their particular characteristics, and the Duke has no compunction in shaving in full view of the narrator's mother, because, 'grand seigneur' that he is, neighbours are merely vassals whom one does not take into account [176]. But the frequency with which Marcel is allowed glimpses into the private life of others, and the apparent simplicity with which he does so, introduces an artificial note into the narrative, because certain episodes can have no other purpose than to admit the narrator into spheres which would normally be denied to him. Walking through Doncières on his way to join Saint-Loup and his friends, Marcel has the opportunity to observe intimate scenes through the windows, all apparently unshuttered, that he passes; he sees, for example:

> ... deux sous-officiers, leurs ceinturons posés sur des chaises (et qui) jouaient aux cartes *sans se douter qu'un magicien les faisait surgir de la nuit, comme dans une apparition de théâtre...* [177]

Marcel—for it is he who is the magician—sometimes drops his magic cloak and is present in situations where one would hardly expect to find him—an unembarassed third, for example, at Rachel and Saint-Loup's tête-à-tête in a private room, to which they had retired to make up a quarrel [178]. Proust seems to have been fond of creating situations in which Marcel can spy upon his fellows. Much of the material Proust incorporated into *Sodome et Gomorrhe* raises the problem of the personalised narrator's relationship to events which Proust himself continually described as scandalous and indecent [179], and in order to isolate Marcel from the implications of the scenes he witnesses but to give him an ideal viewpoint from which to transmit them to the reader, Proust makes Marcel spy on others.

In the apologia, on which the introduction to *Sodome et Gomorrhe* ends, the narrator warns us that we are entering a world, where for many "les romans d'aventure les plus invraisemblables semblent vrais, car dans cette vie d'un romanesque anachronique, l'ambassadeur est ami du forçat" [180] ; nevertheless, it is not this kind of implausibility which is in question when we discover how remarkably practical is

---

[175] *ARTP*, II, ibid.

[176] *ARTP*, II, p. 31.

[177] *ARTP*, II, p. 96. My italics.

[178] *ARTP*, II, p. 170. Professor Green, on the other hand, sees this scene as a strikingly original treatment of the best friend, "appreciating the peculiarly difficult rôle of this unfortunate confidant, usually so scurvily and obliquely presented by writers of fiction". F.C. Green, *op. cit.*, p. 130.

[179] "Il est possible qu'à cause de l'extrême indécence de cet ouvrage je ne maintienne pas cette dédicace" *Lettres à la NRF, Cahier Marcel Proust VI*, p. 97.

[180] *ARTP*, II, p. 67.

Marcel's hiding place [181] which allows him to track Jupien's movements without averting suspicion, and consider Mme de Villeparisis's miraculously apposite recovery [182], the extraordinary chance which allows Marcel to hide in a room next to Jupien's shop, and that, no less unexpected, of finding a ladder which the duc de Guermantes had accidentally left there [183]—a combination of circumstances which allows the hero to hear every word of the conversation between Jupin and the Baron, and to follow every movement.

No less astonishing is a passage added by the editors of the 1954 edition [184] where we find the same kind of unconvincing circumstances, arranged this time so that Marcel can hear and observe Charlus' interview with a 'contrôleur d'omnibus'. He returns no less than three times to the waiting cab in which this interview takes place, after following the Baron (on the Princesse de Guermantes' instructions) to give him a letter from the Princess [185]. He finds the same kind of hiding place as before, which allows him to see and hear everything— 'car on avait fait placer le fiacre dans un coin sombre, à l'angle d'une impasse entièrement noire. J'entrai dans celle-ci pour que M. de Charlus ne me vît pas [186]. The baron obligingly leaves the window open, thus further helping his hidden observer [187]. W.L. Hodson has referred to the presence throughout Proust's writing of this spying, or 'voyeur' technique, and it is remarkable that, crude though it is, it remains fundamentally unchanged, appearing in *La Confession d'une jeune fille* and *La Fin de la jalousie* and the final volumes of *A la Recherche* alike [188]. There is little attempt to do more than arrange a situation capable of revealing certain information that Marcel would not normally possess, involving almost always a concordance of circumstances often lacking in plausibility. Proust's own techniques are here to blame ; the plausible impossibility recommended by Aristotle becomes in Proust's hands an unconvincing possibility, and the arbitrary engineering of events makes their likelihood—however near they are to autobiographical truth—difficult to accept.

---

[181] *ARTP*, II, 602.

[182] *ARTP*, II, p. 603.

[183] *ARTP*, II, p. 609.

[184] *ARTP*, II, pp. 1184-1190.

[185] *ARTP*, II, p. 1188.

[186] *ARTP*, II, p. 1186.

[187] *ARTP*, II, p. 1187. It can hardly have been the implausibility of the situation which made Proust omit this passage, as it bears similarities to other passages, notably the scene in Jupien's hotel in *Temps Retrouvé*, where more unlikely events occur. The edition's conclusion that Proust did not have time to complete it is probably correct.

[188] W.L. Hodson: "Proust's methods of Character Presentation in *Les Plaisirs et les Jours* and *Jean Santeuil*" *M.L.R.* January 1962, and cf. the curious link with Balzac's ending for *La Peau de Chagrin* where Raphael, jealous of Foedora says: "pour la connaître enfin tout entière, je résolus de passer une nuit chez elle, dans sa chambre, à son insu". Ed. Nelson, 1958, p. 206.

Other solutions to the problem of Marcel's contact with the society Proust wishes to observe are more successful. Proust occasionally introduces a character whose function is really that of a second narrator, particularly when he wishes to describe characters and situations in a wider perspective than Marcel's [189]. The description of one of Saint-Loup's friends' attitude to the Dreyfus affair, for example, is conveyed by one of the officers during a dinner at Doncières. He is able, with his more intimate knowledge of the friend concerned, to describe his attitude and conclusions with a precision and accuracy Marcel could not have achieved [190].

Occasionally Proust introduces letters into the narrative, a device which allows him, while ostensibly doing no more than reproduce correspondence between two characters, to vary the narrative viewpoint, obtain perfect omniscience and dispense with an external or even implicit narrator. Such are the advantages of the letter-technique, which was so widely used in 18th century fiction; but Proust's reasons for using it are more simple. The letter Aimé shows Marcel simply allows Proust to present the 'revers de la médaille' once again, adding new information about a situation which has already occurred. Charlus' presence outside the restaurant where Saint-Loup dined with Rachel and Marcel is now explained in a letter he addresses to Aimé, who worked there; at the same time, the reader is introduced to a scene which Marcel is totally absent, and which is reenacted in the letter. Charlus comes to life, and we witness his peroration to an astonished Aimé—completing a picture already begun in the famous scene between Charlus and Marcel [191]. The inclusion of letters to present different aspects of the changing circumstances caused by Albertine's flight continues for a while in *La fugitive* [192], but at no time does the correspondence become the basis for the narrative, and it remains an accessory means of illustrating the difficulty of communication between individuals, and takes the place of conversation which is made impossible by Albertine's disappearance from Paris.

Another method introduced to include events in which Marcel has taken no part is that of 'double narration'. In the description of the princesse de Guermantes' fete in *Sodome et Gomorrhe,* an interesting case of double narration occurs which illustrates the lengths to which Proust is prepared to go in order to 'report' a scene between Swann and the prince de Guermantes, in which Marcel's only interest is that of curiosity. How is the episode included? The device used to do so seems self-explanatory as Swann remarks to Marcel:

Voici mot pour mot, me dit-il, quand nous fûmes seuls, ma conversation avec le prince [193].

---

189 *ARTP,* I, pp. 754, 755, 807.
190 *ARTP,* II, p. 105.
191 *ARTP,* II, p. 992.
192 *ARTP, III,* pp. 452-456; 468-470; 477-8; 515; 525.
193 *ARTP,* II, p. 705.

However, the scene assumes such proportions that eventually Proust comes near to losing all control over it, and manifests his anxiety in the narrative that the reader be unable to follow the complicated shifts of narration it involves. The first delegation of reporting occurs when Marcel lets Swann take over the relating of his conversation; his interjections and comments on the situation he unfolds are transferred into the first person:

> ... (Je ne m'en étais nullement aperçu, étant malade et fuyant moi-même tout le monde)... [194]

A second change of narrator occurs when the Prince takes over from Swann, and begins to recount a conversation he had learned about between his wife and the Prince of Sweden. Thus, like images in an infinitely reflecting mirror, the Prince of Sweden's conversation is reported by the prince de Guermantes, the prince de Guermantes' by Swann, and Swann's by Marcel. This triple degree of narration is maintained and the Prince of Sweden is replaced successively by Beauserfeuil and the abbé Poiré [195]. Proust aware of the intricacy of the situation, takes steps to present the narrative from becoming incomprehensible. He interrupts the Swann/Marcel conversation from time to time, plunging the reader back into the turbulent atmosphere of the Guermantes fête [196] in order to remind us that the main narrator is still Swann:

> "... Je demandai ce jour-là à l'abbé Poiré s'il pourrait dire le lendemain ma messe pour Dreyfus". Allons, bon! s'écria Swann à mi-voix en s'interrompant. [197]

At one stage, he also makes it quite expilcit exactly who is speaking. For during the successive substitutions of one narrator to another, the first person has passed, like the mythical godess's eye, from Marcel to Swann, thence to the prince de Guermantes, to the prince de Suède and to the abbé Poiré. In order to prevent any misunderstanding, Proust makes Swann interrupt his story once more.

> "Non, me répondit l'abbé (je vous dis 'me' me dit Swann, parce que c'est le Prince qui me parle, vous comprenez?)... [198].

Thus, in order to work into the narrative the report of events far removed from Marcel's personal experience, Proust has been obliged to create a situation where he has two entirely passive narrators— Swann and Marcel—reporting 'silently' on events in which they play only a nominal part, and at which each is in reality a silent observer.

Finally, Proust uses techniques to draw significant parallels in his description of society which belong strictly to third-person narration.

---

[194] *ARTP*, II, ibid.
[195] *ARTP*, II, p. 709.
[196] *ARTP*, II, pp. 706-8, 709-710.
[197] *ARTP*, II, 709.
[198] *ARTP*, II, p. 711.

One of the properties of the latter is that the narrator, bound by restrictions neither of time nor place, can present actions occuring simultaneously. Yet, in the first person narrative of *Temps Retrouvé,* the sudden switch from the Guermantes hôtel in the avenue du Bois to La Berma's Salon, is the epitome of omniscient third-person reporting, in a position where it is most unexpected. Accompanied by the complete entering of certain character's thoughts and emotions, the simultaneous scenes in the two salons indicate once again that first-person narrative is insufficient for the treatment in *A la Recherche* of the society theme [199].

The fictional plot of *A la Recherche,* then, with its necessary implication that Marcel is to be the focus and reflecting image of the sum of experience it stands for, creates difficulties in two spheres: when faced with including material about homosexuality Proust has to find methods of replacing Marcel by another reflecting image, in order to shield his personality. When faced with relating Marcel to the wide backcloth of society he wishes to include, on the other hand, he finds his focus limiting and is forced to resort to techniques which project a more comprehensive view of society than is possible by using the fictional hero he has created. The whole question of Marcel's rôle and personality has been raised in this context and we shall now examine his function in relation to Proust's use of first-person narrative.

THE RÔLE AND PERSONALITY OF THE FIRST-PERSON NARRATOR

The consideration of Marcel's personality was made the starting point (in 1943) [200] for a fascinating essay by Louis Martin-Chauffier, who found that "At no time is the hero, Marcel, presented to us as a living character; nor is he made palpable, or even described. The only portrait which is missing is his own" [201]. On the other hand "what matters", he continues, "is the narrator, the one who has discovered the secret of (his) sensations; and having discovered it, regulates not his life but his art, writes not a biography, but assembles a universe, depicts not a life in progress, but rather, starting from the data presented to him, elucidates the general laws of truth" [102].

Louis Martin-Chauffier has put his finger on the narrator's two main functions, which spring from the two main sources of inspiration in *A la Recherche*: the setting of a *moralist*'s range of observations and conclusions within a *fictional* and dramatic framework borrowed from the traditional novel. The narrator is thus Proust's means of relating the non-fictional element to the fictional plot of *A la Recherche,*

---

[199] *ARTP,* III, p. 995 ff.
[200] Translated as "Proust and the Double 'I'", in *Partisan Review,* 1949, Vol. XVI, N° 10, pp. 1011-1027, to which references in this chapter are made.
[201] Martin-Chauffier, *op. cit.,* p. 1015.
[202] Martin-Chauffier, *op. cit.,* pp. 1016-7.

and acts simultaneously as the fictitious hero around whom this plot is arranged. Martin-Chauffier's ingenious conclusion that Marcel the hero, as distinct from Marcel the observer-narrator, is personality-less because his function is to depict the emptiness of a life "which has not assumed its meaning" is difficult to reconcile with the conclusions we have been forced to draw from the same hero-narrator relationship as it appears in *Jean Santeuil*; Frederic Moreau is in many ways as indeterminate as the pre-revelation Marcel, and his tragedy is that he never finds his reason for living. Yet his rôle as a fictional character is not neglected by Flaubert in the way that Marcel is simply forgotten by Proust, or Jean in *Jean Santeuil*. Moreover, the novel, *A la Recherche,* is arranged deliberately around a central hero, and it is unlikely that the powerful climax of *Temps Retrouvé,* with its wealth of careful preparation, would be applied to a character whom the author deliberately effaced from the narrative.

The answer, suggested by the analogous 'disappearance' of the hero in *Jean Santeuil,* is rather that the fictional element, involving the hero, is often abandoned for the moralist element, involving the later narrator, and that the pattern of the early works continues in *A la Recherche.*

In order to give ample treatment to Marcel's two functions, Proust must create situations in which Marcel can come in contact with the spheres of activity he wishes to describe, or find some other means of coveying them to the reader. Very often, the situations which he imagines satisfy one aspect of Marcel's rôle, but not the other. The result is that Marcel is often the passive spectator of an event at which he is nominally present, but in which he plays no part. Marcel the hero is sacrificed for Marcel the narrator. In *Le côté de Guermantes* one scene illustrates the successful combination of Marcel's two functions: structurally, the Opéra passage divides into a classic ternary movement

(i) observation of the society making up the audience, and particularly of the Guermantes box (II, 37-44).

(ii) description of La Berma in an act from *Phèdre,* and the reactions she produces in Marcel, compared with his earlier disappointment on seeing the same actors in the same play several years before (II, 44-52).

(iii) return to the observation of the princesse and the duchesse de Guermantes (II, 52-58).

In the first and third sections Marcel's function is that of the static, passive observer who plays no personal part in the scene, where his rôle is that of a camera, not an actor. As he himself points out, he is seated among 'des snobs ou des curieux qui voulaient contempler des gens qu'ils n'auraient pas d'autre occasion de voir de près' [203]—a

---

[203] *ARTP,* II, p. 38.

situation which allows him to observe, like them, 'leur vraie vie mondaine habituellement cachée'. The passages of description which follow
are all reflected through the spectrum of the narrator, whose function
it is to observe, but not to participate. In the second and central
section, however, Marcel exchanges his passive rôle for one that is
more active. Instead of the Guermantes being the centre of interest,
and the narrator the intermediary between them and the reader, the
narrator moves into the centre of the stage, as La Berma appears, and
the reflecting spectrum which before had served to show the spectacle
of the Guermantes world suddenly becomes a source of vibrating
energy, as a new world of comprehension opens for Marcel:

> ... tout cela, voix, attitudes, gestes, voiles, n'était, autour de ce corps
> d'une idée qu'est un vers (...), que des enveloppes supplémentaires qui,
> au lieu de la cacher, rendaient plus splendidement l'âme qui se les était
> assimilées et s'y était répandue ... [204]

The final paragraph admirably sums up the narrator's dual function
as, when Marcel turns back to examine the duchesse de Guermantes
after the disappearance of la Berma, the relationship previously
established between Marcel and the Guermantes changes, and he is
acknowledged by the Duchess [205].

At other times, however, Marcel's two functions are not simultaneously present in the narrative. As his reflexions on literature and
the artist's duty develop in *Temps Retrouvé,* the fictional scene fades
into the background—this time, although recalled from time to time,
('Cela me fit ressouvenir où j'étais') [206] never to return; the commenting,
analysing narrator's reflexions occupy the reader exclusively, who finds
himself reading a kind of discourse on literature and art, complete
with quotations from Chateaubriand and Saint-Simon [207], until they
finally free themselves for ever from the fictional scenes which gave
rise to them.

Most often, Marcel is uneasily present in the narrative, and it is
this shadowy existence which Martin-Chauffier has reacted against.
One of the greatest differences between Saint-Simon and Proust in
their presentation of society is involved here. In the *Mémoires* not the
least interesting feature is the strongly felt personality of the fiery
Duke, but in *A la Recherche,* the individual character of the author is
less apparent in the drawing of portraits than in the evocation of
sensation and atmosphere. The memorialist is present in *A la
Recherche* but plays virtually no part in the proceedings, and the
narrator/hero's commenting function is accentuated at the expense of
his physical and dynamic participation in the course of events.

Two main results can be noticed: the presence of the fictitious
Marcel becomes mainly theoretical, and, with the virtual dispensing

---

[204] *ARTP,* II, pp. 48-49.
[205] *ARTP,* II, p. 58.
[206] *ARTP,* III, p. 918.
[207] *ARTP,* III, pp. 919, 961.

with the personalised hero, the later narrative tone develops in a way hardly to be reconciled with the character of Marcel. A strange 'division' of personality results: the later narrator is not only disinterested, but also cynical, sarcastic and bitter. His humour, for example, is strangely detached from the emotions Marcel is later represented as having felt at the time. While the presence of two distinct viewpoints is the basis of the 'double vision' technique referred to earler, the later narrator's description of Dieulafoy as an 'espèce de notaire', playing

> ... un rôle aussi original que le raisonneur, le scaramouche ou le père noble, et qui était de venir constater l'agonie ou la mort [208].

hardly prepares us for the moment when Proust, remembering that Marcel is nominally still present in the room, describes his emotion on kissing his grandmother for the last time [209]. The noticeable disproportion between narrator and hero, or between the two separate functions of the combined narrator/hero, recalls efforts in *Jean Santeuil* to strike a balance between the same two narrative elements.

It is in the principal episode of *Le côté de Guermantes,* the first dinner-party that Marcel attends in the latter's hôtel, that this disproportion strikes the reader most forcibly. It is true that, from time to time, the hero Marcel is placed in the same perspective as other characters. He comments on Mme d'Arpajon's conception of Hugo [210], and occasionally ventures a remark which figures in the conversation [211], but in general his physical presence is reduced to a minimum. He does not answer, for example, when he is spoken to [212]; his conversation, when it exists, is mostly paraphrased, and reported indirectly, in direct contrast with the dialogue of the other characters [213]; if it is not paraphrased, it is taken for granted:

> Je compris que la princesse de Luxembourg elle-même, en ayant l'air de défendre son neveu, fournissait des armes pour l'attaquer. "Vous avez tort de le défendre", me dit M. de Guermantes comme avait fait Saint-Loup [214].

Not only is Marcel's function as the fictional hero neglected in essentially visual scenes, like the Guermantes dinner-party, but, as the novel progresses, the later narrator figures more largely in the story and Marcel's fictional personality correspondingly diminishes in stature. His presence in many of the scenes he has to describe is purely negative; if he participates at Charlus' 'execution' by the Verdurins,

---

[208] *ARTP,* II, p. 342.
[209] *ARTP,* II, p. 344.
[210] *ARTP,* II, p. 492.
[211] *ARTP,* II, p. 490.
[212] *ARTP,* II, pp. 497-501.
[213] *ARTP,* II, p. 500.
[214] *ARTP,* II, p. 533.

he is scarcely notireable beside the other characters, and the rare occasions when Marcel plays a definite part, or states a definite preference are always accompanied by surprise. Such is the case when we are unexpectedly introduced to his opinion of Morel—all the more astounding since he has watched Jupien and Charlus with a botanist's detachment in scenes far more disturbing than that between Morel and Jupien's niece, which draws the following unexpected comment:

> J'avais tremblé qu'allant dans la même maison, à quelques minutes, il ne me demandât de le conduire, et je me rappelais trop la scène de l'après-midi pour ne pas éprouver quelque dégoût à avoir Morel auprès de moi pendant le trajet [215].

Accompanying Proust's tendency to ignore Marcel's fictional rôle is an inevitable depreciation in his personality and an immobility and passivety matched by no other character, not even 'tante Léonie', in *A la Recherche*. Particularly noticeable is the fact that, to judge from the hero's indifference to his hosts throughout the work, there seems to be no relation between the taciturn, inward-looking narrator, who afterwards furnishes us with minutely-observed 'portraits' of Prince Von or the princesse de Luxembourg, and the brilliant young guest who is invited to all the Guermantes functions as he himself perhaps too complacently remarks:

> Je ne devais plus cesser par la suite d'être continuellement invité... [216]

These are largely technical problems; because of his choice of construction and the subsequent adoption of first-person reporting, Proust must make his hero participate in, or be present at, all the action contained in *A la Recherche,* although he has repeatedly shown himself careless of the use of the novelist's art. The care which should have been lavished on the transformation of an uncommitted observer (as in *Jean Santeuil*) into a fictional character on whom depends the climax of *Temps Retrouvé* is lacking, while the technical necessity of including the hero remains. Hence his 'passivity', and hence his lack of identity with the commenting observer, who receives much of the attention the fictional hero lacks. The plan and construction suffer visibly through Proust's inability to sustain the use of conventional fictional techniques throughout a work based largely upon them.

What conclusions can we draw from Proust's use of first-person narrative? He prefers to use it rather than third-person narrative, for the advantages in his demonstrations of the subjectivity of experience it gives him; his conception of the gradual unfolding of the richness of life is best presented through the subjective viewpoint of his hero. At the same time, he is uncomfortable in the restricting framework it

---

[215] *ARTP,* III, p. 197.
[216] *ARTP,* II, p. 512, certain other traces of social snobbery remain: i.e., I, p. 735.

gives him in which to include portraits of an objectively observed society, and when he comes to treat the problem of omniscience his disregard of certain basic considerations of fictional writing sometimes mar the technical brilliance with which he engineers situations and characters. The same disregard for conventional fictional composition harms the creation of his first-person hero, and though Proust writes naturally in a form of continuous commentary, the tendency is to make the commenting element of the narrator/hero overshadow the latter's traditional rôle and function. However, the reader scarcely notices them. The contradictions in the sudden appropriating of other characters' thoughts by the personal narrator are rarely apparent, and in no way harm the general presentation of Proust's character theories. Only in the inclusion of homosexual elements does Proust's use of first-person narrative invite open criticism. The author's failure to devise methods of circumventing Marcel, and the ambiguous position he occupies as a result, are unfortunate. But all such disadvantages are outweighed by the positive superiority of first-person narrative for Proust's main purpose: the demonstration of the subjectivity of personal experience, as seen through the eyes of a first-person narrator.

DRAMATIC STRUCTURE

One of the most paradoxical features of Proust's writing before *A la Recherche* was the continual appearance of highly-dramatic scenes, prepared with the care and techniques of the 'traditional' nineteenth-century novelists, irregularly spaced out among long stretches of narrative whose most marked characteristic was the author's disinclination to transpose observations and personal experience into fictional terms of any kind. The introduction of drama was successful but intermittent and the reader was left with the impression that, if he was adept in using fictional devices to heighten interest in the story, Proust was unsure himself what function they should be given in the work of art.

With the elaboration of a fictional and dramatic plot in *A la Recherche,* this uncertainty disappears, and Proust evolves methods of combining less obviously 'fictional' means of presenting the narrative with those techniques we have seen being gradually perfected in *Jean Santeuil,* and of which the chapter *La classe de philosophie* is a striking example. Thus, once again, the structural pattern of the work combines Proust's two main tendencies in composition, the 'moralist's' observation of manners, and the techniques it implies, and the novelist's preoccupation with the recreation of personal experience in fictional terms.

The 'plot' of *A la Recherche* concerns the accidental discovery by the hero of a means of triumphing over the series of bitter disappointments which has marked his career. An emotional climate is carefully introduced: as disappointment and disillusion succeed each other, the hero becomes more and more depressed, and his opinions on life more and more bleak; until, suddenly, disappointment gives way to joy and confidence, and Marcel finds that all his previous disillusions have been a mistake, and that he has discovered a way of converting this mistake into a positive source of value for himself and others. The discovery of *Temps Retrouvé,* the revelation of the final chapters, the dramatic reversal of circumstances they introduce, all depend for their effect upon traditional techniques, creating suspense, surprise and preparing a climax. Proust therefore casts his work in a form which will make use of traditional techniques.

The Disappearance of "Dramatic" Scenes

The careful placing of individual, dramatic scenes within the dramatic framework of *A la Recherche* helps to present the changing emotional climate on which it depends. The series of episodes linking Marcel's childhood with the final period of despair immediately preceding the 'revelation' is remarkable for the gradual disappearance of dramatic scenes. Events which, at the beginning of the hero's life, were presented as dramatic become, with his growing disenchantment, much less so, and Marcel's attitude to life, the gradual decline in his confidence in the excitement and reality of experience, is translated by an accompanying change in narrative presentation.

This accompanying change in the presentation of significant events in Marcel's life is best illustrated by comparing an important upheaval in his childhood, and a no less traumatic experience which occurs in later life. Each profoundly marks the hero's sensibility, but, since they both occur at different stages in the evolution of that sensibility, their presentation is very different. The first has one kind of immediate impact upon Marcel, the second an impact of quite another order, each demanding a different approach, and different techniques.

The terror the child Marcel experiences at the thought of going to bed without the 'viatique' of his mother's goodnight kiss is presented in the most dramatic form possible. The whole episode is constructed around his preoccupation with the consequences of leaving her:

> A Combray, tous les jours dès la fin de l'après-midi, longtemps avant le moment où il faudrait me mettre au lit et rester, sans dormir, loin de ma mère et de ma grand-mère, *ma chambre à coucher redevenait le point fixe et douloureux* de mes préoccupations [217].

Two themes, the bedroom and the anxiety it symbolises, run right through the episode, and are still present at the end, when, though for one night his anxiety has been calmed, he knows that tomorrow it will all begin again:

> Je savais qu'une telle nuit ne pourrait se renouveler... Demain mes angoisses reprendraient et mamant ne resterait pas là [218].

Within the framework these two themes create, Proust arranges all the events, associated in Marcel's mind with the 'drame du coucher', around a central scene. Art and beauty, in the magic lantern episode, merely heighten the child's craving for his mother [219], Swann by his very presence becomes the 'auteur inconscient de (ses) tristesses [220], and occurring at intervals throughout the passages describing the great-

---

[217] *ARTP*, I, p. 9.
[218] *ARTP*, I, p. 43.
[219] *ARTP*, I, p. 10.
[220] *ARTP*, I, p. 43.

aunts and the grandmother, references to the boy's anxiety form a kind of ground-bass to the action, each new appearance emphasising the importance of the goodnight kiss:

> Ma seule consolation, quand je montais me coucher, était que maman viendrait *m'embrasser* quand je serais dans mon lit. Mais ce *bonsoir*... De sorte que *ce bonsoir que j'aimais tant*... Quelquefois quand, après m'avoir embrassé... l'habitude... de lui demander, quand elle était déjà sur le pas de la porte, *un baiser de plus.* [221]

Not only does each restatement of the theme emphasise the importance of the goodnight kiss, it also creates a mounting tension. Descriptions of evenings when the mother's presence calms the child give place to accounts of more painful occasions when she never came, and the climax to the whole episode is dramatically prepared. Having already associated Swann with his dread of quitting his mother, Marcel notes all the family's reactions to his visit; the grandfather sees it as a chance to talk politics, the great-aunts as an opportunity to thank him for a present, Marcel's own mother to talk about his daughter, but for Marcel himself it is the sure indication that he will go to bed alone, as he remarks with dramatic finality:

> Mais le seul d'entre nous pour qui la venue de Swann devint l'objet d'une préoccupation douloureuse, ce fut moi [222].

Then one fatal evening is described; Proust narrows the spotlight of his attention to the one mark on the canvas of the disillusioned narrator's memory which has been undimmed by Time. The order of events is presented dramatically. Accompanied by the knell of the dinner bell, Marcel is sent to bed, his last attempts to kiss his mother brutally interrupted, and his feelings disregarded:

> Je voulus embrasser maman, à cet instant on entendit la cloche du dîner. "Mais non, voyons, laisse ta mère, vous vous êtes assez dit bonsoir comme cela, ces manifestations sont ridicules. Allons, monte!" [223]

The whole episode, moreover, falls into the traditional form of preparation, reaction, climax and anti-climax. The preparation scene in the garden is long and developed with great care. The reaction, the sending of Marcel to bed, is short, sharp and violent. The climax, the arrival of the father in the midst of Marcel's and his mother's 'illegal' embrace, gives way to an anti-climax: the father's anger, feared by both the guilty parties alike, is in reality no more than bewildered indulgence, and the episode closes on a return to the note of calm which had preceded the anguish of bedtime, thus marking a full circle in Marcel's emotions.

---

[221] *ARTP*, I, p. 13.
[222] *ARTP*, I, p. 23.
[223] *ARTP*, I, p. 27.

Aesthetically, too, the whole passage is perfectly constructed, mainly because certain events are consciously highlighted, and others subordinated to the central theme, while the whole is deliberately conceived with a view to creating a dramatic effect. A comparison with the same theme, as it appears in *Jean Santeuil,* shows that Proust has lavished attention on detail and presentation. The scene is much longer in *A la Recherche,* prepared with more regard to tension and drama, and benefits consequently from increased importance. Moreover the commentary provided by the later narrator in *A la Recherche,* emphasises the consciously dramatic quality Proust wishes to bring out, with terms like 'décor', 'drame' and 'théâtre' [224] and the author's comparison between this memory and a searchlight playing on one spot [225].

How different is the recounting of Albertine's death in *La Fugitive.* Here there is a deliberate avoidance of all the techniques—preparation, construction, creation of suspense and climax—which characterise the Combray episode. Yet the importance of the later event is enormous; Marcel's whole existence is for a long time as profoundly marked by it as by the abdication of his will-power in the 'baiser du soir' sequence. Nevertheless the presentation of the *event* provides a sharp contrast with the events in *Combray,* narrator and author's attention now being firmly centred elsewhere.

First, it is true to say that elements of climax and anti-climax persist. On the point of sacrificing everything in order to persuade Albertine to return to him, 'lui demandant de revenir à n'importe quelles conditions' [226], Marcel suddenly receives a telegram informing him of her death. To this first element of surprise is added another: he receives two letters from Albertine, posted just before her death, and begging to be allowed to return. Nevertheless, a reading of this passage does not convey the same kind of terrified anxiety which is so apparent in the 'baiser du soir' episode. This is all the more noticeable because the narrator has earlier specifically related the emotions present in these two scenes: each is based on the 'angoisse' which characterises both the childhood yearning for the mother, and the lover's desire for his mistress, and which 'emigrates' from one to the other [227]. But the main difference is one of presentation and emphasis. The arrival of the telegram now loses all importance, and the emotions its contents awaken alone receive detailed attention. Yet earlier, the father's arrival in the *Combray* episode, the flickering of his candle, the shadow it cast on the wall—all were made to accentuate an emotion. In the description of Albertine's telegram, the same emotion is present, but it is no longer 'mounted' on traditional techniques, such as the inclusion of significant detail. Only so much of the background situation is

---

[224] *ARTP,* I, p. 44.
[225] *ARTP,* I, p. 43.
[226] *ARTP,* III, p. 476.
[227] *ARTP,* I, p. 30.

presented as is necessary for the reader to share Marcel's reactions. It is no longer presented dramatically, but as a matter of course, and the spotlight of the 'drame du coucher' becomes a magnifying glass, as the narrator scrutinises the slightest nuances and implications of a basic emotion, whose growth and individual circumstances no longer interest him. For between the childhood scenes of *Combray* and episodes set like this one in Marcel's adult life a change has taken place. Marcel's preoccupations have now shifted from a belief in life's intrinsic value, to centre around the psychological reactions he can register, within himself, to external reality, whereas earlier at a different stage in his career, external reality presented an attraction greater than that of psychological analysis. The consequences in the presentation of experience are clear. There is no longer any attempt to heighten 'artificially' the significance of certain events, to make them stand out from personal analysis. The narrator, breaking off for a moment from his painful self-interrogation, remarks briefly:

> (Albertine) ne revint jamais. Mon télégramme venait de partir que j'en reçus un. Il était de Madame Bontemps. [228]

—and after these laconic, unemotional lines, and the reproduction of the telegram, the current of psychological questioning, begun before the news of Albertine's death, reported in the telegram, is quietly resumed, and the emotions arising from the change of circumstances simply add a difference of detail to an already-existing current of thought:

> Non, pas la suppression de la souffrance, mais une souffrance inconnue, celle d'apprendre qu'elle ne reviendrait pas. Mais ne m'étais-je pas dit plusieurs fois qu'elle ne reviendrait peut-être pas? Je me l'étais dit en effet... [229]

We never leave the world contained within the narrator's mind; interruptions of this kind disturb the balance of his inner monologue from time to time, but never for very long. Events, as such, are not important; their meaning is. Similarly, when the two 'posthumous' letters from Albertine arrive, there is a noticeable reticence to present the eminently dramatic situation they create in dramatic terms. Just as in *Les Plaisirs et les Jours* Proust refers retrospectively to past events and avoids including them in the narrative [230], so as *A la Recherche* progresses, he refers to emotion from a safe distance, calmly:

> Je sentis, après, que j'avais dû avoir les yeux de quelqu'un dont l'esprit perd l'équilibre. Je ne fus même pas heureux, ni incrédule. J'étais comme quelqu'un qui voit la même place de sa chambre occupée par un canapé et par une grotte [231].

---

[228] *ARTP,* III, p. 476.
[229] *ARTP,* III, iibd
[230] Cf. page 20.
[231] *ARTP,* III, p. 477.

The overall impression left by Proust's recounting of the death of Albertine is curious. The tide of the narrator's monologue, dramatic and full of tension as it is, almost completely engulfs the material facts of the arrival of both telegram and letters. For the narrator their physical existence is important only insofar as they have a bearing on his inner life. Once this bearing is established, they disappear from his, and from the reader's notice.

The use, in the earlier sections, of traditional and dramatic narrative presentation techniques, and their deliberate avoidance in later episodes, corresponds with the general decline in Marcel's spontaneous reaction to the mysteries of existence. As this decline is brought about, however, a new interst begins to emerge not dependent on 'dramatic' presentation: an interest in psychological observation and analysis which, in the discoveries about art in *Temps Retrouvé,* will be given its due importance in the 'ingredients' of the projected work. As the narrator, step by step, rejects his subjective idealism in his progress toward middle-age, he discovers a new field of interest in the observation of himself and his friends. Thus the increasing rarity of conventionally-prepared dramatic scenes has its part to play in the overall structure of *A la Recherche.* Proust is able, by relating dramatic narrative presentation to the plot of his novel, to combine his undoubted mastery over traditional techniques with his insistence on non-fictional observation and commentary, in the form of self-analysis. One further example will illustrate the close relationship which Proust thus establishes between narrative presentation and structure.

All the 'classic' means of creating tension had been used to describe Marcel's mysterious contact with the "trois arbres d'Hudimesnil". This passage [232] with its deliberate references to the Combray reading episode [233] is one of the most dramatic in *A la Recherche,* and the familiar scheme of preparation, climax and anti-climax, often to be found at the root of the 'prepared' scenes in the novel, is strikingly apparent. Such is far from being the case, however, when the disillusioned narrator returns to Paris, and by chance catches sight of a similar line of trees. This time there is no dramatic presentation, no preparation and build-up, and inevitably, no climax. The description of the trees is not coloured by any emotional excitement, but is factual and cold. There is no attempt to 'mount' this scene of spiritual barenness; at no point is Marcel's disappointment dramatised in order to emphasise his indifference to natural beauty. Here, one might have thought, was a perfect opportunity for Proust to make use of his favorite device, anticlimax, but the references to the trees are casual, not 'arranged' to demonstrate Marcel's impotence, and the whole incident is recounted briefly, almost as an anecdote:

C'était, je me le rappelle, à un arrêt du train... [234]

---

[232] *ARTP,* I, pp. 717-719.
[233] *ARTP,* III, p. 855.
[234] *Ibid.*

The tension created in the earlier scene by a rapid succession of unanswered questions [235] is absent. There is no sustained emotional progression, there is no beginning, no end. There is no drama.

Within a conventionally dramatic narrative framework, then, building up towards a significant climax as it draws to a close, Proust inserts a number of individual dramatic scenes which highlight the spiritual decline of the hero by their increasing rarity, until, in the mood of final depression, drama no longer has a place in the novel.

DRAMA AND THE LESSON OF LE TEMPS RETROUVÉ

Proust's tendency to present the narrative without the aid of the traditional novelist's technique takes its place in the conception and aesthetic of *A la Recherche* too. The author uses his undramatic methods of telling often dramatic parts of his story to underline the ideas behind the 'demonstration' the whole work constitutes. When, in the course of *La Recherche,* we come across a scene where a long-awaited event, instead of being endorsed and underlined, is only casually referred to while its consequences are minutely-examined, there is always a reason. When Marcel, obliged to stay indoors because of the harmful effect on his health of the Champs Elysées, hopes vainly for a letter from Gilberte, with whom all future contact seems impossible, the actual arrival of that letter constitutes an important element of surprise and may be considered as a climax to the hours of waiting described so minutely. Yet Marcel's reaction on receiving his letter in no way contributes to this conception of climax. The possibility of its arrival, explains the narrator, had not been forseen by his imagination, with the result that the author's presentation of the situation reflects and translates the lack of emotional drama it produces in Marcel's imagination. Instead of dramatically highlighting the scene— as Balzac would conceivably have done—it is presented in an off-hand manner. At the foot of the page, Marcel notices Gilberte's signature, yet the narrative tone is cold and unemotional:

> ... ce fut justement la signature de Gilberte que je vis. Mais parce que je la savais impossible dans une lettre adressée à moi, cette vue, non accompanée de croyance, ne me causa pas de joie [236].

His first reaction to the event is contained in the long series of reflexions which, outside the context of *A la Recherche,* might be those of a handwriting expert or a museum curator commenting on a famous auto-graph:

> Or, au bas du papier, timbré d'un sceau d'argent représentant un chevalier casqué sous lequel contournait cette devise: "Per viam rectam", au-dessous d'une lettre, d'une grande écriture, et où presque toutes les

---

[235] *ARTP,* III, pp. 718-719.
[236] *ARTP,* I, p. 500.

phrases semblaient soulignées, simplement parce que la barre des 't' étant tracée non au travers d'eux, mais au-dessus, mettait un trait sous le mot correspondant de la ligne supérieure, ... [237]

Proust shapes the narrative so that it exactly recreates Marcel's first impressions. The arrival of the letter is not accentuated because it has no importance. But gradually Marcel's certainty that a letter from Gilberte is, in any case, impossible, is replaced by an awareness of the reality of the situation. The intelligence grasps more quickly than the emotions the fact that Gilberte has written to him, and the transcription of the letter, by the intelligence, the unemotional observation of her signature and curious handwriting, marks this stage. Only finally, when Marcel at last realises all the implications of the situation does the presentation of the scene alter. The anonymous 'feuille de papier couverte de caractères' disappears, and Marcel gives himself up, in possession now of a *letter from Gilberte,* to the delighted contemplation of his life 'semée de ces miracles que peuvent toujours espérer les personnes qui aiment' [238].

The narrative presentation is made to translate Proust's conception of experience as an intangible essence which disintegrates in the eroding atmosphere of Time, and it is the intangibility of the 'reality' of Gilberte's letter with which we are first presented. The gradual realisation of his happiness is summed up in this way:

> Le bonheur, le bonheur par Gilberte, c'était une chose à laquelle j'avais constamment songé, une chose toute en pensées, c'était comme disait Léonard de la peinture, "cosa mentale". Une feuille de papier couverte de caractères la pensée ne s'assimile pas cela tout de suite. Mais dès que j'eus terminé la lettre, je pensai à elle, elle devint un objet de rêverie, elle devint, elle aussi, "cosa mentale" et je l'aimais déjà tant que toutes les cinq minutes il me la fallait relire, l'embrasser. Alors je connus mon bonheur. [239]

The action loses its importance and the effect of the narrative presentation is to show how experience has always to be converted into its emotional equivalent before we realise the happiness it can bring.

Thus the unemotional and essentially undramatic presentation of many situations in the course of *A la Recherche* is carefully premeditated. The supreme example, perhaps, of this 'technique' is the recounting of Albertine's death, where the conversion of an event, presented at first as almost insignificant, into "cosa mentale" occupies most of *La Fugitive.* Not only does the dramatic structure of *A la Recherche* necessitate a series of dramatic scenes, but their scrupulous positioning within the structure, and their gradual replacement by non-dramatic scenes, such as Gilberte's letter arriving at Marcel's

---

[237] *ARTP,* I, pp. 499-500.
[238] *ARTP,* I, p. 500.
[239] *ARTP,* I, ibid.

bedside, or Mme Bontemps' telegram, announcing Albertine's death, translates the essential conception of experience which *A la Recherche* is designed to demonstrate.

THE EFFECT UPON THE NOVEL

What is the effect upon the work, as a whole, of the gradual replacement of dramatic scenes by situations demonstrating the idea of 'cosa mentale'? *A la Recherche* is constructed as a novel, and is supported by techniques proper to that medium. The need to provide, as we have seen, plot, situations and characters is essential to the shape of the work. Writing to René Blum in 1913, Proust referred to his own conception of *A la Recherche* "as a work deviating least from the novel form".[240] Yet, insofar as it does deviate from the traditional conception of the novel, the structure supporting the whole remains fundamentally traditional, and the combination of elements not proper to the conventional novel with the traditional novelist's aims and techniques often has a strange effect upon the work which results.

First, the structure is weakened by the tendency to by-pass events for an examination of their significance, since these events are meant to contribute to the story of Marcel's vocation. Similarly the hero's passivity and insignificance help to undermine the 'plot' designed to demonstrate the theories of *A la Recherche*. Action, demanded by the structure and plot, is included as part of the novel's basic elements, yet belittled as being less important than the 'radiographie au moins sommaire de la réalité insoupçonnable' which must accompany it[241]. The use of the fictional form as a demonstration of ideas which implicitly contradict in part much of conventional fiction's stock-in-trade is the paradox constituted by *A la Recherche*[242].

Second, the 'évolution d'une pensée' is not always perfectly served by the traditional framework designed to contain it. Proust tends, as the novel grows in length, to consider the emotions he wishes to describe in preference to the fictional story in which he has set out to insert them. He states quite plainly at the beginnnig of the second part of *A l'Ombre des jeunes filles en fleurs* that the principle of artistic creation is primarily one of abstraction, a process demanding an effect of 'nudité', resulting from the 'dépouillement de toutes particularités' of the basic emotion or idea[243]. An impression of immobility is the inevitable consequence: the deliberate casting aside of 'décor' essential to the traditional framework of the work, prevents the reader from establishing in his mind the essential reference points he expects

---

[240] Proust to René Blum, February 24th, 1913.
[241] *ARTP*, I, p. 588.
[242] There are many reasons, this one being among the most potent, for seeing Proust as a forerunner of the 'nouveau roman' movement.
[243] *ARTP*, I, p. 645.

to find, and which he needs to help him plot the hero's career, and sometimes Proust finds himself forced to insert short passages of explanation, in order to balance the hero's physical evolution with his intellectual and spiritual 'advance' [244].

The same impression of immobility results from the independent, organic development of 'moraliste' observations, which sometimes run counter to the traditional framework given to the work. The fact that many of Proust's observations interrupt the basic line of thought to such an extent that it only becomes comprehensible if they are removed from the body of the text and included as foot-notes, is proof of their incompatibility with the fictional structure. An example of such a development rooted, in the beginning, in a fictional situation dependent on the plot and moving away from it by means of a generalisation towards a conclusion far removed from the original starting-point, is furnished by a passage, reduced by the editors to a foot-note, in *Temps Retrouvé* [245]. The three stages it contains are very clear:

(i) the continuation of the fictional basis of *A la Recherche* in the recounting of an episode concerned with Saint-Loup, giving rise to additional comment on M. Nissim Bernard.

(ii) a generalisation, arising directly from the preceding indident:

Ainsi par compensation, tandis que des jeunes gens vertueux s'abandonnent, l'âge venu, aux passions dont ils ont enfin pris conscience, des adolescents faciles deviennent des hommes à principes contre lesquels des Charlus... se heurtent désagréablement.

(iii) a final conclusion, having little bearing at first sight on the fictional point of departure, to which it can only be attached through the middle, intermediary stage: Tout est affaire de chronologie.

This marginal note which Proust added to the original manuscript shows clearly the organic and episodic nature of many of his demonstrations, and the changes they represent in leading too far away from the starting point. Its presence, with others, in the last sections of the novel proves that such developments, worked into the text more successfully in earlier parts of *A la Recherche* than in *Jean Santeuil,* are a permanent characteristic and appear in so obvious a form in the final stages of the work only because of the unfinished nature of the manuscript. The basic, fictional progression of the plot is suspended, action further reduced in importance, and a static, immobile effect produced.

The tendency for the novel to break up into fragmentary episodes, a tendency already apparent in *Jean Santeuil,* also reflects the curious application of a traditional plot and structure to demonstrations hardly suited to the framework they imply. It is in the form of a

---

[244] *ARTP,* I, p. 647.
[245] *ARTP,* III, p. 737.

digression, introduced into the middle of a description of Marcel's walks with Albertine and her friends, that Elstir's influence on Marcel is referred to. There is no attempt to relate the digression rigorously to the fictional hero's story ; his visit to the painter's studio is placed vaguely in the past:

> C'est qu'avec mes amies nous étions quelquefois allés voir Elstir [246]

and the scene this reflexion evokes merges into the general resurrection of an idyllic past [247]. Similarly, Proust inserts future as well as past scenes in order to demonstrate opinions or more rigorous laws. To prove that

> ... les souvenirs d'amour ne font pas exception aux lois générales de la mémoire, elles-mêmes régies par les lois plus générales de l'habitude [248].

the narrator, though he has not yet left Paris for Balbec, includes a scene which took place there clearly much later in time:

> Par exemple, pour anticiper sur mon séjour en Normandie... [249]

—manipulating the order of events arbitrarily from his later position in time, not to present his gradual development chronologically, but in the light of conclusions formulated afterwards. A few pages further on, Marcel, sitting in the train which finally takes him to Balbec, anticipates the new aspects of art appreciation he will learn there from Elstir, in order, this time, to illustrate his own theories on the presentation of reality according to 'l'ordre de nos perceptions' rather than the technique 'de les expliquer d'abord par leur cause' [250]. The overall effect obtained in all these examples of chronological transposition for reasons other than those directly connected with the traditional progression of the hero's career, is one of immobility, as the fictional story, always present in the background, is abandoned for other considerations not always coinciding with it. In *La Prisonnière, La Fugitive* and *Le Temps Retrouvé,* the author's primary concern with the narration of the background story begins increasingly to give way to his interest in pursuing intellectual and non-fictional developments. Again the narrative takes on an episodic quality: a simple event in the hero's life may call for long comment from the narrator, who strengthens the case for his general observations by creating new, parallel situations from which to draw universal implications. Marcel wakes one morning with the intention of working on his novel when his thoughts are led astray by the special quality of the weather [251]. Immediately the fictional scene constructed around Marcel is forgotten,

---

[246] *ARTP,* I, p. 897.
[247] *ARTP,* I, pp. 899-912.
[248] *ARTP,* I, p. 643.
[249] *ARTP,* I, p. 643.
[250] *ARTP,* I, p. 653.
[251] *ARTP,* III, pp. 82-83.

and though the narrator first refers to his own 'paresse', the generalising tone of the passage soon converts the fictional hero into a kind of subsidiary illustration for a general observation of humanity:

> ... une de ces journées remplies de tant de changements de temps, d'incidents aériens, d'orages, que *le paresseux* ne croit pas les avoir perdues parce qu'il s'est intéressé à l'activité qu'à défaut de lui l'atmosphère... a déployée; [252]

Soon a whole new scene is introduced, centred around, not Marcel, but another example of 'le paresseux'—'l'écolier délaissant sa classe' [253], which in turn gives way to another describing a duel in early morning. None of these scenes is illustrative of Marcel's state of mind within the fictional context of *A la Recherche,* but each one develops a particular situation which the hero happens to have illustrated in the course of the narrative. The inclusion of extended developments of this kind, which leave the fictional story of the hero far behind, contributes to the break-up of the narrative into a series of episodic and fragmentary sections. Charlus is not only the symbol of a general kind of human behaviour, demanding the coining of new words [254], as Marcel himself is 'le paresseux', but also provides an excuse for Proust to include illustrations drawn from Virgil and Theocritus [255], while the conclusions he eventually draws are a long way from the initial fictional situation, and instead of the Baron de Charlus, it is with a lament for the psychiatrist that the long development occasioned by the Baron comes to an end! [256].

The fictional basis of *A la Recherche,* then, is often disregarded, wholesale developments of accessory ideas and observations conceal it entirely from time to time. Proust is fully aware of the problem of reconciling form and content, and takes care to re-assert the fictional element when it seems in danger of being submerged by commentary and accessory illustration. Remarks such as:

> Mais il est temps de rattraper le baron... [257]

and

> Pour en revenir à M. de Charlus ... [258]

indicate Proust's desire to re-assert the novel's fictional basis. The devices he uses to do so, however, are often insufficient. Only by careful investigation does it become apparent that Mme Verdurin's

---

[252] *ARTP,* III, p. 82. My italics.
[253] *ARTP,* III, ibid.
[254] "les Charlus", III, pp. 212, 217 ; le Charlisme, III, p. 2444 etc.
[255] *ARTP,* III, pp. 206-7.
[256] *ARTP,* III, p. 207.
[257] *ARTP,* III, p. 216.
[258] *ARTP,* III, p. 237.

remark on page 244 of *La Prisonnière* refers directly to another made thirteen pages earlier [259], and Professor Guichard, indicating several other examples of what he calls "la difficulté que l'on éprouve à suivre le fil de l'histoire", estimates that in one instance 2,500 pages separate one allusion from its logical antecedent [260]. The restating of the fictional situation becomes more common as Proust places more emphasis on the 'moralist' element in the later chapters, and the neglected fictional structure demands constant shoring-up. The long passage which the later narrator adds to give all the possible reasons why Mme Verdurin should precipitate Charlus' downfall [261] necessarily entails the eclipse of the actual situation the explanation is designed to serve, and Proust returns three times to the basic situation—thus rendered completely immobile as each re-statement shows that it has not advanced in the slightest—in order to keep it present in the background:

(i) 'Cependant Mme Verdurin était en grande conférence avec Cottard... (III, 228)

(ii) 'Mme Verdurin attendait donc les invités du baron avec une certaine émotion. (III, 238).

(iii) 'En attendant, Mme Verdurin se consultait avec les fidèles... (III, 238).

Proust's choice of an overall structure, therefore, while serving to combine practically all his purposes, nevertheless cannot provide a completely satisfactory framework for all his aims. The fictional element suffers to some extent, but so resiliant is the main construction that it can accommodate material which, strictly speaking, does not always fit perfectly. But if he discovers that the flexibility of this construction can be used to cover up accessory developments without harming the basic conception of the work, Proust also takes advantage of its resilience to include elements which he does not take the trouble to 'convert' into any kind of spiritual reality. The autobiographical references in later sections of *A la Recherche* abound, and their inclusion is not altogether happy.

Towards the end of *Sodome et Gomorrhe* a new narrative tone appears which is none other than the voice of the invalid Proust, no longer delegating opinions to fictional characters or integrating them into fictional scenes and situations. It is a different voice from that of the later Marcel, implementing his decision after the 'revelation' to include general observation in his projected novel. On the contrary, it is an intensly, personal voice, audible from time to time, whose rasping tones come often as a shock to the reader, used to the calmer and more rational attitude of Marcel. It is true that some of this same irratibility is translated into fictional terms and the hero fulminates against the lift-boy's speech [262] and certain mannerisms be-

---

[259] "Je trouve que ce serait de notre devoir de l'éclairer," finds its antecedent on p. 230: "Mme Verdurin était furieuse et décidée à 'éclairer' Morel".
[260] Léon Guichard: *Introduction à Proust*, pp. 25-28. Prof. Guichard's references are to the NRF 15-volume edition.
[261] *ARTP*, III, pp. 228-238.
[262] *ARTP*, II, p. 491.

longing to the Cambremer's lawyer friend [263]. But more often it is the author himself who interrupts the narrative to record a private grievance—often about medicine and doctors [264], often about the noise he complains of elsewhere in his correspondence so bitterly:

> J'entendais quelqu'un jouer avec moelleux des morceaux de Schumann. Certes il arrive que les gens, mêmes ceux que nous aimons le mieux, se saturent de la tristesse ou de l'agacement qui émane de nous. Il y a pourtant quelque chose qui est capable d'un pouvoir d'exaspérer où n'atteindra jamais une personne: c'est un piano [265].

Sometimes it becomes confused with the narrator's general 'laws' of behaviour, with the result that what is intended to underline a universal pattern of behaviour sometimes has the reverse effect. One of Proust's explanations of the origin of love, described by means of a comparison with a particular medicine, whose properties are wrongly interpreted by an invalid, is of this kind. It may contain some truth in a limited field of experience, but its validity as an indication of universal human behaviour is questionable [266].

At the same time as the introduction of a hypochondriac note into the novel, comes the inclusion of personal memories in such a way that they never lose all their autobiographical flavour. A case in point is the portrait of the two sisters, Marie Gineste and Céleste Albaret, whose inclusion breaks not only a carefully-prepared emotional climate, but also a logical thought-progression [267].

The structure of *A la Recherche* with its heavy reliance on traditional techniques, the function it creates within the work for individual "supporting" scenes and the freedom it gives Proust to modify and vary dramatic and non-dramatic presentation of events according to both the fictional, emotional climate and new conception of experience and the way it should be presented—all combine to create a wholly new kind of novel. For novel *A la Recherche* remains, through its traditional framework. It is a kind of novel which creates its own rules, and which accommodates elements normally excluded from the traditional recounting of events in chronological order, and which combines them more satisfactorily than cruder attempts—by Marivaux, for example—to merge two 'genres' into one. *A la Recherche* manages to combine the 17C. French 'moralists' genre into the framework of a traditional 19C. novel. The degree of succes is, and always has been, debatable. The characteristic feature of the work is that it tends to generate a stifling quality of immobility, not only due to the circumstances in which most of it was written, but traceable to the interaction of two quite different sets of aims and techniques.

---

263 *ARTP*, II, p. 806.
264 *ARTP*, II, p. 796.
265 *ARTP*, II, p. 789.
266 *ARTP*, II, p. 798.
267 *ARTP*, II, pp. 846-850.

PART THREE

———————

THE RE-CREATION AND TRANSCRIPTION
OF INDIVIDUAL EXPERIENCE IN
A LA RECHERCHE DU TEMPS PERDU

CHAPTER ONE

A la Recherche, the new conception of the novel, demanded new techniques. In order to combine a variety of different elements—portrait-painting and minute analysis of character, for example, psychological investigation and the examination of forgotten states of feeling—new methods had to be evolved to embrace an enquiry, carried on on several different levels, into all the aspects of experience which Proust wanted to incarnate in his book. We have seen how the plan and structure themselves create new techniques, like that of the alternating narrative viewpoint, which reflect the author's fundamental attitude to certain of these aspects. But the peculiar advantages of Proust's narrative plan, with his commenting narrator, serve his intellectual enquiries—self examination, examination of social attitudes—better than the recreation of deeply-felt emotional states which forms the basis of his quest for lost time, emotional, 'sentimental' enquiries. It is with the perfection of trends, whose presence throughout all the earlier works we have noticed, and their adaptation to the overall pattern of A la Recherche, that the other major aspect of Proust's 'sum' of experience is included.

A-CHRONOLOGICAL PATTERNS

In most of his writing before A la Recherche, Proust shows a concern with chronology which remains a marked characteristic of the final work. The overall plan, as we have seen, concerns the recounting by an unidentified narrator of his past life up to the moment of narration. The emphasis is placed on his emotional and spiritual development, by the strategic positioning of the several involuntary memory episodes, whose importance at the beginning and end of the work, (the 'madeleine' incident imperfectly understood in Du côté de chez Swann preparing and giving way to the completely assimilated experiences in Le Temps Retrouvé), overrides that of the purely chronological development of the boy Marcel. In order to underline the gap which often separates these two sides of the narrator's past life, Proust deliberately manipulates the ordering of the events, substituting a new order for the more straightforward chronological pattern closely associated with the 'traditional' novel.

The recreation of a series of different worlds involves Proust in the successive evocation of a number of different emotional climates. In contributing to the background each demands, Proust has no hesitation in introducing episodes which, chronologically, follow no particular order, but which contribute to a special atmosphere or series of memories, of which they form an essential part. Part of the 'real' Balbec for the narrator is the memory of the fatal evening when he first arrived there, and all his later attempts to accustom himself to the strange new world in which he found himself. Thus, in order to indicate this gradual adaptation to the atmosphere of the Grand Hotel, Proust gathers together to form a single block the various scenes connected with Marcel's arrival, and later, repeated scenes, emotionally rather than chronologically attached to them. The result is that two episodes, separated in time but connected through their emotional significance for the narrator, fuse to form a single homogeneous memory. The recounting of Marcel's anguish on his first evening[1] immediately evokes later scenes where his grandmother provides a steadying, calming influence:

> Et, en effet, ce soir-là, je frappai trois coups — que, une semaine plus tard, quand je fus souffrant, je renouvelai pendant quelques jours tous les matins ... [2]

These scenes are developed almost independently, all the sensations they recall being minutely described, even though they are not rationally connected with the theme of anxiety which binds them to Marcel's arrival: the sudden recollection of effects of sunlight comes flooding back, helping to re-create the real world of Balbec:

> à l'annexe en saillie de l'hôtel, le soleil était installé sur les toits comme un couvreur matinal qui commence tôt son ouvrage et l'accomplit en silence pour ne pas réveiller la ville qui dort encore... [3]

Then the anguish of the first evening returns, and the emotional link connecting all the different memories reappears:

> Mais cette première nuit d'arrivée, quand ma grand-mère m'eut quitté, je recommençai à souffrir, comme j'avais déjà souffert à Paris au moment de quitter la maison. [4]

Thus traditional chronological progression is sacrificed for emotional unity, the importance of which is stressed to the detriment of Marcel's physical development. Blocks of memories, composite fragments of the past which have crystalised in time to form a complete whole, are presented in all the apparent confusion of their significance to the narrator, but linked by a real emotional undercurrent.

---

[1] *ARTP*, I, p. 668.
[2] *ARTP*, I, pp. 668-669.
[3] *ARTP*, I, p. 669.
[4] *ARTP*, I, p. 670. My italics.

Sometimes chronological presentation is interrupted for different reasons; in order to obtain a descriptive effect, depending mainly on the evocation of changes of season and the modifications of light they bring, Proust breaks off from the recounting of Marcel's efforts to meet Albertine, whom he knows only as 'la petite Simonet', to review the various changes of light on the scenery around Balbec, not simply at that time, but at a series of different moments in his entire stay there. Instead of including the series of modifications it undergoes throughout his stay as they occur chronologically, spaced out at appropriate intervals. Proust brings them all together, to obtain an effect of poetry mainly achieved by the juxtaposition of descriptions normally separated in time:

> J'entrai dans ma chambre. Au fur et à mesure que la saison s'avança, changea le tableau que j'y trouvais dans la fenêtre. D'abord, il faisait grand jour... [5]

The description of the sea which follows, with its 'triangles empennés d'une immobile écume' [6] soon gives way to a later evocation, with a different 'lighting effect', and a different impression:

> ... la mer déjà froide et bleue comme le poisson appelé mulet... [7]

A review of all the different views, associated with the sea 'sertie entre les montants de fer de ma croisée' [8] and the hotel bedroom finally ends when the season was so far advanced that light and view had disappeared altogether [9]. Here too narrative patterns are being elaborated simultaneously. Inserted into the straightforward recounting of Marcel's liaison with Albertine is an a-chronological description of scenes which embrace much of the period covered by the first pattern: Marcel is still waiting for a list of new arrivals to the hotel, which will, he hopes, advance his projects of making Albertine's acquaintance, yet the description inserted at this point include moments at which Marcel and she were fast friends. The sudden return to the original point in the narrator's 'listes d'étrangers' comes as a surprise. Proust's narrative plan obliges him to strike a balance between the recounting of Marcel's physical life and the development of his artistic and spiritual appreciation of experience. In this instance each aim is well represented; only the slight shock as the train of thought veers in a new direction indicates the two quite different narrative patterns being employed.

These two examples serve to illustrate the unconventionality of the narrative presentation of *A la Recherche*. The conception of individual thought and memory processes dictating the ordering of the narrative

---

[5] *ARTP*, I, p. 802.
[6] *ARTP*, I, p. 803.
[7] *ARTP*, I, p. 803.
[8] *ARTP*, I, ibid.
[9] *ARTP*, I, p. 806.

arises directly from the meditation on art and literature in *Temps Retrouvé* and we shall refer to its application to Proust's novel as a whole in the following chapters. Meanwhile we can see how far a disregard for conventional chronology serves Proust's purpose, both in creating the series of 'worlds' which the plot of *A la Recherche* demands, and in giving him the opportunity to create effects of poetry within the framework of the plot.

ANALOGY

Another feature of *A la Recherche* is the presence of significant analogies which announce and sum up important changes in the narrator's life. Just before la Berma's appearance in one act from *Phèdre* at the Opéra, Marcel tries vainly to remember a line from the play, but cannot succeed in making the words he thinks make up the particular quotation form the pattern demanded by the metre. Suddenly the complete line appears, and the narrator's relief is described in terms which seem exaggerated for so inconsequential an incident:

> Mais tout à coup je me le rappelai, *les irréductibles aspérités d'un monde inhumain s'anéantirent magiquement*; les syllabes du vers remplirent aussitôt la mesure d'un alexandrin, ce qu'il avait de trop se dégagea avec autant d'aisance et de souplesse qu'une bulle d'air qui vient crever à la surface de l'eau [10].

In the passages which follow, however, Marcel's discovery that la Berma is a great actress has an identical effect of creating order and harmony in a certain aspect of his understanding of art and reality. The perception of a 'rayon central et prisonnier' colouring all the accessories of the actress' art is the exact analogy of the remembering of the one metrical foot which was necessary to transform the chaos of a half-forgotten line into something of great beauty. In this way, an apparently unconnected passage prepares for another which is to follow it.

In *Sodome et Gomorrhe* another analogical passage occurs. Marcel goes to observe Mme de Guermantes' special plant, which can be fertilised only by a particular kind of insect:

> ... (je) regardais par les volets de l'escalier le petit arbuste de la duchesse et la plante précieuse exposés dans la cour avec cette insistance qu'on met à faire sortir les jeunes gens à marier, et je me demandais si l'insecte improbable viendrait, par un hasard providentiel, visiter le pistil ouvert et délaissé [11].

Immediately follows the encounter between Charlus and Jupien, an example of a 'providential' meeting of two like specimens. This time

---

[10] *ARTP*, II, p. 38.
[11] *ARTP*, II, pp. 601-602.

the analogy is not left understood, as in the example of the line in *Phèdre*, but is explicitly stated. M. de Charlus becomes a 'bourdon' [12] and the laws Marcel has learned about botanical and vegetable fertilisation are applied to him: the 'behaviour' of the plant is transferred to Jupien [13], the activity of the insect to M. de Charlus [14]. Finally, just as the 'conjonction' of Jupien and the Baron really takes place, so a real 'bourdon' arrives to fertilise the Duchess' plant, thus making the analogy complete [15].

Less obvious, though again in part explained by the narrator, is the symbolic appearance of the aeroplane in a later passage of *Sodome et Gomorrhe*; this time an event occurs which brings home to the reader many of the implications of a situation which is never so explicitly stated. Marcel feels unconsciously that were he able to rid himself of the habit-forming presence of Albertine, he might at last begin to work seriously, and this feeling is indicated to the reader by the sudden appearance of an aeroplane in the sky above Marcel's head. Marcel, in his imagination has replaced the real countryside around him with the imaginative countryside he remembers from one of Elstir's paintings [16], and half expects to meet some fabulous, mythological creature when, instead of this happening, the aeroplane appears, bringing a sudden and inexplicable rush of emotion to him. Identifying himself with the glorious freedom which the airman enjoys, and which he feels he could attain without Albertine, he watches spellbound:

> Cependant l'aviateur sembla hésiter sur sa voie; je sentais ouvertes devant lui, — devant moi, si l'habitude ne m'avait pas fait prisonnier — toutes les routes de l'espace, de la vie; [17]

At the same time as explaining the hero's situation, it prefigures—as in the two earlier examples—what is to follow: by painfully freeing himself from Albertine's presence, even after she is dead, his vocation eventually asserts itself and leads him in *Temps Retrouvé*, as the aeroplane led its pilot, 'droit vers le ciel' [18].

The most striking of all such analogies is the extended analogy constituted by the section entitled *Les intermittences du cœur*. Describing how suffering does not always accompany the incident which creates it, Marcel recalls how he only really felt the loss of his grandmother after she had died, and then in a particular circumstance. Finally this pain gives way to intermittent pangs of regret and then complete oblivion. Immediately afterwards begins the final stage of the Albertine story, the cementing together of two people

---

[12] *ARTP*, II, p. 606.
[13] *ARTP*, II, pp. 602 and 604.
[14] *ARTP*, II, p. 604.
[15] *ARTP*, II, p. 606.
[16] *ARTP*, II, p. 1029.
[17] *ARTP*, II, ibid.
[18] *ARTP*, II, ibid.

whose separation is later to be so painful. As the grandmother fades into the background, Albertine's image is brought into focus, and the deliberate juxtaposition of the two episodes is intended to have the same effect as the line from Phèdre, the 'bourdon' analogy, and the aeroplane; it is a sign:

> Seulement je ne trouvais plus chez ma grand'mère la riche spontanéité d'autrefois [19]. Ses paroles n'étaient qu'une réponse affaiblie, docile, presque un simple écho de mes paroles; elle n'était plus que le reflet de ma propre pensée.
>
> Incapable comme je l'étais encore d'éprouver à nouveau un désir physique, Albertine recommençait cependant à m'inspirer comme un désir de bonheur... [20]

The implication is that the same pattern of events, heralded in *Les intermittences du cœur,* will repeat itself in the Albertine story, and *La Prisonnière* and *La Fugitive* clearly bring out this implication.

THE "TWO WAYS"

The presence of analogical examples and the new grouping of events into homogenous 'blocks' combine in the almost independent structure of the episodes grouped around the sleeping narrator evoked right at the beginning of *Du côté de chez Swann.* In the evocation of the *Deux côtés,* the two walks which Marcel came to associate with whole aspects of experience which he discovered there for the first time, the whole pattern of much of his later career is laid down and subtly pointed out by the later narrator to the perspicacious reader. This pattern is compactly fitted into the references to the memories which would come flooding back to him, at one point in his life, by the now confident and happy Marcel, who has understood the message of *Le Temps Retrouvé.* By examining the part played in the construction of *A la Recherche* by the *Two ways,* we shall be able to see how the two new important trends which we have briefly indicated come to form an integral part of the very fibre of the finished work.

The 'two ways' contribute not only to the creation of a 'vase clos', an atmosphere, a world, which the later Marcel of *Temps Retrouvé* will try to rediscover, but they also illustrate the associations set out in the second evocation of Combray, and show the entire range of Marcel's future quest, indicating as they do so some of the reasons why he will take so long to reach his goal.

The first of the two walks, Swann's way, as it is known to the world of Combray, is divided into three main parts—Tansonville, Roussainville and Montjouvain—and each marks a stage of his childhood memories [21]. If we follow his progress along the two ways, we

---

[19] i.e. in his imagination.
[20] *ARTP,* II, p. 782.
[21] *ARTP,* I, p. 84.

see that this central belief in the value of art becomes associated in his youthful imagination with love, and in the boy's mind there begins to grow a confusion between spiritual and non-spiritual values; the thought of Gilberte associates itself with the contemplation of natural beauty:

> Et déjà le charme dont son nom avait encensé cette place sous les épines roses où il avait été entendu ensemble par elle et par moi, allait gagner, enduire, embaumer tout ce qui l'approchait [22].

An initial set-back immediately gives rise to the rhythm of all the subsequent love-cycles: love, jealousy and hatred:

> ... mon cœur humilié voulait se mettre de niveau avec Gilberte ou l'abaisser jusqu'à lui. Je l'aimais, je regrettais de ne pas avoir eu le temps et l'inspiration de l'offenser, de lui faire mal, et de la forcer à se souvenir de moi [23].

The strange identification of Gilbert's name with 'des jasmins et des giroflées' establishes itself firmly as a result, and the whole Tansonville passage ends with the complete statement of the fusion of love and art. The hawthorns, so closely connected with Gilberte's image almost *become* Gilbert, and the narrator's emotions, resulting from the ecstasy of their contemplation and that of Gilberte Swann, fuse to form a single sentiment:

> ... ma mère me trouva en larmes... en train de dire adieu aux aubépines, entourant de mes bras les branches piquantes... "O mes pauvres petites aubépines, disais-je en pleurant, ce n'est pas vous qui voudriez me faire du chagrin, me forcer à partir. Vous, vous ne m'avez jamais fait de peine! Aussi je vous aimerai toujours" [24].

Roussainville pushes the association still further: the belief in the absolute beauty and mystery of the countryside around this small village and the adolescent boy's stirring physical desires complement each other, until Marcel comes to think of the latter as holding the key to the world of spiritual values. Art and natural beauty spontaneously give birth to a belief in correspondingly implicit values in love:

> la passante qu'appelait mon désir me semblait être non un exemplaire quelconque de ce type général: la femme, mais un **produit nécessaire et** naturel de ce sol [25],

and so complete is their identification that the possession of the one without the other is always disappointing:

> Mais errer ainsi dans les bois de Roussainville sans une paysanne à embrasser, c'était ne pas connaître de ces bois le trésor caché, *la beauté profonde* [26].

---

[22] *ARTP*, I, pp. 142-143.
[23] *ARTP*, I, p. 142.
[24] *ARTP*, I, p. 145.
[25] *ARTP*, I, pp. 156-157.
[26] *ARTP*, I, p. 157.

This inevitable disappointment leads to a rejection both of love and its desires—"les créations purement subjectives, impuissantes, illusoires, de mon tempérament [27]—and of nature and beauty too:

> ... la réalité qui dès lors perdait tout charme et toute signification et n'était plus à ma vie qu'un cadre conventionnel... [28]

Montjouvain adds no more than a 'sadistic' element to the idea of love which is firmly associated in Marcel's mind with spiritual values.

Thus *Swann's Way* is a symbolic preparation for the narrator's later quest: all the mistakes he will make before his discovery of Time Lost are here indicated: the association of love and art which will become the Gilberte and Albertine love cycles; the rejection of art and beauty, which will become the long period of depression before *Temps Retrouvé*; the introduction to the world of Montjouvain, which will become *Sodome et Gomorrhe*. Similarly *Le côté de Guermantes* completes the symbolic prelude to *A la Recherche*. The intermittent theme of Marcel's vocation is introduced for the first time, and the way in which the child responds to it again indicates the whole pattern of his later life. Just as in *Du côté de chez Swann,* love seems to hold the key to 'truth', so the *Côté de Guermantes* seems to contain the essence of literary creation and the essence of nature, upon which the prestige of literature has played its dazzling colours. The powerful attraction of the Guermantes family itself comes to symbolise Marcel's growing literary ambition:

> Je rêvais que Mme de Guermantes m'y faisait venir, éprise pour moi d'un soudain caprice; tout le jour elle y pêchait la truite avec moi... Elle me faisait lui dire le sujet des poèmes que j'avais l'intention de composer [29].

This arbitrary fusion of two distinct ambitions, social and artistic, leads, inevitably to disappointment; the impossibility of finding the key to aesthetic creation through the duchesse de Guermantes, whom he does not know, and the inability of the deam-world, he has created to contain her, to furnish ready-made literary and philosophical subjects lead him to renounce the values of literature in general. They have no more meaning than the countryside which becomes a 'sol stérile, terre épuisée' [30] when the 'paysanne de Roussainville' fails to materialise from his dreams. The reality which he instinctively believes to exist disappears:

> ... ma vie actuelle... m'apparaissait au contraire. comme comprise dans une réalité qui n'était pas faite pour moi, contre laquelle je n'avais pas d'allié, qui ne cachait rien au-delà d'elle-même [31].

---

[27] *ARTP,* I, pp. 158-9.
[28] *ARTP,* I, p. 159.
[29] *ARTP,* I, p. 172.
[30] *ARTP,* I, p. 158.
[31] *ARTP,* I, p. 173.

Literature, deprived of its essential support, belief in the absolute value of art, loses all prestige:

> Aussi, découragé, je renonçais à jamais à la littérature, malgré les encouragements que m'avait donnés Bloch [32].

and the narrator accepts the 'néant de sa pensée' [33]. The spiritual span of the narrator's life then, is indicated: from the youthful enthusiasm of Combray, through the disappointments of love and society, the magic of names, the belief in the intrinsic value of far-off countries, to the weary disillusionment, when the mistakes bring about the ruin of his belief in art,—the whole progression of thought is included. Marcel mistakes Gilberte's attraction for the real attraction of nature: the love cycles of *A la Recherche* turn the narrator aside from his quest for an artistic vocation. Marcel pursues his instinct to create into the alien world of the Guermantes: the society episodes of *A la Recherche* drain the narrator's desire and faculty to write in an endless round of meaningless parties. The whole section is an allegorical preparation for the life which is about to be recounted, compactly fitted around the sleeping narrator, who recalls the two ways as being part of a past only visible from time to time, but which he evokes when he cannot sleep. This past forms a single emotional unity, just as the nights at Balbec, though separated in time, are fused together to form a compact block. Thus the tendency to create a-chronological sections as major parts of the narrative, and to give some of these sections a preparatory, allegorical function in the structure of the work continue to form the whole of the first episode of *Du côté de chez Swann* and lay down the subsequent course of development for the rest of the novel. Proust has constructed his novel upon a traditional 'plot', but has evolved original methods of putting the plot in action and ordering its various parts.

OLD TECHNIQUES IN NEW SETTINGS

A la Recherche sees the final evolution of methods of narrative presentation which have been used intermittently in earlier works, and whose presence in the final work we have already briefly indicated. The perfection of techniques designed to present experience in the light of the laws of memory and sense association, drawing upon all the experimental works, involves Proust in an amalgamation of a number of different tendencies, always present in his writing, geared now to the 'aesthetic' of *Le Temps Retrouvé*.

Let us briefly recall the results of Proust's attempts to write in fictional forms, and the conclusions these attempts lead him to adopt. As a writer, Proust only works comfortably with techniques which allow him to dispense with all the traditional trappings of narrative

---

[32] *ARTP*, I, pp. 173-4.
[33] *ARTP*, I, p. 174.

presentation . The careful building up of scenes, the minute preparation of fictional backgrounds to accompany them, the scrupulous choice of significant detail—all these appear in the course of *Jean Santeuil,* but are, in fact, rarely used. Throughout his first novel Proust shows himself impatient of such fundamental considerations, and concentrates as a result upon the emotions in the scenes, rather than upon the scenes themselves. The fictional 'platforms' intended to provide "jumping-off places" for the all-important description of sensations and impressions, are often mis-handled or slipshod, betraying the author's impatience with them, and, worse, his inability to create convincing fictional situations, by rapidly imagining a framework into which the particular effect he wanted to describe might be worked in. The new techniques must take this into account, and evolve methods which will concentrate legitimately upon the sensation or impression, and allow him to work back to the particular situation which gave rise to it. Sensation and emotion must somehow be made the kernel of the narrative, so that, having provided the most important element of the situation, Proust has only to sketch in rapidly the few indispensable external details too intimately linked with them not to have become intimately associated with the impression itself.

The new techniques must also take into account Proust's gift for the transcription of the spoken word. From the earliest stories in *Les Plaisirs et les Jours* dialogue appears, either as part of the construction of the passage, or simply as a means of reproducing individual traits and characteristics. By somehow working dialogue into the painting of the different "worlds" of Marcel's life, so that it leaves the description of impressions supreme but at the same time makes use of this valuable way of individualising characters and groups of characters, Proust can combine this one element of 'traditional' fiction—the spoken word transcribed into written dialogue— with others which (like the description of atmosphere) have no need of conventional 'mounting'.

Proust's journalistic essays had helped develop his individual method of jumping from one topic to another, often making wide use of anecdotes to do so. Often these had been used, moreover, as a means of recreating a past which has now disappeared, and the recounting of stories about the Princesse Mathilde for example, helps to bring alive the essence of a 'salon' which no longer functions. In a letter he wrote to Robert Dreyfus [34] Proust points out the limitations of the anecdotic novel:

> Mais la même raison qui me fait penser que l'importance de la réalité suprasensible de l'art empêche certains romans anecdotiques, si agréables qu'ils soient, de mériter tout à fait le rang où tu sembles les placer (l'art étant quelque chose de trop supérieur à la vie, telle que nous la jugeons par l'intelligence et la dépeignons dans la conversation, pour se contenter de la contrefaire), — cette même raison ne me permet pas

---

[34] *Correspondance générale,* t. 4, n° XXXVIII.

de faire dépendre la réalité d'un rêve d'art, de raisons elles aussi anec-
dotiques et trop tirées de la vie pour ne pas participer à sa contingence
et à son irréalité. (16th May, 1908).

Nevertheless, by using anecdotes in the same way as dialogue, subor-
dinating both to the central sensation or memory, but at the same time
preserving a method of composition, which clearly suits his individual
approach, Proust can re-cast a whole technique in the light of the new
aesthetic of *Temps Retrouvé,* so that it gives certain of his talents an
opportunity to display themselves, while preserving the artist's duty
of capturing the 'essence' of the past.

Thus Proust 'new' techniques will hardly be new at all: they will
be the amalgamation of a set of long-established tendencies, but set
in the new framework and perspective of the final work. They will
differ from traditional techniques, as Proust's writing has always tended
to veer away from traditional fictional devices; they will incorporate
elements which Proust has always found particularly to his liking, like
dialogue and anecdote, and the new function such elements will be
given alters his previous disapproval of them as inferior means of
achieving 'la réalité d'un rêve d'art' [35]. It is the re-thinking of the
whole process of literary composition, the review of past experiments,
and the light shed upon both by the confident realisation of his 'duty'
as an artist, that crystallise an already instinctive groping towards
certain kinds of narrative presentation, and produce the individual
quality of the author's presentation of 'l'histoire d'une vocation'.

If the elements of the 'new' techniques, waiting like pieces of a
jig-saw puzzle to fall into place, are composed of almost instinctive
ways of presenting narrative, what of the crystallising agent which will
take these fragmentary pieces and transform them into a coherent
whole? Having considered the 'ingredients' we must now examine the
'recipe' in which they are used, to preserve the culinary images used
by Proust himself in his description of Marcel's projected novel [36].
The conception of the artist's function is clearly set out in *Le Temps
Retrouvé.*

In the narrator's long consideration of the properties of literature,
one theme constantly recurs: Proust's scorn for writers who do not
evolve their own, personal theories and methods, authors who

> ... n'ont même pas eu la force d'esprit de se débarrasser de toutes les
> banalités de forme acquise par l'imitation [37]

while the other 'leit-motif' which reappears continually, during the
final pages of *Temps Retrouvé,* is his assertion that

> l'art recompose la vie... [38]

---

[35] *Ibid.*
[36] cf. "... ne ferais-je pas mon Livre de la façon que Françoise faisait ce
bœuf mode, apprécié par M. de Norpois..." *ARTP,* III, p. 1035.
[37] *ARTP,* III, p. 898.
[38] *ARTP,* III, ibid.

The work of art must be the individual reflection of the writer's conception of experience; the narrative which results must make the reader aware of this writer's personal interpretation of life. The artistic duty, then, is to evolve methods which will give the reader the impression that he is sharing not only one individual's conclusions about life in general, but that he is present at the formation of that conception of life. The author's most intimate reactions must somehow be made to reflect his particular viewpoint. If he remembers scenes and episodes from the past in some strange, and highly personal manner, this highly-personal order of memories must be translated into terms which the reader can understand. If Proust wishes to share with his reader the extraordinary sensations associated with unbidden memories of the past, he must find a way of transcribing both the memories—as they appeared to him—and the sensation which arose directly from them. An intellectual and rationalised account cannot perform this function: an abstract concept of the artist's experience would result, not the recreation within the reader of the same experience. Marcel's groping for the true image of the past must be so presented that the reader becomes Marcel, his experience the reader's experience. A method of "translation" is the key to this most intimate communication of author and reader:

> Il est la révélation, *qui serait impossible par des moyens directs et conscients*, de la différence qualitative qu'il y a dans la façon dont nous apparaît le monde, différence qui, s'il n'y avait pas l'art, resterait le secret éternel de chacun [39].

With all the ingredients at his disposal, with an all-embracing concept of the artist's duty as a guide, Proust completely combines his theories and his talents as a writer for the first time in *A la Recherche*. For the first time the latter are made to serve a coherent vision of the world, and to establish the artist's function within that world. A highly individual technique results, a technique based firmly upon Proust's conviction that

> ... l'art recompose la vie [40].

The basis of Proust's description of his narrator's first contact with a rediscovered past in *Du côté de chez Swann* is the establishment of a new order of preference; supreme importance is given to the essence of the individual impression; intellectual reconstructions which use straightforward chronological patterns, and rational reconstitutions which isolate the inherent emotions from the particular situation have no place in the translation of Marcel's experience. An order of preference, designed to recreate the author's original reactions and emotions, is carefully presented. One memory unfolds to reveal another; the passage from one association to another depends upon the author's

---

[39] *ARTP*, III, p. 895.
[40] *ARTP*, III, p. 898.

individual personality and experience, and the connection between memories, sensations and impressions is so arranged in the description of Marcel's first rediscovery of the past, that the individual personality and experience are inherent in the account of his discovery. His vision of the world directs its presentation.

Consider, for example, the chain of memories and sensations which follows the taste of the 'madeleine' dipped in tea. The gradual unfolding of a whole section of the past is directed by the narrator's search to identify the impression he so strongly feels. A glimpse into the private, intimate regions of this one individual's world results: guided by a sure instinct, he turns his attention to his past life. Suddenly he remembers a little town associated in his mind with the Easter holidays [41]; memories of certain streets come rushing back, as Marcel tries to place the memory conjured up by the 'madeleine', then the memory of one particular house presents itself, one room in the house, the immobile occupant of that room, one particular incident binding him to her, finally, at the very heart of all these successive layers of memory, he rediscovers the impression which the 'madeleine' had so tantalisingly suggested [42].

The identification of the central impression, buried deep under layers of memory which can only be penetrated by the tortuous following of associations and irrational thought-processes, illustrates the new order of preference . The brief memories of the town, the street, tante Léonie's room with its

> ... odeurs naturelles encore, certes, et couleur du temps comme celle de la campagne voisine, mais déjà casanières, humaines et renfermées, gelée exquise, industrieuse et limpide de tous les fruits de l'année qui ont quitté le verger pour l'armoire; [43]

—the penetrating of forgotten worlds of sensation and memory, which in their turn spontaneously evoke others, all pass rapidly through the narrator's mind, threaded together, as it were, on the string of the all-powerful impression which has evoked them all. In this way a whole world is conjured up, but in minute snatches of memory; tiny scenes are evoked which immediately give way to others; careful scene-setting, the detailed provision of contextual explanations, are super-fluous. Memory, sensation and impressions provide all the context necessary, and the result is the presentation of an individual world in an individual way.

This individual world is shown as it is remembered by the narrator, sensitive to the associations it had for him, aware of personal and private implications inherent within it. When he wishes the reader to know what the church in the same village represents for him, the narrator evokes a highly personal *impression* of this church, seen

---

[41] *ARTP*, I, p. 48.
[42] *ARTP*, I, p. 52.
[43] *ARTP*, I, p. 49.

through the perspective of his childhood, associated with often fortuitous memories, coloured by his personal contact with it. The first impressions are vague and general—the result of many visits to a familiar building: he recalls the porch, the slabs of stone marking the tombs of former dignitaries, the windows and their reflections, when suddenly a vivid memory presents itself: Mme Sazerat praying all alone in the church, with a little parcel of 'petits fours' placed on the chair next to her. Logically, Mme Sazerat has no business to be suddenly included in the narrator's description of the nave, yet so intimately is this memory connected with his general impressions, that the one cannot be recalled without the other [44]. Similarly, the narrator, describing at one point the total impression he used to have of the church, with its many different architectural styles, suddenly includes a visit he made to the crypt with Theodore and his sister [45], while the memory of the apse gives rise to an equally unexpected account of later experiences connected with seeing similar buildings [46].

The recreation of an individual conception of the past involves Proust in the evocation of a number of private memories which colour the events he recalls in a highly personal way. The narrative is alive and positively bristles with tiny, ever-changing scenes, built often upon dialogue; the spoken word is all-important, the necessary 'stage directions' implicit in the whole direction of the narrator's thoughts and the absence of 'conventional' preparation allow one scene to melt into another, just as one memory melts into another, taking no account of time and the ordinary spatial restrictions of more 'realist' works of art. Proust 'translates' these sudden flashes of memory by using one of the novelist's most vivid techniques: the direct transcription of dialogue and conversation. The rôle given to dialogue and also to anecdote, as many of the interrelated scenes are cast in anecdotic form, is clear. Each is an accessory means of recreating the 'essence' of experience, and helps to illustrate the general impressions being recalled. As he reviews his memories of Combray, for example, the image of Bloch suddenly appears, and, with it, a little scene involving him and Marcel's father, cast entirely in the form of a dialogue between them:

> Il avait commencé par agacer mon père qui, le voyant mouillé, lui avait dit avec intérêt:
> — Mais, monsieur Bloch, quel temps fait-il donc? est-ce qu'il a plu? Je n'y comprends rien, le baromètre était excellent.
> Il n'en avait tiré que cette réponse:
> — Monsieur, je ne puis absolument vous dire s'il a plu. Je vis si résolument en dehors des contingences physiques que mes sens ne prennent pas la peine de me les notifier.

---

44 *ARTP*, I, pp. 59-60.
45 *ARTP*, I, pp. 61-62.
46 *ARTP*, I, p. 62.

— Mais, mon pauvre fils, il est idiot ton ami, m'avait dit mon père quand Bloch fut parti. Comment! il ne peut même pas me dire le temps qu'il fait! Mais il n'y a rien de plus intéressant! C'est un imbécile. [47]

The circumstances surrounding this tiny scene are never explained, no more than the most general context supplied. Yet, placed in the flow of memories surrounding Combray, the vividness of the episode is striking, and the impression of Combray itself considerably heightened.

Not only are small scenes of this kind introduced into the narrative in order to represent the individual thought-processes at work behind the recreation of the past, but much longer episodes are included, as they occur to the narrator—prompted by a chance association of memories. As Marcel thinks back to one special incident which forms part of his memories of Combray, the time when he mortally offended his uncle Adolphe, he suddenly recalls a whole set of associated incidents, which the first memory gives birth to. First, Adolphe's 'cabinet de repos' recalls the occasion of the latter's quarrel with the boy's parents and the reason why Marcel never went into the pavillion as he used to when his uncle was still on good terms with them. Then, in order to contain the flood of memories that come surging forth, the narrator is forced to envelop one set of incidents within another, and to repeat the process until the whole story, with all the different times and places it calls up, is unfolded. Thus, the ordering of the narrative, based upon the links provided by memory and association, is made to represent the following of the narrator's individual thought-processes. The narrator describes his periodic visits to uncle Adolphe's house in Paris—memories indissolubly linked with the 'cabinet de repos' at Combray [48]. The general atmosphere surrounding this period of time gives rise to a new set of memories: 'à cette époque j'avais l'amour du théâtre', and the *Opéra comique*'s play bills, printed in green, flash before the narrator's mind, along with memories of conversations at school about actors [49]. Then, another incident is recalled, a different scene, still in Paris, in which Marcel makes the acquaintance of the 'dame en rose' [50]. Finally the connection between this new acquaintance, Adolphe, the 'cabinet de repos' at Combray, and Marcel's parents is made clear and this long 'digression' prompted by the chance memory of Adolphe's deserted 'pavillon' in the garden at Combray comes to an end [51].

The internal ordering of this series of scenes is complex. The impression it gives is that the narrator is jumping haphazardly from one memory to another—the impression often given by the articles of *Chroniques,* when Proust's individual methods of composition were

---

[47] *ARTP,* I, p. 92.
[48] *ARTP,* I, pp. 72-73.
[49] *ARTP,* I, pp. 73-4.
[50] *ARTP,* I, pp. 75-80.
[51] "Aussi je n'entrais plus dans le cabinet de repos... de mon oncle." *ARTP,* I, p. 80.

first given full rein. It is, of course, the effect Proust wishes to create, since the following of an individual's sometimes idiosycrtaic thought-processes is closely connected with the 'aesthetic' of *Temps Retrouvé* which demands in art 'un certain rapport entre ces sensations et ces souvenirs qui nous entourent simultanément[52]. Yet, the whole 'digression' is carefully designed. Not only does each related incident contribute to a new glimpse into a part of Marcel's life that the reader would not otherwise have known, but each leads back to the memory which gave rise to the whole digression. The sequence begins and ends symmetrically with Adolphe, his quarrel with Marcel's parents and the latter's part in it. The apparently unconnected episodes, when we see Marcel running to the 'colonne Morris'[53], engaged in conversation with school friends, or watching for a famous actor's appearance outside a theatre[54], are in fact carefully included, and arranged so as to contribute to a planned climax. For the boy Marcel's memories at school, at college, the relating of the different episodes connected with the theatre—all prepare for the scene between Marcel, his uncle and the 'dame en rose', the central scene which is the purpose of the whole 'digression'. They provide an emotional climate, and the narrative becomes dramatic:

> Je classais par ordre de talent les plus illustres (actrices): Sarah Bernhardt, la Berma, Bartet, Madeleine Brohan, Jeanne Samary, mais toutes m'intéressaient. Or mon oncle en connaissait beaucoup, et aussi des cocottes que je ne distinguais pas nettement des actrices... Aussi... je sortis et au lieu d'aller regarder la colonne d'affiches, pour quoi on me laissait aller seul, je courus jusqu'à lui[55].

The scene which follows leads back to Combray and the starting-point of the long train of thought to which it gave rise, and the whole episode is brought neatly to a close.

Proust is, therefore, not simply 'reproducing' his individual thought-processes and making them the basis of a flow of unconnected episodes. Behind the studied incoherence of the story, a master intelligence is at work, carefully weighing one element of the narrative against another. juxtaposing incidents for effect, engineering climax and atmosphere as part of an overall plan. The guidance of the intelligence makes itself felt in the very ordering of the memories, the careful insertion of tiny scenes, the rearrangement of anecdotes which appear as part of a memory pursued by the narrator, but which serve the double purpose of contributing towards the individual poetry of the past, by evoking all the attendant, illogical associations surrounding it, and of forming a dramatic backcloth for more important scenes which they prepare. The guidance, scarcely perceptible as the reader moves from

---

[52] *ARTP*, III, p. 889.
[53] *ARTP*, I, p. 73.
[54] *ARTP*, I, p. 74.
[55] *ARTP*, I, p. 75.

episode to episode, is also present in the wider organisation of the different memories. Starting from the impressions and associaitons which lie at the heart of the narrator's personality, Proust creates a series of interlocking sequences, carefully planned and constructed. The whole Combray chapter is built up in this way; The impression conjured up by the 'madeleine' was made, as we have seen, the centre of a mass of overlapping sensations. On a larger scale, the whole of the second evocation of Combray is an attempt to insert among a mass of enveloping associations, one central passage which conjures up, more than any of the other memories, the 'essence' of the childhood Marcel spent at Combray. The result is that all the other independent and self-contained unities of memory, with their central impression or sensation [56], become *themselves* the accessory sensations and impressions which accompany all facets of experience. For the ordering of sensations around a significant episode is exactly the same as the discovery of the flavour of the 'madeleine' hidden in the mass of enveloping memories which had to be pushed aside before the actual sensation appeared. The one vital episode in the second evocation of Combray repeats this characteristic pattern.

The celebrated reading passage [57] is the focal point of the whole Combray chapter, and all the memories surrounding it are equivalent to the 'layers' of memory hiding the madeleine image from the narrator's mind earlier. It is carefully prepared, following closely on the first long conversation between Léonie and Françoise, and immediately preceding the second between Léonie, Eulalie and the curé [58]. It contains the 'centre' of the Combray childhood, and its physical position in the chapter emphasises its symbolic importance.

Sometimes the intelligence at work behind the ordering of the narrative makes itself felt in the binding together, within an all-embracing image, of several of the apparently disconnected memories. Thus, when the child Marcel is aroused from his wicker chair by the noise of army manœuvres, one dominant image is introduced at the beginning to be picked up later as part of a unifying theme, similar to the extended metaphors of the stained-glass windows, in *Contre Sainte-Beuve*. As the 'cuirassiers' draw near Marcel's garden, the image of a mountain stream is suggested:

> ... quand les cuirassiers défilaient rue Sainte-Hildegarde, ils en remplissaient toute la largeur, et le galop des chevaux rasait les maisons, couvrent les trottoirs submergés comme des berges qui offrent un lit trop étroit à un torrent déchaîné [59].

---

[56] or blocks of memory connected by an image or theme, like the theme of the *'inconnu'* which links several episodes, pp. 56-59.

[57] *ARTP*, I, pp. 83-88.

[58] *ARTP*, I, pp. 54-59; 100-108.

[59] *ARTP*, I, p. 88.

while their departure transfers the idea of water receding to a receding tide:

> ... Et devant chaque maison... les domestiques ou même les maîtres, assis en regardant, festonnaient le seuil d'un liseré capricieux et sombre comme celui des algues et des coquilles dont une forte marée laisse le crêpe et la broderie au rivage après qu'elle s'est éloignée.

Sometimes, on the contrary, links of this kind between sets of memories are more prolonged and much of Marcel's image of Combray is fitted into a loose pattern, which is flexible enough to embrace the 'digressions' of sense-association, but constructed so as to give some form to the different episodes it contains. The description of Combray church, we discover, follows a loose plan made up by the family's Sunday routine. Marcel relates his general impressions to a background never formally described but sufficient to give a certain order to his memories. The porch, then, is associated with Sunday mornings, when he accompanied his parents to church, and the reader insensibly follows them as they enter:

> Son vieux porche *par lequel nous entrions,* noir grêlé comme un écumoir, était dévié et profondément creusé aux angles... [60]

draw near the choir; whose:

> ... pierres tombales, sous lesquelles la noble poussière des abbés de Combray, enterrés là, faisaient au chœur comme un pavage spirituel... [61]

walk down the nave, with its stained-glass windows, casting a light

> ... qui tremblait et ondulait en une pluie flamboyante et fantastique, qui dégouttait du haut de la voûte sombre et rocheuse, le long des parois humides, comme si c'était dans la nef de quelque grotte irisée de sinueuses stalactites *que je suivais mes parents...* [62]

and finally, the service over, leave, turning round to look up at the tower [63], and calling in at the pâtisserie on the way home [64].

The beginning of *Du côté de Chez Swann,* then, with its account of Marcel's first contact with involuntary memory, illustrates in general the methods Proust employed to convey the impressions he felt when he plunged into a forgotten world of memories and sensations, where conventional rules of chronology and rational argument have no place. The sets of memories unleashed through the evocative power of affective memory unfold at intervals to reveal *deeper* layers of memory, connected to the first by a multitude of sensations, whether

---

[60] *ARTP,* I, p. 59.
[61] *ARTP,* I, ibid.
[62] *ARTP,* I, p. 60.
[63] *ARTP,* I, p. 63.
[64] *ARTP,* I, p. 65.

in the tracing of the 'madeleine' flavour, or the rediscovery of the pleasure of reading and a belief in art; the whole pattern of the Combray episode is the rolling away of the accessory recollections surrounding the reading passage, conjuring up the vision of a vague, ideal time, whose sensations are still present, but which nonetheless depend entirely for their presence in the narrator's mind on the chance associations of an individual thought process. The studied inconsistency of the narrative, the lengthy 'digressions' reproduce the idiosyncratic quality of this individual world, while the memories themselves have enough general appeal to translate this world into something of universal value. The lack of formal technical preparation of scenes, the inclusion of significant moments in anecdote and dialogue, and, above all, the individual way of moving freely from one topic, or memory, to another—all these marks of the early works contribute to the presentation of a narrative whose value has now been understood, accepted and deliberately reinforced by the author of *Le Temps Retrouvé*.

THE ADAPTATION OF THE NEW TECHNIQUES TO THE TELLING OF A STORY

Unlike the object of *Combray,* which was to evoke past states of awareness and emotion, the principal interest of *Un Amour de Swann* lies in its recounting of a psychological upheaval in the mind of the central character. Thus, from the painting of a static past, Proust moves into the realm of action and movement, as he recounts the progression made from one state to another in the course of Swann's affair with Odette, and the contrasts it produces—illustrations of theories he is anxious to demonstrate. In *Jean Santeuil,* change and movement were for the most part avoided; in *Combray* change played little part in the penetration of forgotten memories of an ideal past. In *Un Amour de Swann,* however, the basic technique of enveloping incidents and sensations in a cocoon of related associations remains at the heart of the telling of Swann's story and continues to do so for the remainder of *A la Recherche.*

The 'action' of *Un Amour de Swann* can in certain respects be compared to that of a Racine play. In the case both of *Bérénice,* for example, and of *Swann* the interest lies in the different relationships which evolve during the course of the 'plot', while the events precipitating the evolution of these relationships are secondary to the effects they produce on the characters, confronted with a series of 'faits accomplis'. Thus the progression of 'events' in *Un Amour de Swann* is transformed into the examination of a series of states, and the observation of behaviour in general, and the analysis of love and jealousy in particular, form the basis of the narrative.

A typical example of the characteristic narrative pattern of *Un Amour de Swann* is Swann's reaction to the Vinteuil sonata; the emotions awakened in Swann spread over several different occasions and, as in the evocation of Combray, ordinary spatial and temporal limitations disappear as a central emotion is pursued, bringing with it several different scenes unconnected in time, but part of a single emotional unity. The reader is suddenly transported back to the time when Swann first heard the Vinteuil sonata[65], then the emotions

---

[65] *ARTP,* I, pp. 208-211.

awakened at the Verdurin soirée are added to it, bridging the chrono-logical gap between his first evening at the home of Odette's friends and the moment, 'l'année précédente, dans une soirée' when he was first made aware of the music's evocative power. Similarly the sonata is 'buried' among the layers of conversation and small-talk, which emanate from the soirée at which he hears the sonata, and which are alien to the emotions Swann experiences. The 'essence' of his expe-rience is not separated from its attendant circumstances and the général de Forcheville's un-artistic conversation, and Mme Verdurin's inept comments ("on ne perd pas son temps à couper les cheveux en quatre ici... [66]) accompany the profound impression the sonata makes on Swann.

The study of the different, but immobile stages of the liaison con-tinues the method Proust has already introduced of illustrating general evocations of atmosphere with snatches of dialogue, vivid scenes and significant anecdotes. Thus, describing Swann's hesitancy in proposing certain projects to Odette, a general atmosphere is first drawn up:

> ... Mme Verdurin donnait parfois à Swann ce qui seul pouvait constituer pour lui le bonheur; [67]

which is followed by a host of different illustrations:

> ... Mme Verdurin lui apportait la paix et la joie en disant spontanément: 'Odette, vous allez ramener M. Swann, n'est-ce pas?' comme cet été qui venait et où il s'était d'abord demandé avec inquiétude si Odette ne s'absenterait pas sans lui, s'il pourrait continuer à la voir tous les jours. Mme Verdurin allait les inviter à le passer tous deux, chez elle à la campagne... [68]

and the different scenes of dialogue contribute to the exact 'atmosphere' of the general situation being portrayed.

From time to time, however, change is indicated in the telling of Swann's story by introducing a number, relatively small, of convention-ally prepared 'key' scenes, in which past states are recapitulated and future developments precipitated. They form generally part of the series of big social scenes, which run throughout the whole length of *A la Recherche*. *Un Amour de Swann* is constructed, almost symme-trically, on a rising and falling motion created by the waxing and waning of the love affair. Within this symmetrical plan, the 'key' scenes are carefully positioned: Swann's anxious search for Odette in the streets of a deserted Paris, for example, represents the climax of the 'waxing' of the affair, the Sainte-Euverte soirée the crystallisation of Swann's suspicions that it is all over. Each is presented dramatically, as a vivid scene; Swann's tortured search is vividly described:

---

[66] *ARTP*, I, p. 213.
[67] *ARTP*, I, p. 248.
[68] *ARTP*, I, p. 248.

> Il poussa jusqu'à la Maison Dorée, enra deux fois chez Tortoni et, sans l'avoir vue davantage, venait de ressortir du Café Anglais, marchant à grands pas, l'air hagard, pour rejoindre sa voiture qui l'attendait au coin du boulevard des Italiens, quand il heurta une personne qui venait en sens contraire: c'était Odette; [69]

and the climax of the Sainte-Euverte evening is cast in no less a dramatic form:

> Il souffrait de rester enfermé au milieu de ces gens.. il souffrait surtout... de prolonger son exil dans ce lieu où Odette ne viendrait jamais, où personne, où rien ne la connaissait, d'où elle était entièrement absente. [70]

Both mark a significant stage in the succession of emotional states being described and form a deliberate contrast to the long stretches of analysis and commentary which make up the majority of *Un Amour de Swann*.

An analysis of the different elements of the narrative, therefore, reveals three distinct strata:

(i) *the basic structure*: the later narrator's intellectual rationalisations of a series of past situations, describing states and emotions, providing analysis and observation and contributing a continuous commentary from an objective viewpoint.

(ii) *a layer of fictional, illustrative scenes*: the direct result of the commentary and analysis, providing concrete examples, drawn from different times and places, of the narrator's observations. They often consist of short passages of dialogue, with little or no surrounding description, and represent the subordination of the fictional element to the basic, rational structure, which they illustrate and highlight, but do not influence.

(iii) *a number of 'key' scenes*: these act upon the intellectual basis of the narrative and have the power to direct it on a new course. Often of great length, carefully prepared and containing elements of drama, these scenes depend less on dialogue than the illustrative passages, and include descriptions which themselves in turn evoke commentary from the narrator.

All Proust's different tendencies as a writer take their place in the narrative scheme: the basic function of the artist, that of recreating the past, is performed by the 'Combray technique', the ordering of events according to the laws of memory and association; this is inserted into a fictional story which advances rationally, according to an overall plan, by means of the final narrator's guiding commentary, and the actual inclusion of certain key incidents in the life being recounted.

---

[69] *ARTP*, I, p. 231.
[70] *ARTP*, I, pp. 344-345.

Both the static and the dynamic elements of all the earlier works are combined to make up the whole.

The static quality of the work continues to be manifest in both the 'rational' basis and the key scenes, since the latter give rise themselves to commentary and observations which accompany the more direct presentation of events in Marcel's life. The impression of immobility increases with the growing interest in former states and emotions, the preponderent place given to moralist observation and commentary, the lack of interest in traditional fictional techniques, the insufficiently-developed narrator/hero and the increasing interest, as the work progresses, in the psychological analysis of action, rather than in the action itself. Thus it is clear that the different strata of the narrative tend to pay more attention to the rational and intellectual basis of *A la Recherche,* although the work is conceived as a fictional story. Towards the end of the Albertine cycle, the purely rational account of the three stages which mark the narrator's return to a state of indifference to his dead lover occupies a large section of *La Fugitive* and the argumentative basis of the novel becomes more and more apparent.

Nevertheless, the fictional scenes are carefully composed and constructed; they concentrate many abstract elements of social observation into fictional episodes, and give the story of Marcel's vocation a clearly defined progression. The living demonstration by figures like the marquise de Gallardon or M. de Norpois of rational observations of human types ensures the assimilation of the 'moraliste' tradition Proust continues to keep alive into the story of Marcel's vocation, by making the 'key' scenes the depository of social and sociological observation as well as giving them a function within the narrative. The central scene, dealing with the dinner given by the narrator's parents for Norpois fulfills several functions. Through the conversation of Norpois himself the end of *Un Amour de Swann* is introduced to the reader [71], the vocation theme is introduced in the episode concerning the prose-poem on the Martinville spires, while the description of the ex-ambassador's conversation, the dialogue and the pertinent observations of the narrator contribute to the creation of a setting for all the different elements. The episode is also the excuse to recount Marcel's remarkable first visit to the theatre, and is at the same time a demonstration of a 'law':

> ... en causant avec M. de Norpois, je me rendis compte tout d'un coup... combien les sentiments éveillés en moi par tout ce qui concernait Gilberte Swann et ses parents différaient de ceux que cette même famille faisait éprouver à n'importe quelle autre personne [72].

Another way in which much apparently accessory detail and observation is assimilated into the general narrative pattern is in the development of the style of *A la Recherche.* Much of Proust's general

---

[71] *ARTP,* I, pp. 465-478.
[72] *ARTP,* I, p. 438.

observation of manners forms the basis of many of the illustrative scenes, or the 'key' social scenes placed strategically through the work. But it is also true that the weight of observations and comments, so detrimental to the coherent ordering of *Jean Santeuil* finds another form of escape in *A la Recherche,* provided by the style. Many of the images which characterise Proust's mature style undoubtedly originate from the kind of pointed comparisons which 17th century moralists delighted in making to illustrate their observations of contemporary society and behaviour. It is exactly this kind of parallel which forms the basis of much of the richly-imaged style of *A la Recherche.* For example, what, in *Jean Santeuil,* would have formed a lengthy digression on a character's habit of migrating easily from one love affair to another is, in *A la Recherche,* compressed succintly into a single image:

> (Swann) ne s'enfermait pas dans *l'édifice de ses relations,* mais en avait fait, pour pouvoir le reconstruire à pied d'œuvre sur de nouveaux frais partout où une femme lui avait plu, *une de ces tentes démontables comme les explorateurs en emportent avec eux* [73].

Defending his constant use of metaphor, Proust declares it to be the only means of reconstituting the exact impression he wants to convey, since language has become too blunt an instrument to provide an exact notation of individual expressions. Yet, here, and in many other cases, the value of the metaphor lies in the unexpected accuracy of the parallel, and in the evidence it betrays of a keen observer of human nature. The whole description of Swann's questionable use of his privileges as a member of the exclusive faubourg Saint-Germain is concentrated into a single extended metaphor, evolving around the perfectly seventeenth-century parallel between social position and money. His social standing thus becomes 'une sorte de valeur d'échange, de lettre de crédit, dénuée de prix en elle-même' [74], while the idea of bartering is implicit in the imagery:

> Pour ce qui n'était pas transportable ou échangeable contre un plaisir nouveau, il l'eût donné pour rien, si enviable que cela parût à d'autres [75]

and the vocabulary is consciously ambigous: 'crédit' and 'désir accumulé depuis des années' suggesting money, while a transaction closes the illustration:

> ... comme ferait un affamé qui troquerait un diamant contre un morceau de pain [76].

When he sets out to describe the peculiar ornament to the family apartment constituted by Françoise's expressions, a parallel again is introduced, but, again, is compressed into an image:

---

[73] *ARTP,* I, p. 192.
[74] *ARTP,* I, p. 191.
[75] *ARTP,* I, pp. 192-193.
[76] *ARTP,* I, p. 193.

> Comme la vitrine d'un musée régional l'est par ces curieux ouvrages que les paysannes exécutent et parsementent encore dans certains provinces, notre appartement parisien était décoré par les paroles de Françoise inspirées d'un sentiment traditionnel et local et qui obéissaient à des règles très anciennes [77].

Many similar examples can be found throughout the novel [78] and there is little doubt that the final evolution of Proust's style assimilates many of the comparisons and parallels which before were used as parts of the story itself.

The beginning of *La Prisonnière* contains a passage which describes perfectly the basic narrative technique developed in *Combray,* and, by virtue of its position in the later stages of the novel, casts a significant light on the modifications brought about by the increasing insistence on the 'laws' of behaviour upon the technique. Lying in bed, the narrator describes how his imagination leads him from one topic to another, and according to what criteria:

> Remontant paresseusement de jour en jour comme sur une barque, et voyant apparaître devant moi toujours de nouveaux souvenirs enchantés, que je ne choisissais pas, qui l'instant d'avant m'étaient invisibles et que ma mémoire me présentait l'un après l'autre sans que je pusse les choisir, je poursuivais paresseusement sur ces espaces unis ma promenade au soleil. [79]

The link between the different memories which occur to Marcel is sensation, and it is this, which, as we have seen, creates a unity out of a series of otherwise totally unconnected episodes. In the later stages of the work, we can make the same observations as Professor Feuillerat, without necessarily accepting all his conclusions: namely that the emphasis on the power of sensation and memory to conjure up the past decreases as the interest in the behaviour of individuals and social groups increases [80]. We have already seen that this change of emphasis fits perfectly into the downward-moving emotional climate demanded by the fictional plot of *A la Recherche.* But what of the techniques evolved in order to reproduce the past according to the laws of memory, which as the novel progresses, receive less and less attention?

One factor is common both to the pursuit of a sensation which recalls a forgotten past and to the pusuit of laws which reveal the essence of human behaviour: dual pursuits whose aim is to discover

> Notre vie, et aussi la vie des autres; [81]

---

[77] *ARTP*, II, p. 64.
[78] i.e. *ARTP*, I, pp. 779; 791; 794; 795-6-7-8; 802 — II, pp. 28; 45; 48; 320; 371, etc.
[79] *ARTP*, III, p. 84.
[80] Albert Feuillerat: *Comment Marcel Proust a composé son roman,* New Haven, Yale University Press, 1934.
[81] *ARTP*, III, p. 895.

This factor is the unifying element common to a number of completely different situations. When Marcel drank his tea and ate his 'madeleine', the bridge between the moment in time when he did so and the moment in time which remained associated with the taste was a sensation. In precisely the same way, when Marcel points out that Mme Verdurin, in the same circumstances, uses an expression which links her indissolubly with Françoise whom she has never met, the bridge between them, two otherwise unconnected people, is a 'law' of human behaviour [82],—just as Proust is able to use the link of memory and sensation as a means of presenting a narrative to illustrate the inner pattern of *collective* experience. The rôle of the 'laws' is, in fact, identical to that played by sensation.

When, therefore, the narrator remarks in *La Prisonnière:*

> ... (mon attention) n'eût pu être fixée que par l'appel de quelque réalité s'adressant à mon imagination... ou *quelque élément général, commun à plusieurs apparences et plus vrai qu'elles, qui de lui-même éveillait toujours un esprit intérieur et habituellement ensommeillé...* [83]

he is referring to the element which 'converts' the Combray technique of moving freely from one field of emotion to another, at the dictates of memory, into one which allows the narrator to move freely from one demonstration of human behaviour to another, according to the dictates of 'laws' connecting the most disparate anecdotes and incidents. To take a typical example, when Proust wishes to illustrate how one fundamental law of behaviour dictates Charlus' reactions in a number of quite different circumstances, he procedes in exactly the same way as if he were demonstrating how a single sensation can bring together a number of quite different moments in time. The insertion of a host of small scenes, independent of fictional preparation, based often on dialogue, performs the same function in demonstrating the power of the law as in demonstrating the power of memory. Sometimes the scenes are hypothetical, and arranged to underline a particular part of the law:

> Présentait-on au baron un jeune compositeur de tournure agréable, c'était dans les talents de Morel qu'il cherchait l'occasion de faire une politesse au nouveau venu [84]

but the dialogues, which form the basic element in these, as in the scenes inter-connected by sensation, are rarely missing:

> 'Vous devriez, lui disait-il, m'apporter de vos compositions pour que Morel les joue au concert ou en tournée. Il y a si peu de musique agréable écrite pour le violon!...' [85]

---

[82] *ARTP*, I, p. 285.
[83] *ARTP*, III, p. 284, elsewhere refered to as: 'quelque essence générale, commune à plusieurs choses'. III, p. 718.
[84] *ARTP*, III, p. 218.
[85] *ARTP*, III, ibid.

This particular scene is presented in conjunction with the Baron's remarks to Marcel at the Verdurin's and though the relationship and the external circumstances are totally different, (just as those of Françoise and Mme Verdurin are different, though both exclaim 'Sale bête' under similar provocation), nevertheless the Baron's behaviour is in each case the same—an opportunity for Proust to point to the 'law' which the Baron is unwittingly obeying [86]. Mme Verdurin's behaviour, too, provides him with a chance to insert into the narrative several little scenes reproducing the Patronne's gestures of speech, in order to show how the same basic reaction can be found in many different circumstances. For instance, her admiration for Vinteuil is expressed in the same terms as her hypothetical fear that her carpet might be burned if her guests smoked [87].

Thus Proust's instinctive habit of moving from one topic to another, following his own individual line of thought suits his interest in human behaviour as well as his interest in past states and emotions. The 'essence générale' which connects different moments in time and different sections of humanity provides the basis for an enquiry which draws imperiously on the whole of Proust's experience, bringing together past events, incidents, shedding new light on banal anecdotes, making use of his observation of manners in exactly the same way as his analysis of his own thought-processes. The laws dictate the arrangement of the narrative just as sensation and memory recall events which, as Marcel remarks, 'm'étaient invisibles et que ma mémoire me présentait l'un après l'autre sans que je pusse les choisir' [88].

Another example of the way in which the 'laws' are used to re-arrange the presentation of the narrative occurs in *La Fugitive*. The long 'digression' on the change in Gilberte's social status after the death of Swann is not simply a series of gratuitous anecdotes included to exemplify certain social theories [89]. Instead Proust pursues the social and psychological laws which are brought into play by Gilberte, and traces their repercussions on different 'worlds' noting their effect on different people's attitudes, just as his persuance of memory brings fresh worlds and atmosphere flooding back. Moreover, just as the sudden entry into Marcel's wearisome existence of a powerful sensation can make him abandon the reality around him for one infinitely more satisfying [90], so the sudden irruption into his world of a series of 'laws' incarnated by the person of Gilberte (and later by her daughter, Mlle de Saint-Loup) makes the immediate reality of the Guermantes fête dissolve before the evocation of different social situations suddenly illuminated by the narrator's intelligence.

---

[86] *ARTP*, III, ibid.
[87] *ARTP*, III, pp. 240-241.
[88] *ARTP*, III, p. 84.
[89] *ARTP*, III, pp. 574-582.
[90] i.e. the incident in *Temps Retrouvé*, when Marcel is transported back in imagination to Balbec, and which gives rise to the comment: '*l'impression fut si forte que le moment que je vivais me sembla être le moment actuel*', III, p. 868.

The close parallel which it is possible to draw between the 'treatment' of sensation and of psychological and sociological observation is interesting. In *Le Temps Retrouvé,* the narrator comes to the conclusion that the 'vérités de l'intelligence' can perform an important, if subsidiary rôle in the work he is planning to write:

> ... ces vérités que l'intelligence dégage directement de la réalité ne sont pas à dédaigner entièrement [91]...

—yet *A la Recherche* itself relies more heavily on the discovery of such 'truths' than on the pursuance of past impressions, and the technique of presenting scenes from a forgotten past according to the laws of memory and association is far more amply illustrated by the following of the 'laws' and their effect upon different people. Nevertheless the very fact that the same technique is adapted to convey both aspects of what Proust considers as essentially the same enquiry is particularly significant. Whatever intellectual and rational loopholes there may be in his project of equating intelligence and the fruits of anti-intellectual impressions in his allegory designed to illustrate the *fallibility* of intelligence [92], there can be no doubt that, in practice, the balance is more than equal in *A la Recherche,* and the importance given to the laws, and their assimilation into Proust's instinctive methods of composition reveals that for Proust they both constituted legitimate ways of discovering the true essence of all experience.

The effect upon the general narrative flow of the elaboration of the laws is similar to that created by the pursuance of impressions. Explanations of certain changes of attitude from which Gilberte has benefited in her meteoric social elevation, for example, give rise to often lengthy comments on similar or slightly different results of the same basic phenomenon elsewhere. Such 'accessory' demonstrations, like the accessory scenes conjured up by the involontary memory, often lead the narrator far away from the original starting point: the inclusion of explanations for human reactions which arises from Mme de Guermantes' initial refusal to meet Swann's daughter leads us away to far-removed, but fundamentally parallel example of the same truth

> ... quelle que soit l'image, depuis la truite à manger au coucher du soleil qui décide un homme sédentaire à prendre le train [93]...

—just as the pursuit of the basic thread of emotion, with its accessory images and memories, leads the narrator away from the basic fictional scene of Combray.

The method of including the illustrations themselves, in the case of the sensation link or the observation link, is identical too. Dialogue is introduced to conjure up a series of otherwise unsupported images

---

[91] *ARTP,* III, p. 898.
[92] see particularly J.M. Cocking, *op. cit.,* p. 37.
[93] *ARTP,* III, p. 575.

and scenes, in which the essence of the particular atmosphere Proust is anxious to convey to his reader, or the demonstration of the socio-logical law he is putting forward, is captured briefly. The Duchess's refusal to receive Gilberte is captured in this way, the snatch of dia-logue introduced to do so illustrating not only Mme de Guermantes' mannerisms, but part of the whole structure of social snobbery:

'Babal, disait-elle, prétend que nous sommes les deux personnes les plus élégantes de Paris, parce qu'il n'y a que moi et lui qui ne nous laissons pas saluer par Mme et Mlle Swann. Or il assure que l'élégance est de ne pas connaître Mme Swann'. Et la duchesse riait de tout son cœur [94].

Thus, it is clear, that, in evolving techniques to translate his theories on sensation and memory, social observation and the formulation of 'universal' laws, Proust admitted no difference between the two fields of activity which they represent. Each is present, as we have attempted to show, throughout the whole of his output, and only in the crystal-lising form of *A la Recherche* do they combine to form part of a single enquiry. The inclusion of the laws naturally superimposes itself onto the technique already evolved to demonstrate the power of sense-association, and the basic property of each, the pursuit of 'quelque élément général, commun à plusieurs apparences et plus vrai qu'elles' instinctively brings into play the same techniques and methods, whether that element be the intuitive linking of different moments in time, or the intellectual linking of different aspects of human behaviour.

It is difficult to talk of *digressions* when discussing Proust's novel, since the word implies a departure from a main theme or subject, and we have seen that what seem to be digressions in the ordinary sense of the term are, in fact, the result of a rigorous following of a central theme. Inevitably, techniques which consist in recalling apparently unconnected incidents, often with a strongly anecdotic flavour, tend to make the narrative seem formless and, indeed, the later stages of *A la Recherche* often give the impression that Proust has reverted to the shapeless narrative of *Jean Santeuil*; this is far from being the case, however, since the shapelessness of *Jean Santeuil* is due entirely to a lack of direction and inability to control the material at the author's disposal, whereas the narrative of *A la Recherche* is the inevitable and logical final stage of a technique, based, as we have seen, upon care-fully-reasoned theories, which subsitutes sensation and sense-associa-tion for humdrum chronology, and which demonstrates the universality of a small number of basic patterns of human behaviour. Dispensing with time, place and conventional settings, it introduces a highly indi-vidual order of narrative presentation, which can be fully understood only in conjunction with the theories formulated in *Le Temps Retrouvé*.

Nevertheless, the whole of *A la Recherche* does not fit so easily into this pattern, and many passages exist which merit the name of digres-

---

[94] *ARTP,* III, p. 577.

sions. They occur mostly when Proust is carried away by the topic on which he has embarked, and develops it out of all proportion. There is no profound 'law' to be deduced from the Courvoisier's reaction to examples of 'l'esprit d'Oriane'; there is, on the other hand, an obvious pleasure in simply including the reactions for their own sake to which Proust was not insensible. Many of the descriptions in *Le côté de Guermantes* betray the author's evident pleasure in illustrating his characters:

> Quand (la duchesse) 'imitait' le duc de Limoges, les Courvoisier protestaient: — Oh! non, il ne parle tout de même pas comme cela, tandis que les Guermantes un peu cultivés s'écriaient: 'Dieu, qu'Oriane est drolatique! Le plus fort c'est que pendant qu'elle l'imite, elle lui ressemble! Je crois l'entendre, Oriane, encore un peu Limoges!' [95]

The long 'digression' or the respective attitudes of the Guermantes and Courvoisier families is, according to the 'preface' to *Le côté de Guermantes,* a means of demonstrating that reality never lives up to the demands of the imagination [96] but Proust becomes so engrossed in the fascinating characters which emerge from his pen that the point of the 'moral' is lost in the sheer delight the reader experiences in picking his way through the extraordinary world presented for his edification.

Sometimes, there is an obvious attempt to 'tidy up' the narrative. Thus, in *Sodome et Gomorrhe,* Proust makes use of the little train which takes Marcel and Albertine to and from the Verdurins to introduce anecdotes, 'potins', into the text; the train is transformed into an image, capable of providing a link between the various incidents he wishes to record, and which he has found no other way of incorporating into the story. Since Marcel's first stay at Balbec, the inconsistent nature of the 'tortillard' had been emphasised, and just as the line it follows veers sharply from time to time to call at some unexpected station, so the line of the narrative, reproducing the vagaries of the train, twists and turns in order to accomodate the various anecdotes Proust wishes to include. Outwardly, the different stops at the stations are the excuse to include memories which the particular locations evoke in the narrator's memory:

> Mais déjà les souvenirs de ce qu'on m'avait raconté à ce sujet sont remplacés par d'autres, car le B.C.N. reprenant sa marche de 'tacot', continue de déposer ou de prendre les voyageurs aux stations suivantes [97].

But, as the train moves on, the different stops are seen merely to be an excuse for the narrator to add one anecdote onto another, sometimes with no reference to the stations along the line at all. The 'palace' at Maineville leads to a series of anecdotes about Morel's relationship

---

[95] *ARTP,* II, p. 461.
[96] *ARTP,* II, p. 11.
[97] *ARTP,* II, p. 1028.

with various members of the Guermantes family but they are not presented in the order associated with the memory processes of Combray: on the contrary it is evident that the only order is that created by Proust's desire to include as much information as he can. For example, the 'incident relatif à Morel et à M. de Charlus' which the stop at Maineville recalls [98] is left on one side while another is recounted ('Avant d'en parler, je dois dire...') and, when one anecdote has been included, and the narrator makes a reference to his original intention, he puts it off once more, in order to add more information about Morel, information which has nothing to do with the 'incident' so long promised ('Mais avant de dire en quoi Maineville a quelque rapport dans ma mémoire avec Morel et M. de Charlus, il me faut noter... [99]). Finally, the incident is recounted and the narrator, with the 'tacot', moves on [100]. The appearance of the comte de Crécy at Grattevast is the excuse to include stories about Aimé [101], in addition to those concerning Odette's first husband, introduced here in preparation for the later revelation of their marriage. The longest digressions are, however, inserted in the symbolic countryside between Hermenonville and Deauville, an opportunity for Proust to include scenes illustrating the Cambremer's quarrel with the Verdurins. Here there is no longer any pretence at linking the anecdotes with the train image, and they take on proportions which outgrow the image which the latter provides as a framework [102].

Thus even deliberately planned internal constructions such as this are not always proof against Proust's tendency to stray from a discernible narrative thread, and as the novel draws to a close, the narrator's remarks become more and more to resemble straightforward digressions, and to be less and less connected to Marcel's spiritual progress towards *Le Temps Retrouvé,* by significant emotional links.

Sometimes, the 'disorder' of the narrative is countered by virtually replacing Marcel by another character, who assumes the function of proposing the recurrent 'laws' of behaviour. The long conversation he has with Marcel in *Le Temps Retrouvé* reveals Charlus commenting, in what is almost a monologue, on the situation around him, in exactly the same tones as the narrator himself. Though reference is made from time to time to the conversational basis of the passage [103], Marcel disappears, and the general observations which the later narrator introduces into the narrative are all placed neatly in the mouth of the obliging M. de Charlus:

> Quand je lis: 'Nous luttons contre un ennemi implacable et cruel jusqu'à ce que nous ayons obtenu une paix qui nous garantisse à l'avenir de

---

[98] *ARTP,* II, p. 1075.
[99] *ARTP,* II, p. 1076.
[100] *ARTP,* II, p. 1078.
[101] *ARTP,* II, p. 1084.
[102] *ARTP,* II, pp. 1086-1095.
[103] *ARTP,* III, p. 795.

toute agression et pour que le sang de nos braves soldats n'ait pas coulé en vain', ... je ne sais pas si cette phrase est de l'Empereur Guillaume ou de M. Poincaré, car ils l'ont, à quelques variantes près, prononcée vingt fois l'un et l'autre... [104]

The elliptical turns of phrase, with their often subtle and complex reasoning, are all present:

La France n'aurait peut-être pas tenu tant à prolonger la guerre si elle était restée faible, mais surtout l'Allemagne n'aurait peut-être pas été si pressée de la finir si elle n'avait pas cessé d'être forte [105].

It is true that this conversation brilliantly illustrates Charlus' own personality too, and that the laws and observations he is made to formulate are limited to the war and other considerations particularly dear to Charlus, with his special 'goûts'. Yet the basically digressive nature of the demonstrations finds here a particularly convincing form in the shape of conversation. The personal choice of direction which the observations follow is admirably conveyed in reported speech, reflecting not so much formal reasoning as the character of the person speaking.

The two tendencies which run through all of Proust's work, then, the interest in observation of humanity, in the French moralist's tradition, and the desire to write a straightforward work of fiction never completely combine in A la Recherche.

The fictional element is treated uncertainly; at times it is the necessary but subordinate element of a general demonstration of laws of behaviour, at times the legitimate basis for later interpretation and comment. Proust evolves methods of combining various different aims in a truly fictional pattern, discarding the cruder demonstrations of Jean Santeuil and Contre Sainte-Beuve, to create wholly convincing characters to support the illusion of life and reality. Nevertheless his Bergsonian 'philosophy', the re-creation of individual and personal experience, leads him to reject normal narrative and fictional techniques, although he never goes so far as to dispense with them altogether. Instead, A la Recherche is an attempt to combine two completely different attitudes towards fictional composition. The plan of the work relies heavily on fundamentally traditional narrative techniques. the contents, on the other hand, rely equally heavily on abstract reasoning and observation, particularly as the work progresses, and circumstances prevented its author from shaping the later sections as carefully as the earlier.

A successful attempt is made to create a 'new' narrative technique, which is the result of the viewing, in a new perspective, of all the results of preliminary experiments. It not only 'translates' the author's vision, but uses to advantage Proust's particular talents as a writer,

---

[104] *ARTP*, III, p. 798.
[105] *ARTP*, III, pp. 798-799.

master of the spoken word and adept at creating atmosphere, while dispensing with 'routine' fictional devices such as scene-setting, accessory description and documentation. This technique, used equally to elaborate the laws furnished by rational observation, has the effect, however, of placing the fictional element on the same level of importance as the 'moraliste' aspect of *A la Recherche* as the latter grows in importance to become an essential part with involontary memory, in the artist's salvation.

The result is that the traditional, dramatic conception of *A la Recherche* is quite seriously damaged by the consistent disregard of ancillary but necessary fictional techniques in the writing of the work. While the detective story aspect of *A la Recherche* is, as we have seen, successfully maintained, nevertheless the absence of a real hero in Marcel is hard to reconcile with the massive emotional and spiritual emphasis placed upon him in *Le Temps Retrouvé*. The continual use, too, of such techniques as the spying or 'voyeur' device detracts considerably from the credibility of the fiction, and points rather too often to the design behind the scene, a reversal to the conception of fiction as a subordinate element, introduced to prove a point or to complete an abstract demonstration.

It would be wrong to see *A la Recherche* as the completely successful culmination of all the experiments embodied in the earlier works. This is true of the combination and elaboration of certain techniques, theories and ideas which were still evolving in the early works, and which receive final treatment during the course of the novel. Yet the same hesitancy which characterises not only the writer's uncertainty whether fictional or non-fictional 'genres' were best fitted to his aims and talents, but the internal lack of conviction in the use of either, obvious in the essays on Sainte-Beuve and the novel of *Jean Santeuil*, continues in *A la Recherche*. Too often the fictional scene is forgotten both by the reader and by Proust. Not all the inconsistencies of the narrative can be attributed to faulty editing or incomplete manuscripts. Proust's chronic lack of interest in the ingredients necessary to make up a work of fiction, present in all his writings, reappears to influence the direction and emphasis of *A la Recherche du Temps Perdu*. The uncertainty whether to concentrate, in the third-person narrative of *Jean Santeuil*, on the fictitious hero or the autobiographical narrator is not resolved by combining both in the composite creation of Marcel, since the funcitons each perform divide Marcel himself into two persons, as clearly as Jean was separate from the narrator. Although the fictional plan of *A la Recherche* outwardly ensures the complete fusion of the subjective and objective Marcels, nevertheless, we have seen that the narrative 'tones' cannot always be traced to either, but sometimes to a Saint-Simon-like memorialist, the Proust of the correspondance, or the Proust subject to violent but warped emotional desires. It can be argued that, had the conception of *A la Recherche*, as it was planned to appear in Grasset's publication, ever been accomplished, and the pattern of Combray consistently followed in *L'Adoration per-*

pétuelle, then, the two opposing fictional and moralist-like trends might have been reconciled. Proust was perhaps fortunate in evolving a plan which allowed him to take advantage of the lessons of the early works, but less so, certainly, in discovering that this same plan gave him complete freedom to continue making the same 'mistakes' or, at least, never perfectly solving basic confusions, while ostensibly gearing everything to a pattern which suggests that he had done so.

CONCLUSION

The distinguished German critic, Curtius, in an article on Balzac published twelve years ago, drew attention to the extensive changes which have taken place in the French novel since Proust:

> N'oublions pas que, depuis 1919, la situation du roman français s'est complètement transformée, à la suite de la venue de Proust. L'arrivée d'un nouvel artiste de génie éclaire l'art, même l'art du passé, d'une lumière nouvelle. C'est un phénomène constant et nécessaire, dont la critique littéraire ne se rend pas compte suffisamment [106].

Proustian criticism in general has preoccupied itself, as we suggested at the beginning, with the 'fond' rather than with the 'forme' of *A la Recherche*, yet it is in form and technique that Proust's influence has been the most widespread. In the one article which has so far appeared on the narrative techniques of *A la Recherche du Temps Perdu*, some progress is made, but the conclusions reached are disappointing. Referring to the final Guermantes matinée, for example, J.P. Houston [107] remarks that the most convenient way of summing up Proust's techniques of re-arranging facts and events is to see the novel as a series of focal points: ... *we must think of the Princess's 'soirée' as the magnetic field which holds together all this indispensable information.* It is true that one of Proust's most clearly identifiable methods of fashioning his rich and complex material into something which *deviates least from the novel form* [108] is to regroup the narrative according to well-defined criteria, but the writer's claim, on Proust's behalf, that by doing so he achieves "maximum coherence" is wide of the mark. Some of the *digressions,* as we have seen, are there to prove the author's theories about life, some, seen in the perspective of the new narrative technique, are not digressions at all. But even a cursory reading of *A la Recherche du Temps Perdu* makes it quite clear that Proust never found a way of coherently including them all.

The final work, *A la Recherche* itself, is not the completely successful culmination of the experiments that led up to it that some would

---

[106] Ernst Curtius, *Nouvelle Rencontre avec Balzac,* 1950, p. 104.
[107] *Op. cit.*
[108] Letter to René Blum, February 24, 1913.

have us believe. The study of Proust's constantly evolving approach to fictional composition, however, and the techniques he evolved to fit in both with this approach and with his own strengths and weaknesses as a writer, provide a fascinating illumination of the writer's quest, throughout his life, for a form. This quest, as real as Marcel's own symbolic quest, for an art form sufficiently complex and original to overturn conventional attitudes towards life and art, bears great similarity to the allegory of *A la Recherche* itself. Knowing from the beginning that his work would deviate sharply from the 'classical novel' [109], Proust struggled for a long time with a variety of different influences, just as his hero Marcel has to combat a number of deceptive ennemies before attaining his goal. A born snob, in his youth Proust eagerly seized on literature as a means of humiliating social enemies, just as Marcel, early in Combray days, confused the glamour of Mme de Guermantes with the purer appeal of literature. One of the most striking differences between the immature *Jean Santeuil* and *A la Recherche* is the absence in the latter of this frivolous attitude to art. The narrator of the final work does not draw the same kind of gratuitous pleasure from artificially arranged situations as the self-important hero of '*L'affront*' and '*Reparation*'; indeed, now events are engineered not to satisfy the author's self-esteem, but to serve the laws of human behaviour, and it is characteristic that the older Proust does not hesitate to apply those laws to himself. Never could he have given the calm and rational explanation of Marcel's superiority over his social rivals which he furnishes in '*Sodome et Gomorrhe* [110]. *A la Recherche* is the illustration of his own remark that true artists are those who have been able to discipline themselves [111].

Proust's struggle to master both himself and the novel form results in a series of sometimes contradictory but always profitable experiments. Just as Marcel could not realise the value of a life which seemed to consist of a series of disappointing blind-alleys, so the series of failures which precede *A la Recherche* have little value until they are all seen to be tributary channels leading to the final work. The stories of *Les Plaisirs et les Jours* were a pleasant distraction, but did not lead very far; *Jean Santeuil* was abandoned after the author had worked on it for about five years, and there can have been little regret at turning aside from a work that the author describes as a *heap of ruins*. Proust's 'infatuation' with Ruskin fizzled out damply, and translation and pastiche were in their turn abandoned for critical studies. Only in one major aspect does the allegory of Marcel's quest differ from Proust's real one. Love, in *A la Recherche,* is presented as an obstacle to the fulfilment of the hero's destiny, whereas there is no indication that it

---

[109] Proust to Louis de Robert, October 1912.

[110] *ARTP,* II, p. 823.

[111] Referring to a lawyer who has accompanied the marquise de Cambremer to Marcel's hotel at Balbec, the narrator remarks that 'il parlait bien des livres, mais non de ceux des *vrais maîtres,* de ceux qui se sont maîtrisés'. *ARTP,* II, p. 806.

was so in reality. Proust discreetly engineers autobiographical affairs into the 'plot' and, rather than be misled by them, he builds upon them to the greater glory of his literary career. It is interesting to note that sometimes, in the course of this quest, which bears so close a relationship to the quest of the fictional hero of *A la Recherche,* the advance in technical mastery overtakes that in the attitude to life itself. At times, nothing seems to be holding the writer back, save a lack of practical experience in the art of writing fiction; on other occasions, the techniques glitter emptily, and the riches of thought which they ought to introduce are curiously lacking. Proust's incursion into fashionable journalism, like Marcel's journey along the *Guermantes Way,* contributed towards the goal, as yet unforseen, of *A la Recherche.* It also provides an interesting sidelight on the power that the novel form continually exercised over Proust. Though he never accepted many of the conventions which for others it necessarily implied, nonetheless even when setting out to write in quite a different 'genre' he instinctively introduced many of the attitudes and techniques proper to fiction alone. The *Figaro* articles become short stories, the literary reviews nostalgic evocations of the past.

Proust's often clumsy search for a form and technique, complicated by the special preoccupations with Balzac and Ruskin, nevertheless led him into fields which often yield a surprisingly rich harvest, even if they do not represent the goal the writer was progressing towards. The freedom of journalistic writing is transformed into the distinctive rambling but coherently organized probings into the past. The pastiches are brought to a triumphant climax with the imaginary Goncourt Journal in *Le Temps Retrouvé,* and even the critical articles are echoed in the pedantic illustration of theories and attitudes by quotation and allusion [112]. *A la Recherche* is a 'summum' both of Proust's thought and of his experiments in composition.

Contre Sainte-Beuve marks the final, crystallising stage. It is a work, begun by a writer knowing exactly what to say, but unsure of how to say it, and abandoned as soon as he realises what form his work should ideally take. But comparisons between *Contre Sainte-Beuve* and *A la Recherche* emphasise an essential point which must be made to qualify all that we have said about the relationship between the final work and the experiments which preceded it. In many respects *A la Recherche* created material organically, generating its own energy, as it were, to enrich ideas and concepts which are not to be found in the earlier works. The discovery and elaboration of a plan dictated by the intelligence to demonstrate the superiority of sensation over the intelligence has the effect of opening new perspectives which the conventionality of *Les Plaisirs et les Jours* the formlessness of *Jean Santeuil,* and the ambiguity of *Contre Sainte-Beuve* could not provide. Proust recognised the advantages of a set, initial plan, remarking that:

---

[112] *ARTP,* II, pp. 843, 845, etc.

Un écrivain peut se mettre sans crainte à un long travail. Que l'intelli-
ence commence son ouvrage, en cours de cette route surviendront bien
assez de chagrins qui se chargeront de le finir [113].

The multiplicity of incidents it embraces and the adaptability of the
form to the personal life of the writer both give birth to entirely new
material, which takes its place within the outlines of the original plan,
to which it owes its very conception. Once *A la Recherche* had been
rationally envisaged, it came to life of its own accord and onto the
accumulated riches of the author's experience it heaped the discoveries
produced by the act of writing. Proust's final mode of intercourse with
his reader produced fruits which he could not have forseen in his earlier
attempts to establish contact with him.

The gradual self-mastery, reflected in the advances in technical
sureness and originality, led finally to *A la Recherche du Temps Perdu*.
From the beginning, Proust had been dealing with material drawn
from two principal sources: autobiographical memories and personal
experience, and general comments on life and behaviour, following
in the tradition of the seventeenth and eighteenth century moralists.
The strong tendency to comment and observe which the latter implies
prevented the anti-fictional trends from being completely integrated
into a work of fiction, while the inability to transfer personal experience
into the realm of fiction had a similar effect on the autobiographical
material. Nevertheless, interest in purely fictional techniques and attitudes hardened, and the attempts of *Jean Santeuil* to transpose both
general demonstrations of laws and personal theories about time and
spiritual experience into fictional terms result in the elaboration in
A la Recherche of a complete plan, assimilating conventional and
dramatic elements of the novel into a carefully-composed narrative
framework. A brief comparison between Proust's two 'novels', spanning
over a quarter of a century between them, illustrates most completely
the advance in the writer's technical confidence, which we have been
plotting. In the first novel, Proust has not yet found any completely
satisfactory formula for combining the two threads of his inspiration,
one fictional, the other non-fictional. The confused handling of the
narrative is, as we have seen, a proof of this. The ready attraction of
a first person narrative suitable for presenting personal experience, is
abandoned after the preface, and the purely technical problems that it
raises do not receive very scrupulous attention. Conventional third-
person narrative, on the other hand, cannot satisfy the latent desire
to comment and demonstrate—a desire strong enough to transform
objective narration into first-person narrative, by grossly inflating the
narrator's rôle to the detriment of the hero's. Proust's 17th century
attitude to the spectacle of humanity necessarily implies a secondary
place for fictional scenes, as illustrations of abstract argument, clashing
with the implications of third-person narrative which depends for its
effect more heavily on the recounting of a fictional story arranged

---

[113] *ARTP*, III, p. 907.

around a fictional hero. Nevertheless, this experimental novel, though abandoned for translations of Ruskin, is not without relevance to subsequent attempts to build a lasting edifice upon the heaps of ruins Proust described himself as ammassing. The ambitious young writer, as yet unsure of the very ideas he wished to express, was brought face to face with the problems facing all novelists, and in particular the kind of novelists whose confused and dimly-glimpsed ideals lead them far beyond the limits of the conventional 'genres' in which they set out to compose. Proust himself discovered, while writing *Jean Santeuil,* that the presence of a continuous, commenting element was essential to his purpose, and, at the same time, how the neglect of straight-forward fictional accessories threatened the ruin of his whole conception of the novel. Consequently, he developed techniques which place great importance on visual scenes, striving to adapt his personal vision to the limitations of the nineteenth century novel tradition. When, in spite of everything, these limitations proved too great, he abandoned a work, which, uncertain of the direction his material might take, he had set upon one course, while all his instincts as a writer made it veer away onto another.

Most important of the lessons learned in the writing of *Jean Santeuil,* was the realisation of the possibilities presented by a narrator who is both detached *and* personally involved in the recounting of a story: a function performed only partially by an omniscient narrator. The tendency to construct a series of episodic fragments rather than to compose a continuous narrative also leads Proust to experiment with internal structural forms, which serve later on, both to create the plan of *A la Recherche,* and to give its narrative a coherent shape when it threatens to overflow the carefully-constructed banks of the plan. *Jean Santeuil* is valuable in that it gives Proust his first major opportunity to experiment with a new ordering of scenes, regardless of strict chronological patterns, laying the foundations of a new technique, where sensation is made to provide a link between the different sections of a story. The informal way that *Jean Santeuil* meanders on its course, representing, as Proust remarks, a sum of experience 'garnered' rather than 'made', favours this kind of experimentation which traces its roots back to the earliest stories of *Les Plaisirs et les Jours,* with their interest in chronological transposition, and which must be considered as Proust's instinctive method of composition.

By relating the different elements of *Jean Santeuil* to the two main driving forces of Proust's inspiration, it is possible to trace the evolution of certain trends apparent in later writings and in *A la Recherche* particularly. The presence of 'portraits' in the introduction of characters, instantly recalling memorable pages from *Les Caractères* or the *Mémoires* of Saint-Simon, is grafted onto the Balzac-inspired technique of reintroducing characters into, and allied with, an evolving theory later known as that of the multiple personality. The introduction of certain characters into *A la Recherche,* those, for example who appear in the long digression on the Courvoisier family, can be directly traced to the ambiguous use of fiction as both the apparent basis of

Jean Santeuil and as the secondary illustrative element in its general demonstrations. Certain 'hors-d'œuvre' which never disappear from *A la Recherche* are due to the same double attitude, expressed more clearly in *Jean Santeuil* than in *A la Recherche,* where a formula has been created to combine fictional and non-fictional elements more successfully than in the first novel, where the absence of such a formula, allowing the narrative to advance simultaneously in two different directions, prevents it from ever achieving real homogeneity.

Technical comparisons between *Jean Santeuil* and *A la Recherche* reveal a basic confusion in the attitude towards the function, in the work of art, of the fictional element. The use of fictional techniques and the skill with which they are applied evolves independently of this confusion, however. There is, as is natural, a general confusion and mis-handling of still-evolving methods, aggravated by the incomplete form of the concepts they are being designed to express. Again Proust often shows a strange disregard for essential technical considerations alongside great ingenuity and technical mastery, upon which he draws from time to time with considerable effect. Nevertheless, in some fields, *Jean Santeuil* solves problems with which the more complicated patterns of *A la Recherche* are incapable of dealing. The use of third-person narrative when discussing homosexual incidents is often more convincing than corresponding efforts to do the same in the first-person narrative of *A la Recherche.* Marcel's naiveté is greatly abused in the latter and the whole question of the narrator/hero's ambiguous attitude is obscure. In *Jean Santeuil,* on the other hand the technical separation of hero and narrator is a boon to Proust when he wishes to present characters later to be unmasked as homosexuals, involving techniques whereby all the clues are planted so as to make the retrospective revelation convincing, while ensuring that the hero remains in ignorance of the true facts. Here the omniscient narrator can both plant the clues and make Jean's naiveté convincing, when reporting his false conclusions, whereas in *A la Recherche* the problem is complicated by the fact that hero and narrator are one and the same person. The observations in *Jean Santeuil* are the narrator's as well as Jean's, and, given the limited knowledge at the latter's disposal, his reactions appear normal. Moreover the reader is admirably situated, having enough evidence to form conclusions independent of Jean's while still taking these into account. The greatest advantage that third-person narrative offers Proust is the opportunity it offords him of obtaining a wide, overall view of situations, which suits his commenting, observing tendency, and which he later introduces bodily into *A la Recherche—* exceeding the limits of first-person narrative to do so. Yet the most striking feature of *Jean Santeuil* remains its lack of direction; confusion exists everywhere, in the choice of narrative form, in the attitude to, and use of certain techniques, in the centre of interest itself. All these hesitations are traceable to the presence within the narrative of two mutually-excluding attitudes to fictional writing, determining the choice of a narrative form suitable in some ways for certain of Proust's intentions, quite unsatisfactory for others.

The handling of first-person narrative in the fictional transposition of material reported almost unchanged in *Jean Santeuil* is masterly in *A la Recherche*. The subtle interweaving and super-imposition of two narrative viewpoints is carried out with great ingenuity—less obviously than by Gide in *Les Faux Monnayeurs,* for example, where the deliberate change from direct reporting to a different transcription of the same incident in Edouard's *Journal* often entails artificial breaks in the narrative. Proust hardly ever resorts to such evident devices as journals and letters, but gains from the complete freedom and ease with which he imperceptibly changes the perspective, gives the kaleidoscope a slight shake, and alters the reader's vision of Marcel's experience completely, without ever drawing his attention to the change which he has brought about. So subtly is it effected that the reader is often aware of a different emphasis only on a third or fourth reading. Nonetheless, examination reveals an almost continual substitution of subjective for objective reporting and vive-versa. The result in the drawing of characters is to create remarkably solid and lifelike personalities, who turn slowly before the reader's eyes, as the perspective chosen by the author widens or narrows. Processes which Stendhal invented to show his characters in the round, making the reader see them from different angles, are developed by Proust and perfected with remarkable skill. The occasional 'breaking of the rules' of first-person story telling in the society sections seems unimportant compared with the intricate incorporation into the many-sided narrative of all the elements which contribute to the exultant climax of *Le Temps Retrouvé*. The dramatic conception of the plan reacts upon the use to which the narrative is put and on the emphasis accorded to the narrator's different viewpoints. There are noticeable attempts to integrate the moralist's conclusions about life into the scheme of *A la Recherche,* by attaching them to the changing Marcel, and by projecting them through the subjective voice of the continually-evolving narrator; in the same way, prepared, dramatic scenes are integrated into the plot to illustrate the decline in Marcel's spiritual life.

The actual techniques employed reflect the fundamental division of interest in *A la Recherche*. The real preoccupation with the manipulation of chronology becomes an integral part of the new technique, which makes sensation and laws of behaviour the link between moments separated in time and space. The equally real interest in traditional techniques is accorded a function in the recording of certain episodes, and in the construction of the plan, which reposes on the pillars of involontary memory, besides playing a part in the key scenes which record and precipitate action. Yet traditional narrative techniques fade beside the anti-fictional commentary of the later narrator and the introspection of the later Marcel, while action itself is subordinated to the reactions it calls up in the narrator, resulting in an often curiously tenuous narrative thread, while the accessory developments arising from that thread grow in importance until they threaten to snap it altogether. The paradox of *A la Recherche* lies in its attempt to gather into a single structure the two opposing trends: Proust relies heavily for the

full force of his demonstration of the fallibility of the intelligence on the dramatic revelations at the Princess de Guermantes' matinée, yet many of the ingredients necessary to make the drama work are missing during the whole length of the novel. The demonstration itself suffers in consequence since its means are often at loggerheads with its main purpose, and the transcription of experience in an undramatic way clashes with the very conventional dramatic revelation which serves to bring about the moral of the piece.

Two of the most interesting points to emerge from this study of Proust's narrative techniques are the relative importance, in the methods evolved to present them in *A la Recherche,* of the anti-conceptual impressions and the intellectual and reasoned laws; and the importance attached to the intelligence in the construction of an allegory aimed at undermining its power.

The new techniques, evolved naturally to translate Proust's belief in the power of involuntary memory and irrational sense-associations to resurrect the true past, are applied also to the demonstration of the *grandes lois humaines.* This coupling of two different attitudes is the same as the narrator's admission in *Le Temps Retrouvé,* that the rational, psychological observation of humanity is a legitimate way for the artist to transcend the usual limitations imposed by an incomplete vision *and understanding* of experience. The use of a sensation, or an observation, applicable to several contexts, as links in a chain of otherwise unrelated scenes probably arose naturally from Proust's own instinctive habit of moving easily from one topic to another, grouping digressions around a central theme. Both sensation, with involuntary memory, and general intellectual observation, with its universal overtones, lend themselves well to this instinctive approach. The presence of the laws in *A la Recherche,* and their manner of presentation, are far more natural seen in the light of the techniques introduced to include them, than the explanation in *Le Temps Retrouvé* of their function, which is intellectually dishonest. It is probable that Proust found himself using the same approach for both, and worked out the rational explanation for doing so later.

What, then, is to be made of the demonstration of the weakness and impotence of the intelligence, faced with the task of providing the artist's means of salvation from the unutterable boredom of life? The overall structure of *A la Recherche,* designed to give weight to this demonstration, is most conveniently seen as a useful means of bringing together a number of different elements in one framework. But in few works of French fiction has the intelligence been put to greater service than in Proust's apologia of anti-intellectual sensations. Are the narrator's impressions of a forgotten past, for example, as he slowly savours the madeleine's taste, Proust's own experiences, or the bathing of an indefinable experience in the light of his cool and lucid intelligence, recasting, re-shaping, distorting, twisting original feelings so that the reader might begin to understand, not the original experience, but something akin to that experience? The rôle of the

intelligence in the recreation and translation of sensations is as important as the sensations themselves. Not only are Proust's celebrated 'leit-motifs' an obvious example of the way the intelligence creates a 'pastiche' of the original sensation, by painstakingly building up an allegorical representation of it, but the careful, symbolic preparation of future events, the planting of clues to subsequent developments, the telling in miniature of the whole of Marcel's career in the opening pages—all emphasise the preponderant rôle alloted to the intelligence, and an intelligence of the highest order, in *A la Recherche*. Proust's work changed direction as it was being written. Starting as a simple, three-stage demonstration of the belief in the fallibility of human reasoning, the 'moraliste' soon gave the novel a wholly different emphasis, inflating it, though not so dangerously as to destroy the elastic structure holding it up, until not only does the author come to admit that he has written his novel mainly with the help of rational observation, but that the very pursuit of intellectual and abstract concepts has contributed to his 'salvation' as a writer as much as the discovery of a forgotten past. The way in which his inquiry naturally embraces the examination of observable phenomena, borrowing the attitude and vocabulary of science to do so, and the way in which it uses exactly the same narrative techniques to include them as those used to reproduce his anti-intellectual memories, hardly suggests a writer scornful of the validity of all but involuntary memory. And yet this is the hypothesis on which the entire work is founded.

Proust's place in the history of the novel is fairly and squarely at the end of the great nineteenth-century tradition . His techniques reveal him to be a worthy successor to Balzac, Flaubert and Stendhal, modifying their attitudes towards the presentation of reality in the light of the symbolists in general and Baudelaire in particular, but still retaining to a surprisingly large degree many of their tried and proven techniques. Nonetheless he evolves new ones of his own, and always inserts borrowed ones into a new setting. His constant effort to present the narrative so that the reader may share a greater illusion of reality than is often found in Balzac, or even Flaubert, by turning characters and situations inside out, by placing the greatest importance on the individual impression of experience, by deliberately suppressing all but the reaction of the individual and unforgettably colouring the reader's own awareness—in all these ways Proust evolves techniques which were to pave the way for a whole new trend in the development of the French novel. Realising his ideal, at the end of a quest no less hasardous than that of his own fictional hero, of transcribing an original experience, of analysing the self and the factors bearing on the self, seen collectively or otherwise, Proust finally produced a novel whose technique was revolutionary, and whose impact was to modify the entire problem of fictional composition.

PART FOUR

BIBLIOGRAPHY

A. WORKS OF MARCEL PROUST

A la Recherche du temps perdu, Paris, Bibliothèque de la Pléiade, 1954, 3 volumes.
  1) *Du côté de chez Swann — A l'ombre des jeunes filles en fleurs.*
  2) *Le côté de Guermantes — Sodome et Gomorrhe.*
  3) *La Prisonnière — La Fugitive — Le Temps Retrouvé.*
Chroniques, Paris, Gallimard, 1927.
Contre Sainte-Beuve, suivi de Nouveaux Mélanges, Paris, Gallimard, 1954. This edition incorporates *Le Balzac de Monsieur de Guermantes* previously published separately at Neuchâtel, Ides et Calendes, 1950.
Jean Santeuil, Paris, Gallimard, 1951, Three volumes.
La Bible d'Amiens, Paris, Mercure de France, 1926, Translation, preface and notes by Proust.
Les Plaisirs et les Jours, Paris, Gallimard, 1924.
Pastiches et mélanges, Paris, Gallimard, 1919.
Sésame et les lys, Paris, Mercure de France, 1926. Translation, preface and notes by Proust.

B. CORRESPONDENCE CONSULTED

Autour de soixante lettres de Marcel Proust, Lucien Daudet, Paris, 1929.
Correspondance avec sa mère (1887-1905), Paris, Plon, 1953.
Correspondance générale, Paris, Plon, 1930-1936.
  Volumes 1-5 published by Robert Proust and Paul Brach.
  Volume 6 published by Suzy Proust-Mante and Paul Brach.
Lettres à André Gide, Paris, Ides et Calendes, 1949.
Lettres à la NRF, Paris, Gallimard, 1932. (Volume 6 of the *Cahiers Marcel Proust.*)
Lettres à Maurice Duplay, La Revue Nouvelle XLVIII, 1929.
Lettres à Mme C(atusse), Paris, J.B. Janin, 1946.
Lettres à un ami, Georges de Lauris, Paris, 1948.
Lettres à une amie, Manchester, Editions du Calame, 1942.
Marcel Proust et Jacques Rivière — Correspondance 1914-1922, présentée et annotée par Philip Kolb, Paris, 1955.
Letters of Marcel Proust translated by Mina Curtiss. Introduction by Harry Levin. New York, Random House, 1949.
La Correspondance de Marcel Proust (Chronologie et commentaire critique) Philip Kolb, University of Illinois Press, 1949.

C. GENERAL WORKS CONSULTED

Abantagel, Louis: *Marcel Proust et la musique,* Paris, Imprimerie des Orphelins Apprentis d'Auteil, 1939.

Abraham, Pierre: *Proust: Recherches sur la création intellectuelle,* Paris, Rieder, 1930.

Alden, Douglas W.: *Marcel Proust and his French critics,* Los Angeles, Lymanhouse, 1940.

Autret, Jean: *L'influence de Ruskin sur la vie, les idées et l'œuvre de Marcel Proust,* Genève, Droz, 1955.

Beckett, Samuel: *Proust,* London, Chatto & Windus, 1931.

Béguin, Albert: *L'âme romantique et le rêve,* Paris, José Corti, 1946.

Bell, Clive: *Proust,* New York, Harcourt, Brace and Company, 1929.

Bibesco, Princesse: *Au bal avec Marcel Proust,* Gallimard, Paris, 1928.
— *Le Voyageur voilé,* La Palatine, Genève, 1947.

Bonnet, Henri: *Deux études sur Marcel Proust,* Paris, Le Rouge et le Noir, 1930.
— *Le Progrès spirituel dans l'œuvre de Marcel Proust le monde, l'amour et l'amitié,* Paris, Vrin, 1946.
— *Roman et poésie: Essai sur l'esthétique des genres,* Paris, Nizet, 1915.
— *Marcel Proust de 1907 à 1914,* Paris, Nizet, 1959.

Brée, Germaine: *Du Temps perdu au temps retrouvé,* Paris, Société d'édition 'Les Belles Lettres', 1950.

Cattaui, Georges: *Marcel Proust,* with preface by Daniel-Rops, Paris, Julliard, 1952.
— *Marcel Proust,* avant-propos by P. de Boisdeffre, Paris, Editions Universitaires, 1958.

Cazamian, L.: *A history of French Literature,* Oxford, Clarendon Press, 1955.

Celly, Raoul: *Répertoire des thèmes de Marcel Proust,* Paris, Gallimard, 1935 (Volume VII of the *Cahiers de Marcel Proust*).

Chardon, Pierre: *Expliquez-moi Proust,* Paris, Foucher, 1949.

Cochet, Marie-Anne: *L'Ame proustienne,* Bruxelles, Imprimerie des Etablissements Collignon, 1929.

Cocking, J.M.: *Proust: Studies in Modern European Literature and Thought,* London, Bowes and Bowes, 1956.

Crémieux, Benjamin: *Du côté de Marcel Proust,* Paris, Lemarget 1929. *Vingtième Siècle, Ire série,* Paris, Gallimard, 1924.

Curtius, Ernst-Robert: *Französischer Geist im neuen Europa,* Stuttgart, Deutsche Verlags-Anstalt, 1925.

Dandieu, Arnaud: *Marcel Proust, sa révélation psychologique,* Paris, Firmin-Didot, 1930.

Daudet, Charles: *Répertoire des personnages de 'A la Recherche du Temps perdu',* Paris, Gallimard, 1928 (Vol. II of the *Cahiers de Marcel Proust*).

Du Bos, Charles: *Approximations I,* Paris, Plon, 1922, pp. 58-116.

Fallois, Bernard de: *Preface to 'Contre Sainte-Beuve',* Paris, Gallimard, 1954.

Fernandez, Ramon: *Messages,* Paris, Gallimard, **1926.**
— *La vie sociale dans l'œuvre de Proust,* Paris, 1927.
— *A la gloire de... Proust,* Paris, Nouvelle Revue Critique, 1943.

Ferré, André: *La Géographie de Marcel Proust,* Paris, Editions du Sagittaire, 1939.

Feuillerat, Albert: *Comment Marcel Proust a composé son roman,* New Haven, Yale University Press, 1934.

Gabory, Georges: *Essai sur Marcel Proust,* Paris, Le Livre, 1926.

Guichard, Léon: *Introduction à la lecture de Proust,* Paris, Nizet, 1956.

Green, F.C.: *The Mind of Proust,* Cambridge, Cambridge University Press, 1949.

Hommage à Marcel Proust, Paris, Gallimard, 1927 (Volume I of the *Cahiers Marcel Proust*).

Hommage à Marcel Proust, Special number of *Le Rouge et le Noir,* April, 1928.

Hommage à Marcel Proust, Special number of *Le Disque vert,* Paris-Brussels, 1952.

Leon, Derrick: *Introduction to Proust,* London, K. Paul, Trench and Trubner, 1940.

Lubbock, Percy: *The craft of Fiction,* London, 1955.

March, Harold: *The Two Worlds of Marcel Proust,* Philadelphia, University of Pennsylvania Press, 1948.

Massis, Henri: *Le Drame de Marcel Proust,* Paris, Grasset, 1937.

Mauriac, Claude: *Marcel Proust par lui-même,* Paris, Editions du Seuil, 1953.

Maurois, André: *A la recherche de Marcel Proust,* Paris, Hachette, 1949.

Meyerhaff, Hans: *Time in Literature,* Berkely, University of California Press, 1955.

Mouton, Jean: *Le Style de Marcel Proust,* Paris, Editions Corrêa, 1948.

O'Brien, Justin: *The Maxims of Marcel Proust,* New York, Columbia University Press, 1948.

Painter, George: *Marcel Proust, a biography,* Vol. I, London, Chatto and Windus, 1959.

Peyre, Henri: *Hommes et œuvres du XXe siècle,* Paris, Corrêa, 1938.
— *The Contemporary French Novel,* New York, Oxford University Press, 1955.

Pierre-Quint, Léon: *Comment parut 'Du côté de chez Swann',* Paris, Kra, 1930.
— *Comment travaillait Marcel Proust,* Paris, Editions des Cahiers libres. 1928.
— *Marcel Proust, sa vie, son œuvre,* Paris, Editions du Sagittaire, 1946.
— *Proust et la stratégie littéraire,* Paris, Corrêa, 1954.

Pommier, Jean: *La Mystique de Proust,* Paris, Droz, 1939.

Pourtalès, Guy de: *De Hamlet à Swann,* Paris, 1924.

Revel, Jean-François: *Sur Proust, remarques sur à la Recherche du Temps Perdu,* Paris, Julliard, 1960.

Robert, Louis de: *Comment débuta Marcel Proust,* Paris, Editions de la NRF, 1925.
— *De Loti à Proust,* Paris, Flammarion, 1938.

Saurat, Denis: *Tendances*, Paris, Editions du Monde Moderne, 1928.

Seillière, Ernst: *Marcel Proust*, Paris, Editions de la Nouvelle Revue critique, 1931.

Souday, Paul: *Marcel Proust*, Paris, Kra, 1927.

Souza, Sybil de: *L'influence de Ruskin sur Proust*, Montpellier, Imprimerie de la Manufacture de la Charité, 1932.

Spitzer, Léon: *Zum Stil Marcel Prousts, Stilstudien II*, pp. 365-497, Munich, M. Hueber, 1928.

Thibaudet, Albert: *Réflexions sur le roman*, Paris, Gallimard, 1938.

— *Réflexions sur la critique*, Paris, Gallimard, 1939.

Ullmann, Stephen: *Style in the French Novel*, Cambridge, Cambridge University Press, 1957.

Wilson, Edmund: *Axel's Castle*, New York, Scribner, 1936.

D. ARTICLES CONSULTED

Arland, Marcel: "Les années d'apprentissage de Proust", *Arts*, 10-16 juillet, 1952.

Bataille, Georges: '*Jean Santeuil*', *Critique*, July 1952.

Bisson, L.A. 'Marcel Proust in 1947', *French Studies* I, pp. 191-217, 1947.

— 'Proust, Bergson and George Eliot', *Modern Language Review* 40: 104-114, 1945.

Blanchot, Maurice: '*Jean Santeuil*', *Nouvelle Revue Française*, 1st. september 1954.

Bonnet, Henri: 'Une étude allemande sur Proust à la rechecrhe de la conception du roman', *Revue d'Esthétique*, July-September, pp. 312-321, 1956: analysis of Hans Robert Jauss's article originally in Romanische Forschungen: "Proust auf der Suche nach seiner Konzeption des Romans".

Brée, Germaine: 'Marcel Proust et Maurice Barrès', *Romanic Review* 40, pp. 93-105, April 1949.

— 'New Trends in Proust Criticism', *Symposium* 5: 62-71, May 1951.

Cabeen, D.C.: 'Saint-Simon and Proust', *Publications of the Modern Language Association* 46: 608-618, 1931.

Cattaui, Georges: 'Proust après trente ans', *Critique*, I, March, 1954; II, November 1954; III, December 1954.

— 'L'œuvre de Proust', *Critique*, March 1958.

Chaix-Ruy: 'Les thèmes d'*A la Recherche du Temps Perdu* dans le roman autobiographique de Marcel Proust: *Jean Santeuil*', *Synthèses*, August-Septembre 1953.

Etiemble, René: 'Le Style de Marcel Proust', *Les Temps Modernes* 2, No. 20, pp. 1488-1496, 1947.

Fallois, Bernard de: 'Le Roman inédit de Marcel Proust, *Jean Santeuil*', *Opéra*, 26 septembre 1951.

Ferré, André: 'Etat des études proustiennes', *L'Ecole Littéraire*, 13 March, 1953.

Garver, M.: 'A Bibliographical note on Proust', *Modern Language Notes 47*, pp. 176-179, 1932.

Gide, André: 'Billet à Angèle', *Nouvelle Revue Française*, 16, pp. 586-591, 1921.

Hodson, W.L.: 'Proust's methods of Character Presentation in *Les Plaisirs et les Jours*, and *Jean Santeuil*', *Modern Language Review*, January 1962, pp. 41-46.

Houston, J.P.: 'Temporal Patterns in *A la Recherche du Temps Perdu*', *French Studies* XVI, No. 1, pp. 33-44, 1962.

Ironside, R.: 'The Artistic Vision of Proust', *Horizon* IV, No. 19, 1941, pp. 28-42.

Jackson, Elizabeth R.: 'The Genesis of the involuntary memory in Proust's early works', *Publications of the Modern Language Association*, December 1961.

Johannet, René: 'Les Prédécesseurs de Proust', *Revue universelle* 22, pp. 487-491, 1925.

Jones, Stanley: 'Two unknown articles by Marcel Proust', *French Studies* 4, 239,251, 1950.

Kanters, R.: 'Le petit et le grand œuvre de Proust', *Gazette des Lettres*, 15 July 1952.

Kneller, John: 'The Musical Structure of Proust's *Swann*', *Yale French Studies* II, No. 2, pp. 55-62, 1949.

Kolb, Philip: 'An unknown critical Item by Proust', *French Studies* 24, pp. 105-110, December 1950.
— 'Inadvertent Repetitions of material in *A la Recherche du Temps Perdu*', *Publications of the Modern Language Association 51*, No. 1, March 1936.

Le Bidois: 'Le Langage parlé de Proust,' *France Moderne*, 1939.

Lynes, C.: 'Proust and Albertine on the limits of Autobiography and of psychological truth in the novel', *Journal of Ethics and Art Criticism*, 1952.

Madaule, J.: 'Marcel Proust et le drame de la vocation poétique', *Age Nouvelle*, 22, pp. 9-16, 1947.

March, Harold: 'The Artist as Seer' Notes on the Esthetic Vision *Yale French Studies*, 2, pp. 44-54.

Martin-Chauffier, Louis: 'Le côté de Guermantes par Marcel Proust', *Nouvelle Revue Française*, XVI, pp. 204-208, 1921.
— 'Proust and the Double I', *Partisan Review*, October 1949, pp. 1011-1026.

Mauriac, Claude.: 'Jean Santeuil et Marcel Proust', *La Table Ronde*, August 1952.

Maurois, André: 'Les Esquisses des maîtres', *Les Nouvelles Littéraires*, 25 October 1951.

Nadeau: 'Proust contre Sainte-Beuve', *Les Lettres Françaises*, November 1954.

O'Brien, Justin: 'La Mémoire involontaire avant Marcel Proust', *Revue de Littérature comparée* 19, pp. 19-36, January 1939.
— 'The wisdom of the young Proust', *Romanic Review*, April 1954.

Pascal, Roy: Tense and Novel, article based on Dr. Kate Hamburger's 'Die Logik der Dichtung', *Modern Language Review*, 57, No. 1, pp. 1-11, january 1962.

Pommier, Jean: 'Marcel Proust et Sainte-Beuve', *Revue d'Histoire littéraire de la France*, Oct.-Dec. 1954.

Rambaud, Henri: 'Le Premier Livre de Marcel Proust', *Revue universelle* 19, pp. 232-237, October 15, 1924.

Rhodes, S.A.: 'The Guermantes Fêtes in *Le Temps Retrouvé*', *Philological Quarterly* 17, 1932.

Rivières, Jacques: 'Marcel Proust et la tradition classique', *Nouvelle Revue Française*, 7, pp. 192-200, Feb. 1st, 1920.

Rousset, J.: 'Notes sur la structure d'*A la Recherche du Temps Perdu*', *Revue des sciences humaines*, July-September 1955.

Saint-Jean, R. de: 'Quelques livres sur Proust', *Revue Hebdomadaire*, II, pp. 231-238, 1929.

Souza, Sybil de: 'The rôle of Odette de Crécy in *A la Recherche du Temps Perdu*', *The Windmill*, II, No. 5, 1946, pp. 103-110.

Thibaudet, Albert: 'Marcel Proust and the analytical novel', *The London Mercury*, IV, 1920.

Vigneron, Robert: 'Genèse de *Swann*', *Revue d'histoire de la Philosophie et d'histoire de la Civilisation*, 15 January 1937, pp. 67-115.

— 'Marcel Proust ou l'angoisse créatrice', *Modern Philology*, XLII, No. 4, May 1945, pp. 212-230.

— 'Structure de *Swann*: Balzac, Wagner et Proust', *The French Review*, 19, No. 6, May 1946, pp. 370-384.

— 'Structure de *Swann*: prétentions et défaillances', *Modern Philology*, 44, No. 2, November 1946, pp. 102-128.

— 'Structude de *Swann*: Combray ou le cercle parfait', *Modern Philology*, 45, No. 3, February 1948, pp. 185-207.

INDEX

ACHEVÉ D'IMPRIMER

AUX « PRESSES DE SAVOIE », AMBILLY-ANNEMASSE (H.-S.),

EN MARS 1965.

174

192 3 1238

in a row. Gertie Millar, a talented former mill girl (her first husband composed the songs for *Our Miss Gibbs*) became Countess of Dudley. "Ella Gray" might not be destined to become the next Sarah Bernhardt or Ellen Terry, but she could still look beyond the limited options of a touring chorus girl.

IN 1977, WHEN Jean Rhys was old and famous, she asked a new friend, a respected young actor, to make up her face with grease paint. Peter Eyre did his best. Rhys, elegantly dressed and sipping a martini, watched him closely in the mirror. There was no small talk. She simply observed. And then, so Eyre recalls, she just as simply asked him to depart. "I left her there alone, staring at herself in the mirror. And honestly, I still don't have a clue what it was all about."[7]

Perhaps, contemplating her rouged lips and cheeks through the eyes of the newcomer to the stage that she had once been, Rhys was wondering at her stamina in having survived those early years on tour. Perhaps she was remembering the noisy camaraderie and saucy jokes that brightened life in the restricted number of provincial lodging houses open to touring actors, often regarded as both immoral and unreliable payers of their bills. Was she recalling a chivalrously paternal old admirer called Colonel Mainwaring who had carried her off for a countryside tour in his clanking prewar motor car? Or might a frail old woman have been remembering an incident—one which she included in *Smile Please*'s light-hearted account of her years on tour—when she and a dancer pal leaped out of a bedroom window into a snowdrift and ran away from their lodgings, to escape paying an overcharged bill?

Like Colette, of whose 1910 novel about life on stage, *The Vagabond*, she would later become an ardent admirer, Rhys often conflated fact and fiction. In *Smile Please*, Rhys denied that reading formed any significant part of her life as a chorus girl. "I never felt the least desire to read anything . . . I think this indifference lasted a long time."[8] Reminiscing to her daughter, however, Rhys recalled in 1959 that the best part of a drizzly afternoon on tour was to curl up with a book: "There is always a fog or mist, so that warmth and a book indoors are heaven. All this was long ago when I was young and tough."[9]

Rhys was a well-read woman, but she took peculiar care to conceal it. Writing her memoir, she would insist that she and the other chorus girls had spent their spare time reading one book, and one book only: *The Forest Lovers*. A hasty reader of *Smile Please* might assume that she was referring to an Edwardian page-turner of the frothiest sort.

Written by Maurice Hewlett, *The Forest Lovers* was nothing of the kind. A long, earnest and faintly ghoulish pastiche of a medieval romance, Hewlett's novel follows the woodland adventures of Prosper le Gai who, having rescued a country maiden from being hanged as a witch by the simple act of marrying her, compels the unfortunate Isolt to earn his love by undergoing endless acts of submission. Her acquiescence borders on masochism. Was Rhys making sly use of Hewlett's fiction to revisit Mr. Howard's abusive games of submission, out in Roseau, or did she feel some troubled affinity to Hewlett's compliant heroine? Impossible though it is to guess why Rhys singled out this justly forgotten novel for mention in her memoir, we shouldn't assume that *The Forest Lovers* was the only work she devoured during those drizzly afternoons on tour, when losing herself in a book was "heaven."

Our Miss Gibbs was not a production that demanded a great deal from its chorus. Lionel Monckton's songs were beguiling; the dance steps were uncomplicated. Gwen enjoyed the chance to experiment with make-up; the exquisite dresses and spectacular hats for which the production was celebrated confirmed her lifelong love affair with millinery and pretty clothes. In *Smile Please*, Rhys would write that the other young actresses had disliked her and that the wardrobe mistress hated her. The jokes and banter that she had evoked over forty years earlier in *Voyage in the Dark* suggest otherwise. Reminiscing to a theatre-loving friend in the 1960s, a septuagenarian Rhys could still warble a cockney ditty from Ella Gray's backstage days. It doesn't sound plaintive.

'E doesn't wear a collar
Or a shirt all white
'E wears a tidy muffler
And 'e looks all right
'E pays his little tanner
In the gallery with Anna.[10]

Ella—as the nineteen-year-old Rhys now became known to all her new friends—had been lucky to join Sir George Dance's second touring company in July, at a time when *Our Miss Gibbs* was about to start visiting seaside towns along England's sunny south coast. Ella's summers, always the jolliest season for the hardworking chorus girls, were followed by a retreat to Clarice's cottage at St. Asaph—or else to "The Cats Home," a dingy London hostel for actresses who were short of cash—until the onset of the gruelling winter tour. Oldham; Leeds; Manchester; Southport; Newcastle (where Ella, like Anna Morgan in *Voyage*, got sick with pleurisy and had to be left behind for a grim three weeks): Rhys had good reason never to return to the north of England after visiting Leeds and Newcastle with *Our Miss Gibbs*. She liked the company of the funny, tough-talking girls whose life she shared. She grew tired of wearing handed-down dresses and of being treated as a second-class citizen: in short, as a chorus girl acting in the provinces. The touring chorus was where Rhys began; apart from a moment of relative glory, when she played one of three bold Irish colleens who briefly share centre-stage with Miss Mary Gibbs and her suitor, Lord Eynsford, the chorus was where she would remain.

Why did she carry on? An abundance of youthful optimism was the answer that Rhys would offer in her memoir: "Going from room to room in this cold dark country, I never knew what it was that spurred me on and gave me an absolute certainty that there would be something else before long . . . I was so sure."[11]

A more prosaic reason for persisting with her chorus work was the sudden death of Dr. Rees Williams, her adored father, in the summer of 1910. Bereft of his presence in Dominica, Rhys had no incentive to return home and no hope of receiving help from a destitute and suddenly isolated widow who still had a fifteen-year-old daughter on her hands. Owen had left the island in disgrace after the revelation of his second family (by a young woman who worked at the Amelia estate); Edward was travelling the world as an army medical officer. In England, a conspicuously unsuccessful young chorus girl now stood alone, helped only by an occasional handout from her kindly aunt in Wales. Uncle Neville, up in Yorkshire, had already made his disapproval of her life plain by severing all connection to his niece.

Tenacity was a quality that would always enable Jean Rhys to survive. What she never admitted in her memoir was how hard she had to struggle to stay afloat during those early years. Unable to afford time off after her second summer season with *Our Miss Gibbs*, Ella Gray snagged herself a walk-on role in a London pantomime before reluctantly applying to join a music-hall company touring the north through the dead of winter. Her role marked a new low in Rhys's short-lived career on stage. For a sketch designed to entertain an undemanding audience, a comic twist had been added to *Chantecler*, a respected French play by Edmond de Rostand. "Chantecler or High Cockalorum: a Feathered Fantasy in Three Fits" required the feather-costumed actresses to imitate hens. Audiences from northern England's coalpits and steelworks proved unappreciative; pretending to lay an egg onstage troubled Rhys less than the thump of clogs as dissatisfied gallery-goers headed for the exit. With unfortunate timing, one mortified "hen" turned tail and pattered off stage on the night that the show's manager was monitoring the performance. Sacked on the spot and despatched to London on the early morning train, a chastened Ella was taken in by the only member of the Rees Williams family who still had a genuinely soft spot for her: Clarice.

The future at that moment, early in 1911, must have appeared peculiarly grim. The contract with Blackmore's ensured that Miss Gray could, if she so wished, continue dancing in a travelling show for another twenty years. The option wasn't a tempting one. Desperate

Rhys identified this image of herself (*right*) in her touring days of the ill-fated *Chanteclair* production, but the pretty hats are more likely to have been worn for *Our Miss Gibbs*, a musical celebrated for gorgeous millinery, rather than for a sketch in which the chorus girls were dressed as hens. (*McFarlin*)

to avoid another brutal season of touring (one late story, "Before the Deluge," mentions the unfortunate chorus girls being shipped off to Cork on a cattle boat), Rhys jumped at the possibility of filling a tiny spot in the London chorus of Franz Lehár's charming new operetta, *The Count of Luxembourg*. Daisie Irving, a beautiful new friend who was standing in for the play's star (the dazzling Lily Elsie had been taken ill, according to Rhys's story), was willing to give the play's director a gentle nudge.

The part was hers. Rhys's appearance in *The Count of Luxembourg* marked the climax of her stage career. On the opening night in May 1911, Lehár himself was conducting the orchestra at Daly's Theatre, and King George V and Queen Mary were watching from the royal box.

Seated below them in the stalls was a forty-year-old bachelor, a highly successful stockbroker whose well-connected father had recently been appointed Governor of the Bank of England. His name was Lancelot Hugh Smith.

4

Fact and Fiction:
A London Life (1911–13)

"He was a dream come true for me and one doesn't question dreams, or envy them."

—Jean Rhys, "The Interval," *Smile Please* (1979)

RHYS'S FIRST LOVER was named after one of England's best-known eighteenth-century landscape designers. Lancelot "Capability" Brown had laid out the gardens at Mount Clare, the handsome house at Roehampton in which Lancelot, third son of the Hugh Smiths, was born in 1870.

Lancelot (always "Lancey" to his colleagues and clients), had grown up in a world of order and great wealth. The closest friends of his parents were the Hambros and Junius Morgan, father of the legendary John Pierpont Morgan himself. The Hugh Smiths were connected to the Martin Smiths, the Ridley Smiths and the Abel Smiths: all were members of a quietly powerful clan that helped to control, and even to dictate, Britain's finances. Theirs was a world of cool discretion in which a gentleman's returned cheque—as with Christopher Tietjens in Ford Madox Ford's *Parade's End*—could immediately destroy his reputation. So might a misjudged marriage.

Writing her unpublished recollections of a flawlessly dull life, Lancey's mother Constance (Lady Hugh Smith) identified only one outsider

"Lancey" Hugh Smith photographed with his dog at a sports event a few years before he met Rhys. *(Used with permission of the Smith family)*

in the cosily integrated world of Surrey bankers who ranked among her family's closest friends. Grove House—it adjoined Mount Clare— belonged to the widow of Mr. Lyne Stephens, a banker who had left the whole of his fortune to his wife. Her enormous inheritance included a manor house in Norfolk, a magnificent home in Paris and a collection of art fine enough to rival those of the Wallace and the Frick. The reason that nobody called upon the wealthy little widow was simply this: the former Yolande Duvernoy had once been a dancer. Occasionally, the Hugh Smith children skated—with the lonely old lady's permission—upon her garden pond; breaking the strict code of ostracism upheld by Roehampton's banking matrons in order to express her gratitude, Constance thought she had never encountered a woman with a sadder face than Yolande Lyne Stephens. Her funeral, which Lady Hugh Smith described from hearsay, was singularly modest: nobody of consequence had attended.[1]

Lancey was obsessed by Mount Clare (of which he would eventually become the proud custodian) and by social position. The awful consequences of Mr. Lyne Stephens's imprudent alliance were still in his

mind when, as a middle-aged and cautious man of the world, he began
his own discreet courtship of a chorus girl.

———————

DISCRETION WAS ESSENTIAL to a man with powerful clients; we need
not wonder why Lancey himself preserved no trace of an imprudent
love affair. Rhys destroyed everything except for a couple of affectionate notes despatched from the Bishopsgate office of Rowe & Pitman,
the stockbroking firm which twenty-six-year-old Lancey had joined
in 1895. Shrewdly, Rhys's first biographer Carole Angier connected
Mr. Hugh Smith to "Neil James," the affable former lover to whom
the perennially hard-up Julia Martin knows she can always resort for
a handout in Rhys's second novel, *After Leaving Mr Mackenzie* (1931).
While drawing more deeply upon memories of her first love affair for
Voyage in the Dark (1934), Rhys would remain carefully circumspect.
It was never her intention that Lancey's grand friends should identify
him as Walter Jeffries, the mildly seedy protector of Anna Morgan,
an innocent young woman who ends by sleeping with men for money.

Rhys's realistic description of Jeffries has nevertheless provided her
biographers and critics with a convincing story line. Reading *Voyage* as
autobiography, a reader can easily assume that the novelist herself had
first encountered a mildly sleazy financier while taking a day off from
performing at the King's Theatre in the summer of 1911, to stroll along
the promenade at jolly, raffish Southsea (a seaside extension of the naval
town of Portsmouth). It's at Southsea that an admiring Walter Jeffries
treats Anna Morgan to some cotton stockings before making his first
attempt to seduce her in a London brothel masquerading as a plush-
mantled restaurant. But Rhys flags up the contrast between Anna and
Emile Zola's worldly Nana on the first page. Nana is at ease in such
places. Anna—her name is a deliberately unsubtle anagram—is not.
And neither was Rhys. Restaurants of the kind described in *Voyage in
the Dark* had almost vanished from view by 1911, the year in which
the twenty-one-year-old Jean, still known to all her friends as Ella,
embarked on her first serious love affair.

Walter's encounter with Anna is a biographical red herring. A more convincing start to Rhys's own liaison emerges from "Before the Deluge," a short story that Jean only began to write many years after her lover's death. Rhys's stories contain far more autobiographical detail than her novels. Here, quite casually, the narrator lets drop the fact that her friend Daisie Irving often swept her off to the smart supper parties at which admirers feted the pretty stand-in star of *The Count of Luxembourg*. Rhys's official role was to carry Daisie's armful of bouquets, but she was also a welcome guest at the dinners held in Daisie's honour. Snobbish, conventional Lancey would neither have slummed it at Southsea, nor gone shopping for ladies' stockings. He certainly wouldn't have objected to escorting the star of a musical that had received the royal seal of approval at its premiere to a supper at Romano's or the Savoy, chaperoned by Daisie's pretty attendant.

As with Anna Morgan at Walter's "Green Street" home, it was probably in the bedroom of Lancey's Mayfair home at 30 Charles Street (now part of the Saudi Embassy) that Jean Rhys lost her virginity. Penniless, and with no home of her own, she had little option but to become a fond and generous man's kept mistress. ("He had money. I had none," she would bluntly explain, many years later, in *Smile Please*.) Settled by her lover into pleasant lodgings close to Primrose Hill, a lavish dress allowance enabled Lancey's pretty "kitten"—as he liked to call her—to dress in style for elegant suppers out. "I was for sleeping with—not for talking to," Julia Martin dryly remarks of her past affair with Neil James; Rhys herself remembered Lancey asking with genuine interest about her early life in the West Indies and (quite uselessly) attempting to act as her financial advisor. Bewitched by his courtesy and kindness ("He was like all the men in all the books I had ever read about London," she recollected in *Smile Please*[2]), Rhys saw nothing humiliating about the fact that she was never allowed to spend a night at Lancey's bachelor home, or to visit Mount Clare. "I was never envious," she would write with touching defensiveness in her memoir. "It was right, I felt."[3]

Voyage in the Dark offered readers a carefully misleading account of its author's first encounter with Lancey. Nevertheless, discreet though Rhys would always try to be for the sake of a shy, proud man to whom she remained enduringly attached, fictionalised accounts of actual events do appear within *Voyage*. It's here that we read of a romantic weekend for four spent at a hotel in Wiltshire's glorious Savernake Forest; remembering that escapade with Lancey and two friends (the tall green trees had reminded her of Dominica), the older Rhys would often reminisce to friends about the beauty of Savernake's glades and valleys.

Rhys's personal memories of the jaunt may have been pleasant. She kept until the end of her life a long, high-necked and clinging flower-printed dress that is fondly identified in *Voyage* as Anna Morgan's chosen costume for her first evening at the hotel. But the novel also makes the hotel at Savernake the place in which Walter Jeffries casually reveals that he and his young cousin Vincent will shortly be off to New York on a business trip. Vincent, rather than Walter, brutally advises a shocked Anna to start making plans for a life alone. "The new show at Daly's," he tells her in a slyly hidden authorial reference to the very theatre where Lancey had first seen Rhys dancing in *The Count of Luxembourg*. "You ought to be able to warble like what's her name after all those singing lessons."[4]

Whether or not the actual break-up began during a Wiltshire weekend, there's no doubt that Rhys based her portrait of Vincent on the only member of Lancey's family who knew about his affair. Julian Martin Smith, Lancey's handsome eighteen-year-old cousin and favourite protégé, was perceived by Rhys as her nemesis. Lancey, she would always persuade herself, had truly loved her. As the product of a rigidly conservative colonial world, she may for a time have aspired no higher than marriage to her wealthy and generous protector; a man of whose grand family home she had not been permitted so much as a glimpse. She would always believe that it was Julian—the look in Vincent's eyes is compared by a dispirited Anna Morgan to "a high, smooth, unclimbable wall. No communication possible"—who had destroyed their love affair.

Julian Martin Smith, Lancey's cousin and protégé. Rhys put the young stockbroker in *Voyage in the Dark* as Vincent. *(Used with permission of the Smith family)*

While it's unlikely that Lancelot Hugh Smith ever considered marrying Rhys—he remained a bachelor until his death—it's clear that he did recruit Julian Martin Smith as his broker and spokesman during the delicate process of disentanglement. Writing *Smile Please* decades after both Lancey and his young cousin were dead, Rhys described the condescending visits that Julian (whom she identified in print, but only by his first name) had made as Lancey's proxy. The sense of barely suppressed rage is almost palpable in Rhys's description of Julian's demanding the return of her lover's letters and smoothly producing in exchange the cash for an abortion (described in her memoir as "an illegal operation") to which she had already declared her opposition.

The rules of severance had always been explicit. When a Marylebone landlady ordered Miss Ella Gray to leave the elegant suite of rooms that Lancey had recently taken on her behalf—abortions were bad for business—Rhys obediently posted her forwarding address, not to the baby's father, but to Julian Martin Smith (who thoughtfully arranged a quiet seaside holiday at Ramsgate as a reward for her compliance). When a letter arrived to explain that she could rely upon a monthly stipend, a cheque payable via a solicitor's office, Lancey presented it as a joint decision, taken by Julian and himself. " 'We thought that perhaps this was the best way . . . (I thought: '*we*—yes, I thought so.')"[5] Explaining to readers of her memoir why she had accepted the pay-off, the elderly Rhys justified the continued allowance as a symbolic bond: "The man still cared what became of me and the bond was still there."[6] Tellingly, when she came to write *After Leaving Mr Mackenzie*, Jean Rhys named the least empathetic of her female protagonists "Julia Martin." Reading his former girlfriend's novel, as we can confidently assume that he did, Lancey must have winced at the memories revived by her bold hijacking of his adored young cousin's name.[*]

"I KNOW HOW ghastly it is to be stranded when you're young," Rhys would write to a woman friend in 1950.[7] In *Smile Please*, Rhys described herself as withdrawing from the world during the autumn weeks that followed her abortion and seaside recuperation. She went for long, solitary walks, neglected her appearance and slept for fifteen hours at a time. Solitude and sleep; sleep and solitude. "I am talking," Rhys wrote in the section of her memoir called "Christmas Day," "about sadness." Anna, in *Voyage*, falls swiftly into prostitution after Walter Jeffries rejects her final, desperate overture. All Rhys herself could remember having done during those bleak months was to earn some money as a movie extra: girls deemed to be pretty were always welcome for crowd scenes in the early years of film-making.

Lancey, who still took his desolate girlfriend out to an occasional supper, at which he talked and she cried, sent along a miniature star-crowned tree for his Christmas gift at the end of the affair, laden with prettily wrapped trinkets and accompanied by an unsigned card. The reminder of happier times brought no comfort; after donating it to the Children's Hospital on Great Ormond Street, Rhys sat alone in her room, pondering whether life was still worth living. Later, Jean Rhys would claim that she only once made a serious attempt to kill herself, by slitting her wrists in a warm bath. On this earlier occasion, accord-

---

[*] Lancey's interest in the development of his former girlfriend's career as a writer appears in two notes that Rhys preserved from 1927.

ing to *Smile Please*, one of the unhappy young woman's film-extra girl-friends, an artist's model, turned up in time to stop her jumping out of a window and to suggest—over a shared bottle of gin—the possibility of making a new start. Why stay in and mope when she could be out having fun in rackety, sociable Chelsea?

Not every detail of Jean Rhys's early life made its way into either her memoir or her fiction. *Voyage in the Dark* invites us to see her as having followed Anna Morgan's tragic course, sliding down the ladder of despair—from being Walter Jeffries' mistress, to a job as a hope-lessly inept manicurist, before Anna finally sleepwalks into prostitu-tion. *Smile Please*, in contrast, moves straight from the sad little episode on Christmas Day 1911 to Rhys's discovery of herself as a writer, while leading a solitary life in Chelsea. Neither version offers an accurate portrait.

It seems to have been around the beginning of 1912 that an enter-prising Rhys tried her hand at manufacturing cold cream in her lodgings, before she took a job selling the pretty hats made by a deft-fingered girlfriend (identified only as Dawn). According to the story told by Rhys to her daughter almost forty years later, Dawn dispensed with her assistance after finding that her partner, instead of pushing the sale of their most expensive hats, was sweetly encouraging clients to buy only what they could easily afford.[8]

More significant, and more than a little puzzling, is the absence from any of Rhys's accounts of the fascinatingly odd man who befriended her during the year 1912. His memorable name was Arthur Fox Strangways.

Born in 1859, "Foxie," as a sensitive and intensely musical man was always known to his friends, was old enough to have been Rhys's father, and it was as a paternal figure that Rhys adored him. A respected public-school teacher at Wellington during the first half of his life, Fox Strangways retired early, after suffering a breakdown. Following a year in India, during which he became close to the Bengal-born poet Rabindranath Tagore, he returned to London late in 1911 and settled into a bachelor flat on King's Bench Walk in the Temple, just north of Blackfriars Bridge. When Rhys met him in 1912, Strangways had become a respected music critic, writing both for the *Musical Times* and the *Observer*, while acting as Tagore's representative in London.

Rhys's first biographer Carole Angier has speculated that the nymph-like "Ella" became Fox Strangways' mistress.[9] More plausibly, at a time when Rhys was still bruised and miserable about the end of her affair with Lancey, this touchingly old-fashioned Englishman offered the reassurance of a cultured and unthreatening friendship.

Questioned a little patronisingly in later years about her fondness for popular songs, Rhys murmured that she was "not quite indifferent to better things."[10] Stravinsky and Nijinsky were electrifying London audiences during the prewar years; Rhys's enduringly romantic taste suggests that Strangways took his young friend to hear the less revolutionary music that was usually on offer at the drab but acoustically superb Queen's Hall in Langham Place, first home of the Proms. As a man who counted George Moore among his close friends, "Foxie" may also have introduced an avid bookworm to one singularly bleak novel for which Rhys formed an abiding passion. Published in 1894, Moore's *Esther Waters* was years ahead of its time, with its story of a hard-working woman who bravely decides to keep her baby after an accidental pregnancy. Was Rhys's initial admiration for Esther connected to her own regretted abortion, or was it Esther's quiet courage which she always found so sustaining? In her old age, Rhys told friends that she could no longer recall how many times she had reread Moore's book.

───────────

DIANA ATHILL, THE editor whose difficult task was to chivvy along the memoir that Jean Rhys produced with painful slowness in her final years, thought the chapter of *Smile Please* set on the fringes of Chelsea and titled "World's End and a Beginning" was a triumph. So it is, if we are seeking only to know when Rhys felt herself ready to become a writer.

It was on the very first day that she moved into lodgings in Fulham, according to *Smile Please*, that Jean Rhys (still Ella to her London friends) set off to explore the neighbourhood and find a plant to brighten the work table in her room. Walking into a stationer's shop on the nearby King's Road, she impulsively purchased some thick exercise books, a handful of brightly coloured pens and nibs ("the sort I liked") and took them home. Following her habitual modest supper of bread, cheese and a glass of milk, Rhys felt a curious tingling in her fingers. "I remembered everything that happened to me in the last year and a half. I remembered what he'd said, what I'd felt. I wrote on late into the night . . ." After filling almost four exercise books, she set down a single, striking sentence that would later surface in the voice of Anna Morgan: "Oh God, I'm only twenty and I'll have to go on living and living and living."[11] Rhys herself, at the opening of 1913, was twenty-two.

There is no reason to doubt that this vividly described experience was largely true, as was the unanticipated sense of emotional release. (Rhys recalled that the irate lodger downstairs threatened to hand in his notice because of the sobs and laughs and pacing feet as she herself scribbled on late into the night, unconscious of the passing days.) But this discovery of a vocation was not all that occurred during Ella's stay in Chelsea. A glimpse of her lively social existence there emerges from the unpublished memoir written by the artist Adrian Allinson (and lodged at the McFarlin Library, together with Rhys's archive). In "A Painter's Pilgrimage," Allinson describes how he met "Ella, a fair young Englishwoman born in the West Indies" at a Chelsea studio party, and how affected he immediately felt by her "tender loveliness."

Chelsea, just before the outbreak of war, offered a headily adventurous experience to a young, single woman. The annual Chelsea Arts Ball, raising funds for artists' charities, was a famously riotous affair. Women were welcome at the Arts Club on Old Church Street, while a mass of new cinemas had recently opened, including two "Electric Theatres" and a "Palace of Varieties" on the King's Road. One of Allinson's fellow artists shot his young mistress in the Chelsea room they shared.

Life in Chelsea was unpredictable. Fresh from Adelaide and comfortably supported by a family allowance, Stella Bowen was startled to find herself living in a Chelsea flat where a late partygoer might casually scramble through her bedroom window at 3 a.m., having missed a late train to the suburbs. Stella soon settled in, teaching a nimble-footed Ezra Pound new dance steps and attending his weekly dinner club in Soho, while taking occasional lessons from Walter Sickert at the Westminster School of Art, chief rival to the Slade.[12] Nina Hamnett, renting her first Chelsea studio in 1911 when she was just twenty-one, would fondly recall a young Mark Gertler bringing to tea a golden-thatched Dora Carrington, wearing one red shoe and one blue; it felt, Hamnett reminisced, "as if I had invited a god and goddess . . . I preserved Gertler's tea-cup intact and unwashed on the mantlepiece."[13] A little later, Nina fell in love with Henri Gaudier-Brzeska—and wept after discovering that the fierce young woman who shared the French sculptor's penurious life in a Fulham Road studio was not his sister, but his mistress.

Sickert; Yeats; Epstein; Pound; Wyndham Lewis and even the theatrically creepy Aleister Crowley; these are the names that ripple through the pages of Hamnett and Bowen's recollections of prewar life in Chelsea and Fitzrovia (as the most consciously artistic quarter of Bloomsbury became known). This was the remarkable world into which Jean Rhys ventured in 1913. Adrian Allinson's recollection of meeting her at a studio party in Chelsea suggests that a shy and uncommonly beautiful young woman soon ceased to be an outsider.

Generous though Hugh Smith's monthly allowance proved to be, extra funds could always be raised by modelling for artists. Unfazed by posing nude for a "classical" work if no strings were attached, Rhys gladly agreed to model for the elderly and eminently respectable Sir Edward Poynter. Later, Rhys drew upon personal memories of her modelling work for the immensely successful and sexually unscrupulous Sir William Orpen when she wrote (in an early, unpublished work called "Suzy Tells" and then, "Triple Sec") about a flirtatious society artist whom she named "Tommie." After Tommie ardently embraces his alluring new model in a taxi, the narrator asks for money. Relieved by the modesty of the requested sum, Tommie obliges—and promptly resumes the attack. Ordered to stop, he withdraws. "I know now that I have a certain power," the narrator remarks, "and yet, how mean, how mean."

Was Rhys conveying outrage at an attempted rape in this early and unpublished work of fiction? With Jean Rhys—who would one day describe Mr. Howard as having recognised and responded to the secret fantasies of an adolescent girl's wicked self, in the Botanical Gardens of Roseau—it's impossible ever to be certain precisely where the blame is being laid.

5

London in Wartime (1913–19)

"I'm hanged if I didn't fall in love with her."

—Adrian Allinson, "A Painter's Pilgrimage"[1]

"I pulled a chair up to the table, opened an exercise book, and wrote: *This is my Diary*. But it wasn't a diary . . ."

—Jean Rhys, "World's End and a Beginning," *Smile Please*

NO EARLIER DRAFTS or manuscripts survive to contradict Jean Rhys's assertion in *Smile Please* that she first began writing seriously during her prewar life in Chelsea. Although she doesn't say what happened next, it is clear that these early writings continued through the war and that they were later cobbled together as the episodic, unpublished work named "Triple Sec" by Rhys's first literary patron after the dry, crystal-clear and unexpectedly potent French liqueur.

"Triple Sec," previously dubbed "Suzy Tells" by another of Rhys's literary mentors, is narrated by a young woman. While the tough but vulnerable Suzy speaks for her creator, certain true-life experiences that she undergoes have been embellished and rearranged to produce a fictitious outcome. "Triple Sec" cannot be treated as pure autobiography, but it does offer some helpful clues about Rhys's personal life before and during the war.

THE YEAR 1913 had been a testing time for Rhys, crushed by the sense, aged twenty-three, that she had failed in both her stage career, and in love. In April 1914, however, her life grew brighter after a clever and party-loving political journalist called Alan Bott (he later helped to create the Folio Society and Pan Books) enrolled his new friend as member of a private nightclub that had recently opened in Soho.

The Crabtree was founded as a congenial meeting place for his friends by the Welsh painter and draughtsman Augustus John, then at the height of his fame, and financed by John's affable and literary-minded patron, Lord Howard de Walden. Three rickety flights of stairs up from a narrow doorway on Greek Street, the little club was cheerily shabby. Stella Bowen, disapproving of the Crabtree's lack of formality (women wearing trousers, worryingly unmanly men and "*nobody* in evening dress!"), was equally unimpressed by its decor: "Beer marks on plain deal tables, wooden benches, and a small platform on which a moonfaced youth made music for a bevy of gyratory couples."[2] Informal boxing matches were sometimes held here; two good-looking singers of the time, Betty May and Lilliane Shelley, offered impromptu cabaret turns. On one occasion, a baffled Stella Bowen heard the futurist poet Marinetti orating one of his "zoom-bang" songs in Italian at the Crabtree; on another, one of the club's two rival crooners performed an early form of pole-dance by shinning up the wobbly fruit-topped post from which the club derived its name.

The Crabtree's scruffy furnishings were unimportant. Paul Nash, Henri Gaudier Brzeska, Wyndham Lewis, Nina Hamnett, Mark Gertler, Jacob Epstein, Marie Beerbohm, Henry Lamb, Compton Mackenzie: the list of its members reads like a guide to prewar bohemia. A crucial reason for the club's appeal to this youthful group was that basic food and hard liquor were cheap (an honesty box was provided by the door) and members could loiter until dawn—the Crabtree didn't even open its doors until midnight—to dance or to lounge and chat. In *After Leaving Mr Mackenzie*, Julia Martin and George Horsfield visit a club clearly based on the Crabtree. Julia settles in straight away and starts dancing with a stranger; sober George looks on, feeling awkwardly out of place.

Clubs were starting up all over London in an era when writers regularly lunched at Soho's accommodating Eiffel Tower (its sparsely furnished bedrooms were in great demand), while a skittish young Nina Hamnett swigged iced crème de menthe beneath the blind stare of the Café Royal's gilded caryatids. August Strindberg's widow presided over "The Cave of the Golden Calf" in a lavishly decorated basement near Piccadilly Circus, until it went bankrupt in 1914; Jean Rhys preferred the noisy little rooms high above Greek Street. I like to imagine seductive Ella whirling around the floor with my grandfather, the generous, art-loving peer whose deep pockets helped to keep that jolly little club afloat. More certainly, it was during an early visit to the Crabtree that the "tender loveliness" (Adrian Allinson's striking words) of Jean Rhys's appearance caught the eye of one of Alan Bott's fellow journalists.

Maxwell Hayes Macartney, an artist's son and the brother of a political historian, had trained as a lawyer, before switching professions to become a specialist on European affairs at *The Times*, where he worked alongside Bott. Ten years older than Rhys, Macartney was instantly smitten by the delicate features and wistful expression of a young woman who could imaginably have been painted by Botticelli. It was during a teatime feast in Macartney's rooms, where hot buttered toast and sponge cake were appreciatively consumed by a hungry visitor, that Rhys received an impulsive proposal of marriage. Acting from honour or reluctance, she discouraged her host with lurid tales of her life on stage and in Chelsea.* Despite his subsequent hesitation about setting a precise wedding date, Macartney persisted. An agreement to marry was reached, but theirs—so Rhys would nonchalantly comment in *Smile Please* (she never identified either Macartney or Hugh Smith by name)—would remain an "on-and-off" engagement.

Rhys was a little more forthcoming about Macartney (lightly disguised as "Ronald") in "Triple Sec." There, while describing the flat where she visits "Ronald" in the Temple, Rhys fused it with the

---

* "Triple Sec" includes a long confession by Suzy of her unworthiness to become "Ronald's" wife.

nearby home of Arthur "Foxie" Strangways. Located in an area popular with lawyers and conveniently close to Fleet Street for journalists, Macartney's Temple rooms were crammed with books, while signed photographs and informal sketches of Chesterton and Shaw hinted at illustrious friendships. Like the old-fashioned "Foxie," Macartney dressed in tweeds and washed his lean limbs in a tin hip-bath. Unlike Fox Strangways, he also played golf and expected to be cheered on by his sports-averse fiancée.

In July 1914, shortly after meeting her new beau, Miss Ella Gray returned to the stage, playing one of the besieged inhabitants of Renaissance Pisa in Maurice Maeterlinck's scandalous *Monna Vanna* (first performed in 1902). The source of outrage—and full houses—was a scene in which the playwright required Monna Vanna (played by a voluptuous Constance Collier in an all-concealing cloak) to appear naked onstage. A ban on evening performances—in case the mere thought of Collier's body beneath her strategic mantle might incite turmoil in the stalls of the Queen's Theatre—enabled Rhys to continue dancing and drinking long after midnight at the Crabtree. She was heading for the club with her fiancé on the night when they spotted, in Leicester Square, a news-stand poster announcing the assassination of an Austrian archduke at Sarajevo. The consequences of that disastrous event would sink in gradually, less when Macartney went out to France in November as a war correspondent ("Suzy" remembered sadly packing her fiancé's favourite tweed suit), than when Rhys's beloved Crabtree closed its doors in December 1914, "for the duration." We don't know if the news reached her, or whether she cared, that Lancey's adored young cousin Julian Martin Smith had been the first volunteer officer to die in action.

THE AGGRESSIVE LOYALTY to Britain and the Empire which Rhys displayed during the First World War suggests that she had always managed to maintain vestigial contact with her family in Dominica. Out in the Antilles, the belligerent jingoism of the white settlers was

infectious. Only a few stalwarts of the all-white Dominica Club sailed home to enlist; it came as a shock to the patriotic village youths who signed up to fight for king and country when they found themselves assigned to an all-black West Indian regiment in an army that had promised equality to every creed and colour within its enlisted ranks.*
In London, Rhys felt strongly enough about the war to declare that any man who failed to fight for England was a coward. Her views helped to influence Macartney's courageous exchange of his role as one of the war's most respected correspondents—like the fictitious "Suzy," Rhys conscientiously followed her lover's bulletins in *The Times*—for that of a middle-aged soldier at the front.

Macartney's flat felt cosily safe from the German zeppelins which began to launch raids on London in 1915. (Nina Hamnett, who once narrowly escaped stepping aboard a bus that was promptly blown to bits by a zeppelin bomb, later recalled a night when she tiptoed ankle-deep through shattered glass along the Strand to keep a date at the Café Royal.[3]) Perhaps Jean grew guilty about lolling among her fiancé's volumes of Chesterton and Wells while, outside the flat's rattling Georgian windows, the city was besieged. Still aged only twenty-four, she volunteered to work long daily shifts at an army canteen that had been set up at Euston Station, where soldiers travelling down from Scotland and the north made their connection to Charing Cross for the last leg of their journey to the Channel ports.

Lightly though Rhys dismissed her war work in *Smile Please*, her self-imposed assignment was a tough one. Organised by a couple of formidable army wives, the Euston canteen's soberly dressed female staff (gloves and neat black hats were mandatory) committed themselves to frying up plates of hearty food and offering encouragement to their soldier clients. By early 1915, at least 600 men were being shunted

---

* Most of the young islanders who enlisted were served up as cannon fodder. Dominica's most respected modern historian argues that it was the British Army's segregation of black recruits in the First World War which spawned the island's first move towards independence in the early 1930s (Dr. Lennox Honychurch to author, 15 February 2019).

through the station every day; on Platform 12, eighteen camp beds were kept ready for injured and disabled soldiers returning home. Anybody working at the canteen as Rhys did, for nine hours a day, over a period of almost two years, became a witness to the horrors of war.

MACARTNEY'S LONG ABSENCES in France enabled Jean to take a relaxed view of what might be expected of herself as a deserted fiancée, living under his roof. In the summer of 1915, she gladly accepted an invitation from the lovesick Adrian Allinson to come and spend a few off-duty weeks at a cottage in the Vale of Evesham, deep in the bucolic Gloucestershire countryside and close to Crickley Hill. Sweet though Allinson's personality was, and greatly though she admired the earnest young man's uncompromisingly realistic paintings (he had helped to found the London Group, after studying at the Slade alongside Gertler and Stanley Spencer and spending two years on the Continent), Rhys felt no sexual spark. It was the prospect of free hospitality and fresh country air which made Allinson's suggestion irresistible, together with the news that their companion at the cottage would be Philip Heseltine. She may not have expected a brilliant young man, better known for his poetry than his music at that stage of his life, to be accompanied by his beautiful girlfriend, an artist's model called Minnie Channing.

Tall, fair and athletic, with exceptionally blue eyes and a disturbing reputation for physical violence, Philip Heseltine came from a privileged background of wealth, as did Allinson, with whom he had gone on several mountaineering expeditions during their prewar months on the Continent. Rhys was uncertain what to make of him, but the forcefulness of Heseltine's personality made him impossible to ignore. On one well-attested occasion, after dinner, Heseltine suddenly stripped off his clothes, jumped onto his motorbike and roared off, stark naked, up a moonlit Crickley Hill. In the moments when he wasn't squabbling with Minnie (known as "Puma" for her fierce temper), he might either whistle plaintively as a curlew, or serenade his housemates with some melody from Frederick Delius, a British-born composer with a

The charismatic young composer Philip Heseltine, who later took the name Peter Warlock, photographed at the country cottage which he shared with Rhys and two friends in the summer of 1915.

German mother, whose reputation was unjustly clouded by the war. Heseltine worshipped Delius, whom he had first met personally during his schooldays at Eton, and who treated him as a pet protégé. While Allinson was earning a living in wartime by designing sets for Sir Thomas Beecham's opera company and doing sketches for the *Daily Express*, Heseltine had taken a five-month job in 1915 as a music critic for the warmongering *Daily Mail*, largely in order to promote the temporarily banned compositions of his hero.

The best-known account of what happened during Rhys's stay at the Gloucestershire cottage would eventually be published in 1960, in a story which had passed through many stages of careful revision. "Till September Petronella" mixes fact with fiction as bewilderingly as does the account of this same country holiday that Rhys had earlier described in the unpublished "Triple Sec." Only by comparing both of these versions of events with a third—the more artless account offered in Adrian Allinson's unpublished memoir, "A Painter's Pilgrimage"— can we glimpse what actually took place at the crowded cottage.

"A Painter's Pilgrimage" records a memorably unsatisfactory episode in Allinson's life from the point of view of a half-German artist, a sensitive and rather brilliant young man who shared his friend Heseltine's passionate hatred of war. Viewed with hindsight by Allinson, the holiday was doomed from the start. Heseltine and Minnie Channing formed an instant bond of dislike for Adrian's vociferously bellicose girlfriend; urged to pack her bags and take her beastly opinions back to London, "Ella" displayed what Allinson would describe as "a streak of hard determination oddly at variance with her outer frailty." When Philip and Minnie said they couldn't even bear to eat in her presence, his guest calmly retreated to her bedroom, where she seemed content to spend hours rubbing creams into her face, languidly combing her hair and—as always when left on her own—reading. The more that the couple attacked her, the more firmly Ella withdrew. When Allinson, still a virgin at 24, sought sexual favours in return for his own resolute loyalty, Ella coolly announced that she was tired—and closed her door.

"Triple Sec" is less trustworthy than "A Painter's Pilgrimage." The relationship with Allinson is coyly presented here in the format of "a semi demi love affair"; unlike Allinson's Ella, Rhys's "Suzy" walks out on her squabbling housemates. On the contentious issue of war, however, "Triple Sec" proves enlightening. Confident of the rightness of her views, Suzy becomes forthright and even rude. "Why aren't you at the war anyway?" she demands; a white-faced Forrester (unmistakably based upon Heseltine) leaves the room at once. Here, there is no doubt that Suzy's own aggression was the cause for the "instantaneous and violent" hostility to which she (like Rhys) has been exposed.

"Triple Sec" provided the embryo for one of Rhys's finest stories. Parts of "Till September Petronella" are fictitious. Allinson's offended girlfriend did not flee the cottage with the help of a sympathetic "Marston" (the name Rhys eventually picked for the Allinson figure in her published story). Philip Heseltine ("Julian Oakes" in "Till Septem-

ber Petronella") may not have mocked Rhys's voice as "a female pipe,"
but certain of Julian's cruel remarks do sound authentic: the vicious-
tongued Heseltine was entirely capable of having called Allinson's jin-
goistic girlfriend "a female spider" and even "a ghastly cross between a
barmaid and a chorus girl." In Rhys's version of the past, Julian Oakes's
hatred is fuelled by the suspicion that Petronella Gray is only interested
in his pal (described here by Rhys as one of England's finest young artists) because of Marston's wealth. While it's beyond proof that Heseltine expressed such a cynical view at the Crickley cottage, it's certainly
not beyond belief.

Rhys admired Heseltine's musical gift and—perhaps—his devotion
to Delius. "He *is* the great Julian," she allows Marston to say in defence
of his brilliant but volatile friend. "He's going to be very important, so
far as an English musician can be important." But those words were
written long after Heseltine, having renamed himself Peter Warlock
in mocking acknowledgement of his interest in diabolism, had taken
his life by gassing himself in 1930, aged only thirty-six. While Rhys's
story recognises Heseltine's musical artistry, it also honourably records
her absolute failure to please or impress him during the Crickley cottage holiday.

Returning to London from a disquieting month in the country, Rhys
gladly resumed her perch in Macartney's flat during his own continued
absence at the front. A restful home richly supplied with books offered
a welcome refuge after her long days at the Euston station canteen. Or
perhaps not: Julia, in *After Leaving Mr Mackenzie*, alludes to "the mad
things one did" during the war. If Rhys, too, did "mad things," she kept ·
them to herself.

———————

ASSIGNING DATES TO Rhys's wartime life is difficult. Circumstantial
evidence suggests that it was after the closure of the canteen in 1917
that "Ella Gray" contacted Blackmore's Agency once again, hoping for
work in the surprisingly active world of wartime theatre. Soon after
this, Rhys fell ill. Details are scant. "Triple Sec" refers only to "a slight

operation," but it was serious enough to require three weeks at a London nursing home (for which Lancey Hugh Smith, still paying Rhys a regular allowance, may have footed the bill), followed by a short recuperative holiday in the country.

Despite the fact that "Triple Sec" expressed gratitude to the sister of Maxwell Macartney for looking after her during this second, convalescent stage, it was at this vulnerable time that Rhys's fiancé broke off their engagement. "Suzy" describes "Ronald's" haggard appearance when he returned on leave. Macartney may have been shellshocked: the effect of exchanging work as a prominent war correspondent for life under fire must have been devastating to a man in his mid-thirties. Accused of bringing "numerous men friends" back to her fiancé's flat, Suzy is brusquely ordered to get out. (So far as is known, Rhys herself never saw Macartney again.) In "Triple Sec," a narcissistic Suzy describes the impact on her own fragile sensibility. "I'm one of the weak ones and I'll always be hurt," she states, and—a few lines later: "Lay thinking of nothing at all—just tired. Self confidence blown out like a candle."

Rhys herself always responded well in a crisis. While still recovering from her "slight operation," she moved into cheap lodgings in Bloomsbury before making a final attempt to relaunch her stalled stage career. Suzy's dance teacher (Madame Zara) is sufficiently pleased by her pupil's progress to predict a bright future in "acrobatic" ballet (a form of near-nude but tastefully static classical dancing not far removed from Emma Hamilton's notorious "attitudes"). Rhys herself was still taking ballet lessons when she found more conventional work as a sifter of war-related correspondence at the newly founded Ministry of Pensions.

How did an untrained former chorus girl obtain such a job? The answer probably lies with the well-connected Lancey Hugh Smith. Operating out of the Royal Hospital in Chelsea, the government's brand-new ministry had been put in charge of organising the payment of pensions to members of families affected by the war. More employees were urgently required; Rhys was a well-dressed and softly spoken young woman who may have arrived carrying a personal recommenda-

tion from the influential Mr. Hugh Smith. She made a welcome addition to the busy team of sixty women whose challenging daily task it
was to read and assess the sackfuls of heartrending appeals submitted
by maimed soldiers and destitute widows.

The work was both hard and bleak. Britain's new coalition government favoured a more egalitarian approach, but the system of which
Rhys now gained first-hand experience still consistently favoured the
privileged above the deserving. The size of a widow's pension was dictated by her husband's rank, as were the education grants grudgingly
doled out to his sons. In the navy, only the widow of an admiral was
eligible for a government handout. In the army, a soldier's death from
disease was shockingly and regularly blamed on personal "negligence":
no question of a pension for *his* widow. The family of a soldier released
because of a war injury qualified for a pension only after—and if—he
died within seven years of his resignation.[4]

Such disillusioning daily employment, combined with the shabby
way she felt she had been treated by Lancey and Macartney, ended
Rhys's colonial fantasy of an innocent England. She didn't move to a
cheap attic room in Torrington Square for safety—a zeppelin bomb
destroyed lives in neighbouring Endell Street—but because the double-
fronted Bloomsbury lodging house was packed with refugees from
abroad; aliens, like herself. The landlady ran a tight ship; rebuked (once
again) for an excessive use of the household's hot water supply for her
baths, a mortified Ella was defended by a friendly fellow lodger.

Rhys would write with unusual tenderness in the English section of
Smile Please about her chivalrous supporter. Camille (the only name by
which we know him) was a university-educated émigré from Bruges.
Little jokes about robbing the bank for which he worked as a cashier
in order to fund their elopement were light-hearted banter between
friends; Rhys knew how devoted the calm, bespectacled Belgian was
to the elderly wife who co-hosted their weekly "nursery teas," held
in a welcoming room filled with interesting people. Camille, in his
spare time, was writing a book about the Noh theatre of Japan. One
guest was an Icelandic poet; another was a dark, tousle-haired and fine-

featured young man whom Camille introduced as Jean Lenglet (pronounced "Leng-lett").

Camille identified his twenty-eight-year-old friend as Belgian; Lenglet, a man of mystery from the very start, described himself as Franco-
Dutch. Asked out to lunch, Ella decided that this intriguingly reticent
man with sensitive hands was both kind—he rebuked her for using the
chorus girl's cheap trick of drawing attention to a plainer woman in
order to highlight her own attractiveness—and generous: years later,
Rhys would fondly recall Lenglet's purchase of an expensive box of her
favourite Egyptian cigarettes, a large bottle of exotic scent and—at
her own special request—a glass pot of kohl with which to outline her
immense blue eyes. Escorted back to Torrington Square, or possibly to
a dance lesson with Madame Zara (he was sceptical about Ella's stage
future), she was baffled when Lenglet simply shook her hand and left.
Such sedate behaviour was unusual in wartime London. Lenglet's reticence greatly increased his allure.

Smile Please jumps straight from that memorable first date to Lenglet's proposal of marriage. Between times, Camille, Lenglet and Rhys
often spent their evenings drinking at the Café Royal. Here, the seemingly wealthy Lenglet talked about himself, but only on prescribed topics. He captivated francophile Ella with stories of running away from
his strict Jesuit school to become a teenage *chansonnier* in Montmartre;
he may have mentioned penning the occasional article about Montmartre for the Paris-based *New York Herald Tribune*. But his story of
leaving a family home in the Netherlands in order to join the French
Foreign Legion failed to disclose that he had served for just one month.
No explanation was offered for his presence in England; no mention
was made of the second wife, Marie Pollart—he had married her predecessor in Antwerp in order to legitimise a baby son—with whom
Lenglet lived in Paris until 1913, while sharing rooms with her widowed mother.

At the end of 1917, the landlady of Torrington Square invited her
lodgers to a fancy-dress party. A scraggy roasted fowl was served as a
suppertime treat. ("Don't laugh," kind Camille whispered to Ella as she

began to giggle: "she's awfully proud of having got that chicken."⁵) The star of the party was one Simone David, a young Frenchwoman whose large bedroom on the first floor was filled with pretty clothes and dashing hats.* Perhaps it was Simone who loaned her admiring friend the black-and-white Pierrette costume that Rhys remembered having worn that momentous night.

In her memoir, Rhys would relate the evening's events in fairy-tale style. Leading her outside—where, naturally, a huge full moon waited to beam approval—Lenglet took Ella by the hand and asked her to marry him. Only because of her—he now explained—had he courted danger by remaining in London. He didn't say why he was in peril, only that he must leave the country the following morning. Later, when the war was over, he would send word for Ella to join him in his beloved Paris. Could she wait? "It came to me in a flash that here it was, what I had been waiting for, for so long. Now I could see escape." His gentle kiss seemed to promise an enchanted Rhys that she would be forever cherished by this romantic man. Her acceptance was unhesitating.⁶ Fuelled by fantasies of adventure and escape, she was impatient for her summons to come.

Not everybody shared the newly abandoned Ella's sense of excitement. At the boarding house, only Camille was encouraging. A three-page letter arrived from Rhys's younger sister, Brenda, out in Dominica, warning her against such folly.† It is unclear which members of the family actually succeeded in visiting her in London in 1918, or what was said, but it's evident that a mysterious stranger from the Continent was not regarded as a marvellous catch.

The end of the war ushers in a curious silence in Rhys's life. If a young woman disillusioned by her own work at the Ministry of Pen-

---

* The same attractive lodger would feature as "Estelle" in "Till September Petronella."

† In a later draft of "Leaving England" (a chapter in *Smile Please*), Rhys crossed out the word "sister" and bitterly substituted the phrase: "someone who didn't care whether I lived or died."

Previously thought to be of Brenda Rees Williams as a young woman at school in London. Brenda's schooling was cut short by the war. More likely, this dates from the year when Brenda wrote from Dominica to censure her older sister's choice of fiancé. *(McFarlin)*

sions chose to join the three days of celebrations when the Armistice was announced in November 1918, she kept that fact to herself. Early in 1919, however, as steamers began to resume their normal cross-Channel traffic, Rhys agreed to join Lenglet at The Hague. Joyfully, she wrote to tell Lancey to stop paying the solicitor's cheques.

The news that Lancey wanted an urgent meeting caused a flicker of apprehension. Aged twenty-nine, Rhys remained in awe of her first lover; reluctantly, she agreed to meet him for lunch at the smartly conventional Piccadilly Grill.

The cruelly premature death, back in 1914, of Julian Martin Smith had devastated Lancelot Hugh Smith. He himself had gone on to enjoy what is known as a "good" war. His negotiating skills had helped to keep Norway and Sweden free from the grasp of the Central Powers and in 1917, he became one of the very first recipients of a CBE. Politically, as in the world of finance, he was uncommonly well connected. Seen from the perspective of a nervous lunch guest—as Lancey steered a carefully neutral conversation towards her plans—Mr. Hugh Smith appeared to know everybody, and everything.

What emerges from this encounter—and from Lancey's urgent entreaties that "Ella" should break off her relationship with Jean Lenglet—is that this shrewd, conventional and quietly unhappy man remained on some deep level in love with his "kitten," the enchanting young woman he himself had refused to marry, and that Rhys herself had lost none of her reverence for him. Quietly, she listened as Lancelot revealed all that he had ascertained. None of his news was good. Lenglet's passport was invalid (due to the critical loss of his Dutch citizenship when he had impetuously joined the French Foreign Legion). In England, he had apparently been working as a spy for the French. Several of his friends had been arrested; Lenglet had fled from England at the close of 1917 only because the police were after him. By marrying such a man, Rhys would be putting herself at grave risk.

The one thing Lancey seems to have chosen not to convey to his guest—perhaps he was unaware of Lenglet's second marriage—was that her fiancé had a wife still living in Paris; perhaps, he thought enough had already been said. Rhys, to his astonishment, was undeterred. Risks, as she calmly reminded him, were what she most enjoyed. Didn't he remember that she thrived on danger? "He gave a little nod." Only after Lancey had gained her promise to stay in touch—and then kissed her goodbye—did she break down. Rhys wrote in her memoir that she went home in tears.

Danger did excite Rhys; Hugh Smith's warnings were all ignored. In the spring of 1919, too overjoyed at the prospect of escaping from a country she had grown to detest to care about any possible mishaps, Jean Rhys set sail for the Netherlands—and the start of a new European life.

III

A EUROPEAN LIFE
Madame Jean Lenglet

"He [Jean Lenglet] influenced me greatly and for keeps . . . Far more than anyone else ever has done, or will do."

—Jean Rhys to Francis Wyndham, 5 June 1964, *Letters*

6

A Paris Marriage (1919–25)

"From 1917 onwards a gap. He seemed very prosperous when I met him in London, but now no money—nix. What happened? He doesn't tell me."

—Jean Rhys, *Good Morning, Midnight*, Part Three (1939)

ON 30 APRIL 1919, in front of two local witnesses at The Hague, Ella Gwendoline Rees Williams married Willem Johan Marie Lenglet ("of no fixed profession"). Lenglet saw no need to explain to his bride why the ceremony needed to be conducted outside France—where Rhys's bridegroom remained the legal husband of the abandoned and presumably uncontacted Marie Pollart.

Knowing only that she had married a man who loved poetry, sang charmingly and with whom life always felt exciting, Jean Rhys was happy in the five months that she spent living with Lenglet in the pretty old town of The Hague. She kept the photographs that prove it; little black-and-white images showing the Lenglets larking about on Scheveningen Beach, together with a burly male friend. One snap shows a demure Rhys kneeling down in a neatly pleated skirt as she waits for Lenglet to place an imaginary crown on her head; in another, the couple pretend to be having a fight. They both look marvellously carefree.[1] Before the Lenglets left for Paris—her longed-for Paris—Rhys knew that she was pregnant.

The news that her husband's lack of a valid passport meant they

Marked by Jean in her old age as "Austria," these happy snaps more convincingly belong to the Lenglets' honeymoon months at The Hague, when Scheveningen beach was nearby. Their friend is unidentified. *(McFarlin)*

would be entering France illegally came as a shock. In *Good Morning, Midnight*, for which Rhys would draw upon her early memories of The Hague, Sasha Jensen undertakes a similarly illicit journey, curled up like a cat on a third-class luggage rack in order to escape attention. ("I didn't think it would be like this," she sighs.) Recording her own journey in one of her coloured exercise books, Rhys would remember Lenglet's insouciance and her own terror. How could they possibly escape being captured by patrolling guards? As always, her husband had the answer ready: "How? Just by walking over the frontier. By walking along the road between quiet rows of poplar trees at night. A quiet night with the moon up. Walking along until you get past the sentry & finding yourself in Dunkirk in the early morning and so tired so tired ... And the fear. ..."[2]

By early September, safely arrived in a Paris that had just liberated itself from the massive encircling stone walls erected in the previous century, the Lenglets had settled into a low-ceilinged fourth-floor hotel room on rue Lamartine, in the pleasant area south of Gare du Nord known—ever since the arrival of the flamboyant Palais Garnier—as Opéra. Today, still sporting an entrance door crowned by reclining nymphs, the Lenglets' first French home has become part of the Hotel des Plumes, although Rhys's name does not yet feature among the famous writers—Verlaine, Rimbaud, Wilde—proudly recorded in its brochure. An old-fashioned spiral staircase leads up to the couple's snug home; beyond the bedroom window, overlooking a nineteenth-century *école de filles*, a hotel guest can still glimpse the narrow iron balcony on which the newlyweds used to drink white wine and smoke Jean's favourite Egyptian cigarettes. The room itself was simply furnished (the largely fictitious *Good Morning, Midnight* provides the lovers with a large bed and a cosy red eiderdown), but it became a happy nest for two people who were very much in love. The Lenglets returned there whenever they could afford the hotel's modest charges.

For Jean Rhys, born on an island where a creolised form of French was in daily use, Paris felt like a homecoming. She loved the pink glow of the long summer days and the subtler menace of the sea-blue dusks when tugboats whistled to each other along the Seine; she instinctively preferred the casual commerce of quiet neighbourhood bars to the noisy self-consciousness of the big brasseries of Montparnasse that were already being taken over by tourists from abroad. Each day, she revelled in her escape from the invisible social traps of London, a chillier, greyer city that had always seemed to Rhys to be intent upon crushing the spirit of a sensitive outsider.

Once, sitting alone in a boulevard cafe, an intrigued Rhys watched a Creole girl—"a lovely, vicious little thing"*—break away from her older, more sedate companions. "*J'en ai marre*" (I'm fed up), the girl shrilled as she whirled herself into a dance. Carelessly, she lifted her skirt: "Obviously the red dress was her only garment; obviously too, she was exquisite beneath it." Delighting in how the girl strutted around to the song, listening to the seductive and familiar lilt of her island-bred

The balcony of the Lenglets' beloved attic bedroom in Paris on rue Lamartine. *(Author picture)*

---

* "Vicious" is used here in its French sense, *vicieuse*, meaning depraved, amoral (Jean Rhys, "Trio," 1927, in *Collected Short Stories*, Penguin).

voice, Rhys felt a moment of secret affinity. In London, she had struggled to repress her emotions in order to fit in. In Paris, she and this fiercely independent youngster had found their home.

Rhys's time was not all her own. Shortly after arriving in Paris with her husband, she answered an advertisement in *Le Figaro* for a teacher of English to children. Asked to call at 3 rue Rabelais, just off the Champs Elysées, a mildly awed Rhys was ushered by a uniformed maid into the presence of a slight, dark-haired and smiling woman. She introduced herself as Germaine Richelot, unmarried aunt to the four little cousins with whom Madame Lenglet would be expected to converse only in English, a language with which the young Bragadirs and Lemierres were already familiar. Rhys's acceptance was seemingly taken for granted; invited to stay for a family lunch, she was instantly welcomed as a friend, not an employee.

Rhys's recollections of her three months working for the family of Dr. Louis Gustave Richelot, a respected figure in the French medical world, carry no barb or hint of discontent. Each day, she dined with the family in a room hung with beautiful tapestries and guarded by one of the doctor's greatest treasures: a serene wooden Madonna. The mornings were reserved for English conversation with the children; during the afternoons, Germaine insisted that the pregnant "Ella" should rest herself in one of the Richelots' favourite rooms, a light-filled studio. Sometimes, she heard Germaine's musical sister, Yvonne Bragadir, practising for a concert off in some distant room, or softly chatting with the young women's third sister, Jeanne Lemierre, the wife of an eminent physician who lived in a neighbouring street.[3]

Rhys liked and admired all the Richelot family, but it was Germaine who sought to become her particular friend. Germaine confided that she was a secret socialist. She longed to get rid of the family Daimler. Covertly, she attended political meetings. During the war, she had learned terrible things from her voluntary work as a *marraine de guerre* (a soldier's correspondent and comforter). Germaine talked; Rhys, so it seems, was usually the listener in the intimate discussions that continued until, eight months into her pregnancy, the long daily trek from rue Lamartine became too demanding. Gratefully, Rhys promised to stay in touch, and always to consider herself one of the family. Since Dr. Richelot was a gynaecologist, it is to be supposed that this generous family helped to locate (and perhaps even paid the bills for) a hospital suitable for the birth of Rhys's first child.

Born on 29 December 1919, William Owen Lenglet was proudly named—though not baptised, since Jean Lenglet did not believe in baptism—after Rhys's late father, and after Owen, the brother closest in age to herself. Perhaps the attic bedroom at rue Lamartine was draughty; the baby caught pneumonia. On 19 January 1920, the Lenglets' small son died, aged just three weeks, at a convent hospital in rue Denfert-Rochereau.

Later, recalling the tragedy in *Smile Please* with an undertow of self-reproach that no careful reader can ignore, Rhys wrote that she and Lenglet had been patching up a quarrel (about her desire to baptise her sick baby) by drinking champagne with a friend at the *exact* moment that their tiny son had died, alone. "We were all laughing," she wrote. The nuns at the hospital had told her, when she asked, the precise hour of the baby's death. "He was dying, or was already dead, while we were drinking champagne."

Rhys could not forgive herself. She had not been there and she had let her little boy die bereft of proper religious rites. The convent sisters assured her that a baptism had taken place; how could she be certain that they weren't simply consoling her? The baby was hastily buried at Bagnieux, just outside Paris. Privately, Rhys attempted some form of atonement by writing—the date is unknown—a poem which she named "Prayer to the Sun."

A wistful short prayer to a higher power, Rhys's unpublished and affectingly bleak little poem (it consists of fifteen short, unrhymed lines) refers to the loss of a child; a loss for which the poem's author seeks absolution. The speaker is imprisoned within a coffin-like chamber. Poignant allusion is made to the absent consolation of trees, tranquillity, and running rivers. Outside the door, the city continues on its indifferent way; "alien voices" provide a remote background noise.

Beginning and ending with a prayer for deliverance, the poem suggests that Rhys did not recover quickly from the death of her first-born child. She always initially wrote by hand, but this little poem has evidently been revised and typed out in what may have been a final form.[4]

A swift change of location was welcome at such a desolate moment; the Richelots stepped in to help by finding Monsieur Lenglet (whom they had never met) a lucrative position as interpreter for the Japanese section of the Inter-Allied Commission being hastily set up in devastated postwar Vienna. The job required the bereaved father to leave Paris at once; Rhys's distraught state is apparent from the fact that, having found herself another English-speaking job to earn some money before following Lenglet to Vienna, she somehow managed, on her first day of employment, to lose her way from child-friendly Parc Monceau back to her pupil's nearby home on avenue Wagram. That particular stroll takes a pedestrian less than three minutes; Rhys ended by dragging a weeping little boy halfway across Paris before flagging down a taxi to take them home. Refunded the fare by the child's angry mother, Rhys was also sacked on the spot. A week or so later, Germaine waved her sad-faced friend off on the train to Vienna.

THE LENGLETS, PARTLY due to some quiet currency trading of the sort that became common after the war, now grew rich. The citizens of "Red Vienna," so named for its vigorous new postwar policy of social reform, were starving; Rhys, for once, was on the winning side. While the Japanese officers took up residence at Sacher's Hotel, the Lenglets and their friend "André" (Rhys's pseudonym for a romantic young French bachelor regarded as the Inter-Allied Commission's wild card), moved into the Imperial, after lodging with a family of Austrian aristocrats who had lost everything but their grand address on the elegant Favoritenstrasse. You could always tell what a lady Madame de Heuske was, Rhys would confess with self-damning insouciance, from "the faraway look" with which she complied with Madame Lenglet's request for a restorative personal massage of her back and chest.[5] The hypersensitive Rhys was conscious of an implied criticism of herself in the fact that the de Heuskes forbade their daughter Blanca to apply cosmetics to her own fine, transparent skin. Rhys, by contrast, dyed her hair red and paid weekly visits to a beautician. Passers-by, so she would sardonically recall, sometimes compared her to a doll made from the purest white Saxon china (*"la poupée de porcelaine de saxe"*).

"Funny how it's slipped away, Vienna," Rhys would ruminate in the marvellous short story "Vienne," which she would write during the next few years. Living in a world that placed a high value on looks, Rhys lingered on the extraordinary beauty of a Viennese dancer coveted by the city's visiting officers, who nevertheless fear that she may be "too expensive."

> A fragile child's body, a fluff of black skirt ending far above the knee. Silver straps over that beautiful back, the wonderful legs in black stockings and little satin shoes, short hair, cheeky little face . . . Ugly humanity, I'd always thought. I saw people differently afterwards—because for once I'd met sheer loveliness with a flame inside . . . Finally she disappeared. Went back to Budapest where afterwards we heard of her . . . Married to a barber. Rum.[6]

For the dancing girls, as Rhys was quick to recognise in a passage that suggests the influence of Colette on her early work, the visiting officers represented only money; a way out of poverty. For Rhys herself, the city offered an escape from the swift and painfully remembered death of her baby son. "Vienne" describes 1920 as a time when "Frances" (or "Francine") feels "cracky with joy in life"; a later and far more elaborately constructed story titled "Temps Perdi" catalogues every one of the ravishing dresses that a newly rich Lenglet had personally selected for his wife's Austrian wardrobe. Ruffled white muslins; rustling organzas; brilliantly coloured prints in cornflower blue and buttercup gold: all that Rhys would omit from that loving retrospective inventory was a magnificent astrakhan coat, purchased to keep out the bitter cold of Viennese winters. The coat from Vienna would haunt the future novels of Jean Rhys as a symbol of bad times (when it went to the pawn shop) and adventurous times (when it cloaked what Rhys once privately and savagely described as her treacherous body's "little trot" along the sidewalk, nostrils flared, picking up the scent of sex in the spring air: "Trust me, trust me, says the body—But trust it, never."[7])

The Inter-Allied Commission remained in Vienna for over a year. On Rhys's thirtieth birthday, the Japanese officers held a splendid dinner in honour of "Ella et Jean," from which she preserved an autographed menu card, one which would earn a brief mention from Julia Martin in Rhys's second novel. The city enchanted Rhys; she was disappointed to learn in 1921 that it was time for the commission to move on to Budapest where—following two waves of terror, during which many Hungarians had fled abroad—a regent, Miklós Horthy, had replaced an exiled king.

Rhys in Vienna, wearing what may have been the famous fur coat which would feature in her novels, where it sometimes acquired an astrakhan collar.
(McFarlin)

As with Vienna, Rhys experienced Budapest from within a cocoon of wealth. Jean Lenglet had profited handsomely from his currency trans-actions back in Vienna. Rhys kept a photograph of the couple's Austro-Daimler with their uniformed chauffeur chubbily ensconced behind the wheel; it was—did the thought ever cross her mind?—precisely the kind of car that Germaine Richelot despised.

It is likely that the Lenglets were housed in Pest, the livelier of the yoked cities that confront each other across the Danube; certainly, they felt at home in a shadily romantic city crowded with leafy little squares and Parisian-style cafes. The Hungarian women were beautiful, but none were lovelier—as doubtless Lenglet reassured his wife—than her own petted and cherished self. It may have been a desire to flaunt that shapely, well-dressed body before the sceptical Lancey Hugh Smith that caused Ella Lenglet, during the late summer of 1921, to make an impulsive brief visit to London.

The Lenglets at home during their year with the Inter-Allied Commission in Vienna and Budapest. *(McFarlin)*

The conjecture that Rhys was seizing an opportunity to parade her successful marriage to a mistrustful former lover is prompted by her choice of hotel. The Berkeley stood within spitting distance of Lancey's own discreet abode in Charles Street: the home in which a conventional man had never permitted his young mistress to spend a single night. It's unlikely that Rhys was invited to do so now. The friendship survived, but their affair was over.

Rhys may also have been summoned to London by a needy family. Following the death of Dr. Rees Williams, his widow had fallen on hard times in Dominica. By the summer of 1921, there were no white Lockharts left on the island. Proud Minna, having grown up in the Great House at Geneva, was living in cramped conditions at 28 Woodgrange Avenue in Acton, west London. Crowded in beneath the same gabled roof were Minna's unmarried twin, their widowed sister, two daughters and a devoted nurse companion called Miss Woolgar. By 1921, Jean Rhys's mother had already become bedridden; by 1927, the year in which she died, a series of strokes had rendered Minna Rees Williams unable to communicate, or even to sign her own name.

The account of an awkward family reunion which Rhys would put into her second novel, *After Leaving Mr Mackenzie*, appears to draw upon and combine two separate visits to Acton, of which this was the first. Grudgingly conscious of her younger sister's stoic heroism, Julia Martin compares Norah Griffiths to a character in an unidentified Russian tragedy, "moving, dark, tranquil, and beautiful, across a background of yellowish snow." Entering the bedroom in which her mother now lies prostrate, every day, all day long, Julia imagines that she has attracted a flicker of recognition: "Then it was like seeing a spark go out and the eyes were again bloodshot, animal eyes."[8]

Rhys's description of Julia Martin's cool reception by her family at Acton may only slightly exaggerate the contempt with which selfish, well-dressed "Gwen" was received by an impoverished family of reluctant exiles. Julia, however, is broke and importunate. Rhys, in 1921, was riding high.

Back in Budapest for her third autumn out of England, Rhys discovered that she was once again pregnant. Shortly afterwards, Lenglet confessed that he had gambled and lost a small fortune embezzled from his superiors in the commission. Now, penniless and terrified of arrest, he was ready to kill himself.

In life, as in the short story "Vienne" that she would soon base upon her continental adventures, Rhys took pride in her cool-headed behaviour in times of crisis.* Loyal Lancey would never let his erring kitten down: "My plan of going to London to borrow money was already complete in my head," Rhys makes "Francine" say in "Vienne." "One thinks quickly sometimes." The need to escape from Budapest was imperative—but not before a last celebration. Like Lenglet, perhaps, "Pierre" in "Vienne" orders a last, splendidly ostentatious bedroom dinner of wild duck and two bottles of champagne; touching Pierre's arm as if to draw his newfound bravado into herself, Francine feels her own courage wane. "Horrible to feel that henceforth and for ever one would live with the huge machine of law, order, respectability against one. Horrible to be certain that one was not strong enough to face it."⁹

Preparing to leave London for The Hague, back in the early spring of 1919, Rhys had boasted to prudent Lancey that she revelled in taking risks. Fleeing from Hungary in 1921 in the Daimler driven by their stolid chauffeur, her relish for danger was put to the test. "Vienne" fictionalises a frightening moment in the Lenglets' flight at the Czech border, where Pierre is taken into a patrol hut for interrogation. Emerging at last, he shouts to the chauffeur to get moving. "The car jumped forward like a spurred horse," Rhys recalled in her story. "I imagined for one thrilling moment that we would be fired on . . ." On they flew, towards Prague—and then off again.

> "Faster! Faster! Make the damn thing go!"
> We were doing a hundred . . .
> "Get on! . . . Get on! . . ."

* The autobiographical nature of "Vienne" is confirmed by the fact that the protagonists were initially named "Ella" and "Jean."

We slowed up.

"You're drunk, Frances," said Pierre severely.[10]

"Vienne" ends breathlessly in November 1921 outside Prague, on the verge of a last flight to England ("It was: *Nach* London!"). At this point, Rhys's private life vanishes from view until the birth, on 22 May 1922, of Maryvonne Lenglet, in Ukkel, Belgium. By July, following a further request to Lancey for help and a subsequent seaside holiday at Knokke-sur-mer, the vagabonds were safely back in their attic room at the little hotel on rue Lamartine. This was no place in which to bring up a child. Helped by Germaine Richelot, the Lenglets reluctantly arranged for Maryvonne to be cared for at a series of baby shelters or orphanages (each bore some saccharine name like "The Cradle"), from which she could be whisked back home at whim. This seemingly heartless practice was not uncommon. By 1922, two years before he encountered Jean Rhys in Paris, the English novelist Ford Madox Ford had deposited his adored baby daughter by Stella Bowen in a damp little cottage on the edge of the city, where Julie was cared for by a nurse while her unmarried parents resided in Montparnasse.

In the autumn of 1922, a further catastrophe struck the Lenglets when the French police showed up at rue Lamartine, demanding Lenglet's immediate return to his lawful wife. Loyal though Rhys would remain to a husband who seemed habitually to live on the wrong side of the law, the revelation of his bigamy marked the beginning of an erosion of trust from which the couple's relationship would never entirely recover. Over the next two years, Lenglet occupied the twilight world of a fugitive, one from which he would sporadically emerge and seek Rhys out; essentially, she faced life alone.

Other than the saintly Richelots and an occasional handout from Lancey (with whom she remained in irregular contact until at least 1925), Rhys now had no resources. Her story "Hunger" dryly reports the number of days—five—for which a young woman in similar circumstances can survive on bread and coffee.

"Hunger" and the three bitter stories which follow it in *The Left*

Bank, Rhys's first published collection, may well be based upon actual memories of this challenging period. In the first of the three, the narrator withholds her pity from a starving friend who not only continues to rouge her lips and to wear silk stockings, but dares to be flippant about it. ("What did you say?" the narrator asks before repeating the starving woman's retort in dull disbelief: " . . . You cannot buy special clothes to starve in. Naturally not.") In the next, "A Night," where the (once again) penniless narrator wonders whether a lover's tenderness might be enough to keep her from killing herself by drowning or gunshot, Rhys uses the speaker to voice the nonspecific hatred which will become a feature of her work: "It is as if something in me is shivering right away from humanity. Their eyes are mean and cruel." In the third and least successful, "In the Rue de l'Arrivée," a stony-broke and slightly drunk Englishwoman learns to accept pity from someone even unluckier than herself. "*Pauvre petite, va*," murmurs the sinister-looking man who might have been about to pick her up or murder her, after he catches sight of her face. That night, in Miss Dorothy Dufreyne's troubled dreams, the same stranger returns disguised as an angel, about to carry her off to hell: "But what if it were heaven when one got there?" Sentiment still smudges the sharp edges of Rhys's prose, but here, very faintly apparent, are the first traces of Rhys's fourth and finest novel, *Good Morning, Midnight*.

How *did* Jean Rhys survive two years—autumn 1922 to the autumn of 1924—of poverty and unwelcome independence? The wealth that Lenglet had accrued in Vienna and Budapest had vanished, leaving only a cupboard filled with exquisite clothes to inspire "Illusion," one of Rhys's most whimsical early stories (about an outwardly dowdy English woman whose Parisian wardrobe is filled with improbably exotic dresses that include "a carnival costume complete with mask"). Scraps of paper surviving from that bleak period bear the names of various Paris hotels, often in grim areas like the then-notorious wasteland of Place Dauphine. Did Rhys prefer to hole up in some hideaway where she could read and write, to begging from the small group of expatriate friends who had known her in London, before the war? Was this the time when she began to read Colette (for whose early books about the great novelist's years in vaudeville Rhys would retain an enduring admiration) and the remarkable Pierre Mac Orlan, whose stylistically brilliant and often witty Parisian novel about a modern-day Faust and a pure-hearted prostitute, *Marguerite de la Nuit* (1924), became one of her most cherished volumes?

Rhys's only known employer during a period of daunting challenges (met with characteristic defiance) was Violet Dreschfeld, a Jewish sculptor living in Paris. In *Quartet*, Rhys's first and most directly autobiographical novel, Dreschfeld is represented by the gauntly anxious Esther de Solla; in *After Leaving Mr Mackenzie*, a similar character called Ruth owns a Modigliani print—a tigerish, lounging nude with which Julia Martin feels a troubled affinity. Esther and Ruth are mature women, but Violet was close in age to Rhys herself. Their personal relationship is unclear, but Rhys—who would preserve almost no souvenirs from this period of her life—did keep one small photographic record of Violet's work; it presents a modestly dressed "Ella" seated on a rock, her head bowed in thought. Dreschfeld never married and seems to have formed no other significant relationships. We can't know whether she became Rhys's lover for a time, or simply provided a bit of badly needed income, or both. Rhys's relationships with women remain one of her best-kept secrets, but she writes about the female body with an appreciation of physical beauty that seems to go well beyond self-regard.

IT WAS DURING the last quarter of 1924 that a dramatic change occurred in Rhys's life. Lenglet had managed to rejoin her in Paris. Money remained desperately short. It was her own idea (or so Rhys would recall in *Smile Please*) to turn her husband's colourful past to commercial use. Lenglet had worked both as a journalist and a singer in his prewar life; Mac Orlan had written about his own experiences as a chanteur at *Le Lapin Agile*; surely it wouldn't take her husband long to dash off a few racy vignettes about his nights as a teenage heartthrob at Montmartre's famous club? Lenglet complied. Theirs would always be an affectionately collaborative partnership where writing was concerned; after translating and sharpening her husband's submissions, Rhys took them along to the offices of the Continental *Daily Mail*. Courteously informed that Lenglet's anecdotal pieces were a bit old-fashioned for the *Mail*'s readers, Rhys rejected the compensatory offer made to herself on the spot to become an interviewer of celebrities, working from the paper's office in Rome.

In Rhys's retrospective account of the sequence of events, it was an editor at the *Daily Mail* who then suggested that she might show her husband's stories to Helen Pearl Adam, an American journalist whose husband had previously worked in London alongside Maxwell Macartney at *The Times*. "I was very nervous as I'd only met Mrs Adam once," Rhys would write in *Smile Please*, "and I wondered if she'd remember me."[11] Pearl was already aware of Rhys's ambitions as a writer, however; she may even have been told about a work in progress. And so, having rejected Lenglet's anecdotes, Adam apparently asked to see something written by Rhys herself. Playing her cards with care, and conscious of the urgent need to show something marketable to a seasoned journalist, Rhys held back the accomplished stories that she had been working on in Paris during Lenglet's long absences. Instead, she handed over the raunchier and still unnamed episodic novel that had started life in Chelsea in a handful of large-sized notebooks, a year before the war.

Pearl Adam liked what she read, enough so to offer to edit the material and give it a catchy title. "Suzy Tells" would offer a knowing nod both to one of Paris's best-known drinks (a "Suze Fine" was Pernod-based) and to Suzy's, a famous brothel that was celebrated later by the photographer Brassaï.

What happened next would change Rhys's life. Having divided "Suzy Tells" into sections, each headed by a man's name, Pearl Adam decided that Rhys's scandalous manuscript was original enough to interest Ford Madox Ford, editor of Paris's respected literary magazine for English-speaking expatriates, the *transatlantic review*. She was right; Ford was intrigued. Nevertheless, a few days after reading "Suzy Tells" and then renaming it "Triple Sec," Ford set the typescript aside. Instead, he told Pearl Adam that he wanted to see more of this writer's work. Moreover, he wanted to meet such a gifted young author in person.

"*L'affaire Ford*"* (1924–26)

" 'The snow was all over Ireland, falling on the living and the
dead.' Who used to read James Joyce to me? I forget."

—Jean Rhys, misquoting in her old age a line from the famous
closing paragraph of Joyce's story "The Dead," from *Dubliners*ⁱ

RHYS HAD MOST likely first met Ford's partner, Stella Bowen, in London, shortly after her arrival from Adelaide, Australia. Back before
the war, Bowen and Rhys briefly belonged to the same Chelsea-based
group of bohemians. Stella was studying art; Rhys was beginning to
write "Triple Sec," while picking up cash by posing as an artist's model.
In 1918, the year after the twenty-eight-year-old Rhys met Jean Lenglet in London, Stella, aged twenty-four, fell for Major Ford. A highly
educated officer, half German on his father's side, Ford had recently
returned to England from a war that left him temporarily shellshocked
and suffering from memory lapses.

Nobody has ever described Ford as handsome, but nobody who
knew him has questioned his ability to charm women, or his gift both
as a writer and editor, one who had collaborated with Joseph Conrad
and who published his own widely admired novel, *The Good Soldier*, in

* The phrase used by Rhys for a long retrospective account of her relationship with
Ford, to which she referred when dictating the Paris section of her memoir to the novelist David Plante (McFarlin, 007-14.5.f5).

1916. Ford's generous nature had never been constrained by a perpetual lack of funds; neither had a concern for facts impeded his genius for telling stories. At work, he pumped out what were often magnificent novels at the rate of some manic teleprinting machine. Winding down at night, he knocked back red wine with as much gusto as he (very badly) danced and (very enchantingly) talked. Like his own most auto-biographical creation, Christopher Tietjens in the sequence of novels called *Parade's End*, Ford would always seem larger in spirit than the world he was obliged to inhabit.

"Silenus in tweeds"—according to the great war artist Paul Nash, who knew him pretty well—Ford was too gentle in manner ever to appear predatory.[2] Stella, a darkly attractive and culture-hungry young woman with a talent for organising other people's lives, found this brilliant and deceptively helpless man irresistible. An age gap of twenty years was vaulted as easily as the fact that her lover was still entangled with the writer Violet Hunt (for whom Ford had previously abandoned

Stella Bowen (*left*) lived in Chelsea at the same time as Rhys and visited the Crabtree Club with considerably less pleasure. Later, she formed a relationship with Ford Madox Ford (*right*) and moved to France.

his wife and two children). Two years later, Stella gave birth to Julie
(Ford's adored "*petite princesse*"), with whom the couple migrated in
1922 to the south of France—and who was later left to the care of a
dependable nurse in their country cottage close to the capital. Often
though the "Fords," as the unmarried couple were always known in
France, would return to the then unspoiled Riviera coast, Paris exerted
a powerful attraction over an astonishingly well-read francophile who
thrived on discovering talented new writers.

By the autumn of 1924, when Jean Rhys entered his life, Ford stood
at the heart of the expatriate and (thanks to spectacular exchange rates)
uncharacteristically affluent literary world that thronged the brasseries
of Montparnasse. Ford himself, despite regular injections of funds from
Stella's Australian investment trust, was always strapped for cash, in
part because of his generous impulse to subsidise needy poets like the
reticent Ralph Cheever Dunning, a starving opium addict whose sour
warning against the acceptance of charity was taken by Jean Rhys as
the prefatory heading for her own first novel, *Quartet*. By September
1924, the imminent closure of Ford's cherished year-old creation, the
transatlantic review, was already on the cards.

After their fashion, Stella and Ford did their best to economise. In
the country, they rented the stone-walled labourer's cottage at Guermantes where little Julie was lodged; in the city, they occupied a minute
apartment at 16 avenue Denfert-Rochereau. Meanwhile, Ford encouraged his magazine's illustrious contributors to buy their own drinks
at the impromptu weekly evenings he hosted at the Bal du Printemps,
a tiny cafe-restaurant squirrelled away in the winding streets behind
the Panthéon. More student-style partying took place in the dungeon-
like premises that the *transatlantic review's* headquarters shared with
Bill Bird's illustrious Three Mountains Press on Ile Saint Louis's quai
d'Anjou. The setting was as dingy as the menu, but the dancing was
wild and the guests included everybody from Ernest Hemingway to
a majestic Gertrude Stein. Hemingway, Ford's first and prodigiously
gifted literary beneficiary in Paris—he was even allowed to edit an
issue of the magazine in which Ford published the young American's

work—paved the way for Jean Rhys as she joined this exhilarating coterie, shortly after her first encounter with Ford in September 1924.

Recalling the events of the next two years in her memoir, *Drawn from Life* (1941), Stella Bowen would describe an unnamed but entirely identifiable Rhys as having first appeared on their doorstep toting a battered suitcase that contained "an unpublishably sordid novel." Bowen's recollection doesn't square with the account in *Smile Please* of Pearl Adam having already edited and submitted "Suzy Tells" to Ford; what Rhys had produced from her shabby holdall at that first meeting with Ford was the manuscript of a recent—and far more accomplished—short story. Reading "Vienne," Ford thought it so remarkable that he instantly offered to publish the opening six pages (unpaid, of course) in the final, December issue of *transatlantic review*. He might have published more, but Rhys, while willing to undergo another change of name—"Ella Lenglet" did not meet with her new patron's approval—insisted on withholding the part of the story dealing with the couple's ignominious flight from Budapest. The rapid choice of the name "Jean" for herself—no other explanation sounds convincing—may have struck Ella as a way, following the embarrassing rejection by the *Mail* and Pearl Adam of her cultured husband's own, less remarkable stories, to grant Monsieur Jean Lenglet a role in her new literary life.

For Rhys, the news could not have been better. The extract from "Vienne" was to appear in Ford's distinguished magazine alongside contributions from Hemingway, Stein, Tristan Tzara, Robert McAlmon and Ford himself (publishing a tender homage to his old friend Joseph Conrad, who had died in August). No aspiring young writer could have hoped for a more auspicious debut.

Rhys's good fortune seemed infectious. In that same month, September 1924, Lenglet obtained a well-paid job with Exprinter, a Paris tourist bureau. Elated, the Lenglets took their two-year-old daughter out of her latest foster home and away to Tours for a celebratory holiday. Many years later, Rhys would tenderly remind a middle-aged Maryvonne of the visit to Tours with "my sweety pie baby." An informal snap from the trip, presumably taken by a fond Lenglet, shows

Rhys laughing up at the photographer as she nuzzles the elegant canine snout of a new friend's German shepherd. Aged thirty-four, Rhys still looked like a carefree twenty-year-old, one whose serene features belied the writer's evident familiarity with a world of fathomless darkness. It's easy to see why both Ford and Stella were intrigued and—from the very start—a little smitten.

Throughout that golden autumn of 1924, a triangle was established from which Jean Lenglet's demanding new job excluded him. Later, Jean Rhys would say little about this period. It is possible that the relationship between herself and Ford—and possibly Stella—was sexual from the start. Publicly, nothing was said by anybody. It was Stella herself who later coined the phrase "Ford's girl" to suggest how scornfully the gifted intruder was regarded by their friends. Hemingway, who attended the same parties, and worked on editing the *transatlantic review* alongside one of Rhys's new chums, the Midwestern poet, Ivan Beede, never mentioned Rhys once. James Joyce, indebted to Ford for his unfaltering support in publishing the Irish novelist's most experimental work, recalled only having been asked to zip up Miss Rhys's dress while sharing a lift. A lift? An unzipped dress? Clearly, Joyce was flagging up an assignation at a hotel, but Ford is not named, only the vulnerable young outsider from whom a slightly malicious Joyce had nothing to fear.[3]

Ignored in the memoirs of the novelists and poets and painters who flocked to Paris during the 1920s, Rhys herself would maintain a maddening discretion. She didn't want to betray Ford and Stella, her friends and patrons. She hated the idea of dropping famous names. Years later, when asked about Joyce, Rhys acknowledged having met him, but not that Ford had taught her to read his early stories as carefully as she would do *Ulysses* and *Finnegans Wake*. Asked for anecdotes about Ernest Hemingway, the older Rhys recalled an unassuming young man who came to life only when he was dancing. Subjected to more persistent interrogation, she grew vaguer still. *Had* Ford really introduced her to Gertrude Stein? She might have visited. Miss Stein's companion, Alice Toklas (Rhys added with an almost wilful satisfaction at her own elusiveness), had certainly made herself friendly.[4]

The newly named writer "Jean Rhys" at the time of her affair with Ford. Out of sight at her side here is Germaine Richelot, among the most loyal of Rhys's friends in Paris. *(McFarlin)*

Always evasive in public about what was clearly a passionate love affair ("I love him. Terribly," Marya Zelli says about Hugo Heidler in Rhys's unashamedly autobiographical first novel, *Quartet*), Rhys never failed to honour Ford as her literary mentor. Rattling off a florid introduction in 1927 to his brilliant protégée's first publication, a collection of short stories, Ford himself was equally careful to distance himself, pointing out that Miss Rhys had always known better than to take his advice. Rhys, while she didn't disagree, credited Ford with broadening her knowledge of the great French and Russian authors from whom she learned so much.

The absence of almost any documentation before 1931 in the form of letters makes it nearly impossible to chart Rhys's reading habits in Paris during the Twenties. Then, as now, books were always easily available from the *bouquinistes* beside the Seine, but it's likely that Ford, a widely read man who treated Rhys as his pupil, gave her access to his own extensive library. Her husband, the ardent admirer of one of France's most revered modern novelists, had already introduced Ella to the novels of Anatole France, whose vast public funeral the couple attended in 1924. French poetry had come into her life through the nuns at the Virgo Fidelis convent in Roseau. Adoring Mallarmé and Rimbaud, Rhys's strongest affinity was still with Baudelaire, in whose sensual but also condescending celebrations of his beautiful Haitian-born mistress, Jeanne Duval, she perhaps sensed the beginning of her long journey to reclaim a place in history for Mr. Rochester's mistreated Creole wife, the madwoman in the Thornfield attic of *Jane Eyre*. Perhaps: we can only conjecture.

Ford made Rhys aware of some of the writers who would become her touchstones as she strove to create a style—and a world—of her own. Her admiration of Guy de Maupassant, frequently mentioned in her later letters as a master storyteller, is apparent in "La Grosse Fifi." This story of an older woman's brutal murder by her young gigolo lover stands alongside "Vienne" as a minor masterpiece in Rhys's early work. Maupassant's influence was still in evidence in the 1950s, when she planned to call a later story "Fort comme la Mort" in homage to Maupassant's work of the same name. The novella, about an older man's passion for a much younger woman, had been Ford's favourite of all Maupassant's writings. But Ford also introduced Rhys to the novels of his cherished colleague, Joseph Conrad, and to the Russian writers, often in translations made by his friend Constance Garnett. One of the bleakest moments in Rhys's later life would come when a shortage of money and space obliged her to sell her treasured Russian novels. Putting them up for sale in the 1950s, she got only a few pounds in return.

———

WHILE RHYS WAS being introduced to a world of writers, poets and painters in the halcyon autumn of 1924, her husband made a reckless attempt to improve their family circumstances by speculating with money that had been entrusted to him by the tourist agency, earmarked for a specific commercial transaction. Arrested for an *abus de confiance* (premeditated felony) and taken on 28 December to the grim Parisian holding prison of La Santé, pending his trial, a distraught Lenglet begged Germaine Richelot to help him to get legal assistance. Curiously, he made no mention of Rhys, although Germaine's swift response expressed a pointed concern for "your poor little wife." It's possible that Lenglet already felt confident that Rhys would be protected by her powerful new friends.

Quartet, the novel published by Rhys in 1928, relates how a dismayed Marya Zelli is abruptly summoned into the back room of the cheap hotel in Montmartre where she and her husband have been staying. Informed by the hotel's owners that the police have taken Zelli to an undisclosed address, Marya remains in Paris. Rhys herself did not. During the late afternoon of 28 December (the very day of Lenglet's arrest), Ford chaperoned his protégée to the Gare de Lyon; there, the two of them were observed having a heated argument in the station brasserie. It seems likely that Rhys was disputing Ford's hasty decision to get her out of Paris before news of the scandal broke. Later that same evening, a wheezing Ford clambered onto the night train to the French Riviera to beg a favour of the artist Paul Nash and his remarkable wife, Margaret Odeh, a Jerusalem-born radical feminist with—it was said— clairvoyant powers. Ford may not have known that the Nashes had witnessed his quarrel with Rhys; now, he wanted to know if they, too, were travelling down to Cros de Cagnes? If so, could they take care of the suitcase keys which his young friend had inadvertently left behind her in the brasserie as she rushed to secure a seat—somewhere; he couldn't find her—on the Riviera-bound train? The Nashes knew Ford well enough to conclude that the lost passenger was a cast-off mistress. They gave him their word.

Settled into the main hotel at Cros de Cagnes, the Nashes waited for Ford's mystery friend to appear. When Rhys arrived, pale with dismay after spending the night at what she had assumed to be a pension (it proved to be a brothel) the Nashes invited her to supper and arranged for a room: "*Ah, les anglaises,*" tittered the hotel manager, swiftly assuming that Nash was sleeping with both women. No sooner was Rhys settled in than she asked Margaret to cover the cost of her return ticket to Paris. And that was that: the young woman "disappeared from our lives in the same ghost-like way in which she had appeared," Margaret Odeh Nash wrote in her unpublished memoir.[5]

Confirmation of the encounter at Cros de Cagnes—and evidence of Rhys's discomfort—would later surface in an unflattering portrait of the Nashes as the stiffly correct Olsens in "La Grosse Fifi," a story which Rhys wrote in the mid-Twenties and set on the French Riviera. "How rum some English people are!" the central character, Roseau, exclaims. "They ask to be shocked and long to be shocked, but if you really shock them . . . how shocked they are!"[6] The Nashes had not been shocked, but they were certainly intrigued. Setting out the subjects for a future chapter of his marvelous and sadly unfinished memoir, *Outline*, Paul Nash made an opaque reference to a Riviera encounter with the "blonde legacy from Ford."

Seeing her convicted husband was a prime reason for Rhys's return to Paris and she visited Lenglet as loyally as Marya Zelli would do in *Quartet*. At that stage, however, there was nothing Rhys could do for Lenglet (and almost as little to help herself). Like Marya, she sold her pretty Viennese dresses; possibly, Rhys begged assistance from her Aunt Clarice in Wales and received a modest sum, together with advice to seek help from some British clergymen settled in Paris. ("You could easily find out the address of one of them, or I could find out and send it to you," counsels Marya's kindly aunt, Maria Hughes, in *Quartet*.) Marya is taken to live with the Heidlers in their village home at Brunoy; Ford swept Rhys off to the cold little cottage at Guermantes where—as he disclosed to his new agent, William Bradley—the poor young woman became too ill even to work on her writing. Stella was also reported to be sick; a resigned Ford found himself acting as cook, cleaner and nurse, all amidst struggling to complete the second part of his great tetralogy, *Parade's End.*[7]

On 10 February 1925, Rhys learned that her husband had been found guilty of the planned felony charge. Jean Lenglet was condemned to spend two years in the notoriously brutal prison of Fresnes, and then to depart from France. Germaine Richelot advised Rhys to seek a divorce;

instead, a destitute Rhys turned for help to her new patrons. According to Stella Bowen's recollection, their unfortunate friend possessed only a few francs along with her precious writings; there was no question but that they would take her in. The flat on avenue Denfert-Rochereau contained a small spare room; there, Rhys could sleep and write while, for the foreseeable future, Ford and Stella acted as her providers and joint guardians. All they asked in return was that she should be compliant and discreet. As Rhys would later remark of this humiliating episode in her life, she really had no other option.

AS WITH MARYA ZELLI, Rhys's life now developed its own melancholy pattern. Once a week, she went to Versailles to visit little Maryvonne at the most recent orphanage to have been located by Germaine Richelot. Once a fortnight, she took a tram out to Fresnes. Seated opposite Lenglet in one of the square booths that reminded her of roofless telephone boxes, Rhys noticed how thin and nervous her husband had become. They still cared about each other; it was a fact which nobody else seemed to understand.

But Rhys had also fallen in love with Ford, and he with her, as he helped her to revise the short, almost sketch-like stories that she was writing about Paris and Dominica. Sometimes—which gave her pleasure—Ford would snatch up one of her pencilled scrawls and read it aloud, shaking his head when he stumbled over a banality ("Cliché! Cliché!") and putting on a solemn voice for passages that he admired. The praise felt good, and so did the reassurance of being loved. Stella worked on a portrait of their guest; Ford praised her mind and took her to bed with comforting enthusiasm. If Stella knew—as, despite her later, published protestations of ignorance, she probably did—she turned a blind eye to an affair which she had no power to prevent. Sometimes, when Rhys drank too much and felt that the couple were playing a cruel game of their own with her emotions, she lost control and screamed or even spat. This aspect of their emotional guest alarmed her hosts. Neither Ford nor Stella relished the dramas upon which Rhys seemed to thrive. Their highly strung protégée could write as much as she pleased about violence and despair without bringing her anger into what was, despite their bohemian friendships, an outwardly conventional household. They didn't want a fuss. Tensions grew.

Lenglet's prison sentence was shortened, due to good behaviour and the need for space in the large but always overcrowded prison of Fresnes. Released after four months, a shivering ghost of his former charming self, he was granted a few days of freedom before his enforced departure from France. In his largely autobiographical novel *Sous les verrous* (Under Lock and Key) published in 1933, Lenglet described Stania and Hubner (Rhys and Ford) coming to the station to wave him off to Belgium: Hubner, eager to see him gone after sitting through one disastrous dinner out for the four of them, even paid for his rival's rail ticket. Legally, Lenglet was exiled for life. The risks he took to return to his wife speak for the strength of his love for Jean.

And what, meanwhile, was to be done with "Ford's girl" and her inconvenient rages? Ford was still like a man under a spell, but Stella, on whose financial support and organisational skills he relied, was sick of being expected to play the calm, capable wife, as opposed to Rhys the victim—"the poor, brave and desperate beggar who was doomed to be let down by the bourgeoisie."[8] Their experimental ménage à trois had failed, and—as even Rhys had become aware—"it was high time I got away from Montparnasse."[9]

The solution arrived in the form of a potentially undemanding job in the south of France. Winifred Shaughnessy Hudnut, the languidly elegant wife of America's first cosmetics magnate, was the mother-in-law to Rudolph Valentino and—thanks to Hudnut's well-marketed products—the proud owner of the palatial Château Juan-les-Pins on the French Riviera. She was also an ardent spiritualist. In the summer of 1925, Mrs. Hudnut despatched a representative to Paris to seek out some writer gifted enough to assist her in writing a book about the importance of dressing in the spirit—so to speak—of one's previous incarnation.

The energy with which both Stella and Ford represented Jean Rhys as the perfect candidate for Winifred Hudnut's bizarre project reveals how eager they were to be rid of Rhys. Stella provided a glowing character reference for their friend; Ford went further and actually forged a couple of stories intended to showcase Rhys's vast knowledge of the eighteenth century (Mrs. Hudnut's favourite period) and of Russian folklore. (Ford's faux-Serbian folk tale has not survived, but doubtless contained much about reincarnation.) Their efforts were rewarded: on a hot afternoon in July 1925, for the second time in five months, Ford escorted his protégée to a train that was bound for the Riviera.

IT'S A SHAME that Ford kept none of the lively letters in which Rhys regaled him with tales of chateau life at Juan-les-Pins, but her two fictional accounts offer rich compensation. "At the Villa d'Or," a story published in Rhys's first collection, lightly disguises the lecherous and sprightly Mr. Hudnut as Robert B. Valentine, a vegetarian plutocrat who hatches plans to seduce his guest, a curvaceous young singer named only as "Sara of Montparnasse." The ethereal Mrs. Valentine, fiddling with her long strings of beads while she lolls on a cushioned sofa among her pekineses, ponders the merits of rice over ham ("I'm dead sick of rice, Bobbie"); Charles, her obsequious manservant, is fashionably English ("like the armchairs"). Sara, the Rhysian visitor, revels serenely in the chateau's luxury: "Very nice too," is her calm response to an opulent bathroom glittering with crystal bottles of scents and oils.

A Riviera palace had no place in the despairing life Rhys constructed for Marya Zelli in *Quartet*. A decade later, however, Rhys would return to her sojourn with the Hudnuts in *Good Morning, Midnight* (1939). There, in one of her fourth novel's most oddly tender scenes, Sasha Jensen and her suitor, René (a quick-witted gigolo whose history and appearance bear a striking resemblance to those of Jean Lenglet), share a moment of emotional connection in the discovery that they have been guests at the very same chateau: "Here are the palm trees. Here are the entrance steps. That terrible English butler they had—do you remember?" Briefly, Sasha and her dubious companion become cheerful allies in their memories of an absurd but privileged life.

Rhys's three months at Château Juan-les-Pins were far from wretched. Winifred Hudnut took her to Monte Carlo to hear the ageing Russian bass, Chaliapin, growling his way through a concert, while her husband preferred to take an attractive young woman to watch her lecherous host gambling at the casino. During the day, when not required to assist with Winifred's writing project, Rhys retired to her room to work over the collection of stories for which Ford had promised to find publishers in England and America. Sometimes, she went wandering. It was during an impulsive excursion to the deserted nearby beach at La Napoule that Rhys experienced a rare moment of bliss; a feeling of being at one with the world and filled with joy, "not only for me, but for everyone." Such moments never fooled Rhys for long; later, reshaping her exquisite epiphany as a story in draft form, she cynically named it: "The Forlorn Hope."[10]

Rhys's abrupt return to Paris was engineered by Ford. Winifred Hudnut had been displeased to learn from a sharp-eyed chauffeur that her husband had been coaxing kisses from their guest during their drives to Monte Carlo; what vexed her more was a complaint from Ford that a gifted writer was being asked to work unpaid on Winifred's second literary venture. Rhys had grumbled to her mentor about the lack of payment; she had not expected Ford to seize an excuse to summon her back to himself. Escorted to Paris by her irate employer, Rhys was greeted at the station by a beaming Ford. As for her own feelings: conducted by Ford to a grim hotel near Gare Montparnasse: "I thought of the Chateau Juan les Pins and very nearly burst into tears."[11]

"GOD SAVE ME I perish SOS SOS I am so alone."[12] That heartfelt wail most convincingly belongs to a period that would be vividly evoked in *Quartet* when Marya moves from the Heidlers' home into the Hotel du Bosphore, a sour reference by the well-read Rhys to the archly self-forgiving title of Ford's "Mr Bosphorus and the Muses."

At the chateau, Rhys had grown accustomed to luxury; in Paris, she became a poor dependent, isolated from the literary world to which Ford had introduced her, confined to a lonely room in which she wrote and drank and drowned herself in narcotics-induced sleep. Ford moved her to a nearby hotel on rue Vavin. He visited her once a week; he paid the bills. Rhys had become his part-time mistress—his private toy. It was better than nothing for a woman who remained, as *Quartet* would make painfully apparent, in love with this improbable Casanova. Her role now was that of the grateful dependent. Her lover called the shots. Plausible public encounters were conducted for Stella's benefit, to keep up the pretence of a conventional friendship between the three of them. Later, Rhys would remember the humiliation of being ordered by a lofty Stella to sit on the *strapontin*, the inferior seat, her back to the carriage driver, whenever the three of them shared a cab. Showing a quiet face to the world, she burned with rage and wounded pride.

Alone, Rhys visited her daughter. Occasionally, she ventured out with Ivan Beede, the friendly young novelist and poet from the American Midwest who had worked as Ford's assistant on the *transatlantic review*. Beede disapproved of what he saw as Ford's manipulative hold over Rhys. If *Quartet* can be believed (Beede appears there lightly disguised as "Cairn"), he was even prepared to borrow funds and give them to Rhys, simply to get her out of Ford's clutches. Marya Zelli turns Cairn's offer down. Jean Rhys did not stop seeing Ford.

At the centre of Rhys's life—throughout the bleak months that followed her return to Paris—stood her writing, a resource that is entirely absent from the lives of the women she describes in her novels. Glimpses of the world through which she drifted—a flâneur's habit that Rhys shared with her female protagonists and borrowed from Baudelaire—appear in the stories that now began to take their final form from pages of urgently scrawled notes. Sometimes, as in "Mixing Cocktails"—one of two sketches about her Caribbean childhood—she looked back, remembering the melancholy mountains of Dominica, the hammock where she lay dreaming at Bona Vista, the chirping voice of her visiting aunt, Clarice ("That *sea* . . . Could anything be

more lovely?"). Sometimes, evoking Parisian life among the down but
not quite out, Rhys trained a cold stare on her present self, mocking Miss Dorothy Dufreyne of "In the Rue de L'Arrivée" as the fallen
"Lady" (Rhys's own awkward term) who drinks a brandy and soda at
every second cafe she passes, while erroneously congratulating herself on not yet—despite the waiters' "curious stares"—appearing to be
entirely drunk. Sometimes, as in "The Sidi," Rhys would crib and recreate a story from one of Lenglet's eloquent accounts of his terrible four
months at Fresnes. She knew he wouldn't mind. Their shared passion
for writing (and above all, for *her* writing) would always remain a bond.
Lenglet was yet to understand how devastated his wife had been to see
her attractive husband transformed into the trembling ghost of himself that he became at Fresnes, or how intense and complex were her
feelings for Ford.

STELLA AND FORD were away at Avignon in July 1926, when Jean Lenglet stole back across the French border to secretly rejoin his wife in
Paris, while hiding away in the quiet suburb of Clamart. The Lenglets
had evidently remained in touch during his absence from France,[13] and
it's clear from the clandestine reunion that Rhys still cared about a husband who was willing to take such risks to be with her.

On 4 August, Lenglet was hunted down and once again expelled
from France (following a further miserable week-long stay at the for-
tress-like prison of La Santé). In mid-September, spurred by the fear of
losing his wife, Lenglet returned once more. Ford now tried yet again
to ship an unhappy Jean Rhys off to the Riviera, out of the reach of a
man he believed was endangering his protégée's literary future. She
refused to go. According to the fictional accounts subsequently provided by both Lenglet and Rhys herself, this was the moment when
Ford announced that he had personally endured enough. As a writer,
he would always support her; as a lover, he could take no more drama.
Rhys must have been distraught; ordered by a hysterical Lenglet to

choose between her lover and her husband, she refused to renounce Ford.

Quartet, at this moment of climax, permits an enraged Stephan Zelli to murder his wife with a cool *"Voila pour toi"* and then flee, accompanied by another, intriguingly available woman. In reality, a distraught Lenglet armed himself with a revolver and raced off with the crazed intention of killing his portly rival. The police had already learned enough to intercept the would-be assassin. Briefly thrown back into La Santé on 16 September, Lenglet was released only when he promised to leave France for ever.[14]

How had the gendarmes known where to find Lenglet, or that he planned to murder Ford? The most likely source of information was Stella Bowen, whose jealous anger still rang out when she described Rhys, in a memoir written fifteen years after these events, as a "doomed soul, violent and demoralised . . . She nearly sank our ship!"[15]

If Stella did go to the police, Ford did not discourage her. Emotionally, he was done with both women: as Ford sailed away to undertake a lucrative American lecture tour, Stella was left to comfort herself with a flowery public assurance of his enduring devotion. (It took the form of a dedicatory letter prefacing Ford's own new French translation of his finest novel, *The Good Soldier*). Professionally, as Rhys was aware, her faithless lover was still determined to promote her career. The difficulty that Ford now faced was how to offer continued literary support while closing the door on what had proved to be an exhausting and sometimes alarming love affair. It wouldn't be easy.

8

Hunger, and Hope (1926–28)

"The cardinal fact is that a woman cannot earn a decent living ... I'm going into wages and facts. They are utterly dependent on their sexual attraction for salvation."

—Patrick Hamilton to his brother Bruce Hamilton, May 1927[1]

RHYS WOULD OFTEN write about women who sold their bodies for sex. By the time that her affair with Ford had ended, she already knew that writing—not sex—was going to be her own salvation and that Ford, fuelled by guilt in addition to his unswerving belief in her talent, would do everything he could to help her obtain it. And he did. When Rhys travelled to London in the autumn of 1926, she had in her pocket two important introductions. One was to Joseph Conrad's devoted friend Edward Garnett, the éminence grise of Jonathan Cape, who—advised by Garnett—expressed a gratifying willingness to publish an unknown writer's collection of stories about low life in Paris, especially since they came with the guarantee of a preface by Ford, one of the most respected writers of the day. The second letter was to Leslie Tilden Smith, a publisher's reader and freelance editor who had written to Ford in Paris, asking for the names of any up-and-coming authors whom he might represent as their agent in London. Ford had promised to put him in touch with Jean Rhys.

In Paris, anxious to distance his own name from that of Rhys, Ford arranged (with Stella's reluctant consent) for Germaine Richelot to post copies of their talented friend's stories to a handpicked group of newspaper editors in the city: he knew that the advance publication of a tale in the fiction pages of a respected paper would help to promote Rhys's work, ahead of her British debut. The responses were respectful. One letter, which Richelot passed along to Rhys at her latest Montparnasse address (6 rue du Maine), came from Valentine Williams, the Paris editor of the *Daily Mail*. Writing back to praise the unnamed author in January 1927, Williams singled out Rhys's gift for sharpening descriptions by focusing on "unusual features." Perhaps Williams remembered Rhys visiting the *Mail* with her husband's stories and guessed at Ford's involvement; slyly, he suggested—at a time when Ford was commuting between Chicago and New York—that the most likely takers would be the *Chicago Tribune* and the *New York Times*.[2]

In America, where the promiscuous Ford had wasted no time in embarking upon new romantic liaisons, he made contact early in 1927 with a Chicago publisher, Pascal Covici, about a daring new novel. *Perversité* had been hopefully presented to Ford by its author, Francis Carco, just before his autumn departure for America. Ford liked Carco, a former wartime lover of Katherine Mansfield's; he admired the poems and novels in which Carco—like Pierre Mac Orlan, the writer so admired by Rhys—dealt with themes of passion, exploitation and abuse, set in a Parisian underworld. *Perversité* tells of a brother's incestuous desire, which ends in murder. It's uncertain whether the novel was discussed in the (presumably) professional letters which Ford continued, from abroad, to exchange with Rhys, but it is clear that he believed his hard-up protégée would make a sympathetic translator. Covici, who assumed that Ford himself would be doing the translation, was willing to pay a generous $250 in two instalments. Ford, although he could ill afford it in the early spring of 1927, advanced the entire sum to Rhys from his own pocket, while pretending the payment had come from Covici.

Ford's munificence was based on a shrewd calculation. Before leaving Paris, he had persuaded Stella Bowen and Germaine Richelot to collaborate on a discreet plan to assist the penniless Rhys after her husband's final banishment from France. From October 1926 until at least the end of February 1927, when Ford returned to France and cut off the payments, a weekly cheque for 400 francs was paid by Stella and transmitted to Rhys by Germaine.*³ As Ford hoped, Rhys assumed that she was being helped out by the kind-hearted Richelots. The translation payment was intended by Ford to fill the gap left by the terminated allowance.

Ford's keenness to stop subsidising Rhys was sharpened by his having to deal with Stella's suspicions. Dutifully forwarding Rhys's unopened bulletins to Ford's New York address, Stella told him that she imagined Rhys's report of her visit to London contained "a good deal" that was not professional. He made no response. A week or so later, Stella raised the subject with Ford once more ("You might let me know something of the affairs in that quarter"); sending along what she surmised was yet another billet-doux, she reproached Ford for remaining so annoyingly uncommunicative "on that subject." Close to the start of his American trip, Stella had pointedly hoped that Ford wouldn't bring home any more blondes: "I can't bear any more Fair Hair," she told her philandering lover. There wasn't much comfort in learning that a buxom and newly bewitched Mrs. Rene Wright was a brunette.⁴

Visiting London in the autumn of 1926 (as Ford sailed to New York), Rhys had kept away both from Lancey and from her unhappy family in Acton. This was to be a business trip. While Ford prevailed on Harper and Row in the US to publish his protégée's collected stories in the autumn of 1927, Rhys introduced herself to Edward Garnett. Having established that Jonathan Cape would publish *The Left Bank* in the spring of 1927, she arranged to meet Leslie Tilden Smith. Her arrival proved timely. Leslie, who worked for the Curtis Brown agency alongside his wife, Katherine Millard, had recently been left by Katherine for another man. In the autumn of 1926, a still devastated Tilden Smith was working for Hughes Massie, a split-off from the Curtis Brown

---

* In 1927, 400 francs was equivalent to just over £180 today. As a point of comparison, Ford and Stella were paying their daughter's full-time nanny 500 francs a year.

firm, while sharing a modest flat in west London with his seventeen-year-old daughter, Phyllis Antoinette.

Rhys's chief model for the gentlemanly George Horsfield in *After Leaving Mr Mackenzie*, Leslie Tilden Smith was the well-read and Oxford-educated son of a clergyman. Leslie's pale skin and an unexpectedly wide, white smile would lead Rhys, late in life, unkindly to compare him to the villainous and whitely smiling Mr. Carker of Dickens's *Dombey and Son*. (Rhys called her story about Leslie "The Joey Bagstock Smile," but it's clear that Rhys was remembering the odious Mr. Carker rather than roguish Major Bagstock, a character singular for the fact that he laughs, but never smiles at all.) Back in 1926, Rhys noticed Leslie's marmoreal skin and arctic beam less than his admiration for her work and his readiness to support her in a male-dominated publishing world where she could no longer depend upon Ford.

Leslie himself was enchanted by Rhys. So was his pretty daughter, especially when Rhys presented the teenage Antoinette with a ravishing black dress from a suitcase filled with Parisian clothes. Rhys's outward appearance, chic as a fashion model, formed a poignant contrast to her unconcealed anxiety about the cost of London hotels. A chivalrous Leslie insisted during this first visit both on finding his new client lodgings and paying for them himself; later, as they embarked on what Jean coyly described as a "50–50 affair," Tilden Smith invited her to treat his London home as her own.

In London, conscious of her indebtedness to Ford for the all-important introduction to her first publisher, Rhys managed to keep her anger under control. Back in Paris later that autumn, and unaware that Ford and Stella were paying her allowance, her rage finally bubbled over. In a fury fuelled by the alcohol upon which she was becoming increasingly reliant, Rhys dashed off a ferocious little story. "Houdia," which remains unpublished, tells of a sculptor who uses her sharp chisel to stab the eyes of her creation before attempting to shoot the sitter, her married lover. Rhys then set about turning her experiences with Ford, Stella and Lenglet into a play about which, in late November 1926, she sought the opinion of her old friend, Pearl Adam. Pearl, conscious of

Rhys's recent relationship with Ford, expressed herself with caution. She thought that "Iris" (representing Rhys herself) should be made more helpless; the portrait of Stella (as the knowingly deceived wife) was deemed too insubstantial to convince.[5]

Here, in a play now lost or destroyed, Rhys planted the bitter seeds from which her vengeful first novel would grow. The high degree of drama in *Quartet*, as compared to its relatively plotless successors, owes much to the fact that Rhys imagined it being performed on stage. Impossible though it is to prove—she kept none of Lenglet's letters from that time—Rhys's hostile attitude to Ford and Stella was likely to have been encouraged and stimulated by her absent husband.

Jean Lenglet's whereabouts during the autumn of 1926 remain unknown. In February 1927, however, he at last regained the Dutch citizenship that had been forfeited when he joined the French Foreign Legion. After months of extreme poverty, Lenglet thus became eligible for state care in the Netherlands and able to enter the country's equivalent of a workhouse. A man possessed of immense charisma and determination, Lenglet improved his position with remarkable speed. By the end of April, he was in charge of the poorhouse's library; by the end of the summer, he had been placed in charge of the institution itself.

Lenglet had not forgiven Ford. To him, it seemed clear that his marriage had been undermined by a powerful man's determination to seduce his wife; he was haunted by the memory of the deliberately humiliating occasion (Rhys would make good use of it in *Quartet*) on which Ford and Bowen had invited the couple to a restaurant dinner, during which he had been treated—as both the Lenglets agreed—like a common felon. Ford and Bowen had stage-managed Lenglet's final arrest; together, they had destroyed his happiness. When Rhys consented only to visit the poorhouse for a single late-winter fortnight— the paupers were enchanted by their visitor's wistful grace—Lenglet found himself once again, however irrationally, blaming his former rival. He was only partially comforted to learn from Rhys that Ford was in America and that she foresaw no likelihood of ever meeting him again.

Early in 1927, Rhys travelled to London for her mother's funeral. No details survive of the occasion. In *After Leaving Mr Mackenzie*, published four years later, Rhys offered an unsparing portrait of Julia Martin's shift from emotional breakdown during the crematorium service to a truculent verbal attack, back at the family house in Acton, on her sister, Norah. "You're jealous of me, jealous, jealous," Julia screams at the quietly provocative Norah, before informing their complacent Uncle Neville, who has just finished lecturing his bereaved nieces about, life, literature and Dostoevsky, that he himself is "an abominable old man." Later, seeing Julia walking jerkily down the road in a way that attracts curious looks, Uncle Neville wonders what will become of her. "And with decision, he crossed over to the other side of the street."⁶ An exaggeration, no doubt, but it may have been how Rhys recalled a bizarre day on which she herself had relished the chance for a battle with Brenda, the younger sister whom she had grown to both despise and envy.

Rhys spent most of the early spring of 1927 in Paris translating *Perversité*, a short novel by a writer whom she admired and with whose world, as Ford had been quick to appreciate, her own writings shared an affinity. She herself would almost certainly have written the book from the perspective of Irma, the doomed prostitute who is murdered by her brother, but Carco's nocturnal world of gaudy fairgrounds and seedy bars, similar to that depicted in Mac Orlan's wittier novel, *Marguerite de la Nuit*, was one on which Rhys had also drawn for her first Parisian stories.

Rhys's treatment of Carco's *Perversité* provides valuable glimpses of her own development as a novelist. She took artistic liberties, breaking Carco's twenty-two chapters into four parts—much as she would do in her own fiction—with subtitles emphasising a unifying element within each section. She strengthened Carco's menacing emphasis on the colour red—symbolising bloodshed—and his powerful use of shadows. Songs were left in the original French, as in "La Grosse Fifi," a tale in which Rhys had imbued Carco's fictional world of violence and sudden death with her own sardonic wit.

She worked fast, completing the translation of Carco's novella of 127 pages in under six weeks. The pride Rhys took in her achievement is clear from the fact that she allowed Germaine to read chapters of her work aloud to an admiring old Madame Richelot before the finished work was despatched to Ford. In March 1927, on the verge of her own first book's publication in England, Rhys experienced a moment of calm satisfaction. She had done well to be chosen by Jonathan Cape and to find herself an agent who was prepared to type out her manuscripts while offering shrewd advice and—as part of a seemingly affectionate sexual transaction—free accommodation. Translating a fine and intriguingly dangerous writer would do no harm at all to her burgeoning career.

Rhys had already received her payment in full. She was not to know that Ford would hang onto *Perversity* for three months. In June, while passing it along to Covici from the French summer home that he still occasionally shared with Stella, Ford casually announced that he himself had given the translation a few tweaks. Ford's intentions remain ambivalent, but it was just what an unscrupulous publisher needed to hear. Jean Rhys was unknown; Ford Madox Ford, in 1927, was one of the most celebrated writers in North America. Ford, not Rhys, would be announced from its first publication until the present time as the sole translator of Carco's novel.

THE LEFT BANK: *Sketches and Studies of Present-Day Bohemian Paris* was published by Jonathan Cape in March 1927. The announcement "With a Preface by Ford Madox Ford" dominated a stark cover which presented the black-and-white image of a dejected tramp seated beside the Seine. Turning the page, the reader found sixteen pages of meandering evocation, not of Rhys's Paris, but of Ford's own, rifled from his recently published collection of memories: *A Mirror to France*. Instead of praising Rhys's stories, Ford entertained Jean Rhys's first readers in England with his musings on the Parisian underworld, complete with a Carco-esque recollection of being chased home one night by a gang

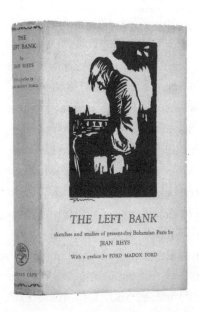

Jonathan Cape's cover for Rhys's first published work was resolutely downbeat. The artist is unknown.
(Used with permission of Peter Harrington Antiquarian Books)

of thugs. A braver editor might have told Ford to quit writing about himself. Unfortunately, neither Jonathan Cape nor Edward Garnett possessed sufficient gumption.

Twelve pages in, and still on a roll, Ford finally recalled the purpose of his preface. "Coming from the Antilles," he wrote:

> Miss Rhys has let her pen loose on the Left Banks of the Old World—on its gaols, its studios, its salons, its cafes, its criminals, its midinettes . . . One likes [. . .] to be connected to something good, and Miss Rhys's work seems to me to be so very good, so vivid, so extraordinarily distinguished by the rendering of passion, and so true, that I wish to be connected with it.

The author's vivid style and subject matter, as Ford was keen to explain in his interminable preface, were far from his own—"No! . . . Her business was with passion, hardship, emotion." Unlike himself, although similarly possessed of "remarkable technical gifts" and a "singular interest for form," the exotic Miss Rhys had a "terrific—an almost lurid!—passion for stating the case of the underdog."

So far, so painfully condescending. But Ford did admire Rhys's work, and he concluded by expressing the hope that when "hundreds of years hence!—her [Rhys's] ashes are translated to the Pantheon . . . a grain or so of my scattered and forgotten dust may go too, in the folds." Such extravagant hyperbole failed to sweeten Rhys's bitterness.

Rhys, still unaware of the fate of her translation of Carco's novel, felt swindled by Ford's hijacking of her collection of stories to promote his own work. Nevertheless, Ford's long-winded introduction drew attention to an unknown author whose "sketches and studies" might otherwise have sunk without trace. *The Left Bank*'s English reviewers didn't go overboard, but they were willing to allow that Miss Rhys's depiction of the underworld of Paris was alarmingly convincing. Hints were dropped that her subject matter was not quite ladylike, but her prose was praised for its originality. "Vienne" and "La Grosse Fifi" attracted particular praise in England. The *New York Times*, reviewing the Harper's publication towards the close of 1927, opined that her style was "singular." A little surprisingly, not one of the reviewers drew comparisons to Katherine Mansfield, a writer to whose more conventional stories of Paris Jean Rhys had been introduced by Ford.

Coming from Jonathan Cape and heralded by a tribute from Ford, *The Left Bank*'s resolute determination not to glamorise Paris helped to place Jean Rhys's name on London's literary map, during the year that Virginia Woolf published *To the Lighthouse*. In May 1927, Rhys received a letter from an old friend, who addressed her as "My dear Kitten," before carefully folding down the top of his note to conceal that tender endearment from the eyes of his work colleagues.[7]

Clearly, the former lovers had maintained some degree of communication; Lancey knew Rhys's French address and regretted not having seen her over Easter, when he had spent a day in Paris. "Is all well [*sic*] write and tell me Lancey." Writing again three weeks later and signing off with "Great Affection," Lancey expressed his frustration at not having yet read her allegedly daring book. "Has it [*The Left Bank*] been stopped by the Censor?" he wondered. "Anyway I am longing to see it. One day you will tell me about the past two years . . . "[8]

Did she? No evidence of a further correspondence has survived, but the presence of a Lancey-like figure four years later in *After Leaving Mr Mackenzie* (1931)—affably remote, but always ready to sign a cheque when required—suggests that the former lovers remained in touch. Rhys's portrait of Mr. Neil James, a connoisseur of fine art, courting Julia Martin's opinion on his most recent acquisitions, makes sad fun of a mismatched affair which had led, in life, to an abortion, an attempted suicide and the humiliation to a proud but poor young woman of being paid off. "[Mr. James] was anxious because he did not want to love the wrong thing," Rhys wrote, mocking Lancey. "Fancy wanting to be told what you should love!"[9]

By May, Rhys had resumed work on *Quartet*. The novel's chief character, Marya Zelli, lives in seedy hotels; Rhys's working conditions were far less bleak. In the autumn of 1926, she had occupied a room on rue du Maine; Lancey wrote to his "kitten" the following May at 9 rue Victor Cousin. These were pleasant side streets in Montparnasse; Germaine was probably paying the rent. The Richelots never lacked money; Germaine took pleasure in helping a friend in whose ability to write a great novel she had complete faith—"even if" (as she gently teased) "you do prefer short stories."[10]

For Rhys herself, it took a long struggle to advance beyond creating a simple record of the past. All she knew was that her novel—she toyed with calling it "Masquerade"—would explore the predicament of an impoverished young woman whose husband is jailed and whose protectors betray her. In the summer of 1927, her puppets had not yet wriggled free of their strings. Her progress—when she was not half-heartedly working in undemanding jobs at fashion houses or cosmetics stores, obtained through glowing testimonials from Germaine—remained slow.[11]

The reason why Germaine and Rhys fell out remains unclear. One cause was Rhys's discovery of her friend's compliance in hiding the source of an allowance that had been paid to Jean for six months by Ford and Stella. But Germaine could also be controlling. It wasn't agreeable to be lectured on the need to obtain a divorce from Jean

Lenglet, for whom Rhys's feelings remained both loving and protective. Neither was it easy for a proud woman to accept that Germaine was both choosing the series of Catholic orphanages at which little Maryvonne still regularly lodged, and paying for the child's clothes and uniforms. The Richelots had even ventured to raise the possibility of adopting Maryvonne themselves. Putting aside her troublesome novel for a few weeks, Rhys vented her altered feelings about the Richelots in a savage little story. Provisionally titled "Susan and Suzanne," it presented a young mother (Susan Helder) who is mistakenly shot while attempting to steal jewellery from her employer. The employer, who adopts Susan's orphaned child, is called Madame Brega. Germaine's sister was Madame Bragadir.[12]

Though it's unlikely that Rhys showed this particular unpublished story to her friend, she certainly made her anger felt. In September 1927, Germaine made a dignified attempt to put things right. "I see that you still have much bitterness against me," she wrote after receiving what appears to have been a grudging apology. But: "My dear Ella, I have nothing to forgive (had I anything to forgive you would be forgiven long ago, as you are unhappy, and because I did love you)."[13]

Jean Lenglet left his job on the same September day that Germaine despatched her kindly message to Rhys. Sacked for appropriating funds intended for the poorhouse library, Lenglet returned to The Hague where—somehow—he acquired a pleasant home at 3 Esdoornstraat, close to the city's broad beaches and nature reserve. This, from October 1927 until early the following year, was the home of the reunited Lenglets and their five-year-old Maryvonne. The reunion, though relatively brief, was evidently successful, since they repeated it in the summer of 1928.

Rhys was still with Lenglet at The Hague when news reached her of what appeared to be an act of incredible treachery. *Perversity* had been published in the US in her translation, but under Ford's name. She may never have known about the frantic letters of protest that Ford had fired off to Covici, but the apparent betrayal stoked a fierce resentment that Lenglet did nothing to dampen as his indignant wife worked on *Quartet*, with her husband at her shoulder.

Was Lenglet a sympathetic listener, or was he himself contributing to the novel? The question arises because Lenglet would later surprisingly claim in the Dutch press, where his word was accepted as the truth, that he had co-written Rhys's first three publications. Certainly, their relationship as writers had always been one of friendly collaboration. *The Left Bank* had included "From a French Prison" and "The Sidi," based on Lenglet's account of the tragic death of a sensitive young Arab at Fresnes. Yet Rhys would always state that it was she alone who wrote her books, and there's no reason to doubt her. What Lenglet did contribute to the writing of *Quartet* was faith in his wife's ability, combined with a shared memory of key moments—like the restaurant encounter with Ford and Stella that had followed his release—on which his wife intended to draw.

"MASQUERADE" REMAINED THE working title for a darkly satiric novel about appearances and their deceptions. Visiting a new restaurant, Marya Zelli finds "no *patronne*, but the patron was beautifully made up." Warning Marya against the English in Paris, the friendly artist Esther de Solla tells her: "They touch life with their gloves on. They're pretending all the time."[14] Rhys's prose glitters with irony on every page, especially when she writes about Stella Bowen, easily recognisable as the opinionated and commanding Lois Heidler. The angry contempt of Bowen's subsequent portrait of Rhys in *Drawn from Life* was an understandable response to the vicious way that Stella had found her cultural aspirations lampooned in *Quartet*. Here, in one of the milder passages, Lois is painting Marya, her guest. Lois, as usual, is holding forth:

> The movement of her head was oddly like that of a bird picking
> up crumbs. She talked volubly . . . and it was evident that she took

Montparnasse very seriously indeed. She thought of it as a possible stepping-stone to higher things and she liked explaining,
classifying, fitting the inhabitants (that is to say, of course, the
Anglo-Saxon inhabitants) into their proper place in the scheme
of things.

Ford is more gently treated. We see Heidler striding "masterfully" up
and down the room as his amiably elephantine contribution to a dancing party given by his alter ego, Mr. Rolls. Later, Heidler asks Marya
(his mistress) to save Lois from embarrassment by pretending to maintain a friendship: "You've got to play the game." Heidler lays out his
conditions—the helpless Marya will be cared for, and loved, so long as
she agrees to abandon her convicted husband. In the end, it is Marya
whose heart is broken, when Heidler leaves her and returns to Lois.
"I loved him too," Marya proclaims to her husband in the awkwardly
melodramatic last pages of the book.[15] Rhys herself remained publicly
silent about her feelings for Ford throughout her life.

What evidently bothered Rhys most about her relationship with
Ford and Stella, as she worked on *Quartet*, was the persistent recollection of being robbed of her freedom. Released from prison, Stephan
Zelli describes liberty as an illusion: "When you come out—but you
don't come out. Nobody ever comes out." Ordered back into captiv-
ity with the Heidlers by their friend Miss Nicholson, Marya identifies her own situation with that of an entrapped fox. "Up and down it
ran . . . Up and down, up and down, ceaselessly. A horrible sight, really.
"Sweet thing," said Miss Nicholson."[16]

The novel which Rhys brought back to London from Holland in
the summer of 1928 was typed out from her habitual scrawl by a painstaking Leslie Tilden Smith. Offered to Jonathan Cape, it was rejected
on the grounds that Rhys's portrait of Ford Madox Ford as Heidler
was libellous. Jonathan Cape's nervousness was understandable; he was
already taking a considerable risk in publishing Radclyffe Hall's sensational lesbian novel, *The Well of Loneliness*, over which he would lose an
expensive lawsuit later that year. Rhys's novel also contained troubling

hints of same-sex relationships; reassuring her jealous husband about the way Lois clasps her hand beneath a restaurant table, Marya shrugs it off: "Oh, she often does that."[17]

When Jonathan Cape turned Rhys's book down, his colleague Edward Garnett stepped in to recommend her novel to Frank Swinnerton, his discerning colleague at a rival firm. Retitled *Postures* to highlight her treatment of disguise and pretence, Rhys's first full-length work of fiction was published in the autumn of 1928 by Chatto. Friends were enthusiastic. Germaine Richelot hurried to congratulate Rhys: "I know enough of your life, dear Ella, to feel I was "reliving" it with you as I reread the book."[18] Ivan Beede praised the novel's poetic language. Like an admiring Leslie Tilden Smith, Beede was put in mind by Rhys's Paris scenes of T. S. Eliot's ability to conjure up the echoing vacancies of a nocturnal metropolis; Beede mentioned Eliot's "Portrait of a Lady," while Tilden Smith compared *Postures* (favourably) to "Prufrock."

The reviewers—they were predominantly male—hedged their bets. Admiring Rhys's laconic style and the originality of her voice, they deplored—as in the *Left Bank* stories—the way she dwelt upon "squalor." True, the glamorous Kiki of Montparnasse (Alice Prin) and her lover, Foujita, could be glimpsed in a passing reference to "Cri-cri" with the Japanese companion whom Lois Heidler longs to lure to her parties. But where was the exhilarating city of Josephine Baker, and frantic jazz and flirtations? What were they to make of a protagonist who brazenly declared her intention of becoming "so drunk that I can't see"? Wasn't Heidler stating the obvious (Rhys's irony went clean over their heads) when he said that "nobody owes a fair deal to a prostitute. It isn't done"?[19] While conceding with majestic reluctance that the author was "an artist," the *Manchester Guardian* opined that "a great deal depends on what she does next."[20]

For the 1928 reviewer, knowing nothing about Jean Rhys's life, it would have been impossible to appreciate the art with which Rhys had transferred her own experiences into the life of a less educated heroine. By excluding the literary aspect of her own connection to Ford from the novel, Rhys was able to alter the relationship between the characters. Marya has only her body to offer, as a model for a bewitched Lois, and as a mistress for a quietly oppressive Heidler. Far more passive than her creator, she is as much of a prisoner as her incarcerated spouse. Only occasionally—it seems to be an authorial lapse when Marya quotes Edouard Dujardin's famous novella's title "*Les lauriers sont coupés*" (usually translated as "We'll go to the woods no more), as Heidler prises open her bedroom door—does the sophisticated sensibility of Jean Rhys glint through the simpler, sadder personality of a young woman whose increasing reliance upon alcohol is firmly connected by Rhys to Marya's relationship with the worldly, hard-drinking Heidler.

Quartet is by no means artistically perfect. The shifts in points of view are executed as unsubtly as the moments in which Lois expresses her jealousy of Marya ("she ought to sing for her supper; that's what she's here for, isn't it"),[21] or when "HJ" (Rhys seems to be mocking Ford's reverence for Henry James) bluntly spells out the novel's theme of imprisonment by remarking that: "One's caught in a sort of trap." Nevertheless, Rhys had taken a remarkable leap forward from the sharply observed sketches of 1927 to the well-planned structure and confidently ironic tone of 1928. Leslie Tilden Smith now felt ready to devote himself entirely to encouraging and promoting such an exceptional talent.

Shortly after reading the reviews of *Quartet*, Rhys carried Maryvonne away from her father in Holland for a promised three-month holiday, beginning with a happy stay at Bandol in the south of France. It was the first time since leaving Paris that Rhys had been alone with her daughter. Lenglet, regarding himself as the more devoted parent, criticised her for negligence. "*Elle desire jouer, courir, discuter meme* ['She needs to play, run about, chat']," he scolded his wife on 21 February 1929. Given that Lenglet himself welcomed Maryvonne back to Holland by installing her at the home of a certain Madame van der Heyden, this seems unjust.[22]

Tireless though both Rhys and Lenglet now became about creating delightful stories for their daughter's amusement (several of Lenglet's

Maryvonne Lenglet and her father in Holland, c. 1929. Dutch was her first language, and would remain so. *(McFarlin)*

small hand-bound texts survive, as do Rhys's regular gifts of classic children's books like *Treasure Island*), they had abandoned Maryvonne during her early years. More lavish presents helped assuage Rhys's conscience. Such indulgence became easier for Rhys in 1929 after Simon & Schuster agreed to publish *Postures* in America, where they retitled it *Quartet*.

Why the sudden transatlantic interest in an almost unknown writer? It is possible that Ford (perhaps still feeling guilty about Covici's blushless naming of himself as the translator of Carco's novel) mentioned Rhys to the literary agent Paul Revere Reynolds, a shrewd, slow-spoken

New Englander who had represented everybody from Joseph Conrad to Lytton Strachey, and who now, unexpectedly, took Jean Rhys on as his client.

Reynolds was famous for getting good deals for his authors. Encouraged by their own inhouse reader's praise for the newly named *Quartet* as a work of "Flaubertian economy," Simon & Schuster offered a generous advance which also owed something to their hope that Rhys's daring novel would follow the runaway success of *Bad Girl*, Viña Delmar's racy 1928 tale of life in Harlem.[23]

By the summer of 1929, Rhys was finally enjoying the ease of a little financial freedom with which to work on a second novel. Not yet wholly committed to a personal relationship with Leslie Tilden Smith, she used her American advance to return to Paris.

IV

THE RHYS WOMAN
Jean Rhys

"Every day is a new day. Every day you are a new person."

—Jean Rhys, *After Leaving Mr Mackenzie*

9

Two Tunes:
Past and Present (1929–36)

> "When you were a child, you put your hand on the trunk of a tree and you were comforted . . . you knew that it was friendly to you, or at least, not hostile. But of people you were always a little afraid."
>
> —Jean Rhys, *After Leaving Mr Mackenzie* (1931)

AFTER LEAVING MR MACKENZIE was written in Paris and London over a period of two years from 1929. During that time, Rhys unexpectedly found herself having to care for Maryvonne on her own for several months while Lenglet—no explanation was provided for his abrupt departure—disappeared from Holland. Much though Rhys loved her solemn little girl, the frustration proved considerable of having to combine child care with the demands of writing a novel. Thankfully returning to Leslie Tilden Smith's mews flat in Holland Park from the hated south London convent school at which she briefly boarded (it was the mother branch of the Virgo Fidelis convent formerly attended by Rhys in Dominica), Maryvonne witnessed enough drama to decide that she herself would never attempt to become a writer.*

---

* "This was idiotic of me," Rhys later told Sonia Orwell of the impulsive decision to send her daughter to the school in South Norwood. "Because I'd liked my convent

Rhys's difficulties with producing her second and more carefully crafted novel are still apparent in the draft that survives at the British Library. Sometimes, only a few words were scribbled across a sheet of paper; insistent repetitions and carefully indicated gaps show how fully the novel needed to take shape in Rhys's mind before she felt ready to commit any readable writing to a page.

Although less directly autobiographical than its predecessor, *After Leaving Mr Mackenzie* contains many links to Rhys's own life. Some are easily spotted: Julia Martin, the narrator, remembers having been frightened and fascinated by masks as a child growing up in a hot and distant country. Her family live in Acton. She has had two unsatisfactory love affairs. She even occupies rooms in a cheap hotel on the Quai des Grands-Augustins, where Rhys began working on the novel in 1929. Unlike Julia, however, Rhys was typing out an English student's doctoral thesis in order to pay the rent.[*] Mr. Mackenzie is a pompous caricature of Ford, but Rhys is playing games with the reader by allowing Julia to discover him tucking into a dish of veau Clamart: Clamart was where Lenglet had skulked while hiding from the Paris gendarmerie. Another example of Rhys's layering and game-playing is the way in which she signals *Mackenzie*'s debt to Katherine Mansfield's "The Daughters of the Late Colonel" (especially in the portrayal of Julia and Norah as two fatherless sisters well past girlhood). Rhys winks her acknowledgement to Mansfield's story when Julia's cautious admirer, George Horsfield, follows the announcement of his father's military rank with a troubling non sequitur: "Pa was a colonel. I was

---

I imagined that a convent was a kind and pleasant place to be" (Jean Rhys to Sonia Orwell, 3 May 1971, McFarlin 2.8.f6).

[*] In 1929, Elsie Phare (later Elsie Duncan Jones) spent a few months in Paris, where she met Samuel Beckett and also Jean Rhys, who unexpectedly volunteered to type out her dissertation on English Royalists in exile. Later, Elsie blamed Rhys's abysmal typing for her failure to gain a fellowship (Elsie Duncan Jones obituary, *Independent*, 23 October 2011; Professor Peter Davidson, her former pupil, confirms the details: Davidson to author, 20 December 2020).

seduced by a clergyman at a garden-party. Pa shot him. Heavens, how the blighter bled!"¹ Mansfield's story of a colonel's two daughters had appeared in a collection called *The Garden Party* in 1922.

Finding the biographical clues hidden within a Rhys novel is always fun. Echoes and parallels can be filleted out; resemblances and points of difference can swiftly be established between the fiction and the life of its creator. Entertaining though the enterprise may be, it's a pursuit which undermines appreciation of Rhys's uncanny ability to engage with readers who know nothing about her personal circumstances.

While connected to *Quartet* in its use of the third person and abruptly shifting points of view, Rhys's second novel is more sophisticated in the way that it separates the imagined Julia from the actual Jean. Although close to Rhys in her obsession with appearance, her vulnerability, lightning rages and casual reliance upon alcohol for a boost, Julia Martin—like Marya Zelli—is neither a writer nor even especially cultured. The "Rolling down to Rio" rhyme that haunts Julia—and neatly flags up her Brazilian childhood—comes from Kipling's popular children's book, the *Just So Stories*. Modigliani's brazenly exposed nude, with which Julia registers a disturbing affinity when she first sees it, is feebly described by her as "a rum picture." A reference to Joseph Conrad's early novel, *Almayer's Folly*—to which Rhys had been introduced by Ford—arises from the consciousness not of Julia, but of her quietly valiant sister, Norah Griffiths. Julia—it's clear—wouldn't know who Conrad was. Unlike Rhys, who hated the sense of being indebted, Julia Martin is a habitual parasite, a woman who takes money without shame from anyone she can persuade to bestow it. (She meets her match in Uncle Griffiths, the affluent but tight-fisted relative who stumps up a pound, but only to ensure his embarrassing niece's immediate departure from England.)

Rhys's genius—still not fully flowered in her fortieth year, but growing at an astonishing rate—lay in her unfailing ability to create, within fewer than 150 pages, a world that is both uniquely alien and recognisably mundane. The grim outline of Julia's future life is visible from the bald opening statement ("After she had parted from Mr Mackenzie, Julia went to live in a cheap hotel on the Quai des Grands Augustins"[2]) to their second farewell at the novel's disturbingly inconclusive ending:

> "Goodbye," said Mr Mackenzie.
>
> The street was cool and full of grey shadows. Lights were beginning to come out in the cafes. It was the hour between dog and wolf, as they say.[3]

RHYS WOULD SOMETIMES describe *Mackenzie* as her best novel. The unshowy but always telling vocabulary (Uncle Griffiths sounds "alarmed and annoyed"; Julia speaks to her inert mother in a "frightened, hopeful" voice) reminds us that Ford had introduced his protégée to the early work of James Joyce; she could always quote lines from *Dubliners*. Shafts of sardonic wit lighten the darkness: a landlady is briskly skewered on her notion of acceptable behaviour in a female lodger: "A man, yes; a bottle, no,"[4] while Mr. Mackenzie's tips are "not always in proportion with the benevolence of his stomach."[5] Julia's stingy uncle greets his penniless niece with utter disbelief: "as he might have said: 'A zebra? A giraffe?' "[6]

Of less interest to her first readers than to students of literature is the way in which—far more than in *Quartet*—Rhys held herself apart from the imaginary Julia Martin. Rhys's appearance remained exceptionally youthful and attractive. It is unlikely that any man reacted to her as a hopeful stroller does after a swift backward glance at Julia's haggard face in the novel's closing chapter, "Last." ("*Oh la la*," he said. "*Ah, non alors*"). Rhys's sharp eye, not Julia's, notices how the host of a certain Parisian restaurant always positions himself on the kitchen stairs, in order to leer up the skirts of female customers. Rhys, not Julia, undercuts the consideration shown by Mr. James (modelled upon the business-like Lancey) when he announces the precise number of minutes he can allot to a meeting with his former mistress. ("I've got loads of time—heaps of time. Nearly three-quarters of an hour.")[7] Rhys, not

Julia, skilfully prefigures a suicidal moment beside the Seine through a deftly planted reference to Mr. James's vase of drooping tulips.* Dying, "with curved grace in their death,"[8] the flowers will return as sirens of the night river, shadows that "thrust out long, curved, snake-like arms and beckoned."[9] Here, far more than in *Quartet*, Rhys's prose approaches poetry in its evocative use of images—like the suggestive vase of tulips—to conjure up Julia's thoughts.

JONATHAN CAPE PUBLISHED *After Leaving Mr Mackenzie* early in 1931. The times were commercially challenging; the novel's jazzily bright pink and yellow jacket—it showed Parisian-style houses bordering the Seine—was directed at a broader market than *The Left Bank*'s heroically gloomy cover (from the same publishing house).

American publication by Knopf followed in June, but only after Rhys's unflattering portrait of Ford, a major figure in the States, as Mr. Mackenzie had caused a nervous Max Schuster to reject the novel which his publishing firm had been keenly anticipating since 1929. Reviewers were unanimous in praising the exceptional quality of Rhys's writing: the critics for the *Observer* and the *Daily Telegraph* described it as "flawless" and "superb," while America's *Saturday Review* astutely praised Rhys's prose for possessing "the balance and beauty of verse."[10] Militating against any hope of popular success on either side of the Atlantic for Rhys's second novel were the vociferous objections made to a morally dubious heroine and—once again—a "squalid" tale. The point was rammed home when *The Times* and the *Times Literary Supplement* simultaneously published an anonymous review in which *Mackenzie* was dismissed as "a waste of talent," expended on "a sordid little story."[11] Rebecca West, while assuring readers of the *Telegraph*

---

* Rhys's first working title, "Wintry Orchids," hinted through its glacial invocation of a famously sexual flower (the courtesan Odette in Proust's novel wears a corsage of orchids) at Mr. James's chilling kindness to Julia, his former mistress. Possibly, a vase of orchids had preceded the drooping tulips she sees in her lover's Mayfair home after he—once again—bails her out.

that Rhys was among the finest writers of her generation, regretted that such an interesting writer should be "enamoured of gloom to an incredible degree."[12]

By 1931, Leslie Tilden Smith was working in a freelance capacity for his friend Jamie (Hamish was his given name) Hamilton's new London publishing firm, with connections in the States provided by Hamilton's second job as a scout for Cass Canfield, head of Harper's. Editors and publishers talk among themselves; overheard trade gossip may have led even Rhys's devoted supporter at home to question the darkness of her subject matter. "My father had tremendous faith in her writing . . . he did all the typing and correcting," Leslie's daughter would inform Diana Athill in 1967.[13] Within the privacy of her notebooks, however, Rhys jotted angry notes about observations made by a certain "Mr Smith," who considers that the only kind of writing to succeed "is written to make money," and that authors who "drink and starve and all the rest are mad." Elsewhere in the same black exercise book, Rhys recorded a quarrel during which "L" warned her that "a writer is always to be identified with the kind of person he or she writes about." Defending herself, Rhys had begun to shout. "Well then said L, enjoying himself in his quiet way . . . Yes he said now don't get excited and don't use that awful language."[14]

Behind what read like fragments from actual discussions lies the

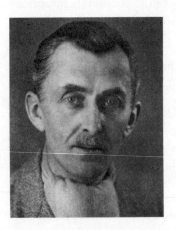

Leslie Tilden Smith, Rhys's second husband. *(McFarlin)*

sense of Rhys's personal anxiety. She didn't need to be warned that novels like *Quartet* and *Mackenzie* would never make her rich. The problem of distinguishing herself from the women about whom she wrote would become a lifelong concern. She was, and still too often is, judged by the fictitious alter egos whom she created, but only in part resembled.

In 1929, when Rhys started work on her second novel, one of the few fictional characters comparable to Rhys's wayward Marya Zelli and Julia Martin was the surrealist poet André Breton's Nadja, a woman who (in Breton's words) "enjoyed being nowhere but in the streets, the only region of valid experience for her." Breton had published *Nadja* in 1928, just before the UK publication of *Postures* (*Quartet*). It is unclear when Rhys first read the book, but she could still hold a discussion with a fellow admirer in her eighties about the merits of *Nadja*.[15] Writing to a new American friend in June 1931, Rhys confessed that she liked *Mackenzie* above anything she had yet achieved. Seeking a French publisher, she sent a copy to Ford's Paris agent, William Bradley.[*] Her pride was justified; *Mackenzie* reached a significant group of admirers. They included a talented Irish writer whose own wild personality matched that of Rhys at full tilt, but Norah Hoult—unlike Peggy Kirkaldy, Evelyn Scott and Norah's own husband, Oliver Stonor, a novelist writing under the pseudonym of a Devon village, Morchard Bishop—was never to become a personal friend.

Peggy Kirkaldy (born Margaret Jacks) was a tiny and kind-hearted woman with a hot temper, a weakness for the racecourse and a devastatingly sharp tongue. Among writers, she was on good terms with Elizabeth Bowen, Jocelyn Brooke and Denton Welch, but her closest and most long-standing literary friendship was with Dorothy Richardson, author of the *Pilgrimage* cycle of novels. Always hopeful of becoming a writer herself, Peggy divided her time between socialising

---

[*] Bradley's friendship with Ford did not stop him talking to Rhys, when she visited Paris in September the following year, about a publisher for "Triple Sec." Rhys excused herself, claiming that she had "borrowed enough" from it for her work-in-progress (*Voyage in the Dark*) to render the original unsaleable (JR to WB, 3 February 1931; 21 September 1932; 1 October 1932, William H Bradley papers, HRC).

at her London house, and self-imposed seclusion—she felt that solitude helped her writing—at an isolated home on the Norfolk Broads.

By 1931, when Peggy first made contact with her, Rhys was living with Leslie Tilden Smith in Elgin Crescent, west London. Peggy paid a visit to the flat; the two women hit it off. Growing chummy over a glass—or two or three—Jean discovered a sympathetic listener to whom she could groan about Leslie's sporadic attempts to restrict her drinking. Writing to Peggy later, Jean was treacherously frank about Leslie's gift of an "awful" hat during a damp, joint excursion to Cambridge. Conscious that Peggy had smart friends, Rhys put on airs. Cambridge was described as "rather a darling place"; one early letter was signed "*A bientot*, as they say" (this from a woman who spoke impeccable French). More candidly, Rhys expressed her urgent hope of making some money with a third novel, one on which she had just embarked. Income was needed; when Rhys first met him, Leslie was already running short after borrowing heavily against his future inheritance (his clergyman father planned to divide a modest legacy equally between a prudent daughter and a spendthrift son). Freelance editing for a burgeoning publisher, however kind-hearted a one, was not well paid.[16]

The friendship which Rhys formed with the strong-willed and beautiful Evelyn Scott and her second husband, John Metcalfe, promised to be more important to Rhys's career. A respected novelist and exceptional critic, Scott's literary fame by the late Twenties was so great that her reader's report on William Faulkner's *The Sound and the Fury* (1928) had been published as a preface to a limited edition of the novel, together with its editor's prediction that Mr. Faulkner's star might one day rise high enough to glitter alongside Scott's own. James Joyce had personally written to thank Evelyn for a discerning early review of *Ulysses* in *The Dial*.

Scott's private life was equally remarkable. Three years younger than Rhys, she had eloped in 1913, aged twenty, swapping a shabbily grand life in Tennessee for a lonely hut in the wilds of Brazil. While there, Scott's unhappy mother showed up and stayed on to create a

An arresting portrait of Rhys's influential American admirer, the novelist Evelyn Scott. *(Used with permission of Denise Scott Fears)*

threesome with Evelyn and her married—and much older—partner from the South, a promiscuous author, playwright and physician in tropical medicine called Frederick Creighton Wellman. Returning to New York, her affairs with Waldo Frank and William Carlos Williams had done nothing to hinder Evelyn Scott's ascent in the literary world before her second marriage, in 1930, to the English-born Metcalfe.

In June 1931, writing to Rhys from the steamer bound for New York aboard which she and Metcalfe had been devouring *Mackenzie*, Scott announced her intention of winning American recognition for such a "rare, subtle and sensitive talent."[17] For a writer who had just begun work on her third novel with no certainty of which brave editor, during increasingly straitened times, would publish another unsparing tale of life on a downward curve, this was splendid news. Rhys wrote back on the same day that she received Scott's enthusiastic letter, expressing gratitude and pleasure. The exchange marked the start of a friendship based upon mutual admiration: "My God, what a fine writer you are," Rhys would exclaim after reading Scott's fiercely strange novel, *Eva Gay* (1933). More than warm-hearted Peggy Kirkaldy, Scott became a valued literary advisor, while John Metcalfe (himself a writer of fascinatingly macabre short stories), a man who lived predominantly in

England, would quietly establish his own close friendship with Rhys and Tilden Smith.

———————

WRITING AN AFFECTIONATE letter to Leslie Tilden Smith's daughter in 1968, Maryvonne described how dependent she had been upon Leslie's kindness during the childhood holidays she spent with her volatile mother. He was "a marvellous man . . . I really loved him," Maryvonne told Antoinette.[18] But this declaration was made to Leslie's own loving daughter. Elsewhere, Maryvonne would go out of her way to explain what fun her mother had been as a companion on the riverside excursions and camping holidays which formed a regular feature of Maryvonne's annual summers in England. In 1931, when Maryvonne turned nine, the trio left London for a long summer spell at a rented bungalow beside the River Wye. Rhys was always happy in the Welsh borderlands which reminded her of her father's attachment to Wales; the chuckle of the Wye's clear water flowing steadily over a stony bed reminded a homesick writer of Dominica's enchanting rivers. By the autumn, however, Maryvonne was back in Holland; shortly before Christmas, Rhys visited Lenglet and Maryvonne in Amsterdam.

The presence of Jean Rhys in her estranged husband's home was unusually welcome. Jean Lenglet had spent much of his year of absence from Holland working on *Sous les Verrous* (Under Lock and Key), his own take on the Ford affair. "I found him . . . very unhappy," Rhys remembered later. "He'd finished this very long and, yes, autobiographical mostly, novel in French, but made no attempt to publish it. So I took the mss back to London and worked at it with rage, fury and devotion."[19]

Rhys went over her husband's novel (which Lenglet, contrary to her later recollection, had already translated into awkward English), with all the scrupulous care she had lavished upon Carco's *Perversité*. The use of prison imagery in her own *Quartet* inspired her choice for its English title: *Barred*. Honourably, since the novel did not present Rhys herself in a glowing light, she made only a few alterations to

Lenglet's portrait of his wife as Stania, a weaker and more subservient character than *Quartet*'s Marya Zelli. Rhys did, however, take care to establish that Stania never lived with her "protectors," the Hubners, as she herself had lived with Stella and Ford. Given the libellous portrait that Ford had painted of Rhys as Lola Porter, a tempestuous and highly sexed Creole writer, in his most recent book, *When The Wicked Man* (1931)—and it's difficult to suppose that the well-read Rhys was unaware of such a sensational fiction—she was generous to tone down the harshness of Lenglet's portrait of her former lover.* Perhaps Rhys was seeking to redress what she later described remorsefully as the "spite" of *Quartet*.

Published in the spring of 1932 by Desmond Harmsworth (following a string of rejections), *Barred* inspired a rave from Compton Mackenzie and drew respectful reviews from J. B. Priestley, Frank Swinnerton and one of Rhys's most ardent admirers, Norah Hoult. Rebecca West declined to supply a review, pointedly saying that she looked forward soon to reading another of Jean Rhys's *own* works. Rhys's involvement in her husband's novel was no secret: Lenglet had added a touching foreword under his pen name of Edouard de Nève, in which he thanked Jean Rhys, as the author of two "beautiful" novels, for sparing the time to foster "this gloomy child of mine."

Translating *Barred* drew Rhys away from working at her third novel. Provisionally, she named it "Two Tunes," a reference to its dazzlingly persuasive exposition of her growing belief that the dreamworld of the past and the activity of the present co-exist, simultaneously, within a single conscious realm. In *After Leaving Mr Mackenzie*, Julia Martin vividly recollects a moment from her Brazilian childhood (the memory, of course, belonged to Rhys's own and ever-vivid Domini-

---

* Rhys's first biographer, Carole Angier, suggests that Ford's curious novel *When The Wicked Man* (1931) balanced his vicious fictionalisation of a creole character who displays all of Rhys's intemperate violence and rage with a gentler presentation of her, within the same novel, as Henrietta Felise. Ford's biographer, Max Saunders, has convincingly since shown that Henrietta Felise was based upon Ford's later lover, Elizabeth Cheetham (Max Saunders, *Ford Madox Ford*, Vol. II, OUP, 1996, pp. 296–7).

can past) when a terrified child scents invisible danger in a sunlit forest glade. Now, in the novel that would become *Voyage in the Dark*,
Rhys dived more deeply into her Caribbean past, exploring the episodes and images that she could best employ to haunt—and eventually, overwhelm—young Anna Morgan. Rhys's use of the first person
marked a technical advance in her ability to forge an immediate connection with her reader. The eerie authenticity of Anna's voice conceals
from our eyes the chasm that lies between Rhys, the creator, and the
tragic, untutored girl.

Voyage in the Dark was written during the long aftermath of the US
stock market crash when Leslie became almost as penniless as Rhys.
Money problems were behind the couple's impulsive decision to move
to Berlin; in Germany, the exchange rates would work in their favour.
The plan fell through when the Tilden Smiths' Jewish contact ominously vanished from view. As a result, Leslie and Rhys were still living in London early in 1933, when Lenglet asked for a quick divorce
in order to marry an attractive and intelligent Dutch writer. Well
regarded as a novelist in her day, Henriëtte van Eyk shared Lenglet's
admiration for Rhys's work.

Rhys gave her consent, but not without reluctance. Lenglet had been
the first to encourage her to write. He was part of her life, the father
both of her lost baby son and of the living, loving Maryvonne. Granting a divorce felt especially strange at a moment when she had just finished translating and revising *Barred*, Lenglet's own account of their
shared past.

The news of Lenglet's marriage plans came at a time when Rhys
was struggling to maintain authorial control of the emotions stirred
up by her deep immersion in the past. Before *Voyage in the Dark*, Jean
had never written with such passionate intensity about Dominica, an
island which grew ever more alluring to her amidst the angry despair
and cynicism of England in the early Thirties. "It was as if a curtain
had fallen," she wrote in *Voyage*'s opening line, recalling London's cool
disdain for a gauche little girl newly arrived from an outpost of the

Empire. A few pages later, Rhys used the same consciously dramatic image to set her two stages, past and present. "A curtain fell and then I was here."[20]

The dipping, gliding past–present progress of *Voyage in the Dark* is impeccably managed from the first moment of shy embarkation—the pick-up of a couple of chorus girls on a promenade at an English seaside town—to its unflinchingly bleak destination. "This thing here—I can't believe it's the same sun, I simply can't believe it," Anna tells herself in the midst of remembering how, as a child whose closest friend was a free-spirited black girl, she had hated the colour of her own white skin.[21] Taken to England's Savernake Forest by her well-meaning lover—Walter Jeffries imagines it will remind her of the tropics—Anna does indeed slip back into her earlier life on the edge of a wilder, virgin forest in the Caribbean. ("We used to sit on the veranda with the night coming in, huge. And the way it smelt of all flowers.")[22] Finally, as Anna undergoes a botched abortion—the operation would end Miss Morgan's short life in Rhys's preferred first version—the past sweeps the present away in a bravura passage which runs all Anna's distant memories together, pulling her under while the treacherous voice of her protector rings like a hollow bell through the rising dark. "*My darling mustn't worry my darling mustn't be sad . . . he said it's nearly four o'clock perhaps you ought to be going . . . You ought to be going he said.*"[23] Rhys's debt to James Joyce, as apparent here as in the extraordinary conclusion to her fourth novel, *Good Morning, Midnight*, reminds us that an early section of *Finnegans Wake* was published as "Work in Progress" in the *transatlantic review*. Copies of Ford's cherished magazine had been Rhys's intimate companions for at least a year during her affair with him in Paris.

In later years, trying to explain her writing process, Rhys cited Charlotte Brontë's famous description of the novelist (or poet, since Brontë was thinking of her sister, Emily) whose duty it is to work passively, "under dictates you neither delivered nor could question."[24] Omitted from this romantic view of inspiration guiding the pen was the considerable emotional strain that writing imposed. *Voyage in the Dark* would become Rhys's finest achievement yet; it was also by far her most demanding.

Drink, always a reliable source of brief good cheer, impeded the novel's progress towards its end. Desperate to reach completion, Rhys turned down an invitation to join Lenglet and Maryvonne for a last family week in Holland during the spring of 1933. Instead, leaving Leslie to spend some welcome time with his own daughter at the still unmarried couple's new flat on Adelaide Road, just north of Regent's Park, Jean retreated alone to the quiet Sussex seaside town of Rottingdean.

As a cure for booze and the blues, Rhys's industrious month in a room above a seaside teashop was a success. Having arrived "crazy with depression," she slept well in the sea air and read nothing more stressful than P. G. Wodehouse's latest contribution to the Blandings Castle series while she worked at *Voyage*. "If I could make one more effort I could finish it I think," she wrote to a sympathetic Evelyn Scott. "One more—You know—You do know don't you."[25]

Scott, a heavy drinker herself, did know, and sympathised. "Haven't touched a drop for a month," Rhys bragged at the end of her seaside vacation—but then undercut the boast: "Won't it be fine when I do."[26] Rhys never concealed her fondness for alcohol and she never renounced it for more than a few weeks—just long enough to demonstrate her iron will.

The Thirties was a decade remarkable for the heaviness of the drinking that went on, especially in Prohibition America. Nobody thought any the worse of Rhys for getting drunk, until drink unleashed her demons. "I'm not one to whine like some women do," she told a writing friend in later life: "I attack."[27] Attacking could mean delivering a punch, a string of expletives or a sudden disgusted jet of saliva. Leslie, a heavy drinker himself, tried to subdue her by silent disapproval, a tactic which Rhys angrily described as "his hanging judge's face."[28] When that failed—and it invariably did—Tilden Smith reverted to screaming back at her. Sometimes, their verbal battles ended in blows. "She [Rhys] and my father had terrible rows," his daughter later confirmed.[29]

In September 1933, the Lenglets' divorce was finalised. Tilden Smith would wait until February 1934 to propose. Rhys, who accepted at once, remembered both the proposal and the quiet ceremony at a London registry office as times of rare, unqualified joy. While marriage did not mark an end to her professional relationship with Lenglet, an active supporter of her writings, the wedding signalled Leslie's personal commitment to his Ella as a beloved partner, as well as a writer of extraordinary talent. Their squabbles continued. Until the very end of her long life, Jean Rhys preserved an undated scrap of paper recording the conclusion to one of the many physical and verbal battles that rifted her marriage to Leslie, but never broke it. "To an afflicted one," it read. "Nothing have I to give for you. Only my heart, my true heart—forgiving and loving Leslie."[30]

LESLIE, WHO TYPED out the new novel, faced the difficult task of finding a publisher for a work which demonstrated that Jean Rhys had defied the requests of her reviewers for a little less squalor and gloom. Jonathan Cape rejected *Voyage* (still called "Two Tunes" at that point) as too depressing, while Jamie Hamilton—despite an enduring respect for Jean's work—asked for cuts that Rhys felt would wreck her delicately calibrated book. As a devoted supporter of Patrick Hamilton, the hard-drinking author best known today for *Hangover Square*, Michael Sadleir of Constable was used to publishing bleak books: his friend's most recent fiction had borne the unappetising title: *Plains of Cement*. Sadleir took Rhys's novel, scheduling it for the autumn of 1934, prior to the US publication in March 1935. He imposed two conditions: he wanted 2,500 words cut from the elaborate Joycean sequence at the end and he wanted Anna Morgan to be kept alive.

Rhys complied about the deletion, but it seems likely that—after preserving and obsessively revising the original manuscript—she later made use of the omitted pages for her descriptions of madness in *Wide Sargasso Sea*.[31] She disagreed more strongly with the publisher's insistence that Anna should survive her last grim ordeal. Artfully, she subverted Sadleir's wishes by her deft use of the ray of light—a crucial last image—that is visible from Anna's sickbed. To Anna, the light appears as a sword: "the last thrust of remembering before everything is blotted out." In the novel's closing words, she weighs hopefulness against despair. "I lay and watched it and thought about starting all over again. And about being new and fresh. And about mornings, and misty days, when anything might happen. And about starting all over again, all over again . . . "[32]

As Rhys's revision subtly intimates, death has already reached poor Anna and death will strike her down.

WHILE LESLIE SEARCHED for a willing publisher, the couple's resources dwindled. It was not for family feeling alone that—shortly after their winter wedding ceremony—Rhys introduced Leslie to her favourite brother, Owen Rees Williams, who was back in London after unsuccessfully attempting to set up a fruit farm in Australia. Charmed both by Rhys's delicate beauty and by her unexpected willingness to sit down on the floor and play trains with their small son, Owen's wife Dorothy revised her initial opinion when Rhys asked for a loan. Speaking to Rhys's first biographer, Carole Angier, Dorothy Rees Williams recalled how she had warned her easy-going husband that she would walk out on him rather than give his sister a single cent. ("If you send that woman one penny I go out that door and never come back.")[33] Dorothy, the most forthcoming interviewee that Angier spoke to in Jean's family, missed no opportunity to condemn her sister-in-law after that first unfortunate encounter.

Leslie and Rhys had never lived grandly. In the first months of their marriage, they struggled to cover the modest rent for two adjoining bedsits in Bloomsbury's dilapidated Brunswick Square. During the summer of 1934, they took a further step down the property ladder by moving out of town to "Luxor," a tiny bungalow near Shepperton, on muddy little Pharaoh's Island (presented to Horatio Nelson as a fishing retreat on the Thames after his victory on the Nile). "Luxor" lay between "Rameses" and "Assouan." Writing to Evelyn Scott on 10 June, Rhys playfully commented on a disrespectful homage to the Egyptian gods: an image of Osiris painted by a previous inhabitant onto their new home's lavatory door.

To Maryvonne, now twelve, this was a time of uncomplicated happiness. Her mother had married a kind and affectionate man; she liked living at Luxor; a late summer camping excursion to Wales's Brecon Beacons was remembered for wonderful family games of charades. It might be hard to imagine—Maryvonne would proudly comment on a radio programme, almost fifty years later—just how brilliant her late mother had been at playing roles. She could even do Long John Silver! But "you can't imagine her like that. No, she was an actress really."[34]

Constable paid only £25 for "Two Tunes" in July 1934, but the death of Rhys's maternal Aunt Brenda netted her a welcome £100 (most of Brenda's modest legacy went to the younger niece and namesake who had taken care of her in Acton), while the death of Leslie's mother at the end of that same summer produced a welcome financial injection of £2,500 (£180,000 in today's money). Always materially generous when she could afford to be, Rhys lavished treats upon her daughter—"everything a child could wish for," Maryvonne later recalled: "books and ballet, music, pantomime and circus."[35] Shortly before Christmas, Rhys went into Harrods, bought smart pyjamas for Leslie and a much-coveted mouth organ for her daughter—and then forgetfully left them behind, on a cloakroom chair. Not surprisingly, they disappeared. And her thoughtful gifts were to have been such a surprise! Twenty years later, Rhys still felt mortified.

Lost presents sound like an oversight, but Rhys's mind may have been unsettled by disappointment. The autumn reviews of *Voyage in the Dark*, the most compassionate, understanding and tragic portrait of a woman that she had yet created, were the best and most extensive that Rhys had so far received. One perceptive fellow novelist, Clemence Dane, writing in *Dublin Magazine* (January 1935), singled out the author's power "to express the emotions and bewilderments of the inarticulate" which is central to Rhys's presentation of Anna, the most innocent of her heroines. Nevertheless, while *The Lady*'s reviewer (8 November 1934) believed it would give that magazine's readers a clearer understanding of how even a "nice" girl might be driven into prostitution, regret was still persistently being expressed at such a fine female writer's obsession with "dreadful" and "difficult" subjects. For the future, Rhys's own literary voyage looked to be heading into uncharted waters.

A more likely explanation for Rhys's odd act of carelessness in Harrods was that she had begun drinking so heavily during 1934 that she couldn't write.[36] And without her writing, she went to pieces.

Rhys's distraught state militated against new opportunities to establish herself in the London literary world. Rosamond Lehmann was among the keenest admirers of *Voyage in the Dark*. At the beginning of 1935, Lehmann wrote Rhys a flattering letter, suggesting that they should meet. This was an opportunity that was not to be passed up. Lehmann's own first novel, *Dusty Answer* (1927), had been an instant bestseller; since then, she had become a force to be reckoned with in the publishing world. Invited to visit the Oxfordshire home which Rosamond shared with her husband, Wogan Philipps, and their baby girl, Rhys was initially hesitant. Reassured by Leslie that the meeting would be well worth the difficulties of an elaborate cross-country journey by train and bus, she agreed to make the trip.

Eagerly anticipated by Rosamond, Rhys's visit to Oxfordshire was a disaster. All ready with their questions, Rosamond, her actress sister Beatrix, and their friend, the widowed, elegant and sharply intelligent Violet Hammersley, together let fly like a firing squad. An unnerved Rhys, fidgeting unhappily with the gloves which she considered essential for a lady's social visit, provided her terse responses in a carefully enunciated whisper. After an awkward hour, she asked to be taken back to the railway station.

Rosamond's second attempt to befriend Rhys was equally unsuccessful. Set for May 1935, it conflicted with celebrations being held to honour George V's twenty-fifth (and penultimate) year on the throne. Rhys, whose face bore alarming bruise marks from an unmentioned battle with Leslie when she finally showed up, seemed obsessed by the pros and cons of showing the royal procession to the nation on Pathé newsreels. Books, to Lehmann's disappointment, were not discussed, and neither were the bruises. A further encounter, scheduled for 14 June at the popular Café Royal, brought a new setback when a dishevelled Leslie Tilden Smith shambled through the cafe's elegant doors to offer Rosamond a rambling tale about a car crash. Although unharmed, Rhys was said to be too distraught for a social outing. Empathising— she, too, had recently been in a motor accident—Lehmann sent best wishes for a speedy recovery.

Plainly, Rhys liked Rosamond or she would not herself have proposed a further attempt at establishing a friendship. Invited for an early autumn visit to the flat on Bury Street, just off Piccadilly, into which the Tilden Smiths had recently moved from their faux-Egyptian bungalow on the Thames, Rosamond was greeted by a wan-faced Leslie. Ushered in, the immaculately dressed visitor found herself staring at a dishevelled Jean, sprawled across a sofa, glass in hand as she taunted her silent husband for looking—as well he might—downhearted. "Poor Leslie," she kept saying, "poor, poor Leslie. He looks so miserable and wretched and ill. . . ."[37]

Departing as swiftly as she could, Lehmann felt more sympathy for an embarrassed Leslie than his intoxicated wife. She didn't know the couple well enough to wonder whether perhaps Leslie had been playing an unkind game of his own when he ushered her into the flat, rather than sending their visitor away with a polite excuse. If his wife shamed him, so could he shame her.

Lehmann never learned the truth about that second cancelled meeting with Rhys at the Café Royal. There had been no car crash. On 13 June, the Tilden Smiths had been arrested for causing a disturbance (by fighting each other) in Soho's shabby Wardour Street at four in the morning. It seems that the gentle Leslie could hit back. The mutual damage inflicted by punches and flailing fists was bad enough for a doctor to be called to the police station where the couple were jailed for the rest of a short night. Charged at Bow Street the following morning, Rhys pleaded not guilty to the charge and signed herself as "Ella Tilden Smith, Journalist" before a thirty-shilling penalty was handed down. Leslie, after chivalrously taking full responsibility for the incident, paid the fine.

Twenty years later, Rhys would combine the jubilee celebrations of 1935 with her humiliating arrest as she set to work on one of her finest short stories: "Tigers are Better-Looking." But it was the Leslie-like "Mr Severn" whom she chose to despatch to prison for a night, adding only a cryptic "GR" on the wall of his cell to signify his creator as the former Gwen Rees.

A COMPLETE ABSENCE of documentation in the form of letters or diaries makes it impossible to know how much responsibility for the couple's rows can be assigned to Rhys, and how much to her outwardly calm husband. Confirmation of Rhys's own volatility emerges earlier in 1935, and from an unexpected quarter. Bringing his daughter to England for the Easter holidays, Jean Lenglet had spent a few days at "Luxor." Any ménage à trois is risky; emotions at the house ran high. Fictionalising the occasion in a 1937 novel, *Schuwe Vogels* (*Shy Birds* was not published in England and may never have been seen by Rhys), Lenglet characterised Rhys as a violent and obscene-tongued wife whose alcoholic depression culminates in her death (by drowning in a river). Tilden Smith's daughter, Antoinette, who visited the island hideaway during Lenglet's stay, later confirmed that tempers had indeed run high. Peace was temporarily restored after Lenglet's departure; back in England for the summer holidays, Maryvonne was carried off to south Wales's beautiful and isolated Gower Peninsula in a newly purchased car for what she would remember as an idyllic week alone with her mother and Leslie.

The death of Leslie's father in September 1935 unlocked the remaining portion of his son's inheritance. "Luxor" was promptly abandoned for the Bury Street flat—just off Piccadilly—to which Rosamond Lehmann paid her memorable visit. The flat was well located, but neither a new home nor Leslie's decision to spend his newfound wealth on taking his wife back to the Caribbean could shake off Rhys's despair. The drinking continued—and so did the rows. Jamie Hamilton, acting in his capacity as Leslie's part-time employer, visited discreetly while Rhys was on her own. He mentioned remarks that had been made at the office about Leslie's battered face; prospective clients were not favourably impressed when greeted by bruises and black eyes.

The hint of a threat hung in the air. Reluctant to sack an excellent editor and literary advisor, Hamilton decided instead to provide a diversion. In June, he had asked Leslie to edit a memoir written by two nephews of Winston Churchill. Based in part on their recent experiences of public school, and laced with anecdotes about an eccentric upbringing, *Out of Bounds* was co-authored by Giles and Esmond Romilly. Leslie and young Esmond had got on rather well. It was Hamilton's idea that Esmond should become a paying guest at Bury Street.

Aged seventeen, their new lodger enchanted Rhys. Handsome, wilful and clever enough to dazzle her with his political views, Esmond had recently got himself thrown out of a fascist rally for causing a disturbance. Later, he would elope with Oswald Mosley's adamantly left-wing sister-in-law, Jessica Mitford. Rhys was working on an early draft of "Till September Petronella" when Esmond arrived at Bury Street. Might her characterisation in that long short story of the charismatic composer Philip Heseltine as the captivating but also dangerous Julian Oakes offer readers a glimpse of the way Rhys responded to wild young Romilly? Working on her fiction always improved her spirits, but it's likely that Esmond himself helped to effect a change of mood as the year drew to a close. But the real boost for Rhys came from the prospect of returning, at last, to her island birthplace.

———

VOYAGE IN THE DARK had provided the spur to Leslie's generous impulse to splash out on a Caribbean adventure. How could anybody who had lived at Rhys's side as she lovingly recreated a Caribbean past for Anna Morgan not believe that a return to Dominica would make her happy? First-class tickets were purchased for a passenger ship leaving Southampton in February 1936. Just back from seeing her sick daughter (Maryvonne had contracted measles) at her new convent school in Holland, Rhys wrote a farewell from Bury Street to Evelyn Scott. As usual, all was in chaos. A fused light had plunged the couple into darkness; they were packing by the erratic glimmer of a few candles that Leslie had wedged into a biscuit tin.[38]

Rhys's letter to Scott doesn't disclose whether Esmond was still with the Tilden Smiths at the time of their departure from England; by the time they returned, the young man had left England himself, to fight against Franco in the Spanish Civil War. It's unknown whether Rhys read at the time of his premature death in 1941, when Romilly's plane vanished over the North Sea while undertaking a raid on Germany, but she always spoke of him with tenderness. Her own son, had he lived, would have been just two years younger than Esmond.

10

A la recherche, or *Temps Perdi* (1936)

> "I suppose going back to Dominica is foolhardy but I want to
> so much—I can't help risking it. You can imagine the wild and
> fantastic plans and hopes."
>
> —Jean Rhys to Evelyn Scott, December 1935[1]

WAVING THE TILDEN SMITHS off at Southampton—the port where
Rhys had first stepped foot on English soil nearly twenty years earlier—
were members of both their families: Leslie's recently married daughter
arrived with her husband, while Rhys was given bouquets of flowers
by her two sisters and brother, Owen (Edward, the eldest, was still
working abroad as an army medical officer). Rhys struck them all as
unusually animated and happy; judging by her boast to Evelyn Scott of
"fantastic plans and hopes," she may have dreamed that day of returning to Dominica for good.

Most of what we know of the couple's journey comes from two long
typewritten letters sent by Leslie to his daughter back in England. He
reported the voyage out as tranquil, marred only by Rhys's suspicion
that one of the SS *Cuba*'s passengers, a boisterous young Italian woman,
was making fun of the Tilden Smiths. After steaming through the Sargasso Sea, rank with the floating brown *sargassum* weed from which
it takes its name, the Tilden Smiths disembarked at the exuberantly

colourful town of Fort-de-France in Martinique, where they met up
with the Irish novelist Liam O'Flaherty, "typing away for dear life,"
Jean reported to Evelyn, "and delighted with the West Indies, the only
place left not yet written up he said."[2] The following week, the couple
sailed on to St. Lucia, where the widowed Evelina Lockhart—a cherished young bride when Rhys last saw her—welcomed them to the little
hotel which she was being paid to run by its absentee owner.

Leslie's letters read as though he would gladly have prolonged their
stay at Hotel Antoine, where Rhys showed at her best as a valued literary advisor to a mildly eccentric young cousin, Emily (always known as
Lily) Lockhart, who proudly displayed a magazine to which she herself
was the sole contributor.[3] But Rhys, understandably, was impatient to
reach Roseau. She hadn't been home for twenty years; how much would
remain unchanged?

To Leslie, settling into the best rooms at the La Paz—the town's
only hotel—Roseau appeared charming, with its wide harbour, busy
market square and the tranquil Botanical Gardens. To Rhys, change
was visible everywhere. Her family's house was boarded up; Kingsland
House, the elegant former home of her father's medical colleague, Sir
Henry Nicholls, had been converted by his daughters into a pension
from which—to Rhys's dismay—a visiting lady writer despatched invi-
tations for literary chat. The haughtily exclusive Dominica Club looked
but a ghost of its former self; almost all the white pioneer settlers who
had once regarded themselves as lords of the island had sold up and
left. One resident told the visitors the curious story of Mr. Ramage
(someone whom Rhys had known as a child), who was found dead at his
remote property during the 1920s, still clasping a shotgun. Mr. Ramage's mysterious death followed a mob attack, allegedly triggered by the
frightened crowd's ghostly encounter with a "white zombi."[4] The eerie
image of a tall, pale old settler, brandishing a gun, stayed with Rhys. It
seems to lie behind her account of the English Mr. Mason's confrontation with an angry mob of arsonists in one of the most dramatic scenes
in *Wide Sargasso Sea*.

Alone, Rhys visited the old Victoria library where as a girl she had loved to sit reading on the shady veranda; here, a distant cousin still wearily presided over the massive desk to which books were brought by the island's schoolchildren to be stamped. The building, although unchanged, was overshadowed by the larger and adjacent Carnegie-funded library which had been built during the year that Rhys left the island to the design of Dominica's former administrator, Sir Henry Hesketh Bell. Alone still, she visited her former school to take tea with a greatly aged Mother Mount Calvary, the nun who had formerly been in charge of the convent. Here, too, everything—including her welcoming hostess—seemed diminished. Wishing to please an elegant visitor dressed in her best hat and gloves for the occasion, the old lady reminisced about the various ways that Rhys's father had always assisted the convent. Later that day, standing beside the Celtic cross that marked his neglected grave in the nearby churchyard, the doctor's daughter thought of the many ways in which kind, easy-going Willie Rees Williams had helped islanders and settlers alike. Nothing was recorded; all was forgotten. In her memoir, years later, Rhys confessed that she had shed tears that day.

Creating a careful map of the island for his daughter's benefit and his own amusement, Leslie had to rely upon Rhys's memory for the accurate placing of his two careful "x's," marking her father's two hill-country estates up on the island's west coast. No one could direct the Tilden Smiths to Amelia, nor Bona Vista; the little plantations of Rhys's girlhood lay buried under two decades of luxuriant, smothering forest. But Geneva: surely Mitcham House must survive? Having hired the grandest available car in Roseau for a pilgrimage to the old Lockhart home, Rhys was advised to employ a guide. "I thought, "A guide to Geneva for me. How ridiculous." However, there was a guide, we went quickly by car, and he seemed to know exactly where to take me."*⁵

It may have been from their guide that Rhys first heard about the

---

* Leslie's retrospective account to his daughter suggests the Geneva visit took place towards the end of their stay, but it's hard to believe Rhys had resisted the temptation while staying in Roseau.

ruinous changes that had taken place on the island. Some of these distressed her more than others. Hurricanes and crop disease had devastated Dominica's fragile economy during the postwar years; growing racial anger had been fuelled by the brutally insensitive act of segregation meted out by the British Army to the black islanders who had crossed the world in 1915 to fight—and die—for Britain and the Empire. Rhys was surprised but relatively unconcerned to learn that a new non-white middle class had taken charge of the island, while the white plantocracy, its regime never so secure as those of the sugar barons of Barbados and Jamaica, had shrivelled away. Phyllis Shand Allfrey, the niece of Rhys's childhood sweetheart Willie Nicholls, had briefly returned to Dominica in 1931 only to discover, as she would write in her autobiographical novel, *The Orchid House* (1953), that her own class had become "the poor whites, we no longer have any power."[6]

The chief cause of distress for Rhys came from discovering the recent fate of her own family home. Four years before her return, there had been outrage when it was discovered that the British Colonial Office was increasing taxes on the island's black population to subsidise generous salaries paid to the handful of white officials who remained at Roseau. Following a mass resignation by the angry members of Dominica's legislative (all black) council, the British administrator invited two white planters to take their place. Within a month of his new appointment, Rhys's cousin, Norman Lockhart, the white owner of Geneva, was taught a harsh lesson when Mitcham House was raided and torched.

Some tokens of the old Geneva estate survived for a shocked Rhys to see: a mounting block; a few blackened walls; the sugar works' massive iron wheel, shipped out in the 1820s from Derby, England. The rest had gone: "There was nothing, nothing. Nothing to look at. Nothing to say. . . ." When Rhys knelt by a river to scoop a palmful of clear water into her mouth, the guide warned her: "Very dirty, not like you remember it."[7]

Following this wrenching experience, Rhys found it distressing to remain close to the places she had remembered best. A Lockhart connection still carried weight among the island's tiny white community. Strings were pulled; funds were tendered: by the end of March, the Tilden Smiths had bought themselves six weeks of isolation on a partly abandoned estate in the far north of the island, complete with maid, cook and overseer, and its own spectacular beach. The estate was called Hampstead.

———

WRITING *WIDE SARGASSO SEA* two decades later, and conflating the ruined Geneva of 1936 with the events that she believed had taken place there back in the 1830s, Rhys would also draw upon other and far less melancholy memories, of Hampstead. For here, to her astonishment, she discovered an almost exact replica of her lost home. Even the history carried startling echoes: once again, the Swiss family of Bertrand had been supplanted by members of the Lockhart family. Inscribing each of the little holiday snaps taken by Leslie of his wife (flaunting a faultless figure in her chic one-piece bathing suit), Rhys carefully recorded the fact that the beautiful beach at Hampstead was still called Bertrand Bay.

Despite Hampstead's isolated position, it was within reach of a couple of white families who were keen to welcome visitors from England. The Aspittels of Melville Hall proved pleasant but unexciting; a more interesting encounter was promised by an invitation from the Napiers of Pointe Baptiste.

Rhys had been fascinated by the exotic past history of Evelyn Scott. She showed less interest in the backstory of headstrong Elma Gordon Cumming, daughter of one of Scotland's largest landowners, who left her husband to run away with Lennox Napier, a literary-minded outcast from her own world who had spent time in Tahiti. Disgraced by their notorious affair, the Napiers had fled from England, eventually settling in Dominica because—in part—of their need for a warm climate. (Lennox was more fragile than his sturdy wife.)

Pointe Baptiste, the house that the Napiers had lovingly created to overlook twin beaches—one was of black sand, one of the finest

pale coral—was and is like nowhere else on Dominica. Distinguished
visitors—from Noël Coward to Patrick Leigh Fermor—would fall
under the spell of the immense sea-facing veranda that fronts a light-
filled, beautifully proportioned house packed with unexpected treasures: carved masks from Tahiti; a screen painted by the polymathic
French chef Marcel Boulestin; a library stocked with French literature, including (the small volumes still sit on the library shelves) a well-
thumbed first edition of Proust's *A la recherche du temps perdu*. Here,
surely, Rhys would feel herself perfectly at home?

The reason for the Napiers' hospitality soon became clear. Elma
Napier was in search of a publisher. Jamie Hamilton had sent her—at
the autocratic Mrs. Napier's insistence—the negative fiction-reader's
report on which his rejection of her recently submitted novel, *Duet
in Discord*, had been based. Mrs. Napier had since gleaned that Leslie
Tilden Smith was an editor (but not that he worked for Hamilton);
Leslie, not his wife, was the object of Elma's lavish attention during the
Tilden Smiths' visit to Pointe Baptiste. The price of a delicious lunch
was made explicit: Mr. Smith must provide a glowing report for Mrs.
Napier to flourish before reluctant publishers. It's unclear whether Leslie complied, but Elma's novel was published by Arthur Barker—under
the pseudonym Elizabeth Garner—a few months after their encounter.

Rhys was understandably displeased by Mrs. Napier's attentiveness
to Leslie, while ignoring his wife. Unburdening herself in a letter to
Evelyn Scott, she wrote with withering scorn of a neighbour who is "by
way of being literary" and who has "done her war dance at me. (Toma-
hawk in hand, smile on face)." There was one piece of good news: "She's
going to England next week thank God."[8] Elma Napier was equally
scathing. Responding over a decade later to a query from Alec Waugh
about Rhys's literary reputation in Dominica, Elma promised to "try
and read her. None of us has ever heard of her."[9] The hiss of poison-
tipped arrows is almost audible.

Rhys's happiness at Hampstead glows out of Leslie's tender photograph of his wife gazing down at him from a tree-strung hammock.
A continued exchange of friendly cards between Rhys and Dora, the

Rhys at Bertrand Bay, now known as Hampstead Bay (*left*), and relaxing in a hammock (*right*). Leslie was the admiring photographer. (*McFarlin*)

Hampstead housekeeper, suggests that a comfortable relationship had been established; Leslie's lengthy letters to his daughter communicate an ease-filled sense of peace. Ella was working again, he reported with evident relief, adding that she was really well (his code for sober) and "simply loving the place."[10]

Rhys, nevertheless, had set her heart on undertaking two major expeditions during their long stay in the north. She wanted to visit the territory that had been granted to the island's earliest settlers—the Amerindian Caribs now known as Kalinago—back in 1903. And she wanted to cross the island on the great Imperial Road which everybody claimed (wrongly, so a stubborn Rhys would enduringly assert) had never been completed.

Ever since childhood, Jean Rhys had been intrigued by the fate of Dominica's earliest surviving inhabitants. Following her return, she had learned about the Caribs' recent exposure to what they reasonably perceived as insulting behaviour. In 1930, after two Caribs were erroneously shot for suspected smuggling, their people's compensation had been, not the badly needed hospital they requested, but a police station from which to spy on them. When a handful of angry protesters burned the station down, the British navy retaliated by flashing searchlights across the Caribs' terrain each night from the deck of an offshore warship. Feelings of resentment ran high.

It's reasonable to suppose that Rhys gave an accurate account of her visit to the Carib community in "Temps Perdi," a story she first began to contemplate during her final weeks at Hampstead. Arriving on horseback at a circle of thatched Carib huts, the Tilden Smiths were advised on how best to conduct themselves:

> "There is a beautiful Carib girl," the policeman said, "in the house over there—the one with the red roof. Everybody goes to see her and photographs her. She and her mother will be vexed if you don't go. Give her a little present, of course. She is very beautiful but she can't walk. It's a pity that."[11]

Anger at the policeman's condescension simmers beneath the surface of Rhys's prose. Later, the disillusioned visitor tells the reader that a stiff drink helps fend off any compassionate impulse. After a swig of rum, "nothing dismays you; you know the password and the Open Sesame. You drink a second; then you understand everything—the sun, the flamboyance, the girl crawling (because she could not walk) across the floor to be photographed."[12]

Rhys's second expedition, with a compliant Leslie tagging along behind their two local guides, began with a drive south down the island's east coast to Hatton Garden, one of the island's many abandoned estates. It was here, a few miles beyond the site of the modern airport, that Rhys believed the final stretch of the Imperial Road had emerged from the tropical jungle. Signs of an old *pavé*, or paved track, a leftover from Dominica's eighteenth-century French past, strengthened her argument. Off the travellers set, plodding alongside the brown–green waters of the winding Pagua river, advancing ever deeper into the island's seemingly impenetrable forest. Leslie grew silent. Rhys fell and twisted her foot. Relentless rain poured down from a dark sky. The sense of her own folly grew unbearable, but Rhys could not bear to yield: "Nothing left of the Imperial Road? Nothing? It just wasn't possible."[13]

It seems that Rhys did convince her husband of the road's existence, however irritable the long-suffering Leslie must have grown during a pilgrimage along muddy paths that had to be hacked out of the jungle by the cutlasses wielded by their quietly disdainful guides. Seventeen miles short of Roseau, the exhausted group finally reached the original road's end at Bassinville; and still, Rhys remained adamant. Completing his island map and anxious not to anger his wife, Leslie dutifully represented an Imperial Road that had almost spanned the island.[14]

Back in Roseau, and on the verge of making their first—and last—visit to America, the Tilden Smiths were called upon by the island-born children of Rhys's brother Owen. Leslie was proud to report to his daughter that Rhys had confronted an "awkward" family situation with uncommon grace. Approached by Ena, the oldest of her unknown nieces, his wife had been affectionate and—insofar as Leslie's rapidly shrinking funds permitted—generous. Oscar, the oldest boy, asked for more. He had grown "downright beastly," but Rhys had "marvellously kept her temper." Bringing the interview to an end, Ella had presented Oscar's younger sister with a generous handful of notes and coins. "And you," she had instructed her disgruntled nephew, "can go."[15]

EN ROUTE TO New York in the early summer, the Tilden Smiths were full of hope. Evelyn Scott had already helped Rhys to move from Paul Revere Reynolds (with whom she had fallen out) to another leading American agent, Carol Hill; writing to Leslie, Scott had expressed a determination to do her very best for the writer whom she felt most proud to know. It's probable that the two women had met up in England during 1935, when Evelyn was spending much of her time with John Metcalfe at a Suffolk cottage in Walberswick (affectionately known at the time as Bloomsbury-by-the-Sea); by February 1936, Scott had temporarily rejoined her previous husband, Creighton Wellman, in New York. Since then, she had been urging Rhys to visit and promising to arrange useful introductions. Having helped John Metcalfe only a couple of years earlier to whip through a windfall legacy of £20,000, Evelyn was unlikely to have encouraged the Tilden Smiths to curb what had become an enjoyably spendthrift existence.

Arriving in New York in June for a three-week stay, the Tilden Smiths rented a suite at the top of a charmingly Frenchified hotel near Washington Square. Rhys got all her teeth crowned and went shopping for the expensive clothes which always provided her protective armour against a (seemingly) critical world. Evelyn, meanwhile, arranged a cavalcade of social events, leaving little time for the quiet restaurant suppers which were an unsociable writer's preferred form of entertainment.

Having stumbled and twisted her ankle while trying to find the Imperial Road, Rhys now suffered a second and more serious fall. It seems likely to have taken place during the very last days of her visit to New York, when she was increasingly relying on alcohol to get her through the ordeal of a hectic social schedule. Groups, however courteous their intentions—and the New Yorkers were eager to welcome Evelyn's friend—always frightened Rhys. ("The damned way they look at you, and their damned voices," she had made Anna Morgan say of the English in *Voyage*.) Performing on stage had never inhibited her (except, understandably, when she was asked to mimic a hen laying an egg). The prospect of putting herself on display in society required courage of a kind Rhys lacked: "as a well-trained social animal I'm certainly not the goods," she would ruefully confess to Evelyn after her return to England.[16]

It may have been the combination of physical pain, drink and nervousness that caused Rhys's volatile temper to erupt during the final week of her visit. Piecing together what happened from the few letters

that Evelyn Scott and Rhys exchanged thereafter, it seems that the
Tilden Smiths were invited to Evelyn's home for a farewell family supper. Evelyn believed that she heard Rhys say something casually brutal
about the misshapen hand of Manly, Wellman's son; Rhys remembered
only that Manly had been combative and that Evelyn took his side.
"So I blew up," Rhys wrote in the plaintive half-apology she sent from
London in August, and "once I got going old griefs and grievances
overwhelmed me."[17]

The explosion may not have been entirely Rhys's fault. In 1936, Scott
herself was going through a personal crisis, exacerbated by the fact that
her much-loved second husband John Metcalfe, back in England, had
entered a period of severe depression. Money was short and—following
a cool reception for her most recent novel—Scott was fighting her
own emotional battles. During the same year of her rift with Rhys,
Evelyn also quarrelled with one of her closest American friends, Lola
Ridge. Writing to Emma Goldman during the following spring, Scott
acknowledged with sorrow that, "between the near tragedies in personal affairs, the intensive labour and pressure about livelihood, I have
simply dropped interchanges of correspondence with even my dearest
friends."[18]

It seems that both Rhys and Scott were at fault. Their friendship, one
of the most significant in the prewar period of Rhys's literary life, was
never resumed, after a last volley of angry exchanges in the late summer
of 1936, and by 1942, Scott, suffering from increasingly severe bouts
of mental illness, had almost no allies left. To those who remained,
including her loyal husband, Evelyn Scott always expressed pride in
having known and helped such a remarkable writer as Jean Rhys.

11

Good Morning, Midnight
(1936–39)

"It is only lately that I answer unkindness with a raving hate—
because I've got weaker. My will is quite weakened because I
drink too much."

—Jean Rhys, Green Exercise Book[1]

DEFENDING HER OUTBURST in Evelyn Scott's apartment in a letter
sent from London in August 1936, Rhys admitted to her friend that she
had drunk "a hell of a lot" during the last days of her stay. Reminiscing
about that same New York visit many years later, Rhys said that she
hadn't been sober in Manhattan "for one instant."[2] It's quite likely that
she did the damage to her foot in New York through a tipsy stumble,
but it's also conceivable that she was given an angry shove after launching into one of her unpredictable and vitriolic tirades. The injury, following her tumble while searching for the Imperial Road on Dominica,
was serious enough to confine her to the Tilden Smiths' twin-bedded
cabin on the liner transporting them home to England.

Back in London by early June, Rhys found that the persistent physical pain of a badly swollen foot did nothing to improve her mood, nor
to reduce her reliance on alcohol. While holidaying in her beloved
Wales with Leslie and Maryvonne in late July—Lenglet had meanwhile joined the anti-fascist cause in Spain as a reporter—Rhys was

rushed into a tiny local hospital: a "most alarming experience." Back again in London, Leslie settled his wife into an expensive (and alcohol-free) nursing home off the Cromwell Road: "of all terrible streets," an unappreciative Rhys complained. Depressed by her surroundings ("grim, clean, hard, cheerless, smug, smirking etc.") and the unwelcome absence of drink, Rhys mordantly quipped to Evelyn that amputation would save trouble, while doubtless adding to "my chic. . . ."[3]

Leslie, meanwhile, was forced to face the consequences of their extravagant holiday. By the late summer of 1936, the legacy from his father had almost run out, as had the Bury Street lease. Fortunately, the prudent and relatively wealthy Muriel Tilden Smith was ready to support her improvident but beloved sibling. By mid-August, Rhys was able to exchange her nursing home for the snug Chelsea flat which, thanks to Muriel's discreet generosity, Leslie and his wife would occupy for the next three years.

A blue plaque now records Rhys's residence at 22 Paultons House, which was then a smart new building in bright red brick that stood at the shabbier end of the King's Road in Chelsea. Today, Rhys sleuths may savour her posthumous blue-plaqued proximity to the smart townhouse in Paultons Square where Lancelot Hugh Smith's favourite niece—a sculptor—has added some of her own equestrian bronzes to a legacy of her uncle's collection of eighteenth-century porcelain and paintings. This was never Lancey's home; back at the time when Rhys lived at Paultons House, her former lover had recently exchanged his family's mansion in Roehampton for Garboldisham Hall, a handsome old Norfolk manor house within easier reach of Sandringham. While an ageing bachelor entertained the young princesses whose royal parents had been grateful beneficiaries of Lancey's shrewd financial advice, Rhys found solace in strengthening connections to her Creole past.

IN AUGUST, ENGAGED in a war of words with Evelyn Scott, Rhys was told by a still furious Scott that she held a "distorted" view of how people behave. Responding on 10 August, Rhys carefully excluded Evelyn and her American friends before launching into a ferocious condemnation of English society's "mean bloody awful hatred of everything that isn't exactly like your mean self."[4]

Rhys had picked quarrels with many friends since her return to England. She was also anxiously adrift in her search for a subject for her next novel. Installed at the new flat, she felt the daily reproach of a private study and writing desk that a thoughtful husband had provided for her use.

Two women provided consolation to Rhys during this fallow and unhappy period; it's striking that they both had deep connections to the West Indies, where women were not judged irrational—or even insane—if they had a temper that sparked out like a lightning flash: "like a hurricane like a creole" as Antoinette Cosway remarks of her mother in *Wide Sargasso Sea*.

Phyllis Shand Allfrey, a generation younger than Jean Rhys, was the granddaughter of Dr. Rees Williams's medical colleague, Sir Henry Nicholls; her 1953 novel, *The Orchid House*, would take its name from Sir Henry's abiding passion for growing orchids. Back in 1936, returning to England after a short time in America, Phyllis became an assistant to Naomi Mitchison, the formidably well-connected author and activist through whom she met many left-wing intellectuals (including George Orwell), while becoming a regular contributor of poetry and articles to the new Labour Party-sponsored magazine, *Tribune*.

Years later, as founder and editor of the *Dominica Star*, Phyllis would appoint herself as Rhys's personal Caribbean informant. Back in the Thirties, however, politics played little or no part in their friendship. Admiring Phyllis's slender fairness and quiet elegance without sharing her political views, Rhys was delighted to find a London neighbour with whom to share her memories of the vanishing Dominica of her youth. Phyllis enjoyed telling island stories of her own; possibly, some of these tales inspired Rhys's plans for a historical play set in Antigua, the island where Robert Shand Allfrey, Phyllis's disappointingly unemployable white husband, had grown up.[5] Rhys herself had briefly visited

Antigua during the voyage out to Dominica: just long enough to decide that it was both flat and dull: "*not* a beautiful island."[6]

Questioned in her later years about the writer whose literary fame—a little to her mortification—by then far outshone Phyllis's own, Allfrey gave nothing away about Rhys's drinking and her temper, preferring to recall the ballet treat her friend had bestowed on a thrilled seventeen-year-old Maryvonne by sweeping her daughter off to Moira Shearer's stage debut in *Endymion* in 1939. Phyllis did, however, let slip one incident which betrayed—as she was perfectly aware when she disclosed the episode—Rhys's enduring social insecurity. Invited to dine at Paultons House one night, Phyllis had dropped some casual remark about the commonness of the name Smith; a standoff about what was perceived to be a deliberate put-down of the Tilden Smiths (and perhaps even of the Hugh Smiths) had ended with Rhys's angry refusal to cook dinner for their honoured guest that night.[7]

It would seem obvious for Rhys to have discussed with Phyllis her brother Owen's mixed-race children, as three of Phyllis's uncles, including Willie, Rhys's childhood beau, had been rebuked or exiled for fathering children by island women. The likelihood is that Rhys preferred to discuss Owen's illicit relationships with Eileen Bliss.

Rhys always described this as her favourite photograph of Maryvonne, her uncomplaining and long-suffering daughter. *(McFarlin)*

Unlike Phyllis, who never forgot the social superiority of Sir Henry Alford Nicholls to a mere Dr. Rees Williams, Eileen was a woman with whom Rhys could reveal and revel in being her own true self.

The initial approach had been made by Bliss, an admirer of Rhys's novels who obtained a personal introduction by applying to Horace Gregory, a scholarly poet and translator who had successfully experimented with reading sections from Rhys's prose work aloud to his American college students at Sarah Lawrence.* In September 1936, shortly after the Tilden Smiths moved to Paultons House, the thirty-three-year-old Bliss paid Rhys her first visit. The friendship that instantly sprang up between the two women would prove robust enough to last a lifetime.

———————

ELIOT BLISS (Eileen renamed herself in homage to George and T. S. Eliot) was born and bred to English parents in Jamaica before moving to England, where the publication of her second novel, *Luminous Isle* (1934), had been sponsored by Vita Sackville-West.

A volatile depressive who suffered from long periods of illness, Bliss was a lesbian who wore her hair in an unfashionably close-cut crop, and who wrestled, like Rhys, with yearnings for a Caribbean world in which, as both women were acutely aware by the time they met, they possessed no authentic home. "When I try to explain the feeling I find I cannot or do not wish to," Rhys once confessed to her orange exercise book, although she was happy to describe in her memoir the desire she had felt to lose her own pallid skin tone along with her inhibitions when she watched, as a child, the dark-skinned carnival dancers leaping and prancing along the streets of Roseau.[8]

Phyllis Shand Allfrey regarded herself, always, as Rhys's social and intellectual superior; Eliot, from her very first encounter with Jean

* Gregory evidently appreciated the kinship to poetry in Rhys's prose. His students were fortunate; her work is best experienced when read aloud, either in English or French.

Rhys, was a shamelessly adoring fan. Everything about the writer and her Chelsea home had been perfect, Bliss told Rhys's first biographer back in the 1980s, from the green bedsheets to the lovely portraits of Jean that decorated the walls; from the evident devotion of a tactfully invisible husband to the tasteful hair rinse (blue) that complemented the chicly dressed Miss Rhys's sapphire eyes. Rapturously, Eliot reminisced to Angier about the delicious Caribbean meals cooked by her hostess; ruefully, she admitted that Rhys often drank more than was prudent. Perhaps unwisely, Bliss also recalled that kind Leslie had always been on hand to scoop the ladies off the floor at an evening's end and carry them safely off to bed. Further details were neither sought nor provided.[9]

"GREAT IS THE truth, and truth will prevail," Rhys inscribed in the copy of *Quartet* which she gave to Eliot Bliss, echoing the dog-Latin motto she had once drunkenly scrawled for Eliot across a bedroom mirror at Paultons House. This was Rhys's abiding creed: *to tell the truth.* She saw it as her only chance to draw upon and survive the growing darkness within her: "the bitter peace" that she would describe in *Good Morning, Midnight* as standing very close "to hate," and even, to death.[10] The feeling was there; what eluded Rhys still, in the summer of 1937, was the way in which to give form to that theme.

"It's hard to harbour illusions in a room by the month hotel." That line might have come from *Good Morning, Midnight*, in which Rhys's ageing avatar hides from the cruel eyes of Paris in just such a room. Rhys herself had read it in Louis-Ferdinand Céline's first novel, published in 1932. *Voyage to the End of Night* became one of her touchstone books; it was one of the few that she would always keep close to her.

Céline's reputation as a racist bigot has obscured the wit, humanity and elan of his earliest work. Celebrated for the dazzling originality of Céline's style, *Voyage to the End of Night* takes its readers into the depths of Paris and its heights. From the gloomy grey piers of the old encircling city walls, up to a Walpurgis Night fantasy above Sacre

Coeur, out to the bravura description of the Seine and its fleets of tugboats with which the novel ends, Céline reinvented a Paris that Rhys
drew upon as she created her own extraordinary version of a city that
is both real and imagined. But it may also have been Céline's use of a
compellingly intimate narrator's voice that Rhys was hearing as she
began to think of how Sasha should speak. Fiercely; bitterly; wittily;
suspiciously: it was Céline's Bardamu who taught Rhys the difficult art
of shifting moods in the space of a sentence.

Diary of a Country Priest, the novel written in 1935 by one of Céline's
greatest admirers, Georges Bernanos, exerted a more direct influence on the creation of Sasha's personality than elements of Rhys
herself. Recommending one of her most cherished French books to
a literary friend in 1953, Rhys quoted Bernanos on an author's need
for scrupulous honesty. *"Il faudrait parler de soi-meme avec un rigueur
inflexible"*—"It's essential to be inflexibly truthful about oneself"—the
lonely parish priest writes in his self-excoriating diary. Rhys's patron
saint was Teresa of Ávila, with her clarion call to rise above despair; the
priest's touchstone is Saint Thérèse of Lisieux, who preached the doc-
trine of universal grace. "Grace is everywhere," are the young priest's
dying words; reaching up for the final embrace of a sinister lover whose
white dressing gown is insistently compared to a priest's robe, Rhys's
narrator is allowed to find her own cruel form of grace in death.

Rhys went to Paris alone in the autumn of 1937, while she was still
planning her unwritten novel. She was just in time to catch the tail
end of the International Exhibition that was housed in and around the
new Palais de Chaillot. Today, the 1937 world fair is best remembered
for *Guernica*, Picasso's passionate elegy for the massacre—in the anni-
hilation of an entire town—of his Basque compatriots. At the time,
the crowds were drawn to an art-deco railway pavilion and a hangar-
like Palais de L'Air, rather than to Le Corbusier's city of the future
by Porte Maillot, or the looming symbols of Nazi Germany (Speer's
gigantic tower crowned by eagle and swastika) and of Soviet Russia
(two massive farmworkers). Rhys arrived in October, just as the fair
was starting to close down. She returned to London with a portrait of

a melancholy-eyed banjo player painted by a new friend, Simon Segal: the Russian-born émigré had sold everything he put on show in Paris in 1936 to a single buyer, an achievement which Rhys's novel fondly recorded for her "Serge Rubin." But Rhys also brought back to London a unifying image for her book. The International Exhibition provides a ghostly backdrop to a key scene in *Good Morning, Midnight*, but what is on show instead throughout the novel is Mrs. Sasha Jansen, formerly "wild Sophia": the woman who—ludicrously, unflinchingly and entirely self-aware—escorts the reader to the dreary, predestined setting for her death.

Marya Zelli died at the end of *Quartet*; no hope gleams from the knife-like band of light that shines under Anna Morgan's door at the end of *Voyage in the Dark*. Older, better-educated and superficially more worldly than her predecessors, Sasha Jansen is shown sleepwalking through a dying world—Rhys was not oblivious to international events—towards an equally bleak conclusion. ("So good night, Day!" is how the second stanza of Emily Dickinson's 1838 poem "Good Morning, Midnight!" ends, in a gloom that leaves no room for doubt that it has reached its terminus.)

Rhys herself evidently knew Dickinson's work well. Mrs. Jansen never mentions the poem, but it's made apparent that she's aware, from the moment that she chooses a hotel that overlooks a dead-end street ("an impasse"), precisely where she's headed. ("Quite like old times," the room seems to jeer. "Yes? No?"[11]) The question Sasha faces is merely of method: how to reach her own dead end without too much indecorum, without too many of the sobbing fits that can never bring adequate relief. Her survival of a difficult past has evidently owed more to luck than to will: when she speaks of the good fortune of being saved ("rescued, fished-up, half-drowned, out of the deep, dark river").[12] Sasha already knows that "the real thing," when it comes, will be when no friends are on hand to help: "When you sink you sink to the accompaniment of loud laughter."[13]

Raw-nerved herself, Rhys endowed Sasha Jansen with her own paranoia. Everything and everybody becomes Mrs. Jansen's cold-eyed judge. A clock, seeming to belch, giggles at her; windows distort into sneering eyes. It's a shock to discover that she, in her once elegant fur coat (the coat from Vienna was becoming Rhys's literary trademark), has faded into the shabby old soak perceived by others as *"la vieille"*: age haunts her like a vengeful spectre. Mirrors are as pitiless as the judging gaze of strangers: "Fly, fly, run from these atrocious voices, these abominable eyes. . . ."[14] But Mrs. Jansen always holds the advantage over her perceived judges. Sometimes, she uses a witty form of mockery to strike back. "He arrives," she comments of the man who will cause her to be sacked from her job at a fashion house, "Bowler-hat, majestic trousers, oh-my-God expression, ha-ha eyes . . . I know him at once."[15] Sometimes, as with the quietly spoken Rhys herself, Sasha's anger knocks the reader backwards with the force of a physical blow:

> One day, quite suddenly, when you're not expecting it, I'll take a hammer from the folds of my dark cloak and crack your little skull like an egg-shell. Crack it will go, the egg-shell; out they will stream, the blood, the brains. One day, one day . . . One day the fierce wolf that walks at my side will spring on you and rip your abominable guts out . . . One day, one day. Now, now, gently, quietly, quietly . . . [16]

While it's not difficult to identify the resemblance to Rhys in Mrs. Jansen's savage self-knowledge and the violence of her imagination, it's naive to attribute to the author herself what Judith Thurman once interestingly described as a "squalid complicity" between Rhys's narrator and Sasha's predators: "their company, their protection, their money—in exchange for the pleasure she can give them as a victim."[17] Another early feminist critic, Judy Froshaug, proved equally illuminating when she praised Rhys's uncanny understanding of minds that teeter on the border of insanity: "women who spend their lives balanced between despair and a sort of frantic hopefulness, women alone, women who beg to be loved but expect to be rejected."[18] For this aspect of Sasha, Rhys was drawing upon the darkest aspect of the only person of whom she knew enough to tell the truth: herself.

While Mrs. Jansen's final days in Paris place her at an unquestionable distance from her creator, elements of Rhys's own experiences are apparent throughout the novel. An account of Sasha's loss of her baby boy enables us to glimpse how deeply Rhys grieved when her own son perished. The retrospective narrative which comprises Part Three of the adroitly structured four sections of *Good Morning, Midnight* summons up all the tenderness, innocence and anxieties of Rhys's early married life with Jean Lenglet (the Dutchman Enno Jansen in the novel) in Paris and at The Hague.

Beyond all this, however, it's rash to read *Good Morning, Midnight* as an artless account of Rhys herself, or even as a vision of the woman she feared she might become. Like her predecessors, Sasha Jansen is, rather, that ideal surrogate memorably posited in Rhys's private exercise books as the damaged spirit to whom we can all relate: "the I who is everybody." The casual reader might suppose that Rhys—who relished her comforts and liked pretty surroundings—had visited the Paris Exhibition while spending her nights among the brooms and mops of the servants' floor at a down-at-heel hotel. (*"Quatrième à gauche*, and mind you don't trip on the hole in the carpet. That's me," says Sasha.")[19] The likelihood is that Rhys stayed with a disapproving but always loving friend. Germaine Richelot is recognisable in the novel as Sidonie, whose kind attempt to find her hard-drinking friend a suitable room is interpreted by thin-skinned Sasha Jansen as condescension. ("God, it's an insult when you come to think about it!"[20])

Deceptively concise—a mere 190 pages—*Good Morning, Midnight* reveals better than any other of Rhys's novels the chasm that divided Jean's chaotic life from the disciplined clarity of her writing. Behind *Good Morning, Midnight*, even more skilfully concealed than in *Voyage in the Dark*, lies the wealth of a cultivated mind. *"Belle comme une fleur de verre"* . . . *"Belle comme une fleur de terre,"*[21] the words Sasha casually summons to describe two young fashion models, first appear in a poem by the surrealist writer, Robert Desnos. Rhys's startling image of mascara-fringed, staring eyes, set on a whirling wheel of lights, is placed towards the end of the novel, presaging Sasha's self-sought death. It derives from Man Ray's *Les Larmes* (1932), the Paris-based artist's close-up photograph of a heavily lashed eye weeping glass tears. Sasha's long nocturnal strolls remind us of Rhys's admiration for Baudelaire, Céline and George Moore, in whose finest novel, *Esther Waters*, she had read of the "strange mingling of enchantment and alienation that people experience in the city streets."[22] Rhys herself was also recalling the wanderings of the ghostly woman at the centre of *Nadja*, André Breton's avant-garde novel of 1928. Rhys, not Sasha, was quietly referencing both Bernanos's gift of universal grace to his dying priest and Molly Bloom's celebrated monologue in *Ulysses*, in the final affirmative that the less literary Mrs. Jansen whispers as she reaches exaltedly up from the darkness of her bed for the last time: "Then I put my arms round him and pull him down on to the bed, saying: "Yes—yes—yes . . . "[23]

A Beckett-like vein of black comedy and occasionally, pure slapstick, provides a steady counterpoint to the vortex of Jansen's descent. Its presence is evident from Rhys's opening page, when Sasha encounters a woman cheerily humming the tune of "Gloomy Sunday" while reading its score and tapping out the song's rhythm on the tabletop. In 1939, Rhys didn't need to inform readers that the melancholy Hungarian hit song of 1932 (later recorded by Billie Holliday) was known as "The Suicide Song." At times, the jokes in *Good Morning, Midnight* are delightfully silly: "Very light," remarks a chambermaid as she flicks on the switch in a sombre little room that faces an exterior wall. (Jansen had requested "a light room.")[24] "They add, of course, a macintosh,"[25] Sasha quips when describing the penchant of Englishmen for making love while fully dressed. René, the gigolo with whom Mrs. Jansen develops an unexpectedly satisfying relationship, describes to her a house so grand that even the lavatory chain, when pulled, plays a tune. "Rich people," he sighs. "You have to be sorry for them."[26] Dropping her guard for just one moment, Sasha laughs with him, not at him.

Briefly, their author permits two characters to enjoy a moment of perfect harmony.

BACK AT PAULTONS HOUSE early in 1938, Rhys began work on the novel almost at once. She kept at it for just under a year. Simon Segal wrote to urge his new friend (it's unclear whether they had become lovers in Paris) not to despair and to keep in mind Baudelaire's words about the strength born of grief. "*Moi aussi je souffre souvent—toujours, beaucoup, croyez moi,*" he comforted her. "*Mais je l'aime, cette souffrance, car elle seule ne me trahit jamais, me donne courage et la belle colère . . .*" ['I too suffer often—all the time, and deeply, believe me . . . But I love my suffering, for alone of all things it never betrays me, it gives me courage, and my blessed rage'].[27] Rhys's magpie mind seized upon the quotation and compulsively twisted it into another maxim, muttered by Sasha as she sits alone with her ghosts in her room, after turning down a promising teatime date at the Dome: "*La tristesse vaut mieux que la joie*" ("So sadness has it over joy").[28]

Distractions were few, but it was impossible, living in London in 1938, to be unaware of the shocking events that were taking place in Europe, or of the growing inevitability of war, something that can only have darkened the mood of a woman whose only child lived for much of the year on the Continent. Neither Rhys nor her daughter attended the funeral of Rhys's Aunt Clarice, who died that year, but Maryvonne still enjoyed the long school holidays she spent travelling and camping with Leslie and her mother in Scotland, Wales and—just the once—Ireland: holidays on which her volatile mother, with her writing set to one side, always seemed to be happy and relaxed. Maryvonne would also remember 1938 as the year in which she was finally introduced to her mother's wistful sisters: Minna, by then suffering from advanced Parkinson's disease, was being looked after in Acton by the same sturdy nurse who had nursed Minna and Brenda's mother, and who still shared their home. It's unclear whether Maryvonne also met luckless Owen and his hardworking wife, or her great-uncle, Neville, husbanding his frugally issued pennies up in Harrogate.

Replying years later to one of *Good Morning, Midnight*'s most ardent admirers, Rhys recalled that ending the novel had been her greatest challenge: "I tried and rewrote and rewrote but no use." A bottle of wine had, so she airily claimed in 1956, produced the solution "from Heaven knows where" in the form of "the Man in the Dressing Gown."[29] It's a warning never to take writers at their word about the mysteries of the creative process. In fact, the sinister role that Sasha's top-floor neighbour would play had been woven into the fabric of Rhys's novel from its opening pages, when his "immaculately white robe" presents him both as "the ghost of the landing" and "the priest of some obscene, half-understood religion."[30] His significance as a bringer of death is intentional, and clear.

Always a perfectionist, Rhys was reluctant to let go of her novel. Furious arguments took place. At one point, having threatened to destroy the manuscript, she hurled Leslie's typewriter out of a window. Smith only dared carry the pages to the waiting publisher, Michael Sadleir of Constable, after his wife had fallen asleep. When Sadleir sent a contract for her signature, the couple were still quarrelling, or so Rhys would enjoy telling the story to close friends.[31]

Published in April 1939, on the eve of war across Europe, *Good Morning, Midnight* received dismal reviews. In America, it was summarily rejected and remained unpublished until late in Rhys's life. Jean Lenglet, who admired the novel enough to translate it into Dutch, secured his former wife a valuable new critical admirer in Victor de Vriesland. In France, however, both Lenglet and Rosamund Lehmann's brother John failed to find Rhys a publisher. Editors at Plon and Stock were not alone in raising their hands in horror: *"le sujet (en ce moment surtout) effroye tout editeur"*—"The subject matter (especially at this time) appals them all"—Lenglet wryly reported to his former wife. In England, Frank Swinnerton expressed his distaste for a novel which neither Norah Hoult nor Rebecca West, two of Rhys's most loyal admirers, were prepared to review. "Oh dear—how sad, how painful it is to read," Violet Hammersley protested to Rhys on 22 May.[32]

Today, Rhys's fourth novel is regarded by many as her finest work. Touchingly, the only two men who seem to have recognised *Good Morning, Midnight* as a work of genius at the time of its publication were its author's husbands, both present and past. Home comfort was not enough. Almost thirty years would pass before Rhys would feel able to relinquish a novel into the hands of a publisher.

———————

A FEW PERCEPTIVE reviews might have made all the difference to the career of Jean Rhys. In 1938 she had begun to collect ideas for a next novel. The fascinating evidence survives, both in a group of fictional recreations of her childhood that she scrawled within a much-used black exercise book, as well as in a seven-page typescript dating back to 4 December 1938. Revised over a period of almost three decades, "Mr Howard's House" was typed on the onion-skin reverse sheets of what seems to have been Rhys's final draft of *Good Morning, Midnight*. Here, in the cold cruelty of "Mr Howard," and in a troubling dream of sacrifice and rejection, were planted the seeds of *Wide Sargasso Sea*. Rhys called this group of fictionalised childhood memories, simply "Creole."[33]

Rhys's return to Dominica in 1936 had stirred up many of her old memories. Buried deep within *Good Morning, Midnight*, one of Sasha Jansen's strangest recollections is a reimagining of fourteen-year-old Gwen Williams's encounters with her parent's married friend, "Mr Howard," in the Botanical Gardens at Roseau:

> A man is standing with his back to me, whistling that tune and cleaning his shoes. I am wearing a black dress, very short, and heel-less slippers. My legs are bare. I am watching for the expression on the man's face when he turns round. Now he ill-treats me, now he betrays me. He often brings home other women and I have to wait on them, and I don't like that.[34]

Unpursued in *Midnight*, this same trauma of sexual coercion resurfaced in the notes for "Creole"; it is possible that the account that Rhys gave here of her abuse by "Mr Howard" caused an older Rhys protectively to scribble across the top of "Creole"'s opening page: "Don't on any account," and then, with unexplained relief: "Thank God."

The episode which follows directly on from "Mr Howard" in Rhys's exercise-book notes towards "Creole" reveals that, long before Rhys began work on her fifth and final novel, she was pondering the injustice done by Charlotte Brontë to Mr Rochester's first wife, a "mad" Caribbean heiress, in *Jane Eyre*. Her emotional return to Dominica in 1936 had provided a possible title from her voyage across the treacherous waters of the Sargasso Sea.

Rhys had first read Brontë's novel as a schoolgirl at the Perse. She read it again in 1938. Pondering "Creole," Rhys began to blend elements of the sinister Mr. Howard with "Raworth," her own interpretation of Edward Rochester. Privately, she set down her idea of a troubling dream in which a young girl sees herself in bridal white, trustfully following a beckoning gentleman into a forest. Within the wood, without warning, the man turns on her; his face is "black with hatred." The dream ends abruptly as the girl's mother rouses her daughter from sleep.

Over three decades later, following the publication of *Wide Sargasso Sea*, Rhys acknowledged that she had embarked upon a first version of that novel (provisionally named "Le Revenant") before the Second World War, commenting that Leslie had been very excited by what he then read. In October 1945, Rhys confided to Peggy Kirkaldy that she regarded "Le Revenant" as "the one work I've written that's of much use."[35]

"Revenant" is generally taken to mean somebody who has returned from the dead: a zombie. All that survives from another idea Rhys had in the late Thirties, "Wedding in the Carib Quarter," is a one-page plan of headings for chapters. A hint of that vanished work's transgressive content survives in the words Rhys scrawled across the head of the page: "& a fearful warning too! That was! It went for keeps." She added what seems to have been a similar warning to her future critics and biographer: "Attention Miss! Or Madam. No playing around with ME."[36]

"Le Revenant" vanished—ripped up during a marital squabble, Rhys would sometimes claim—but it's significant that she squirrelled away two chapters for future use. One contained the dream encounter in the forest which had found its first form in the notes towards "Creole." Eventually, that dream would play a crucial role in *Wide Sargasso Sea*.

HOLIDAYS HELPED ASSUAGE the bitter disappointment with which Rhys read the reviews of *Good Morning, Midnight* in April 1939. Following a visit to Wales and a brief summer sojourn at Taplow, a sleepy little town beside the Thames, she and Leslie returned to Chelsea. Seventeen-year-old Maryvonne was staying with them when war was announced by Neville Chamberlain on 3 September. Offered the choice of remaining in England or rejoining her father, she opted for Holland. Appreciative though she was of Leslie's kindness and of her mother's affectionate impulses, Maryvonne's first language was Dutch and her first loyalty, at a time of potential crisis, was to the father she adored.

The farewells between mother and daughter were not dramatic: in the early autumn of 1939, nobody could imagine what horrors lay ahead.

V

DARKNESS AT NOON
Mrs. Max Hamer

"A harsh word could kill her, imagined insults lurked in
chance encounters. A vulnerable complex organism,
she was made to be hurt.'

—Peggy Kirkaldy, "Portrait of a Lost Friend"[1]

12

At War with the World
(1940–45)

"Pressed flat against the cellar wall, they listened to the inexorable throbbing of the planes. And above them, the house waited . . . "

—Jean Rhys, "A Solid House"[1]

AGED FIFTY-FIVE IN 1940, Leslie Tilden Smith was too old to fly combat aircraft as he had done in the first war. Gallantly determined to do his bit for England, he volunteered and was commissioned as a pilot officer, a modest desk job ranking just above a midshipman in the naval equivalent. Evelyn Scott's middle-aged English husband followed the same patriotic route: it's possible that the Tilden Smiths met up with John Metcalfe after their move in February 1940 to Bircham Newton, an RAF base in the flatlands of north Norfolk. It was there, three months later, that Jean Rhys learned of the fate of the Netherlands.

Rhys had remained in touch with her daughter and Jean Lenglet for some months after Maryvonne's return to Amsterdam in the autumn of 1939. Lenglet's regretful letter about his failure to secure a French publisher for *Good Morning, Midnight* reached his former wife early in 1940; probably, he added a copy of an article written the previous summer in which "Edouard de Néve" (Lenglet's pseudonym) had praised

Rhys as a shamefully unrecognised novelist, one who regarded isolation as essential to her work: *"cette solitude imposée à elle-même."*[2]

Lenglet had approved of Maryvonne's return from England shortly after war was declared, believing that his own country was safe. On 10 May 1940, Hitler invaded the Netherlands. By the end of the month, the German occupation of the country was complete and all lines of communication were abruptly severed. Jean Rhys now daily faced the possibility that both her adored first husband and her only child were dead.

The first sign that Rhys was under stress emerged at Bircham Newton shortly after news of the German occupation of Holland. Laura, the protagonist in one of Rhys's wartime stories, "I Spy a Stranger," violently rounds on an officious male visitor for claiming that the WAAFS up at the station smelled. Rhys's fiery real-life response to such an offensive comment may have been what proved her undoing.

No details survive, but while Leslie remained at the base, Rhys was hastily banished to West Beckham, a pretty little north Norfolk village situated close to woodlands and the coast—and also to a bomber-detecting radar station. Three village houses had been requisitioned for military use; Rhys was consigned to the former home of the housemaster at a local school. She was living there alone in the summer of 1940 when the first German bombers streamed overhead, targeting Norwich. Gazing upwards, how could Rhys not think of the bombs that Hitler had already dropped on Holland? Watching her—as wartime villagers would have watched the solitary, book-reading woman who now lived at the schoolmaster's house—how could they not become suspicious?

Rhys had lived within the comforting anonymity of cities for all of her adult life. Even at Bircham Newton, however out of place she had felt there, she occupied the protected role of a spouse attached to the glowingly patriotic world of the Royal Air Force until—for whatever reason—she had disgraced herself. At West Beckham, Rhys felt more under scrutiny than Sasha Jansen had ever sardonically perceived herself to be in the Parisian bars of *Good Morning, Midnight*. Laura, spoken of as "that crazy foreigner" in "I Spy a Stranger," suspects passing strangers of stopping to "gape" at her house and peer into her room ("or I think they can"). At West Beckham, Rhys shut herself in, closing the window curtains and—more practically—draping blankets over the doors: even in summer, Norfolk's east wind carries the sting of a salted whip. She could not rid herself of the sense that the villagers, and even the house itself, were watching her—"seeing me as I really am."[3]

The growing darkness of Rhys's mood in 1940 emerges from the jungle of angry notes which she jotted to herself while living at the village house she renamed "Rolvenden" in the story "Temps Perdi." One furious outburst was triggered by a cleaning woman's failure to return Rhys's greeting: "servants are much the worst, I always think," snapped the thin-skinned colonial outsider, adding that "90% of the English have the souls of servants and the manners too." Elsewhere, Rhys cursed the entire nation of England—"rot its mean soul of shit"— before trying to obliterate words that, if discovered, might incriminate her as the enemy. In three disjointed pages, headed: "The Kingdoms of the Human Ants, part of a lecture delivered when I was drunk from sadness," she bitterly compared the innocence of young women ("beautiful & eager with a touching humility and charm") to the harridans they must become: "drab spiteful cruel . . . you think how can I let these girls grow into these women." Confiding her thoughts to these same private pages, Rhys noted her consciousness of being disliked and added a final prayer: "Let me not be like my father and mother do let me not they were so unhappy so dead. I want to be happy."[4]

Later, reworking these thoughts into stories that were among the best she ever wrote, Rhys would acknowledge that most of her suspicions were groundless. "They don't think or say anything that I would imagine they think or say," she admitted of her West Beckham neighbours in the finished version of "Temps Perdi." But the hostility that she sensed was real. On 1 August 1940, a Norwich newspaper published a tasty snippet about a woman who had pleaded guilty to the charge of behaving in a drunk and disorderly fashion on a public highway. Rhys's

married name was given in full; so was the location. So was the fact that
an upstanding member of the West Beckham community had doused
the obstreperous female with a bucket of cold water.[5]

Looking down at the soberly dressed woman in the dock, the magistrate heard that Mrs. Tilden Smith, prior to her arrest, had proclaimed
herself a proud West Indian and denounced the English as "a b——
mean and dirty lot." A compassionate man, the justice gathered that
she was distraught about the fate of her daughter, out in Nazi-occupied
Holland. He imposed no fine. Rhys's punishment was bad enough:
she must continue to live among the villagers who had witnessed her
arrest—and who noted that Mrs. Smith's husband seemed in no hurry
to join his wife.

In February 1941, following a modest promotion to the desk-
bound rank of flying officer, Leslie was relocated to work with the
radar-detection unit near West Beckham. By March, for undisclosed reasons, Rhys had moved to lodgings in the Chapelfield area of Norwich. It
was to escape her seemingly self-imposed isolation that she impulsively
travelled south to the Colchester home of her old friend Peggy Kirkaldy.

The visit was not a success. Some friend of Peggy's let slip a malicious comment about the Jamaican-born Eliot Bliss as exuding a certain odour. Eliot was a friend of Peggy's, but it was Rhys who took
loyal offence at a blatant ethnic sneer about her Caribbean compatriot.
Evidently, there was a heated exchange with her hostess; certainly, by
the time Rhys wrote to plead for understanding, and to lament her
"hideous" life in Norfolk, Peggy felt no duty to respond. The result
would be four years of silence.

Rhys returned to Norwich from Colchester on 20 March. Reading
The Times a few days later, she came across a respectful obituary of
one of the country's leading financial figures. Lancey had played no
part in Rhys's life in Norfolk, where he himself lived in old-fashioned
splendour at Garboldisham Hall, but she was still in possession of his
friendly notes to her in Paris. She kept a couple of them, along with
a flowing, high-waisted and prettily flowered robe to which she had
granted a brief appearance in *Voyage in the Dark*, as Anna Morgan's din-

ner-gown at the hotel in Savernake Forest. The dress, still in her wardrobe when Rhys reached her eighties, was a last reminder of the days
when young Ella had imagined herself becoming Mrs. Hugh Smith:
a genuine English lady; the cherished spouse of a rich and generous
English gentleman: his petted kitten. Another time; another world.

Rhys would always maintain discretion about her periods of mental
crisis. Some partly destroyed letters, drafted into the back of a diary
that she kept after the war, suggest that she held her younger sibling
Brenda responsible for despatching her to an asylum on the outskirts of
Norwich.[6] It's conceivable that Rhys—like Laura in "I Spy a Stranger"
and Teresa in "A Solid House"—had deteriorated enough by April
1941 to have been briefly committed by Leslie, with the consent of
Rhys's sister, to the gloomy mental hospital of St. Andrew's in Thorpe,
although the hospital had largely been handed over for the care of
injured soldiers. No records survive from this period of the hospital's
history to allow Rhys's claim to be checked.*

Rhys was either due for release from St. Andrew's, or was lodging
elsewhere in Thorpe, when she begged her practical and well-connected
friend Phyllis Shand Allfrey to find her some quiet sanctuary, away from
a city under siege from the air. Phyllis gave the request careful thought
before recommending an unusually literate Norfolk vicar, whose family were already housing several evacuees. His name was Willis Feast
and his abiding interest was in modernist poetry. An informal drawing
of Feast in 1940 by Wyndham Lewis (held in the Norwich Gallery
Archive) shows a quizzical, intelligent-looking young man with slanting
eyes set above high cheekbones and a narrow-lipped, appealing smile.

Phyllis had probably warned the Feasts that her friend was in need of
a rest. It's unclear whether she herself knew about the gravity of Rhys's
breakdown, but the Feasts went out of their way to make their visitor
feel welcome. Rhys was housed in the best bedroom at Booton rectory,

---

* Some of the diary's torn pages were addressed to Edward Rees Williams. Evidently,
Rhys intended to share her suspicions of Brenda with their older brother, following his
return from service in India as an army medical officer.

its long windows overlooking an old-fashioned garden shaded by the tall green trees that always reminded her of Dominica. Meals were brought to her room on a tray so that she could work in solitude. Later, in the afternoons, the visitor lounged under the low boughs of a garden elm (according to the recollection of Barbara, the vicar's thirteen-year-old daughter), slowly leafing through *For Whom the Bell Tolls*, Hemingway's newly published novel about the Spanish Civil War. A cake was baked at the rectory to honour a birthday which the age-conscious and still girlish-looking Rhys is unlikely to have admitted was her fifty-first. Young Barbara Feast thought that a real lady would have buttoned her dress a little higher when visitors dropped by. She wondered, as all the household did, how anybody should be so astonishingly languid.[7]

Rhys's indolence was not the only cause for concern at the rectory. Mr. Feast's gentle enquiry about her real reason for going into the garden one day provoked a burst of rage that escalated to hysteria until the vicar's wife, acting with imaginable satisfaction, gave their unapologetically contrary guest a hard slap across the face.[8] By the middle of September, Rhys was back in Norwich, where a vicar from one of Willis Feast's neighbouring parishes was taken to visit her. Although "hellishly angry" when the two priests arrived, a shared bottle of gin had apparently worked wonders. Rhys, after a drink or two, proved to be irresistible. Departing in a spirit of genuine regret, Eric Griffiths felt that he understood why Willis had been looking so dreamy of late: he had been hosting an enchantress.[9]

Rhys remained alone in Norwich throughout the autumn of 1941, dependent on the goodwill of hard-pressed and sharp-tongued wartime landladies, a breed whom she detested in part because she always felt that they were judging her. Teresa, in Rhys's story "A Solid House," is transfixed by "the hard bright glitter" of her landlady's eyes; the English can seem friendly, Teresa reflects after a conversation with her fellow lodger, Captain Roper: "but hidden away, what continents of distrust, what icy seas of silence. Voyage to the Arctic regions. . . ."[10] Teresa is said to be recovering from an attempt to kill herself; of Rhys, we know only that she was being seen by a doctor during her last months in Norwich. Louis Rose had trained as a doctor, but by 1940, he was living in Norwich while working as honorary psychiatrist to the Lowestoft and North Suffolk Hospital.[11] Rhys's striking description of the twin spirits, one passive and meek, the other discordant and angry, who wrestle within two of the women in her wartime stories, Audrey in "The Insect World," and Inez in "Outside the Machine," suggests that a professionally trained view of her personality may have influenced the writer's view of herself for a time. If so, it didn't last.

In February 1942, Leslie and Rhys were reunited at West Beckham just long enough for Rhys to get her husband into serious trouble by shouting "Heil Hitler" while drinking in a country pub. Her outburst, especially shocking for emerging from such a reserved, softly spoken woman, was reported. Leslie's superiors promptly removed him from Norfolk, packing him off to Bristol and then to picturesque Ludlow, once the capital of Wales. It seems that he was asked to leave the RAF; nevertheless, spending a summer holiday together at Oxwich Bay on the Gower Peninsula, Leslie and Rhys enjoyed a rare period of untroubled serenity. This particular part of Wales could always cast a spell: straying one summer afternoon into a field thick with golden cowslips, Rhys felt that she never wanted to leave.[12] A month later, the Tilden Smiths moved back to London.

———————

FROM THE AUTUMN of 1942, Leslie and Rhys occupied (Leslie's loyal sister, Muriel, paid their rent) an airy top-floor flat on Steele's Road, a broad and pretty street near Primrose Hill in north-west London. Leslie resumed his old freelance job as a publisher's reader for Jamie Hamilton. Rhys was still drinking heavily; while nervously discouraging his married daughter from paying visits, Leslie represented himself to an impressed Antoinette as "working for the Air Ministry."

Primrose Hill wasn't a reassuring area of London to inhabit during wartime. Long-barrelled defence guns, mounted on top of the ancient hill, offered scant protection from the bombs that regularly fell on neighbouring streets. Rhys was evidently recalling one of these devastated locations when she described Audrey in "The Insect World" as walking home past a ghostly street of "skeleton houses," where front doorsteps "looked as though they were hanging by a thread."[13] At night, blackout curtains kept out the light, but not the sound, of a besieged city under fire.

It was during the two years that the Tilden Smiths spent together at Steele's Road that Rhys resumed her writing. Work continued on "The Revenant," but her chief preoccupation was with an auto-biographical group of stories, each of which examines the fate of a vulnerable woman—always alone; always adrift—trapped within a wartime world where anything less than noisy patriotism will be perceived as treachery; it's a world in which they have no place and can find no refuge.

Rich in black humour, Rhys's wartime stories focus on the experience of exclusion. While "A Solid House," "Temps Perdi," "The Insect World" and "I Spy a Stranger" are the most well known of the group, the behaviour of Inez Best in "Outside the Machine," which takes place in the women's ward of a hospital near Versailles, suggests that this story, although set in an earlier time, was also written or intensively revised at Steele's Road. Inez exhibits all the resentment and barely contained fury of Rhys's wartime women. Like them—and like Rhys herself—she exults in every chance to speak her mind. "Don't underrate me," Inez thinks as she listens to two of her condescending fellow patients calling for another member of the ward to be hanged (for the crime of trying to kill herself): suddenly, Best lets fly, calling them out as "a pair of bitches":

> "Who was speaking to you?" Pat said.
>
> Inez heard words coming round and full and satisfying out of her mouth—exactly what she thought about them, exactly what they were . . .
>
> "Disgusting," said Mrs. Wilson. "I *told* you so," she added triumphantly. "I knew it. I knew the sort she was from the first."[14]

A simmering rage bubbles through these stories, boiling into eruption when least expected. "Damn you don't call me that," shrieks twenty-nine-year-old Audrey when innocently addressed by her cheery flatmate as "Old Girl" in "The Insect World." "Damn your soul to everlasting hell *don't call me that. . . .*" In "I Spy a Stranger," Laura—the most akin to Rhys herself of all the author's wartime women characters—explodes with more justification when her cousin's husband tries to hustle her out of their house and off to an asylum:

> "Come along, old girl," Ricky said. "It's moving day." He put his hand on her arm and gave her a tug. That was a mistake . . . It was when he touched her that she started to scream at the top of her voice. And swear—oh my dear, it was awful. He got nasty, too. He dragged her along and she clung to the banisters and shrieked and cursed. He hit her and kicked her, and she kept on cursing—oh, I've *never* heard such curses.[15]

Truths were being told and Rhys went out of her way to signal her own connection to the wilful, violent-minded women she described. Packing her cherished possessions to leave her cousin's home, Laura even provides the reader with an italicised inventory of Rhys's most sacred personal treasures ("the bracelet bought in Florence . . . the old flowered workbox with coloured reels of cotton and silk"). Having mentioned a jewellery box with a golden key, Laura/Rhys adds a blatant pun on the Lockharts' family name: "I'm going to lock my heart and throw away the key." Nothing here is accidental; every connection is intended. *Here I am*, the author seems to say. Make of me what you will. It's all in view, but on my terms, reader, never on yours.

———————

SOMETIME IN 1944, Leslie and Rhys walked up Primrose Hill together and said a prayer—although neither of them was conventionally religious—for the safety of Maryvonne Lenglet.

And sometime in the spring of 1945, Leslie felt confident enough about his wife's improved behaviour to permit his married daughter to pay a first visit to the flat in Steele's Road. (No mention is ever made either by Leslie or Rhys of the son, Anthony, who had taken his mother's side in the Tilden Smiths' divorce.) To Antoinette's relief, Rhys greeted her cheerfully before showing off a room which she had been painting—she intended it to become Leslie's study—in a blaze of vibrant colours.

What was going on?

A plausible guess might be that Leslie had decided it was safe enough for his daughter to visit after his wife's dark mood had been lifted by unexpected and joyful news from the Netherlands: a letter had arrived explaining that Maryvonne was safe, well—and a married woman with a husband she adored.

The fuller story which reached Rhys later—direct communication with the Netherlands remained difficult throughout 1945 and Maryvonne was slow to reveal all the details—filled her with wonder and pride. In 1941, aged nineteen, Maryvonne had gone to work for the country's resistance movement, contributing to *Vrij Nederland*, an underground paper, while her father, one of the best brains of the Dutch resistance, daringly helped at least thirteen RAF pilots to evade capture and return safely to England. Within five months, both of the Lenglets were arrested. Lenglet, due to the swift intervention of Henriëtte van Eyk's brother, had been able to escape death by pleading insanity. His colleagues were shot. All that Maryvonne knew in 1945 was that her father, having escaped from an asylum and then a series of Dutch prisons, had eventually been deported—twice—to Sachsenhausen, one of Germany's most brutal concentration camps. His son, Maryvonne's older half-brother, had meanwhile fought on the side of the Nazis.

Lenglet's ultimate fate was still unknown to his daughter when Maryvonne first managed to get a letter to London. It's unclear when Rhys learned the fact that her first husband, having survived the camp's notorious death march from Sachsenhausen to the north-west of Germany in the spring of 1945, had rescued a destitute Polish aristocrat who—following Lenglet's swift divorce from Henriëtte van Eyk—became this remarkable man's fifth and final wife. Reporting the brief fact of her recent marriage to Job Moerman (on Valentine's Day), Maryvonne omitted to mention that the risk for two resistance workers of being recognised by a German registrar had been so great that the bride smuggled five grenades into the ceremony in her pocket, while Job carried a pistol under his jacket. Later, Rhys would learn that her heroic daughter, released shortly after her arrest in 1941 on account of her youth, had continued her father's work of helping downed British pilots evade capture. She performed this task while sheltering with a beloved family friend, a woman who was shielding twenty-five Jews in her Amsterdam attic. (Henriëtte, who was also working with the resis-tance, but on a different basis, had been nervous of the consequences of taking Maryvonne back into her home.) It was during this period that Rhys's intrepid daughter had met Job Moerman, an undercover expert in the gathering of intelligence about the enemy.[16]

What mattered most to Rhys in the final months of war was to learn that her lost daughter was safe. Peace was announced on 2 September. It's reasonable to suppose that the Tilden Smiths were feeling happy, relieved and in need of a rest when they decided to spend the month of October at a rented property on Dartmoor.

THE COTTAGE, ALTHOUGH set in a beautiful landscape, close to one of Dartmoor's many rivers, was remote and spartan. The journey had been long and the middle-aged Tilden Smiths were both in poor health. Rhys was recovering from a summer bout of flu; Leslie, now sixty, looked pale and gaunt. Writing to her husband's daughter a short time later, Rhys said Leslie kept remembering his mother's sudden and premature death; Rhys herself was full of unease. Fictionalising the Dartmoor visit in one of her most troubling tales, "The Sound of the

River," she made use of a brooding landscape, the wind, dark trees and a silent river which finally gushes free of its banks, to create a haunting sense of inevitability.

The end came with terrible swiftness on 2 October 1945, the first full day of their visit. Leslie had seemed fragile when they arrived; now, he complained of spasms and violent pain in his chest and arm. By the time Rhys had returned from her second anxious trek to the hostel where their landlord was staying nearby, having broken a glass pane in the front door in order to reach the telephone and summon medical assistance, Leslie was dead.

> "Wake up," she said and shook him. As soon as she touched him her heart swelled till it reached her throat. It swelled and grew jagged claws and the claws clutched her driving in deep. "Oh God," she said . . . and knelt by the bed with his hand in her two hands and not speaking not thinking any longer.[17]

To some, such a sudden and isolated death from a heart attack (the cause given on the death certificate) did not look natural in a man of only sixty. Rumours buzzed. Leslie's daughter told the doctor who had eventually visited the cottage that she believed Rhys might have killed her father; Rhys's unsympathetic younger sibling imagined that her sister had calmly sat by, doing nothing, while Leslie died in the adjacent room. Writing to a shocked Antoinette to explain that she would not attend a London memorial service, Rhys was devastatingly candid. Yes, she had often treated Leslie badly when she was working on her books. "I did love him though," Rhys wrote, adding wistfully that she thought her husband had "sometimes" been happy in her company. She was being honest—not intentionally cruel—when she told Antoinette that her chief sensation during the Devon cremation had been of empathy and even gratitude: "I had all the time the feeling that Leslie had *escaped*—from me, from everyone and was free at last."[18]

But Rhys's feelings ran deeper than this. "He was smiling as if he knew what she had been thinking," she wrote (in "The Sound of the

River"), when describing her husband's last living look at his wife.[19] Praising Leslie's gentleness and patience to Peggy Kirkaldy—it was the first time Rhys had communicated with her friend since their falling-out in 1941—Rhys allowed her misery to show in a sudden outburst of candour: "Oh Peggy I'd give all my idiotic life for an hour to say good-bye to him."[20] Years later, however, Rhys would use "The Joey Bag-stock Smile" to portray Leslie, not as Dickens's slyly lecherous Major Bagstock in *Dombey & Son*, but as Mr. Carker, the novel's pallid-faced and perpetually smiling villain. The sense of a meditated payback is strong; the reason for Rhys's grudge towards a man who had devoted himself unstintingly to the service of his wife and her fiction remains a mystery.

THE DEVON DOCTOR shared the dark suspicions of Leslie's daughter. He may have insisted upon a post-mortem only because Rhys freely admitted to having tried to ease Leslie's pain with her own prescription pills, but he had also heard gossip from the couple who lived in a neigh-bouring cottage. They stated that a quarrel had taken place on the first evening of the Tilden Smiths' arrival; the noise had been loud enough to penetrate their own closed doors and thick stone walls. More tell-ing, and in Rhys's favour, is the fact that these same loquacious neigh-bours took Rhys in for the first night after Leslie's death and—at her request—contacted Leslie's devoted sister, Muriel, and Edward, Rhys's eldest brother. The fact that they did so without hesitation hardly sug-gests that the couple saw their unhappy guest as a murderess.

Evidently, Rhys knew where her long-absent brother now lived; was Edward's presence in Devon the reason that the Tilden Smiths had elected to take a holiday on nearby Dartmoor? Desperate for money, it's entirely possible that Leslie and Rhys had hoped to obtain a loan; childless, retired from his career as an army medical officer and com-fortably established in the family home of his well-off wife, Gertrude, at Budleigh Salterton, Rhys's eldest brother might command resources upon which less well-heeled relatives could conceivably draw. (Rhys's

younger sister had made a similarly late and far more prosperous marriage during the war, but by 1945, Rhys was conscious that Brenda's
goodwill was no longer to be relied upon for further handouts.)

Colonel Edward Rees Williams was a man with a strong sense of
duty. It was he who paid the outstanding month's rent on the Dartmoor cottage, arranged for Leslie's cremation, escorted Rhys to the
ceremony and then drove her back to Knottsfield, Gertrude's house in
Budleigh Salterton.

Interviewing various members of the Rhys family in the 1980s,
Carole Angier was offered a lurid account of Rhys's short, unhappy
stay at the home of a stiffly respectable sister-in-law determined, however reluctantly, to behave well in difficult circumstances. Leslie's son,
Anthony, had visited Knottsfield for just long enough to note that his
(almost unknown) stepmother was lolling in bed, while Colonel Rees
Williams meekly gathered up her dirty laundry for the wash. Rhys
herself was desperate not to be sent away: "I've a *horror* of London,"
she wailed to Peggy Kirkaldy. "I will go to pieces there." Another family connection told Angier that—rather than leave—Rhys had actually
used the bedsheets to fasten herself to the bed. Edward lost his temper;
Rhys produced one of her terrifying screaming fits; the police were
called in.[21] True? The details are eerily close to Laura's wild behaviour
in the story "I Spy a Stranger," when her cousin's officious husband
tries to bundle her out of the house. Rhys was never afraid to draw
upon shaming episodes in her life if she saw a chance to make them
serve her art.

Undoubtedly, Rhys's sudden widowhood presented her family with a
problem. Leslie's will bestowed nothing but debts; Rhys had no money
of her own. Usefully, Edward Rees Williams persuaded his sister Brenda's rich and fair-minded husband, Robert Powell, to contribute to a
small weekly allowance for his sister, while Muriel Tilden Smith volunteered to cover the rent on Steele's Road for a few more months. Given
the difficult circumstances—a coldly furious wife (Gertrude Rees Williams apparently refused ever again to have Rhys in her home), and the
harsh austerity of postwar Britain—the long-suffering Edward must

have felt that he had done his best by an errant sibling whom he had not set eyes on for forty years. And so he had: in later years, Jean Rhys would always praise her brother for his kindness.

———————

EDWARD HAD NO knowledge as yet of his sister's remarkable capacity for survival. Paying a short courtesy visit to an unknown mother-in-law during the summer of 1946 (Maryvonne had remained in the Netherlands), Job Moerman was intrigued to be greeted at the door of 3 Steele's Road by a short, lively and sturdily built man. He said that he was helping Mrs. Tilden Smith to smarten up the flat. Rhys introduced this cheerful individual to Job as her late husband's cousin and executor. His name was Max Hamer.

13

Beckenham Blues (1946–50)

"If the law says you're dangerous, you're dangerous. If the law
says you're mad, you're mad. Then God help me."

—Jean Rhys, Orange Exercise Book, *c*.1950[1]

FEW COUSINS CAN have had less in common than Leslie Tilden
Smith and Max Hamer. Leslie was bookish and—except when he
got drunk and quarrelled with his wife—quiet; Max was outspoken,
exuberant and—when he first met the widowed Rhys—unashamedly
indifferent to culture. A good raconteur in possession of a pack of
yarns, he regaled Rhys with comic stories about the early years he had
spent at sea before his embarkation (following a decade of unemploy-
ment) on a less adventurous career as a trainee solicitor. It was probably
Max's employers who had encouraged a somewhat imprudent man in
his mid-fifties, equipped with a wife and young daughter, to invest in
property. And so, at some point between 1930 and 1938, Max Hamer
took out a mortgage in order to purchase a three-storey gabled Victorian house in the new south London borough of Beckenham, formerly
a village in Kent. Plans to move there were forestalled by war: Beckenham lay on "Doodlebug Alley," a firm favourite with the Luftwaffe.

Like Leslie, Max had signed up once again, despite his mature
years, to do his bit against Hitler. (Max was eight years older than
Rhys, although he may never have known it.) In 1945, the sixty-three-
year-old Lieutenant Commander Hamer's impressive title concealed a

Rhys's third husband,
Max Hamer (pronounced
"Hay-mer"), was a cousin
of Leslie Tilden Smith, a
roguish charmer who made
Rhys laugh. *(McFarlin)*

humdrum job supervising the issue of barrage balloons and kites from
HMS *Aeolus*, a warehouse staidly anchored behind the high street of
Tring, in Hertfordshire.

The attraction of Max as a potential husband—he was not forgiven
by his wife of over thirty years for starting divorce proceedings shortly
after he met Rhys—was considerable. Dapper, funny and well spoken,
he was a far more sexual man than Leslie. On a more practical level, he
owned a house; Rhys, when her sister-in-law ceased to pay the rent at
Steele's Road, was going to be without a home. But what a shy, intro-
verted woman, one who was prone to despair and self-doubt, valued
above all in Max Hamer was his unquenchable cheeriness. He made
her happy.

Max's optimistic temperament meant a lot to Rhys in 1946, the year
in which she turned fifty-six. The end of war had ushered in a period
of continued rationing and relentless hardship for most of the British population, half a million of whom lost their uninsured homes to
bombing raids. Rhys's own spirits were not lifted by the difficult task
of revising her wartime stories, among the darkest that she would ever
write. Pushing herself even harder, she was determined to create a fic-

tional record of the mysterious portents that had preceded Leslie's sudden death.

Writing "The Sound of the River" so soon after the loss of her husband brought Rhys close to a complete breakdown: she told Peggy Kirkaldy that she couldn't even bear to listen to certain music or to read her favourite French poets. She believed this story to be among her best work. She showed her faith by insisting that "The Sound of the River" should provide the title for the short and stark collection that she proudly submitted in March 1946 to Michael Sadleir of Constable. "It's been the hardest thing I've ever done in my life," Rhys had admitted to Peggy in February. By July, the publisher had turned it down, and hope had fled. "No one does believe in me," she sadly wrote.[2]

Sadleir's response was dismaying, but understandable. Having already been burned by the poor reception and negligible sales for *Good Morning, Midnight*, he shunned the patent risk of publishing an even more disquieting production, and in bleaker times. In 1946, English book-buyers wanted entertainment, not anguish. Crime fiction sold well (Sadleir's own historical thriller, *Fanny by Gaslight*, had recently been filmed); war-weary readers lapped up the romantic novels being written by Georgette Heyer and Daphne du Maurier. How could Jean Rhys's savage vision of a country at war, observed by her group of vociferously unpatriotic outsiders, hope to match the sales of Elizabeth Goodge's sweetly fantastic *The Little White Horse*, or even Nancy Mitford's acidly funny portrait of the declining ruling class at play, *The Pursuit of Love*?

Widowhood; lack of money; rejection; the encroaching spectre of old age: for all these reasons, an always reckless woman embraced the comforting attentions of a sensual, entertaining and delightfully hopeful man. Job Moerman, preoccupied by his postwar work with British intelligence—he would spend the following year back in the Netherlands, teaching the art of information-gathering to army officers stationed at Breda—didn't have time to fret over why a singularly well-read novelist was living with a man who shared none of her intellectual curiosity.[3] (Rhys had begun the year by lending Peggy a smuggled copy

of *Tropic of Cancer*, while begging for its return.) Reporting back to a
relieved Maryvonne, Job merely said that Rhys—still always referred
to as Ella by her family—seemed in good heart.

Max asked Jean to marry him even before he became free; Rhys
bridged an awkward hiatus by changing her legal name to Hamer by
deed poll. By the time her third marriage took place on 2 October
1947 (two years to the day after Leslie's death, and just two weeks after
Max obtained a divorce involving substantial alimony payments), Rhys
had already exchanged her flat on Steele's Road for life on the breezier
heights of Beckenham.

———————

BACK IN THE 1940s, the proud new borough of Beckenham was an
exceptionally decorous suburb. Civic parades were opened by sensibly
shod ladies with large hats and double-barrelled names; the local tennis
club and sports grounds, sponsored by Beckenham's sturdy new row of
provincial banks, were well attended. So was the old grey church of St.
George's, which stood guard high above Beckenham's winding hillside
high street. No church-goer herself, Mrs. Hamer's preferred weekly
appointment was with the local hairdresser to whom she repaired for a
shampoo and set whenever a disquietingly flirtatious husband seemed
about to stray.

The trouble with Max, as Jean later explained to Peggy Kirkaldy,
was that while she herself might often "look potty, he *is* potty."[4] Evidence of her partner's unreliability became apparent as soon as they
moved into 35 Southend Road. The house itself was large but damp;
a rickety iron balcony overlooked the fruit trees and brambles in a
small, neglected garden at the back. A cavernous cellar had become
a wartime home to an army of rats, while the cast-iron water pipes
were rusted beyond use. A builder selected by Max for his friendly
manner requested a down-payment of £400 in cash (£15,000 today)
and promptly disappeared. Max's postwar return to work as a solicitor
had been short-lived. Newly unemployed, he decided to raise money
by joining forces with a well-spoken former jailbird who urged Max

to take a punt on nightclubs. Such a speculative investment naturally required many evenings of careful research; Rhys was left at home, alone. "Clinging vines aren't in it," she later sighed to Peggy when reviewing her passive acceptance of her fate.[5]

Rhys wasn't drinking much during her first months at Beckenham. The chief consolations of an often solitary life were her cherished collection of English, French and Russian books, her writing (however unpublishable) and the company of her three cats. Black-coated Mr. Wu was a sleek and fiercely handsome fellow, closely followed in his mistress's affections by pretty Gaby and, lastly, Mi-Kat, a keen mouser who kept the cellar rats at bay. When the next-door couple's guard dog killed both Mr. Wu and Gaby, Jean reacted with predictable fury. Summoned to Bromley magistrates' court in April 1948, she was charged with throwing a brick through her neighbours' window and threatening to do so again.[6] Found guilty of having wantonly destroyed an apparently historic piece of stained window-glass, Rhys was ordered to pay £5 (£175 today) compensation to Mrs. Hardiman, proud wife of a respected shoemaker and a figure of conscious importance in Beckenham society.

Characteristically, Jean Rhys would soon put her legal defeat to good use: Selina Davis, a free-spirited mixed-race woman living in Notting Hill, is found guilty of precisely the same crime in one of Rhys's best-known postwar stories, "Let Them Call It Jazz." At the time, however, Jean simply retreated behind a set of newly ordered Venetian blinds, which she kept pulled down all day. Screened windows only provoked further suspicion; from April, until the day of her ultimate departure from Southend Road, Mrs. Hamer was kept under close scrutiny by the local residents.

Larger worries than dead cats or hostile neighbours were preying upon Jean's mind in the summer of 1948. Maryvonne, bringing along her baby girl for a first visit to Southend Road, broke to her dismayed mother the news that the two of them, accompanied by Hock, their pet chow, were about to follow Job out to Java. Born in Indonesia, Job Moerman had gained a position as clerk to the largest Dutch shipping line in the East Indies. The post was a risky one since it was offered at a time when Indonesia was seeking to assert independence from the Dutch empire, and when armed combat was threatened. Maryvonne did her best to make light of the potential danger. Nevertheless, having so recently become accustomed to the fact that her daughter was still alive and well, Jean grew anxious. Six months later, while making light of friction with her Beckenham neighbours (the court case went unmentioned), she apologised to Maryvonne for having been so poor a mother, one who had never "helped you enough or been the right sort of person for you."[7]

———————————

WRITING TO PEGGY KIRKALDY in 1950 about her unhappy life at Beckenham, Rhys explained that it was then, when she went "all of a doo-dah," that she had once again started to drink.[8]

One theory about Jean Rhys's hard-drinking habit holds that it was driven by her body's need for a sugar boost; Rhys's granddaughter, Dr. Ellen Moerman, points to the fact that her own mother, during her later life, was diagnosed with diabetes.[9] While it's true that Rhys favoured sugar-laden drinks and often drank sweet wine early in the day, an unidentified diabetic condition would have made it unlikely for her to go at times for several months without a drink, while betraying no signs of ill health or unusual lassitude. In calmer periods, Jean was often happy only to sip a glass or two of wine at supper and exhibited no ill effects; when anxious or unhappy, alcohol comforted Rhys and she drank fast, in order to get drunk. Despite the pride she always showed in having a strong head, it never took long.

By the end of her first year at Beckenham, Rhys needed the comfort of drink to blot out her worry about Maryvonne, out in the East Indies, and to deal with the grim realisation that her hopeful, gullible Max was an easy target for any silver-tongued crook whom he happened to meet. By the autumn of 1948, she was threatening to leave him; instead, Max made a surprisingly practical suggestion. The house on Southend Road was built for family use; why not raise revenue without risk by renting out the underused upper floors? Two couples, the Bezants and the Daniells, moved in during November. Recent Jewish emigrants, the new tenants may already have been friends when they arrived at Southend Road; if not, they certainly became so during their stay. An in-house alliance of refugees from Germany boded less than well for a temperamental landlady who had already been cautioned in Norfolk for saluting Hitler.

The comforting prospect of a steady rental income was offset for Rhys by the news that her enterprising husband had discovered a new route to prosperity. The source was to be a certain Mr. Roberts, an inventor whose plans required investment in the form of substantial loans from his new partner. More reassuringly, Max found himself a day job in March 1949, working as managing clerk for a family firm of solicitors. Cohen & Cohen were an unusual outfit (the father lived at a hotel on Park Lane, while his playboy son preferred chasing women to pursuing legal cases) and Max's work proved undemanding. Unfortunately, his new annual salary of £400 attracted the keen interest of Mr. Roberts, a man who, like Max's previous business partner, preferred to do business after hours. Left alone all day and for a great many evenings, Rhys continued with her project for a prequel to *Jane Eyre*, with Bertha Mason as the central character. In the spring of 1949, she planned to locate "The First Mrs Rochester" (as Rhys now named the reworked "Revenant") at the ultra-English naval port that she had already used for a discarded historical screenplay set on Antigua and titled "English Harbour." The period in which to set her "West Indian" story remained unsettled; in October 1949, Rhys told Peggy Kirkaldy that she was considering placing "a novel half done" in the 1780s. The rest, she believed, was "safely in my head."[10]

Work never calmed Rhys; in the spring of 1949, she was still worried about Mr. Roberts' money-making schemes and terrified by the dangers to which Maryvonne, and her year-old granddaughter, might be exposed in politically turbulent postwar Java. She was already drinking heavily when her first serious confrontation took place with the upstairs tenants. The fault was largely Jean's own: writing a long confessional letter to Peggy Kirkaldy, she later admitted "I couldn't have behaved worse or with less tact."[11]

The trigger seems to have been an evening party held in the Bezants' flat on 11 April, in rooms just above where Rhys was trying to write, despite a racket which distracted, irritated and finally maddened her. The guests left an hour before midnight. A few minutes later, Rhys stormed up the stairs, shouted at Mrs. Bezant and then slapped—or perhaps punched—her husband. When the angry couple called in the police, as the tenants were always quick to do when she flared up, Rhys rashly called the constable "a dirty Jew." After hitting and even biting him, she accused the bewildered officer of belonging to the Gestapo.[*]

Max, a former solicitor, represented his wife at her second appearance in Bromley magistrates' court on 25 April. (Rhys had been bailed after pleading not guilty at the first.) A fair-minded magistrate awarded £3 to the injured policeman and a pound to Mr. Bezant. Mrs. Hamer was put on warning to keep the peace for a year.

Peace lasted less than a day. Back at Southend Road after her trial (Max had gone straight from the courtroom to the Cohens' city office), Jean found that she had locked herself out of the house. A helpful policeman fetched her a plank of wood, via which she managed to clamber in through an open window, but not before taking a tumble. Humiliated, bruised and distressed by her morning at court, Rhys found herself confronted by all four of her tenants. A golden opportunity to point out that Mrs. Hamer's saviour had been a member of the very constabulary she had recently abused was doubtless seized. The result was that Jean flew at Mr. Bezant.

Back in court on 6 May 1949, Rhys again pleaded not guilty. A claim that she had attacked Mrs. Bezant and Mrs. Daniell was briskly dis-

---

[*] Jean Rhys's insults were frequently anti-Semitic but almost always inconsistent and contradictory. Six months after her row with the Bezants in April 1949, she described her Jewish tenants to Maryvonne as "a little nest of Nazis" (Rhys to Maryvonne, 24 October 1949, in Francis Wyndham and Diana Melly (eds.), *Jean Rhys Letters*, André Deutsch, 1984, p. 265).

missed; the charge of an assault on Mr. Bezant was allowed to stand. As with the magistrate on the occasion of her wartime summons in Norfolk, the prosecuting council sympathised with the gentle, well-spoken lady in the dock. Agreement was swiftly reached that a token fine would be paid and that a psychiatrist would provide, at the end of three weeks, his assessment of the defendant.

On 27 May, Mr. Bezant appeared in court to declare that he had heard "nothing but screaming, shouting and abuse four times a week from this woman."[12] A warrant was served in her absence for Mrs. Hamer's arrest. On 24 June, Max informed the court that his wife was not well enough to undertake the ten-minute bus journey to Bromley. Three days later, having finally complied with the psychiatrist after over a month's delay, Mrs. Hamer showed up at the gloomy red-brick court building in person. It sounds as though Rhys had primed herself for the ordeal with a drink. "He [the magistrate] asked me if I had anything to say," Jean later told Peggy Kirkaldy. "So I said it." Having begun by objecting to being called hysterical by the psychiatrist, she found herself unable to stop. ("I hear myself talking loud and I see my hands wave in the air," Selina says in "Let Them Call It Jazz.")[13] Rhys was finally silenced by the magistrate who abruptly sentenced her to five days in Holloway prison's hospital wing, pending two years on probation and a further medical report. It's unclear whether Max was present to see his sobbing wife led out of court and taken away in a black police wagon.

———————

RHYS ENTERED HOLLOWAY through what appeared to be the gate-house of a fortified castle; above the smoke-blackened archway, an inscribed motto prayed to God that *this place be a terror to evil doers.* Her experiences as a prisoner provided first-hand material for "Black Castle" (later retitled "Let Them Call It Jazz"), the story which Rhys began to write soon after her release. Her talismanic cosmetics and jewellery were removed; her clothes and shoes were replaced by flat brogues and a loose black tunic that distinguished the prisoners from the trimly pinafored female guards.

Being sent to prison was a terrible humiliation, but Rhys was not cruelly treated and the wing reserved for mentally and physically sick inmates was situated far away from Holloway's "lifers"—although not far enough to block out the sobs and shrieks that haunted a newcomer's nights. The dreariness of a postwar prison diet was compensated for by the opportunity to read—Rhys had learned the value of prison libraries from Lenglet—and, curiously, to rest.

Rhys got on well with the prisoners whom she met in Holloway. A cheerful old lag introduced her to the art of collecting "doggins" (the "dog-ends" or stubs of discarded cigarettes) and reminisced about her former life outside in "the Smoke." A seasoned younger inmate advised Rhys to say as little as possible about herself to the woman doctor in charge of her case. Like Selina in her short story, Jean seems to have heeded a prudent warning.

It was the misery that got under Rhys's skin during her stay at Holloway. "But oh Lord why wasn't the place bombed?" she wrote that autumn to Peggy Kirkaldy: "If you could see the unfortunate prisoners crawling about like half-dead flies you'd understand how I feel. I did think about the Suffragettes. Result of all their sacrifices? The woman doctor!!! Really human effort is futile."[14]

Selina contemplates killing herself by jumping off a high wall into the prison's drill ground. If Rhys had similar thoughts, she suppressed them. Writing to Maryvonne on 10 July, during the week that she was pronounced sane and fit for release (although in prescribed need, for two years, of psychiatric observation), Jean mentioned only that she had been briefly in hospital. Brightly, she wrote of sitting out with Max on their little iron balcony and of picking fruit and berries in the neglected back garden. If Maryvonne was puzzled by her mother's insistent tone when Rhys wrote on 16 August 1949 that "*I am all right dear*," heavily underlining her words of reassurance, there was nothing that a faraway daughter could do.

The shock and disgrace of imprisonment had been too great for a brief summer jaunt out of town to raise Rhys's spirits. Writing to Peggy on 4 October, Rhys confessed that she had temporarily lost the will to write. To Maryvonne, she had already confided her fears about Max's most recent friend, a man who was promising him "heaven and earth."[15] Max, unknowingly, had met his nemesis.

WHAT MICHAEL DONN lacked in integrity—and it would seem that he had none—was masked by an abundance of charm. Young, charismatic and unscrupulous, he had no difficulty in persuading the gullible Max Hamer to find him a job with Cohen & Cohen. Convinced by his personable manner, the family lawyers took him on. Rhys, to her credit, was never deluded for a second about Michael Donn's criminal streak, but Max started to behave with increasing recklessness, disappearing to Paris with Donn for five days before returning home via Jean's bedroom window, late at night. Maryvonne heard that Max was "very optimistic"; sometimes, longing for a happy outcome, Rhys allowed herself to share her husband's fantasies about finding a crock of gold which could be used to help poor, faraway Maryvonne and her baby daughter. Writing again provided a more reliable source of comfort; on 24 October, Jean urged her daughter to keep a diary or a notebook, adding that "writing can be (among other things) a safety valve."[16]

Rhys liked to claim that it was only left-wing Max who read their weekly copy of the *New Statesman*; (Hamer often teased his wife about her old-fashioned conservative views). If so, it may have been Max who, on 5 November 1949, found in the magazine's back pages a small announcement requesting "Jean Rhys" to contact a certain Dr. Hans Egli in Hampstead. Dr. Egli proved to be the London economics correspondent for the Swiss newspaper *Neue Zürcher Zeitung*; it was Hans's actress wife, Selma Vaz Dias, who had placed the advertisement and who instantly responded to Rhys's letter.

Jean must have felt dazed when she read in Selma Vaz Dias's bold hand that the actress had come across *Good Morning, Midnight* in Paris,

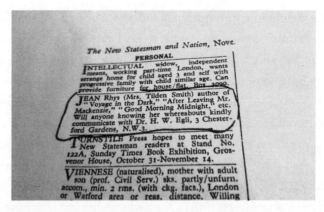

The *New Statesman* advertisement which changed the course of Rhys's life. *(McFarlin)*

read it and fallen instantly in love with the book. As a first step towards performing it on the BBC (Miss Vaz Dias enclosed her adaptation, written for a single narrating voice), she was giving a ticketed reading to a carefully selected audience on 10 November. An admired actress and gifted promoter of new European playwrights to English audiences, Selma did not need permission to give a reading. What she had sought to discover before approaching the BBC with her project was whether Jean Rhys was still alive.

We don't know whether it startled Rhys to learn that she was assumed to be dead. We do know that she liked the adaptation; the news that Selma also intended to talk about her earlier novels on the BBC reduced an emotional woman to tears. Writing back on 9 November, she told the gratified Vaz Dias that the actress had worked a miracle; such discerning enthusiasm had lifted "the numb hopeless feeling" that had paralysed her for so long. Now, filled with fresh hope, she could return to work.

Rhys blamed flu rather than nerves for her absence from the powerful reading that Selma gave to an appreciative audience—it included an admiring Max—at the Anglo-French Centre in St. John's Wood. She was not too ill to proclaim her triumph in disdainful Beckenham. Haughty Mrs. Hardiman, still nourishing a grudge against her brick-throwing neighbour, promptly spread the word that Ella Hamer, a common criminal, was pretending to be a famous writer. Doubtless, she shared the joke with Rhys's tenants; it's clear that they seized the chance to have some sport.

On 16 November, Mrs. Daniell, having barged her way into her landlady's bedroom at midday, offered her thoughts about the fact that the supposed great writer was still lolling in bed with a drink in her hand. Jean screamed at her. When Mrs. Daniell responded by tipping a rubbish bin—perhaps it was only a wastepaper basket—over Rhys's head, Jean lost any last shred of prudence. Still in her nightclothes and clutching Selma's letter as proof, she ran out into Southend Road, proclaiming her identity and shouting that her work was going to be performed on the radio.

Back at Bromley Magistrates' Court, on a charge of causing a public disturbance and holding up traffic on what was never a bustling thoroughfare, Jean was ably defended by Max. The case was dismissed. Rhys's tussles, however, were making excellent copy for the local press. "Mrs Hamer Agitated" ran the headline in bold black print which appeared on 24 November in the *Beckenham and Penge Advertiser*; as luck would have it, this was the very day on which Selma had arranged to visit her heroine in Beckenham.

Selma did not see the newspaper article, although she might have wondered why her distracted hostess poured out a cup of boiling water when her visitor had asked for coffee. Unconscious of the undertow of anxiety, Selma stayed on late into the evening, praising Rhys's work and promising her a golden future. Everything, in Selma's breezy view, was going to turn out splendidly. The Hamers, both of them, were enchanted by their new friend.

———————

WHO WAS SELMA? Why were the Hamers so enthralled? Tara Fraser remembers her grandmother well enough to conjure up Selma's throaty announcement to Rhys as she first sailed into view: "Darling, I want to be the first to tell you: your work is *glorious!*"[17]

Jean Rhys's biographers and editors have been harsh judges of Selma

Selma Vaz Dias, the charismatic woman who entered Rhys's life in 1949.
(*Used with permission of Tara Fraser*)

Vaz Dias. The time has come to redress that critical imbalance and to understand why Rhys was enduringly grateful and loyal to this extraordinary woman.

Born in Amsterdam in 1911 (Selma's old-fashioned Dutch was good enough for her to attempt to correspond with Maryvonne in Mrs. Moerman's first language), Selma Vaz Dias had suffered a tragic loss during the Second World War when her adored brother Sieg was executed for his courageous work with the Dutch resistance. Exotic, passionate and widely read, Selma had won her first major role—acting alongside John Gielgud in a Russian play, *Red Rust*—at the age of sixteen, straight out of RADA, where she had been awarded the prestigious annual Gold Medal. Married since 1936 to a respected journalist, a dapper president of the Foreign Press Association known for his vehemently anti-Nazi views, Selma's bright star was still in the ascendant when Rhys entered her orbit.

Today, it's difficult to appreciate that Selma, back in 1949, appeared a far more significant figure than Jean Rhys. Since the war, she had been working closely with the BBC on plays and short stories selected and often translated by Selma herself, while introducing English audiences to the work of Genet and Lorca through the readings in the original languages that she regularly gave at the prestigious Anglo-French Centre. Shortly after meeting Rhys, Selma would join forces with Peggy Ramsay (not yet the formidable theatrical agent she would become), in order to form the First Stage Society.

Like Rhys, Vaz Dias possessed a volatile personality. Her brother's death had triggered a breakdown, leading to electroshock treatment. On the day of her Beckenham visit, however, the actress was elated by the warm reception that had been given to her latest reading. Having described her triumph to Rhys, Selma expanded on her plans to perform *Good Morning, Midnight* in her own adaptation, on the Third Programme. BBC radio drama was still in its first decade and the idea of one woman occupying airtime for almost an hour was unthinkable. But Selma's faith in her project was absolute. The play would happen. She knew it.

And so, having painted her bright vision and filled Rhys with hope, Selma swept splendidly away into the night.

————————————

THE EXCITED EXPECTATIONS aroused by Selma's predictions were short-lived. On 14 January 1950, Max Hamer was charged with attempted fraud for abetting the stealing of seven cheques, to a value of £3,000 (£105,000 today), from the offices of Cohen & Cohen.

After months of worrying about the hold that Michael Donn appeared to have exerted over her naive husband, the awfulness of the reality caused Rhys's fragile control to snap. On the same night that Max was charged, she squabbled with the most belligerent of her tenants, Mr. Daniell; the following day, a furious Rhys was thrown out of Beckenham police station after referring to Daniell as "a dirty, stinking Jew."* Fined only £1 on this occasion, she was back at Bromley Court within days, following further allegations by her tenants of offensive behaviour.

On 30 March, Bromley Court decided to adopt the drastic course

* Mr. Daniell was still nursing a grudge against Rhys thirty years later, when he wrote to her editor, having read of Rhys's death, to inform Diana Athill of his former landlady's insulting behaviour.

of banishing a conspicuously absent Mrs. Hamer from living in Beckenham. The mortgage company had moved more swiftly. By the end
of March 1950, 35 Southend Road had been repossessed. All that was
left in the Hamers' former home, as the magistrates now learned, were
two Chinese vases, a divan bed and the quietly vindicated (or perhaps
noisily triumphant) tenants.

The owners themselves had disappeared.

14

The Lady Vanishes* (1950–56)

"Her life was tragic; her courage quite indomitable."

—Peggy Kirkaldy to Selma Vaz Dias, 4 May 1957

IN THE EARLY spring of 1950, the mortgage company's repossession of 35 Southend Road left Max and Rhys without a home. The couple had not been entirely friendless in Beckenham: the last to survive of Jean's cherished trio of cats was hastily bestowed upon a good-natured young neighbour, while another local resident provided temporary storage for her clothes and—crucially—shelf space for a few favourite books. Selling off the majority of her books in order to raise money was a far more painful process for Rhys than it had been to relinquish (for the same purpose) Leslie's library after his death. Later, she recalled having had to part with the bulk of her cherished French and Russian novels. They fetched almost nothing. Among the handful that she kept back—they included works by Sartre, Beckett, Bernanos, Colette and Céline—was *Esther Waters*. The calm and stalwart Esther was always Rhys's touchstone in trying times: in 1953, she would tell one friend that she had read Moore's novel sixty times.[1]

---

* Selma Vaz Dias had appeared in cameo as a train passenger in the film *The Lady Vanishes* in 1938, but Hitchcock's title also seems fitting for Jean Rhys's disappearance from public view after Max's trial.

From March 1950 until Max's trial at the Old Bailey in May, the Hamers rented a single room at a London boarding house in Stanhope Gardens, South Kensington. When Max was not being summoned to meetings by the ever-optimistic and persuasive Michael Donn, the couple wandered like strangers through the unfeeling and stony (as Rhys felt it to be) city. Forlorn and guilt-ridden, Max allowed himself to be dragged by his culture-hungry wife to a film-showing of Jean Cocteau's *Les Parents Terribles* and on tours of London's monuments. Visiting Westminster Cathedral, Rhys fantasised about seeking refuge in a kindly Catholic retreat. "I'm so tired," she sighed to a sympathetic Peggy Kirkaldy that March.[2] Drifting through the Victoria and Albert's echoing galleries, she drew comfort from the archaic smile of a wooden Madonna; it revived happy memories of the Richelots' charming home in Paris (usurped and looted, as a shocked Rhys would overhear by chance in a hairdresser's salon one day, during the Nazi occupation of her favourite city).

The Madonna's smile offered private solace to Rhys at a time when her cheerful husband was understandably edgy and bad-tempered. A domestic row at the National Portrait Gallery about the relative merits of Jacob Epstein (intriguingly singled out for praise by Max) and James Tissot's gentle paintings of Parisian scenes (admired by romantic Rhys) ended with Max flying into a rage about Winston Churchill: "so it all ended badly as usual," Jean confided in one of the long confessional letters within which, during this sojourn in a London limboland, she unburdened herself to Peggy.[3]

An unexpected source of relief during a miserable three months arrived in the form of a mysterious benefactor. A letter from a London firm of solicitors announced that a modest sum of money would be provided to Rhys for an undetermined period; while this form of charity was not entirely welcome to a woman who hated to feel indebted, the Hamers were undeniably short of ready cash. Max thought that the anonymous donor might be the altruistic Earl of Listowel, Secretary of State to the Colonies, with whom the Hamer family claimed some distant link. Lord Listowel was well known for his charitable deeds;

nobody else comes to mind unless kind-hearted Peggy Kirkaldy was trying to help without offending Rhys's prickly sense of pride.

On two points, Rhys did not waver. Maryvonne was not to be told the truth and Max was not to be abandoned: "I couldn't give Max away," Jean told Peggy, and again, in the same letter of 21 April: "I don't want to leave Max (Mrs Micawber)."[4] Rhys could—and did—often quarrel with Max, but her loyalty to him never faltered.

On 22 May 1950, following a public trial at the Old Bailey that lasted a fortnight, Max Hamer, aged sixty-eight, was found guilty: his two-year sentence was to be served at Maidstone Prison in Kent. Michael Donn, already in possession of a substantial criminal record, was given four years at a different jail. Despite all that she had suffered through Max's association with Donn, Rhys warmed to the young man's mother: "a very simple, kind soul [who] says this is killing her," she told Peggy, adding that Mrs. Donn, who spoke almost no English, looked very frail.[5]

Max, to his wife's astonishment, wanted her to share a home with Mrs. Donn; instead, Rhys went to ground for several months at an old-fashioned Welsh inn owned by Peggy Kirkaldy's bookish friend, Edith Colley. "He [Max] doesn't know how I like trees, shadows, a shaded light," she had lamented to Peggy during her pre-trial sojourn in west London.[6] Staying at the Half Moon Inn in Llanthony, Rhys enjoyed a tranquil view of the misleadingly named Black Mountains' leaf-green hillsides; perhaps they reminded her of Dominica.

Far from London and the shock of Max's harsh sentence, Rhys took stock of her situation. She stopped drinking. And, despite her keen and recent interest in the story of an heiress with a "defective mind" who is locked away by her husband to slowly starve to death (Jean had been reading Elizabeth Jenkins's fact-based gothic novel, *Harriet*), Rhys set aside her own plans for a book about the imprisoned first wife of Charlotte Brontë's Mr. Rochester.[*] Instead, haunted by the loss of her own pre-

---

[*] Jenkins's well-received novel was based upon an actual case, but her debt to Brontë's *Jane Eyre* is apparent. What clearly interested Rhys about a book she called "a horrible and sinister thing" was that—unlike Brontë's crude characterisation of Bertha

cious library, Rhys began work on the story of how two Roseau childhood friends, a girl and a boy, rescue just two books from suffering a similar fate. The boy's "coloured" mother sets about the destruction of the library acquired by her late husband, a condescending white man. The books that are saved are revealing. The boy, modelled upon a sickly, studious child whom Rhys had befriended during her own childhood in Roseau, rescues Kipling's *Kim*, a favourite with Jean's father. The girl snatches up *Fort comme la Mort*, the novel by Maupassant from which Rhys had taken the idea of an older lover's passion for a younger partner for an earlier story: "La Grosse Fifi." Maupassant ended his short novel with a letter-burning scene; perhaps it was that conflagration which suggested to Rhys her own eventual title for a story called "The Day They Burned the Books."

By March 1951, Rhys had moved from Wales to Maidstone, the county town of Kent, better known then for the nauseatingly sweet smell of its toffee factory than for the faux-medieval prison building within which Max started saving up his prisoner's rations to buy chocolates for the sweet-toothed and loyal wife he must have feared he had lost.[7] Rhys changed lodgings twice more before finally settling into rooms above a friendly Maidstone pub.

As at the Welsh inn, the fragile-looking Rhys was welcomed with genuine kindness. The family who owned the Ropemakers' Arms sometimes got on her nerves (Jean grumbled in her journal that the innkeeper's daughter-in-law always sang as she went about her household chores: "that dreadful sobbing break in the middle of the voice"), but the proprietor's wife was quick to realise that their softly spoken lady lodger was something out of the ordinary. On one occasion, returning from "my obligation walk," Rhys found that her sitting-room table had been spread with books evidently bought from a local stall; none was to her taste, but she appreciated a thoughtful gesture. (Rhys's private reading at the time included Sartre's witty plays and Koestler's *The Age of Longing*, a futuristic novel set in Paris). Guiltily, she with-

---

Mason—Jenkins represented the unfortunate Harriet as a sympathetic character, one with whom the reader could identify.

drew her grumbles about the singing daughter-in-law—"as a woman, she is much better than I am. That girl who yowls so horribly is neat, clean, hardworking . . . She runs lightly up and down the stairs without touching the bannister. Light of foot and heart is she!"[8]

That passage appears in a remarkable document that was eventually employed to bulk out Rhys's posthumously published memoir, *Smile Please*. Written in a small brown exercise book, "The Rope-Makers' Arms Diary"* opens with the enigmatic words: "Death before the Fact," remembered by Rhys from a favourite passage in Teresa of Ávila's *Meditations*. The diarist then instructs herself: no chance will be permitted to revise or to have second thoughts. "Down it shall go. Already I am terrified."[9] What follows takes the form of a day in court, with Rhys challenging herself as she stands in the dock.

Trials and confinements had, over the past few years, played an increasingly significant role in Rhys's life; here, however, she took control of her fate. At first, the questions are put by an anonymous interrogator; later, a knowing prosecutor (*"There you are! Didn't take long, did it?"*) is replaced by a more understanding counsel for the defence (*"Did you in your youth have a great love and pity for others?"* Yes, I think so. *"Especially for the poor and the unfortunate?"* Yes.) These external voices are replaced by that of the author as she searches for a reason to go on living—and finds it in her writings.

Phrases in what was evidently always meant to be a private piece of work ("Oh the relief of words," and "How clumsily I'm writing. Start again") suggest that this extraordinary confessional marked Rhys's first nervous step towards resuming literary work since her arrival in Maidstone. Writing, she told herself in the journal, was what she must do in order to justify her existence. "If I stop writing my life will have been an abject failure," she wrote. "I will not have earned death."[10]

---

* "Diary" is an inexact description. Rhys interspersed the fictional trial of herself with personal responses to her life in Maidstone (the audience at a cinema matinee; the owners of the pub; her rooms) and sudden time shifts into reminiscences of Dominica and her first years in England.

Much emerges from this intimate, heroically honest document. It's clear that Rhys had not lost her sardonic sense of humour ("O.K. O.K. That brings me to my bedroom in waltz time") or her courage, presented in the half-remembered words of her beloved Saint Teresa: "At the cost of a long death before the fact, I shall conquer this world that is ever new, ever young. Dare to follow me and you will see." She isn't afraid here to convict herself of all the mortal sins—drunkenness is included—except for one that she adds only to clear herself of the charge: coolness of heart. Neither will Rhys permit the probing voice in her head to convict her of committing what she terms, in the Catholic fashion learned at her convent school, "the venial sins." After identifying these lesser, forgivable sins as spite, malice, gluttony, envy, avarice, stupidity, caution and cruelty, the diary-keeper sweeps her self-made list of minor crimes away, more grandly than any judge: "I cannot any longer accept all this. *Do you mean that you are guiltless of the venial sins?* Well. Guiltless!"

The evidence that Rhys never intended to publish such a private record is clear: she used that same small exercise book to draft—and then tear out—the letters that accused her sister of trying to lock her away in an asylum. But Diana Athill was right to add "The Ropemakers' Arms Diary" to her author's posthumously published memoir; nothing Rhys ever wrote was more bravely revealing.

DISGRACED AND PERMANENTLY disbarred from his profession, Max Hamer was an unemployable man of seventy when he walked out of Maidstone prison in May 1952. His wife, aged almost sixty-two, had not published a word for thirteen years. Their mysterious benefactor's assistance had ceased. Rhys was living on the modest allowance provided by her surviving siblings,* to which members of the Hamer fam-

---

* Edward Rees Williams had prudently invested a small sum in government gilts in order to provide his sister with a reliable source of income; Robert Powell (married to Rhys's younger sister) was also continuing to make regular contributions.

ily added a small annual payment in compensation for the modest naval allowance that was cancelled when Max was convicted. (Typically, for an always improvident man, Max Hamer had no pension.)

Life in the centre of London was beyond the Hamers' economic reach; instead, they squeezed themselves into a couple of small rooms in a shared house on Milestone Road in Upper Norwood, just north of the enormous, landscaped park that surrounded the burned-out remains of Joseph Paxton's Crystal Palace.* Writing to Maryvonne in June, and again in August, Jean was valiantly cheerful. A Polish co-tenant was doing a splendid job on the minute garden. The pond was filled with goldfish and the roses were glorious. Just one heartfelt statement offered a glimpse of what Rhys had endured during her husband's prison sentence: "I like so much not being alone."[11]

Rhys's response to a change of home was always the same. Beginning in euphoria, she rapidly plunged into gloom. Six months after their move to Norwood, Max—he was almost certainly prompted by Jean—sought advice from the former husband of Norah Hoult, one of his wife's earliest literary admirers. Oliver Stonor had remarried and moved to Devon, where the cost of living was low when compared to London. Did "Mr Bishop" (Stonor's literary pseudonym) remember having praised Miss Rhys's work? Max wondered. Now, his wife had a new novel "all planned out" and needed only a quiet country home in which to write. Might Mr. Stonor know of such a place in Devon?[12]

Sadly, Oliver Stonor was unable to help, and Jean's prudent older brother ruled out hare-brained plans for the couple to live in a caravan. Nevertheless, Rhys struck up a literary correspondence with Stonor who, as she was quick to appreciate, was an unusually well-read man. (He had recently published a short and erudite study of William Blake.) Max was not greatly interested in books; Rhys's letters to Stonor glow with all her old passion for the one world—other than her Dominican girlhood—in which she could always take refuge. Here was a man who

---

* Space restrictions at Milestone Road are apparent from Rhys's doleful references to "The Iron Maiden," a fold-up bed which frequently threatened to trap her fingers.

shared her admiration for the technique of Maupassant's short stories and understood why, in January 1953, she rated Hemingway's 1927 short story "Hills Like White Elephants" above his highly praised and recently published novella, *The Old Man and the Sea*.[13]

Hemingway had become one of the world's best-known writers. Rhys's novels were known only to a discerning few. On 5 March 1953, while confined to her bed by flu, she comforted a despairing Stonor about the future of his own work: "You have fifteen long years probably to be still at your best," she reassured him. "As a writer longer." All that really matters, as she was well positioned to advise her friend, is to endure: "I don't believe in the individual Writer so much as in Writing. It uses you and throws you away when you are not useful any longer. But it does not do this until you are useless and quite useless too. Meanwhile there is nothing to do but plod along line upon line."[14]

Apologising for her earnestness ("Max says I alarm people because I am so serious"), Rhys turned down Stonor's suggestion that the two of them should meet. "I'm a bit afraid of people now," Jean confessed, before slipping away into chatter about her cousin Lily, now living in London and composing Creole calypsos and songs "better than anyone . . . a natural born money maker 1953—I feel it in my bones."[15]

THE ABSENCE OF an obvious market may have contributed to Rhys's decision to drop work on a Caribbean prequel to *Jane Eyre* (the novel which Max had confidently described to Stonor as "all planned out"). Instead, she turned her thoughts to radio plays.

Back in the early 1950s, growing rivalry with television was making BBC radio hungry for innovative new work. The pay was generous and a successful drama was usually granted a paid repeat. Rhys herself had no connection with the BBC, but she knew someone who did. Selma Vaz Dias's career had been prospering since her well-remembered visit to Beckenham. She had played a leading role in the London-based French production of Jean Genet's *The Maids* in 1952; in 1953, Selma was booked to appear both on stage at the Embassy Theatre, and on the radio as Lady Macbeth. Her influence within the BBC at that time was considerable.

From January 1953, Jean Rhys spent six months pursuing Selma with an urgency that betrays how badly she needed to earn some money. A promised dramatisation of *Quartet*, with a role for Selma herself, was followed by a flood of poems and stories, including some very early work ("Houdia" and "Susan and Suzanne" both pre-dated *Quartet*) and the more recently completed "The Day They Burned the Books" (for which a nervous Rhys expressed little hope since "most people find it dull."*)[16] All came to nothing; by June—having also failed to interest the BBC in Lily Lockhart's calypsos—Selma was forced to discourage her. Rhys struggled to sound insouciant: "Really I am not worried about the BBC. It would have been a miracle if they approved of anything I write or wrote and I do think you were a heroine to try. Thank you." Rhys's appeal for communication ("Ring me up if ever you feel like it") seems not to have evoked a response.[17]

Consolation arrived in September in the form of a long-promised visit from Maryvonne and Job Moerman with their five-year-old child. The Moermans were briefly back from Jakarta and spending time in Holland with a fragile Jean Lenglet, to whom a concerned Rhys sent her "best love," and his equally frail Polish wife, Elizabeth Kassakowska.[18] Rhys plotted out their route for a quick late-summer tour of England, ensuring that her little family saw Cambridge and Ely cathedral as well as Savernake Forest and the pretty village of Burford, wistfully remembered by Jean for its exceptional tranquillity. The Moermans also made time for two expeditions to Milestone Road. "I was bursting with pleasure, my darling," Rhys wrote after their first visit and, following their second: "I send hugs and kisses as many as you want, and my best and deepest love."[19] However poor a mother Rhys judged herself to have been, she never lacked affec-

---

* Rhys's reference to the number of people to whom she has been showing her work reminds us that she was never so entirely out of touch with the literary world as her myth suggests.

tion for a daughter to whom she regularly wrote two or three letters a week.

In October, the Hamers undertook a disastrous experiment. Yacht *Atlast*—permanently moored at Haverfordwest in a remote and very English corner of south Wales—took their fancy because of the Welsh location and because the rent was low. The reason swiftly became apparent; the boat's only habitable cabins were buried in a dark hold at the foot of a rope ladder, within a space dimly lit by a series of unworkable gadgets. The washbasin taps didn't function; for company, the unhappy tenants had a frisky troop of mice. Rhys, clambering down the swaying ladder one night, missed a rung and fell. By January 1954, the couple were back in central London; by April, Rhys was airily joking to her daughter that she looked (in the opinion of one candid doctor) as though a horse had stamped on her face. Her fall had been serious; back problems would plague Rhys for many years to come.[20]

While the Moermans returned to the East Indies and to an even more dangerous posting—Makassar, capital of the island of Celebes, was notorious for its violence—the Hamers themselves settled in the spring of 1954 at a shabby, half-empty London hotel on Lancaster Terrace, close to Hyde Park. Charges were modest in an area that had been badly damaged by wartime bombing. Rhys blocked out a view of blitzed house fronts with bright yellow window curtains; two cherished blue-glass fish were placed where they could best catch the light. The Hamers remained at the Elizabeth Hotel for a year and a half; the need to live even more economically took them next down to Cornwall, where they settled close to Bude, near the Devon border, in the autumn of 1955.

The move to Cornwall's rugged north coast was not an immediate success. After six chilly months in an isolated clifftop bungalow intended for summer lets (the sea view across the aptly named Widemouth Bay was spectacular), "Bellair" was hopefully exchanged by the Hamers for "Garden Bungalow" at the nearby hamlet of Upton. Here, gardenless, and under constant patrol from a vigilant landlord, the carless couple still had to take a mile-long windswept walk along the cliffs in order to shop at Bude. By July, Rhys and Max had moved again. Their new home consisted of two rented rooms and a kitchen at 4 Cartaret Street—a small and featureless hilltop road close to the post office, Somerleaze Downs and Bude's most recently added attraction, a vast concrete "seapool" for outdoor swimming. Perhaps Jean sauntered down from Cartaret Street to bathe there (Rhys always firmly distinguished "bathing," which she loved, from swimming, which she disliked) while listening to the mighty roar of Atlantic breakers, out beyond Bude's expansive tidal beach. The sound brought back memories of when she first heard that same majestic Atlantic roar competing against the soft sigh of the Caribbean, on either side of a narrow isthmus jutting out from the south-west coast of Dominica at Scott's Head.

Rhys had learned that her daughter was ill, but not that she had been taken into hospital while out in the East Indies. (Tuberculosis was diagnosed later, following the Moermans' return to Holland.) Not worrying Maryvonne was, nevertheless, an evident objective of the long, chatty letters that Jean regularly despatched from Bude to distant Makassar. Nothing too negative was mentioned; instead, Rhys joked about their Cartaret Street landlady's persistent attempts to sell her untreasured knick-knacks to a reluctant tenant. Painting in words a comic picture of her own ageing self as she scuttled along a cliff path in a high wind, "chasing my poor old hat, swearing all the time," Jean went out of her way to praise Max for his irrepressible kindness and good cheer.[21] Sometimes, between grumbles about the dismal supply of books available at Bude's railway bookstore—there was no other—she mentioned what she was reading. In 1955, she had taken the trouble to post Maryvonne one of her own firm favourites, Stevie Smith's *Novel on Yellow Paper*. Published in 1936, Smith's first novel shared Rhys's unusual combination of a poet's ear with a bleakly sardonic perception of the difficulty for an outspoken, strong-willed woman to inhabit a world of conventional views. "We carry our own wilderness within us," Smith remarked in her second novel, *Over the Frontier* (1938). Rhys would have agreed.

And, at last, in the autumn of 1956, there was good news to report.

The BBC had succeeded in making contact with Rhys about the long-deferred adaptation of her novel; Sasha Moorsom, a talented young poet and producer, and an ardent fan of Rhys's work, was eager to bring her finest novel to a wider audience.

"I feel sure that I have to thank you," an excited Rhys wrote to Selma Vaz Dias on 16 October; six days later, she reported the change in her fortunes to Maryvonne, by then living in Surabaya. "It *has* come off! The BBC are going to do *Good Morning [Midnight]*. Just in time! I was nearly done."[22]

Rhys's gratitude to Vaz Dias was not misplaced. In the autumn of 1956, nobody at the BBC seems to have known whether Jean Rhys was still alive or—if this were the case—where to find her. Neither, when Moorsom contacted the actress, who was then appearing in the first English production of Jean Genet's *The Maids*, did Selma.* On 19 October, Vaz Dias revealed to Rhys the various routes by which she herself had fruitlessly tried to track down her elusive friend for Miss Moorsom. A letter to Lily Lockhart was returned unopened from an out-of-date address; Rhys's most recent publisher, Constable, thought she was dead; Peggy Kirkaldy hadn't heard a word from Rhys for four years, after refusing her request for a loan. Finally, Selma had suggested that Miss Moorsom might place an advertisement in the *New Statesman*, just as she herself had done seven years earlier. An unnamed friend of Rhys's had noticed the ad and had passed along the news to Bude.[23]

Selma's generous warmth—and the knowledge that she had not, after all, been quite forgotten—filled Jean with hope and energy. Between October 1956 and February 1957, Rhys advised Selma on how best to shorten her adaptation of *Good Morning, Midnight* for its airing in May. Their correspondence was outspoken, but companionable. When Selma insisted on using the word "rustle" for the swish of a silk

---

* Selma was reprising the performance as Solange (in English) that she had given (in French) in 1952. This was her Genet moment; in April 1957, she played Madame Irma in the world premiere of *The Balcony*, directed once again by Peter Zadek.

dressing gown, as Sasha Jensen's sinister last lover slips into her darkened hotel room, Rhys raised only a tentative protest ("she must *hear* it and it isn't quite right for a man's dressing gown somehow. Do you think?") before deciding to let Selma have her way.[24]

Towards the end of February 1957, just as the Hamers were at last preparing to move out of their town lodgings and into a more remote home of their own on the far side of Bude's tidal beach, news came of a preliminary reading—the first of two—which were to be given at the BBC. Rhys was determined to be present; a gratified Selma invited the Hamers to dine with her family at home after the performance.

The lengthy preliminary reading—in 1957, it was the longest play ever to have been performed on radio by a single actress—was a success. Always easily moved to tears, Rhys wept as she listened to the caustic, insidious murmur with which Vaz Dias seemed to inhabit Sasha Jansen's personality, body and soul. Rhys often told Selma that she thought of *Good Morning, Midnight* as belonging to them both. Having listened, mesmerised, to the recording of Selma's extraordinary interpretation which survives in Tulsa's McFarlin collection, I can understand why.

Seated in the Eglis' cosy Hampstead kitchen later that same evening while Selma's family toasted the actress's successful rehearsal performance, Jean Rhys spoke as if for the very first time of her ideas for a novel that would explore the earlier life of Jane Eyre's Creole predecessor, the mad first wife whom Mr. Rochester had locked away in a Thornfield attic. And so it was, as both Selma and Rhys would always agree, that *Wide Sargasso Sea*—still provisionally named "Mrs Rochester"—came into being at the candlelit table in the Eglis' kitchen, assisted by a sense of tremendous good cheer about the BBC's production and by liberal quantities of Hans Egli's wine: "it's the nicest thing that's happened to me, for years and weary years," Rhys wrote to Selma from her new home in Bude on 7 March 1957.

Excited though Rhys was ("I came back [from London] brimful of ideas," she told Selma on 18 March), she still hesitated before committing herself to the novel that she had been pondering for so many years. Instead, eager for another radio success, Rhys sent Selma her old idea for an eighteenth-century naval drama set at Antigua's English Harbour, suggesting its suitability for broadcasting, while presenting it as a current work which "ought to be ready in a day or two."[5] Silence followed: evidently, neither Selma nor Sasha Moorsom was keen to pursue the project.

ON 3 MAY, a week ahead of the public broadcast of *Good Morning, Midnight*, the *Radio Times* ran a puff piece by Selma under the enticing title: "In Quest of a Missing Author." Nobody could have known how close its content was to the impassioned piece that Selma had been preparing to write back in 1949, before she first made contact with Jean Rhys. Five days later, Rhys opened a letter from an eloquent admirer who had read Selma's article. His name was Francis Wyndham and he wanted to know whether Miss Rhys might have a work in progress. If so, might she care to grant an option on it to the publishing company with whom he worked?

Wyndham's timing was impeccable. Selma's broadcast on 10 May— repeated the following evening—was widely heard and admired. Within days, Rhys had heard from several fans and another interested publisher. But Wyndham had got there first and the prospect of being paid for an option on the spot was irresistible. So Rhys said yes.

On 1 June 1957, Jean wrote to thank Francis Wyndham's female colleague at André Deutsch for the cheque which sealed her commitment. Twenty-five pounds was a paltry sum to offer for the rights to an unsubmitted work, as Diana Athill, the colleague in question, would later readily admit. On the other hand, Jean Rhys had published nothing for a very long time. Rhys herself was delighted. Having assured the unknown Miss Athill that her new novel was already progressing well, she promised to deliver a completed manuscript before the end of the year.

VI

THE PHOENIX RISES
Jean Rhys

"With this eye I see and no other. I cannot see with other people's eyes. With my own eyes I must see. I cannot help what I see . . . When I let go of what I have seen I am lost in a world so black and deadly that I am crazy with fear."

—Jean Rhys, Green Exercise Book[1]

15

A House by the Sea (1957–60)

"The shadow is yourself that follows you, watching."

—Jean Rhys to her daughter, Maryvonne,
14 January 1958, quoting from her own unpublished
fragment of a children's story for Maryvonne

Rhys's view from Rocket House, Bude: the causeway which connects
Breakwater Road to the Atlantic. What inspiration did Rhys draw from
seeing views like this while she worked on early drafts of *Wide Sargasso
Sea*? (*A souvenir postcard owned by the author*)

AT THE TIME that Francis Wyndham's letter reached Jean Rhys, the Hamers had been living for three uncomfortable months at Rocket House, their new canal-side home in Bude.* Rhys had been initially attracted by the little modern house's romantic perch against a wall of black rock; just beyond it, the narrow strip of Breakwater Road broadens into a causeway of large, smooth stones, built to hold back a fierce and often dangerous sea. The large windows on the lower floor of Rocket House offered dramatic views across broad, sea-swept sands to a towering cliff and, set into the protective curve of a hillside, the town of Bude.

The move to Rocket House had started badly when Max slipped and cut open his head on a steep flight of stone steps leading up to Breakwater Road from an iron bridge that crosses the canal. In May, when Francis's letter arrived at this challenging abode (the Hamers only remained at Rocket House for as long as they did because the rent was so low), Max was still slow on his feet and troublingly shaky.

Rhys's excitement about her new home was short-lived. After three months at Rocket House, she began complaining to faraway friends and family—never to her West Country neighbours—about the house's chief drawback for an antisocial woman. Bude, in the days when it was easily reached by rail, was a popular seaside resort. From May through until the end of summer, Breakwater Road—leading up to the pretty and popular cliff route to Widemouth—offered one of Bude's favourite walking paths for holidaymakers and day-trippers. The windows which offered fine views across the beach also offered a chance for curious passers-by to peer in.

By 1957, many of Rhys's friends had died. One of the few who remained was Peggy Kirkaldy, with whom Rhys had recently renewed contact, but Peggy had terminal cancer. Cheerful as ever, Mrs.

---

* "Rocket House" suggests that the site had originally been used to alert the local lifeboat service when a ship was in distress. The house still stands, above the broad canal along which mineral-rich sea sand used to be carried inland, to use as a fertiliser for fields.

Kirkaldy wanted to know how Rhys's unwritten novel was progressing. "Dear girl you *must* do your book," Peggy wrote, urging Rhys not to fight against the impulse to settle down to work: "it is not to be denied." We no longer possess all the kind letters from Rhys in which, in turn, she tried to prepare her dying friend for the inevitable. "You comfort me," Peggy told her on 4 September, adding, pathetically: "—I am so scared."²

The late 1950s proved to be one of the most challenging periods in a life that was seldom easy for Rhys. True, Selma Vaz Dias's broadcast had been widely heard and admired; true, it had inspired a brief flurry of interest and curiosity about an author widely assumed to be dead: "very *tactless* of me to be alive," Rhys dryly commented to Selma in November 1957. "No *savoir faire*. (Dam [sic] little *savoir vivre* either.)"³ In 1957, Rhys herself was sixty-seven years old. She was poor, she was isolated—and she was burdened with the care of a seventy-five-year-old man whose health was failing. A friendship of the quietly nurturing kind that Francis Wyndham now began to provide offered her a lifeline.

Rhys was not a habitual preserver of other people's letters: a shame, since her lost first exchanges with Francis Wyndham might have told us how much her new friend disclosed about the long history of his interest in her work. Wyndham's introduction to it had come back in 1948, while talking with two artist friends, Anne Dunn and Lucian Freud; Dunn had read *Voyage in the Dark* in Paris, before reading it aloud (in Ireland) to an enthralled Freud and then sharing their excitement with Francis.⁴ Copies of Rhys's novels had become rare during the postwar years, but in 1949, another close friend of Wyndham's, Jennifer Fry, picked up for him (once again, in Paris) a used copy of *Good Morning, Midnight*, a novel to which she also introduced her husband, Alan Ross.

By the end of the Forties, a discriminating clique of admirers of Rhys's work had formed (another fan was the novelist Julian Maclaren-Ross); encouraged by them, the twenty-six-year-old Francis Wyndham decided to draw attention to a forgotten—and possibly dead—writer, one whose work he had come to revere. His essay, "An Inconvenient

Novelist," published in December 1950 in *Tribune*, remains one of the shrewdest appraisals of Rhys that we possess and the first to point out how integral a blackly deadpan, self-decrying wit is to *Good Morning, Midnight*, the darkest of Rhys's novels. Having hidden herself away in Wales after Max's conviction, Rhys had been unconscious of that generous appreciation before she started, seven years later, to correspond with its author.

As meticulous as Rhys herself, and even more restricted in his output (a novel, a collection of essays, two books of short stories), Wyndham was a writer and editor who almost seems destined to have become Rhys's staunchest ally. A carefully critical reader, he shared Rhys's passion for French literature. (Wyndham's Francophile great-uncle, Sydney Schiff, translated the last volume of Proust's masterpiece under the pseudonym Stephen Hudson.) Having joined André Deutsch as a literary advisor shortly after the firm's modest birth in 1954, Wyndham, by 1957, had persuaded Deutsch—as well as André's long-suffering

An uncharacteristically dapper Francis Wyndham, teacup in hand. *(Used with permission of James Fox)*

colleague (and former lover), the steely and intelligent Diana Athill—
to publish the first works of another Caribbean writer, V. S. Naipaul.
Much though Athill often later liked to claim the credit for discovering
both Naipaul and Rhys, the original impetus had come from Francis;
it was Wyndham, rather than Athill, whom Rhys would slowly learn to
regard as her most trusted literary confidant.

Looking back on his long friendship with Jean Rhys after her death,
Wyndham fondly recalled the shared—and sharply ludicrous—sense
of humour which lay at the heart of his relationship with a woman easily old enough to have been his mother. Only in her correspondence
with Francis—to whom amphetamines were as much a daily necessity
as whisky had become to Rhys—could Jean feel free to be smartly
flippant about her life in Bude. In one characteristic letter, she compared Carson McCullers's celebrated novel to dismal Rocket House
(a very sad former cafe indeed), before pondering how best to conceal
a recent and substantial deposit of empty whisky bottles from public
view. Diana Athill would prove to be patient, thoughtful and talented;
(her well-received collection of short stories and her fine first memoir
of a doomed wartime romance, *Instead of a Letter*, would be published
before *Wide Sargasso Sea* appeared). But it was to Francis, between jokes
and confidences, that Jean Rhys first began unfolding thoughts and
ideas about how best to shape her own slow-growing novel, almost as if
in conversation with a second self.

By March 1958, a year after the move to Rocket House, a little progress had been made with Rhys's still untitled work. "Mr Wyndham"
was informed that the first two parts would be set in the Caribbean,
shortly after the abolition of slavery: "Part III England. Grace Poole,
the nurse or keeper speaking." The voices were still eluding Rhys, but
she was evidently optimistic about the unwritten novel's progress: "Can
you give me this year?"[5] Francis's response does not survive, but it's certain that he remained encouraging rather than directive. As a younger
protégé of Wyndham's would later explain, what really mattered was
to earn his approval: "his praise, his excitement and his responsiveness

to the book meant more than anything."[6] Wyndham's responsive and unstinting support for what would sometimes seem to be a hopeless project meant everything to Jean Rhys.

The news that Francis was to leave Deutsch in 1959 was far from being the devastating blow that an apprehensive Rhys initially supposed. Employed for five years at *Queen*—where he doubled as both theatre critic and literary editor—before joining the newly formed *Sunday Times* magazine in 1964, Wyndham made use of his formidable array of friendly connections to operate as Rhys's unpaid agent and publicist. Rosamund Lehmann's brother John, editor of the *London Magazine*, was already himself a warm admirer of Rhys's work. To Francis, it was clear that the publication in such a respected literary magazine of a handful of Rhys's short stories—a genre in which he rightly felt that she excelled—would help to ensure a warm future reception for her still unfinished novel. For Rhys, the fact that John Lehmann was ready to pay her forty guineas for a single story would prove especially alluring.

The only other source of money to be looked for in hard times was the BBC. Even after the 50 per cent division of proceeds with Selma Vaz Dias (a division which both women considered fair), Rhys's share of the performance and repeat of *Good Morning, Midnight* had been handsome. Jean may have wondered why Peggy Ramsay thought Selma (her client) should be identified as the work's sole author for a German production the following year.* What mattered in the immediate future was that Selma, possessed of invaluable contacts at the BBC, was willing to act as her advocate.[7]

These were still the honeymoon years of Rhys's complex relationship with Vaz Dias. While she readily supported Selma's plan to adapt another of her already published novels (*Voyage in the Dark*) for a radio performance, her friend's persistent interest in the unwritten *Wide Sargasso Sea* was becoming more problematic. Rhys herself never doubted

---

* The 1958 Radio Bremen production was rewritten and shaped for performance by a large cast.

that what she was writing would be a novel, but Selma always insisted on seeing "Mrs Rochester" as a work for radio, with herself in the leading role. These contrary perceptions of what Rhys was engaged in doing are apparent in the ongoing correspondence between two strong-willed women; so is the fact that Jean was anxious to do almost anything to avoid a confrontation. Somehow, she evidently hoped, the predicament would resolve itself. Selma would adapt *Voyage*; Rhys, meanwhile, would complete her novel: all would be well.

Writing about her personal life to Selma, Jean confessed her despair about the dire living conditions (damp was the worst problem in a concrete-walled building) at Rocket House. Writing to her beleaguered daughter in Amsterdam, she struggled to sound cheerful. Job Moerman's abrupt decision to leave his final posting to Surabaya in July 1957 had been well advised; a few months later, 40,000 Dutch citizens were expelled from the newly independent Indonesia by President Sukarno. The price of that hasty departure was the loss of Job's employment and all sources of income, while treatment for Maryvonne's recurrent lung disease incurred substantial medical bills. By 1958, when Job finally found work in Rotterdam, the Moermans were penniless; Maryvonne started working night shifts at a mail sorting office, while caring for a nine-year-old daughter and helping Jean Lenglet's ageing Polish wife to nurse her ailing husband. (Lenglet never fully recovered his health, following his experiences during the war.)[8]

In the autumn of 1957, shortly before her hospitalisation, Maryvonne managed to save enough money for a short visit to Rocket House, just long enough for a relieved Jean to report to Selma that her long absent daughter was "nice and not a bit like her mum—*thank God*."[9] In her subsequent letters out to Rotterdam, Rhys stayed carefully light-hearted. Playfully, she lamented the absence of warmth on what she mistakenly called the "Cornish Riviera," or else shared the wonders of a new hair cream with a daughter whose own thatch of light brown hair had begun to turn grey as she neared forty.[10] Mocking her own folly, Rhys described her just reward for buying herself a cheap sundress to bask in an English summer: "at once the sun went in and a wind blew from the Arctic—(Good morning midnight!)'[11] Cheerfully, she relayed Max's endearing naivety about her use of hair dye. "This morning the first thing he said was "Your hair is getting back to its natural colour. Thank heaven"! Natural!! So I shook the bottle and put on some more natural brown."[12]

When thinking about her granddaughter, Rhys always identified little "Ruthie" with her own younger self. "About Ruthie, she's there in my head all the time," she told Maryvonne (much as Julia Martin had remarked of her own remembered childhood in *After Leaving Mr Mackenzie*). Learning in the spring of 1958 that a new school in Amsterdam would expose her grandchild to an unknown group, this sense of empathy overpowered her. "I hate them," she wrote back to her daughter in April (meaning not friends, but groups) "and fear them like I hated termite nests at home."[13] On such occasions, Maryvonne refrained from comment. Perhaps, she understood how impossible Rhys found it ever to banish the memory of childhood terrors which time had magnified.

Surviving letters do not suggest that Maryvonne heard much about her mother's new novel. Francis Wyndham, during the late 1950s, received sporadic progress reports. Selma, alone, was allowed an occasional glimpse of the truth. "I will not disappoint you," Rhys had reassured her in the spring of 1958.[14] Nine months later, she had settled into a bizarre but productive working routine: "One day drunk, two days hangover regular as clockwork." The result—at last—was a first draft: "*The first draft*, you'll think. After nearly two years." Regrettably, no early draft survives.[15]

In March 1958, while asking Francis if she could defer submission for another year, Rhys had described the embryonic book as being divided into three parts, the first two of which would be set in the West Indies during the 1840s. By May 1959, she had changed her mind. Part Two had shifted to the attic at Thornfield Hall in which Antoinette Cosway, like Bertha Antoinette Mason in *Jane Eyre*, is eventually incarcerated. Rhys now envisaged this central section as an episode of ominous darkness: " 'the slow approach of night' in that awful room," Rhys wrote to Selma, casually misquoting Milton.[16]

Rhys's dark vision of Part Two owed something to the atmosphere of gloom at home. Two years on, Max had not recovered from his plunge on the steep stone steps below Rocket House; in June 1959, Rhys gratefully assented to Selma's offer to nurse him back to health for a fortnight at the hospitable Eglis' London home, a suggestion which Max—he hated ever being separated from his wife—firmly declined.[17] Instead, acting on the persistent prompting of her brother-in-law, Rhys offered Selma the more congenial task of acting as a literary advisor to the charming and quietly ambitious Alec Hamer.

Two years younger than his brother Max, and often confined to his London home by the need to care for a disabled daughter, Alec had kept well clear of the Hamers during Max's imprisonment at Maidstone. Alec nurtured writing ambitions of his own, however, and it may have been the broadcast of *Good Morning, Midnight* which caused him to renew the fraternal connection. By January 1959, the relationship had grown friendly enough for Alec Hamer to offer to act—and to be accepted—as Rhys's informal editorial advisor.[18] Rhys clearly valued Alec's judgement; he would be the first person permitted to read the first (lost) draft of *Wide Sargasso Sea*. When her brother-in-law asked for help in getting some of his own stories adapted for broadcasting, Rhys didn't hesitate. Selma never did succeed in getting any of Alec's works on air, but the two of them became close friends. "Fred"—the name by which Frederick Alexander Hamer was always known to Vaz Dias—became such a regular feature of Selma's letters to Rhys that it's tempting to wonder about the exact nature of the relationship between an aspiring London-based writer and a glamorous actress whose marriage (according to her daughter and granddaughter) had never been exactly monogamous. Certainly, when Selma visited her in the summer of 1963, Rhys thought it quite natural to suggest that she should bring along Alec, not her husband.

A pleasing distraction from Rhys's struggle with the novel emerged towards the end of the summer of 1959; Francis was able to report that John Lehmann was eager to publish "Till September Petronella." (It appeared in the January 1960 issue of the *London Magazine*.) The novel-length story Rhys based upon her awkward 1915 holiday with Adrian Allinson, Philip Heseltine and Philip's girlfriend had already been drastically cut by Rhys. Heseltine had died back in 1930, but Rhys took care to protect the reputation of his surviving fellow pacifist and conscientious objector by pre-dating events to the summer of 1914. Francis, meanwhile, seized the opportunity offered by Lehmann to publish an accompanying glowing tribute to the story's author. Sent a first draft of Wyndham's introduction, Rhys offered only one proud correction: "I am not a Scot at all. My father was Welsh—very."[19]

By December 1959, Rhys had returned to plotting (and re-plotting) her novel. Scant but intriguing evidence that she had consciously begun to connect her own Lockhart ancestry to the life of Antoinette Cosway emerges from the compelling fact that she suddenly sent Selma a Christmas clutch of annotated photographs of Bertrand Bay, dating from her stay at the Hampstead estate, in the north of Dominica, in 1936. It is from the ominously deserted huts of former slaves at "Bertrand Bay" that Antoinette and her stepfather, Mr. Mason, ride back at sunset to Coulibri, the house that will be destroyed by fire that night. The house at Hampstead, rather than the charred remains of Geneva, offered Rhys her blueprint for Coulibri, the troubled, atmospheric island home in which readers first encounter the young Antoinette. Progress, however gradual, was being made.

―――――――――――

IN FEBRUARY, 1960, the Hamers left Rocket House for good. The final straw had come the previous spring when a local woman suddenly dug up all the pretty wild flowers that Rhys had loved to see growing close to her door. "Oh she's a devil," an indignant, nature-loving Rhys wrote to her old friend Eliot Bliss. "How glad I shall be to depart."[20]

Fifty miles south-west of Bude, along the north coast of Cornwall, lies Perranporth, the home of Winston Graham, who was putting the little seaside resort into his fourth novel about Poldark during the unhappy six months that Rhys and Max spent as his neighbours. Graham never met the Hamers, and thus escaped the potential difficulty of being entertained in a minute and pitifully inadequate house that poor Rhys once jauntily compared to a horsebox. Unheated, "The Chalet's" sole washing facility was a small handbasin. Outside, cold March rain fell in driving sheets onto flat land which—as Rhys discovered with dismay—had recently been approved for a social housing development. A modest row of village shops lay half a mile away, at the far end of a muddy track across treeless fields.

This was not what advertisements for a sunny and warm garden home had led the ever-hopeful Hamers to expect. To Selma, Jean admitted that "a terrible weariness" was preventing her from working on the novel; to Francis, while hoping for his eventual opinion on "a chapter here and there," she only sighed about the incessant wind and rain. Maryvonne, approached as a potential typist for the ten-year-old story which her mother had partly set at Holloway prison (John Lehmann, having accepted both "Till September Petronella" and "The Day They Burned the Books," was eager to publish more of her work), heard about Rhys's terror of causing a local scandal: "the people here are terribly narrow-minded," Rhys confided to her daughter, "and they gossip like crazy."[21]

Four months at Perranporth drove Rhys, in final desperation, to seek help. Edward and Gertrude Rees Williams, arriving in May after a testing hundred-mile drive from Budleigh Salterton on tiny, winding lanes, found the Hamers penniless and on the verge of collapse. Rhys was in tears, Max was ill and the Chalet's roof was leaking.

Edward Rees Williams was not an imaginative man, but he did have a strongly developed sense of duty. Rhys was taken out to a comforting lunch in Perranporth by Gertrude, who then delighted her sister-in-law by buying her a pretty broad-brimmed hat; Edward, meanwhile, sat down for a manly chat with Max. Before returning home, Rhys's brother gave her his solemn promise of help, an oath which he made good on within a month. By July, a home for the Hamers had been purchased on the outskirts of Cheriton Fitzpaine, a rural north Devon village lying within an hour's drive of Budleigh Salterton.

Economy, as well as the need for rapid action, had influenced

Edward's purchase. Six Landboat Bungalows was a bargain only because it had recently been deemed unfit for habitation, a flaw which Edward promptly set out to remedy. Jean, learning that she would soon have her own kitchen and even a bathroom, grew as happy as a child. The yet unseen bungalow was immediately renamed "The Ark." Joyful letters were despatched to Selma, Francis and Maryvonne about romantic plans to embellish "The New Jerusalem" with sumptuous bargain fabrics of crimson and gold. "I do think Edward has been kind," Rhys enthused to Maryvonne in October 1960, adding what now became the mantra of her letters, that a perfect nest had been provided in which to complete the hatching of her novel.[22]

The novel's progress at Perranporth had not only been delayed by poor accommodation. In May 1960, just before Edward's errand of mercy, Rhys had suggested that Francis might show the *London Magazine* "Let Them Call It Jazz," "a bit of a crazy story" which she artlessly represented as a new work. A delay in revisions, together with the magazine's dismaying loss (by Charles Osborne, an office junior with a bright future) of another submission, "Tigers are Better-Looking," meant that neither story would appear in the magazine until 1962. In the meantime, Rhys's spirits were lifted by the news that Francis had successfully placed another story, "Outside the Machine," in a respected annual collection called *Winter's Tales*. William Sansom, a writer whose style Rhys admired, had apparently sent Francis an enthusiastic letter about "Till September Petronella." The poet and highly regarded founder-editor of *New Verse*, Geoffrey Grigson, intended to include Rhys in a new twentieth-century survey of world literature.[*] Better still, over in the US, both Simon & Schuster and Viking had expressed an interest in acquiring *Good Morning, Midnight*.[†]

"I don't know how to *start* thanking you, but I do indeed feel so very grateful," Rhys wrote to Francis on 31 May, before blithely

---

[*] Grigson's ambitious project seems not to have been completed.

[†] US interest evaporated and *Good Morning, Midnight* remained unpublished there until 1970.

announcing that she intended to set the novel aside and to work, instead, on a series of Caribbean stories set in the time of her childhood.[23] An old and frequently rewritten story about her father's former friend, Mr. Ramage—eventually to be published under the ironic title "Pioneers, Oh, Pioneers"—was now presented as a recent discovery among her papers.*

Francis Wyndham rarely put his foot down, but he did so now. On 14 July 1960, while still living at Perranporth, a chastened Rhys promised to desist. "I do understand that the book 'Sargasso Sea' is what is wanted," she wrote. "As soon as I am safe and sound" (at the bungalow purchased by Edward), "I will work very hard and finish it. Not too late I hope." As for writing a collection of Dominica-related stories: "I won't talk about it any more."[24]

---

* Nine years later, Wyndham negotiated the story's first appearance (as "My dear darling Mr Ramage") in *The Times Saturday Review*, 28 June 1969.

16

Cheriton Fitzpaine

"More discontents I never had
Since I was born, than here,
Where I have been, and still am, sad,
In this dull Devonshire . . . "

— Robert Herrick, "Discontents in Devon," *c.*1640[1]

JEAN RHYS SPENT her first seventeen years in Dominica because that was where her family lived. But what persuaded her to spend the last nineteen years of her life in a village of which she spoke to her London friends with a gloom to match that of the London-bred Civil War poet Robert Herrick? If she hated life at Cheriton Fitzpaine so much, why did she choose to remain there?

IMAGINING CHERITON FITZPAINE from afar, you should place this north Devon village midway between the towns of Tiverton and Crediton. Narrow the focus; cradle it amidst small, hilly fields, of which the nearest to the village are separated by narrow and winding lanes guarded by towering hedges. Out beyond the fields, to either side of this landlocked world of farming communities, lie the high and open heathlands of Exmoor and Dartmoor. Within, it's hard to shake off the feeling of having entered a parallel universe, one in which time remains suspended somewhere between the wars. Driving down the

steeply twisting little roads that lead the visitor past a neat row of former almshouses to the church, the open green and the long, thatched
schoolhouse that lie at the centre of Cheriton Fitzpaine, you wouldn't
feel surprised to encounter a gaunt young farm-boy, limping home
from the trenches of 1918.

Visiting to form my own impressions of the village in which Edward
Rees Williams purchased a home for his sister in the summer of 1960, I
met a rosy-cheeked man who'd liked growing up here enough to move
back to Cheriton in early middle age. Roy Stettiford was among the
youngest of a family who lived in the single-storey house next to the

Cheriton Fitzpaine, the secluded Devon village in which Rhys spent the
last nineteen years of her life. *(Used with permission of Piers Howell)*

Hamers for many years. He remembers peeping through their window one day and seeing Rhys (an old lady, in his child's eyes) sitting in front of a television and drinking, straight from the bottle, all by herself. "She were hard on her husband, we thought," remains his only criticism. Roy's memory of Max Hamer is of a friendly, pale, shortish man with a white forked beard "like a nanny-goat," whose wool beret, pulled low over a balding pate, gave him a bit of a foreign air: French, they thought.[2]

The most radical change about life in Cheriton Fitzpaine—after Bude and Perranporth—was that on Cornwall's north coast, the Hamers had lived among people who were used to the regular influx of strangers who visited every summer. Cheriton has never—until Rhys became famous—attracted tourists. Here, Jean and Max found themselves dwelling among conservative Devon families of modest means, people who tended to view as an outsider anybody who came from farther away than Exeter or Plymouth. The Hamers' nearest neighbours felt at home living alongside the fields that belonged to Landboat Farm, owned and run by the Carrs, a staunchly Methodist young couple who didn't drink and who cared about land, not books. Max and Jean thought differently. They were, and would remain, apart.

Edward Rees Williams had seen no reason to brief anybody other than Cheriton's vicar about his sister's unpredictable moods. The sudden bursts of rage that Rhys's drinking habit often engendered shocked her new neighbours and sometimes frightened them. Many stories are still recalled of the kindnesses that were regularly performed for the Hamers, especially as Max became increasingly infirm and his wife less able to care for him at home. Nevertheless, it remains an uncomfortable fact that a handful of village families did encourage their small sons to persecute an elderly woman whom they regarded as a stranger and a witch. "I am envied and hated," Rhys reported to Selma Vaz Dias in the autumn of 1963, adding, two months later, more nervously: "the gossip is dreadful. . . ."[3]

Viewed on a bright summer morning, the centre of Cheriton Fitzpaine looks idyllically pretty. The long walls of the schoolhouse gleam white under its steep roof of thatch; standing beside the rectory, a visitor can easily spot where the tower of St. Matthew's rises into view, solid and reassuring. Walking beside me along a hillside lane flecked with mud and cow dung, Roy Stettiford talks in a soft Devon accent about the village his parents first knew. Back then, Cheriton Fitzpaine was a thriving little community with its own post office, butcher's and grocer's shops. Hard times had shrunk the village; arriving in the late summer of 1960, Rhys and Max found themselves dependent for all necessities on two pubs and a small store for general supplies. For books, Rhys relied for several unsatisfactory years on the fortnightly visits to the village of a mobile library van.

I hadn't expected Cheriton's rectory to be so old or so appealing, but Roy Stettiford explains that the house was once home to the Arundells, a family of public-minded rector-squires who put on plays for the village and rewarded good Sunday-school pupils with an occasional outing to the Tiverton picture house. An older villager, Ken Sanford, remembers games of tennis, always in whites, taking place on the high flat lawn that lies behind the rectory; Roy remembers scrumping for apples in the orchard. In 1964, Rhys told Selma Vaz Dias of the pleasure she always derived from watching the huntsmen trotting past on a bright winter's morning; a last trace of the days when the Arundells hosted the Eggesford Meet, an annual gathering of hounds, horses and their riders that took place in the heart of the village.

The rectory played an important role in Rhys's life at Cheriton. By 1960, the Arundells had been replaced by Alwynne Woodard, the only person among the villagers who swiftly understood that an exceptional writer was living in their midst.

Woodard was a remarkable priest—"a dear, the real McCoy," as Rhys gratefully wrote to Diana Athill in the late summer of 1963.[4] The grandson of a Victorian canon who had founded a group of evangelical schools, Alwynne was educated at one of them, Lancing. Returning there as a young schoolmaster, he taught classics and English to Evelyn Waugh. Unjustly dismissed by a headmaster who was then himself forced to leave, Woodard spent many years doubling as a rural dean

The Reverend Alwynne
Woodard, the cultured,
compassionate and broad-
minded vicar who came to
Rhys's help while she was
struggling to write *Wide
Sargasso Sea*.

and the well-liked chaplain to a psychiatric hospital in Surrey, before settling into the less demanding role of vicar to a tiny parish of which only a small percentage were regular churchgoers.

A bookish, dreamy man, Woodard was married to a conscientious and necessarily patient woman who supervised weekly basket-weaving classes in the rectory's front room, while one of their four daughters amused herself by painting saucy murals above the staircase. The vicar's vagueness was notorious. (On one occasion, the absent-minded Alwynne actually allowed his spouse to fall out of their car, while driving inattentively on.) But it was the Reverend Woodard's goodness of heart that Roy Stettiford and Ken Sanford both singled out to me for praise: "He were always kind, a very kind gentleman indeed."[5]

Woodard's first recorded encounter with the Hamers was unfortunate. A few months after the couple's arrival, Rhys had been enraged by the erection of a barbed wire sheep-fence close to the bedroom window of their new home. A neighbour, alarmed by the wildness Rhys displayed when her blood was up, summoned the vicar to arbitrate; Rhys, on this occasion, was both drunk and furious. Nevertheless, while trying to soothe her, Woodard felt an unanticipated sense of rapport.

It was shortly after this incident in the spring of 1961 that the vicar started to make occasional afternoon visits to the intriguing Hamers. Sometimes, to the consternation of a watchful village, he took along a bottle of whisky and shared its contents with a woman whose mind had struck him from the first as being out of the ordinary. Keeping clear of the topic of difficult neighbours, they talked about books. It seemed that Cheriton's odd new resident was trying to complete a novel. The vicar loaned her *Tom Jones*, which she didn't much care for; his response remains unknown to the copy which Rhys despatched to him of Orwell's *Animal Farm*.

Woodard's appreciation of Rhys as a writer began on an autumn evening in 1961 when, informed by his sobbing friend that she had destroyed her novel, he decided to gather up the scrawled sheets of paper that lay in heaps around the room. Back at the rectory, Woodard persuaded one of his daughters to help assemble the semi-legible handwritten pages into some kind of an order. Helen Woodard eventually retired to bed; the vicar, having spent most of the night patiently collating pages, managed to decipher enough of Parts One and Two of *Wide Sargasso Sea* to recognise that the work in progress was exceptional. From then on, Woodard paid regular and sometimes daily visits to the Hamers' home. He "cheered me up when I was at my last gasp," Jean would tell Diana Athill in August 1963, marvelling at Woodard's kindness to a non-churchgoing member of a community by whom "I've been given up as a bad job I fear."[6]

TODAY, JEAN RHYS's home is the last still standing of a small row of undistinguished one-storey properties: the rest have been destroyed. Across the lane, a hillside field has already disappeared under a new, larger hamlet of residential homes.

The cottage (a word suggestive of a quaint charm that Rhys's home lacks) is now and always was screened from the curious eyes of passersby, protected by a dense green hedge. To the back of the bungalow, beyond a muddy plot from which Rhys struggled to create a flower garden, she could glimpse cattle and sheep as they roamed the hillside fields. This was Rhys's favourite outlook. Writing to Francis Wyndham in the summer of 1967, at the time of her proposed departure for the less remote Essex flat that had been selected for her future home by Diana Athill, she lovingly recorded all that she could see from her small sitting-room's window: two successively flowering lilacs, a honey-suckle, two apple trees, peonies, Michaelmas daisies, "and so on." That careful inventory spelled out what Rhys could not quite bring herself to admit to her London friends. Despite Miss Athill's kind endeavours to improve her lot, she really did not want to leave Devon.[7]

Rhys was not a skilled plantswoman, but there's no doubt that she loved her Landboat plot. Writing to her daughter in July 1961, Rhys tried to explain the restorative effect on her spirits of digging in the garden: "I like the smell of earth and grass . . ." Two days later, she told Maryvonne of the pleasure she had derived from bringing into the house a single unidentified crimson flower: "not to be believed it is so beautiful."[8] In later years, chatting with her celebrated Devon neigh-bour, William Trevor, Rhys only ever wanted to talk about one subject: gardening. Encountering the elderly lady out walking in her long coat and neatly knotted headscarf, the younger writer always supposed that the wicker basket on Rhys's arm was for the purpose of gathering flow-ers. Villagers knew better: Jean's basket was used to carry her bottles home from the local pub.[9]

I revisited Cheriton in 2021 and met Sam Moss, the proud owner since 2004 of Rhys's former home. Like Rhys, Sam often hears scrab-blings from the cottage's attic and doesn't relish making an investiga-tion.[10] In their early days at Landboat, one of her sons used to see an old lady sitting by his bed: photographs identified her as Jean Rhys. Today, Sam is good-humouredly used to being approached by Rhys's fans. The most regular visitors to Cheriton are Dutch. We agree that it's time the cottage had a plaque to honour Rhys's nineteen years of residence.

Despite improvements having been made during the last years that Rhys lived here—and many more since Samantha Moss moved in—everything within Landboat Cottage (as it is named today) feels cramped and undersized. Back in 1960, the year of the Hamers' arrival, a tiny bathroom stood just beyond the door: "a delightful thing to have

one," Rhys crowed to Maryvonne: "a luxe."[11] To the right, an equally
small kitchen became her workroom. Here, an open oven door kept
Rhys warm while she wrote at a table covered—Caribbean style—with
a bright square of chequered oilcloth. Overhead, a naked orange light
bulb provided a luridly inadequate substitute for the dazzling sunlight
of a Caribbean childhood.

Space was always limited. Behind the bathroom, a minute spare
room became a store for the battered suitcases in which Rhys kept
old manuscripts and drafts. Beyond the kitchen, the Hamers' bedroom
was dominated by the old-fashioned dressing table at which, throughout her life in Devon, daily court was held by Jean with her reflected
image, reddening pursed lips, blueing lowered eyelids, blotting out the
evidence of many a sleepless night. From the sitting-room to the rear
of the cottage, little windows stared across the garden plot to where a
distant line of scrubby trees stood beyond the first hillside field. Rhys
evoked this view in one of the many poems that she despatched at
irregular intervals to Francis Wyndham. She called it: "A field where
sheep are feeding"—and acknowledged an evident debt to Longfellow's
The Song of Hiawatha.

> The silent field powdered with moonlight,
> And the low hills
> The low, meek unaspiring hills.
> And the tall trees
> The tall proud dark trees
> Leaning down to shallow water
> Looking into shallow water.[12]

Rhys's enduring grievances were not with the smallness and inconve-
nience of a house in which water from burst pipes frequently dripped or
cascaded through the low ceilings, but with a ramshackle iron-roofed
shed. Large enough to house Edward's car when he drove over either
to deliver a Christmas capon, or to make peace with an irate Landboat neighbour, the empty shed also offered a perfect nesting place

for mice. Rhys's attitude to animals could be capricious: a dog lover in earlier years, she was terrified by the pale-eyed mongrel sheepdogs that sometimes roamed the lanes in Cheriton. Cows might be endured (*"They know* who to shy at," Rhys joked to the resolutely urban Francis Wyndham[13]). Mice were another matter. Rats were worse.

During the nineteen years she spent at Landboat, Rhys's correspondence makes it almost possible to predict the onset of a mental health crisis by the increase in her allusions to the unwelcome presence of largely imaginary rodents. In September 1963, writing to Selma Vaz Dias, Rhys claimed that an invasion of mice had caused her—not for the first time—to tear up a chapter of the ongoing novel. ("But that's no excuse.") Writing to Francis Wyndham in October, she darkly noted her growing terror of "my mouse-haunted kitchen" and her creation of a barrier of wood and stones to keep vermin at bay: "quite

This may be the second-hand caravan Rhys bought with Jo Batterham in the last years of her life. Its grim appearance nicely conveys the imagined horror of the sinister shed which forms such a feature of her letters from Devon. *(McFarlin)*

useless of course. Also there are alarming sounds from above where the hot water pipes are. (Things larger than mice?)."[14] Edward Rees Williams became sufficiently worried about his sister's state of mind to pay an inspection visit that same autumn; what he saw in her did not reassure him.

––––––––––

WHEN CORRESPONDING WITH an increasing number of friends and admirers in London, Rhys seldom missed an opportunity to voice her dislike for Cheriton Fitzpaine. In December 1960, while writing about the "marooned" Cosways in her novel, she described herself to an anxious Maryvonne as "simply marooned." Like the unhappy young priest at Ambricourt in Georges Bernanos' celebrated novel—*Diary of a Country Priest* was a book that seldom left Rhys's side—she felt that the village was watching her, cat-like, with suspicious eyes. Reaching a particularly low ebb in the early autumn of 1963, when Max was away in hospital, Rhys wailed to Selma Vaz Dias that the villagers hated her "because I try to write . . . More than half the population think I am a *witch*! And that I do harm!!"[15] A follow-up letter identified the vicar's wife—no fan of Rhys—as having relayed the village's suspicions of witchcraft. Mrs. Woodard had added that her husband was praying for Mrs. Hamer's redemption.

"This is not a place to be alone in," Rhys wrote to Selma in that troubled autumn of 1963. The words were heavily underlined; the letter described her home of three years as "stupid," "ugly," "beastly" and even "evil."[16] In some part of her mind, Rhys believed it all. "Sleep It Off Lady," the unnerving title story of her last collection, represented Rhys herself in the guise of "Miss Verney," an overimaginative and often intoxicated old lady who—having been perused and told to "sleep it off lady" by Deena, the cold-eyed child of a disapproving neighbour—is left helplessly lying on open ground in the chilly air of approaching night.[*]

––––––––––

[*]   Rhys's description of the malevolent child is often assumed to have been an unkind

Bad things did happen in the village during Rhys's time there. In 1966, Diana Athill brought back to London an unnerving tale of having been robbed as she lay awake in Rhys's newly built annex by a night visitor who used his long-handled hook to reach through the window and snatch her purse.[17] Athill's tale was true: the thief, a local boy, was subsequently arrested. Miss Verney's miserable death of overnight exposure was the product of Rhys's imagination. So, to a certain degree, was Rhys's much proclaimed loneliness. Evidence abounds, both in the villagers' memories and in Rhys's own letters, of endless acts of kindness towards an eccentric outsider who had settled for good in a village that was neither ugly nor evil. Miss Verney's occasional and gently outspoken visitor, "Mr Slade," is a thinly disguised portrait of Rhys's friend Alan Greenslade, her regular taxi driver and—through his always available telephone—her principal contact with the outside world. Mrs. Greenslade and Roy Stettiford's mother often cooked meals when Rhys wasn't eating, and helped to care for Max. Women like Joy Haslehurst, who never featured in Jean Rhys's plaintive letters to London, were always around to join Mrs. Hamer for a drink at the pub and to see her safely home. Kind Devon friends took Rhys on day outings to local landmarks and beauty spots. Alwynne Woodard watched over her and would summon Edward whenever further help was required. Joan Butler, the prototype for cliché-prone "Letty Baker" in Rhys's story of Miss Verney, paid regular visits. Rhys habitually misrepresented her situation at Cheriton when sharing her thoughts with the outside world. Loneliness was always more a state of mind than a fact of her existence.

Jean Rhys did not love Cheriton Fitzpaine, but it was the place to which she always chose to return. In 1964, on the brink of making her first visit to London in seven years, Rhys admitted to Eliot Bliss that she was already plotting her escape back to Devon: "I've been down

---

representation of the daughter of one of her Landboat neighbours. She was also drawing on Georges Bernanos' troubled Seraphita, the farm child who, in his *Diary of a Country Priest*, identifies the priest's drinking habit and tells malicious stories about him.

here too long and have almost taken root," she confided before adding with typical bravado: "– though not quite!"[18]

CHOOSING HER WORDS with care for a modest 2017 leaflet that records Jean Rhys's nineteen-year residence in Cheriton Fitzpaine, Diana Athill concluded it by saying that "here it was that by her own choice, Rhys came to the end of her days."

The words sound a little grudging (Athill would certainly not have chosen Cheriton for her own final years), but they are accurate. For Rhys, a recluse who believed that she must "earn" her death by her writing, a quiet retreat in the tedious, secluded depths of Devon was ideal. Robert Herrick, a poet and priest who elected to return to Dean Prior after being ousted from his Devon parish during the English Civil War, would have agreed:

> Yet, justly too, I must confess
> I ne'er invented such
> Ennobled numbers for the press
> Than where I loathed so much.[19]

17

The Madness of Perfection
(1960–63)

"The difficult thing is the only worthwhile thing."

—Jean Rhys to Selma Vaz Dias, September 1963[1]

HOW LONG HAD *Wide Sargasso Sea* been gestating within Jean Rhys? The truest answer might be all of her life. A more specific answer would be that Rhys's first references to the Sargasso Sea and its depths, beneath a rank cargo of floating, brownish weed, date back to 1936, the year she returned to her homeland, Dominica. At Bude, memories may have been triggered by a similar brownish weed that still floats on dark water above what Rhys described as a "weir" separating Rocket House from the little resort's tidal beach.

In the autumn of 1960, just after the Hamers' move to Cheriton Fitzpaine, when gently pressed about the progress of her novel, Rhys sounded a note of cautious optimism. "It may go better here," she wrote to Francis Wyndham (who had by then left André Deutsch to work for *Queen* magazine).[2]

Wide Sargasso Sea's rebirth at Bude in 1957 had coincided with Max's deterioration in health. Having suffered what seems to have been a first stroke in 1958, he grew much worse in 1959, during the couple's final months at Rocket House. The subsequent move to Landboat Bunga-lows had brought no improvement; it wasn't long before Max was having to spend weeks—and sometimes months—at the nearby hospital in Tiverton (formerly the town workhouse) and in its recovery wing for convalescents, the Belmont. National Health Service care for the elderly was far from perfect in 1960s Britain. Inevitably, Max's growing unhappiness affected a wife who still loved him. Slapping down a well-meaning but occasionally tactless Diana Athill with less than her usual courtesy, Rhys once snapped back that—whatever Miss Athill might suppose—Max was "not a bundle of old rags to me—he is Max. (Nice. Was. A stoic.)"[3]

In December 1960, contemplating what would become a typical Devon winter—with a sick husband, a view across vacant and water-logged fields and icicles hanging by the bathroom wall—Rhys valiantly joked to Maryvonne about being perceived as a comic old eccentric, one who might scandalise her daughter by suddenly showing up in Rotterdam in a bright red wig and purple dress.*

To Selma, whose career by then had begun to ebb, Rhys argued that sadness ("the shadow of light as it were, this black melancholy") was the necessary price of life and experience. "I know it so well, my God, it goes everywhere with me—but almost despair my dear," she added. "Though never quite."[4]

Although disheartened by the lack of easy access in Cheriton either to books or whisky ("Woe. Woe."), Rhys's spirits were lifted by Francis Wyndham's good news in the new year of 1961: the *Sunday Times* and the *TLS*, when reviewing *Winter's Tales*, the annual anthology in which Francis had managed to place one of a clutch of stories Rhys had sent him, had both praised "Outside the Machine" as an exceptional work. Reassured, she sent Francis her revision of "Let Them Call It Jazz." The story was still in her handwriting: the experiences of a mixed-race woman in Holloway prison hadn't seemed prudent material to

---

* Rhys just beat Jenny Joseph to it with her comic image: Joseph's celebrated poem, "Warning," with the now famous opening about an older woman wearing purple and a red hat, was published the following year, in 1961 (Jenny Joseph, *Selected Poems*, Bloodaxe, 1992).

share with any local typist, even back in Perranporth (where Rhys had tried to recruit Maryvonne as an overseas secretary), and certainly not in conservative Cheriton. Understanding her concern, Francis—who rarely performed such a service for a friend, however gifted—typed it out himself.

Rhys's fierce dispute with the local farmer about his obstructive fence had opened the way for a new friendship when Alwynne Woodard stepped in to make peace. The vicar's calming visits had helped Rhys to resume her writing. By the beginning of the autumn of 1961, she had grown confident enough to show—and even read aloud—the opening of her work-in-progress to her brother-in-law. The orderly Alec Hamer, while shocked by the chaos in which Rhys habitually wrote—"it's the way I work—always," she explained to Francis on 11 October—had liked what he heard. Nevertheless, as Rhys admitted, the novel remained a long way from completion. Each week, so Francis gathered, she formed the intention of despatching a chapter to London. "But. Well, but—"[5]

Wyndham, while pleased by the evidence that progress was being made, was disturbed by the news that Rhys was in low spirits. "I've been seeing a lot of the collective face that killed a thousand thoughts lately," she admitted in this same October letter, "and sometimes there is blue murder in my wicked heart."[6]

Rhys chose not to tell Francis Wyndham that she had again been drinking heavily. Within a day or so of writing to him, she had ripped up a chapter of the novel. Alarmed by one of her lightning outbursts of rage—when angered, the ageing Rhys could still spit, bite or scratch a perceived opponent—Gladys Raymond (a postmistress who lived in one of the Landboat bungalows) summoned the vicar.

It was this visit which had led to Alwynne Woodard's decision, after reading some of Rhys's handwritten pages, to help their author in any way he could. By 17 October, Rhys was cheerfully telling Wyndham about her renewed determination to "fix the book up, write it legibly and sooner than you'd believe."[7] The cause was some "wonderful" pep pills that a sympathetic doctor—presumably the helpful vicar's own physician son-in-law—had recommended.

Mandatory drug regulation was still in its infancy during the early 1960s. Jean Rhys was not the only creative person who became innocently addicted to prescribed anti-depressants and amphetamines: Selma Vaz Dias suffered noticeable and adverse effects after being given "Marplan" (an anti-depressant) by the controversial psychiatrist William Sargant.[8] From the first, Rhys spoke gratefully of the "bright red pills" and the immediate surge of energy—she compared the sensation to flying—that they produced. In December 1961, she relied on them as she struggled to cope with a double blow. It was while Rhys was facing her husband's first protracted absence (Max was referred to Tiverton Hospital for examination and rest by the same kindly doctor who had prescribed her medication) that sad news reached her from Holland. Jean Lenglet, the father of her only child, the fascinating, brave and literary-minded man whom she had loved most enduringly, the loyal supporter of her work long after their marriage had ended, was dead. Although long anticipated, the shock of his loss was deeply felt by Rhys at a time of actual and emotional isolation. Pills helped; in need of more, she had only to ask for a repeat. When Max was released from hospital at the end of December—a concerned Edward Rees Williams had been paying regular visits to his sister during her weeks alone at Landboat—Rhys welcomed him wearing a bright red dress to match her uplifting scarlet pills.

It's impossible to know how much the improvement in Rhys's spirits resulted from her new medication, but by the spring of 1962, despite bad flu and a harsh winter that had frozen all the pipes and flooded the streets of nearby Tiverton, she was back at work on the novel. Doubtless, she had also been cheered by the knowledge that some of her finest stories were at last appearing in print. Alan Ross was now editing the *London Magazine*, subsidised by his rich and cultured wife, Jennifer Fry. "Let Them Call It Jazz" had appeared there in February, while later in the year—following its long disappearance within the magazine's office files—the rediscovered story "Tigers are Better-Looking" was finally due for publication.

Alan Ross unwittingly provided Rhys with a fresh source of stimulation for the novel she was at last identifying regularly as "Wide Sargasso Sea." As part of a collection of commissioned essays about how various writers had found their vocation, Ross encouraged Rhys to contribute a brief article on her early years in England. Provisionally titled "Leaving School," the piece would evolve into one of Rhys's most directly autobiographical stories, "Overture and Beginners Please," while laying the ground for her long-planned memoir. Ross had promised a generous fee. More importantly, the subject matter had the unanticipated effect of forcing Rhys to confront her own first response to *Jane Eyre*.

Charlotte Brontë's novel had been a set book at the Perse School in Cambridge—half a century ago—when Rhys first read it. Even in her seventies, Rhys still remembered with pain how she herself had been nicknamed "West Indies" and treated by her fellow pupils as "a Savage from the Cannibal Islands."[9] A hurtful parallel was easily established by thoughtlessly cruel schoolgirls between an easily riled young "Savage" from Dominica and Bertha Antoinette Mason, bred in Jamaica and crudely portrayed by Brontë as a red-eyed and bestial creature who "snatched and growled like some wild animal."[10]

Mining her memories of the Perse for "Leaving School," Rhys thought often and hard about the crass injustice of Brontë's representation of Bertha Mason. Rhys did not, as she explained in several long letters to Francis Wyndham, deny that calculated alliances were historically made between English fortune-hunters and Creole heiresses, or that some of those unfortunate young brides had proved to be emotionally unstable. Her own identification was with Bertha's role as an outsider. "Creole of pure English descent she may be," Rochester remarks of Antoinette, "but they are not English or European either."[11]

Unstated but implicit in Rhys's letters to Francis Wyndham and Diana Athill in 1962–63 was the growing evidence that the writer's own delicately calibrated mental stability increased her empathy with

Antoinette (or "Bertha," as Antoinette's husband in Rhys's novel inexplicably insists upon renaming her). A hint of the depths and complexity of Rhys's feelings emerges from the fact that her own private title for *Wide Sargasso Sea* for a long time was "Before I Was Set Free." Freedom, for the twenty-year-old Antoinette, is to be gained only when she dreams of leaping from her husband's blazing roof into the waiting arms of Tia, her dark twin and nemesis: " . . . I saw the pool at Coulibri. Tia was there. She beckoned to me. And when I hesitated, she laughed. I heard her say, You frightened?"[12]

"Bravo!" wrote Rhys in a letter, after describing her heroine's dream of a self-willed death. "You must earn death," Jean had instructed herself in her diary at the Ropemakers' Arms. Here, in the final pages of her novel, as she transforms Bertha Mason's gothic death-plunge into an act of courage, Rhys and her character appear to merge into a single being. "Now at last I know why I was brought here and what I have to do," Antoinette asserts in the book's last lines as she wakes from a dream of setting Thornfield on fire. The words she uses offer an unmistakeable echo of those in which Rhys would regularly pledge her own solemn purpose and vocation: to write and—like Bernanos—to write with unflinching honesty about the only truth she knew. Her self.

WRITING HER NOVEL still felt "like pulling a cart up a very steep hill," Rhys sighed to Maryvonne in March 1962. By now, however, she had at last secured access to a typist who was prepared to take dictation—a new experience for Rhys—while helping to transcribe her shambolic pages of manuscript.

Alwynne Woodard had been the negotiator of this new arrangement. While taking bottles of whisky to Rhys's cottage to add cheer to their long and often daily chats, the vicar had realised how much of his new friend's time was taken up by the difficulty of revising almost indecipherable handwritten drafts of her own work. During the autumn of 1961, Woodard thought he had discovered a solution. Morris Brown, an aspiring television playwright, had rented Pond Cottage, a stone-walled farmhouse at nearby Witheridge, as a quiet occasional retreat for himself and his wife while he worked on a life of Jesus for the BBC. Katherine Brown, marooned on an isolated Devon hilltop, had time on her hands. Intrigued by Woodard's accounts of a local author who was at work on a remarkable novel, she offered to act as Miss Rhys's unpaid typist.

All began well. In December 1961, Woodard conducted Rhys to the Browns' farmhouse. The couple were warm and welcoming; Jean, gloved, hatted and smiling, was at her courteous best. An arrangement was set up for day-long visits, during which Rhys read aloud from her handwritten draft. A patient and efficient typist, Katherine Brown admired what she heard enough to suggest introducing Rhys to their Yorkshire-born friend Olwyn Hughes, should she ever need an agent (a recommendation which Olwyn herself would follow up some four years later). Less wisely, she and her husband began contributing ideas to the novel-in-progress. This was unacceptable. In September 1962, Rhys sheepishly admitted to Francis Wyndham that her latest handwritten submissions were the result of a row after the well-meaning Browns had started "suggesting this and that—I just ran away (*as usual!*)."[13]

The winter of 1962/63 proved to be one of the coldest on record; trapped in a small, cold house with thin walls, the Hamers quarrelled furiously. Early in April, Max's doctor despatched his patient to a quiet clinic on the south Devon coast. "Whatever you call me I love you and only you and always shall," a forlorn Max wrote in the only note to his wife which she chose to preserve.[14]

Jean Rhys, throughout that harsh winter and bitter spring, continued recklessly popping red pills, washed down with whisky while she tried to combine work on her novel with a long first draft of the autobiographical "Leaving School" for the *London Magazine*. Writing belatedly to thank Eliot Bliss for her welcome Christmas gift of cash, Rhys admitted that she had come "damn near a complete crack up for the first time in my life."[15] One unfortunate outcome of that "crack up" seems to have been that Rhys—having renewed the connection—finally lost the services of her friendly typist.

No clear account exists of what went wrong with the convenient arrangement that Alwynne Woodard had set up with Katherine Brown. Writing to Diana Athill in May 1963, Rhys began by suggesting that Morris Brown had been shocked by overhearing her dictate Mr. Rochester's seduction of his wife's maid (described to Athill as "that very tame affair with the coloured girl.") Less disingenuously, she admitted that Katherine Brown's husband had annoyed *her* by his habit of walking in and interrupting her attempts to dictate. Angry words were apparently exchanged. Brown nobly agreed to banish both Christ and himself to a remote garden shed, but the initial warmth had gone. When Rhys attempted to renew the arrangement with Pond Cottage towards the end of May, she was fobbed off by the Browns with weak excuses.[16]

Given the circumstances, Francis Wyndham must have been astonished to receive at last and without warning what he described to Diana Athill on 4 May 1963 as "the makings of an extraordinary book."[17] The "makings": Athill, while sharing her former colleague's delight in the exceptional quality of the novel's opening section (Mrs. Brown had typed out the chapters leading up to Antoinette's marriage), agreed with Francis that the rest (the long honeymoon section set on an unnamed Dominica had not yet been written) remained unresolved. Publication, despite André Deutsch's own unconcealed impatience— following six years of Rhys's unfulfilled promises—would have to wait.

Max, sent home in May, suffered another stroke. Back once more at the Tiverton Hospital that June, her husband grew so thin and forlorn that Rhys, making one of her weekly visits, burst into tears. "How could the nurses be so inhuman?" she stormed to Selma Vaz Dias on 24 June; why wouldn't they let the poor man smoke in bed? It comforted her to learn that life-enhancing, exuberant Selma and Alec Hamer— anxious to see his brother again after Rhys's alarming reports about Max's failing health—aimed to visit Cheriton together at the start of July. Diana Athill had meanwhile contrived a temporary typing solution: her younger colleague, Esther Whitby, had volunteered to go to Cheriton in late July, in order to work with Rhys on her latest revisions. Conscious of her author's drinking habits, Diana Athill thoughtfully supplied Esther with an escape from unwelcome pressure; Mrs. Whitby, Athill imaginatively explained in advance, was suffering from a temporary allergy to alcohol.

Selma and Alec suffered from no such constraint; to Rhys, their visit from 3–5 July 1963 was an unqualified delight. Her guests—they stayed at the Ring of Bells, the prettier of Cheriton's two inns—seemed to enjoy each other's company as much as they took pleasure in hers, although Alec, finally visiting the hospital in Tiverton, was appalled by his brother's decline. Rather than discussing progress on her current novel, as Rhys had dreaded, Selma wanted only to talk about her persistent hope of adapting, for a multi-voiced broadcast on the BBC, *Voyage in the Dark*.*

Intent upon making *Voyage* sound authentic, Selma had brought along Clifton Parker, a suave and well-regarded composer for whom she wanted Rhys to sing the old Kwéyòl songs that flicker through Anna Morgan's memory in the novel.

Mr. Parker put his considerable charm to good use during his visit to Rhys's home. The tape recording that he made at Cheriton survives in the Rhys collection held at the McFarlin Library in Tulsa. Eerily and sweetly, a light and lilting voice quavers out into the dusty air, hesitates, then starts again. "It's not quite right," Rhys says. Her voice sounds plaintive; evidently, she's on the verge of tears. Parker's voice speaks gently, reassuring the singer about how well she's doing. "You got every word absolutely right, except *bon dieu*," Selma's richer voice chimes in. "I know," says Jean. "I know." Comforted, she begins to sing: "*My belle ka di* . . . no, that's not right." Silence falls. The tape whirrs, crackling. Unexpectedly, the tremulous voice gathers new strength, before Rhys changes her tone and bursts into a rollicking ditty; the words tell the story of a bad, greedy woman from Grenada who's being told to take her gold earrings, pack her bags and go home. "*Doggee doggee go bone*"

---

* It's possible that Selma had been influenced by hearing the multi-voiced performance of *Good Morning, Midnight* on Radio Bremen in 1958.

runs the chorus and, halfway through it, Rhys bursts into giggles. "I don't know . . . something like that . . ." She pauses with a question in her voice, hesitating, waiting for the approval that will surely come, like a child.

But she's *performing*, I suddenly realise; she's an actress, performing for an actress. And, sitting quite alone in the University of Tulsa's dimly lit McFarlin Library, in the late afternoon, listening to the soft and charming voice of a seventy-two-year-old woman who is also—very definitely—conscious of a flattering masculine presence in the room, I find myself smiling in delighted recognition. "A siren" was how Francis Wyndham once described Jean Rhys; just for a moment, I understand exactly what he meant.[18]

———————

THE SUCCESS OF Selma Vaz Dias's visit to a friend she hadn't seen for six years had much to do with the fact that—following three years of a shrinking stage career, illness and a period of depression treated by therapy and heavy medication—the actress appeared to be restored to her impulsive and charming best. Giddy with relief that she was not to be persecuted about her unfinished novel and well plied with whisky, Rhys thought nothing of signing a scrap of handwritten paper which assigned to her friend 50 per cent of any future payments for the use of Rhys's work, together with the right to exert complete artistic control.

The financial division was unusual only in extending beyond Selma's personal involvement;* far rarer was the case of a writer handing over artistic control to a single person. At the time, in a blur of drink and euphoria, it all seemed to make perfect sense. In 1963, Rhys's own name was still only known to an elite group of admirers; armed with her hastily scrawled signature, and still at ease in a world to which

———

* In 1957, for example, Peggy Ramsay drew up what was then regarded as a standard contract, dividing 50 per cent of the rights to Tito Strozzi's *Play for Two* between Strozzi's translator, Smylka Perovic, and the adapter, Selma Vaz Dias, who became one of Peggy's first clients (private collection).

Rhys's own connections were limited, Selma promised to become a zealous promotor of her less celebrated friend's work.

And so—for a short time—Vaz Dias proved to be. Immediately after her return from Devon, an elated Selma began talks with the BBC about her ongoing adaptation of *Voyage*, while warning a naive Rhys not to go signing agreements with anyone until a suitable literary agent had been located by her truest friend. Finding one didn't take long; within a fortnight of her Devon visit, Selma had persuaded John Smith of the well-regarded Christy & Moore agency—their clients included Georgette Heyer and George Orwell—to visit Rhys at Cheriton. A letter written by Smith on his return to London advised Selma to expect a percentage from the forthcoming publication in a Hungarian magazine of "Let Them Call It Jazz"; Rhys's new agent evidently foresaw no difficulties with the financial division that had been—however informally—agreed between a pair of friendly ladies.

Shortly after Selma's visit, her blithely announced decision to mould together two of *Voyage*'s most dissimilar characters caused Rhys to regret that impulsive relinquishing of her own right to artistic control. If Selma failed to distinguish between "Laurie"—a tough call girl whom Rhys, in 1963, compared to Mandy Rice-Davies, a star witness in the trial of Stephen Ward—and "Maudie," a soft-hearted chorus girl aspiring to a quietly respectable marriage, what might she not do to destroy poor, half-formed Antoinette? Rhys's pleas on behalf of Laurie and Maudie were ignored; so were the comparisons of herself to an anxious mother cat trying to protect her kittens with which Rhys resisted sending any part of the unfinished novel to her persistent friend. Rhys underrated Selma's determination. "Mrs Rochester" was *their* baby, in Selma's view, and Vaz Dias was determined to have her share in that precious infant's future.

Selma had already left Devon when—following Rhys's insistence—a greatly weakened Max Hamer arrived home from the Tiverton clinic on 11 July. "I do not forsake people," Rhys wrote the following day to the daughter she had so often abandoned in orphanages. To Diana Athill she wrote that it was impossible to leave Max in a place where he was so unhappy: "Besides I miss him."[19] Nevertheless, and not only for her own sake, Rhys returned Max to the Belmont clinic for a few days at the beginning of August. She was about to be visited by Esther Whitby, an unknown editor from André Deutsch. Max, a proud man, would hate to be identified by a stranger as a mere bedridden invalid.

The morning after Mrs. Whitby's arrival—the Woodards had offered to lodge Esther at the rectory—the vicar drove his guest up the narrow lane to Landboat Farm.

Almost sixty years later, Esther remembers her sense of shock that such a frail old lady could endure such a home: "the wretched little back-to-front bungalow was entirely charmless." The visitor's first day was spent in creating a working copy out of the litter of unnumbered pages that lay in scattered heaps around and about Jean Rhys's chair. The second and third days were given over entirely to taking dictation as Rhys read in a tiny voice from the illegibly scrawled (and over-scrawled) pages of manuscript. The intensity of Rhys's quest for the perfect phrase was no less remarkable, in Esther's view, than the obstinacy with which the author refused to relinquish a single page.[20]

Back in London, Mrs. Whitby was eagerly interrogated. Selma Vaz Dias, invited to lunch with Diana Athill and Francis Wyndham shortly before her own summer visit to Cheriton, had represented Jean Rhys as a tall, thin, gothic-looking woman. (Selma's bizarre account was almost unchanged from the one she had written for the *Radio Times* back in 1957.) Their faith in Selma's veracity waned after Esther described a small, pale, white-haired and neatly dressed lady who cried often and lunched—if at all—on chocolates. Pressed further by Diana about Rhys's eating habits, Mrs. Whitby thought she remembered having seen an unwashed egg cup by the sink. Their intriguing author apparently drank very little; she had not at any time—as Esther took care to stress—been drunk.[21]

Esther Whitby's industry paid off; a month after her visit, a provisionally complete version of Part One of the tripartite "Wide Sargasso Sea" reached London. Rhys herself, however, was entering a period of acute paranoia.

The summer of 1963 was the first time that Rhys had been exposed to long periods of isolation while living within a watchful village since her unhappy wartime months at West Beckham. Writing to Selma on 6 September, she expressed her fervent longing for Max to return from hospital and help stave off "this terrible anxiety and loneliness." As at West Beckham, it seemed that everything and everyone was against her: she felt convinced that she was "hated."[22] Maryvonne, urgently summoned from Holland, found her mother tearing up pages of manuscript and constructing barriers against invisible rodents (a detail put to good use later in Rhys's portrait of lonely Miss Verney in "Sleep It Off Lady"). Edward, seeking a medical opinion, was advised that his sister was not insane, but in need of a rest-cure. Rhys agreed. "*Je suis cassé*" [*sic*] (I'm worn out) she informed Francis. A rest was all that was required.[23]

Francis Wyndham did his best to help stave off the encroaching darkness. Accompanying his generous personal gift of a cheque for £100 (£2,100 today), intended to pay for a fortnight at a rest home, he produced what should have been a delightful piece of news. *Art and Literature*, a new international cultural magazine, was funded by Anne Dunn, the wealthy friend who had first introduced Wyndham to Rhys's work. Now, Dunn and her editorial colleagues (John Ashbery, Rodrigo Moynihan and Sonia Orwell) were requesting something by Rhys for their first issue (March 1964). Francis's suggestion that they should publish the opening section of "Wide Sargasso Sea," together with an introduction written by himself to Rhys's work, was received by the magazine's board with delight.[24]

Rhys's reaction was disappointing. Ignoring the purpose of Wyndham's cheque, she set it aside as a future gift for her hard-up and overworked daughter, out in Holland. The idea of a magazine's publishing what she herself considered to be unfinished work goaded Rhys to a whole new level of hysteria. Innumerable revisions must immediately be made—but how? Should she attempt to continue working amidst the scandal and hatred that she firmly believed now surrounded her in Cheriton? Should she abandon Max (still in hospital) and accept Selma's tempting offer of a quiet workroom at her comfortable Hampstead home? How (crescendo) should she find the *time!*

Haunted by worries about invading vermin, scandal-spreading neighbours, extensive revisions and the need to be on hand for poor Max, Rhys dithered. "We long to receive you into the bosom of our family," Selma cooed soothingly from her London home on 21 November; five days later, however, she rashly instructed Rhys to bring with her the long-awaited extract from "Mrs Rochester." Alarmed, Rhys backed off, pleading that she could only work at home; besides: "*I am ill.*"[25]

A well-meant invitation soon developed into a battle royal; in the early spring of 1964, the projected visit to Hampstead was still being discussed when Selma abruptly accused her friend of betrayed promises, while an aggrieved Jean pointed out that her suitcase had been packed for the journey to London since before Christmas. The fault was not of her making, Rhys concluded in a tone that brooked no dispute: "the only definite dates *were cancelled. By you. By wire.*"[26] The sense of injustice was angry and mutual; silence descended between the two women for the next nine months.

Always meticulous, Rhys was still frantically correcting Part One of her novel and firing off entreaties for more time when John Ashbery wrote to explain that her latest list of changes had missed the new magazine's deadline. The extract (edited by Sonia Orwell) was published in the March edition of *Art & Literature*; while it is close to the final version of *Wide Sargasso Sea*, Rhys had yet to introduce several key episodes, including the visit subsequently paid by Antoinette to her imprisoned and deranged mother. Wyndham's accompanying introduction made mention of Ford Madox Ford's admiration for Rhys's style, while Francis himself drew attention to the fact that "the elegant surface and the paranoid content, the brutal honesty of the feminine psychology and the muted nostalgia for lost beauty, all create an effect which is peculiarly modern."[27]

The ground had been prepared: all that was necessary now was for

Rhys to complete her novel. Jean's valiant effort to meet that challenge was impeded by a despair that neither pills nor whisky could assuage. Max had spent the Christmas of 1963 in hospital; alone once more, his wife's sense of being trapped within a hostile and judgemental community escalated into hysteria. Off in London, both Francis and Diana were besieged by wild, voluminous letters, a bombardment that they struggled to answer and did not always even bother to keep.

Once again, the understanding Alwynne Woodard came to the rescue. Early in March 1964, a distraught Rhys was carried off to the rectory and encouraged—to the considerable irritation of Woodard's wife—to treat it as she would a hotel. As at the kindly Willis Feast's Norfolk rectory, meals were left outside a cherished guest's door; Rhys's time was all her own. After dinner, escorted to Woodard's study and snugly installed beside a crackling fire, Rhys talked about her novel. She had been missing male company; warmed by the vicar's understanding manner and encouraged by his intelligent interest in her progress, she blossomed.

Diana Athill had already made the suggestion that Rhys should create a period of happiness for Rochester and Antoinette before an estrangement which, in the novel's original version, had struck both Wyndham and Athill as too abrupt to carry conviction. Talking the novel through with Woodard, Rhys came to appreciate the shrewdness of Athill's observation. Part Two, rewritten in Rochester's voice and showing that he was initially consumed with passion—but never love—for his beautiful young bride, was first worked out during these pleasant evenings at the rectory. By the end of March, Rhys felt cheerful enough to satirise her slow progress to an anxious Francis by borrowing an apt line from Oscar Wilde's best-known play. "I never knew anybody take so long to dress," Algy twits his friend Ernest, "and with so little result." (Rhys was by then aware that Francis's grandmother, Ada Leverson, had been the playwright's beloved "Sphinx.")[28]

That April, back at the bungalow, Rhys sat up all night, every night, either at the kitchen table or huddled in bed, navigating her way through the "wild sea of wrecks" that had floated into her mind in the form of the latest and most powerful of her spontaneous poems. Writing "Obeah Night"—so Rhys disclosed to Francis Wyndham on 14 April 1964, in a letter containing that long, remarkable work in full—had finally enabled her to look through the eyes of Rochester at his bride, the young woman whose mind forever flutters, like Rhys's own, on the dark brink of madness.

Narrated by the man Rhys still called both "Rochester" and "Raworth," "Obeah Night" is the self-aware poem in which Antoinette's husband justifies his own cruel plan to lock his white Creole bride away, after her suspected transformation into a zombie. (*"Did* you come back I wonder," Rochester asks himself after his anxious young wife visits her old nurse, Christophine, in order to obtain a love potion: "Did I ever see you again?")[29]

Later, Rhys would shift the cause of Rochester's altered view of his wife onto the stories he is told by Antoinette's malevolent older cousin. It's from the embittered Daniel Cosway that he first hears tales of rumoured madness in Antoinette's family;* tales, even, of her affair with an islander: "a *terrible* thing for a white girl to do" in those times, as Rhys explained to Francis Wyndham in that same impassioned letter of 14 April. "Not to be forgiven."[30]

By April, Rhys was living entirely within the world of her novel; the present-day world entered her letters rarely, when she grumbled at hearing dustbins being emptied outside. Weeds grew up over the windowsills. A kitchen chair was propped under the inside handle to the front door to keep well-meaning neighbours out. Max Hamer lay mute and unvisited inside the hospital that he would never again leave. His wife couldn't bear even to take time off to buy herself food. She simply could not stop.

All the signs of another approaching crack-up are apparent in Rhys's letters, as both Wyndham and Athill must surely have seen with dismay. "Yes I need a holiday," she admitted to Francis in her long, wild

---

* Rhys never forgot having heard such tales in her own family. It was said that one of her mother's aunts had been "insane."

letter of 14 April; "all this *write write write all night* and food such a bore," she told Athill two weeks later. "Not so-o good."[31]

Even under pressure, Rhys could prove surprisingly efficient where work was concerned. When Diana announced that she had found a competent typist in London, Rhys laid down the law, insisting that Mrs. Kloegman must always submit three copies, ready to be marked up with her own ongoing (and seemingly, never-ending) revisions. Advised that Deutsch intended to republish two of her novels, she somehow managed to complete a light edit of both *Voyage in the Dark* and *Good Morning, Midnight* within a single week.[*]

Such moments of clarity were becoming rare and Rhys knew it. On 15 July 1964, she told Francis about having been "in a very blue mood lately," with "awful pits of despair."[32] A few days later, she attacked one of her Landboat neighbours. Difficult though it is to imagine a small woman in her mid-seventies endangering anyone's life, Rhys's behaviour seemed crazy enough to raise the alarm. Edward was summoned for an urgent discussion by a concerned Alwynne Woodard. By the middle of July, acting on professional medical advice, Edward had reluctantly consigned his sister to the Belvedere clinic (formerly Ward 12) at the Exminster branch of the Exe Vale Hospital, still better known by its old name as the Devon County Lunatic Asylum. The decision had been "sad but inevitable," Edward wrote to a dismayed Diana Athill. At this dark stage, he could not predict whether his sister would ever resume work on her novel. "But let's hope . . ."[33]

---

[*] Deutsch's sudden interest in republishing the earlier novels before the appearance of *Wide Sargasso Sea* was prompted by Alan Ross's interest in doing just that himself (possibly at the suggestion of Francis Wyndham, who was eager to build awareness of Rhys). When Ross dropped the project, so—until the publication of *Wide Sargasso Sea* had secured a market for their client's work—did André Deutsch.

18

An End and a Beginning
(1964–66)

"Disaster seems to be so much her element."

—Diana Athill to Alec Hamer, 3 March 1966[1]

RHYS'S CAPACITY TO endure hardship, ill health and mental breakdowns was remarkable and would remain so until the end of her life. On 28 July 1964, the same day that her brother wrote despairingly to Diana Athill about the remote chances of the novel ever being completed, Rhys wrote to her daughter from the Exe Vale Hospital to announce that, despite having felt "rather rotten for some time," she was now on the mend.

Gruesome stories about Britain's recently nationalised asylums in the 1960s aren't hard to find, but Rhys was not insane and—as earlier at Holloway prison's psychiatric wing—she was treated reasonably well. By 2 September, defying medical advice to convalesce, Rhys was back at her bungalow and hatching plans to travel to London. No mention was made of staying with Selma Vaz Dias after their falling-out; instead, a Kensington hotel was booked by Diana Athill, who also made plans for a celebratory lunch with her author. Determined to keep the visit short, Rhys left Cheriton accompanied only by a small suitcase and her latest revisions to the efficient Mrs. Kloegman's typescript.

The day after Rhys's arrival in London, she had a heart attack. Giving Diana the bad news, the hotel in Kensington reported that Rhys had almost died. She spent the next month in a west London hospital; visitors included her cousin Lily Lockhart, a worried Maryvonne, and Esther Whitby, who had not forgotten the stubborn old lady she'd met in Devon. Selma, anxious to make legal her informal agreement with Rhys, gained only a whispered apology from a patient who felt "too rotten" for a business discussion.[2] Visiting the hospital on that same day, Diana Athill later claimed that she heard Vaz Dias describe their mutual friend as a former prostitute. While it's reasonable to suppose that Rhys had occasionally accepted cash for favours when she was hard-up, would a singularly broad-minded woman really have described her stricken friend in such a way? Might Selma merely have suggested a link between Rhys and vulnerable, desperate Anna Morgan at a time when she herself was adapting *Voyage* for radio? Whatever was actually said, it gave Rhys's forceful editor a reason to turn against Vaz Dias for good.[3]

Rhys's condition was serious—she would require heart medication for the rest of her life—and the process of recovery was slow. Writing to Diana Athill from a pleasant nursing home at Caterham in Surrey towards the end of the year, Rhys mentioned a bundle of corrected pages for Part Two (the honeymoon section which is set on Dominica) that had been left behind at the bungalow. Fearing that the long-awaited novel might never reach completion, Athill asked Edward Rees Williams to collect whatever he could find and bring it to London for her to edit. Presented by him with a jumbled bagful of indecipherable pages (Rhys took an almost wilful pride in the fact that nobody but herself could read her drafts), Miss Athill conceded defeat. The bag of papers was silently returned to Cheriton after Edward's visit to his sister's sickbed. Rhys was never told.[4]

By the end of January 1965, Rhys was installed at the Caroline Nursing Home in Exmouth, a seaside town within easy reach of her brother's home at Budleigh Salterton. Complaining to Maryvonne on 25 February about Edward's thoughtlessness at expecting her to share a room with two strangers (economy had played its part), Rhys sounded what would become a wearyingly familiar note. How much she would have preferred to pay a loyal daughter to become her mother's nurse! Surely Job Moerman could spare his wife in a time of such maternal need?

Rhys had not lost her wits, but her health remained precarious. John Smith, the agent found for her by Vaz Dias, felt uneasy when a commanding Selma instructed him to prepare a formal written contract between herself and his elderly, ailing client. Cautioned by Smith against signing anything she did not entirely understand, Rhys nevertheless readily put her signature to what now became a legal agreement. Rhys was no businesswoman; she never saw anything wrong with rewarding her friend's endeavours. Only on the subject of "Wide Sargasso Sea," as the novel was now known to all but a stubborn Selma (still clinging to the abandoned title "Mrs Rochester"), did she remain inflexible. Nothing—not a page, not a word—was to be sent to Miss Vaz Dias until the work was complete, and until she herself had authorised the action.

By March 1965, Rhys had returned to Cheriton. Her neighbours were kind. Forthright Mrs. Raymond carried her letters to the post; Mrs. Stettiford and Mrs. Greenslade took turns to cook Rhys's lunches; bunches of spring flowers were left by well-wishers at the bungalow door. If she felt strong enough, Alan Greenslade was always ready with his taxi to drive her over to Tiverton, where Max still lay, unspeaking, scarcely conscious of his grim surroundings. His wife's dutiful visits to the hospital became increasingly rare.

Low in spirits and struggling to continue work on the novel, Rhys received news from an unexpectedly ebullient Selma. While it did not surprise her to learn that the actress's adaptation of *Voyage* had been rejected by the BBC (Rhys herself had never been able to see the novel as a radio play), Jean was delighted to hear that her friend's waning stage career had received an unexpected boost. A controversial new tragi-comedy called *The Killing of Sister George* was due to go on an extensive try-out tour before opening in London. Beryl Reid and

Eileen Atkins were to play the leads as a bizarrely dissimilar same-sex couple: Selma Vaz Dias was cast as their neighbour Madame Xenia, a comic clairvoyant. The role was just what she wanted; life was on the up!

In the summer of 1965, the two old friends were independently pulled into terrible downward spirals. While Selma was enduring the considerable humiliation of appearing, night after night, in what felt to *Sister George*'s beleaguered cast like a doomed production (Frank Marcus's treatment of butch lesbianism, however entertaining, did not go down well in the provinces), Rhys's spirits also plunged, and for reasons she could not explain. Terrified of being returned to the asylum, she retreated into silence. It would take almost a year for her to feel able to refer to "the perfectly awful time between March and October last year." It had been an experience, she would confide in 1966 to a sympathetic Olwyn Hughes, which "I wouldn't live again for millions."[5]

Almost no evidence survives of that long, black summer in Devon. Edward, himself nursing a dying wife, was possibly unaware; concerned letters to Rhys from Diana and Francis were left unanswered. A hint of the depth of Rhys's unhappiness finally emerged in a frantic August appeal to Maryvonne (*"please* if you can come") from a mother who admitted that she had become too sad even to write. That in itself, Rhys wrote, was perhaps the worst part of what had befallen her.[6]

Maryvonne became her mother's sole confidante during an interval of darkness which Rhys described to her daughter on 15 September as like living in a nightmare. By October, somebody had persuaded Rhys to visit a doctor. Armed with new medication (no more scarlet pills), the seventy-five-year-old author struggled to pull herself together with a new regime of early nights and a pre-dawn start, fuelled by strong tea and a nourishing pack of cigarettes.

It helped. Gradually, Rhys became cheerful enough to start weaving fantasies about an entrepreneurial new career for her deft-fingered daughter: why should Maryvonne not make the fortune she lacked (the unfortunate Moermans had remained penniless ever since their return from Indonesia) by opening her own Quant-style boutique! Rhys was only half joking when she put in an early request to be made her own special dress, a very last one, pretty as the ones in Vienna that she had once so adored. Rhys had always believed that beautiful clothes brought her good luck: might the solace of a new outfit restore her will to write? Inspired, she summoned the obliging Alan Greenslade to take her on a clothes shopping visit to Exeter, where she invested in a smartly fashionable trouser suit.[7]

Superstition; a new outfit; different pills: whatever achieved it, the spell had been broken. By 15 November, a relieved Diana Athill was in receipt of a fresh batch of revisions and inserts. Responding, she complimented Rhys on being a "perfect" writer. Athill's admiration had grown all the more heartfelt for witnessing the struggle Jean Rhys had

Diana Athill at her last home in Highgate, two years before her death. The smile and bright clothes marked the point at which she had decided I was worth her time. *(Author picture)*

endured to complete a novel that would ultimately contain no more
evidence of effort than the glitter of light on dark water:

> "Do you think that too," she said, "that I have slept too long in
> the moonlight"?
>
> Her mouth was set in a fixed smile but her eyes were so with-
> drawn and lonely that I put my arms round her, rocked her like a
> child and sang to her. An old song I thought I had forgotten:
>
> > *Hail to the queen of the silent night,*
> > *Shine, shine bright Robin as you die.*
>
> She listened, then sang with me:
>
> > *Shine, shine bright Robin as you die.*[8]

"I SPY A STRANGER," one of Rhys's most troubling and brilliant stories
about madness, was published for the first time by *Art & Literature* in
January 1966: its warm reception heralded what promised to become
a remarkable year. Writing to Francis Wyndham for the first time in
several months, Rhys (still unaware of her friend's role as a literary
adviser to the magazine's board) proudly passed along the joyful news
that the magazine had purchased three more of her stories from the
1940s: "The Sound of the River," "The Lotus" and "Temps Perdi."
Rhys's happiness was increased by the fact that *Art & Literature* paid
unusually generous fees.[9]

Signs were emerging that the hard work put in by both Francis
Wyndham and Diana Athill to raise awareness of Rhys's writing was
paying off. Back in the 1960s, the publishing world remained small
and clubbable; while Francis plotted with the kind and well-connected
Sonia Orwell at *Art & Literature*, Athill made use of the same social
network to ensure that Rhys would be in line for prizes and awards. It
was she who approached the widely loved publisher Jamie Hamilton,

an influential figure who had known Rhys ever since the publication of *Quartet*. Horrified to learn of the financial difficulties amidst which the elderly writer was apparently producing a masterpiece, Hamilton immediately agreed to act as her sponsor. The result, as Diana happily announced to Rhys on 15 February 1966, was that she could now rely upon receiving an annual payment of £300 (worth only a little under £5,000 today) from the Royal Literary Fund.

Grateful though she was (Jean wrote an appreciative note to Hamilton, following an affectionate letter from Leslie Tilden Smith's former employer), Rhys was too engaged in the last stages of revision to pay much attention to events outside the novel. Diana, like Francis, would often be consulted about the best way to tell Antoinette's unhappy story. Rhys herself took the decision, at this late stage, to rip up a scene describing the Thornfield house party. In Brontë's novel, the house party takes place while Bertha Mason is locked away in the attic; for Rhys, writing from Antoinette's perspective, it was not only a distraction, but unsuited to her own and discrete version of Mr. Rochester. Out it must go, reduced to Antoinette's incurious awareness of "strange people in the house . . . laughing and talking in the distance, like birds . . . "[10] The novel was almost done; just a few more days were needed . . .

However deeply immersed in her work Rhys was, she must have been growing aware that the literary world had started to wake up to her existence. Olwyn Hughes, without mentioning that she was the sister of the reclusive widowed poet who lived near Rhys in Devon, had driven down to Cheriton towards the close of 1965, in order to present herself as an agent with excellent connections at the BBC. Selma Vaz Dias had achieved nothing in this particular line since her own visit to Devon in 1963; Rhys, blithely disregarding her previous agreement with Selma, instantly offered Hughes the right to represent both her short stories and her first two novels. Meanwhile, Arthur Mizener, the future biographer of Ford Madox Ford, declared his willingness to help get Rhys's early novels republished in America. Gathering that an elated Jean now seemed to have acquired no fewer than four agents

(Selma Vaz Dias, John Smith, Olwyn Hughes and now Mizener), Francis Wyndham prudently forbore to comment. Rhys, as he had learned, never listened when her spirits were high.

Trouble emerged, not from mild-mannered John Smith, but from the intervention of an unexpectedly furious Selma at what she perceived as an encroachment by Olwyn Hughes on her own legitimate right to represent Rhys to the BBC. True, there had been a signed agreement, but it had led to nothing, Rhys reassured a puzzled Miss Hughes on 25 February; a little guiltily, she added that poor Selma wasn't well. What about a compromise arrangement, one by which Selma could be given first reading rights of any stories that Olwyn could place with the BBC? And, of course, she must have a share of any payments. "I will write to Selma tomorrow," Rhys promised, confident that she could dispel her old friend's rage.

The anger with which Vaz Dias greeted Rhys's proposed defection to Olwyn resulted in part from her own misfortunes. Resoundingly booed from Bristol to Hull and beyond in *The Killing of Sister George*, Eileen Atkins and Beryl Reid gamely stuck by Marcus's play until— during its early London run-up—a carefully selected gay audience finally got the joke. A deadly provincial flop was transformed into one of the hottest tickets in town (and, eventually, a long-running hit). But Selma had been unable to cope with the strain of being jeered at, night after night. By the time the play crawled into London, another actress was playing Madame Xenia. *Sister George* would become a milestone in the ascent of Reid and Atkins; for Selma Vaz Dias, it marked a bitter ending to a prestigious stage career. Apart from a new interest in painting, leading to several well-received exhibitions in Paris and London, Selma now had little left to boast about, other than her starring role as the first discoverer and proud representative of Jean Rhys.

Answering Rhys's hopeful request that Selma should cede her agent's role to the younger and more experienced Olwyn Hughes, Vaz Dias coldly reminded her friend of the legal status of their own agreement. A second pleading letter from Devon went unanswered. In Selma's view, the matter was closed. She was not to be replaced.

Selma's silence coincided with ominous news of Max. On 3 March, a distraught Rhys wrote once more, begging Selma to make peace with Olwyn and relating the Tiverton hospital's warning that Mr. Hamer could die at any moment. "I keep a tight hold of myself," she added pleadingly, "or I'd crack [up] completely—again."[11]

Alec Hamer and Maryvonne reached Cheriton in time to be with Rhys on 7 March, the date on which Max Hamer, a shrivelled ghost of his former sturdy self, died. The cremation—a large number of bouquets testified to Max's popularity in the village—took place at Exeter two days later. The east wind felt sharp as a knife. Back at her kitchen table later that same day, Rhys wrote to Diana Athill. The novel was finished. A dream had revealed it to her as a baby, puny, but safely delivered and lying in its cradle. Rhys's work was done: now, "I don't dream about it any more."[12]

Athill, visiting the bungalow at the end of March to make note of any final revisions before she herself carried the pages back to London, was astonished by Rhys's calmness. Later, back at her cousin Barbara Smith's home in Primrose Hill, where Diana shared a top-floor free flat with the Jamaican playwright Barry Reckord, Athill read "Wide Sargasso Sea" once again. Later still on that same night, she wrote to praise its author as "a rare and splendid creator." She meant it. Talking to me in the last year of her life, Athill emphatically described Jean Rhys as the only "genius" she had ever known. I asked about V. S. Naipaul, another author she felt proud to have helped. Athill paused to consider before granting that "Vidya" was indeed "a bit of a genius. But not the *real* thing. Not like Jean."[13]

And what was Jean's reaction to Max's death? Did his widow grieve? Writing to Diana shortly after the funeral, Rhys admitted only that she was finding it hard to believe that he was gone. She mourned him in her own way and on her own terms. It was during the bleak early spring of 1966 that, according to the Cheriton gossip tree, a few small boys gathered to laugh and throw stones at the little old lady whom they saw standing in the road outside Landboat Bungalows with a row of medals pinned across her chest. "Wings up! Wings up!" she shouted at the sky, before she shuffled out of view behind the high green hedge that screened her home from public view.

Fact or myth? It's a strange story. Why would Rhys shout "Wings up," when Max had served in the navy? Leslie had been a pilot in his youth. Jean Lenglet had helped the fliers of wartime planes to escape the Nazis. Had she conflated three lost husbands in a confused moment? Was she troubled by the giggling children, or even by the handful of stones they flung at her? Possibly. Possibly not. What mattered, seemingly, was the offering of a personal homage to Max Hamer, a man who, for all his faults, had never ceased passionately to love his wife.[*]

---

[*] Rhys herself related this curious incident several years later to her friend David Plante, who included it in the account of his own relationship with the elderly writer which he published in *Difficult Women* (Gollancz, 1983).

VII

UNWELCOME FAME

19

No Orchids for Miss Rhys[*] (1966–69)

"I've always hated personal publicity (Why necessary?). Only the writing matters."

—Jean Rhys to Francis Wyndham, 21 July 1960[1]

"BLOODY BUT UNBOWED," was how Alec Hamer described his sister-in-law to Diana Athill shortly after Max's death in March 1966.[2] Nevertheless, the shock had hit Max's seventy-five-year-old widow hard. Only a miracle could save her now, Rhys informed a still irate Selma Vaz Dias on 18 March; to Maryvonne, who returned to Holland shortly after the funeral, she made a more direct appeal. "I am very lonely . . . perhaps you will be the miracle that will bring me to life."[3]

Valiantly, given her economic circumstances, Maryvonne made three separate visits to England that year. Unable to commit herself to becoming her mother's carer, as Rhys wished, Maryvonne thought

---

[*] The McFarlin archive contains an undated draft letter Rhys wrote in response to an essay George Orwell published in *Horizon*, October 1944. "The Ethics of the Detective Story from Raffles to Miss Blandish" praised James Hadley Chase's gruesomely brilliant novel of 1939, *No Orchids for Miss Blandish*, while describing the extreme violence of its imagined world as the "distillation" of a fascist society in which monstrous deeds, if boldly executed, become the norm. (Jean Rhys to George Orwell, McFarlin, 1.1.f3.)

that books might help to assuage sadness, especially since the travelling library van had stopped visiting Cheriton.

Maryvonne's initial choice, *A Moveable Feast*, failed to please a reader who deplored the self-serving nature of Hemingway's recollections of Paris; V. S. Naipaul's exquisite *A House for Mr Biswas*, sent along by Francis, was greeted with more enthusiasm. Mary McCarthy's *Memories of a Catholic Girlhood* (Athill's choice, after second thoughts about the suitability of Truman Capote's *In Cold Blood*) was pushed aside as Rhys gave thanks for the more welcome arrival of a £50 (£950 today) advance for *Wide Sargasso Sea*, with a further £200 to be paid on publication.

Athill had prudently reserved herself a room at the Ring of Bells inn when she visited Cheriton to gather up the completed "Sargasso" in March 1966. Entering Rhys's bungalow for the first time during that brief descent on Devon, she was shocked. Brought up at Ditchingham Hall in Norfolk—a secure world of nannies, ponies and family prayers—Athill found it impossible to imagine that a recently widowed woman in her early seventies (Jean had long since lopped several years off her true age) would wish to continue living alone in such circumstances. Rhys, always ready to condemn Cheriton to critical outsiders, initially welcomed well-organised Miss Athill's offer to find her a more congenial abode. No time was wasted; by May, Diana was negotiating with the administrators of a new housing development at Chingford, a quiet community on the fringes of Walthamstow in north-east London. Sonia Orwell and Francis Wyndham both approved the scheme, while Edward Rees Williams generously volunteered to cover the required £1,000 deposit (£18,750 today). It occurred to none of them, even though Rhys clearly dreaded the move, that she actually liked being a hermit. "I was never very fond of a mob," Jean admitted to her new confidante Sonia Orwell, in November 1966, adding that of late her attitude had grown more extreme: "I'm really afraid of most people."[4]

Conscious that the Royal Literary Fund's newly agreed annual payment of £300 would not go far in keeping Rhys from penury, the efficient Diana also managed to secure for her pet author the modest pension due to a naval serviceman's widow. Sixty pounds a year wasn't princely, but every penny mattered to a woman who was regularly going without meals in order to fund her weekly purchases from the village pubs. ("Whisky is now a must for me," Rhys informed her disapproving daughter on 4 July, and she meant it.)

Wide Sargasso Sea was to be published in October. From April onwards, Rhys's loyal support team united with Deutsch's ebullient new publicist, the Viennese-born Ilsa Yardley, to plot a campaign that would ensure maximum exposure both for the book and its reticent author. Francis Wyndham, from his influential perch as a commissioning editor of contemporary culture for the new colour supplement at the *Sunday Times*, arranged for Rhys to have her first post-publication interview with Hunter Davies, author of the newspaper's popular *Atticus* column. Sonia Orwell undertook to obtain coverage on "The Critics," the best-known radio review programme of its day. Advance copies were personally delivered by Sonia and Francis into the hands of all the literary opinion-makers whom they knew, together with duplicates of the prescient appraisal of Rhys's significance that Francis had published back in 1950 in *Tribune*. Recipients included Anthony Powell, Cyril Connolly, John Lehmann, Raymond Mortimer and Beatrix Miller, editor of English *Vogue* (and Francis's friend since his days at *Queen*). The word was spread that a remarkable author had seemingly returned from the dead, bringing with her a masterpiece; a work of genius; everything, in fact, was done to ensure that Rhys's name would reach every corner of London's intimate literary world well before the day of *Sargasso*'s publication. Small wonder, then, that Diana Athill told Sonia Orwell on 10 October that *Wide Sargasso Sea* would go "splendidly," or that Sonia shared Diana's optimism about their "well-laid plans."[5]

Selma Vaz Dias, as long promised, received an early proof copy from the publisher; on 30 July, John Smith independently sent an early copy to the formidable Peggy Ramsay, with news that the novel's author was due to become the centre of "a little cult."[6] It's unclear whether Smith was aware that Ramsay already represented Vaz Dias, who meanwhile hastened to send her own copy to the BBC, accompanied by her vision for "Mrs Rochester" as a radio play, starring Selma herself.

The BBC wasted no time in rejecting Selma's proposal. Salt was rubbed into her wounds by a report from Rhys that Olwyn Hughes's approach to *Woman's Hour* had proved more rewarding. A radio abridgement was to be commissioned, but not from Selma; the central role of Antoinette Cosway was to be played by Nicolette Bernard, a talented actress who had recently starred in an award-winning television production, *One Free Man*, with Oliver Reed. For Selma, the final straw was the news that Elizabeth Hart, a young film producer, wanted to option *After Leaving Mr Mackenzie*. Hart did not wish Selma either to write the screenplay or to play Julia Martin.

Pleading to Selma on 16 September that she needed "all the cash I can lay my hands on," while reminding her friend of the half-share in any profits that she would receive, Rhys's tone became nervously conciliatory.[7] Uselessly so; two months later, without consulting Rhys, Selma wrote to inform the disconcerted producer of *Woman's Hour* that she alone controlled all Rhys's dramatic rights. Nicolette Bernard was declared unworthy of the central role; enclosed with Selma's letter was her own taped reading for the part of "Bertha," the name that Vaz Dias still persisted in giving to Antoinette. An equally aggressive letter about the planned filming of *Mackenzie* was seemingly despatched to Elizabeth Hart.

Selma did not achieve her aim, but she did destroy Rhys's moment of opportunity. *Woman's Hour* hastily abandoned their project, while Elizabeth Hart withdrew her offer; John Smith, exhausted by the difficulty of dealing with an emotional Selma's demands, threatened to resign as Rhys's primary agent. Smith relented (Christy & Moore would still be representing Rhys well into the 1970s), but the future for Rhys's work, in any form other than print, did not appear bright.

Solace was on hand. *Wide Sargasso Sea* was to be launched with a conspiracy afoot to ensure that Rhys should enjoy her first taste of public success. Edward offered to pay first-class train fares to London for Rhys and Maryvonne, while Diana booked, for the duration of Rhys's London visit, a smart service flat in Belgravia. Twenty, Chesham Place (now the Hari Hotel) provided access to a pleasant restaurant and—

crucially—an excellent bar. Maryvonne, back in England for the third time since Max's death, passed along reassuring news of the lightened atmosphere at Rhys's bungalow. It was all quite marvellous, she relayed to Diana. Rhys was *so* happy, and Maryvonne herself was willing to do whatever was required of her in order to ensure that everything went smoothly, from running errands to—in rueful acknowledgment of Rhys's volatility—acting as her scapegoat.[8]

Rhys meanwhile busied herself with drawing up a list of the loyal friends whom she wished to receive finished copies of her novel. Gladys Raymond, the robust but goodhearted postmistress whom Rhys had attacked and whose boisterous young family were an ongoing source of complaint, ranked high on the list. Perhaps a proud novelist wanted a sceptical neighbour to know that she wasn't only drinking when she sat up late at night. It's more likely that Rhys's complaints about Mrs. Raymond to urban friends masked a grudging respect for one of the few women able to match Rhys—expletive for expletive—in bandying insults.

No record survives of what form the book launch took or what Rhys decided to wear—pink, lilac and pale blue were the colours she now felt suited her best—but it's certain that she prepared herself with fastidious care: clothes, like make-up and wigs, were increasingly deployed by Rhys as a protective uniform. The occasion was sufficiently crowded for Diana Athill to succeed in keeping a frustrated Selma at bay. Five days later, however, Vaz Dias made a lengthy journey from her new home in Golders Green for the express purpose of visiting Jean Rhys at Chesham Place. Rhys, holding court from her bed, struck her visitor as looking both "decorative and demure"; describing her impressions to Diana Athill, Selma added an ungrudging tribute to her old friend's astonishingly girlish complexion: "What a skin!"[9]

WIDE SARGASSO SEA has become the best known of Rhys's works. An immediate success is easy to assume, especially since an award led to its swift republication as a Book Club choice (adorned with the same crudely lush depiction of a bridal Antoinette imprisoned in a green jungle that André Deutsch had finally chosen—against Rhys's wishes—for the cover of their first edition*). Nevertheless, despite all the careful preparations, reviewers did not rush to embrace *Wide Sargasso Sea*. In the *Guardian*, Shusha Guppy's sensitive praises for "a mirror in which women can see their own inner selves" were undercut by her odd misreading of Antoinette's eventual fate as a consequence of her "predatory temperament." In the *Sunday Times*, Kay Dick dismissed the book as an awkward annotation of Brontë's novel: "only Jean Rhys's grip on tragedy saves *Wide Sargasso Sea* from melodrama." Alan Ross, accustomed to the harsher voice of Rhys's wartime stories, condescended to the book in *The London Magazine* as mere "romantic evocation." Nobody picked Rhys's novel for their Christmas Book of the Year. Instead, Margaret Drabble chose Maureen Duffy's *The Microcosm* (ahead of its day in its portrayal of life in a lesbian club), while Rebecca West opted for *The Journal of Beatrix Potter*. All perfectly nice, as Rhys ruefully reported to Eliot Bliss, but it seemed a shame that only one reviewer of the pack—Rhys didn't say which—had appeared to grasp what her novel was about. Whisky, meanwhile, provided more reliable good cheer than sniping critics—"and what the hell! It isn't what the doctor ordered."[10]

What was it that an evidently disappointed author thought the reviewers had missed?

Rhys's frequently declared intention had been to redress the injury done by Charlotte Brontë to the white Creole class of which Rhys herself was a member. But a prequel novel necessarily set in the years that followed the abolition of slavery had also forced Rhys to confront the question of her own family's complicity in that act of human enslave-

---

* Deutsch never returned the four cherished paintings of Geneva by Brenda Lockhart (Rhys's aunt), which Rhys had sent to Diana Athill for possible use on her novel's front cover. Rhys's frequent claims that the paintings had been stolen from her were dismissed by her friends as histrionics, but her aunt's watercolours were Rhys's very last family link to Dominica. The paintings formed part of Tom Rosenthal's sale of the André Deutsch archive to Tulsa between 1988 and 1994.

ment. Many of the stories upon which Rhys drew derived from her great-aunt Jane Woodcock's unreliable family memories, but the book's deep connection between Antoinette, a slave-owner's daughter brought up in Jamaica, and Rhys herself, whose Lockhart forebears had owned and trafficked slaves on Dominica, is never stated. The critics of 1966, unconscious of Rhys's family history and only vaguely aware of the small, remote island on which she was born, read her novel without subtlety. They saw it as a romantic and deeply felt reworking of an aspect of Brontë's greater work. Today, the richer underlying themes of *Wide Sargasso Sea* are more readily perceived when firmly anchored within the book's colonial context.

The novel's best secret lies in its use of historical names as almost soundless evocations of a hidden past. Rhys's quiet braiding into her narrative of the name of the dispossessed Bertrand family, first owners of Geneva and of Hampstead, seems to weave an imaginative union between "Bertrand" (the gentle "nameless boy" despised by Rochester) and Hampstead's carefully identified "Bertrand Bay" as the settlement from which the novel's Jamaican freed slaves emerge to punish their former owners. Grandbois, Rhys's name for Antoinette's honeymoon retreat on another island which is still patently Dominica, clearly references the old Kwéyòl name, "Gwan Bwa," for the inaccessible refuges of the maroons or escaped slaves, deep within Dominica's interior of mountains and rainforest. Locked away by a husband who scorns and seeks to banish her ("She was only a ghost. A ghost in the grey daylight"), Antoinette refuses to become another in that anonymous throng of nameless sufferers, that nearly inaudible incantation from the depths of the Great Forest.

Rhys devised subtle ways to suggest her family's complicity in slavery and colonial persecutions. "Now we are marooned," Antoinette's mother says, after her horse is poisoned, it would seem, by "the black people [who] stood about in groups to jeer at her, especially after her riding clothes grew shabby (they notice clothes, they know about money)."[11] The use of that word, "marooned," deliberately connects the Cosways to the slave community of maroons who, in Jamaica as in Dominica, fled for refuge to the island's interior. Maillotte Boyd's name—or so Rhys had implied in *Voyage in the Dark*—was picked from an authentic list of the house-slaves who had once worked for Rhys's promiscuous forebear. We learn from Antoinette that her malevolent cousin, Daniel Boyd, has adopted the name Cosway in order to goad the planter who became his mother's white lover;[12] the possibility lurks that Antoinette's closest childhood friend, Maillotte's daughter Tia, may be her own darker-skinned half-sister. When Tia tearfully throws a stone at Antoinette's face after the torching of Coulibri, the Cosways' home, she evokes the crime—the throwing of a stone that merely grazed the cheek of a plantation owner—for which a slave had been hanged in 1844. Alighting at Massacre for his island honeymoon, Rochester—his obtuseness is stressed throughout Rhys's novel—never bothers to discover that the little harbour's name records the slaughter by British and French troops of a hundred indigenous islanders in 1674. It's not by chance that Rhys bestows the name of her father's favourite small estate near Massacre on the "little half-caste servant" Amélie, whom Rochester casually beds in the thinly partitioned room next to that of his wife.[13] Significantly, only the English outsider, Rochester, refers to the girl as a "half-caste." His rape is not only of a vulnerable young girl, but of one of Rhys's favourite homes.

Antoinette herself appears to be less a portrait of the young Jean Rhys than a distilled incarnation of Rhys's intense memories of the fiercely beautiful island to which, in her imaginings, she forever sought to return. That should come as no surprise when we remember that Rhys, throughout the painful decade that she spent labouring over her final novel, was simultaneously writing and revising the handful of Dominica-related stories that would eventually be grouped together in *Sleep It Off Lady* (1976). "Heat"; "Pioneers, Oh, Pioneers"; "Fishy Waters"; "The Bishop's Feast"; "Goodbye Marcus, Goodbye Rose" and the haunting little ghost story, "I Used to Live Here Once": these were the fictional tales which helped Jean Rhys to confront and tame the enduring ghosts of her own past on an island in the East Caribbean.

HUNTER DAVIES, INTERVIEWING Rhys at Chesham Place for the *Sunday Times* in late October 1966, had been forewarned by Francis Wyndham that Jean Rhys was unusually reticent. Even so, ushered into the presence of a smartly dressed old lady (Rhys was now seventy-six), Davies was startled both by the hesitancy of her responses and the extreme quietness of her voice. Miss Rhys was "strange, shy, very dignified," Davies wrote in the *Atticus* column published two weeks after the launch of Rhys's novel; her book struck him—like herself—as interesting but odd. Rhys was better pleased by the accompanying photograph of herself in her heyday, dressed up for a day out in Vienna, than by the article's jaunty heading: "Rip van Rhys."[14]

Widely read at the time, that chatty profile by Davies enabled Joan Butler, a briskly practical widow who lived in Cheriton Fitzpaine, to connect his description to the pale old lady she had often seen tottering alone through the village, shading her face from the sun (or perhaps from inquisitive strangers) with a broad-brimmed hat. Calling at the bungalow for the first time early in 1967, Butler received a cautious welcome. Over time, however, a pattern of fortnightly visits enabled Joan Butler to help supervise Rhys's welfare, while acting as a useful source of information on their friend's well-being to Diana Athill and Sonia Orwell. Intellectually and politically far apart (Butler's views were closer to those of the left-wing Max Hamer's than his widow's), Joan nevertheless established with Rhys an undemanding friendship on which the age-weakened writer would increasingly come to rely.

More welcome to Rhys than Joan Butler's extended hand in the aftermath of her novel's London launch was a typically generous letter from Sonia Orwell asking what sort of an all-paid winter holiday would suit her best. The invitation was thoughtfully accompanied by a bottle of whisky and followed up, to Rhys's delight, by an elegant, tissue-wrapped dress in her favourite shade of pink. Rhys's gratitude was profuse.

Until the launch, Rhys had known George Orwell's widow only as an occasional and kind-hearted correspondent who had proof-read the section of *Wide Sargasso Sea* published in *Art and Literature*, along with several of her best short stories. Meeting Sonia in London in the autumn of 1966, Rhys felt instantly at ease with a generous, intelligent and opinionated woman with blue, slightly bloodshot eyes, a blazing smile and a love of Paris that equalled Rhys's own. Their rapport was immediate; Rhys was never exposed to the more hurtful side of Sonia Orwell's personality, or to that of the occasionally capricious and petulant Francis Wyndham. Francis and Sonia: here were two friendly allies who liked one other and understood Rhys well enough to be outraged when Athill suggested that pretty clothes were wasted on an old woman. A degree of frivolity—as they understood and Diana did not—was essential to Rhys's happiness, and even to her work.[15]

Where Diana Athill excelled was as a wily and intelligent editor who fought Rhys's battles with the skill of a fencing champion. All her considerable adroitness was required to negotiate a way past Rhys's ill-considered—and, by now, greatly regretted—agreement with Selma

Sonia Orwell, whom Rhys regarded as the kindest of all her literary friends.

Vaz Dias. Selma's interference with *Woman's Hour* had proven disastrous; on 1 December, an apprehensive Rhys confided to Athill that Selma, without consulting her, had approached the BBC with a revised adaptation of *Voyage in the Dark*. Remembering Selma's casual attitude towards two of the novel's characters—Maudie and Laurie—Rhys feared sabotage. "I know how easily my books could be utterly spoiled," Jean wrote, forgetting that she had once remarked that she didn't care what became of work that had already been published. She added that she no longer trusted Selma "very far. Not at all!!!" The following day, Rhys expressed bitter regret at having signed away artistic control over her own work; not for the first time, and certainly not for the last, she claimed that the agreement made with Selma was no more than a joke.[16]

To Selma, the agreement was solid and legitimate; the worry for Rhys's publisher was that Vaz Dias's interventions could easily destroy any chance of Rhys's novels ever being staged or filmed. Action had to be taken. While Rhys's thoughts were focused on a post-Christmas holiday at Brighton—Sonia promised her a hotel room stocked with new books (carefully pre-selected by Jennifer Ross), champagne and fresh flowers and (this came "tops" in Jean's opinion) freedom to spend all day in bed—Diana made her move.[17]

It remained a source of pride to Selma that she was still represented by her old friend Peggy Ramsay, then London's best-known theatrical agent. Conscious that no agent likes to relinquish their cut of a deal, Athill cannily opened negotiations by reassuring Ramsay on 2 February 1967 that the financial division agreed between Rhys and her client was not in dispute. Only in the tricky area of artistic control, Athill explained, did Selma need to be kept "right out of the matter."[18]

Diana's masterstroke was simultaneously to sidetrack Selma by deferentially seeking her professional advice on the possible future for Rhys's works on stage and screen. "It seemed to me," the flattered actress wrote to Ramsay on 5 February, while making plans to visit Peggy for further discussions about her own role in Rhys's future, "that you were the most suitable and reliable person to deal with the situation."[19]

Selma's letter arrived too late; by 3 February, alarmed by Diana's account of Selma's reckless interventions, Peggy Ramsay had changed sides. Evidence of her abrupt shift of allegiances survives in an extraor- dinary letter fired off by Peggy on that same day. Writing to Bryan Forbes, she urged the film director to beware of "a madwoman" called Selma Vaz Dias, lest she should wreck his proposed production of *Wide Sargasso Sea* with her preposterous demands. A baffled Forbes wrote back to explain that he had neither read the novel nor considered film- ing it. He had no wish, having read her warnings about the alarming Selma, to make an offer.[20]

Uninformed of these crafty intrigues, Rhys herself learned only from Diana that her worries were over; Selma had agreed to renounce authorial control. What Rhys did not yet know was that Diana had won her a powerful new ally. The impressive bulk of the British Library's Ramsay files concerning Jean Rhys bears witness to the birth of an improbable but enduring friendship.

———————

IT'S SURPRISING TO find that Diana Athill chose Jean Rhys for her confidante in 1967 about her ongoing and increasingly unsatisfactory love affair with Waguih Ghali, a volatile young Egyptian exile whose wittily original novel about life in Cairo, *Beer in the Snooker Club*, she had edited for André Deutsch. Grateful for Diana's help over Selma, Rhys offered her lovelorn editor the consolation—Diana enjoyed lit- erary social events as much as Rhys detested them—of accepting on her behalf the Heinemann Foundation Award, bestowed by the Royal Society of Literature, of which Rhys now became a belated fellow. The ceremony took place in July 1967. Reporting on the august occasion to Rhys, Diana mischievously passed along the news that she and Sonia had listened to Rebecca West going into raptures over a writer she had recently ranked below Beatrix Potter. When an old and celebrated poet got drunk and fell flat on the floor, nobody at this distinguished and mildly eccentric gathering had turned a hair.[21]

While stoical about the lame reviews of *Wide Sargasso Sea*, and pro-
fessedly indifferent to the warmer critical reception of two older novels
(Deutsch had cautiously waited until 1967 to publish Rhys's revised
editions of *Voyage* and *Midnight*), Rhys confessed to Sonia Orwell that
she felt discouraged by the "tepid" response to the new collection of
stories that were published during that same summer.[22] Rhys's disappointment was understandable; *Tigers are Better-Looking* contained
some of her finest wartime writing, but critical interest in Rhys's work
was already—and to her frustration would remain—focused upon the
connection between the author herself and the less literate, more vic-
timised women about whom she wrote in her novels. The idea of "the
Rhys woman" had begun to take root.

Overshadowing the summer of 1967 was the alarming prospect
of leaving Devon for Chingford. Hints were dropped by Rhys of her
growing unease. Maryvonne had repainted the inside of the bungalow, making it appear delightfully bright and cottage-like, her mother
told Sonia, while sighing to Francis at the prospect of leaving her
garden and view of the fields beyond.[23] To Diana, the vigorous organ-
iser of her proposed new life (Diana had even begun to buy suitable
pieces of furniture), Rhys meekly apologised for causing trouble. All
would be worth it to see Rhys living nearer to London, her efficient
editor smiled.

Rhys was unexpectedly rescued from her predicament by eighty-
four-year-old Edward Rees Williams. On 7 October 1967, transpar-
ently relieved, Jean passed the news along to her mortified editor.
Anxious about the fate of his own promised investment, Edward ("kind
man," his sibling cooed) had undertaken a five-hour journey from
Devon to Essex in order to view the Chingford flat. He was guided
around a show apartment before learning that no other had yet been
built and that only Diana and he himself had expressed any interest in
making an advance purchase. Rhys's flat did not, as yet, exist.[24]

Writing to Sonia in late October, Rhys openly rejoiced. The cancel-
lation of her dreaded move was all she could have wished for: "my best

plan now is to stay down here and *take holidays.*"²⁵ The hint was hardly subtle; Sonia promptly invited Rhys to bring her family along for a pre-Christmas holiday at her own agreeable house in west London. The offer was gladly accepted.

THE BIGGEST SURPRISE of 1967 was the news, announced early in the summer, that Raymond Mortimer and Margaret Lane had chosen *Wide Sargasso Sea* for the year's top book award. Winning the £1,000 (£18,270 today) [W. H.] Smith Award guaranteed a prominent week-long display of the chosen novel in every branch of what was then Britain's leading book chain. Telling Diana Athill on 7 October that the Smith award had really "got to" Maryvonne, Rhys wondered whether her daughter might be allowed to accept the prize on her mother's behalf at the customary celebration dinner? The answer—to the disappointment of both Rhys and Maryvonne—was no. Rhys's timid request for Selma Vaz Dias to be invited to the prize-giving dinner was similarly squelched when her publisher (André couldn't stand Selma) instructed her to choose between Miss Vaz Dias or himself.

Back in the 1960s, the [W. H.] Smith Literary Award was as big an event as the Booker or a Pulitzer. Rhys was becoming quite famous. The experience was not one that gave her a superabundance of pleasure: "not fair!" she protested to Francis after being chased into her favourite hairdressing salon by an especially determined photographer.²⁶ Any happiness that she did feel was blighted by her awareness of the growing resentment of Selma Vaz Dias.

An autumn spent witnessing her friend's success had hardened Selma's determination to have what she regarded as her fair share of the spoils. *She* had rediscovered Jean Rhys; jealously, she scanned the papers for any article about Rhys that failed to mention the role that she herself had played in bringing Rhys into the public eye. In mid-December, while Rhys and her family (even Job came over from Holland for a few days) became the appreciative guests of Sonia Orwell at her house on Gloucester Road, Selma accused Francis Wyndham of exploiting Rhys's name for personal gain, while neglecting ever to mention herself. It must have given Francis a moment's quiet satisfaction to inform Miss Vaz Dias that he was not responsible for editorial cuts in newspapers, and that every penny he earned from praising an author he so much admired went straight to Rhys herself.[27] For the moment, Selma was silenced.

Maryvonne's relationship with Selma was more delicate. Initially, Rhys's daughter had been pleased to learn of Selma's Dutch origins and grateful for the offers of cost-free hospitality which Vaz Dias generously continued to extend to her. But Maryvonne shared Francis's distaste for Selma's assumptions about the vast wealth that Rhys had supposedly accrued. Responding to a barrage of accusations in early December, Maryvonne explained that, while money concerns were actually making her mother "incredibly" anxious and tense, what Rhys most lacked now was peace and quiet: " . . . But I expect you have already had a row."[28]

Staying at Sonia Orwell's home in December 1967 proved to be neither peaceful nor quiet. Rhys's granddaughter still recalls her own nervousness at the smartly chattering guests who trooped through Sonia's home or hosted parties for Rhys at their own splendid residences. She points out that Sonia's unstinting kindness had included social coaching for a shy girl of nineteen.[29] It had included a chance to see Tom Stoppard's arrestingly witty play, *Rosencrantz and Guildenstern Are Dead*. Did Sonia want clever Ellen to discover a connection between Rhys's brilliant reinterpretation of an aspect of *Jane Eyre* with Stoppard's artful reworking of *Hamlet*?

The chance for Rhys to spend most of the day at 153 Gloucester Road, resting and reading in a pleasant back bedroom overlooking a garden (while seeing her family splendidly entertained), was restorative and comforting; writing to thank Sonia later, a grateful Rhys said that the room's tranquil outlook had lulled her back into the security of childhood. By February 1968, however, Rhys's overdue receipt of a

£1,200 bursary from the Arts Council* had resulted in her once again being targeted by Selma, declaring that everybody was getting rich "(except me)" from a talent which she, Selma Vaz Dias, had personally "nursed and nurtured and coddled for years."[30]

Admirably, Rhys refused to lose her temper, allowing herself only the secret satisfaction of recommending to her friend a new book about that ultimate drama queen, Sarah Bernhardt. Instructed in return—the tone was almost a command—to buy two paintings by Selma of her "Mrs Rochester" (at forty-five guineas apiece), Rhys made her reluctance clear by asking instead for a flower painting, while adding with patent hopefulness: "(You don't do flowers do you?)." A painting of flowers was immediately despatched; the requested £25 payment was as promptly made. But Selma remained displeased; a full year later, Peggy Ramsay gathered that Rhys had wretchedly underpaid Vaz Dias for the tremendous effort required to produce "my one and only flowerpiece."[31]

Selma's steady drip of complaints had no significant impact on her former friend's spirits. Writing to Francis Wyndham in the spring of 1968 within hours of dealing with one of Vaz Dias's challenging letters, Rhys prattled happily about her current interest in biography— she was reading Henri Troyat's life of Tolstoy (in French) alongside Lytton Strachey's older life of Queen Victoria (in English). To Francis, her favourite literary confidant, Rhys also admitted her worry that her finally completed story "Overture and Beginners Please" had greatly exceeded the London Magazine's request for a lively little reminiscence of her schooldays. Once embarked, she had found the pull of the past impossible to resist.

Autobiography was clearly the direction in which Rhys was now heading. While her market-conscious publishers would have welcomed

---

* Under pressure from Sonia Orwell, this long-promised bursary had been personally signed off in January 1968 by Charles Osborne for the Arts Council. On this occasion, Osborne was quietly making up for the fact that he had mislaid one of Rhys's finest stories, "Tigers are Better-Looking," in the files of the London Magazine, when he was working for the Rosses as an office junior.

another novel, nostalgic short stories and the beginnings of a memoir were all that they seemed likely to cajole from a writer who was nearing eighty. The need to capture and set down her early memories had frequently distracted Rhys from working on *Wide Sargasso Sea*; now, the moment had come to sharpen and perfect those alluring fragments of recollection. Diligently and patiently, Sonia, Francis and Diana united to encourage the ageing author, often typing out her work themselves and always praising what they were shown. At times, perhaps because Rhys's progress was so slow, they were a little too uncritical where her last stories were concerned.

Self-absorption, always essential to Rhys's work, increased as she grew older. Maryvonne, writing to Leslie Tilden Smith's remarried daughter in the spring of 1968, confided that her mother had "a supreme egocentric view of life"; Rhys's daughter nevertheless knew her mother well enough to understand that passionate self-engrossment was "a must for her kind of writing."[32]

An unforgiving solipsism was indeed central to Rhys's work, but it could make her a difficult friend. In May, while affectionately reassuring Rhys about the existence of an eager audience for her planned collection of tales of long-ago Dominica, Francis Wyndham arranged for "Pioneers, Oh, Pioneers" (Rhys's story about the settler Mr. Ramage's retreat into eccentric seclusion) to be typed by himself. Rhys wanted more. Recalling the distant days when little Gwen Williams had used a special "swizzle stick"* to mix evening cocktails for her father and Ramage, she demanded just such a stick for her evening drink. Patiently, Francis tracked down and despatched an expensive glass cocktail stirrer, from Harrods to Cheriton; all wrong! Rhys groused. This was not in the *least* what she wanted! For a start, the stick must be wooden . . .

There were times when even the fondest of Jean Rhys's London

---

* A Caribbean "swizzle," as drunk by Jean Rhys's father and his friends, is made by mixing gin and chartreuse with squeezed lime, sugar, a dash of Angostura bitters—and lots of crushed ice.

friends felt relieved that she preferred to live in distant Devon. Absence made it possible for them to retain real tenderness for a stubborn old woman whose child-like need for sympathy and attention could—and increasingly often, did—become relentless. What almost certainly would have killed off such unstinting affection was the greater trial of daily proximity.

20

Rhys in Retreat (1967–74)

"It's a great effort to chat & I don't do it well."

—Jean Rhys to Oliver Stonor, 3 August 1968[1]

IF ASKED WHAT else she still wanted from life after the publication of *Wide Sargasso Sea*, Jean Rhys would never have requested celebrity. An invitation to talk with Francis Wyndham on television in December 1968 was firmly rejected: "I'd be nervous and self-conscious. However kind you were—this would happen." The following year, Peggy Ramsay approached her about *Late Night Line-Up*, the well-regarded television culture programme on which even the secretive Marcel Duchamp had consented to appear. Rhys turned the opportunity down without a blink.[2]

Away from London, privacy was easier to maintain. As mistress of her own time and—until 1971—with distractions threatened by neither a telephone nor a television, Rhys continued to rise at dawn, now her favourite time for writing. Later in the day, she dutifully responded to a growing stream of letters from young readers who found themselves reflected in her fiction and wanted to visit—some dreamed of coming to live with and care for—their heroine. Such aspirations were courteously discouraged in letters executed in ballpoint on small sheets of paper torn from a block and addressed with the cramped neatness of an aged schoolgirl. Penning them, as Rhys

ruefully confided to one of her earliest interviewers, Marcelle Bernstein, imposed a considerable physical strain.[3]

Huddled under a favourite rug, Rhys might spend a wet afternoon in Devon reading a novel recommended by Francis (vainly
hoping she would share his admiration for Anna Kavan's *Ice*) or
by Sonia (urging Rhys to read the latest work by her close friend,
Marguerite Duras). When Maryvonne and her daughter paid visits,
they, too, brought books; Rhys's granddaughter remembers almost
losing her coursework volumes of stories by Chekhov and Maupassant to her grandmother: "always a sign of approval."[4] An evening sweetened by half a bottle of whisky from the Ring of Bells
("Hells' Bells" to an uncharmed Maryvonne Moerman) was usually followed by an early bed with some less challenging literature.
Marcelle Bernstein wasn't the only interviewer to hear of Rhys's
fondness for reading herself to sleep on a windy night with Marcel
Boulestin's recipes. Appreciative though she was of gourmet food
when it came her way, Rhys may never have attempted to cook any
of the Parisian chef's delicacies on the two-ring stove in her doll-
sized kitchen.

Such, for eleven months of the year, was Jean Rhys's tranquil routine, but her life in the country was less lonely than her letters implied.
Oliver Stonor and his plump, sweet-natured wife Mollie, were the hospitable owners of a picturesque stone cottage at Morebath, close to
Exmoor, where Rhys often went to lunch to meet a few of the couple's restfully undemanding friends. One guest, an older woman, won
Rhys's approval simply by dressing with exceptional elegance; another
was just forgiven for declaring that she lacked only the time to become
a novelist herself. Preferring more youthful company, Rhys was
delighted when the Stonors' friend Christopher Cox, a young Devon
book-dealer, offered to help her to recreate an approximation of her lost
library of novels and poetry. Alexis Lykiard, a poet and translator who
lived close to Cheriton with his model girlfriend, Diane Leigh, was a
well-read young Francophile who introduced Rhys to the self-styled
"Comte de Lautréamont's" influential prose poem on the nature of evil,

Les Chants de Maldorer[*] and some of the more ghostly tales of Sheridan Le Fanu. Apparently, she loved *Carmilla*, the Irish writer's sumptuously creepy novel about a female vampire, pre-dating Bram Stoker's *Dracula* by almost thirty years. Lykiard, noting the way Rhys sometimes rolled her now slightly watery blue eyes towards heaven, and knowing a little about her Caribbean background, wondered if the writer he so admired was of "mixed race."

An unexpected hit at one of the Stonors' lunches for Rhys was Herbert Ronson, a chivalrous travel journalist from Cheshire. Calling at Rhys's bungalow in the summer of 1969, Ronson found his hostess clinging to the side of her open front door with the wistful grace—in his own words—of a tiny deposed queen. Was it by chance that Rhys allowed the belt of her dress to slip to the ground as—while showing the visitor around her garden—she softly wondered whether Herbert might like to arrange a joint trip to Portugal? (This project replaced Rhys's recent plan to visit a new literary admirer, Gerald Brenan, at his home in Andalucía, cancelled in 1968 after Brenan's wife, Gamel, became terminally ill.[†]) Relating his story twenty years later in the pages of the *London Magazine*, Ronson recalled himself as having behaved like a man under a spell; he had been "entirely captivated . . . robbed of volition." There had been many such travel requests; at the last minute, Rhys always changed her mind, but Ronson never lost his desire to grant pleasure to a charming and capricious old lady.[5]

At Cheriton, despite the watchful kindness of neighbours like the Greenslades and friends like the Stonors, Rhys had to look after herself for most of the time. Visiting London each winter, she relied upon

---

[*] Isidore Lucien Ducasse's celebrated phrase in *Maldorer* about the improbable conjunction of a sewing machine and an umbrella on an operating table was later seized upon by André Breton and the surrealists during the 1920s, when Rhys lived in Paris and took an interest in their writings.

[†] Generously quoted in Jonathan Gathorne Hardy's biography, *The Interior Castle* (Sinclair-Stevenson, 1992), Gerald Brenan's correspondence with and about Rhys included an especially shrewd observation (to David Garnett) that her writing "keeps one all the time at the central point of feeling."

Sonia Orwell to organise every aspect of her life and to ensure that it was filled with treats. Sonia did not disappoint. Visits to beauty salons and excitingly modern shops like Biba and Miss Selfridge vied with afternoons at the ballet, where Rhys preferred *Swan Lake* and *Giselle* to more challenging fare. ("I know it's escapist," she wrote to a new young novelist friend, Rachel Ingalls, "but why not? There's such a lot to escape from.")[6]

Less enjoyable, always, were the carefully prepared parties which played a key part in Sonia Orwell's life. Not even the hair-styling and beautiful clothes provided by her thoughtful hostess succeeded in banishing Rhys's nervousness of the strangers who crowded around her and asked clever questions about her work. "It's really a great effort to chat," as she sadly confessed to Oliver Stonor, "& I don't do it well. Never mind. I think a lot."[7]

SONIA'S UNSTINTING GENEROSITY to Rhys's close family helped compensate for her friend's own conscious—and considerable—failings as a parent. A major reason for Rhys's growing unhappiness about the continued division of her income with Selma Vaz Dias was the knowledge that she had deprived her good-humoured, middle-aged daughter of a precious potential source of financial security.

Much of the trouble with the arrangement Rhys had originally made with Selma stemmed from Rhys's complete unworldliness about money. In 1963, she had signed her name to Selma's proposed financial division without a thought; in 1967, following a delightful lunch at the Savoy Grill with a well-spoken American academic, she promised to send Howard Gotlieb the only draft pages that survived of her work on *Wide Sargasso Sea*. On this occasion, Oliver Stonor came to her rescue by instructing Gotlieb either to send back Miss Rhys's chapter or pay £300 (£5,250) for it; the manuscript was swiftly returned. From this point on, Rhys's awareness of the error she had made in signing Selma's document was heightened by the evidence of growing interest in the staging and filming of her work. In 1968, Patrick Garland began planning to stage *Quartet* (Garland was about to make his name directing Alan Bennett's *Forty Years On*); in 1969, Peggy Ramsay was approached for a film option on *Wide Sargasso Sea*. Negotiating with the producer, Ramsay began to have second thoughts about the fact that Selma Vaz Dias, who remained on Peggy's client list, was still legally entitled to receive 50 per cent of everything—stage, film, radio, translations— relating to the work of Jean Rhys.

Normally, Ramsay might have contacted Diana Athill about rene- gotiating Selma's portion. Since Athill was grieving over the suicide in her north London flat of her young Egyptian lover, Peggy decided to deal with the matter herself. On 10 June 1969, Selma was insis- tent about receiving her legal half share; three days later, she agreed to a compromise.[8] By 1 August, the new agreement had been finalised. While far from ideal, Ramsay's renegotiation reduced Selma's share to one third.* Writing to thank Peggy on 18 August, Rhys claimed that the good news had released her from a long period of creative sterility.[9]

The behaviour of Rhys was startlingly similar to that of her old friend in regard to their disputed agreement. Like Selma, Rhys both denied the past and rewrote it, insisting that she had never intended her signature to be binding, while angrily underlining sections of old letters in which Selma had expressed gratitude. A month after thank- ing Peggy for her intervention, she almost lost a powerful supporter by instructing a Devon solicitor to inform Mrs. Ramsay that he could obtain a far better deal from Selma: "We will of course bow out," a livid Peggy informed Rhys, who hastily backed down.

The friendship between Selma and Rhys did not survive Ramsay's efficient negotiations. Rhys grumbled to Francis Wyndham in October 1969 that Selma's deception had been worse than a burglary. Until her own death in 1977, Selma believed that Wyndham and Diana Athill

---

* Selma's husband, Hans Egli, continued to receive her renegotiated third share until 1985, when the Rhys estate unilaterally withdrew from the arrangement. Three of Selma's five grandchildren received a single payment of £100 (£270) apiece in 1988 through a trust created by Selma. No further payments were made to Selma's family, either from the Rhys estate or a Rhys-related trust (Tara Fraser to author, July 2020).

had conspired to efface her role in Rhys's rediscovery—and that an insufficiently grateful Rhys had betrayed her trust.[10]

———————

RHYS DID NOT miss Selma much at a time when she was surrounded by admiring and far less challenging young women. Among these was Marcelle Bernstein, a staff writer whose lengthy article on Rhys for the *Observer Magazine* was published on 1 June 1969.

Opening up during her interview with Bernstein, a perceptive journalist in whom she had already placed her trust, Rhys used a question about early love affairs to distance herself from the women about whom she wrote in her novels. While agreeing that they often underwent similar experiences to their author, and bore an acknowledged resemblance to aspects of her personality, Rhys pointed to a crucial difference. They were victims. She herself was not. "I wasn't always the abandoned one, you know," Rhys told Bernstein, somehow forgetting her unhappy romance with Lancey or all the times in Beckenham that she lay alone at night. And why, if she was the quitter, did she end relationships so impulsively? A shrug. She grew tired of the person, or the place; the spell broke: who could say? Pressed by her sympathetic interviewer for more detail—lovers in Paris? boyfriends during her dancing days?—Rhys retreated behind an inscrutable wall of reserve.[11]

Rhys's correspondence with Bernstein dated back to October 1968, eight months before this major interview was published. Unusually, Rhys liked what Bernstein wrote about her; she also liked Marcelle herself. A perceptive reader of the novels, Bernstein still has fond memories of their long and congenial lunches out (always at Marcelle's expense), and the teas for which the abstemious Bernstein soon learned to bring along a bottle of whisky. In 1973, Rhys suddenly ended the relationship. Letters went unanswered; no explanation was ever provided. Today, recalling what Rhys had said in the interview about her role as the leaver, never the abandoned one, Bernstein still sounds wistful and uncomprehending.[12]

Bernstein was not alone. The photographer Barbara Ker-Seymer earned her spurs as a new friend in 1969 by making a habit of despatching well-reviewed new novels from London to Cheriton Fitzpaine. Rhys seemed delighted. Two years later, Ker-Seymer was ghosted, and again, no explanation was given. Once Rhys had cut the lines of communication, there was no going back.[13]

Barbara Ker-Seymer had first made contact with Rhys through an introduction by Francis Wyndham. It was the well-connected Francis who also introduced Rhys to Antonia Fraser, after much gentle beseeching on Lady Antonia's part. A grand title appealed less to Rhys than the unexpected gaiety of Antonia's spirit; it was hard to resist a beautifully buxom young woman who made jokes about her attempts to slim with "Miss Trim"—plastic leggings that inflated the sweating wearer into an approximation of a poolside lilo.[14] In London, Antonia good-naturedly indulged her heroine's taste for undemanding entertainment. If the future wife of Harold Pinter was disappointed by Rhys's request for a matinee visit to *The Mousetrap*, compensation was on hand. Unusually, while visiting London, Rhys consented to join the younger woman and her family for regular Sunday lunches at their home in Campden Hill Square. Unaware of Rhys's scorn for the concept of reincarnation (Rhys once mischievously remarked that she'd only care to return as a mouse or a crocodile), the Fraser family still remembers the alacrity with which, asked by one of Antonia's daughters whom she might previously have been, their usually reticent guest opted for a doomed princess from the court of Marie Antoinette. ("No hesitation at all," Lady Antonia recalls. "She was absolutely clear."[15])

Is there a connection here to André Breton's *Nadja* (always a firm favourite with Rhys), in which the novel's tragic heroine also dreams of having been a princess at Marie Antoinette's court? Perhaps. Less open to conjecture is the evidence that a part of Rhys's mind still inhabited the Paris through which Nadja—like Rhys herself—had wandered in the blue twilight of the Twenties.

Rhys's novels and short stories entered the French consciousness in 1969. Sympathetically translated by some of the finest practitioners of their craft, Rhys's fictions read almost as if they had emerged from their own language. So, in a significant sense, they had. Chatting with a French interviewer at the beginning of 1970, Rhys explained her mental trick of translating a difficult passage into French before attempting to rewrite her English version. Learned from Ford, along with an enduring respect for the technical skills of Flaubert and Maupassant, the exercise had served Rhys well. Her habit of thinking in French was never entirely dropped. Maryvonne, visiting her eighty-year-old mother in 1970, was an astonished witness to the ease and fluency with which Rhys participated in an interview for a French culture programme.

Among the respectful and admiring letters which reached Devon via Rhys's French publishers, Denoël, the most unexpected came in April 1970 from a prison in Lyon. Having admired Jacqueline Bernard's fine translation of *Good Morning, Midnight*, Rhys's correspondent hoped that the writer who had created such an empathetic victim as Sasha Jansen might sympathise with the situation of a jailed businessman who had been falsely accused of murder. Perhaps Marc Verney's eloquent appeal reminded Rhys of the sentences served by two of her husbands; she wrote at once to her favourite and greatly respected French translator, Pierre Leyris, asking him to find a lawyer willing to look into the case. Verney's eventual fate remains unknown, but in July 1971, he despatched to Devon a tiny pair of sabots that he had carved from wood during his imprisonment. Given Rhys's love of such trinkets, they probably joined the "awfully corny" china cherub candlesticks which held an honoured place on a Landboat mantelpiece.[16]

On 21 May 1970, Sonia Orwell, en route to France to nurse the novelist Marguerite Duras, received an equally startling letter.[17] Here, and in an equally ebullient missive to Maryvonne, Rhys gleefully described how Jan van Houts, a middle-aged Dutch poet and teacher, had tempted her out of the village for a five-day vagabond tour around Devon. Eleven years later, publishing his recollection of their joint escapade, Houts would stress that no romance took place between himself and the elderly writer he admired. He did, nevertheless, emphasise the delightful transformation that he had witnessed during their jaunt, as a quiet, reserved old woman disclosed the skittishly vain and happy siren who had at times in the past—very rarely—revealed herself to Francis Wyndham. Houts made a point in his memoir of describing the Parisian poster of a skilfully twirling girl-skater that he had noticed hanging in Rhys's tiny entrance hall. For him, the image evoked Rhys's own combination of a rigorous discipline with flirtatious charm.[18]

Rhys's fantasy of pursuing a new love affair was abruptly terminated by the death that autumn of her beloved elder brother, Edward. Knottsfield, the house at Budleigh Salterton, had already been sold after the death of Edward's wife, and the ageing widower had moved into a couple of rented rooms, where he was visited at least twice by his favourite sister. On one of these occasions, or during his own last visit to Cheriton at the end of 1969, the childless Edward disclosed his intention of making Maryvonne the principal beneficiary of his modest estate. To Rhys herself, her brother left both the income from a third of his investments and lifetime ownership of the bungalow that he had leased her at a peppercorn rent for the past decade. Chauffeured to Edward's funeral in the faithful Alan Greenslade's new Vauxhall, an inconsolable Rhys dissolved into predictable tears. According to Owen Rees Williams' perennially unsympathetic widow, Rhys's howls drowned out the vicar's words of divine consolation.

Writing to Maryvonne, Rhys admitted that, knowing nobody and overwhelmed by grief, she had asked Mr Greenslade to take her home early, "& he did."[19] Rhys's discomfort, perceived by Owen's hard-up and hostile relict as the typically bad behaviour of overdressed, hysterical "Gwennie" (showing up in a posh chauffeur-driven car), is not hard to understand.[20] Brenda Powell, whose mind was moving slowly towards dementia, could not safely be left alone by her long-suffering husband; the couple's sole representative at the funeral was an adopted son, a nephew whom Rhys had never met. She had encountered Owen's widow just once; she had not seen Owen's English son, John, now forty years old, since his childhood. If Rhys dressed smartly for the funeral, she did so not to outshine unrecognised relations, but to honour a brother who had always been kind.

UNRECORDED IN EARLIER biographies of Rhys is her late and significant friendship with the novelist Rachel Ingalls. Fifty years younger than Rhys, Ingalls was the formidably bright daughter of a Harvard professor of Sanskrit. She was just twenty-five when she arrived in London from New England in 1965. A writer whose stories combine bizarre situations (an unhappy wife is seduced by a towering and sexually insatiable sea creature in "Mrs Caliban") with adversarial dialogue and a ruthlessly economic style, Ingalls was praised by Charles Monteith, her editor at Faber, as "a genius, not a word I use lightly."[21]

Rhys first met Ingalls in the spring of 1970. A self-sufficient young woman, Rachel avoided literary society as zealously as her compatriot and good friend David Plante sought it out. Plante remembers arranging the introduction because he knew how much Ingalls admired Rhys's work; what he did not anticipate was that an immediate bond of recognition would develop into a warm correspondence which was maintained until 1973, when osteoporosis would make writing by hand too difficult a challenge for Rhys to maintain. This problem may also have played a part in a proud woman's abrupt severance of her relationships with Ker-Seymer and Bernstein: we can't be sure.

While the physical process of writing became increasingly arduous as Rhys aged, her imagination remained unrelenting. "I've been having such strong dreams that I must really be feeling guilty," Rhys confided to Ingalls in July 1970 when she was working on one of the two late and disturbing stories to which she gave a Devon setting, "Sleep It Off Lady" and "Who Knows What's Up in the Attic?" A month later, Rhys admitted to her new friend that she was finding it hard to settle down: "as for working, it's grinding out line after line or else lying awake with words rushing through one's head too quickly to catch."[22] Writing the chilling fate of Miss Verney in "Sleep It Off Lady" had, as she admitted to Ingalls, frightened her so much that she had to take a short spell away from her desk.

Holding this unexpected collection of letters in my hands has brought me a little closer to Jean Rhys. As always, she can be relentless, pressing Ingalls to get David Plante to plead with his Rome-based friend Jerry Bauer for a set of author photographs that Rhys is desperate to obtain. (Deutsch—somewhat unusually for a publisher—did nothing to help their authors in this respect.[23]) For the most part, however, the letters are almost maternal, begging Ingalls not to cut her luxuriant, shoulder-length hair ("Dear Rachel your hair is so pretty as it is . . . I've spoilt mine") and saying fondly that Ingalls's cosy gift of a large red shawl is worn in part because it always keeps the "dear" giver in her thoughts. While Rhys took a close and persistent interest in Ingalls's work, she was especially struck by *Theft*, an early novella set in a Southern jail during a riot. Did Rhys look upon Ingalls as her literary heir? The possibility is strengthened by the evidence of her steady reassurances, her regularly expressed hopes for the younger woman of "a prize or two, and all the luck there is," and the tender prediction: "Surely all sorts of nice things—all sorts—are waiting for you."[24])

Unusually in Rhys's long life, she seems to have found in Ingalls— hailed in a recent appraisal for her "hallucinatory realism"—a woman writer whose own disciplined habits she was willing to respect.[25] David Plante—as he himself readily admits—never minded running errands for Rhys (mainly as a service to Sonia Orwell, at whose house he was rewarded by meeting the cream of London's intelligentsia); Ingalls was at nobody's command. She would send Rhys thoughtful gifts (her present of a catalogue from the great Tutankhamun exhibition was better received than Diana Athill's offer to push the supremely self-conscious Rhys round the crowded show in a wheelchair). She would take her elderly friend off to the cinema (a Chaplin film proved more successful than *The French Connection*). Like Rhys herself, she refused to be bullied.

Rhys would have agreed with the tributes that were to be paid, decades later, to an exceptional writer, at the very end of Rachel's life (Ingalls died in 2019). Today, David Plante concedes the justice of Ingalls's anger when she read the portrait of Rhys with which he opened *Difficult Women*, a brilliant but treacherous work published in 1983. From that day on, Ingalls never spoke to him again.[26]

THE YEAR 1971, another unproductive one for Rhys's writing, ended with an unexpected and delightful tribute to the power of her imagination: *Memories of Morning: Night*, a hauntingly evocative monodrama which the widely admired young composer Gordon Crosse based upon *Wide Sargasso Sea*, was given a warm welcome at its premiere at the Royal Festival Hall, with the mezzo-soprano Meriel Dickinson singing the role of Antoinette. Regarded today as one of this sensitive musician's finest works, Crosse's tribute may have seemed to Rhys to be an augury. While 1972 would be darkened by the deaths of her valiantly independent young cousin, Lily Lockhart, and of Max Hamer's brother, Alec (well described by himself, so a grieving Rhys felt, as "a simple soldier"), the year also ushered in a new phase in Rhys's growing fame.

Rhys herself entered 1972 in valedictory mode, paying Sonia Orwell to host what she wistfully described to Rachel Ingalls as her "farewell party" at Gloucester Road. Adieux seemed in order; Patrick Garland had abandoned his attempt to stage *Quartet*, while Rhys's final collection of stories for Deutsch was refusing to come together. A fall, resulting in a cracked rib, was an unkind reminder to Rhys that she was about to turn eighty-two.

Change was in the air. A warm appreciation of *After Leaving Mr Mackenzie* in the *New York Times* was pleasing; the news from Peggy Ramsay that Susan Sontag was chasing an option to film *Good Morning, Midnight* and *Wide Sargasso Sea* sounded intriguing. Neither event prepared Rhys for the glowingly intelligent and sensitive appreciation of her novels which appeared on 18 May 1972 in the *New York Review of Books*.

V. S. Naipaul was a prolific contributor of substantial essays to the *NYRB* in the early Seventies: another from 1972 was an evaluation of the work of Borges. His tribute to Rhys showed the Trinidad-born British novelist at his generous best. "What a stoic thing she makes the act of writing appear," he exclaimed in an appreciation which moved Rhys to tears by what she described to Francis Wyndham as its "marvellous, and a nearly complete understanding of my life." Naipaul also performed the valuable service of distinguishing the writer from her subjects. For the first time, an eminent critic was prepared to consider the women about whom Rhys wrote, not as self-portraits or alter egos, but as independent creations whom Naipaul intuited to be far "cruder, and less gifted than herself." Naipaul identified Rhys's vagabond women as "bohemian, in the toughest sense"; he saw their self-elected rootlessness as part of the author's prescribed journey for her protagonists as they travelled "from one void to another." He understood how important it was to Rhys that they should remain watchful outsiders, "schooled by their society in the arts of survival."[27] The influence of Francis Wyndham, who had stayed close to Naipaul since first persuading André Deutsch to publish the young novelist's work, hovered behind a number of the essay's penetrating observations about Rhys herself.

The effect was immediate, and not entirely welcome. While visits that summer from both Francis and Sonia to Cheriton were rapturously received, Rhys resisted a growing interest in her personal life. A disappointed Peggy Ramsay learned from Diana Athill in August that Michael Lindsay Hogg's proposal for a television documentary interweaving Rhys's life with her novels must be turned down; Rhys would not permit such an invasion.

Rhys completed her two new stories with a Devon setting by the end of the summer of 1972, before she allowed herself the challenge of reading Arthur Mizener's year-old biography of Ford Madox Ford. Her claim to have come across a new and expensive literary biography by accident while visiting Cheriton's poorly stocked mobile library van is unconvincing; more likely, she ordered or asked for it. The book infuriated her. Mizener had not only broadcast the knowledge that Rhys had received an allowance from Ford and Stella for several months, but had included a footnote which suggested that Rhys had given birth to a "love child."

An extant document titled "*L'affaire Ford*" presents Rhys's rambling rebuttal of Mizener's claims.[28] Publicly, Rhys had always praised Ford as a mentor while denying—to all but a chosen few—the existence of their love affair. Now, too upset to continue working on the story collection she had promised to Deutsch, Rhys ranted to close friends about Mizener's allegation with a passion that gave it credence. An intrigued David Plante was not alone in wondering whether Mizener's claim might be true, and why it was that Ford and Stella had been so anxious to pay Rhys off at the end of the affair.[29]

British interest in the reclusive novelist and her sharply contemporary novels was growing almost by the month. Peggy Ramsay's announcement that John Mortimer was to adapt *Voyage in the Dark* for the stage was followed by news that a television version, starring Jacqueline Tong as Anna Morgan and George Baker as Walter Jeffries, was in production. (Watching it on her new television set, Rhys was disappointed; Tong seemed too hard and knowing for her own vulnerable Anna.) Meanwhile, in June 1972, Rhys learned that Glenda Jackson was keen to acquire *Good Morning, Midnight*.[30] No evidence survives of which role was being considered for the twenty-year-old actress who had most recently partnered forty-eight-year-old Marlon Brando in *Last Tango in Paris*, but Francis Wyndham heard in October from a dazzled Rhys that Maria Schneider had proved to be so ravishingly lovely in person—we don't know where they met—that she herself lost her wits and could only mutter "banal things in French."[31] More thrilling still for a recent convert to television, and described by Rhys to Francis as almost the nicest surprise of an astonishing year, was the gift from a friend of the autograph of her favourite television performer, Ronnie Corbett.

For Francis, as for an anxious Diana Athill, the best news from Rhys in the late autumn of 1972 was that she had resumed work on her stories. Encouragement was always required, however, and Francis demonstrated once again that his patience and perseverance were unending when it came to Jean Rhys. It was Wyndham who arranged for "The Insect World" and "Pioneers, Oh, Pioneers," stories which had been obsessively revised and rewritten over decades, to be published in, respectively, the *Sunday Times* and *The Times* as tasters of what was to come. Meanwhile, Francis persuaded Rhys to return to "Night Out," one of her best early tales about Paris, by offering to work over it with her himself. When Francis advised, Rhys listened: she obeyed when he insisted that Rhys's meticulous reworking of an old Lenglet story, "The Chevalier of the Place Blanche," must carry an acknowledgement to its first author.

Other, more recent stories guided Rhys gently forward towards the memoir of her early life that she had been wistfully contemplating for forty years. All she had lacked until now was the voice in which to tell it. And now—miraculously—that voice came into her mind.

"I can still shut my eyes and see Victoria grinding coffee on the pantry steps." These are the simple, declarative words that Jean Rhys used to open an artfully structured reminiscence of her childhood in Dominica that she named: "On Not Shooting Sitting Birds." The slow evolution of "Overture and Beginners Please" from a *London Magazine* request for a short piece on her experiences at school had first focused Rhys's thoughts on a memoir. But it was the little group of Dominica-based stories that found their final shape in the early 1970s which gave Rhys the voice in which to tell it. The voice was clear, strong and strikingly youthful. Her memory and her imaginative power remained intact. The question was whether an octogenarian whose gnarled hands now struggled to clasp a pen retained the physical energy required for such a daunting task.

21

"Mrs Methuselah" (1973–76)

"I rode a swing—swing high, swing low. That's been my life."
—Jean Rhys to Mary Cantwell, *Mademoiselle*, October 1974

THE PERSONAL HIGHLIGHT of Rhys's eighty-third year was the transformation of a barely habitable bungalow in Devon into a cosy cottage. The miracle was worked by freckled, red-haired, outspoken Jo
Batterham—a favourite niece of Francis Wyndham's friend, the landscape and portrait painter Derek Hill—with the help of an attractive
and well-read young woman called Virginia Stevens.

During the colder months of each year, from 1972 onwards, Rhys's
regular perch in London, chosen and paid for by Sonia, became the Portobello Hotel in Stanley Gardens, Notting Hill. First taken there by
Francis to meet a writer whom she and "Gini" Stevens revered (the couple had already—unsuccessfully—attempted to doorstep Rhys during
a visit to Devon), Jo was thrilled to see the painting of a rose hanging
above the writer's bed. The artist, as Batterham explained to her hostess,
was Jo's own father, a notable interior decorator; Rhys had purchased
the picture on impulse a week earlier while visiting John Hill's recently
acquired showroom with the ballet critic, Richard Buckle.* Jo Batterham

---

* John Hill had taken over Abbott & Green, a Wigmore Street shop famous for its
William Morris–style wallpapers.

had inherited her father's talent; before leaving the Portobello that evening, she volunteered her services as an unpaid advisor on the transformation of Rhys's Devon home.

Rhys's initial aspirations were touchingly modest. She wanted bright colours on the walls, to remind her of the Caribbean; she needed a comfortable spare bed for the use of her visiting daughter. Above all, she wanted to see an end put to the gaunt, ramshackle shed which had once served as an occasional garage for Edward's car. Rhys's wish was granted; by the summer of 1974, the hated shed had been demolished and replaced by a sweet-smelling cedarwood sleeping annex that could double as a writing room. A creature of habit, Rhys always preferred to use her kitchen table as a desk.

Rhys could joke about herself to close friends as "Mrs Methuselah," but age was taking its toll. Towards the end of 1973, the year in which she brusquely terminated several handwritten correspondences, rheumatism defeated her ability to operate a pen for longer than a few minutes at a time. This, for a woman who had always written her work by hand, presented a serious problem; Jo's partner Gini Stevens volunteered to do what she could to help solve it. While Jo Batterham, caring for a young son at her Putney home, directed the bungalow's improvements from afar (the village builder, Mr. Martin, carried out her instructions), Gini began driving down to Devon for ten days of each month to work as Rhys's unpaid amanuensis. The task wasn't easy; recalling her role for a magazine article in 1974, Stevens conjured up the relentless commitment of Rhys at work, "dictating version after version to me, sometimes continuing for a five or six hour stretch, ruthlessly paring everything that is not essential."[1] A grant was eventually obtained by Diana Athill to cover Gini's time and travel costs, but it wasn't surprising that the young woman sometimes skipped a visit.

Rhys became extremely fond of Gini. By the summer of 1974, she had found a way to keep Stevens close to her by appointing an enthusiastic amateur to replace the experienced Olwyn Hughes as the agent for her early works and short stories. (John Smith of Christy & Moore continued to represent the later books.) Gini took her new role seriously; within weeks, she had proudly reported to Diana Athill her successful advance sale of the world rights to Rhys's still uncompleted final stories. Untutored in the ways that publishers operate, Gini had no idea that Deutsch themselves expected to sell the tales abroad and take a commission. Scolded by Diana, Gini found an unexpected supporter in Francis. Mistrustful of "stingy publishers," Francis told an apprehensive Rhys that Gini and she should stick to their guns.[2]

Clear evidence of the warmth of Rhys's feelings for her two new friends emerges from the fact that—anxious to escape from chilly Devon in the bitter autumn of 1973, when a rash of strikes and a steep rise in oil prices led to national restrictions on energy use—Rhys invited herself to spend a month at Jo Batterham's spacious home in Putney.[3] Much admired (and still fondly remembered) by Jo's small son, Luke, for her purple hat, her pinkly powdered cheeks and her handsome gift of a £1 note for every drawing that an artistic little boy became unsurprisingly eager to present, Rhys made a charming guest. Away from the usual London pressure to put on a performance, she relaxed. According to Jo Batterham, she drank with enjoyment, but never to excess. Back at the Portobello Hotel for a more challenging post-Christmas sojourn in the city, Rhys relied on alcohol to help her face the ordeal of interviews, photoshoots and—least appealing of all—the literary gatherings her publishers required her to attend. It was—as she well understood—the price to be paid for Sonia's generosity in paying her bills.

Listening to people who remember Rhys's mid-winter residences at the Portobello Hotel during the early 1970s, it's clear that, in England at least, Rhys was becoming a literary cult. Expected to amuse in return for being feted by social networkers, authors and grandees, she often drank too much. Quieter events were always preferable. Rhys loved to dress up for an early-evening hotel visit from Francis or Sonia. She enjoyed going out to a cheerful bistro lunch in Chelsea with David Plante and Rachel Ingalls. She never rejected a chance to be swept around the West End shops and salons by a new young friend, Diana

Melly, owner of a vividly hippified camper van often driven by Diana's boyfriend, Jeremy d'Agapayef.

In a small group, Rhys could always hold her own. Introduced to an admiring Glenda Jackson at an Italian restaurant lunch that was hosted by the actor Peter Eyre, she delighted the actress by unexpectedly praising her consummate comic timing, having become a keen follower of Jackson's appearances on the *Morecambe & Wise Show*. It's likely that Rhys relished a threesome lunch with Edna O'Brien, for which Mrs. Melly's handsome young lover was bidden to stay, while Diana—Rhys's kind chauffeur that day—was blithely dismissed.

Rhys's bookshelves, sharply observed by Alexis Lykiard on his visits to Cheriton Fitzpaine, now included copies of several novels by O'Brien, standing alongside the Liverpool Poets. Did she even notice the absence of poor Diana from the lunch table of O'Brien, a writer who was then being considered as an adapter of one of Rhys's novels for the screen? Self-absorption remained one of Rhys's most striking characteristics. Peter Eyre, the mellifluous-voiced young actor who had arranged the lunch with Glenda Jackson, never forgot the strangeness of carefully painting Rhys's ageing face with theatrical make-up in order that—or so Eyre assumed from her serene farewell when his nerve-racking task was completed—Rhys, seated at her hotel dressing table, drink in hand, might commune alone with the ghostly reflection of a younger stage self. On more sociable occasions, Eyre was permitted to escort Rhys to a ballet matinee or to squire her to Don Luigi, her favourite Chelsea restaurant. The rules for these intimate suppers never changed: Eyre must arrange a corner table, dimly lit, from which an unapologetically inattentive Rhys could weave a romance about herself and one of the other restaurant guests, preferably a distinguished older man, dining alone. She ate, Eyre recalls, with the gusto of a woman of half her age.[4]

One of the most disappointing experiences of Rhys's two visits to London during that chilly winter of fuel rationing in 1973/74 was to be told—after the prolonged but exquisite pleasure of being robed in couture for a *Vogue* profile—that the silk dresses and jackets were mere borrowed plumage, not gifts. Back in Devon at the end of February and grumpily perusing the words for "My Day" that she had written to accompany the profile, Rhys's spirits were lifted by news from Francis Wyndham. A major appreciation of her work was about to be published in the *New York Times Book Review*; an elated Francis was ready to predict the result: "One of those fantastic American successes which mean lots and lots of money."[5]

Al Alvarez was an influential and regular writer for the American literary pages. Published as the *Book Review*'s lead piece on 17 March 1974, his critical assessment of Rhys's work described both *Good Morning, Midnight* and *Wide Sargasso Sea* as masterpieces, before declaring their author to be, quite simply, "the best living English novelist." Wyndham was right; Alvarez's impressive tribute changed his old friend's fortunes in America almost overnight. A fresh flurry of film and interview interest gratified Rhys less than the news of immediate bulk reprints of *Good Morning, Midnight, After Leaving Mr Mackenzie* and *Wide Sargasso Sea. Quartet*, out of print in the US since 1957, was snapped up and reissued; 100,000 copies were hastily printed of *Voyage in the Dark*.

One of my own favourite pictures among the many taken of Rhys in her later years, this accompanied Julie Kavanagh's interview. *(Willie Christie)*

Alvarez had beaten Wyndham to it. Having cannily despatched an advance proof of his appraisal to Rhys in early February, he had received her pleased response four days later. Eager to interview her for Ian Hamilton's magazine *The New Review* (in which "Sleep It Off Lady" was due to make its debut that October), Alvarez paid his first visit to Cheriton Fitzpaine at the end of March. Stockily handsome, with a razor-thin strip of moustache, Alvarez was a man whom Rhys found both empathetic and physically attractive. Rhys had read the poetry of her equally reclusive neighbour, Ted Hughes. She was a greater admirer of the self-laceratingly honest work of his first wife, Sylvia Plath. It's possible that Alvarez and she discussed *The Savage God*, Alvarez's recent book about suicide—notably that of Sylvia Plath; it's more certain that they discovered a shared love of poetry. (Alvarez was one of the few people to whom, during five years of confiding and affectionate friendship, Rhys would regularly send copies of her own poems.) A more personal interest—as Alvarez loved to tell the story—was apparent in the way that Rhys had gazed into his eyes during their first meeting, while insouciantly caressing a slender stockinged calf. His description of glimpsed layers of frothy white petticoats (as Rhys saucily crossed her still elegant legs) was more imaginative. Frilly petticoats were never Rhys's style, but Alvarez's own embroidery nicely captures the hint of flirtation in the air.

THE YEAR 1974 marked the climax of Rhys's success, bringing with it a rush of new requests for interviews. A handful of the supplicants made it through; few of them managed to pierce the armour of their subject's reserve. "I was having rather a troublesome time," was all Rhys would admit to Julie Kavanagh, a bright young journalist interviewing her for the influential US paper, *Women's Wear Daily*, when Kavanagh asked about the years in postwar England during which Rhys had vanished from public view.[6]

Rhys's reticence with Kavanagh may have been due in part to a serious bout of summer flu. Just a month earlier, Mary Cantwell was granted one of the most revealing interviews Rhys ever gave, for *Mademoiselle*, an American magazine that was aimed at a target audience of educated young women who read as avidly as they pursued the latest fashions. (Joan Didion guest-edited one issue; Sylvia Plath drew on her time working as a *Mademoiselle* intern for her boldly autobiographical novel, *The Bell Jar*.)

Cantwell's interview with Rhys in the summer of 1974 coincided with one of Maryvonne's visits to the Devon cottage; Rhys was communicating, however indirectly, with her daughter when she told Mary Cantwell about the "awful misery" she had felt over the loss of her first-born child; her baby son. Cantwell herself was more struck by Rhys's image of herself as a woman who dreaded social gatherings: "I'm a person at a masked ball without a mask" was how she described it. Sipping sweet vermouth and soda while her fingers restlessly flicked the on–off switch of a tiny electric heater, Rhys struggled to explain to an attentive Cantwell how the troubled leading characters in her novels always evaded the net of any conscious plans that she herself had made for them, seeming to act and speak of their own volition. How, then, could Julia Martin, Sasha Jansen or Anna Morgan be seen by readers as mere versions of herself? Perhaps Maryvonne scolded her mother for drinking alcohol outside mealtimes; unexpectedly, Rhys suddenly confessed to her visitor that—having once had what she considered "a good head"—she could no longer drink without consequences.[7]

If none of Rhys's friends picked up on that hint in Cantwell's illuminating interview—it's hard to imagine either Francis Wyndham or Diana Athill as readers of *Mademoiselle*—it may simply have been that they knew better. Rhys had spoken of her characters as moving beyond her control; she herself could not bear to be placed under restraint. Covertly watching the octogenarian writer methodically swilling down a lethal two-handed combination of whisky and champagne, glass after glass, as she sat on a sofa alone, apart from a cluster of chattering party guests, the young writer James Fox (he was one of Wyndham's literary protégés) once caught Rhys's eye. What he saw there disturbed him; it was a "hell-bent, give me more pain and just watch me" stare of black defiance. And up to her lips went yet another glass.[8]

Since 1967, Rhys had resisted all pleas for television interviews; in the early autumn of 1974, she relented. Setting the crown on a remarkable year was Tristram Powell's documentary tribute for *Omnibus*. Shown in late November, with a pensive, slender Eileen Atkins playing an amalgam of the women of the novels, the programme concluded with an interview granted by a visibly nervous Rhys. Powell, who places Rhys alongside Lucian Freud and Beryl Bainbridge as a genuinely reluctant performer, regards that reticence as evidence of a rare artistic integrity.[9]

Rhys's nervousness with such a practised interviewer as Tristram Powell may once again, in an autumn when she was struggling with the aftermath of her summer flu, have owed something to ill health. Shortly after thanking Sonia Orwell, on 15 November 1974, for all her help over the past years ("you are the most generous woman in the world," Rhys would exclaim as Sonia offered to finance the purchase of a west London flat for her young granddaughter), she was rushed into St. Vincent's, a London nursing home where she would spend the next two months. Rhys was still at St. Vincent's when Selma Vaz Dias started threatening a lawsuit over the absence of any reference to herself in Tristram Powell's documentary. Had Francis Wyndham objected to being left out of the programme, an impatient Peggy Ramsay demanded? Wasn't there enough reward for Selma in knowing that she, too, had contributed to the revival of her old friend's career? Perceptively, but with an excess of candour, Peggy commented: "It's as if you want to become Jean Rhys."[10]

Nineteen seventy-four had been a glorious year in terms of recognition, but the occupational hazards of success took Rhys away from her writing. Diana Athill remained anxious about the slow progress of the story collection that her pet author had contracted to supply to Deutsch by the following spring—and to which Gini Stevens had already sold the world rights from under Diana's affronted nose. Athill caused a lengthy delay of her own when she decided at the last moment, in the spring of 1975, that one of Rhys's personal favourites must be excluded. The tale in question was "Imperial Road," Rhys's barely fictionalised account of her quixotic endeavour, back in 1936, to demonstrate the completion of a road that had, in truth, foundered after seventeen treacherous miles.

Rhys had been labouring over various versions of "Imperial Road" for thirty years, but times had changed dramatically in the Caribbean during the 1970s. A house boldly rebuilt upon the scorched foundations of the Lockharts' home at Geneva had recently been burned down; "Black man time is come! White man had his fun!" ran the opening line of a calypso song for Roseau's carnival in 1974.[11] Fired up by the accounts from Dominica that arrived in news clippings sent by Phyllis Shand Allfrey, living out on the island, Rhys nobly urged Francis Wyndham to publicise the environmental threat posed by unscrupulous British timber firms to Dominica's magnificent rainforest;[*] it was not, however, the time to start celebrating Britain's past presence on the island. To Diana, Rhys's clearly autobiographical story read like an endorsement of colonialism. She ruled it out. Rhys, outraged and miserable, ceased to work.

As so often in Rhys's later years, a tricky moment was quietly resolved by Francis Wyndham. While reluctant to get involved in Rhys's championing of her beloved island's rainforest, he promised to get "The Imperial Road" published as an independent story in the *Sunday Times*, for which he worked.[†] Wyndham then offered the services of Sonia and himself as first readers of the stories that Rhys had been

---

[*] Phyllis Shand Allfrey had resumed contact with Rhys in 1973, when a film crew arrived in Dominica to scout locations for *Wide Sargasso Sea*. It would be another twenty years before a film was made, using Jamaican locations. A BBC version followed in 2006.

[†] Although "The Imperial Road" was never published in the *Sunday Times*, it survives in multiple drafts. Rhys intended it to form part of her memoir. Diana Athill, who finished editing *Smile Please* shortly before Rhys's death, decided, once again, to exclude an unfinished work for which her enthusiasm had always been scant.

intermittently dictating over the past two years to Gini Stevens. He chose shrewdly: Sonia Orwell had earned her editorial spurs on Cyril Connolly's *Horizon*—and Jean trusted her.[12]

Soothed by Wyndham's assurance that all would be well, Rhys returned to work on one of her finest late stories in the summer of 1975. Writing to Phyllis Shand Allfrey back on 16 May 1973 about her longing to "lay my bones" in Dominica, Rhys had told her Caribbean-born friend of a poem called "Return," written and then lost during her first lonely months of living at Maidstone. Rhys described "Return" to Phyllis as a poem about going back to Dominica and only realising that she was already dead "when no one recognises or sees me." As always with Rhys, no sign of the long gestation ("I've tried over and over again to rewrite it," she told Shand Allfrey) was visible in "I Used to Live Here Once," the exquisitely simple ghost story of just such a return that she finally dictated to Gini Stevens in the summer of 1975.[13]

The stories for *Sleep It Off Lady* (Rhys's first collection since *Tigers are Better-Looking*, back in 1968) were delivered to an anxious Athill in the autumn of 1975. Alone in Devon, and increasingly prone to anxiety, Rhys started to worry about the large sums of money that her new—and her first—financial advisor, Michael Henshaw, was now handling on her behalf. Henshaw was a charming man who represented a dazzling list of writers and actors, but his methods were often highly unorthodox. Weaving dreadful scenarios in which the cottage was to be confiscated and she herself sent to prison (shades of Jean Lenglet and Max Hamer), Rhys blamed the shock of a dawn raid on the cottage by a sinister—evidently imaginary—official for a fall which cracked one of her ribs. "I was NOT drunk!" she joked to Francis in October, while gallantly declining to add that she was in considerable pain.[14]

Reading on through this same surprisingly cheerful letter, Francis discovered the source of Rhys's good humour. An unnamed literary admirer from New York was courting her. Should she boldly cross the Atlantic? Visiting her with champagne and flowers at the grim West Kensington care home where Sonia had lodged her temporarily incapacitated old friend, a frisky Al Alvarez encouraged Rhys to dream.

Why should a still beautiful woman not set herself up in a comfortable apartment in Manhattan for a while and allow herself to be adored? Alvarez himself would take charge of her social life; her unnamed beau would see to all of the glorious rest. But who *was* he? Rhys wouldn't say.

The identity of Rhys's American suitor remained unrevealed. Conceivably, she misread the courtly manner of Frank Hallman, an American Southerner who was in the process of publishing her *Vogue* piece ("My Day"), together with two autobiographical fragments, in a special edition of 750 copies. To Rhys, Frank's generous flood of gifts (stockings, French scent, silk scarves) may have looked like courtship; it's entirely possible that a grateful Hallman—Rhys had personally managed to sign most of the insert sheets during his brief visit to Devon earlier that year—did encourage the idea of a trip to New York. What Rhys failed to grasp—she perhaps was never told—was that her swain was happily partnered by Richard Schaubeck, his devoted companion until Hallman's tragically premature death in the spring of 1976.

Rhys's plans for New York were pure fantasy; an eighty-five-year-old with a cracked rib was not fit to go travelling anywhere, except in her dreams. In dreary times, however, confined to a hotel for ailing senior citizens, the thought of a solicitous admirer offered consolation. Tongue-in-cheek, Rhys often referred to the unnamed East Coast "suitor" as her last lover.

ONE OF THE oddest items tucked away in the stiff rows of boxes of Rhys-related papers and manuscripts held in the McFarlin Library at Tulsa dates from Rhys's autumn at the Kensington care home. Written in scrawled red biro on lined foolscap paper, it is defiantly titled "Shades of Pink." Closer inspection reveals an unexpected first collaboration between Jean Rhys and David Plante.

Rhys had first encountered Plante's name when they both contributed stories to a Penguin anthology published in 1969. In 1970, when they were introduced to each other by Sonia Orwell, the personable young writer from Provincetown quickly became a friend. *Diffi-*

cult Women, Plante's controversial 1983 character study of himself in his relationship with three extraordinary and forceful women (Sonia Orwell, Germaine Greer and Jean Rhys), opened with the startling episode which took place five years after that first meeting, in December 1975, when he paid his first visit to the dreary west London hotel at which Rhys remained confined. Oddly, Plante had received no warning that Rhys, well prepared for the occasion by Sonia, was expecting a professional meeting at which she would dictate material for her memoir to an obliging friend.

Plante's far-from-artless memoir presented Rhys at the hotel as a recent acquaintance, an ancient mariner who was drinking hard while relating interminable tales of her childhood in the Caribbean. Rhys rambled on; Plante, matching her drink for drink, listened. Eventually, the physically diminished and still disabled Rhys hobbled into the bathroom. The next thing Plante heard was a pitiful wail; Rhys's skinny posterior had been trapped in the well of her own bathroom lavatory. The fault lay with Plante, as he realised too late: having previously made use of the old lady's loo, he had neglected to re-lower the seat.

Eight years later, working up that disastrously mismanaged encounter for public consumption, Plante omitted to mention that his hostess was expecting him to take dictation for her memoir. Instead, he offered a brutally candid portrait of a snorting, spitting, dishevelled Rhys in decline. "Shades of Pink," the unpublished and never completed work on which Rhys invited Plante to collaborate, was her own more generous attempt to wrest a comic story from a mortifying incident, one which had been replete with misunderstandings. Plante himself was transformed into urbane "Maurice Denis," visiting a youthful "Lucy Nicholson" at the recognisably odious hotel. Plante's version dwelt on a puddle of piss on the bathroom floor; the knickers hanging around Rhys's ankles; the "battered" hat perched askew on her lolling head. Rhys's version presents a moment of sheer comic delight as Lucy rises up into her saviour's arms from her porcelain well with buoyant exhilaration: "like a cork out of a bottle."[15] The surviving fragment of "Shades of Pink" offers a late example of Rhys's unique capacity in her fiction both to mock and to transcend herself in portraits that are only ever partially autobiographical. Plante was charmed and a little shamed by Rhys's generous interpretation;[16] Diana Athill was not amused. The project was dropped.

Early in 1976, when Rhys was happily restored to her beloved suite at the Portobello, Plante paid his forgiving old friend a further visit. It was on this occasion that a chastened David (Sonia Orwell had given him a stern dressing-down for his inept handling of Jean at the West London hotel) first volunteered to transcribe Rhys's memoir. Some progress was made until—anxious to establish a logical sequence for the random episodes which Rhys provided—Plante requested an oral chronology. To a sensitive author, it seemed as if a pushy young man was attempting to take control of her most personal project. Rhys lost her temper. All talk of a collaboration was dropped.

Rhys's black mood had lifted when she wrote on 15 February to tell Francis Wyndham that she had been enjoying Antonia Fraser's adaptation of *Rebecca* for radio. Antonia's version of elegant, suave Max de Winter was declared to be Rhys's ideal: "a dream of a man."[17] Romance was on Rhys's mind once more; just as she began researching the possibility of a jaunt to New York and her mystery lover, a second and far more serious fall landed her, first, in hospital and then—to her dismay—back in a London nursing home. The medical report was grave: in addition to four cracked ribs, two dating back to the previous autumn, the X-rays revealed an enlarged heart. Rhys's days of independence were over. From 1976 on, age-friendly accommodation would be required whenever she visited London; down in Devon, discreet feelers were put out for a suitable nurse-companion.

Joan Butler, Jean's country neighbour, produced a solution that would not impinge too much on Rhys's enduring desire for privacy. Janet Bridger was a forthright young Canadian district nurse who, after five years of working for an Inuit community, had settled in Devon. Janet was willing to spend four hours a day at the cottage doing whatever was required, including discreet supervision of Rhys's intake of alcohol. Several visitors to the cottage were startled by Bridger's gauchely truculent manner (Jo Batterham detested her), but there was no doubting Janet's commitment. Her first year with Rhys went quite well.

The problem of where to find West Country help with transcribing the dictated memoir was solved by the discovery in a nearby village of Michael Schwab. Helpful, efficient and handsome to boot, Michael was willing to double as Rhys's driver—Mr. Greenslade had decided to retire after his wife's death—and typist. By July 1976, Rhys was feeling strong enough to dictate the entire section of the memoir that deals with "Meta"—the violent nurse who had so terrified little Gwen Rees Williams—in a single, exhausting session. Like Gini Stevens, Michael Schwab was astonished by the contrast between Rhys's fragile appearance and her capacity to dictate and revise aloud for hours on end.

Every ounce of Rhys's waning creative energy was now devoted to completing the memoir. Diana Athill, having efficiently secured grants to cover Michael Schwab's driving expenses and time, advised the *New Yorker* that the four stories they were planning to publish ahead of *Sleep It Off Lady* would be the very last that they would receive from the weakened author. For Deutsch, to whom Jean Rhys had become a lucrative investment, it was crucial that she should stay alive long enough to finish the memoir; for Sonia, expressing her thoughts discreetly to Diana Athill in March, the time had come to hope for a merciful ending. Aged almost eighty-six, Rhys surely deserved a peaceful death?[18]

A little wishful thinking was involved on Sonia Orwell's part. While Francis Wyndham was increasingly preoccupied by the need to care for his ageing mother, Sonia herself had fallen victim to an unscrupulous accountant. The hospitable house on Gloucester Road was put up for sale; the days of bankrolling Rhys's holidays in London were over. Vaguely conscious that something was amiss, Rhys took good care—as indeed she always had, year after year—to thank her "darling Sonia" for "ALL you've done for me."[19]

Happily, Jean Rhys's own improved financial position meant that she no longer depended on the generosity of friends like Sonia Orwell.

Everything she produced now carried a perceived value and was received accordingly. *Sleep It Off Lady*, published in October 1976 by Deutsch, and in November by Harper & Row in the US, was the first work she had produced since the outstanding collection titled *Tigers are Better-Looking* in 1968. Francis and Sonia had both gone over it, as had Diana Athill; none of them had been able to get around the fact that a collection which included several stories on which Rhys had been working, on and off, for three decades, together with a handful which had been written on various topics over the past five years, did not make for a well-integrated whole. The title story was widely praised, while both William Trevor and the *New York Times Book Review*'s Robie Macauley thought "I Used to Live Here Once" was among the finest, and certainly the most concise, ghost stories they had ever read. (It's a little over 400 words.) *Kirkus Reviews* described the collection as "sketches" and, rather crushingly, a "*force mineure*," while praising the "desolate allure" which their reviewer identified as Rhys's trademark.[20]

Rhys's plans for a memoir had been at the forefront of her mind when she wrote "Overture and Beginners Please" and "Before the Deluge"; these highly personal stories were the only two to describe her first years in England at school and then on tour. Writing, dictating and revising a group of stories that drew upon her Dominica childhood, while feeling her way towards the best voice in which to narrate her memoir, Rhys seems also to have worried about which remembered episodes were suited to which genre. The best answer, as with the almost purely autobiographical "On Not Shooting Sitting Birds"—clearly more appropriate to a memoir than a story collection—was not always found.

Rhys's discretion meant that little was yet known about her early life. Nobody reading the new collection could have been expected to guess that "Good-bye Marcus, Good-bye Rose," Rhys's troubling story of a little girl being molested by a distinguished older gentleman, was based upon fact. Neither were her readers to know how much personal detail had been worked into "Pioneers, Oh, Pioneers," the story of Mr. Ramage on which Rhys had been working on and off ever since her return to Dominica in 1936, when she first heard about the English settler's mysterious death at his isolated home.

A fierce perfectionist, Rhys herself was dissatisfied by the collection. Her comment to an admiring Oliver Stonor about one widely praised late story, "Rapunzel, Rapunzel," was that "I missed it somehow." It reflected her feeling about them all. Writing to Francis (Wyndham shared Stonor's liking for Rhys's odd little tale about the shearing of a plain woman's proudly displayed golden locks) she disparaged the collection as "the 'So-So Stories'" (for which Wyndham scolded her).

Rhys's growing readership disagreed. In America, especially, sales of her novels continued to soar. While Peggy Ramsay's telephone clamoured with requests from Hollywood, American universities had also begun to show a keen interest in Rhys's manuscripts.

Oliver Stonor had been acting on Rhys's behalf for some time as the middleman in sales of her hotchpotch of literary papers to Bertram Rota, the London antiquarian bookseller and dealer. Rota's own book expert, John Byrne, now stepped in to facilitate a more substantial purchase for the McFarlin Library in Tulsa, where an ambitious young academic named Thomas Staley was in the process of creating a centre for women's studies. In the autumn of 1976, while Diana Athill replaced Rhys's trio of agents with one of her own choosing (the erudite and raffishly charming Anthony Shiel), Tom Staley visited London and offered a thousand guineas to acquire the bulk of Rhys's work. Staley was an attractive man. Rhys's granddaughter, who was shooed away from paying a visit of her own when Staley arrived to discuss the details of the deal, suspects that her still flirtatious grandmother feared competition for the attention of a new admirer. Rhys may also have wished to conceal from her hard-up family just how much money was passing into her hands.

Rhys had spent most of her summer in Devon dictating episodes from her memoir to Michael Schwab. Back in London at the end of 1976, and staying in a service flat near Sloane Square, she summoned David Plante back for a second attempt at collaboration. Some progress was made; it seems to have been during this brief interlude that Rhys humbly described herself to Plante (when compared to her beloved Russian authors) as a mere trickle feeding into the great lake of fiction. Once, apparently, she broke into a perfectly conceived evocation of the lost *mornes* (mountains) of her beloved Dominica. To an enthralled Plante, her description sounded improvised; Rhys's habit of careful mental preparation suggests that she already knew every word that she narrated by heart.

The problem for Rhys of working with David Plante was that he, too, was a writer. His first attempt to extract a chronology had appalled her; now, seeking to impose a structure on the flood of episodes with which Rhys inundated him, Plante asked permission to reshape them. Having painstakingly snipped Rhys's sentences apart and reconnected them into a more logical narrative, Plante read her the result aloud. Hearing what he took for a whisper of approval, he carried his revised manuscript home to type it up.

Both Diana Athill and David Plante were good storytellers. Both of them dined out on the drama of their friend's response. Diana, arriving at Rhys's flat later that same evening to see Jean safely into her bed, encountered a wild creature, untameable in her fury, swearing, drunk and sobbing that her book had been stolen from out of her hands. Never again would she work with David Plante![21]

Rhys's attitude to her work was protective; her anguish at the sense that the memoir had been tampered with is not in doubt. No longer impoverished, she was even willing to fork out £500 to pay David off for his forfeited effort. But she did not want to lose Plante's friendship; Diana was specifically instructed to make the payment through Deutsch, as if the decision had been all their own.

Rhys had always been volatile. It was only a matter of weeks before a nervous David was recalled and forgiven. Work resumed; for the time being, there were no more outbursts. Towards the end of February 1977, the partly completed memoir was sealed by Plante within two sturdy envelopes on the outside of which he wrote, under Rhys's directions, that the contents were to be destroyed if anything should happen to their owner. Authorising the statement, Rhys carefully inscribed her name twice over, once as Jean Rhys and then as "E[lla] G[wendoline] Hamer."

Why such an anxious precaution? In 1977, after over thirty years of living entirely in England, Rhys was making preparations to leave the country. Her health was poor; her bones were increasingly brittle; she was in her eighty-seventh year: anything might happen. If disaster struck, an unfinished, orphaned memoir that presented her younger self to the world without the mask of fiction was in need of the best protection that a mother could provide for a work to which Rhys by now felt as tenderly close as a pregnant mother to her unborn child.

VIII

AND YET I FEAR*

*   Written when Rhys was in her mid-eighties, "And Yet I Fear" is her finest unpublished poem. Clearly influenced by one of her favourite poets, Emily Dickinson, Rhys salutes death as a massive hidden power; a welcome force that will sweep her up into the universe, to become one with the wind and the stars and "sweet" eternity. Closing on a Shakespearean image of death at sea, this remarkable fifteen-line poem (it would be interesting to know who typed it out for her) suggests that incapacitating old age, rather than death, was what Rhys feared.

22

"The Old Punk Upstairs"*
(1977–79)

"The more I realise the precariousness of Jean's hold on calm, the more valiant she seems to me."

—Diana Athill to Francis Wyndham, 1 January 1980[1]

JEAN RHYS WAS a woman who compartmentalised her friends. So did Sonia Orwell. This helps to explain why Jo Batterham and Diana Melly only met each other late in 1976, a year during which Sonia, working out a plan with Melly for Rhys's future, organised a rota of volunteers to ensure that Rhys, however physically incapacitated, could continue to enjoy her annual visits to London. Several illustrious artists, poets and writers joined the list, although few of them offered more than lip service.

What Batterham and Melly importantly shared was an understanding of the crucial importance to their old friend of details that less sensitive acquaintances might have overlooked. Jo took endless trouble to see that the latest cottage furnishings were in just the right colour to satisfy the changeable wishes of a peculiarly demanding client; inter-

---

* Borrowed from the title of a 1990 newspaper tribute by jazz musician and memoirist George Melly to his friend Jean Rhys ("The Old Punk Upstairs," *Independent on Sunday*, 28 October 1990).

minable discussions took place over the precise shade of yellow vel-
vet for a chaise longue on which a lame octogenarian author might
regally recline (Rhys was a great admirer of Sarah Bernhardt's receiving mode) when being viewed by inquisitive journalists. Diana Melly,
whose major test of her friendship with Rhys was yet to come, was
already putting herself out to hunt down the perfect dress, the exact
shade of pink lipstick and even the facial masseur whose calming hands
could best restore an illusion of youth to match Rhys's indomitable
spirit. More than any other of Rhys's friends, Melly understood how
anxiously an outwardly successful old woman continued to fret about
her appearance.

Work on Rhys's memoir had progressed well enough in the early
part of 1977 for David Plante to tell Sonia that Rhys was worrying
about having mislaid an incomplete account of her early years in Paris
("*L'affaire Ford*") which she was evidently planning to revise for inclusion in *Smile Please*. The published memoir ends just before Rhys's first
encounter with Ford; the absent section would have let us know—as
perceptive readers might already have guessed from the early novels, in
which Ford's identity was apparent—that there had been a love affair.

The reward that Rhys had chosen for her own hard work was to be a
winter fortnight in Venice, with Diana Melly and Jo Batterham as her
appointed chaperones. Rhys's only prior knowledge of Italy derived
from a few blissful days spent in Florence with Jean Lenglet, when the
couple had visited the Uffizi and gazed at *The Birth of Venus*, the painting that became Rhys's favourite work of art, along with the *Winged
Victory* in the Louvre. Had Lenglet pointed out the younger Rhys's
resemblance to Botticelli's young goddess, skimming the rippling
waves aboard her scallop-shell as detachedly as the pale palaces of Venice's Grand Canal float above their supportive reflections? Maryvonne,
who had visited Italy with her husband, Job, described Venice as the
most enchanting of European cities. Venice, then, it must be.

Shepherded on board for her first—and first-class—aeroplane flight,
a terrified but excited Rhys sipped courage from a mini-bottle of com-

plimentary champagne. Landing, she was conducted to a hotel which had been specially chosen for its romantic associations. Confirmation of Rhys's unquenchably romantic taste comes from Peter Eyre's recollection of being asked, when he visited Cheriton Fitzpaine in 1974, to bring with him recordings of Wagner's *Liebestod* and highlights from *Der Rosenkavalier.* Where, then, in Venice should Jean Rhys stay but at the hotel that had been home to Alfred de Musset, to Marcel Proust and even to Wagner himself?

Passers-by can still glimpse the ornate corner bedroom on the first floor of the old Danieli (not the modern extension) which Rhys occupied during the last week of February and first ten days of March 1977, while Jo and Diana made do with a humbler room next door. Diana's faded travel snaps confirm the state of general enjoyment that glows out of the long, chatty letters despatched by Jo to Sonia in Paris. Here, we see slender, dark-haired Diana and stockier, beaming Jo pushing a crumpled Rhys along in a wheelchair (she was too lame to cross the stepped bridges on foot). There, a careful Diana arranges Rhys's battalions of pills (a task which Diana enjoyed as much as lovingly tidying the five little purses of cosmetics without which the elderly Rhys still never left home). In one image, Rhys waves from the balcony of her high chamber to a throng of tourists, obliviously passing by; in another, a cushioned bolster enables a smiling Jean to gaze at the ravishing city from the back of a gondola.

Life followed an orderly pattern. Rhys's mornings (a leisurely breakfast in bed followed by a lengthy tryst with the hotel's hairdresser) released Diana and Jo from their duties until the stately lunch in the hotel dining room which was Jean's favourite treat of the day. Back at the Danieli after a brisk post-prandial hour of being pushed around the city's chilly *calle* and *campi*, Rhys drowsily read Hemingway's novel of Venice, *Across the River and into the Trees* (renamed "Across the Street and into the Grill" by a mischievous E. B. White). Next door, Jo tapped away, clattering out a daily journal of events for Sonia while Diana, when not busy knitting as she enjoyed a tranquillising joint, studied the

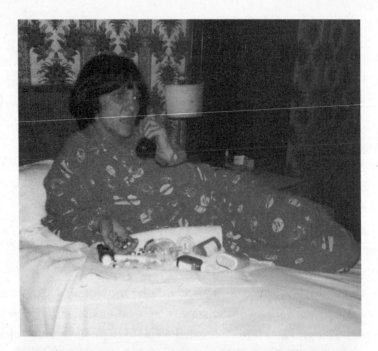

(*Above*) Diana Melly arranges Jean's battalion of medications, a task that pleased her orderly mind. (*Below*) Jo Batterham, pushing a rather depleted Rhys across San Marco in her wheelchair. *(Used with permission of Diana Melly)*

hefty hotel bills. A substantial reduction in their meal and bar charges followed her divulgence to the Danieli's impressed manager that their elderly guest was a writer of international renown.

Evenings began with Negroni cocktails in the hotel bar, where the handsome pianist was always ready to serenade Rhys with one of her favourite old French songs by Piaf or Charles Trenet. Later, after the light snack, glass of cold milk and early bedtime on which Rhys always insisted, Jo and Diana sauntered companionably out, in search of a more vibrant Venice.

Bad moments were rare. "We seem to laugh the whole time, it's in the air," Jo wrote to Sonia—and Jean agreed.[2] Back in Devon and writing to congratulate Melly on the good reviews for her own first novel, *The Girl in the Picture*, a grateful Rhys—she had spent a cheerful week with the Mellys after her return to London—thanked her and Jo again for contributing to her happiness: "You were both so good to me."[3]

Venice gave Rhys a sustained feeling of joy that she had rarely found before, except in an enchanted moment of epiphany. Asked by Tristram Powell, at the end of his television interview with her, whether—had she her life to live over again—she would choose to write, or to be happy, there's no forgetting the pathos with which a yearning Rhys cries out: "Oh, *happiness!*"

———

FOUR MONTHS AFTER the trip to Venice, Diana Melly received a summons to Devon. The University of Kent, a leader in the rapidly expanding field of Commonwealth literature since 1964, ran a course on African and Caribbean-related studies. Rhys's own recent contribution to Caribbean literature was to be acknowledged by the university with an honorary doctorate.[*] The invitation had come from Professor Louis James, who had been visiting Jean since 1975. Since Rhys

———

[*] The influence on Rhys's postwar writing of the distinguished Caribbean authors living in London during the 1950s remains underexplored. It wasn't by chance that Rhys chose to recast her own experiences as those of Selina Davis ("Let Them Call It Jazz"), a light-skinned newcomer to London from the Caribbean.

Rhys returns to her room at the Danieli after waving to the crowds. *(Used with permission of Diana Melly)*

was understandably reluctant to attend the long, formal ceremony at Canterbury, three representatives of the university, including Professor James and Mark Kinkead-Weekes, had decided to visit Cheriton, bringing with them a black gown, a diploma—and a tape recorder.

Rhys's first official sign of academic recognition, while eased by the arrival on the previous night of a tanned Diana Melly (with a sulky-faced boyfriend in tow), proved a less happy experience than her visitors had anticipated. A glass of champagne failed to calm Rhys's nerves, while the discovery that the imposing gown—as with *Vogue*'s dresses— was simply offered on loan lowered her spirits considerably. The real ordeal was yet to come, when Rhys listened to the oration that had been pre-recorded for her imagined pleasure.

On the following morning, 21 July 1977, Rhys wrote to Louis James, author of the recorded oration, to berate him for having dared to suggest that, while her father had always been considerate towards his black patients, he had been any less attentive than to his patients who were white. All were equal in his eyes: this was the point which Rhys wished to stress. She was mollified by the news, resulting from James's own researches, that "all of Roseau" had followed Dr. Rees Williams's coffin through the town.[4]

Diana Melly spent a peaceful night in Rhys's new cedarwood annex before her return to London; Jo Batterham, visiting Rhys a few weeks later to discuss some further improvements to the cottage's decoration, alarmed both Sonia Orwell and Diana Athill by reporting that Janet Bridger was neglecting her duties and showed no concern for poor Jean's appearance. Janet's cooking was denounced as atrocious; worse, Bridger ordered Rhys about. How lucky for their old friend it was (Jo remarked) that she still possessed kind neighbours like the Stettifords and Mrs. Raymond—the Greenslades had both died—to bring in meals and to lock the door each night (a precaution taken after Athill's frightening experience when a boy burglar stole her purse from a bedside table in the new annex).

Jo's mention of the reported death of Brenda Powell, the last survivor of Rhys's immediate family, was added almost as an afterthought to her long letter. Brenda had suffered nearly a decade of slow mental decline and the siblings had not spoken for many years; nevertheless, according to Janet, Rhys had burst into tears when she heard the news. Brenda had belonged to the old Caribbean world in which, endlessly rehearsing the scenes and sentences of her memoir, Rhys now—and perhaps, always—dwelled more intensely than in the present. ("*Swing swing*," Rhys wrote over and again in her notes, seeming to remind herself of the perpetual shift between past and present experience that had formed a key element in the time-shifting structure of *Voyage in the Dark*: "*Swing swing*.")

Dictating her episode-driven recollections to Michael Schwab in the summer of 1977 (David Plante had decamped for a long holiday in Italy), Rhys slipped effortlessly back into the mind of a little girl, the doctor's favourite daughter, growing up in Roseau at the end of the nineteenth century. Titled "The Yellow Flag," and eventually placed in the opening section of *Smile Please*, a fragment of an early draft which survives in the British Library's Rhys Papers describes the abandoned Victorian quarantine station around which Rhys had once played with her friends. The published version quotes a few lines from an old military ditty which the children sang as they rocked to and fro on the "broad and comfortable" seats of their chosen playground's swings.

Rhys's original draft of the song had included the response given to a young maid's naive plea for a husband. "How can I marry such a pretty little girl, / When I haven't got a shirt to put on," the married soldier teases the girl, as she innocently hastens to provide the elegant clothes her dashing suitor claims to lack. "Swing swing," Rhys added at the end (as well as the start) of her draft—and she marked out that second "Swing" with a long, low and suppliant "S," one that looks as if she intended it to represent a small, submissive body. The station was "a safe, bland, self-satisfied place," Rhys wrote in her final version, before adding: "and yet something lurked in the sunlight." As with the childhood memory related in *After Leaving Mr Mackenzie* of a frightened little girl running home from a silent, sunlit place, and never revealing what has scared her, it feels as if Rhys has deliberately placed on view a sinister recollection from the past, as sharply evoked as the unspoken scent of terror that haunts some of Henry James's most troubling works. The connection is not irrelevant; Rhys's letters show that she had read *The Turn of the Screw* at least six times.

Dark thoughts ran deep within Rhys, and never more so than when she was alone in Devon. The Canadian-born Janet Bridger took it calmly when a stone was flung at her one day in Cheriton, a village where outsiders were often viewed with suspicion. Bridger was a good deal more frightened when, following an altercation with Rhys, she found herself locked inside the cottage with its owner, who, elfishly taunting and triumphant, flourished aloft what Rhys imagined to be the only key to the door. Janet's thankful recollection of a spare key, kept in a dresser drawer, flattens the climax of her dramatic tale with her escape into the Devon night, but it also adds plausibility to a disturbing episode.

BY THE LATE summer of 1977, it was becoming apparent to Rhys that she could no longer rely upon friends to take care of her whenever she left Devon. Francis's spare time was occupied by the needs of his dying mother, while Sonia Orwell was frequently absent in Paris. In August, Rhys looked into the possibility of spending time at a Catholic retreat in London, vaguely referred to as "The Blue Nuns." Informing Sonia of the failure of another tentative plan, Rhys confessed a modest dread of imposing her weakened body and its daily needs on the kindness of well-meaning acquaintants. "Between you and Di [Melly] you are really Jean's only hope," Sonia wrote a little desperately from Paris to Jo Batterham on 16 August; three weeks later, Rhys herself echoed that sentiment. "I haven't got many friends in London now," Jean told Jo, "in fact, Diana Melly and yourself are the only ones I'm sure of."[5]

Sonia was acting with the best of intentions when she arranged for Rhys and Janet Bridger to spend the autumn of 1977 together at Oatlands Hotel, an expensive nursing home in Surrey. Grand surroundings—the hotel stood proudly on the site of a royal Tudor palace—failed to disguise the ubiquity of wheelchairs and medical trolleys. Janet fled back to Devon after three dispiriting days; visited by a sympathetic Athill, Rhys glumly joked that one ancient resident's enthusiasm for killing off new germs must be directed at herself, the unwelcome new pest. Of course (as Rhys acknowledged with a giggle), she was being paranoid, but please, couldn't Athill find her a way to escape? Diana did her best, placing a carefully worded advertisement for rooms in a private London home that might suit a "distinguished elderly woman" with independent means and "outside sources of care." An unknown Mrs. Hatch offered an upstairs bedroom with narrow stairs up which her daughters could carry an elderly tenant, when required. *If* they were around. *If* they chose: it's hardly surprising that Rhys turned the offer down.[6]

The obvious solution was for Rhys to be taken in either by Jo Batterham or by the Mellys. But taking Jean in also meant gratifying her expectations, which were often unreasonably high. "I know [clothes] shopping is tiring," the eighty-seven-year old Rhys hopefully advised Jo on 27 October, "but I find it so exciting and it would please me so much." The fact that a distraught Jo felt unable to face the ordeal of conducting a frail old woman around London's finest dress shops had much to do with the fact that her beloved Gini Stevens had just left her to marry an American.[7]

Rhys was unaware that the kind-hearted Mellys were already on her case. George was sympathetic to needy women, especially when they were as interesting as Jean Rhys; Diana relished the idea of rearranging their family home in Gospel Oak—only the first-floor rooms housing George's magnificent collection of surrealist paintings were ruled out of bounds—in order to ensure the happiness of a cherished guest.

The preparations, outlined in an entertaining and moving article which George Melly would publish some thirteen years later, were tremendous. George relinquished his beloved box mattress, the lowest and least dangerous form of bed the Mellys could produce for an unsteady old lady with brittle bones; Diana, moving out of her own airy bedroom on the second storey of a three-floor maisonette at 102 Savernake Road with views of Hampstead Heath, redecorated the entire ensuite in what she knew were Rhys's favourite shades of pink: rosy pink lampshades; sunrise pink curtains; marshmallow pink for the freshly painted wooden floors. The result, so an admiring George recalled with the sad hindsight of 1990, was "incredibly pretty . . . as warm, cosy and mildly exotic as a gypsy caravan." Here, surely, even such a perennially wistful writer as Jean Rhys might allow herself to feel happy? "She would have no practical worries, proper meals, lots of treats and outings, friends when she wanted company, help with her make-up, an important chore . . ." (George had already persuaded the Mellys' friend Mary Quant to send Rhys a bag of her daisy-themed cosmetics during the summer) " . . . and any amount of love and goodwill. We were longing for her arrival."[8]

Of the three months that the octogenarian Rhys would spend under George and Diana's roof, the first two were an almost unqualified success. A document of proof survives in the form of a daily journal kept by the Mellys' lodger. Fresh from reading Oriental Studies at Cambridge, young Sarah Papineau found their guest captivating, demanding, and capricious.[9]

It took a week, so an intrigued Papineau recorded in her diary, for a haphazardly coiffured Miss Rhys (increasingly blind and averse to wearing glasses, Jean often put her pink or white wigs on back to front) to venture down the stairs. A few days later, Sarah attended a kitchen lunch at which a radiant Rhys—Diana had spent the morning shopping on her behalf at *Chic*, an expensive Hampstead boutique—regaled the two of them with memories of her early years in Paris. Publicly, Rhys had always been resolutely discreet; feeling herself to be among friends on this occasion, she opened up. It seemed that she hadn't warmed to the Fitzgeralds, but the dashingly handsome Hemingway, praised for

At home with the Mellys at Savernake Road. *(Used with permission of Diana Melly)*

his matchless skill with dialogue in fiction, was approvingly described as having been "shy and unassuming" in person.* She mentioned an early experiment with opium as a disappointment (it had produced no effect at all), before expressing a shy curiosity about the musky joints that Diana Melly was pleasurably inhaling with her coffee. (A shared spliff would often prove useful when Rhys became emotional.) Still tucking into her toffee pudding, Rhys begged for her appointment with an unknown new doctor to be deferred; she didn't want to be seen looking "awful" by a stranger. "She looked beautiful!" an admiring Sarah added to her journal of a memorable day.[10]

Sarah Papineau swiftly became Diana Melly's dependable supporter in the house, taking Rhys breakfast in bed, helping her to clamber into the bath and sometimes rushing back early from her evening waitressing duties at Ronnie Scott's, just to make sure that their celebrated visitor was safe and snug in her room. On 27 November, in a typical diary entry, Sarah noted that she had carried up the stairs a three-course lunch prepared by herself for their guest. A happy afternoon chatting to Rhys about punk rock had prefaced a warm invitation to Devon. Later that day, after the novelist Bernice Rubens had popped in for a quick visit (Rubens had her own house key to the Mellys' easy-going home), Sarah took Jean's glass of milk upstairs and settled the honoured guest safely into her bed.

The combination of circumstances was extraordinary. Here was a reclusive and frail old lady residing as the acknowledged queen of a household where jazz music, modern art, recreational drug-taking, theatre chat and the Mellys' own complicated love life, created a heady brew. Athill, after dropping in from her nearby home in Primrose Hill, reported to an anxious Sonia that, while "pink and lame," Rhys looked "ravishing" and "happy as a bee."[11]

Events that had been painstakingly arranged for Rhys's enjoyment

---

* Rhys's account adds a little credence to Jean Lenglet's claim in a Dutch publication that she had introduced him to Hemingway, whom he allegedly interviewed for his former employer, the *New York Herald Tribune*.

didn't always go well. George recalled the uncomfortable lunchtime occasion when Jean mischievously informed a disconsolate Penelope Mortimer, the respected author of *The Pumpkin Eater*, that Caroline Blackwood was the only woman writer in England who wasn't actually murdering the language. (Rhys had been devouring *Great Granny Webster*, Blackwood's disturbing and award-winning story of a loveless old grandmother, obtained by Sarah Papineau at Jean's urgent request.) The actor Peter Eyre, arriving for lunch at Savernake Road on a chilly day wrapped in a long, high-collared coat, had to be asked to leave because his appearance reminded a weeping Jean of the doomed aristocrats in the Russian Revolution. Contretemps often proved entertaining: George Melly's mother visibly sulked when Rhys hogged the limelight at a Christmas family lunch, while Al Alvarez was told off after giving a giggling Jean so much champagne that she fell on the floor: "all her recent accidents have been due to that," Sonia Orwell reproachfully reminded Diana Melly from Paris.[12]

Some of the disasters had comic overtones: Rhys once pulled so hard on the lavatory chain that the whole cistern crashed down; on another occasion, Diana Melly crossly compared herself, the forceful Athill and Jo Batterham to limp tea towels as they debated whether to answer angry thumps on the floor above, reminding them that a trapped Rhys wanted a top-up to her drink. Requests were not always so graceful. A polite manner had long concealed the formidable power of Rhys's will. As age stripped away the niceties of courtesy, she grew ever more ruthless about exerting that remarkable faculty to get her way.

By and large, Rhys threw tantrums only in the company of those she knew could be subdued. George, who allowed nobody to subdue him, could spend a tranquil evening watching an old Hitchcock film with their guest, or chatting about books. (A well-read Francophile, George shared Jean's affection for Breton's *Nadja*.) His wife, meanwhile, resigned herself to a volley of screams and curses whenever—which was increasingly often—she failed to please. "The thing is that you never know whether to talk to an old woman or to Jean," Diana Melly sighed to a distant Sonia, while wishing she could do more to make their guest happy. Sometimes, caressingly patted and told that she possessed the Caribbean islanders' gift for creating "magics" (a form of bewitchment) as she perched on the edge of Jean's bed to share a puff of her own late-evening joint, Diana believed for a fleeting moment that she had succeeded.[13]

There were many good times. Rhys loved being taken to Ronnie Scott's to hear George singing with John Chilton's band, the Feet-warmers, for whom she wrote the ruefully ironic lyrics to "Life Without You." But her patient hostess was not alone in feeling the strain. *Take a Girl Like Me*, the admirably candid memoir which Diana Melly published in 2005, recalls the occasions on which a grey-faced David Plante crept down their stairs from a tough two hours of labouring over the smallest details of Rhys's memoir. "I had now heard Jean's stories many times," he would write in *Difficult Women*. Rhys's title—*Smile Please*—was a given; the content now consisted of endless tiny refinements, the same ones being made over and again to the text that he was perpetually being instructed to read aloud. "Shit!" Rhys would shout if David spoke too quickly, or if some unbidden memory caused her pain. And then, out of the blue, just as when she assured Diana Melly that she possessed the power of "magics," there would come a murmured observation that caused all the humiliation and despair to slide away. Today, Plante still remembers how much it meant whenever Jean Rhys spoke to him as a valued colleague, explaining, on one fondly recalled occasion, the difficulty she always had with creating a sense of space around each word. "Yes," he remembers her saying in her soft little voice. "I tried to get that. I thought very hard of each word in itself."[14]

On 7 February 1978, Rhys was chauffeured to Buckingham Palace to receive a CBE from the queen. Diana Athill had persuaded one of the academic world's most adept fixers, Noel Annan, to arrange the honour; it was an award which appeared a perfect way to crown Rhys's achievements. A small celebration lunch was held afterwards in the Mellys' home at which Jean presided, smiling, sober and impeccably dressed. Her conversation with the queen was reported to have been pleasant but brief; it seems unlikely that Her Majesty was one of Rhys's keenest readers.

By February 1978, the dark side of Rhys's volatile personality had begun to emerge once more. Al Alvarez arrived at Savernake Road just in time to dissuade a distraught Jean from tearing up a latest—and last—short story: thanks to Alvarez's intervention, a delicate homage to Dominica and to Rhys's best-liked cousin, Lily Lockhart, "The Whistling Bird," would be published in the *New Yorker* in September that year. Diana Melly reached a point at which, so she recalls, she often felt like physically spitting into the bowl of soup being carried upstairs to their screaming guest. George Melly jokingly suggested that the two unhappy ladies might perhaps like to go in search of the local canal and drown themselves after supper. Plante, shocked by the violence of one of Rhys's rages, took an unkept vow never to visit her again.

What was going on? In part, the problem derived from the fact that Rhys felt both beholden and insecure. Kind though the Mellys had been, they were not her family and, however thoughtful their behaviour, she could imagine herself as their prisoner, shut away in her pretty pink suite. Rhys was also unsettled by the news that had reached her of a biography that Thomas Staley was determined to write. Confiding in his English friend John Byrne on 28 December 1977, Staley admitted that Rhys was reported to be unhappy and even alarmed, but added that he intended to go ahead with a critical work in which only a single chapter would be addressed to her personal life.[15] A chapter was still enough to cause dismay, however; having been distraught by Arthur Mizener's revelations in his biography of Ford, Rhys feared the very worst for herself at the hands of another American academic.

Equally terrifying to an old lady living in a house that was not her own was the prospect of being abandoned. Planning a winter weekend at her Welsh retreat during George's absence on a road trip, Diana Melly persuaded Sarah Papineau to return to act as Rhys's companion at Savernake Road. It was already well known that Jean liked Sarah. All, surely, would go well.

Returning from Wales three days later, Diana was greeted by an exhausted and ashen-faced Sarah. She described Jean as having passed completely beyond reason; entering Rhys's bedroom, Diana was met with such fury that its force seemed to hurl her back against the door. Melly remembers it having been on the following day that Maryvonne Moerman was informed by a wild, knife-wielding Rhys that she would slash George's treasured surrealist paintings to ribbons if her daughter dared to leave the house. According to Diana, the usually stoical Maryvonne passed out from sheer fright.[16]

The change in Rhys at this point was absolute and devastating. Her loving hosts had become the enemy. Everything they did was wrong. Nicknaming her "Johnny Rotten"—after the punk prince of bad behaviour—was George's way of trying to dispel a darkness in which no glimmer of light appeared. All their good times had been blotted out. Rhys ranted to everybody who dared to come near her that she was a helpless victim, deserted for weeks on end by a woman who—the unkindest cut of all—produced hideous clothes which her imprisoned guest was then *compelled* to buy. Even now, Diana was trying to prevent her from going home. Of course, as George wrote in his ruefully honest account of the debacle, the converse was true: "Di could hardly wait."[17]

Sonia, advising the Mellys from Paris, knew Jean Rhys well enough to take her new mood seriously. Writing to Diana, she warned her that "you must, must must protect yourself." Conscious that Diana herself had a fragile psyche and that she was heroically determined to escort Rhys down to Devon, Sonia warned her not to go unaccompanied: "You must not be alone with her at Cheriton Fitz."[18]

Diana did as she was told. A workman joined her for the long journey when, towards the end of February 1978, she escorted a glowering Rhys back home. Reports of heavy snow ahead almost forced their car to turn back; Jean's face conveyed her scepticism. Only the presence of large drifts beside the narrow lanes leading down into Cheriton finally convinced her that "bad weather" was not part of a cunning plan to drag her back to Savernake Road. Flowers sent by Jo Batterham and a warm welcome from her Landboat neighbours were received in silence. Not a word was forthcoming, not even when Diana and her companion thankfully took their leave.

It was difficult for Diana Melly to acknowledge such abject failure, when she herself had tried so hard. The persona she would self-mockingly name "Mrs Perfect" (and even crown with a cartoon halo in her 2005 memoir) had imagined that she possessed the ability to make Jean Rhys feel happy. Writing to Sonia in Paris, Diana sadly admitted that "I can't do that, I can't even make her feel all right."[19]

NORMALLY, A CHANGE of scene could lift Rhys's spirits, but not this time. Visiting Cheriton in May to record Rhys's latest minute revisions to her memoir, David Plante grew so disheartened that he took Joan Butler's advice and left after two days. When Jo Batterham tentatively reminded Rhys that she herself was still owed the cost both for an elegant chaise longue and its expensive upholstery, Rhys rebuked her for preying upon a helpless pauper. And yet, as Batterham sadly recalls, nobody could have been kinder after Gini Stevens's defection than Rhys, who took her out to lunch and—offering a pretty flower across the table—gently reassured her unhappy friend that life would brighten with the coming of spring.[20]

Dictating an essay, commissioned by *Harper's*, to a flattered Janet Bridger (Janet wrote it neatly out by hand on sheets of pink paper, all ready for the typist), Rhys could still rally her powerful gift for sardonic self-scrutiny, even in the last year of her life. "Making Bricks without Straw" offered a darkly comic self-portrait of the author in interview mode, wondering how much eyeshadow to apply and where to place the chaise longue in order to expose her face to the most flattering light. But, once again, the peevish voice of complaint pushed its way to the fore. Why must these well-meaning interviewers always assume that Rhys's own life had been as miserable as the wretched women whom she described? Why must they keep trying to pigeonhole her as a white Creole, or as a feminist?* And why must they regard every careless word she uttered—after the couple of stiff drinks required for the ordeal of being interrogated—as gospel truth?[21]

The essay was written for public consumption. Privately, Rhys recognised that she was fast losing the war between a frail body and her ferocious will. "Well, you are a fighter," remarked one of the nurses who now regularly came in to bathe her, when Rhys refused to make use of her cane to stump back into the bedroom. Maybe so, Rhys pondered in one of her last, painfully executed handwritten notes, but, "What exactly am I fighting for?"[22]

By the end of the summer, professional interviews had become too taxing for Rhys to undertake. Nevertheless, when Olwyn Hughes and Diana Athill mentioned a young book rep who was visiting Exeter and eager to meet her, Rhys managed a handwritten note to welcome Madeline Slade for a visit to the cottage in what would be the last autumn of her life. Feigning surprise when her guest arrived, Rhys was nevertheless beautifully dressed and—as it was mid-afternoon—eager to be poured a gin and vermouth. Dismayed by the cottage's exterior, Slade complimented her hostess on the transformation that had been worked within. ("She told me how hard she had tried to make it look nice.") Once Slade had put away a typed list of questions, Rhys relaxed, asking whether Madeline was a writer, too. ("She got very serious when I said I'd stopped. 'It doesn't do to stop,' she said. 'You need to keep practicing.'") But what remained with Slade most strongly was Rhys's response when a woman neighbour called in. ("They chatted about the woman's young daughter, and Jean was so interested; she wanted to know how the little girl was; everything about her. Just then, when she forgot I was there, I thought that she seemed really happy.")[23]

---

* Rhys steadfastly declined to be a poster girl for feminism. At Holloway, she had expressed her solidarity with the suffragettes who were imprisoned there. But when asked for her thoughts about the brave suffragette who had died after throwing herself in front of a galloping horse on Derby Day in 1913, Rhys, who adored horses, expressed her sympathy for the colt.

ONE OF THE free-standing sections of Rhys's memoir (dictated almost without hesitation to Michael Schwab during the post-Venice summer of 1977) had described "Meta," the abusive nurse whose harsh behaviour and suggestive name (so close to the Latin *mater*) seem to connect her to Rhys's mother. *Smile Please* makes no pretence of a happy relationship between the author and Minna Lockhart. But it was to Minna that Rhys touchingly dedicated the completed pages which reached Diana Athill in November 1978. "This is such a cold, grey country," Julia Martin had imagined her mother sadly saying of England, shortly before her death at Acton in *After Leaving Mr Mackenzie*. "This bouquet I hand to you, my silent mother, who died so unhappily in a cold country," was what Rhys wished her final and most personal work to say, perhaps as a token of apology for her own past lack of sympathy for Minna's loss of her husband, her home, her health and—even—of her difficult daughter. It's always startling to realise the number of years during which a literary perfectionist like Rhys could continue to meditate upon the best way to use a particular phrase, once it had taken root in her mind.

The memoir was already overdue for publication; given Rhys's age and increasing frailty, the risk of waiting for a revised second portion covering the author's life after her arrival in England was deemed too great. Athill decided that the book should be edited immediately and published within six months. Privately, Diana admitted to Anthony Shiel her disappointment at the meagre "Brownie snaps" Rhys had supplied as illustrations; writing to Jean, Athill combined enthusiasm with some practical observations. Two submitted episodes from Rhys's later years didn't sit comfortably, in Athill's view, with the remarkable evocation of her childhood in Dominica. The story of the completed Imperial Road—Rhys's last attempt to smuggle that deeply felt false memory into print—would also have to go. And so—but Athill did not tell Jean this, or offer any explanation—would the words she had specifically chosen as a dedication to her mother. Later, when Diana offered David

Plante the chance to become Rhys's posthumous dedicatee, he refused. David, in his own odd but passionate way, did love Jean Rhys. He knew what Jean herself had wanted.

Unaware of the fate of her carefully worded dedication, an always meticulous Rhys worried that Athill appeared to be less concerned with checking the text than with reshaping the book. (Loosely linked episodes were skilfully rearranged by Athill and assigned titles: "Geneva"; "The Doll"; "Carnival"; "Paris," and so forth.) On 12 December, an apprehensive Rhys wrote to ask Oliver Stonor what she could do about it all. Nothing, was the dispiriting answer. Esther Whitby, who had returned to work part-time at Deutsch, confirms that it was customary practice, when Athill was busy, for any proofreading tasks to be passed along to a colleague. In this case, although Athill was indeed distracted, since her mother was dying, *Smile Please* never left her own possessive hands.

The result of what seems to have been Athill's combination of necessary haste and an uncharacteristic inattentiveness amounted to a flurry of careless errors and misprints in the published text of Rhys's last work. Courteously pointed out to Athill by Oliver Stonor in 1979—his handwritten list survives in the McFarlin archive—they have never been corrected. In her preface to *Smile Please*, Diana poked fun at Rhys for (so Athill claimed) having objected to the absence of a mere "then" and a "quite" from the published text of *Wide Sargasso Sea*. Such a prodigiously careful reviser of her own work would assuredly have been dismayed to see "Brokenhurst (for Brockenhurst), "No Theatre" (for Noh Theatre) and a celebrated Italian play quaintly retitled *Paula and Francesca*, appearing alongside a playwright called Richard Brindsley Sheridan and a piece of sheet music titled "Flora Dora" (a misnaming of the charming Edwardian musical, *Florodora*, which Rhys had artfully slipped into her childhood memories as a foreshadowing of her life on stage). It's a shame. *Smile Please* seems to have been the work that Rhys herself valued more than any other she wrote, perhaps because it was so personal and achieved in such difficult circumstances.

AT THE END of 1978, and still concealing from friends and editors alike her actual age of eighty-eight, Rhys felt vigorous enough to plan a spring trip to London. In February 1979, a "crack-up," Rhys's habitually terse code for a breakdown, took her instead into a nursing home near Exeter. Her appetite had become bird-like. Always conscious of her weight—she had hated it when, during the 1960s, she briefly became a little plump—Rhys boasted to Oliver Stonor of having shrunk to a mere six stone. Addressing a new admirer, Elaine Campbell, she gallantly promised to write the foreword to a planned reissue of Phyllis Shand Allfrey's Caribbean novel, *The Orchid House*.

"Onward and upward," Rhys chirruped to Stonor from hospital. Sure enough, by 11 March, she was home again and feeling strong enough to ask Diana Melly to book her into Blake's (London's most luxurious boutique hotel was a firm favourite with Princess Margaret) for a month of final revisions. Evidently, she intended to regain control of her precious text.

The details have never been entirely clear about the fall which took Rhys into a West Country city hospital rather than to Blake's Hotel in the late spring of 1979. Diana Athill, no fan of Janet Bridger's, wondered whether an obstreperous Rhys might have been given a rough shove before Janet remorsefully settled the dazed old lady into a chair and hastened home. Janet herself claimed that an intoxicated Rhys had been alone when she fell. Urgently recalled to the cottage by one of Rhys's alarmed neighbours, Bridger had summoned the doctor, who diagnosed a fractured hip bone. Immediate attention was required. Rhys was rushed by ambulance to the main hospital in Exeter.[24]

Rhys's ancient body failed the trial of anaesthesia and surgical invasion. For six weeks, disabled and silent, she lay in the Creedy Ward of the Royal Devon and Exeter Hospital. Plans for the spring publication of *Smile Please* were resumed after Athill had paid a brief, unsatisfactory visit to Rhys's bedside. A few days later, George Melly, popping into the hospital on his way to keep a jazz date in Exeter, had trouble in recognising the shrunken features of a patient identified on the information card above her bed as: "Joan."

On 14 May, a sudden impulse caused Jo Batterham, who had taken her son out for lunch from Bryanston School that day, to drive west on a seventy-five-mile detour to Exeter. Having found her way to Creedy Ward, Jo shared George Melly's difficulty in recognising the pale, wigless little figure whom she found clawing at the bedclothes, open-eyed and staring, but unable to speak. The doctor in charge, when questioned, breezily opined that "Joan" might survive another month. Appalled, Batterham left the hospital and drove down to the coast. Walking beside the sea, so Jo says today, she "just willed" her ancient friend to die. Back in the ward, she clasped one of Rhys's restless hands and softly sang the Piaf song that seemed to fit the moment best: "*Non, je ne regrette rien.*" ("And do you think she did regret anything?" I ask. "I doubt it," answered Jo.)[25]

Back in London that same evening, Jo heard the news that Rhys had died and rang Diana Melly. Diana told her that she was looking out of the window, watching a pink cloud sail away, high above the rooftops of north London. "And there goes Jean," Diana said.[26]

The Stonors, who were holidaying in France in the spring of 1979, learned from their young friends, Olive and Christopher Cox, that Rhys's funeral in Exeter had been a muted affair. Maryvonne and her daughter, Ellen, represented the family; friends included Francis Wyndham and the two Dianas (Athill and Melly). Peggy Ramsay sent lavish flowers; Al Alvarez, although absent, wrote an obituary in which he reaffirmed his view of Rhys as one of the most important British writers of the twentieth century, while praising Francis Wyndham (appointed by Rhys as her literary executor) for his unstinting perseverance and enthusiasm. Selma Vaz Dias, two years dead, went unmentioned in the tributes.

Some years after Rhys's cremation, Diana Athill arranged for the placing of the modest memorial—for which Maryvonne chose the wording—which stands in the graveyard of St. Michael's at Cheriton

When the clearance of Rhys's cottage began, this pink mohair shawl, a gift from Sonia Orwell, was still hanging, neatly folded, on the back of her writing chair. *(Used with permission of Carmela Marner)*

Fitzpaine. At present, no stone or plaque commemorates Jean Rhys on the green Caribbean island where she was born and where—speaking to us through Antoinette Cosway in *Wide Sargasso Sea*—she hoped to die. "If you are buried under a flamboyant tree," I said, "your soul is lifted up when it flowers. Everyone wants that."[27]

Following the overnight demolition of her family's Roseau home in 2020, nothing physical survives to connect Rhys to Dominica, the island where she had—more directly than through Antoinette—told Phyllis Shand Allfrey that she wished her bones might be buried. "I Used to Live Here Once," the title of a story completed four years before her death, suggests that Jean Rhys already knew the truth. There would be no return. There was no need. The island that had cast its haunting spell over Rhys's imagination would live on, enduringly, within her work.

Afterlife

JEAN RHYS'S DREAD of publicity, combined with the mass of correspondence that she evidently destroyed, testifies to her fear of being subjected to a biography. Nevertheless, Tom Staley's short critical study of her novels, which appeared in the year of Rhys's death, contained nothing that would have distressed her. As indicated in his 1977 letter to John Byrne, Staley's book contained only a brief prefatory chapter about the author herself, in which a bare outline of the skimpy known facts of Jean Rhys's life was provided. Admirers curious to know more about Rhys turned with interest to *Smile Please*, published in May 1979, the month of her death. Reviews of the memoir were perfunctory; readers felt deprived by the absence of a narrative shape, and disappointed that so little space had been found for a famously reticent author's experiences after leaving Dominica.

Initially governed by Jean Rhys's strong desire for privacy, Francis Wyndham would eventually comply with Diana Athill's wish to permit a young Canadian-born academic, Carole Angier, to deploy her skills as a tenacious researcher to uncover the story of Rhys's life, combining her independent sleuthing with use of the growing archive now held at Tulsa. Angier's generous-spirited and invaluably detailed book was published in 1985, alongside a brief, perceptive study of the novels which Angier contributed to the *Lives of Modern Women* series, edited by Francis Wyndham's friend Emma Tennant.

First, however, came David Plante. Intimations of what was afoot

emerged at a PEN event in January 1980, at which both Jo Batterham
and David Plante took the stage before an audience of Rhys's admirers.
Recalling the evening for me in the summer of 2018, Diana Athill was
as dismissive of Batterham's romantic eulogy as of Plante's shrilly dis-
loyal put-down of his old friend as "a silly, bigoted woman." Like Athill,
Plante recalls the fury with which a protective Harold Pinter verbally
attacked him from his seat beside Lady Antonia Fraser in the front row;
Batterham, writing to Plante in March, did not hold back. Defending
himself, Plante responded that he was only being honest: "Jean would
have understood what a writer must do."[1]

I'm inclined to agree with Plante. The controversial portrait which
he provided in *Difficult Women*, published in 1983, was no crueller about
Rhys than about Plante himself. Today, his book reads as a carefully
stylised presentation of partial or imaginative truths shot through with
moments of wit, compassion and considerable insight. To Rhys's sup-
porters, however, the act of betrayal was unforgivable. Rachel Ingalls
was not the only former friend who never spoke to David Plante again.

Diana Melly and Francis Wyndham meanwhile embarked upon a
selected edition of Rhys's letters which was published in 1984. Frustrat-
ingly truncated because of an absence of almost any correspondence
from the first forty years of Rhys's life, it spans the years 1931 to 1966,
ending on the verge of the publication of *Wide Sargasso Sea*. Equipped
with sensitive linking passages and notes contributed by Wyndham,
the edited *Letters* provided many readers with their first introduction
to Rhys's wilful, witty and laceratingly self-aware personality. Reading
the letters that she wrote to Wyndham himself—I only wish that we
could also read his to her—it's easy to understand why Francis found
Jean Rhys so irresistible.

Wyndham himself approved and admired *The Blue Hour* (2010), an
intuitive and often illuminating short biography of Rhys which was
written with passion and empathy by Lilian Pizzichini. Invited to single out the book which she believes best captures her grandmother in
the context of her work, Ellen Moerman recommends *Genèses d'une folie
créole: Jean Rhys et Jane Eyre* by Catherine Rovera (Hermann, 2015).

A meticulously researched examination of the sources of Rhys's best-known novel, Rovera's eloquent study also illuminates the author's creative processes.

For newcomers to Rhys who want to look beyond the novels, there exists no better introduction than *Smile Please*. Much of what you have read here is grounded in Rhys's own artfully circumspect account of her life, starting out when she first faced a camera on her sixth birthday, and ending as her work was about to be seen and judged by Ford Madox Ford. For a biographer, part of the fascination of *Smile Please* lies in the memoir's conspicuous absences: within its pages, there's no mention of Jean Lenglet's imprisonment; no name for the gentlemanly lover who got Rhys pregnant and broke her heart; no hint that her childhood beau, identified only as "a little boy called Willie," was the son of Roseau's leading doctor, Sir Henry Alford Nicholls (an admission which would implicitly have acknowledged the subordinate role of Rhys's own beloved father).

Against the absences, we can set a quiet store of revelations. *Smile Please* tells us just how young Rhys was when she first started to write for herself; she was still a child in Dominica when she began keeping "my secret poems exercise book" and wrote plays for home performance. Glancing at her subtle reference to "the Sensitive Plant" that grew wild—as it still does—on the hillside at Geneva, we might almost miss the hint of just who that sensitive plant might represent. There's even an alluring suggestion of just how closely the memoir and the story "Sleep It Off Lady" became entwined in the ageing Rhys's thoughts, when she remembers in the memoir that one of the chorus girls in *Our Miss Gibbs* addressed her as "Verney": Miss Verney is also the name of the unfortunate "Lady" of the story. "There were supposed to be rats in the dressing-room," Rhys comments a few lines later in the memoir, "but I never saw one." Miss Verney, in the story Rhys had plotted out alongside the gestating memoir, suffers from a fixation about an imaginary rat.

Is the intertextual echo simply a slip or one of the author's literary tricks? Is it an accident that Antoinette Cosway and young Rhys ride a horse that bears the same name: Preston? We can't be sure. It's seldom useful or enlightening to attempt to overanalyse Rhys's fiction. Neither does it help us to compare Rhys to the writers whom she admired and sometimes challenged. Influences abound in her work, but—like Emily Dickinson, in whose wittily broken lines and ghostly shafts of light Rhys may have found the clearest mirror for a mind that looked always into itself—Rhys demands, and deserves, to stand alone. Writing from pitiless self-knowledge, Jean Rhys addresses the watchful and lonely outsider who lurks within us all. And here, I believe, lies the answer to the enduring power of a novelist whose softly insistent, knowing and *sui generis* voice speaks with more power to our times even than to her own.

Acknowledgements

My thanks for help with Dominica-related material to: Pearle Christian, Peter Harrington, Lennox Honychurch, Sonia Magloire Akba, Gregor Nassief, Polly Pattulo, Marina Warner, and also to the *Observer* for commissioning a travel essay on Jean Rhys's Dominica, which enabled me to visit that unforgettable island before writing a book to which it has contributed so much.

My thanks for help about Rhys's relationship with Lancelot Hugh Smith to: Charles Abel Smith, Dorothy Abel Smith, Andrew Lycett, Elizabeth Macdonald Buchanan, Andrew Martin Smith, Julian Martin Smith, Faith Raven and Victoria Wakefield. Also to Zachary Leader and to Gilly King, both for enabling me to visit Mount Clare at Roehampton and for access to an unpublished memoir by Lady Hugh Smith; and to Jennifer Zulfigar for arranging access to Lancey's former Mayfair home (now part of the Royal Embassy of Saudi Arabia).

My thanks for help in researching Rhys's life and homes in the West Country to: Ellie Babbedge, Frieda Hughes, Alice May, Samantha Moss, David Thorn, Roy Stettiford, Frances Wood.

My thanks for help about Willis Feast's family (Rhys's hosts in Norfolk): to John Bolland.

My thanks to Tara and Nigel Fraser, Gerry Harrison; Judith Landry, Kika Markham and Susannah Stack for their especially generous help about Selma Vaz Dias, and to Hugh Fleetwood and to Kate Pocock, for leading me to Rhys's important friendship with Rachel Ingalls; to Selina Hastings, regarding Rhys's significant connection to Rosamund and John Lehmann; to Richard Schaubeck, regarding her friendship with Frank Hallman; and to Sophie Oliver, especially for sharing images of Rhys's one surviving dress from her first years in London.

My thanks for help with interviews, correspondence, hospitality and—above all—their time: Carole Angier; the late Diana Athill; Gaia Banks; Jo Batterham, Marcelle Bernstein; a mother-daughter contribution from Gwen Burnyeat and Ruth Padel; John Byrne; Helen Carr; Susannah Clapp, Gordon Crosse, Polly Devlin, Meriel (Dickson) Gardner; Anne Dunn; Peter Eyre; Ruth Fainlight; James Fox; Antonia Fraser; Valerie Grove; Glenda Jackson; Alan Judd; Julie Kavanagh; Alexis Lykiard; Diana Melly; Paul Mendez; Sarah Papineau; David Plante; Tristram Powell; Diana Quick; Catherine Rovera; Madeline Slade; Barbara Smith; Hilary Spurling; Tom Staley; David Tobin (Walden Books); Esther Whitby; Rachel Wyndham.

Thanks for translation help to Martine Orsmond (Dutch) and to Stephen Romer (French).

Thanks for access to manuscripts and books are due to the British Library; the London Library; Megan Barnard, Elizabeth Garver, Jim Kuhn and Rick Watson at the Harry Ransom Center in Austin, Texas; and Frank Bowles, Cambridge University Archive, for the papers of Sir Henry Hesketh Bell.

Particular thanks are due to Marc Carlson and his team for all their help at the McFarlin Library, Tulsa, to Sean Latham for arranging for me to give a talk at the library, and to Joli Jenson for arranging everything to make my stay in Tulsa so memorably agreeable.

I am particularly indebted to Helen Carr, Lennox Honychurch, Peter Hulme, Polly Pattulo and Catherine Rovera for undertaking to read parts (and in Peter's case, most kindly, all) of the work in progress and to make useful comments.

I'm grateful to Victoria Dickie for inviting me to a book club discussion of *Wide Sargasso Sea* which enabled me to air a few ideas at an early stage, and to rethink some important points.

More particular and considerable thanks are due to Francis Wyndham's literary executor, Alan Hollinghurst, for a meticulously observed, thoughtful and so generously expressed reading of an almost final version of the book.

My special thanks and love, always, to my dearest Ted: my wise first reader, editor and loving supporter on what has proved to be an unsurprisingly emotional voyage into the often dark corners of an extraordinary woman's mind.

As always, Anthony Goff and George Lucas have been magnificent—and inspiring—agents. My gratitude and unquantifiable thanks are also due to John Glusman and Helen Thomaides at Norton; to Arabella Pike, Kate Johnson and Jo Thompson at HarperCollins, and to Katy Archer, whose project editing has been a model of its kind. My heartfelt thanks to Emma Pidsley, at HarperCollins, and Ingsu Liu and Matt Dorfman, at Norton, for their gorgeous covers; Mark Wells for indexing; and Martin Brown for the map of Dominica. It's been wonderful to be buoyed up by such commitment and enthusiasm for a book that means so much to me.

I am especially grateful to Jean Rhys's granddaughter, Dr. Ellen Moerman, and to Catherine Rovera, separately, for their generous and discrete contributions.

Last, but far from least, my thanks to Anthony Griffiths for the good-humoured and patient tech support and expertise that I could always rely upon to rescue me from disaster.

All mistakes are, of course, my own.

Notes

The following abbreviations are used in the Notes:

AA—Al Alvarez
BL—British Library
DA—Diana Athill
DP—David Plante
EB—Eliot Bliss
EM—Ellen Moerman
ERW—Edward Rees Williams
ES—Evelyn Scott
FW—Francis Wyndham
GR—Germaine Richelot
JL—Jean Lenglet
JR—Jean Rhys
LHS—Lancelot Hugh Smith
LTS—Leslie Tilden Smith
McFarlin—McFarlin Library (Special Collections), University of Tulsa, Oklahoma
MH—Max Hamer
MM—Maryvonne Moerman
OH—Olwyn Hughes
OS—Oliver Stonor
PAS—Phyllis Antoinette Smyser
PK—Peggy Kirkaldy
SO—Sonia Orwell
SVD—Selma Vaz Dias

Foreword

1   Jean Rhys, *Smile Please: an Unfinished Autobiography*, "From a Diary: at the Rope-makers' Arms," André Deutsch, 1979, p. 163.

PART ONE: A WORLD APART

Chapter 1—Wellspring (1890–1907)

1   Jean Rhys, *Wide Sargasso Sea*, Part 2, Penguin, 1966, p. 85.
2   Lizabeth Paravisini-Gebert, *Phyllis Shand Allfrey: A Caribbean Life*, Rutgers University Press, 1996, p. 15. Willie's wildness was further confirmed when he was sentenced to six months' hard labour in an English prison in 1927, after stealing a fellow lodger's suit and defrauding three constables.
3   JR to FW in her poem, "Obeah Night," 14 April 1964, in Francis Wyndham and Diana Melly (eds.), *The Letters of Jean Rhys, 1931–1966*, André Deutsch, 1984, p. 265.
4   Jean Rhys, "The Sound of the River," *Tigers are Better-Looking*, André Deutsch, 1968.
5   Jean Rhys, *After Leaving Mr Mackenzie*, Jonathan Cape, 1931, Part 2, Chapter 12, "Childhood."
6   Catherine Rovera discusses Rhys's reworking of these events in her notebooks, in relation to *Good Morning, Midnight* and the first stirrings of *Wide Sargasso Sea* in: "Jean Rhys's Phantom MSS: 'December 4th 1938. Mr Howard's House. CRE-OLE'," in *Women: A Cultural Review*, 31:2, pp. 187–98, 18 August 2020; online, DOI:10.1080/0957042.2020.17/67836.
7   Rhys, *Wide Sargasso Sea*, Part 2, André Deutsch, 1966, p. 147.
8   Rhys, "Geneva," *Smile Please*, André Deutsch, 1979.
9   Rhys, *Wide Sargasso Sea*, Part 3, André Deutsch, 1966, p. 173.
10 House of Commons reports, 1 July 1844, p. 247.
11 Rhys, *Wide Sargasso Sea*, Part 2, André Deutsch, 1966, p. 155.
12 JR to DP, nd, McFarlin, Plante Papers, 007.15.f2.

Chapter 2—Floggings, School and Sex (1896–1906)

1   Jean Rhys, "My Day: 3 Pieces," in *Invitation to the Dance*, edited by Frank Hallman (New York, 1975).
2   JR to DP, nd, McFarlin, Plante Papers, 007.15.f1.
3   Rhys, "Meta," *Smile Please*.
4   JR, McFarlin 1.6.f11.
5   JR, McFarlin 1.3.f8.
6   JR, McFarlin 1.1.f6.
7   JR, McFarlin 1.1.f16.
8   JR, McFarlin 1.6.f11.

9   JR, McFarlin 1.1.f1.

10   Henry Hesketh Bell, *Glimpses of a Governor's Life from Diaries and Memoranda*,
     Sampson Low, 1946.

11   GBR/0115/Y3011C-N, Sir Henry Hesketh Bell Collection, Royal Commonwealth
     Library, Cambridge University Archive.

12   Rhys, "The Zouaves," *Smile Please.*

13   JR to EM, 11 January 1960, Wyndham and Melly (eds.), *Letters.*

14   Jean Rhys, "Mixing Cocktails," *Jean Rhys: The Collected Short Stories*, Penguin,
     1987, p. 36.

15   Rhys, "Goodbye Marcus, Goodbye Rose," *Collected Short Stories*, p. 278.

16   Rhys, "Goodbye Marcus, Goodbye Rose," *Collected Short Stories*, p. 277.

17   See Chapter 1, n. 6.

18   JR, "Triple Sec," unpublished manuscript, McFarlin 1.5.11-12.

19   JR, Black Exercise Book, McFarlin 1.3.f5 and 1.3.f11.

20   Rhys, "Leaving Dominica," *Smile Please.*

21   Rhys, "First Steps," *Smile Please.*

PART TWO: ENGLAND: A COLD COUNTRY

Chapter 3—Stage-struck (1907–13)

1   Rhys, *Wide Sargasso Sea*, Part 2, Penguin, p. 65.

2   Rhys, *Wide Sargasso Sea*, Part 2, Penguin, p. 70.

3   Rhys, "From a Diary: at the Ropemakers' Arms," published as an appendix to
     Smile Please.

4   Rhys, "First Steps," *Smile Please.*

5   Rhys, "Overture and Beginners," *Collected Short Stories*, p. 307.

6   Rhys, "First Steps," *Smile Please.*

7   Peter Eyre interviews with author, July 2018.

8   Rhys, "Chorus Girls," *Smile Please.*

9   JR to MM, 19 November 1959.

10   JR to FW, 26 October 1961, McFarlin 2.15.f1.

11   Rhys, "Chorus Girls," *Smile Please.*

Chapter 4—Fact and Fiction: A London Life (1911–13)

1   Extract from unpublished memoirs of Constance, Lady Hugh Smith (1900), Roe-
     hampton University Archive, pp. 88–91.

2   Rhys, "The Interval," *Smile Please.*

3   Rhys, "The Interval," *Smile Please.*

4   Jean Rhys, *Voyage in the Dark*, Constable, 1934, Part 1, p. 7.

5   Rhys, "First Steps," "Christmas Day," *Smile Please.*

6   Rhys, "First Steps," "Christmas Day," *Smile Please.*

7   JR to PK, May 1950, Wyndham and Melly (eds.), *Letters.*

8   JR to MM, November 1965, Wyndham and Melly (eds.), *Letters*.
9   Carole Angier, *Jean Rhys, Life and Work*, André Deutsch, 1990, p. 87.
10   JR, McFarlin 1.1.5.f9.
11   Rhys, "World's End and a Beginning," *Smile Please*.
12   Stella Bowen, *Drawn from Life, Reminiscences*, Collins, 1941, p. 37.
13   Nina Hamnett, *Laughing Torso*, Constable, 1932, p. 36.

Chapter 5—London in Wartime (1913–19)

1   Adrian Allinson, "A Painter's Pilgrimage," unpublished memoir in typescript, McFarlin.
2   Bowen, *Drawn from Life*, p. 36.
3   Hamnett, *Laughing Torso*, p. 86.
4   Janie Lomas, "War Widows in British Society 1914–1940," unpublished PhD thesis, appendix A, Table 1, Stafford University.
5   Rhys, "Leaving England," *Smile Please*.
6   Rhys, "Leaving England," *Smile Please*.

PART THREE: A EUROPEAN LIFE

Chapter 6—A Paris Marriage (1919–25)

1   In what seems to have been forgetful old age, Rhys annotated this group of photographs as: "Austria."
2   JR, Green Exercise Book, McFarlin 1.1.2; Jean Rhys, *Good Morning, Midnight*, Constable, 1939, p. 100.
3   Fonds Louis Gustave Richelot (1858–1956), Repertoire numerique detaille, d/AB/XIX/4224-AB/XIX/4227, Archives Nationale de France, 1015.
4   JR, unpublished poem, "Prayer to the Sun," McFarlin 1.2.f10.
5   JR, McFarlin 011.1.f10, from the scattered pages of a typescript titled "And Paris Sinister," later incorporated into Jean Rhys, *The Left Bank: Sketches and Studies of Present-Day Bohemian Paris*, Jonathan Cape, 1927.
6   JR, "Prayer to the Sun," McFarlin 1.2.f10.
7   JR, McFarlin, Plante Papers, 007.15.f5.
8   Jean Rhys, *After Leaving Mr Mackenzie*, Part 2, Chapter 5, "Acton."
9   Rhys, "Vienne," *Collected Short Stories*, p. 110.
10   Rhys, "Vienne," *Collected Short Stories*, p. 118.
11   Rhys, "Paris Again," *Smile Please*.

Chapter 7—"L'affaire Ford" (1924–26)

1   JR, McFarlin 1.5.f9.
2   Paul Nash to Anthony Bertram, 2 March 1925, quoted in Max Saunders, *Ford Madox Ford: A Dual Life: the After World*, Vol. II, OUP, 1996, p. 282.

3 Saunders, *Ford Madox Ford*, p. 284.

4 JR to FW, 16 July 1967, McFarlin 2.14.f1.

5 All details concerning Rhys's departure from Paris and stay in Cros de Cagnes come from the unpublished memoir of Margaret Odeh Nash, and from Paul Nash's subsequent letter to Anthony Bertram, 2 March 1925. Nash papers, quoted in Saunders, *Ford Madox Ford*, p. 282.

6 Rhys, "La Grosse Fifi," *Collected Short Stories*, p. 78.

7 Saunders, *Ford Madox Ford*, pp. 284, 603.

8 Bowen, *Drawn from Life*, p. 167.

9 JR, "L'affaire Ford," McFarlin, Plante Papers, 1981–007 f5.

10 JR, "The Forlorn Hope" (unpublished) was drafted in two versions and related to David Plante in 1977, McFarlin 1.1.f17.

11 JR, "L'affaire Ford," McFarlin, Plante Papers, 1991–007 f5.

12 JR, first page of Black Exercise Book, McFarlin 1.1.f3, later incorporated into the story "Tigers are Better-Looking."

13 JR to JL, nd, McFarlin 2.15.f4.

14 Here, I have followed Max Saunders, since his is the most convincing explanation of a complicated sequence of events, *Ford Madox Ford*, pp. 295–7.

15 Bowen, *Drawn from Life*, pp. 166–7.

Chapter 8—Hunger, and Hope (1926–28)

1 Patrick Hamilton to his brother Bruce Hamilton, May 1927, quoted in Sean French, *Patrick Hamilton: A Life*, Faber, 1993, p. 86.

2 Valentine Williams to GR, 19 January 1927, McFarlin 2.9.f6.

3 Saunders, *Ford Madox Ford*, p. 608.

4 Saunders, *Ford Madox Ford*, p. 608.

5 Pearl Adam to JR, 13 December 1926, McFarlin 2.1.f1.

6 Rhys, *After Leaving Mr Mackenzie*, Part 2, Chapter 5. "Acton," Chapter 9, "Golders Green."

7 LHS to JR, 5 May 1927, McFarlin 2.5.f11. The folded paper is apparent from the fact that the upper part of the words "dear kitten" is missing.

8 LHS to JR, 27 May 1927, McFarlin 2.5.f11.

9 Rhys, *After Leaving Mr Mackenzie*, Part 2, Chapter 6, "Mr James."

10 GR to JR, 18 November 1929, McFarlin 2.9.f11.

11 JR, nd, Green Exercise Book, McFarlin 1.1.f3.

12 BL, Rhys Archive, ad. ms 57859.

13 GR to JR, September 1927, McFarlin 2.9.f6.

14 Jean Rhys, *Quartet*, Chapter 1; GR to JR, September 1927, McFarlin 2.9.f6.

15 Rhys, *Quartet*, Chapter 23.

16 Rhys, *Quartet*, Chapters 18, 21.

17 Rhys, *Quartet*, Chapter 18.

18   GR to JR, 15 November 1928, McFarlin 2.9.f6.

19   Rhys, *Quartet*, Chapter 12.

20   *Manchester Guardian*, 26 October 1928.

21   Rhys, *Quartet*, Chapter 12.

22   JL to JR, 21 February 1929, BL, Rhys Archive, ad. ms 8819.

23   A report from "the inner sanctum of Simon & Schuster, US, by 'M.L.S.'," in the substantial collection of documents copied from the McFarlin Library originals, BL, Rhys Papers, ad. ms 8819.

PART FOUR: THE RHYS WOMAN

Chapter 9—Two Tunes: Past and Present (1929-36)

1   Rhys, *After Leaving Mr Mackenzie*, Part 1, Chapter 3, "Mr Horsfield."

2   Rhys, *After Leaving Mr Mackenzie*, Part 3, Chapter 3, "Last."

3   Rhys, *After Leaving Mr Mackenzie*, Part 1, Chapter 1, "The Hotel on the Quay."

4   Rhys, *After Leaving Mr Mackenzie*, Part 1, Chapter 1, "The Hotel on the Quay."

5   Rhys, *After Leaving Mr Mackenzie*, Part 1, Chapter 2, "Mr Mackenzie."

6   Rhys, *After Leaving Mr Mackenzie*, Part 2, Chapter 3, "Uncle Griffiths."

7   Rhys, *After Leaving Mr Mackenzie*, Part 2, Chapter 6, "Mr James."

8   Rhys, *After Leaving Mr Mackenzie*, Part 2, Chapter 6, "Mr James."

9   Rhys, *After Leaving Mr Mackenzie*, Part 3, Chapter 1, "Île de la Cité."

10   *Observer*, 8 February 1931; *Daily Telegraph*, 30 January 1931; *Saturday Review of Literature*, US, 25 July 1931.

11   *The Times* and *Times Literary Supplement*, 5 March 1931.

12   Rebecca West, *Daily Telegraph*, 30 January 1931.

13   PAS to DA, 27 January 1967, McFarlin 2.4.f7.

14   JR, Black Exercise Book, McFarlin 1.1.1, pp. 12, 98–9.

15   André Breton, *Nadja*, Librairie Gallimard, 1928, p. 142. Rhys's fellow admirer was the francophile musician, George Melly.

16   JR to PK, 4 May 1931, Wyndham and Melly (eds.), *Letters*.

17   ES to JR, 9 June 1931, Wyndham and Melly (eds.), *Letters*.

18   MM to PAS, 30 April 1968, McFarlin 10.2.f1.

19   JR to FW, 19 June 1964, Wyndham and Melly (eds.), *Letters*.

20   Rhys, *Voyage in the Dark*, Part 1, ch. 1.

21   Rhys, *Voyage in the Dark*, Part 1, ch. 6.

22   Rhys, *Voyage in the Dark*, Part 1, ch. 7.

23   Rhys, *Voyage in the Dark*, Part 4, ch. 1.

24   Charlotte Brontë, writing her Introduction to Emily's *Wuthering Heights* as "Currer Bell."

25   JR to ES, 1933, nd, Wyndham and Melly (eds.), *Letters*.

26   JR to ES, 1933, nd, Wyndham and Melly (eds.), *Letters*.

27   JR to AA, 7 September 1974, BL, Alvarez Papers, ad. mss. 88595.

28 JR to AA, 7 September 1974, BL, Alvarez Papers, ad. mss. 88595.

29 PAS to FW, 5 June 1982, McFarlin 10.3.f1.

30 LTS to JR, nd, private collection.

31 Rhys, manuscript of *Voyage in the Dark*, McFarlin 1.5.13.

32 Rhys, *Voyage in the Dark*, Part 4, Chapter1.

33 Angier, *Jean Rhys*, p. 293, quoting from a personal interview with Dorothy Rees Williams.

34 Transcript of Paul Bailey BBC radio interview, 15 April 1981, McFarlin 1.2.f11.

35 MM to DA, nd, McFarlin 2.2.f10.

36 JR to ES on her drinking habits, 18 February 1934, Wyndham and Melly (eds.), *Letters*.

37 Angier, *Jean Rhys*, p. 338, quoting from her interview with Rosamond Lehmann, 1986, p. 701.

38 JR to ES, 16 February 1936, McFarlin 2.9.f11.

Chapter 10 — A la recherche, *or* Temps Perdi *(1936)*

1 JR to ES, December 1935, Wyndham and Melly (eds.), *Letters*.

2 JR to ES, nd, Wyndham and Melly (eds.), *Letters*.

3 LTS to PAS, 19 March 1936, McFarlin 2.10.f1.

4 The term "white zombi" appears in "Pioneers, Oh, Pioneers," a story about Mr. Ramage which Rhys worked on for many years and which was published in her final collection "Sleep It Off Lady." *Collected Short Stories*, pp. 264–73.

5 Rhys, "Geneva," *Smile Please*.

6 Phyllis Shand Allfrey, *The Orchid House*, Rutgers University Press, 1996. Introduction by Lizabeth Paravisini-Gebert, p. xxiv.

7 Rhys, "Geneva," *Smile Please*.

8 JR to ES, nd., "Hampstead," Wyndham and Melly (eds.), *Letters*.

9 Elma Napier to Alec Waugh, 30 January 1949, Waugh Papers, Boston University 20th Century Archive.

10 LR to PAS, 29 February and 18 March 1936, McFarlin 2.10.f1.

11 Rhys, "*Temps Perdi*," *Collected Short Stories*, p. 262.

12 Rhys, "*Temps Perdi*," *Collected Short Stories*, p. 263.

13 Jean Rhys, "The Imperial Road," version 4, *Jean Rhys Review*, 11, 2, Spring 2000.

14 LTS, map, McFarlin 2.10.f1.

15 LTS to PAS, 19 March 1936, McFarlin 2.10.f1.

16 JR to ES, 10 August 1936, Wyndham and Melly (eds.), *Letters*.

17 JR to ES, 1936, nd, Wyndham and Melly (eds.), *Letters*.

18 ES to Emma Goldman, 25 May 1937, quoted in Wyndham and Melly (eds.), *Letters*, p. 34.

Chapter 11—Good Morning, Midnight (1936–39)

1   JR, Green Exercise Book, McFarlin 1.1.2.
2   JR to DA, 29 May 1966, McFarlin 2.3.f5.
3   JR to ES, 10 August 1936, Wyndham and Melly (eds.), *Letters*.
4   JR to ES, 10 August 1936, Wyndham and Melly (eds.), *Letters*.
5   JR, "The Martyr," Orange Exercise Book, McFarlin 1.1.f4.
6   JR to PK, 9 March 1949, Wyndham and Melly (eds.), *Letters*.
7   Paravisini-Gebert, *Phyllis Shand Allfrey: A Caribbean Life*, p. 48.
8   JR, Orange Exercise Book, McFarlin 1.1.f4.
9   Angier, *Jean Rhys*, pp. 361–2.
10 Rhys, *Good Morning, Midnight*, p. 128.
11 Rhys, *Good Morning, Midnight*, Penguin, 2019, p. 3.
12 Rhys, *Good Morning, Midnight*, Penguin, p. 4.
13 Rhys, *Good Morning, Midnight*, Penguin, p. 4.
14 Rhys, *Good Morning, Midnight*, Penguin, p. 17.
15 Rhys, *Good Morning, Midnight*, Penguin, p. 11.
16 Rhys, *Good Morning, Midnight*, Penguin, p. 40.
17 Judith Thurman, "The Mistress and the Mask: Jean Rhys's Fiction," *Ms*, 4, No. 7, January 1976, pp. 51–2.
18 Judy Froshaug, "The Book-Makers," *Nova*, September 1967, p. 45.
19 Rhys, *Good Morning, Midnight*, Penguin, p. 6.
20 Rhys, *Good Morning, Midnight*, Penguin, p. 6.
21 Rhys, *Good Morning, Midnight*, Penguin, p. 15. Stephen Romer points out that Rhys has altered the original line in a poem by Desnos, reading: "Belle, comme une fleur de verre, Belle, comme une fleur de chair" (flesh) to read: "Beautiful, she's beautiful as a flower in glass, Beautiful as a flower in earth."
22 Jean Rhys used these words to describe the tone employed by George Moore in *Esther Waters* in a letter to OS, 5 March 1953, Wyndham and Melly (eds.), *Letters*.
23 Rhys, *Good Morning, Midnight*, Penguin, p. 190.
24 Rhys, *Good Morning, Midnight*, Penguin, p. 27.
25 Rhys, *Good Morning, Midnight*, Penguin, p. 130.
26 Rhys, *Good Morning, Midnight*, Penguin, p. 169.
27 Simon Segal to JR, nd, Wyndham and Melly (eds.), *Letters*, pp. 138–9. With thanks to Stephen Romer for this translation.
28 Rhys, *Good Morning, Midnight*, Penguin, p. 43. With thanks to Stephen Romer for this translation.
29 JR to SVD, 4 November 1956, Wyndham and Melly (eds.), *Letters*.
30 Rhys, *Good Morning, Midnight*, Penguin, pp. 7, 25.
31 JR to FW, 14 May 1964, Wyndham and Melly (eds.), *Letters*.
32 Violet Hammersley to JR, McFarlin 2.5.f8.

33 JR, "Creole," McFarlin 1.3.f5.

34 Rhys, *Good Morning, Midnight*, Penguin, pp. 145–6.

35 JR to PK, [October] 1945, Wyndham and Melly (eds.), *Letters*.

36 Author interviews with Carole Angier (12 September 2019) and David Plante (28 November 2019), to whom Rhys would eventually give her single-sheet plan for "Wedding in the Carib Quarter." I'm also indebted to Catherine Rovera for drawing my attention to her fine essay, "Jean Rhys's Phantom Manuscript: 4 December 1938. Mr Howard's House. CREOLE," *Women: a Cultural Review*, 18 August 2020, 31:2, pp. 187–99.

PART FIVE: DARKNESS AT NOON

1 Peggy Kirkaldy, "Portrait of a Lost Friend," McFarlin 2.7.f1.

Chapter 12—At War with the World (1940–45)

1 Rhys, "A Solid House," *Collected Short Stories*, p. 212.

2 JL to JR, 17.1.1940, McFarlin; Edouard de Néve, "Jean Rhys, romancière inconnu," *Les Nouvelles Litteraires*, August 1939.

3 Rhys, "Temps Perdi," *Collected Short Stories*, p. 249.

4 Rhys, BL, Rhys Archives, ad. mss. 57858.

5 *Norwich Mercury and People's Weekly Journal*, 1 August 1940.

6 Rhys, "From a Diary: at the Ropemakers' Arms," *Smile Please*.

7 Angier, *Jean Rhys*, pp. 442, 707, based upon letters to Carole Angier from Willis Feast's daughter and Eric Griffiths.

8 Angier, *Jean Rhys*, pp. 442, 707; John Bolland to author, 28 June 2021.

9 Angier, *Jean Rhys*, pp. 442, 707; John Bolland to author, 28 June 2021.

10 Rhys, "A Solid House," *Collected Short Stories*, p. 218.

11 Angier, *Jean Rhys* (p. 219) identifies Louis Rose but provides no confirmation that he treated Rhys; John Bolland to author, 28 June 2021, provided further details on Rose.

12 JR, "Cowslips," McFarlin 1.1.f13.

13 Rhys, "The Insect World," *Collected Short Stories*, p. 343.

14 Rhys, "Outside the Machine," *Collected Short Stories*, p. 196.

15 Rhys, "I Spy A Stranger," *Collected Short Stories*, p. 144.

16 Dr. Ellen Moerman kindly supplied or confirmed the information about her mother given in this paragraph.

17 Rhys, "The Sound of the River," *Collected Short Stories*, p. 230.

18 JR to PAS, 10 October 1945, Wyndham and Melly (eds.), *Letters*.

19 Rhys, "The Sound of the River," *Collected Short Stories*, p. 228.

20 JR to PK, [October] 1945, Wyndham and Melly (eds.), *Letters*.

21 Angier, *Jean Rhys*, p. 431, from interviews with DRW.

Chapter 13—Beckenham Blues (1946-50)

1   JR, Orange Exercise Book, McFarlin 1.1.4.
2   JR to PK, 11 February 1946 and 3 July 1946, Wyndham and Melly (eds.), *Letters*.
3   Information about Job kindly supplied by Dr. Ellen Moerman.
4   JR to PK, 21 April 1950, Wyndham and Melly (eds.), *Letters*.
5   JR to PK, 1950, Wyndham and Melly (eds.), *Letters*.
6   *Bromley & West Kent Mercury*, 1 April 1948.
7   JR to MM, 11 January 1949, Wyndham and Melly (eds.), *Letters*.
8   JR to PK, nd, 1950, Wyndham and Melly (eds.), *Letters*.
9   Dr. Ellen Moerman in conversation with author and Gaia Banks (Sheil Land Agency), December 2019.
10 JR to PK, 9 March and [October] 1949, Wyndham and Melly (eds.), *Letters*.
11 JR to PK, nd, 1950, Wyndham and Melly (eds.), *Letters*.
12 *Beckenham Journal*, 27 May 1949.
13 JR to PK, nd., 1950, Wyndham and Melly (eds.), *Letters*, "Let Them Call It Jazz," *Collected Short Stories*, p. 161.
14 JR to PK, 4 October 1949, Wyndham and Melly (eds.), *Letters*.
15 JR to MM, 10 July 1949, Wyndham and Melly (eds.), *Letters*.
16 JR to MM, 24 October 1949, Wyndham and Melly (eds.), *Letters*.
17 Tara Fraser (granddaughter of SVD) to author, 13 July 2018.

Chapter 14—The Lady Vanishes (1950-56)

1   JR to OS, 5 March 1953, Wyndham and Melly (eds.), *Letters*.
2   JR to PK, 10 March 1950, Wyndham and Melly (eds.), *Letters*.
3   JR to PK, 21 April 1950, Wyndham and Melly (eds.), *Letters*.
4   JR to PK, 21 April 1950, Wyndham and Melly (eds.), *Letters*.
5   JR to PK, May 1950, Wyndham and Melly (eds.), *Letters*.
6   JR to PK, 21 April 1950, Wyndham and Melly (eds.), *Letters*.
7   JR to DP, McFarlin 14.2.fi.
8   Rhys, "Ropemakers' Arms," *Smile Please*.
9   Rhys, "Ropemakers' Arms," *Smile Please*.
10 Rhys, "Ropemakers' Arms," *Smile Please*.
11 JR to MM, 22 June and 31 August 1952, Wyndham and Melly (eds.), *Letters*.
12 MH to OS ("Morchard Bishop"), 29 December 1952, Wyndham and Melly (eds.), *Letters*.
13 JR to OS, 27 January 1953, Wyndham and Melly (eds.), *Letters*.
14 JR to OS, 5 March 1953, Wyndham and Melly (eds.), *Letters*.
15 JR to OS, 7 April 1953, Wyndham and Melly (eds.), *Letters*.
16 JR to SVD, 27 March 1953, Wyndham and Melly (eds.), *Letters*.
17 JR to SVD, 8 June 1953, Wyndham and Melly (eds.), *Letters*.

18 JR to MM, 8 June 1953, Wyndham and Melly (eds.), *Letters*.

19 JR to MM, 29 August and 16 September 1953, Wyndham and Melly (eds.), *Letters*.

20 JR to MM, 31 January and 4 April 1954, Wyndham and Melly (eds.), *Letters*.

21 JR to MM, 5 July and 16 October 1956, Wyndham and Melly (eds.), *Letters*.

22 JR to MM, 22 October 1956, Wyndham and Melly (eds.), *Letters*.

23 SVD to JR, 19 October 1956, Wyndham and Melly (eds.), *Letters*.

24 JR to SVD, 12 November 1956, Wyndham and Melly (eds.), *Letters*.

25 JR to SVD, 18 March 1957, Wyndham and Melly (eds.), *Letters*.

PART SIX: THE PHOENIX RISES

1 JR, Green Exercise Book, McFarlin 1.1.2.

Chapter 15—A House by the Sea (1957–60)

1 JR to MM, 14 January 1958, quoting from her own unpublished fragment of a children's story for Maryvonne—and then her granddaughter—about "Mitsou San," Wyndham and Melly (eds.), *Letters*.

2 PK to JR, no date but evidently 1957, McFarlin 2.7.f1. The cache of letters from Rhys to Peggy Kirkaldy published in Wyndham and Melly (eds.), *Letters* was found in a doctor's surgery in Colchester and provided to Rhys's letter-editors in the 1980s.

3 JR to SVD, 6 November 1957, Wyndham and Melly (eds.), *Letters*.

4 Anne Dunn to author, 30 May 2020.

5 JR to FW, 29 March 1958, Wyndham and Melly (eds.), *Letters*.

6 Francis Wyndham's funeral tribute (copy provided by Alan Hollinghurst to author).

7 Margaret (Peggy) Ramsay to SVD, 2 October 1958 (private collection).

8 I'm again indebted here to Dr. Ellen Moerman for details about the Moermans' difficult life in the Netherlands.

9 JR to SVD, 21 December 1957.

10 JR to MM, 4 May 1959; 28 December 1960, Wyndham and Melly (eds.), *Letters*.

11 JR to MM, 4 June 1959, Wyndham and Melly (eds.), *Letters*.

12 JR to MM, 19 November 1959, Wyndham and Melly (eds.), *Letters*.

13 JR to MM, April 1958, Wyndham and Melly (eds.), *Letters*.

14 JR to SVD, 9 April 1958, Wyndham and Melly (eds.), *Letters*.

15 JR to SVD, 10 January 1959, Wyndham and Melly (eds.), *Letters*.

16 JR to SVD, 27 May 1959, Wyndham and Melly (eds.), *Letters*.

17 JR to SVD, 14 June 1959, Wyndham and Melly (eds.), *Letters*.

18 Alec Hamer to JR, 31 January 1959, McFarlin 2.2.f8.

19 JR to FW, 14 September 1959, Wyndham and Melly (eds.), *Letters*. Wyndham had taken the reference to Rhys's Scottish blood—she had distant Scottish forebears on her Lockhart side—from Selma's 1957 article for the *Radio Times*.

20   JR to EB, 2 February 1960, McFarlin 2.1.f4.

21   JR to SVD, 24 February 1960; to FW, 12 April 1960; to MM, 22 June 1960, Wyndham and Melly (eds.), *Letters*.

22   JR to MM, 6 October 1960, Wyndham and Melly (eds.), *Letters*.

23   JR to FW, 31 May 1960, Wyndham and Melly (eds.), *Letters*.

24   JR to FW, 14 July 1960, Wyndham and Melly (eds.), *Letters*.

Chapter 16—Cheriton Fitzpaine

1   Robert Herrick, "Discontents in Devon," in *The Poetical Works of Robert Herrick*, edited by F. W. Moorman, Clarendon Press, Oxford, 1915, p. 19.

2   Author interview with Roy Stettiford, 26 April 2019.

3   JR to SVD, 17 September and 27 November 1963, Wyndham and Melly (eds.), *Letters*.

4   JR to DA, 3 August 1963, McFarlin 2.3.f3.

5   Author visit to Cheriton Fitzpaine, 20 June 2019.

6   JR to DA, 3 August 1963, McFarlin 2.3.f3.

7   JR to FW, 23 July 1967, McFarlin 2.14.f1.

8   JR to MM, 15 and 17 July 1961, Wyndham and Melly (eds.), *Letters*.

9   Frances Wood to author, 27 March 2020. Wood learned about William Trevor's friendship with Rhys when talking to him during a Booker shortlist photoshoot at Hatchards in 2002.

10   Author interview with Samantha Moss, 7 July 2021.

11   JR to MM, 6 October 1960, Wyndham and Melly (eds.), *Letters*.

12   JR to FW, 6 June 1961, Wyndham and Melly (eds.), *Letters*.

13   JR to FW, 23 May 1961, Wyndham and Melly (eds.), *Letters*.

14   JR to SVD, 25 September 1963 and to FW, 16 October 1963, Wyndham and Melly (eds.), *Letters*.

15   JR to SVD, 17 September 1963, Wyndham and Melly (eds.), *Letters*.

16   JR to SVD, 30 September 1963.

17   DA to author, 24 September 2018.

18   JR to EB, 2 October 1964, McFarlin 2.1.f4.

19   Robert Herrick, "Discontents in Devon," *Hesperides* (1647).

Chapter 17—The Madness of Perfection (1960–63)

1   JR to SVD, September 1963, Wyndham and Melly (eds.), *Letters*.

2   JR to FW, 6 October 1960, Wyndham and Melly (eds.), *Letters*.

3   JR to DA, 28 April 1964, Wyndham and Melly (eds.), *Letters*.

4   JR to SVD, 9 January 1961, Wyndham and Melly (eds.), *Letters*.

5   JR to FW, 11 October 1961, Wyndham and Melly (eds.), *Letters*.

6   JR to FW, 11 October 1961, Wyndham and Melly (eds.), *Letters*.

7   JR to FW, 17 October 1961, Wyndham and Melly (eds.), *Letters*.

8   Author interview with Tara Fraser, 8 July 2021.

9   JR to SVD, 9 January 1961, Wyndham and Melly (eds.), *Letters*.

10   Charlotte Brontë, *Jane Eyre, an Autobiography*, Smith, Elder & Co., 1847, Chapter 26.

11   Rhys, *Wide Sargasso Sea*, Part 2, Penguin, p. 40.

12   Rhys, *Wide Sargasso Sea*, Part 3, Penguin, p. 123.

13   JR to FW, 12 September 1962, Wyndham and Melly (eds.), *Letters*.

14   MH to JR, April–May 1963, Angier, *Jean Rhys*, p. 498.

15   JR to EB, 18 April 1963, McFarlin 2.1.f4.

16   JR to DA, 5 June 1963, Wyndham and Melly (eds.), *Letters*.

17   FW to DA, 4 May 1963, McFarlin 2.4.f10.

18   Francis Wyndham, Introduction to Wyndham and Melly (eds.), *Letters*, p. 12.

19   JR to DA, 7 July 1963, Wyndham and Melly (eds.), *Letters*.

20   EW to author, 20 May 2020; Esther Menell, *Loose Connections*, West Hill, 2014, pp. 144–5.

21   EW to author, 20 May 2020.

22   JR to SVD, 6 September 1963, Wyndham and Melly (eds.), *Letters*.

23   JR to FW, 11 October 1963, Wyndham and Melly (eds.), *Letters*.

24   Anne Dunn to author, 30 May 2020.

25   SVD to JR, 21 and 26 November 1963, McFarlin 2.12.f1; JR to SVD, 27 November 1963, Wyndham and Melly (eds.), *Letters*.

26   JR to SVD, March 1964, Wyndham and Melly (eds.), *Letters*.

27   Francis Wyndham, Introduction to *Wide Sargasso Sea*, first published in *Art and Literature*, March 1964.

28   JR to FW, 25 March 1964, Wyndham and Melly (eds.), *Letters*.

29   "Obeah Night," in JR to FW, 14 April 1964, Wyndham and Melly (eds.), *Letters*.

30   JR to FW, 14 April 1964, Wyndham and Melly (eds.), *Letters*.

31   JR to FW, 14 April 1964, Wyndham and Melly (eds.), *Letters*.

32   JR to FW, 15 July 1964, Wyndham and Melly (eds.), *Letters*.

33   ERW to DA, 28 July 1964, Wyndham and Melly (eds.), *Letters*.

Chapter 18—An End and a Beginning (1964–66)

1   DA to Alec Hamer, 3 March 1966, McFarlin 2.2.f8.

2   JR to OH, recalling Selma's 1965 hospital visit, 25 February 1966, Wyndham and Melly (eds.), *Letters*.

3   DA interview with author, 20 July 2018. Tara Fraser to author, 20 September 2021.

4   DA told me this well-honed story in June 2018, but also DA to ERW, 8 January 1965, and ERW to DA 14 January 1964, McFarlin 2.4.f10.

5   JR to OH, 25 February 1966, Wyndham and Melly (eds.), *Letters*.

6   JR to MM, 4 August 1965, Wyndham and Melly (eds.), *Letters*.

7   JR to MM, 9 November 1965, and (nd) November 1965, Wyndham and Melly (eds.), *Letters*.

8   Rhys, *Wide Sargasso Sea*, Part 2, Penguin, p. 70.

9   Anne Dunn telephone interview with author, 30 May 2020.

10 Rhys, *Wide Sargasso Sea*, Part 2, Penguin, p. 149.

11 JR to SVD, 3 March 1966, Wyndham and Melly (eds.), *Letters*.

12 JR to DA, 9 March 1966, Wyndham and Melly (eds.), *Letters*.

13 DA to JR, 28 March 1966; DA to author, 23 July 2018.

PART SEVEN: UNWELCOME FAME

Chapter 19—No Orchids for Miss Rhys (1966–69)

1   JR to FW, 21 July 1960, McFarlin 2.3.f5.

2   Alec Hamer to DA, March 1966, McFarlin 2.2.5.

3   JR to MM, 18 March 1966, Angier, p. 571.

4   JR to SO, 17 November 1966, McFarlin 2.7.f8.

5   DA to SO, 2 October 1966; SO to DA, 13 October 1966, McFarlin 2.5.f9.

6   JS to Margaret (Peggy) Ramsay, 30 July 1966, BL, Ramsay Archive, ad. mss. 88915 1/182/7.

7   JR to SVD, 16 September 1966, McFarlin 2.12.f2.

8   MM to DA, 15 October 1966, McFarlin 2.5.f10.

9   SVD to DA, 1 November 1966, McFarlin 2.4.f9.

10 JR to EB, nd, 1966, McFarlin 2.1.f1.

11 Rhys, *Wide Sargasso Sea*, Part 1, Penguin, p. 16.

12 Rhys, *Wide Sargasso Sea*, Part 2, Penguin, p. 106.

13 Rhys, *Wide Sargasso Sea*, Part 2, Penguin, p. 55.

14 Hunter Davies to author, 21 June 2020. Davies's interview appeared in the *Sunday Times*, 6 November 1966.

15 SO to FW, 11 April 1967, BL, FW archive (not yet catalogued).

16 JR to DA, 1 and 2 December 1966, McFarlin 2.3.f8.

17 JR to SO, 7 January 1967, McFarlin 2.3.f9.

18 DA to Margaret (Peggy) Ramsay, 2 February 1967, BL, Ramsay Archive, ad. mss. 88915 1/182/7.

19 Selma Vaz Dias, 5 February 1967, BL, Ramsay Archive, ad. mss. 88915 15/1/206.

20 MR to Bryan Forbes, 3 February 1967; BF to MR, 6 February 1967, BL, Ramsay Archive, ad. mss. 88915 1/182/7.

21 DA to JR, nd, July 1967, McFarlin 2.3.f10.

22 JR to SO, mid-July, nd, 1967, McFarlin 2.7.f8.

23 JR to FW, 23 July 1967, McFarlin 2.1.f4.

24 JR to DA, 7 October 1967, McFarlin 2.3.f10.

25 JR to SO, 20 October 1967, McFarlin 2.7.f8.

26 JR to FW, 13 December 1967, McFarlin 2.14.f2.

27 FW to SVD, 19 December 1967, McFarlin 2.12.f8.

28 SVD to MM, 6 December 1967; MM to SVD, 8 December 1967, McFarlin 2.12.f8.

29   EM to author, 15 December 2020.

30   SVD to JR, 6 February 1968, McFarlin 2.12.f3.

31   JR to SVD, 6 February and 3 April 1968, McFarlin 2.12.f3; SVD to MR, 10 June 1969, BL, Ramsay Archive, ad. mss. 88915 15/1/206.

32   MM to PAS, 30 April 1968, McFarlin 10.2.f1.

Chapter 20 — Rhys in Retreat (1967–74)

1   JR to OS, 3 August 1968, McFarlin 10.2.f5.

2   JR to FW, 2 December 1968, McFarlin 2.14.f2; JR to MR, 9 August 1969, BL 88915/1/182.

3   Marcelle Bernstein: "The Inscrutable Jean Rhys," *Observer Magazine*, 1 June 1969, and to author, 13 July 2020, and 18 March 2021.

4   EM to author, 12 December 2020.

5   Herbert Ronson, "Meeting Jean," *London Magazine*, July 1988, pp. 75–8.

6   JR to Rachel Ingalls, 20 June 1971, private collection.

7   JR to OS, 3 August 1968, McFarlin 10.2.f5.

8   SVD to MR, 10 June, BL, Ramsay Archive, 88915, 15.1.206.

9   JR to MR, 18 October 1969, McFarlin 2.4.f5.

10   MR to JR, 11 September 1969, BL, Ramsay Archive, 88915/1/182; JR to FW, 22 October 1969, McFarlin 2.14.f5.

11   Marcelle Bernstein, "The Inscrutable Jean Rhys," *Observer Magazine*, 1 June 1969.

12   Marcelle Bernstein to author, 20 June 2020.

13   Barbara Ker-Seymer to JR, 15 January 1969, McFarlin 2.6.f10. A correspondence of fifteen letters between Rhys and Ker-Seymer (1969–70) is in the Tate Archives at Millbank.

14   JR to Antonia Fraser, 26 October 1969, McFarlin 2.5.f7.

15   Antonia Fraser to author, 12 May 2018; 5 September 2018.

16   JR to Rachel Ingalls, 25 July 1971, private collection.

17   JR to SO, 21 May 1970, McFarlin 2.8.f4.

18   Jan van Houts, "The Hole in the Curtain," in Pierrette M. Frickey, *Critical Perspectives on Jean Rhys*, Three Continents, 1990.

19   JR to MM, 26 November 1970, Angier, p. 603.

20   This was how Dorothy Rees Williams described the funeral scene to Carole Angier, *Jean Rhys*, pp. 602–3.

21   David Plante, in an unpublished article about Rachel Ingalls, 2019, and to author, 20 June 2020; Ingalls, *Times* obituary, March 2019.

22   JR to Rachel Ingalls, 25 July and 24 August 1970.

23   Author interview with DA, 23 May 2018.

24   All quotations are from Rhys's privately owned letters to Rachel Ingalls, July 1970 to August 1974.

25   Lidija Haas, "The Hallucinatory Realism of Rachel Ingalls," *New Yorker*, 4 March 2019.

26   Author interview with DP, 9 July 2020.

27   V. S. Naipaul, "Without a Dog's Chance," *New York Review of Books*, 18 May 1972, pp. 29–31.

28   "L'affaire Ford" was drafted out in JR's Green Exercise Book, McFarlin 1.1.1.

29   DP to author, 9 July 2020.

30   FW to JR, 30 June 1972, McFarlin 2.14.f10.

31   JR to FW, 20 October 1972, McFarlin 2.14.f10.

Chapter 21—"Mrs Methuselah" (1973–76)

1   Virginia Stevens, *Radio Times*, 21 November 1974.

2   FW to JR, 17 August 1974, McFarlin 2.15.f1.

3   JR to Jo Batterham, 27 October 1973, private collection.

4   I'm indebted for these details to Glenda Jackson, Alexis Lykiard, Peter Eyre, Diana Melly and Edna O'Brien, in conversations and correspondence during September 2020.

5   FW to JR, 26 February 1974, McFarlin 2.15.f1.

6   Julie Kavanagh to author, 22 and 26 July 2020.

7   Mary Cantwell, "I'm a Person Without a Mask," *Mademoiselle*, October 1974.

8   James Fox to author, 18 January 2019.

9   Tristam Powell to author, 14 January 2019.

10   MR to SVD, 10 December 1974, BL, Ramsay Archive, ad. mss. 88915 15/1/206.

11   Paravisini-Gebert, *Phyllis Shand Allfrey*, p. 243.

12   FW to JR, 25 July 1975, McFarlin 2.15.f2.

13   Paravisini-Gebert, *Phyllis Shand Allfrey*, p. 245.

14   JR to FW, 9 October 1975, McFarlin 2.15.f2.

15   JR, "Shades of Pink," McFarlin, Plante Papers 14.f4.

16   DP to author, 20 April 2020.

17   JR to FW, 15 February 1976, McFarlin 2.15.f2.

18   SO to DA, 2 March 1976, McFarlin 2.2.f12.

19   JR to SO, nd, McFarlin 2.9.f4.

20   *Kirkus Reviews*, review of *Sleep It Off Lady*, 1 November 1976.

21   DP and DA to author 18 and 20 July 2018.

PART EIGHT: AND YET I FEAR

1   Rhys, "And Yet I Fear," BL, Rhys Archives, ad. mss. 57858.

Chapter 22—"The Old Punk Upstairs" (1977–79)

1   DA to FW, 1 January 1980, Wyndham Papers, BL (uncatalogued).

2   JB to SO, 10 March 1977; the rest of the details are from Diana Melly to author, January 2019–January 2020.

3   JR to DA, 29 March 1977, McFarlin 2.3.f8.

4   Louis James, "The Lady is Not a Photograph," *Journal of Caribbean Literatures*, 3 (2003), pp. 175–84.

5   SO to JB, 16 August 1977; JR to JB, 7 September 1977 (private collection).

6   Jo Batterham paraphrased the advertisement to SO, 3 October 1977 (private collection); DA to SO, 1 November 1977, McFarlin 2.2.f13.

7   JR to JB, 27 October 1977 (private collection). JB to author, 1 August 2020.

8   George Melly, "The Old Punk Upstairs," *Independent on Sunday*, 28 October 1990.

9   Sarah Papineau to author, 9 July 2020, with comments and excerpts from her diary for 1977–8 (private collection).

10 From the private collection of Sarah Papineau.

11 DA to SO, 1977, McFarlin 2.2.f9.

12 SO to DM, 22 December 1977, McFarlin 2.7.f1.

13 DM to SO, 6 January 1978, and to author, 15 January 2020.

14 Plante, *Difficult Women: A Memoir of Three*, Gollancz, 1983, pp. 17, 46, 51.

15 Thomas Staley to John Byrne, 28 December 1977 (private collection).

16 DM to author, 15 January 2020.

17 Melly, "The Old Punk Upstairs."

18 SO to DM, February 1978, McFarlin 2.7.f1.

19 Diana Melly, *Take a Girl Like Me: Life with George*, Chatto, 2005, p. 125.

20 JB to author, 18 July 2020.

21 Rhys's "Making Bricks without Straw" was first published in *Harpers*, July 1978. Reprinted in *Vogue* in 1979, it is included in Frickey (ed.), *Critical Perspectives of Jean Rhys*.

22 JR, June 1978, nd, McFarlin 1.3.f7.

23 Madeline Slade interview with author, 8 December 2021.

24 DA to author, 17 June 2018 and also DA to SO, nd, McFarlin 2.2.f9.

25 JB to author, 12 September 2018.

26 JB to author, 12 September 2018.

27 Rhys, *Wide Sargasso Sea*, Part 3, Penguin.

Afterlife

1   DA to author, 20 June 2018; DP to JB, 21 March 1980 (private collection).

Sources and Bibliography

The main collection of Jean Rhys's papers—it includes photographs, official documents, correspondence, poems, four exercise books, manuscript and typed drafts and personal papers—is held in twenty-three boxes at the McFarlin Library (Special Collections) at Tulsa, where Tom Staley, during the 1970s, initiated the library's role as a special collection for women writers. The library also holds the archives of André Deutsch, and the section of David Plante's papers which relates to Jean Rhys in particular.

The British Library also possesses numerous manuscript notes and drafts, together with a substantial collection of copy documents from McFarlin. The Alvarez Papers— including a large number of the reviews of Rhys's work and interviews with her—are also held at the British Library.

WORKS BY JEAN RHYS

The Left Bank: Sketches and Studies of Present-Day Bohemian Paris, Jonathan Cape, 1927; US: Harpers, 1927

Perversity (with the translator's name given as Ford Madox Ford), translated by Jean Rhys from the novel by Francis Carco, US only, Pascal Covici, 1928

Postures, Chatto & Windus, 1928; US: *Quartet*, Simon & Schuster, 1929

"The Christmas Presents of Mynheer van Rooz," *Time and Tide*, 12, November 1931, pp. 1360–1

After Leaving Mr Mackenzie, Jonathan Cape, 1931; US: Knopf, 1931

Barred, translated by Jean Rhys from Jean Lenglet's work as Edouard de Néve, Desmond Harmsworth, 1932

Voyage in the Dark, Constable, 1934; US: William Morrow, 1935

Good Morning, Midnight, Constable, 1939; US: Harpers, 1970

Wide Sargasso Sea, André Deutsch, 1966; US: Norton, 1967

Tigers are Better-Looking, with a Selection from "The Left Bank," André Deutsch, 1968; US: Harpers, 1974

My Day, US: Frank Hallman, 1975

Sleep It Off Lady, André Deutsch, 1976; US: Harpers, 1976

Smile Please: An Unfinished Autobiography, André Deutsch, 1979; US: Harpers, 1980

Jean Rhys: The Collected Short Stories, Penguin, 1987; US: Norton, 1987. Several of Rhys's stories, including "I Spy a Stranger," had not been included in the earlier collections, but were first published during her lifetime in magazines (notably the *London Magazine*, the *New Yorker* and *Art and Literature*) and, less frequently, newspapers.

A SELECTION OF BOOKS AND ARTICLES RELEVANT TO JEAN RHYS

Angier, Carole, *Jean Rhys, Lives of Modern Women*, Penguin, 1985
———. *Jean Rhys, Life and Work*, André Deutsch, 1990
Athill, Diana, *Stet*, Granta, 2000
Atwood, Thomas, *The History of the Island of Dominica*, Joseph Johnson, 1791
Bell, Henry Hesketh, *Obeah, Witchcraft in the West Indies*, Sampson Low, 1889
———. *Glimpses of a Governor's Life*, Sampson Low, 1946
Benstock, Shari, *Women of the Left Bank, 1900–1940*, University of Texas, 1986
Bernabé, Jean, Patrick Chamoiseau and Raphael Confiant, *Eloge de la Creolité*, Gallimard, 1993
Bhaba, Homi K., *The Location of Culture*, Routledge, 1994
Bliss, Eliot, *Luminous Isle*, Cobden-Sanderson, 1934
Bowen, Stella, *Drawn from Life: Reminiscences*, Collins, 1941
Brathwaite, Edward Kamau, *The Development of Creole Society in Jamaica 1770–1820*, Clarendon Press, Oxford, 1971
———. *Contradictory Omens: Cultural Diversity and Integration in the Caribbean*, Mona, Savacou Publications, 1974
Callard, D. A., *Pretty Good for a Woman: The Enigmas of Evelyn Scott*, Norton, 1986
Carr, Helen, *Jean Rhys*, Northcote, 1996
Chambers, Colin (ed.), *Peggy to her Playwrights: The Letters of Margaret Ramsay, Play Agent*, Oberon Books, 2018
Clyde, David, *Two Centuries of Health Care in Dominica*, Pre Printing Press, India, 1981
Curtin, Philip D., *The Rise and Fall of the Plantation Complex: Essays in Atlantic History*, Cambridge University Press, 1992
Devlin, Polly, *Writing Home*, Pimpernel Press, 2019
Elkin, Lauren, *Flaneuse: Women Walk the Streets in London, Paris, New York, Tokyo and Venice*, Chatto & Windus, 2016
Emery, Mary Lou, *Jean Rhys at "World's End": Novels of Colonial and Sexual Exile*, University of Texas, 1990
Frickey, Pierrette M. (ed.), *Critical Perspectives on Jean Rhys*, Three Continents, 1990
Froude, J. M., *The English in the West Indies; or, The Bow of Ulysses*, Cambridge University Press, 1888
Le Gallez, Paula, *The Rhys Woman*, Macmillan, 1990
Gates, Henry Louis, *Writing and Difference*, University of Chicago Press, 1986
Gikandi, Simon, *Writing in Limbo: Modernism and Caribbean Literature*, Cornell University Press, 1992
Gilbert, Sandra M., and Susan Gubar, *The Madwoman in the Attic: The Woman Writer and the Nineteenth-Century Imagination*, Yale University Press, 1980

Glissant, Edouard, *Le Discours Antillais*, Seuil, 1981

Gregg, Veronica Marie, *Jean Rhys's Historical Imagination: Reading and Writing the Creole*, University of North Carolina Press, 1995

Grieve, Symington, *Notes Upon the Island of Dominica*, AC & Black, 1906

Hardwick, Elizabeth, *Seduction and Betrayal* (1974), Faber, 2019

Hearn, Lafcadio, *Two Years in the French West Indies*, Harpers, 1890

Hughes, Richard, *A High Wind in Jamaica*, Penguin, 1947

Hulme, Peter, "The Locked Heart: The Creole Family Romance of *Wide Sargasso Sea*," in F. Barker, P. Hulme and M. Iverson (eds.), *Colonial Discourse/Postcolonial Theory*, Manchester University Press, 1994, pp. 72–88

Hulme, Peter and Neil L. Whitbread (eds.), *Wild Majesty: Encounters with Caribs from Columbus to the Present Day*, Clarendon Press, 1992

James, Louis, *Jean Rhys*, Longman, 1978

Jordis, Christine, *Jean Rhys*, La Manufacture, 1990

———. *Jean Rhys, La Prisonnière*, Stock, 1996

Judd, Alan, *Ford Madox Ford*, Collins, 1990

King, Bruce, *West Indian Literature*, Macmillan, 1979

Kloepfer, Deborah Kelly, *The Unspeakable Mother: Forbidden Discourse in Jean Rhys and H.D.*, Cornell University Press, 1989

Leigh Fermor, Patrick, *The Traveller's Tree*, John Murray, 1950

Lisser, Herbert G. de, *The White Witch of Rosehall* (1958), Macmillan Caribbean, 2007

Ludwig, Ralph (ed.), *Ecrire la "parole de nuit": La nouvelle literature antillaise*, Gallimard, 1994

Lykiard, Alexis, *Jean Rhys Revisited*, Stride, 2000

———. *Jean Rhys: Afterwords*, Shoestring Press, 2006

Maurel, Sylvie, *Jean Rhys: The West Indian Novels*, New York University Press, 1986

———. *Jean Rhys (Women Writers)*, Palgrave Macmillan, 1999

Maximin, Colette, *La Parole aux masques: Litterature, oralité et culture Populaire dans la Caraibe anglophone au XXe siècle*, Editions caribéennes, 1991

Melly, Diana, *Take a Girl Like Me: Life with George*, Chatto, 2005

Menell (Whitby), Esther, *Loose Connections: from Narva Mantee to Great Russell Street*, West Hill Books, 2014

Michie, Elsie B. (ed.), *Charlotte Brontë's* Jane Eyre: *A Casebook*, Oxford University Press, 2006

Moers, Ellen, *Literary Women*, The Women's Press, 1978

Oates, Joyce Carol, "Romance and Anti-Romance: *Jane Eyre* to Rhys's *Wide Sargasso Sea*," *Virginia Quarterly Review*, No. 61 (1), Winter 1985, pp. 44–58

Oliver, Sophie, "Fashion in Jean Rhys/Jean Rhys in Fashion," *Modernist Cultures*, November 2016; curator of a 2016 Exhibition at the British Library on Making the Reputation of Jean Rhys http://blogs.bl.uk/english-and-drama/2016/10/rhys-cycled-.html

Paravisini-Gebert, Lizabeth, *Phyllis Shand Allfrey: A Caribbean Life*, Rutgers University Press, 1996

Pizzichini, Lillian, *The Blue Hour: A Portrait of Jean Rhys*, Bloomsbury, 2010

Plante, David, *Difficult Women: A Memoir of Three*, Gollancz, 1983

Pope-Hennessy, James, *West Indian Summer: A Retrospect*, Batsford, 1943

————. *The Baths of Absalom: A Footnote to Froude*, Allen Wingate, 1954

Raiskin, Judith L., *Snow on the Cane Fields: Women's Writing and Creole Subjectivity*, University of Minnesota Press, 1996

————. *Wide Sargasso Sea, a Critical Edition*, Norton, 1999

Rovera, Catherine, *Genèses d'une folie créole: Jean Rhys et Jane Eyre*, Paris, Editions Hermann, 2015

————. "(Out)Rage against the Machine: "Parasexuality" and Subversion in Jean Rhys's *Voyage in the Dark*," Etudes Brittanniques Contemporaines, September 2013

Saunders, Max, *Ford Madox Ford, A Dual Portrait*, Oxford University Press, 1996

Savory, Elaine, *Jean Rhys*, Cambridge University Press, 1999

Scott, M. A. *The Perse School for Girls: The First Hundred Years, 1881–1981*, Cambridge, 1981

Scura, Dorothy McInnis and Jones, P. C., *Evelyn Scott: Recovering a Lost Modernist*, University of Tennessee Press, 2001

Shand Allfrey, Phyllis, *The Orchid House*, Constable, 1953

————. *It Falls Into Place: the Stories of Phyllis Shand Allfrey*, Papillotte, 2004

————. *Love for an Island: The Collected Poems of Phyllis Shand Allfrey*, Papillote, 2014

Spurling, Hilary, *The Girl from the Fiction Department: A Portrait of Sonia Orwell*, Penguin, 2002

Staley, Thomas F., *Jean Rhys: A Critical Study*, Macmillan, 1979

Thomas, Sue, *The Worlding of Jean Rhys*, Westport Connecticut, 1999

Vreeland, Elizabeth, "Jean Rhys: The Art of Fiction LXIV," *Paris Review*, 76, Autumn 1979, pp. 218–37

Warner, Marina, *Fantastic Metamorphoses, Other Worlds: Ways of Telling the Self*, Clarendon Press, Oxford, 2002

————. *Signs and Wonders: Essays on Literature and Culture*, Chatto, 2003

Waugh, Alec, *The Sugar Islands*, Cassell, 1958

Wilson, Mary and Kerry L. Johnson, *Rhys Matters: New Critical Perspectives*, New Caribbean Studies, 2013

Wyndham, Francis and Diana Melly (eds.), *The Letters of Jean Rhys, 1931–1966*, André Deutsch, 1984

Credits

Many of the letters quoted from in this book are in private collections, as indicated within the notes. Dr Ellen Moerman, Rhys's granddaughter, also retains a collection pertaining to her grandmother, including books which Rhys still owned at her death. A full list of extracts used with permission of Dr Moerman is below:

Extracts from *Good Morning Midnight* reprinted by permission of Dr Ellen Moerman © 1939 (Jean Rhys)

Extracts from *Smile Please: An Unfinished Autobiography* reprinted by permission of Dr Ellen Moerman © 1979 (Jean Rhys)

Extracts from *Collected Short Stories* reprinted by permission of Dr Ellen Moerman © 1987 (Jean Rhys)

Extracts from *Jean Rhys: Collected Letters* reprinted by permission of Dr Ellen Moerman © 1995 (Jean Rhys)

Extract from "Mixing Cocktails," "Vienne," "La Grosse Fifi" and "In the Rue de l'Arrivée" reprinted by permission of Dr Ellen Moerman © 1927 (Jean Rhys)

Extracts from "A Solid House," "Outside the Machine" and "The Sound of the River" reprinted by permission of Dr Ellen Moerman © 1968 (Jean Rhys)

Extracts from "Temps Perdi" and "I Spy a Stranger" reprinted by permission of Dr Ellen Moerman © 1969 (Jean Rhys)

Extracts from "Goodbye Marcus, Goodbye Rose," "The Insect World" and "Overture and Beginners" reprinted by permission of Dr Ellen Moerman © 1976 (Jean Rhys)

I am particularly indebted to the published selection made by Diana Melly and Francis Wyndham (eds), in *The Letters of Jean Rhys, 1931–1966* (André Deutsch, 1984).

Index